Handbook of Research
on the
International Relations of
Latin America and
the Caribbean

───────── ■ ─────────

Handbook of Research on the International Relations of Latin America and the Caribbean

■

G. Pope Atkins

University of Texas at Austin and
United States Naval Academy

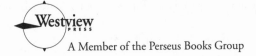

A Member of the Perseus Books Group

Published in 2001 in the United States of America by Westview Press, 5500 Central Avenue, Boulder, Colorado 80301-2877, and in the United Kingdom by Westview Press, 12 Hid's Copse Road, Cumnor Hill, Oxford OX2 9JJ

Find us on the World Wide Web at www.westviewpress.com

Library of Congress Cataloging-in-Publication Data
A CIP catalog record for this book is available from the Library of Congress.
ISBN 0-8133-3379-2

The paper used in this publication meets the requirements of the American National Standard for Permanence of Paper for Printed Library Materials Z39.48-1984.

10   9   8   7   6   5   4   3   2   1

To Louann and Larry

Brief Contents

Preface   XV

1   RESEARCH PATTERNS AND ISSUES   1

2   THE LATIN AMERICAN AND CARIBBEAN REGION   41

3   LATIN AMERICAN AND CARIBBEAN STATES   87

4   NONHEMISPHERIC STATES AND CANADA   143

5   THE UNITED STATES   157

6   INTERSTATE INSTITUTIONS   175

7   WARFARE, INTERVENTION,
    AND DIPLOMACY FOR PEACE   205

8   INTERSTATE AND TRANSNATIONAL PHENOMENA   259

References   309

Notes   397

Contents

1 RESEARCH PATTERNS AND ISSUES   1
   Latin American and Caribbean IR as
      a Field of Study, 1
   Regionalism and Area Studies, 3
   The Latin American–Caribbean Region and the Study of IR, 6
   Intellectual Foundations to 1918, 7
      Nineteenth-Century Characteristics, 7
      Realism and Geopolitics, 8
      Liberalism, 10
      Marxism and Leninism, 12
   The Interbellum Period, 12
   Postwar Developments, 16
      Realism Theorized, 16
      Behavioralism Versus Traditionalism, 17
      The Impact of Postwar Developments, 19
   The Emergence of Multiple Paradigms, 20
      Radical Challengers, 21
      Foreign Policy Analysis, 21
      Neorealism, 23
      Marxism-Leninism, 23
      Developmental, Dependency, and World-System Theories, 24
      Pluralism, 28
      Formal Theory and Rational Choice, 30
      Postpositivism, 33
   Disciplinary Developments, 34
      Developments in the Study of IR, 34
      Developments in Latin American–Caribbean IR Studies, 36

2   THE LATIN AMERICAN AND CARIBBEAN REGION   41
    General Surveys, 41
        International and Diplomatic History, 42
        International Politics, 45
        International Political Economy, 46
    Theories of General Application, 48
        Marxism-Leninism, 48
        Structural Economic Dependency, 49
        Neo-Marxist Dependency Theory, 51
            World-System Theory, 54
        General Commentary, 55
    Colonies and Dependencies, 56
        General Works, 57
        The Spanish–American Empire, 58
        Portuguese Brazil, 60
        The Circum-Caribbean, 61
            General Treatments, 61
            Puerto Rico, 63
            The British West Indies, 66
            The French and Netherlands Antilles, 67
            The Virgin Islands, 68
    Latin American Regional International Relations, 69
    The Subregions, 76
        The Circum-Caribbean, 76
        Central America, 81
        The Commonwealth Caribbean, 83
        South America, 84
        Extrahemispheric Subsystems, 86

3   LATIN AMERICAN AND CARIBBEAN STATES   87
    General and Comparative Studies, 87
    Survey Analyses, 88
        The External Environment, 91
        Decision Making, 92
        Nationalism, 93
        Geopolitical Formulations, 95
        Geographic Levels of Policy and Relations, 97

The Circum-Caribbean, 97
Central America, 98
Commonwealth Caribbean States, 100
South America, 101
Relations with the United States, 102
Argentina, 104
Bolivia, 107
Brazil, 108
Chile, 115
Colombia, 116
Costa Rica, 118
Cuba, 119
Dominican Republic, 124
Ecuador, 126
Haiti, 127
Mexico, 128
Nicaragua, 137
Panama, 138
Paraguay, 138
Peru, 139
Uruguay, 140
Venezuela, 140

4   NONHEMISPHERIC STATES AND CANADA   143
    Studies of a General Nature, 143
    Europe, 144
    The Soviet Union, 149
    Other Extrahemispheric States, 152
    Canada, 154

5   THE UNITED STATES   157
    Historical Surveys, 158
    The Monroe and Other Doctrines, 162
    Foreign Policy Analyses, 165
    Perceptions, 170
    Subregional Policies, 171

6   INTERSTATE INSTITUTIONS   175
    General Works, 175
    Latin American and Caribbean Integration and Association, 176
        Nineteenth-Century Spanish-American Congresses, 176
        Post–World War II Latin American–Caribbean Institutions, 179
        Central American Federation and Integration, 184
    The Inter-American System, 186
        General Treatments, 187
        Inter-American Development Bank, 191
        Principles and Practices, 191
            Codification of International Law, 191
            Nonintervention, 193
            Peace and Security, 193
    Other Inter-American Regimes, 194
        Mexico–United States Border Agreements, 194
            Riverine and Related Arrangements, 194
            Maquiladora Arrangement, 195
        North American Free Trade Agreement, 196
        Western Hemisphere Free Trade, 198
        Transisthmian Canal, 199
    Global and Extrahemispheric Organizations, 202

7   WARFARE, INTERVENTION,
    AND DIPLOMACY FOR PEACE   205
    Latin American Revolutions for Independence, 205
        General Treatments, 206
        Spanish-American Country Studies, 208
        The Case of Cuba, 210
        The Case of Haiti, 211
    Inter–Latin American Conflicts, 212
        General Works, 212
        Boundary and Territorial Disputes, 212
        Interstate Warfare, 216
            Cisplatine War (1825–1828), 216
            Paraguayan War/War of the Triple Alliance (1865–1870), 217
            War of the Pacific (1879–1883), 217
            The Chaco War and the Peace Process (1932–1939), 219

Ecuador-Peru Conflict, 219
Caribbean Conflict, 220
External Interventions, 221
  Mexico and International Conflict, 221
    The Texas Question and War with the United States, 221
    French Occupation, 223
  European Actions in South America, 224
  U.S. Interventions, 225
    Caribbean Imperialism, 225
    Cuba, 226
    Nicaragua, 227
    Haiti, 228
    Dominican Republic, 228
    Cold War Interventions, 229
    Guatemala, 229
    Cuba, 230
    Dominican Republic, 231
    Chile, 232
    Grenada, 232
    Post–Cold War Interventions, 233
World Events, 234
  Spanish-American War, 234
  World War I, 235
  World War II, 235
  Cuban Missile Crisis, 238
  Cuba in Africa, 239
  Argentine-British South Atlantic Conflict, 240
Internal War, 241
  Social Revolutions, 241
    Mexican Revolution of 1910, 241
    Cuban Revolution of 1959, 244
    Nicaraguan Revolution of 1979, 244
  Insurgents and Insurgency, 246
    General Treatments, 246
    The Cuban Model, 248
  Latin American Peace Processes, 251
Central American Conflict and the Peace Process, 251

Internal and Transnational Wars, 251
The Search for Peace, 255
Country Studies, 256
    El Salvador, 256
    Nicaragua, 257
    Guatemala, 258
    Honduras, 258

8   INTERSTATE AND TRANSNATIONAL PHENOMENA   259
    Development Theory in Practice, 260
    Business Enterprise and Multinational Corporations, 266
        General Studies, 266
        Country Studies, 269
            Mexico, 269
            Peru, 271
            Venezuela, 272
            Other Countries, 273
    Economic Policies and Relations, 274
        Trade and Investment, 274
        External Debt, 276
    Environmental Issues, 279
    Political Systems and International Processes, 280
        Democracy and Human Rights, 280
        Armed Forces, Military Rule, and Military Assistance, 284
        Revolutionary Movements, 286
            General Treatments, 286
            International Communism, 288
    Some Transnational Networks, 290
        The Roman Catholic Church, 290
        Protestant Churches, 292
        Subnational Associations, 293
    Intersocietal Phenomena, 294
        Cultural Relations, 294
        Movement of People, 297
        The Drug Traffic, 304

Preface

This handbook is intended to provide a thorough multidisciplinary reference to the literature on the international relations of Latin America and the Caribbean. Although most of the more than 1,600 books cited have appeared since World War II (the scholarly activity over the past four decades has been especially productive), earlier works dating from the nineteenth century are also considered. But this book is not exhaustive in scope. For reasons of both purpose and space, I emphasize scholarly book-length works. Generally not included (there are some exceptions) are monographs, doctoral dissertations, official publications, bibliographies, guides to libraries or archives, documentary collections, and other data sources. Other handbooks dealing with the topic are cited. Given the enormous volume of materials produced on the subject, this handbook is perhaps only suggestive as to where the search may begin. As readers concern themselves with particular themes they will discover an increasing list of new materials. The presentation is organized along the same lines that I have applied in a companion volume, *Latin America and the Caribbean in the International System* (4th ed., Westview Press, 1999). To have included an index seemed unwieldy and superfluous. I attempt to compensate for its lack with a detailed table of contents, many cross-references in the text, and a reference list that provides an index of authors.

I am indebted to professional colleagues who read parts of the manuscript and made valuable comments and suggestions: Henry Dietz, Helen Purkitt, James Roach, and Larman Wilson. I express my appreciation to members of the staff of the Hispanic Division of the Library of Congress who produce the *Handbook of Latin American Studies* (to which I have been a contributing editor for general international relations for more

than a decade). I thank especially Dolores Moyano Martin, recently retired as editor, Sue Mundell, formerly associate editor, and Ann Mulrane,
editorial assistant. I also want to take this opportunity to acknowledge
two superb editors at Westview Press with whom I have enjoyed excellent
professional relationships over the years: Barbara Ellington, who helped
initiate the present work before retiring from the press; and Karl Yambert,
who skillfully and patiently guided it to fruition. Finally, as I have grate-
fully done on numerous occasions in the past, I pay special tribute to my
wife, Joan Jorns Atkins.

G. Pope Atkins

CHAPTER 1

■

Research Patterns and Issues

The study of the international relations (IR) of Latin America and the Caribbean involves several academic complexities. The elements of this undertaking, which are appraised in this introductory chapter, have evolved for more than a century. They have combined to produce an expanding academic domain characterized by increasingly sophisticated research and broadening coverage of expanding phenomena—and by a number of controversial issues.

LATIN AMERICAN AND CARIBBEAN IR AS A FIELD OF STUDY

Various developments have shaped the study of the region's IR. In the United States, pre–World War II pioneering scholars, in addition to producing thorough studies of their own, trained later generations of academics who further advanced the study of Latin America's IR. With the dramatically increased U.S. academic interest in Latin America and the addition of the new Caribbean states after 1960, scholarship reflected the broader and myriad tendencies and debates in the general study of IR. Research by British scholars had been extensive until after World War II when it declined—although the quality of work by the smaller number of Latin Americanist researchers remained high. Scholars in Spain, Germany, France, Italy, the Netherlands, the Scandinavian countries, and

1

Portugal increasingly (to varying degrees) produced works of merit on the region, but their numbers were small. The European Community sponsored the founding of an important research institution devoted to European–Latin American relations. In the Soviet Union, Latin American studies were pursued primarily in Marxian terms. With the end of the cold war, however, and the collapse of communism and dissolution of the Soviet state, Latin American studies in Russia were dramatically reduced. The sustained escalation in the quantity and quality of scholarship by Latin American and Caribbean researchers was particularly notable. Although they were strongly influenced by academic developments in the United States and Europe, they not only adjusted them to serve their own research purposes but developed new theories that reflected their own perceptions of global and regional realities.

Alongside the increasing analytical richness, the study of the region's IR has had its share of publications in all parts of the world that do not merit the status of scholarship. One must acknowledge the excessively nationalistic, impressionistic, polemical, and speculative materials; sensational journalism; and zealous dogmatism in both criticism and advocacy of theory and policy—all of which have appeared with a dearth of evidence or reasoning. The choice of topics to be studied has often followed the rise and fall of ephemeral current events. This problem is not restricted to Latin American–Caribbean studies—a similar statement could be made about the general study of IR, as well as other fields within the various disciplines. And this difficulty does not detract from the significance of the scholarly advances that have been made or of the importance of the phenomena being investigated.

The Latin American–Caribbean field of study is an intricate one, requiring analytic attention on various levels. Latin America has traditionally been geographically defined as that portion of the Western Hemisphere south of the United States. The term "Caribbean" was added in the 1960s to recognize the emergence of former British and Netherlands dependencies (especially the former) as new states within the area. IR concerns range through (1) the global international system within which regional processes operate; (2) the overall Latin American and Caribbean region and its subregions; (3) the foreign policies of the states within the region and of the outside states that interact with them; (4) an assortment of international institutions inside and outside the region; (5) warfare, its approximations, and the search for peace; and (6) an array of other inter-state relations and transnational phenomena (such as economic trade and investment flows, cultural relations, migration of people, and the drug traffic, which involve a myriad of nonstate actors).

Most academic analysts of Latin American–Caribbean IR today are simultaneously members of academic disciplines and part of two multidisciplinary enterprises—the study of IR in general and of Latin America and the Caribbean in particular. The latter effort is a component of the concept and organization of "area studies." Thus, scholars are usually (1) trained in specific disciplines (political science, history, another of the social sciences, or sometimes IR as a separate discipline), (2) instructed in the intellectual traditions of IR, and (3) imbued with the special characteristics of the region. Consequently, they must deal with (1) problems in the relationships among the general field of IR, Latin American–Caribbean studies, and the various disciplines; (2) questions about the position and viability of area studies in both IR and the disciplines; (3) particular intradisciplinary issues; and (4) specific concerns within the Latin Americanist community. Also important are those IR researchers who do not consider themselves Latin American–Caribbean specialists but use regional phenomena for their theoretical, comparative, or case studies.

REGIONALISM AND AREA STUDIES

The concept of the region has long been evident in both the study and practice of IR—first simply as regional elements in world affairs and more recently as subsystems of the international system. The IR context of "area studies" falls within this regional arena. The notion has been reflected in some sense over a long period of time, such as the indirect connection in the voluminous literature on European international relations and in the classic imperial-colonial era with the identification of colonial "areas." But a more general and overt academic concern with regional topics appeared only after World War I and became a strong scholarly enterprise following World War II.

Bryce Wood notes that during and immediately after World War II, governments discovered an alarming shortage of individuals seriously acquainted with languages, cultures, geography, and other characteristics of world areas.[1] Thereafter, cold war hostility inspired the increasing development of scholarly specialization in world areas, such as Latin America, South Asia, East Asia, Western Europe, Eastern Europe, the Middle East, and southern Africa. The Soviet Union, China, and Japan were often separated for special study—as were Mexico and Brazil in the case of Latin America. Government and foundation grants in the United States, Great Britain, France, and elsewhere supported universities in their development of regional scholarly efforts and to establish or broaden existing area studies centers.

Latin American studies (along with Asian studies) was something of an exception to the above. After the mid-nineteenth century, a literature on Latin America of some significance began to develop in the United States, Great Britain, and in Latin America itself. Beginning in the 1880s, with the rise of the Pan American idea and formal organization of what came to be called the Inter-American System, western hemispheric ideas and organizations were added as a continuous object of scholarship. One reason for this regional exception was that by 1830 most of Latin America had emerged as a collection of independent states, of analytic interest to outsiders as well as themselves as new members of the international system. Another reason was the rise of the United States to great power status and, beginning in the late 1890s, its adoption of a Caribbean imperial policy, which generated a great deal of writing. Much of the rest of the world outside of Europe and the Americas (with the major exceptions of Japan and China, as well as of some others) had been subordinated as part of the extensive European empires.

After World War II, the further development of Latin American studies took place in the new environment of the concept, organization, and support for area studies—although Latin America, seemingly safe behind the front lines of the cold war, was slow to receive official recognition compared to most other areas. With the Cuban Revolution of 1959 and its subsequent alliance with the Soviet Union, such recognition and attendant support of Latin American studies was forthcoming—which in time became arguably the largest and professionally best organized of area studies within the Third World category.[2] Even with the end of the cold war and increased awareness of the global forces of transnationalization and globalization, considerable evidence suggests that the Latin American and Caribbean region (as well as those of other parts of the world) have actually increased their cohesion concurrently with the global processes.[3]

Wood says that area centers were formed "on the theory that collaboration is more effective than isolation in advancing knowledge about foreign areas through research, publication, and teaching."[4] Scholars associated with area centers generally hold appointments and teach in various university departments. Centers offer or coordinate undergraduate and graduate academic programs, and deal in different ways with questions about the balance between competence in an individual discipline and in a geographic area. They provide extracurricular endeavors of interest to faculty and student area specialists and sponsor visiting foreign scholars. Field research varies according to discipline and project. But with researchers typically having a strong personal interest in an area and a desire to interact with foreign colleagues, a substantial "on site" familiarity with the region is the norm.

The fundamental proposition underlying area studies, that human beings in a designated geographic portion of the world are a viable division for scholarly analysis, has been and remains a matter of debate. In the case of the study of IR, a legitimate question is whether the independent states within a region form a coherent entity for study or only a convenient geographic contrivance. The literature defines a region within the international system as a set of geographically proximate and regularly interacting states that share to some degree a sense of regional identity and are so perceived by external actors.[5] These same criteria also identify further subsystems within the region. Thus geographic proximity within a physical boundary is a necessary but insufficient characteristic of a regional subsystem. Further requisites are the extent of regional self-perception and the regularity of relationships (both formal and informal) among the regional countries, and the views of the external actors about the region.

With regard to the problem of Latin America and the Caribbean, one must acknowledge that many specialists, seeing the great diversity in numerous aspects among the constituent states, are skeptical of regionwide conceptualizations and generalizations. They prefer to concentrate on the individual countries and subregions. Globalists, in their continuing debate with regionalists, have maintained that the most important international structures and the most critical issues are worldwide in scope; thus, analytic efforts should concentrate on the highest level. In my view, shared with many other area specialists:

An accurate picture of the international relations of Latin America and the Caribbean requires that we recognize and link individual state, subregional, regional, hemispheric, global, and other extrahemispheric levels of interaction. This demanding analytic task is required if we do not accept the idea that one or some levels of analysis offer the key to understanding at the exclusion or slighting of the others. . . . These possibilities may complicate the structure of the Latin American and Caribbean subsystem (as well as the global system) but they do not refute the central regional concept as a point of departure. Latin America and the Caribbean may be set apart as both conceptually defensible and analytically important.[6]

THE LATIN AMERICAN–
CARIBBEAN REGION AND THE STUDY OF IR

The development of the study of the region's IR, although distinguished by particular characteristics, has taken place largely within the evolution of IR as an academic undertaking.[7] The unresolved question of whether IR should or can constitute a separate discipline, or whether it is inherently at best an interdisciplinary or more likely a multidisciplinary enterprise, has been in dispute—although it is no longer as vigorously debated as in the past. Throughout the life of the study until recently, several disciplines had, in fact, contributed to IR, with one or another of them at different times forming the core (but not exclusive) perspectives. History was primary through World War II, supplemented by law and political philosophy; then the study increasingly centered in political science, with history and the other social sciences making specific contributions. Since the mid-1980s, IR has become much more multicentric in disciplinary terms. Furthermore, students have confronted a vast array of data and diverse and sometimes contradictory philosophical, theoretical, and methodological modes of analysis. They have differed in, and strenuously disputed, their approaches to understanding. Scholars have offered a variety of competing paradigms and diverged over what constitutes the substance of IR and the appropriate analysis of it. For some, this situation is the healthy conceptual pluralism of a disparate realm; for many, it is a debilitating fragmentation symptomatic of a field in disarray; for others, it is the inevitable consequence for a field that undertakes analysis of such a vast domain. With these concerns in mind, the following discussion identifies, in summary form, the principal paradigms and disciplinary issues as they have appeared and competed for influence within the multifarious study of IR, and their import for the study of Latin America and the Caribbean.[8]

INTELLECTUAL FOUNDATIONS TO 1918

Analyzing what came to be called international relations is literally an ancient undertaking, as writings on the subject appeared at least as early as the fourth century B.C. The organized and sustained academic study of IR, however, was not taken up until after World War I, making it a relatively new enterprise when compared with other fields of social inquiry. Prior writings in history, international law, political philosophy, and military strategy constitute enduring traditions of thought and analytic perspectives that have been drawn upon to some degree throughout the twentieth century. They are the "classical" ancestries of IR, providing a broad conceptual and methodological heritage.

Real-world developments in the nineteenth century and the accompanying scholarship on international phenomena formed the immediate bases for the post–World War I evolution of the study of IR (the war itself gave profound impetus), including their relevance for the Latin American region. These intellectual developments were occurring as the newly independent Latin American states sought to consolidate internally and to participate as well as they could in the international system.

Nineteenth-Century Characteristics

During the nineteenth century—more precisely, the century between the end of the Napoleonic Wars in 1815 and the outbreak of World War I in 1914—IR scholarship was carried out by international or diplomatic historians, political theorists (philosophers), legal scholars, and military analysts. Together they focused on diplomacy, nationalism, and imperialism; the laws of war, peace, and neutrality; the history and strategy of war; and the state positions and international issues accompanying these phenomena. By the end of the century the enterprise was increasingly undertaken by the newly organized social sciences, especially political science and political economy, which absorbed political theory and elements of law and debated the extent of their linkages to history. Most scholars considered events to be unique and nonrepeating and, therefore, the search for causal explanations infeasible. The historical method was essentially descriptive and interpretive, organizing material according to time, place, and theme and basing primary evidence on thorough archival research. The legal approach analyzed both private and public international law, with the latter usually within the narrow confines of analyzing treaties and legal principles and procedures. Political economy reflected increasing global economic activity and concentrated on government foreign economic policies and their relationship to international economics. The infrequent teaching of IR tended to focus on training professional diplomats in the nature and rules of statecraft and the conduct of diplomacy.[9] The proliferation of memoirs by political leaders, diplomats, and military men continued the eighteenth-century tradition of claiming to know how to make statecraft more effective[10] (a practice continuing to the present day). In conceptual terms, the long-existing competing dichotomy of "realism" and "liberalism" (later transformed into part of "idealism") continued to be prominent. As a dissent to both the realist and liberal modes of thought and action, Marxism and then Leninism appeared; their importance, however, was to be recognized later. These matters were centered in Europe and, to an increasing degree, the United States; Latin Americans also made contributions. Latin American subject matter, although not in the mainstream of IR writing, generally fit into the parameters indicated above. With the newly independent states of Latin America expanding their international activities, and being the object of actions on the part of external states, a literature of some importance developed—especially in the United States, Great Britain, and the Latin American states.

Realism and Geopolitics

Realism, the oldest concept in international theory and practice, formed the dominant perspective. With an ancestry that included Thucydides, Machiavelli, Hobbes, and Clausewitz, realism advocated essentially a mode of operation and expressed only a rudimentary theory of interstate relations. As a pragmatic state-centric view of the world, it focused on the nature of states (their sovereignty, territoriality, and power) and the practices of statecraft (especially diplomacy and war, with consideration of law as a way to regulate power relations). Both state officials and academic analysts widely assumed that state behavior was based on the notions of interests and power and the strategies of interstate balances of power and competitive imperialism. Practices associated with realism were important aspects of the Latin American experience and were reflected in the writings on the region's IR at the time. Many international historians assumed realist motives and power structures in their interpretations and narratives of international phenomena, although they were not necessarily specified overtly.

In the latter part of the nineteenth century, geopolitical thinkers—who stressed the organic nature of the state, the links between geography and power politics, and strategic geopolitical calculations—began to analyze and prescribe for interstate politics. They integrated their geopolitical assumptions and calculations with the realist mode of thinking, inasmuch as they emphasized state interests and power and interstate balances of power. Unlike their realist forebears and colleagues, however, they viewed IR in systematic, global, strategic, and explanatory ("power determinants") terms. Geopolitics began as a European construct in the latter half of the nineteenth century. Among the most influential Europeans was British scholar Sir Halford Mackinder (director of the London School of Economics and Political Science from 1903 to 1908). He expounded his "land-power thesis," arguing that whoever dominated the Eurasian landmass would dominate world politics.

Although European geopoliticians ignored Latin America in their calculations, they strongly influenced Latin American geopolitical writers, who followed the European lead to produce national versions of geopolitics and policy recommendations to political leaders. Latin American analysts of military affairs in particular adopted geopolitical perspectives. They were most prominent in the ambitious competing South American states of Argentina, Brazil, and Chile.[11] In the late nineteenth and early twentieth centuries, U.S. Navy captain (later admiral) Alfred Thayer Mahan joined the geopolitical enterprise and developed his "seapower thesis" regarding state power and control of the sea-lanes (Mahan served a term as president of the American Historical Association). His equations, which prominently addressed the "Caribbean Basin," strongly influenced U.S. officials (the basic intent of his work) as well as certain scholars. Mahanian thinking persisted for many decades in U.S. policies of power politics in the Caribbean. Latin American geopoliticians and Mahan produced the closest thing to a realist-based theory of Latin American IR.

Liberalism

In sharp contrast to realism, liberalism championed the quest for universal international principles and purposes, such as peace, freedom, democracy, justice, and moral behavior. It was not a monolithic "school" but a variety of uncoordinated approaches. Nineteenth-century political and economic liberalism had originated in the seventeenth and eighteenth centuries, stemming especially from the combination of the Enlightenment and the rise of capitalism. Liberalism in international law followed the rationalism of Hugo Grotius (1583–1645), seeking to create "rules of the game" that would mute the violence of war and promote a community of nations. In domestic politics, liberals emphasized constitutionalism, republicanism, limited government, and individual liberty—which Immanuel Kant extended to interstate relations with his theory of the democratic peace (republics did not go to war with each other). In the economic arena, the stress was on Adam Smith's principles of individual initiative, free enterprise, free trade, and minimal state intervention in the economy. During the latter half of the nineteenth century into the twentieth, reform-minded historians and legal scholars went beyond the established confines of their disciplines to prescribe for interstate relations in the traditions of Grotius, Kant, and Smith. They concluded that the industrial and scientific revolutions had made the world both more economically interdependent and militarily dangerous. They called for the advancement of international cooperation through development of international organizations and the rule of law. They applauded The Hague System of international conferences and permanent courts and the emphasis on peaceful settlement of international disputes and disarmament. They claimed that as international economic contacts increased, liberal (free) international trade would serve as a force for world peace. They further assumed that the spread of representative government around the world would facilitate international peace and stability.

The liberal perspective persisted in the inter-American arena. Most fundamentally, the U.S. and Latin American movements for independence found a common philosophical basis in the principles of the Enlightenment—despite the contradictions of slavery and servitude and problems with carrying out the development of socially, politically, and economically equitable republics. Economic liberalism in most of Latin America dated from the middle to the late nineteenth century, when nationalist elites began to lead a conscious thrust for economic modernization. The legal-institutional approach was also postulated in the thinking and writing of advocates for two important interstate institutional efforts. First, the new Spanish-American states made several attempts to form a loose federation, which sought political union, mutual security, and international legal reform. Later, the United States led the formation of a formal inter-American organization (which in time was known as the Inter-American System) emphasizing peaceful settlement of disputes and liberalized trade. Liberal tenets were found in the Latin American participation in The Hague System (they were especially attracted to its emphasis on disarmament, arbitration, and international institutions). They were also reflected in the significant Latin American contributions to international law (they sought in particular the prohibition of external intervention based on a theory of absolute state sovereignty). Latin Americans (and Iberians) considered the father of international law to be the Spaniard Francisco Vitoria (1483–1547) of the University of Salamanca. He founded the naturalist school (asserting that principles of law are inherently the right of human beings), which was later challenged by positivists (concerned with explicit facts and phenomena to the exclusion of speculation about causes and origins). Grotius drew on both schools in his more eclectic approach. Mention should also be made of the prominent research and advocacy of the Carnegie Endowment for International Peace in the inter-American arena. Founded by U.S. industrialist and philanthropist Andrew Carnegie in 1902 (who had a strong and lasting personal interest in inter-American affairs), the endowment thereafter devoted significant attention to the Inter-American System.[12]

Marxism and Leninism

From the mid-nineteenth century through World War I, Marxism and then the Leninist interpretation appeared as ideological-theoretical calls for action against the evils of capitalism and imperialism. Marxism and Leninism dismissed both realism and liberalism, arguing that the functioning of the international system was understood in economic and social terms. They were based on a determinist philosophy of history in which the contemporary stage of capitalism, characterized by class struggle between the proletariat and the bourgeoisie, and inherent, irreconcilable, and fatal contradictions within capitalism itself.

Karl Marx (and his cotheorist Friedrich Engels) were primarily interested in the analysis of class struggle, and within that framework they advocated, under favorable conditions, violent revolution led by the Communist party to overthrow the capitalist system. The party would then create a transitional socialist "dictatorship of the proletariat" and proceed to the attainment of a peaceful, stateless, and classless Communist society. Other than a short pamphlet on Mexico, Marx ignored Latin America. Lenin extended Marx's concepts into a more explicit theory of imperialism, set forth most cogently in his 1912 long essay, *Imperialism—The Highest Stage of Capitalism*. Lenin said that the capitalist states' policies were inevitably imperialist, and the world capitalist system was the driving force behind both colonization and war. Leninism also predicted world revolution and the destruction of the bourgeois state and establishment of proletarian dictatorship. Latin America did not become a part of the Leninist equation until after the Great War.

THE INTERBELLUM PERIOD

The catastrophe of World War I gave profound impetus to the study of IR. The subject was increasingly added to university curricula in Europe (notably the United Kingdom) and the United States. Institutes dedicated to the study of international law and organization were formed in Switzerland, Great Britain, and the United States. Analysts studying IR during the interwar period were collectively concerned with international history, current events and public policy, international law and institutions, diplomacy and power, and ethical philosophy. Historians continued the tradition of describing what they deemed to be unrepeated events and changing situations. Legal scholars persisted in describing and interpreting international law, organizations, conferences, and treaties. A new perspective appeared, called "current events" or "current history," which was largely a reaction to international historians' lack of attention to recent affairs. It was based essentially on factual journalistic descriptions, sometimes accompanied by exhortation. The philosophers' normative work interpreted political thought, the ethics of political action, and notions of international political community. Some scholars searched for the "lessons" of history but their efforts were largely subjective and unsystematic pleas for reform of the international system.

In conceptual terms, idealism and realism provided the competing "grand theories" around which philosophical IR debates revolved; Marxism-Leninism was a lesser part of the mix. Political idealism emerged as the central paradigm in the aftermath of World War I but was increasingly challenged by political realism with the unsettling events of the 1930s.

In a dramatic extension of the prewar legal-institutional-reformist movement, post–World War I idealists further absorbed much of liberalism and reacted against the long-standing dominance of realist practice in interstate relations. Idealism was a representation of things as they might or should be rather than as they necessarily were. The shortcomings of realism, idealists charged, had resulted in the horrors of World War I, the disastrous consequences of the breakdown of the international balance-of-power system. In addition, believing the war had revealed the deficiency of traditional history as a guide to the future, idealists sought to establish a new, independent academic discipline of international relations. It was to be dedicated to the study of international conflict and its peaceful settlement, and the causes of wars and how they could be prevented. Thus idealism, unabashedly subjective and prescriptive, formed the paradigm on which the new discipline was founded. IR had strong normative purposes and explicitly emphasized connections between theory and practice and ends and means. But the overall organization of the study of IR was not so clear-cut; the new academic discipline competed with the extant disciplines within which inquiry was also pursued. The competition was particularly evident among historians, history-oriented political scientists, and legal scholars.[13]

Idealism reached its height in the 1920s to the latter 1930s. Despite certain generally shared assumptions and purposes, idealists prescribed different measures that competed and sometimes disagreed to the extent that they did not make up a unified "school" of thought. Within the designation of idealism were pacifists, world federalists, legal reformers, political and economic liberals, social democrats, humanitarians, and moralists. Particularly prominent were those who ascribed war to wrong-headed reliance on power politics, which they sought to replace with legal-institutional arrangements that would facilitate peace. They advocated a number of actions that states adopted to varying degrees: collective security within the new League of Nations; new emphases on and reforms of international law; disarmament and arms control; and political, social, and economic reforms within the states themselves.

Latin American idealism at this time focused on preferences for states to behave in accordance with international law and within interstate organizations. They favored participation in the League of Nations and reformation of universal international law, primarily as possible ways to restrain U.S. intervention in their affairs. When that effort failed, Latin Americans shifted to advocacy of organization and law on a regional basis within the developing Inter-American System. They championed codification of a distinctly American (western hemispheric) international law and development of measures for mutual security that would replace unilateral U.S. intervention.

The experiences of the 1930s and then World War II heavily influenced the course of realist-idealist competition. Aggressive militarist fascism and its variants in the 1930s—Mussolini's fascism in Italy (where the generic name originated), Hitler's national socialism (Nazism) in Germany, Franco's falangism in Spain, and, with less ideological cover, the militarists' mentality in Japan—challenged the foundations of idealism. The dictators adopted supporting ideologies (which were transferred by like-minded elements to Latin America). Although analysts generally consider fascist forms to be nonsystematic fragments of vague and contradictory ideas without philosophical or ideological consistency, those forms nevertheless influenced IR theory. Nazism adopted an extreme ver-

sion of geopolitics by advocating the single-minded acquisition and assertion of national power and the expansion of strong states at the expense
of weaker ones (retired German army officer Karl Haushofer influenced
Hitler in this regard). Although fascism was anathema to most geopoliticians, its association with fascism discredited the general field of thought
for decades to come—except in South America, where it continued to
thrive.[14] The broader consequence of the 1930s experience was deep disillusionment with idealist prescriptions and to put idealism on the defensive and give renewed impetus to realism.

The realist challenge to idealism proceeded from the mid-1930s to
soon after World War II, when it was consolidated as the primary paradigm in the study of IR. Academic realists made important efforts in the
1930s.[15] They said idealism had been incapable of resisting the rise of the
totalitarian regimes, deterring their aggression, and preventing the world
war. They challenged idealist assumptions about human nature and notions of universal ideals and international community, and discredited the
ability of international organization to deal with raw power and determined aggression. They offered instead a theory saying that the realities
of human nature and of the international system required thinking in
terms of the nature of state power and how international peace and stability depended on balancing that power with countervailing power.

Marxism-Leninism was not ignored in the interbellum period, but it
occupied a decidedly secondary position to the idealist-realist confrontation. As a general matter, during the period leading up to World War I
and extending through World War II, nationalism triumphed over the
expected labor solidarity. Initial Soviet assessments of Latin American society were heavily dependent on Marxist ideas of class struggle. A widely
held view was that both "objective" and "subjective" conditions necessary
for a proletarian revolution were lacking. Latin America was virtually
unique in Marxian terms. Without differentiating among countries,
Marxists saw the region as standing midway between precapitalist and
mature capitalist stages. (Marx and his successors had also seen India far
from any stage of development that would permit much class identification.) Leninism further rationalized the Latin American situation in
terms of "geographic fatalism," a form of geopolitics that perceived the
debilitating disadvantages for communism of the region's physical re-

moteness from the Soviet Union and imperial domination by the United States. Latin American Communist writers tended to adopt Lenin's theses regarding the region.

POSTWAR DEVELOPMENTS

Realism Theorized

The prewar and wartime disillusionment with idealism was carried into the cold war era, when realist theory was consolidated. The postwar realist movement, centered in the United States, extended the prewar efforts and constructed a general theory of political realism in IR. Among the prominent realist theorists were political scientists Hans Morgenthau, Henry Kissinger, and Arnold Wolfers, theologian Reinhold Neibuhr, and diplomat George Kennan. They had matured in a period of international history dominated by the rise of the fascist totalitarian power centers, and came to influence as the world entered the cold war of conflict involving a totalitarian Communist power center. Realists sought to understand state power and interstate power relations and to advise political leaders how to think about such matters.

Hans J. Morgenthau, a refugee from Nazi Germany and professor of political science at the University of Chicago, was the leading theoretician. Along with other German academic exiles and refugees who helped found postwar realism, Morgenthau's thinking was deeply affected by his experience with fascism and Hitler. He outlined his theory as a set of "principles of political realism."[16] Morgenthau asserted that international politics were susceptible to systematic analysis and theoretical generalization. Furthermore, if politics were not studied in terms of the world as it is, not as it ought to be, policies are doomed to failure. Thus, realist theory was both a "guide to understanding" and an "ideal for action." The competitive and often conflictual practices associated with power politics and self-interest is consonant with the objective laws of imperfect human nature, which do not change and can be discovered. Idealist reformers' faith in human progress and institutions and laws is misplaced. Interests and power combine as the "main signpost that helps political realism find its way through the landscape of international politics"—and the balancing of power is the recurring basic pattern of interstate relations. Political realism, Morgenthau said, acknowledges the moral significance of political action. But a tension exists between abstract universal moral principles and the requirements for political success. The same moral dictates for individuals do not prevail among states, where morality must be considered in the concrete circumstances of time and place.

Political realists adopted, as a corollary to their general theory, the rational model of foreign policy decision making. The model assumes the rationality of policymakers who logically, reasonably, and prudently follow (or should follow) an unemotional and consistent plan of state purposes, goals, objectives, and procedures, which are calculated to solve strategic problems related to state interests and power in the context of external power relationships. Thus what went on inside the state in the way of individual psychology or organizational process was of little analytic importance.[17]

Morgenthau had his own view of what constituted a scientific IR theory. He wrote that the role of theory was "to bring order and meaning into a mass of unconnected material and to increase knowledge through the logical development of certain propositions empirically established." IR theory was purposeful, he said. Its ultimate function was "international peace and order to be achieved through scientific precision and predictability in understanding and manipulating international affairs."[18]

Behavioralism Versus Traditionalism

Another group of dissenting scholars who were disappointed with the state of the postwar study of IR pressed for the adoption of political behavioralism. U.S. political scientists had undertaken such efforts in the 1920s but they did not flourish until the 1950s. The behavioral purpose was first and foremost the creation of a science of politics, based on rigorous scientific methods and quantitative techniques already being used in the other social sciences (which had been borrowed from the natural and physical sciences). IR behavioralists sought to reveal causality and uniformities in state behavior and interstate processes. They were dissatisfied with what they saw as the shortcomings of historical and legal-institutional description, philosophical speculation, and the unrigorous methods of both idealism and realism (all of which they grouped together in the single category of "traditionalism").

Behavioralists also differed among themselves over what direction their own efforts should take—a situation that eventually led to schism. At the heart of many disagreements was the continuing debate over inductive versus deductive research—between empirical theory (which logically induces theory on the basis of factual observation and statistical analysis) versus formal theory (which deduces theory based on mathematical logic applied to premises and formalized with mathematical symbols). Behaviorally inclined Latin Americanists clearly favored empirical theory. They dismissed description unguided by appropriate theory as aimless, as well as speculation unsupported by data as futile; thus, their task was to construct a scientifically testable theory-data linkage or continuum. (Formal theory and its unhappy connection to Latin American studies are discussed below.) It may be noted that certain prominent pioneers of behavioral theory in U.S. political science, such as David Easton and David Truman, had promoted a rigorous science of politics without engaging in quantitative methodology, although in time they represented a distinct minority of the movement.

The "behavioral revolution" was accompanied by sharp and often acrimonious controversy. Traditionalists accused behavioralists of triviality, pretension, and unnecessary jargon. Those associated with descriptive and normative methods denied the possibility of a science of politics along the lines advocated by behavioralists. They defended empirically rich case studies and justified the importance of history, law, institutions, and current affairs. Idealists and realists, seeing a lack of practical purpose in behavioral research, reasserted the relevance of normative analysis to policy action.[19]

The disputes between traditionalists and behavioralists and among behavioralists themselves appeared to be not so much about theory as method—behavioralists had dismissed traditionalist methods as unrigorous but had not rejected their theories as such. At the same time, as indicated above, behavioralists had subdivided into empirical and formal theorists. In fact, the complex arguments were (and still are) more fundamentally about epistemology and the meaning of theory. Rather than solely debating method, the contestants disagreed about the origin,

nature, methods, and limits of human knowledge, and over what constituted theory and how to theorize.

The Impact of Postwar Developments

Realism and behavioralism together exerted enduring influences on the
study of IR, and they in some way influenced most analysts who thereafter dealt with IR. Each had demonstrated, in different ways, the possibility of systematic conceptual and theoretical research and analysis of
causation in IR. Scholars increasingly accepted the inseparability of theory and data so as to generalize beyond the flux of ephemeral events. The
behavioral perspective implanted quantitative analysis as a permanent
feature of IR research, although the methodological scene remained pluralist and many scholars preferred verbal theory and data analysis. Policy
implications and normative considerations remained as important elements of the study of IR, although policy analysts increasingly felt
obliged to support their appraisals and prescriptions with databased theoretical insights. Historians tended to remain skeptical of the utility of
models and quantification (a certain number did engage in "behavioral
history"). But historians were increasingly willing to integrate political
conceptual and theoretical insights into their narratives and interpretations.[20] A new mainstream of historians recognized that even unique
events take place within some (perhaps changing) structure. Latin Americanists (and other area specialists) tended to resist quantitative approaches. By the late 1960s, however, Latin Americanists, especially
younger scholars in the United States, had adopted the new approaches—although not in a wholesale manner and more so in comparative than international politics.

   Whether or not IR scholars considered themselves behavioralists, they
adopted many of the concepts and much of the language. A widely accepted behavioral conceptual development was the view of international
politics as a system of activities (part of which involved the distinction between international system and foreign policy analysis). Derived by political scientists from systems theory, this perspective was concerned with
the dynamic structures and processes of the international system. Within
this conceptualization, a subsystemic area of inquiry was found between

individual state actors and the global system. Of particular importance among the various kinds of subsystems was the geographic regional subsystem, such as Latin America and the Caribbean. Subsystem analysis also dealt with state actors (those within the region and outsiders with significant interactions with the region) and with the informal and formal interstate structures and processes having to do with the region.

Although liberalism and idealism never regained their former position of primacy in the study of IR, they continued in theory and practice. They were seldom identified as a single category but were prominent within other groupings as they developed from the late 1950s to the end of the century. Idealists were prominent in peace studies, which arose in the late 1950s.[21] World order studies seeking international peace and justice through law and organization was a clear continuation of the long-standing idealist thrust. From the mid-1970s and then revitalized after the end of the cold war, the rise of interest in nongovernmental organizations, especially the writing on human rights and international norms, was a continuing manifestation of idealist principles and purposes. Among the transnational phenomena, neoliberalism in both its economic and political dimensions loomed large.

THE EMERGENCE OF
MULTIPLE PARADIGMS

The further evolution of the study of IR from the mid-1960s produced a multiplicity of approaches vying for recognition, each of which has in different ways influenced Latin American–Caribbean analysts as well as their generalist colleagues. Both realism and behavioralism underwent significant adjustments and change—and were joined by new competing theoretical standards. Accompanying and inseparable from these trends were further methodological developments and controversies.

The period began with the emergence of radical dissenters unhappy with both traditionalism and behavioralism. As that movement faded in the 1970s, a complex rivalry began to arise among five sets of competing ways to approach the study of IR: (1) foreign policy analysis, which came into its own as a primary and complex behavioral IR subfield; (2) neorealism, which focused even more closely on interstate power structures and placed high value on "parsimonious" theory; (3) dependency and world system theories, sometimes called "globalism" because of their emphasis on the world capitalist system; (4) pluralism, by its nature an especially heterogeneous grouping, and which, among other things, included the revitalization of international political economy as a major IR subfield; and (5) formal theory, which evolved out of behavioralism into a distinctive approach. Later, a loosely connected group of postpositivist theorists, within which feminist theory was most directly relevant to IR, came forward to deny the efficacy of all extant IR theories and to propose distinct alternatives.

Radical Challengers

A new generation of radical IR scholars in the United States and Europe expressed deep dissatisfaction with both traditionalists and behavioralists. Many of them were associated with the Peace Movement and the New Left, so that their "postbehavioralism" was rooted in, and could not be separated from, their opposition to the Vietnam War. Strong dissension was found within the large Latin Americanist community in the United States and was vigorously expressed in the meetings and publications of the Latin American Studies Association. The dissenters argued in ethical, moral, political, and ideological terms. They charged the IR and Latin American studies professions with intellectual irrelevance. They accused behavioralists with mindless quantification, which they said produced a normative sterility that supported the status quo in the guise of science. They objected to realists, whom they detected as part of elite political establishments, and to the conservatism and reactionism of other traditionalists. They were especially hostile to what they saw as a fundamentally imperialist U.S. foreign policy. They demanded that academics and their professional associations should be relevant by actively working to solve social and political problems. During the post-Vietnam period, the movement itself declined. But its influence continued to be felt, especially in the humanities and history but also in the social sciences—and thus in general IR and Latin American–Caribbean IR.

Foreign Policy Analysis

One of the important behavioral conceptual influences on the study of IR was distinguishing between the analysis of foreign policy and of the international system itself. As a consequence, political scientists created the new field of foreign policy analysis, which focused on decision making in the process of formulating and executing policies. They worked in association with cognitive and social psychologists interested in the same phenomenon. Many empirical-behavioral foreign policy theorists saw the rational model associated with the state-centrism of political realism as fundamentally flawed in assuming decisions to be the result of consistent monolithic state processes overseen by logically reasoning decision makers. They constructed alternative competing theories emphasizing the centrality of fallible human beings. They argued that the human element in decision making not only intrudes on but also departs from the rational processes advocated by realists and neorealists. Among the earliest were researchers in comparative foreign policy who developed a "political process model" of decision making (which grew more out of comparative politics than international politics as studied at the time).[22] Latin Americanists in the field favored this approach and its strong empirical content. The model assumed that foreign policy decisions were made within the broad context of the overall political system. It focused on the decision-making agents and the intrasocietal and extrasocietal influences brought to bear on them. In taking into account a wide range of competing internal political and societal actors, comparative foreign policy theorists challenged the realist-rationalist notion of a unitary state actor. They also parted ways with their deep interest in the psychological elements of decision making—particularly how decision makers' motivations and expectations were affected by their perceptions and images of the world, of their own societies, and of themselves. Analysts also applied game theory (mathematical cost-risk analysis), but saw it as one of several forms or aspects of inquiry. Researchers brought to bear different concepts and methods; they were united by a desire to find generalizations about foreign policy decision making across states.

Among comparative foreign policy researchers from the beginning were those who worked with cognitive and social psychological concepts and theories that addressed what and how people perceive, think, and know. They dealt generally with how information is mentally processed, to include concepts of images and perceptions as well as others, such as judgment. They were particularly active in crisis and simulation research. But the results of experimental cognitive and social psychological theories did not come to the general attention of IR researchers until the 1980s, when they emerged as a dominant influence. For a time, prominent theorists advocated bureaucratic and organizational process models (dealing with the psychology of group behavior and institutional interests within competing bureaucracies and other organizations). Critics said the approach was too conceptually narrow to realize its goal of explaining policy decisions, but that it could make a useful corollary to more comprehensive models.

Neorealism

Although realism emerged from the theoretical battles to remain the primary paradigm in the study of IR, the behavioral attack inspired some realists to make their paradigm "more scientific." The result was the creation of "neorealism." (Initially the pejorative label of critics, including other realists, the term came to be generally accepted to identify the revised realist thinking.) The new realists said they had departed from the classic realist school in two fundamental ways: They favored explanation and deemphasized policy prescription and they rejected the need to consider human nature as a causal factor. Neorealists laid primary stress on the balance-of-power structure of the interstate system, as both determinant of and constraint on policy action (hence they were also called "structural realists"). They also emphasized system stability even in a world of change. Neorealists continued to embrace the rational model of foreign policy decision making. Traditional realists and other critics rejected neorealist thinking on the grounds that it was too mechanistic and determinist, thus placing unrealistic constraints on policymakers' freedom of action.[23] Despite the neorealists' rejection of human nature as an analytic variable, their continuing emphasis on rationality, power, and balance of power in fact is an acceptance of the same assumptions about human motivations and interests as their traditionalist forebears and colleagues.

Marxism-Leninism

The major theoretical contestations in IR had largely ignored Marxism-Leninism.[24] Lenin's argument that economic factors dominated the capitalist states' foreign policies and inevitably made them imperialist was the continuing basis for subsequent theorizing.[25] At the same time, traditional Marxism-Leninism was challenged by a number of conflicting interpretations, including Trotskyism, Stalinism, Titoism, Maoism, Castroism, and others. Various guerrilla insurgency doctrines (notably in Latin America—see Chapter 7) and neo-Marxist dependency theory and world-system theory (see below) recalled the earlier propositions. Following World War II, Soviet writers tentatively explored the notion that Latin America shared some common characteristics with the newly independent, precapitalist, non-Communist, underdeveloped Third World in Asia and Africa. In particular, they thought U.S. economic domination offered the possibility of an anti-imperialist revolution, even though Latin America continued to have unique social and economic characteristics and a limiting geographic location. In the mid-1960s they began to detect the decline of U.S. influence in the region. Theoretical Marxism-Leninism declined precipitously with the end of the cold war and associated events—the dissolution of the Soviet Union and the general eclipse of communism and its associated intellectuals.

Developmental, Dependency, and World-System Theories

In the mid-1950s, theorists in comparative politics and development economics were joined by certain historians to create a model of liberal development and modernization. They were designed to explain Third World processes and to serve as the basis for First World (especially United States) foreign assistance policies. They purported to integrate Latin America into the Third World framework. Many Latin Americanists responded that developmental and modernization assumptions were inapplicable to the region and that the theories simply did not explain (and therefore could not prescribe for) Latin American phenomena. The critics identified four fundamental problems: (1) Latin America was not only different from Western Europe and the United States but from Africa and Asia as well; (2) the region itself was far from homogeneous in terms of the theoretical "indicators of development" and did not conform to the assumptions about societal transition from premodern to modern; (3) as a general matter, all countries fit erratically into a model of unilinear, inexorable movement from traditionalism to modernism as the consequence of deterministic "forces of history"; and (4) the theory was ethnocentric with its assertion that developing nations should become like the older, Western, industrialized countries.[26]

Dependency theory developed in part as a reaction to developmentalism, although as a mode of thought it was part of a long intellectual tradition. Dependency theory assumed two forms—structuralist and neo-Marxist. World-system theory grew out of the neo-Marxist perspective to establish an independent paradigm. All three theories are multidisciplinary to differing degrees, combining elements of economics, politics, sociology, and, in the case of world-system theory, world history. All of them challenge the state-centric models of the international system. Structuralism seeks to reform public policy; neo-Marxism is revolutionary; and world-system theory dismisses both efforts as futile.

Latin American economists, led by Raúl Prebisch of Argentina, introduced structuralist theory in the immediate aftermath of World War II. He and his colleagues initially designed the theory with reference to the Latin American region but later expanded it to include the entire Third World. The theory gained increasing favor as the basis for Latin American economic policies, which strongly challenged orthodox monetary and fiscal policies. Although structuralism focused on economic matters, it was clearly aware of political and social ramifications. Structuralists visualized the world economy in terms of a "center-periphery" pattern, with industrialized states forming the center and underdeveloped ones the periphery. This structure, they said, perpetuated a form of colonialism based on economic underdevelopment and unfair terms of trade. In order for Latin American states to break peripheral dependence, structuralists prescribed internal economic as well as political and social reforms, import-substitution industrialization, creation of regional or subregional integration organizations, and participation in commodity agreements with other producers around the globe of primary raw materials.

Latin American, European, and U.S. social scientists from several disciplines developed neo-Marxist dependency theory, which took special interest in Latin America but also generally embraced the Third World.

Neo-Marxist theorists adopted structuralism's core-periphery concept of the international system, but otherwise differed in fundamental ways.

They went beyond the primarily economic parameters of structuralism to construct a general sociopolitical theory of IR; and they rejected the "reform the system" approach and advocated socialist revolution. Their basic premise was that the interests and activities of external capitalist states and multinational corporations operating in the world capitalist market determined Latin American economic development. Latin American economic dependence was the inevitable result of international capitalist power politics, especially those of the United States, over which Latin Americans had little control. A common theme was the impact of foreign capitalist penetration in shaping domestic political, economic, and social systems—that economic dependence was largely responsible for the inequitable domestic social and political structures. Some dependency theorists spoke of "internal colonialism" within Latin American societies, with the minority advanced elite sector allied with foreign capitalists. Neo-Marxists would eliminate the private agricultural system, institute state ownership of large industries, and either exclude foreign investment or allow it to operate only under the strictest controls.

In the 1980s, the status of both structuralism and neo-Marxism began to decline as neoliberal concepts and policies gained favor. Even though the subsequent critical reaction to neoliberalism did not serve to revive either form of dependency theory, they had made a combined long-term impact on the general study of IR and of Latin America and the Caribbean. They had advanced a point of view, a set of concepts, an assortment of empirical critiques of the status quo, and a vocabulary that made permanent contributions to the field. The early dependency theorists especially played a key role in popularizing ideas that are still used today—to justify demands to reform the world trade and financing system and to deal with the gap between rich and poor countries. The dependency concept also spurred thinking about the impact of foreign influences on domestic societal structures and the relationship of domestic political change and foreign policy. Brazilian theorist Fernando Henrique Cardoso (and later president of Brazil), a key figure in creating this form of dependency theory, criticized the adherents in the United States. He said they did not understand that, rather than creating a new paradigm or methodology, the theory grew out of a long-standing intellectual effort in the tradition of Western thought. "Studies of dependency," he said, "constitute part of this constantly renewed effort to reestablish a tradition of analysis of economic structures and structures of domination."[27]

World-system theorists were initially led by sociologist Immanuel Wallerstein. They developed a comprehensive synthesis and framework of world history that grew out of neo-Marxist dependency theory but superseded that declining school and stood on its own terms. Wallerstein himself was also influenced by and drew upon French political-economic writing, not all of which was Marxist—and distinguishes Wallerstein from other neo-Marxists—but was similarly critical of Western capitalism. For world-system theorists, the European discovery of the New World and subsequent domination of the Americas, with Latin America emerging as a separate region, was a defining element in the worldwide spread of capitalism. The appearance of capitalism and the rise of European imperialism were not simply characteristics of a new period in the evolution of interstate power relations revolving around autonomous states and societies; instead, they created a new and increasingly integrated "world-system." This first "world economy" was shaped by the "historically imposed logic" of evolving capital markets and characterized by the Marxian concept of historical materialism. The structure has continued, in changing form, to the present day. The theory asserts a hierarchical political-economic-social structure within which states and societies themselves were defined—a variation of the core-periphery concept. The central core was made up of the most powerful industrialized states led by dominant capitalist classes; the periphery included the weakest and most exploited societies; and the semiperiphery consisted of those with some internal authority but also subordinate to core entities. World-system theorists denied the validity of state-centric models for analysis, since, they said, the state is a mere artifice in the service of the elite capitalist classes who held political power. Development policies were fictions that relied on internal societal dynamics, when in fact "development" was the outcome of global historical forces. They also chided realism for its short-term historical perspective that embraced too little of human experience.

Revisionist world-system theorists have disagreed on how far back in history their basic constructs apply. They have traced economic cycles backward in time and discovered earlier beginnings of the world-system, of which they consider the modern capitalist world-system to be the most recent stage. This proposition raises questions about the neo-Marxist theoretical basis.

Pluralism

At the beginning of the 1970s, a growing pluralist perspective of the international system and its actors emerged as an important theoretical challenge to the dominant realist state-centric model.[28] Pluralists are defined by their mutual discontent with realism for its neglect of transnational phenomena and by their insistence that interstate and transnational perspectives should be combined to produce one of a multicentric global system of "complex interdependence."[29] They generally acknowledge that states remain the most significant actors in world affairs, but maintain that numerous important transnational (nonstate) actors and relations should be integrated in their own right with interstate phenomena. Pluralism appealed to many IR specialists for emphasizing what they saw as crucial but neglected or inadequately recognized phenomena. Latin Americanists had long understood the importance of transnational phenomena, which had always been part of what evolved into the Latin American and Caribbean international subsystem—with the long-standing role of the Roman Catholic Church, foreign business enterprises, the movement of people, outside cultural influences, drug trafficking, and other phenomena. But pluralism languished as the cold war intensified and realism and then neorealism persisted as the primary paradigm, absorbing certain transnational elements into subordinate schematic positions.

With the end of the cold war, the abandonment of associated security concepts, and the rise to prime importance of a host of essentially transnational issues, students of IR and of Latin America revived and expanded pluralist concepts. Pluralists now challenged neorealism for what they saw as misleadingly simplistic rather than beneficially parsimonious international structural theory. They continued to dispute state-centric assumptions that inadequately explained crucial transnational events and relationships. Pluralists admit they have complicated the study of IR but they say pluralism is consonant with the complexities of the international system itself.

Pluralism is not a single theory but an inclusive category of research efforts and conceptual debates that embrace a wide range of transnational phenomena. Consequently, pluralism is broadly interdisciplinary, even fragmented, as contributors from international and comparative politics, economics and international political economy, sociology, anthropology, psychology, and history, as well as (in a more limited way) the humanities and even theology, examine (and perhaps promote) the relevance of various phenomena to the international system. Pluralism attracted certain idealists, behavioralists, and even realists. It embraced as key concepts interdependence, transnationalism, globalism, and neoliberalism. (These pluralist concepts indicate another area in which liberalism and idealism have thrived, influenced by similar normative questions that had preoccupied earlier scholars in terms of an emphasis on political and economic liberalization, nonstate organizations, and international norms.) But pluralism has suffered from a lack of the precise meaning of some of its essential concepts—although the literature is nevertheless abundant in this regard.[30] For pluralism to produce a unifying paradigm or theoretical synthesis of its basic tenets and policy prescriptions, given its inherently decentralized nature, would be a highly difficult undertaking. Thus, although IR specialists of Latin America and the Caribbean and their generalist colleagues assume the significance of transnational phenomena and the need to theorize about them, for the time being they grapple with specific elements within the pluralist boundary.

Numerous aspects of traditional liberalism and idealism were absorbed into the pluralist category, but not as a single or otherwise coordinated effort. Pluralists disagreed, for example, over the relative role or emphasis that should be accorded international governmental organizations (IGOs). Post–World War II realists had accommodated IGOs as actors created and maintained by states, perhaps as a relatively minor element and as another arena where interstate power politics were played out. Pluralists generally came to regard IGOs among transgovernmental actors, or at least with the potential to act independently from the states that created them. Thus neoinstitutionalism, which deals with formal institutions and legal-formal-structural analysis, fits into the pluralist paradigm; it provides a link with traditional idealism in normative terms.

Much of the study of international political economy fits into the broad pluralist category. It was initially a post–World War II revival of the nineteenth-century undertaking. During the 1950s and 1960s, however, international political economy was subordinated to the primary interest in IR with security and related issues; only a few scholars, relatively isolated within political science and economics, were involved.[31] Dramatic and disruptive political-economic events in the 1970s inspired the elevation of the field to continuing prominence. No consensus emerged about the appropriate theoretical paradigm for general understanding or as a basis for public policy prescriptions. Nevertheless, a significant number of political economists ("structural liberals") revived the idea that open economies and free (liberal) trade would not only provide for a stable world economy but also contribute to a more stable, peaceful world.[32] This approach reflects the intense global economic linkages as part of the general interdependence of nation-states and the rise of transnational actors—multinational corporations and certain IGOs prominent among them. Michael Banks notes that nonstate actors "inspired international political economy, on which a wave of 1970s literature gave powerful impetus to the new pluralism."[33]

Formal Theory and Rational Choice

Formal theorists spun off from behavioralism in the early 1980s and formed a separate paradigm. The views of Dina Zinnes, a leading IR behavioralist, summarized formal theorists' thinking in their reexamination of behavioralism at the end of the 1970s. She looked back over two decades of concentrated quantitative scientific study of IR and saw a mixture of disconnected findings, primarily the result of a general disregard for the development of a unifying theoretical framework that would facilitate more coordinated research. For Zinnes, theory referred solely to constructs formalized in mathematical models; all other efforts, even if committed to the theory-data continuum, were at best "ad hoc hypothesis testing" (she did not address extant game theory).[34]

Formal theorists assert that the use of mathematics to derive propositions ensures precise logical consistency, whereas verbal language risks logical inconsistency and vagueness. They further search for universal explanations for political behavior rather than middle level or particularized explorations. To this end, they design mathematical models to represent real-world situations, and to derive solutions they apply the rational choice model, with a strong preference for game theory. Game theory places a priority on logical consistency as a function of rationality and minimizes the need for empirical evidence. Formal theorists imply or assert that their mathematical sophistication and search for universal explanations qualifies them as the only practitioners of a true science of politics, with other approaches being lesser forms of inquiry.[35] In contrast, the goal of many other behavioralists in IR was to establish middle-level "islands" of theory about phenomena, such as the causes of war and the control of international crises. In foreign policy analysis, they sought the determinants of decision making for different types of states, rather than the universal propositions of how states behave.

Formal rational choice theorists made area studies a special target. They argued that true scientific research occurs within their universalist perspective, irrespective of regional boundaries. In any event, they said, area researchers such as Latin Americanists engage largely in atheoretical work. The position of Robert Bates was particularly significant because of his reputation as a leading Africanist scholar. Bates distinguished between "social scientists" and (presumably unscientific) "area specialists." He asserted that the development of rational choice models had finally equipped political science "to handle area knowledge in rigorous ways." He castigated area researchers for rejecting rational choice "while lacking training fully to understand them."[36]

By the 1990s, with the expanding influence of formal theory, considerable contention had also ensued among U.S. political scientists and IR specialists. The formalist challenge had serious implications for IR methodology and foreign policy analysis as well as particular salience for regional specialists as expressed targets of formalism. Stephen Walt, a noted security analyst, offered a balanced critique of formal theory and rational choice with reference to his field of IR research. He saw in formal theory, with its devotion to mathematical logic, more a method of theory construction than theoretical content. He argued that the principal function of social science "is to develop knowledge that is relevant to understanding important social problems" and that "formal techniques facilitate the construction of precise and deductively sound arguments." But recent formalist efforts in security studies had "relatively little to say about contemporary security issues." Even if formalists were able to demonstrate an especially productive approach, he said, "that would hardly mean that alternative research techniques should be entirely discarded."37

Many nonformalist IR researchers and Latin American–Caribbean scholars felt under siege. Stephen Walt, for example, warned that the formal theory–rational choice school had reached such a level of influence that "if the reliance on formal methods becomes the sine qua non of 'scientific' inquiry, then scholars who do not use them will eventually be marginalized within their fields." Specialists in Latin American and Caribbean comparative and international politics also saw dangers in the formalist attack. They pointed to the similar assault in economics some two decades before, as that discipline increasingly emphasized mathematical modeling and universal theoretical goals. The result had been the decline in numbers of Latin Americanist economists and diminishment of their role in the discipline.

Other scholars counseled patience, saying that rational choice researchers will be obliged to face certain issues. In particular, they must address the matter of their conceptual prejudgments. Several of the formalist rational choice assumptions are core beliefs of the realist paradigm. Rational choice theory requires acceptance of both traditional and neorealist assumptions about the rationality of decision makers, state power, the interstate power system, and human nature—all of which are unproven and debatable, no matter how elegant the mathematical models expressing them may be. Thus game theorists must also examine the credibility of simply rejecting the growing body of empirical findings by other theorists, such as about decision making based on cognitive and social psychology.

The formal theory–rational choice complaint about area studies has to do with the very nature of the phenomena that interest and occupy scholars of the region—who are not inclined to agree that their work has little or no value. Latin America–Caribbeanists pursue case and comparative studies focused on the geographic region, not on universal phenomena. They see intellectual, theoretical, and policy value in area expertise, and scholarly richness and relevance in their approaches to these matters. Such scholars feel obliged to deal with a broad range of foreign policy, interstate, and transnational phenomena if they are to understand their chosen field of study. They are eager to develop expertise in the region, subregions, and particular states and societies and to engage in (perhaps extensive) fieldwork. These analysts are likewise broadly pluralist rather than narrowly parsimonious in terms of theory and method, willing to acknowledge the value of a variety of approaches (including formal theory, but not its exclusionist pretensions). They are both theoretical and empirical and use verbal or quantitative language as appropriate, but find abstract mathematical modeling irrelevant to their research purposes. As such, they generally recognize that theories may take different forms (scientific, normative, or policy), which are pursued in accordance with what one is trying to understand. Latin America–Caribbeanists see the increasing diversity in the region and the world presenting intellectual and practical predicaments for conceptualizing and theorizing universal constructs. They are interested in getting on with trying to understand regional real-world phenomena, not in building abstract models or validating a particular paradigm. One must acknowledge that, even with the meaningful advances made in explaining Latin American–Caribbean IR, important gaps continue to exist in our knowledge. One wonders, however, if Latin Americanists have any more theoretical limitations than do IR generalists.

Postpositivism

Postpositivism is a collection of distinct groupings of theorists who, although asserting distinct approaches to IR seeking recognition and influence, are united by their mutual rejection of virtually all other IR paradigms. They are treated briefly because postpositivism does not affect the study of Latin American and Caribbean IR as such, beyond its import for the study of IR in general. As a general matter, postpositivists, despite some claims to the contrary, do not seem to have made a strong attempt to apply their themes to the study of IR. This is not to deny the rich and diverse literature, the serious intellectual challenge of postpositivism, or its impact on other fields of study—it may in time have more influence on IR.

The feminist perspective is an exception with reference to general IR— but it did not take postpositivism to generate or recognize that. In Latin American–Caribbean studies, feminist research is presently concentrated in comparative rather than international politics, although it is gathering momentum in the latter enterprise. The feminist work on women in development in comparative politics is the principal linkage with IR.[38]

The debate in IR is part of a much larger epistemological conflict between philosophers of science and philosophers of postpositivism, all of them found in numerous disciplines in the natural, physical, and social sciences, the humanities, and history. Postpositivists, among them critical theorists, postmodernists, relativists, and social constructionists, challenge the scientists' belief in rational positivism (science) as the way to discern reality and find the truth about it. They charge that a concept of scientific objectivity is deceptive—that in fact ideology and power intrude into scientific conceptualization and experimentation. In IR, postpositivists share the belief that positivism is inadequate for the appropriate study of the world today. They say that resolution of the enormous global problems requires above all a social theory for action aimed at human emancipation. A theory with emancipatory goals of peace and justice requires prevailing over antithetical positivism.[39] Ann Tickner observes about feminist writing, with relevance for postpositivism in general, that the concern with emancipation is often mistakenly seen as part of the idealist tradition of IR. However, she says, Western and Enlightenment theories of universal justice, built on an abstract concept of rationality, "have generally been constructed out of a definition of human nature that excludes or diminishes women and places women in an inferior position, outside the realm of rationality."[40] In sum, the impact on IR of postpositivism, the latest general paradigm to appear in the evolution of the study of IR, remains to be played out.[41]

DISCIPLINARY DEVELOPMENTS

Developments in the Study of IR

Disciplinary developments in the general study of IR over the past half-century directly affected the study of Latin American–Caribbean IR and helped shape its characteristics. Accompanying the debates over paradigms in the 1950s and 1960s was one about the desirability and feasibility of consolidating IR as an autonomous discipline. The effort involved

fundamental questions and contending positions concerning the boundaries and content of the field—its scope, method, purpose, theory, disciplinary orientation, policy relevance, and so on. Specialists who preferred
an autonomous discipline had a modicum of success. Extant university
schools of international relations flourished and new ones were founded,
in the United States, Great Britain, and elsewhere. Some specialists have
continued to the present day to assume or argue for a discipline of IR, or
to regret that the effort to do so had not or could not be sustained.

The virtual abandonment of efforts to create a generally recognized autonomous discipline of IR shifted attention to the individual disciplines
that are party to the study of IR. That study became centered in political
science, with other disciplines more narrowly involved from their particular academic vantage points (in particular history, economics, psychology,
sociology, and anthropology). Part of the shift from history and law to
political science to lead the study of IR was conceptual—the idea that
core concepts of IR were rooted in the study of politics. The state, the
supreme political entity, was the prime mover of international relations
(i.e., the international system was an interstate system). Thus, the analysis
of IR was a specialized form of political analysis, characterized by unique
aspects that made it a distinguishable subfield of politics. Furthermore,
political science was more eclectic than the other disciplines and willing
to acknowledge that the study of international politics had auxiliary connections with other fields of inquiry. Just as influential was the fact that
other disciplines were unwilling (and less able) to take on the task. The
decline of interest in international history on the part of historians, and
the tendency of economists to adopt a restricted definition of politics,
further lodged the study in political science.[42] It may be noted that
younger international historians, including in the Latin American field,
were increasingly attracted to, and divided between, social and cultural
history. The two groups sometimes communicated well, sometimes not.
In time they made efforts to accommodate or synthesize traditional
diplomatic concepts and themes, with mixed results.

As it turned out, the study of IR was increasingly fragmented. The array of disparate international phenomena steadily broadened and inquiry
increasingly divided into subfields within several academic disciplines,
with little coordination among them—and a tendency toward specializa-

tion that encouraged probing ever more deeply but not broadly, which discouraged interdisciplinary interests. The organizing function of political science was thus limited by events and no other discipline was capable of providing an overarching organizing paradigm or felt obliged to do so. Within political science itself, IR no longer constituted a single field but divided into the related undertakings of analysis of the international political system, foreign policy analysis, and international political economy. At the same time, IR analysts were increasingly compelled to include transnational phenomena in all three fields. Furthermore, political scientists strongly disagreed among themselves about the appropriate scope and methods of their own enterprise, as the above survey of the "paradigm wars" amply demonstrates.

Furthering this problem was the tendency for other disciplines (with perhaps the exception of economics and psychology) to fragment internally, with decreasing communication between the fields within them. This was an important trend, in that it fractured the minimum core of essential analytic approaches that young scholars had to know. Thus, unlike the postwar period into the early 1980s, graduate students could complete doctoral programs without taking a common core of courses that defined the field of IR. The result has been the lack of a frame of reference to connect (much less synthesize) the disparate research efforts. It may be that IR, because of its very nature today and because of fundamental disciplinary and inter- and intradisciplinary cleavages, cannot be captured within a common framework.[43]

Developments in Latin American–Caribbean IR Studies

A significant growth in the study of Latin American–Caribbean IR after World War II coincided with the extensive changes in the general study of IR.[44] Until then, it had been the province of a small number of trailblazing scholars, mostly in the United States and Great Britain and a few in continental Europe and Latin America. Given their small numbers, the breadth of coverage was impressive but nevertheless restricted. The dramatic expansion of scholarly attention dated especially from the early 1960s—and has continued apace to the present day. The overall development of scholarly advances in the field, however, has varied in different parts of the world.

In the United States, researchers specializing in Latin America were influenced by the same innovations as other IR scholars. By and large, however, they were not theory designers and were more reluctant to adopt behavioral methods. In time, their scholarship reflected broader disciplinary tendencies and disagreements. The traditional methods, concepts, and often-atheoretical assumptions slowly gave way to the new techniques and broad agreement on the importance of theory (in all its variety). In the United Kingdom, where Latin American studies had long been strong, the volume (but not the quality) of research declined after World War II—along with official interest and government funding.

In the Federal Republic of Germany, scholars renewed the pre–Third Reich German interest in Latin American studies, which continued after German reunification. In France, Italy, the Netherlands, and the Scandinavian countries, more analysts undertook research into the region's IR. Nevertheless, the number of scholars dealing with Latin America and the Caribbean in all of these continental European countries was small. Spaniards had always been interested as the mother country of Spanish America; after the fall of Franco in 1974, they renewed the production of sound works on the region. In Portugal, where some scholars had always had a special interest in Brazil, activity also incrementally increased but remained slight compared with other scholarly undertakings. As Latin American relations became of more interest to the European Community, it sponsored the founding in 1984 of the Institute for European–Latin American Relations in Madrid, which conducted extensive IR-related research. Although juridical, historical, and ideological traditions remained strong in Europe, the mainstream of IR there increasingly converged with (but did not merely copy) U.S. methodological and theoretical trends (quantification and mathematical modeling were not as broadly adopted). European scholarship often reflected dissatisfaction with U.S. government strategic perceptions of Latin America and the power politics it employed, and the desire of European governments and transnational actors to play an independent role in the area.

In the Soviet Union, the volume of academic work on Latin America increased significantly after the Cuban Revolution of 1959, the Soviet

Union's attachment to it, and the subsequent broadening of Soviet relations around the region. Academic work occurred largely in isolation from outside intellectual currents. Almost all Soviet Latin Americanists based their analysis on Marxist concepts. Beginning from a tradition characterized by predictable polemics and unsophisticated ideological propagandizing revealing a low level of understanding of Latin America, attempts were made with some success to engage in serious analysis paying more attention to propositions, evidence, analysis, and logical argument. Most work, however, continued in the old genre and the overall level of scholarship left much to be desired.[45] With the collapse of communism and the demise of the Soviet Union, Latin American studies in Russia continued, but with little vitality and supported by modest resources.

In Latin America itself, IR as a social science was relatively new. Historians, lawyers, and diplomats who emphasized international law and diplomatic history had traditionally carried on the writing. In Spanish America this was largely in the tradition of IR research and teaching at major Spanish universities. By the mid-1970s, however, the broader range of alternatives developed by their U.S. and European counterparts had influenced an increasing number of scholars. It was evident that Latin American and Caribbean social scientists were becoming the source of original conceptual and theoretical contributions. Thereafter they produced some of the best theoretical and policy studies in the field. They not only adjusted the approaches to serve their own research purposes, but adopted new theories that reflected their perceptions of regional realities. On balance, Latin American research remained relatively more traditional than that in the United States and Europe, although decreasingly so.

By the mid-1980s, almost all Latin American countries had set up international relations institutes, which undertook research on general IR, on the region's IR, and on foreign policy problems and processes of their own governments. The Commonwealth Caribbean had its own special characteristics. As dependencies they had long been influenced by British academic traditions; in time they also absorbed developments in the United States. The Institute of International Relations at the University of the West Indies (which served all Commonwealth Caribbean countries) developed a high level of proficiency.[46]

These regional developments were largely a consequence of a growing perception of the relationship of academic expertise to national development, and of a desire for more exact understanding of IR as states increased their activity at all levels of the international system. Consequently, international politics, foreign policy analysis, international political economy, and development economics, with regional and country considerations factored in, made the greatest strides. Academic nationalism—the desire to reduce "knowledge dependency" on the outside world—was part of the mix. At the same time, many graduate students chose to study in the United States, Europe, Canada, or elsewhere in the outside world. Useful collaborative scholarship was carried out, especially with North American and European colleagues.

Regional scholarship confronted problems in its development. Progress was made despite the relatively small number of IR scholars, and was concentrated in countries with the resources and willingness to sustain them. Authoritarian regimes have usually either restricted or suppressed academic activity that they saw as in any way challenging their authority. It must be noted that democracies and partial democracies do not always honor academic freedom, but their negative elements rarely compare with those of dictatorships and military regimes. In addition, the reality of scarce scholarly resources and their maldistribution tend to wear away gains made and to obstruct further progress.

As the twenty-first century begins, Latin American and Caribbean studies in IR are vital and broadly based but, as in IR study at large, fragmented in theoretical and disciplinary terms. Those studies have been more interdisciplinary and less parochial than among the disciplines themselves, and pleas for pluralism probably receive more sympathy among Latin American–Caribbeanists than among their other colleagues within the disciplines. But these attitudes are limited by (1) the fact that regionalist scholars must live within their respective disciplines, which have reward systems that may not encourage such collaboration; (2) the real-world post–cold war situation of rapidly changing circumstances and expanding phenomena requiring investigation; and (3) the lack of a generally agreed-upon paradigm, much less a basic organizing framework, for analysis.

CHAPTER 2

———————— ■ ————————

The Latin American
and Caribbean Region

The overall panorama of the international relations of the Latin American and Caribbean region is the focus of this chapter. It examines studies of a general scope that deal broadly with the structure and conditions of the region and its subregions within the international system. This involves some related phenomena and issues as well as certain more general theoretical perspectives. The chapter also provides points of reference for the particular themes taken up in the rest of the book.[1]

GENERAL SURVEYS

Studies by historians, political scientists, and political economists have detailed general Latin American–Caribbean IR from a regional perspective (although acknowledging the subregional and country components). They fall into two categories: those that deal with the region and the outside world at large, and those that address the more restricted yet expansive arena of inter-American relations. The latter category tends to be on a level of generalization of sufficient breadth to mix together the presentation of the literature in both classifications.[2] Taken together, these surveys identify the essential elements of the international relations of Latin American and Caribbean states and societies.

International and Diplomatic History

The earliest general treatments of Latin America's international relations were in the historical and legal-institutional traditions, which have been carried forward to the present day. The latter efforts, narrower in scope than the history category, are addressed in Chapter 6. An abundance of comprehensive international and diplomatic histories have detailed the broad range of Latin America's international relations on global, hemispheric, and regional planes. The general histories have tended to emphasize interstate relations and have often incorporated legal-institutional matters, with the states' foreign policies treated as adjuncts to interaction processes.

U.S. Latin Americanist John Holladay Latané published *The Diplomatic Relations of the United States and Spanish America* (1900), the earliest significant historical survey of general themes in inter-American relations. Its contents were formal discourses he had presented in the first Albert Shaw Lectures on Diplomatic History at Johns Hopkins University. With deletions, revisions, and additions, a second edition was published in 1920 with a new title: *The United States and Latin America*. Soon after, William Spence Robertson issued *Hispanic-American Relations with the United States* (1923). In accord with the growing practice at the time, he chose not to use the term "Latin America" in favor of "Hispanic America," to designate Spanish America and Brazil (a trend later abandoned, with "Hispanic" correctly referring to things Spanish). The book chronicles events from about 1830 to 1919 on a broad array of subjects: U.S. political influence, the Monroe Doctrine and intervention, peaceful settlement of disputes, commercial relations, U.S. industrial enterprises, educational contacts, scientific explorations, and Pan Americanism. Both books were superseded by the long-lived contribution by history-inclined political scientist Graham H. Stuart, *Latin America and the United States* (6 eds., 1922–1975; the sixth edition was coauthored with James L. Tigner). A lengthy, highly detailed, largely descriptive treatment, it was the standard textbook in the field for many years. In the succeeding editions, Stuart updated events without fundamentally changing the basic themes and organization. His analysis approved of U.S. national values and hesitated to criticize U.S. policies. The 1975 edition included chap-

THE LATIN AMERICAN AND CARIBBEAN REGION   43

ters dealing with Pan Americanism, the Monroe Doctrine, Anglo-American nineteenth-century isthmian diplomacy, developments since the 1930s, and U.S. relations with eight individual Latin American states and with Central America. J. Fred Rippy, *Latin America in World Politics* (3 eds., 1928–1938), is cast on a broader scale. A particularly thorough survey from 1493 to the dates of publication, the contents deal with the principal outside powers and their actions in the Latin American region, intra–Latin American relations, and Latin America's post–World War I change from a largely passive to a participatory role in extrahemispheric affairs. Rippy also asserted that "Latin America" and "Hispanic America" were sufficiently similar in meaning to be used as synonyms. A significant and widely read book by renowned historian Samuel Flagg Bemis, *The Latin American Policy of the United States* (1943), deals extensively with U.S. interactions with Latin America from the early nineteenth century to the date of publication. The work is noted for both its scholarly excellence and confident justification of U.S. actions.

Later significant general international histories in the earlier tradition appeared. J. Lloyd Mecham, *A Survey of United States–Latin American Relations* (1965), a popular college-level textbook by a historian-turned-political-scientist, is a highly detailed and informative treatment divided into two parts: "Policies of General Application" and "Caribbean and Country Relations" (including nine individual states and general Caribbean policies). Although concerned (often subjectively) with U.S. policies and focusing on U.S. strategic concerns, the emphasis is on policy actions and deals to a considerable extent with broad elements of inter-American relations.

Federico G. Gil, *Latin-American–United States Relations* (1971), a well-conceived historical-topical treatment by a political scientist, successfully achieves the purpose of providing for undergraduate students "a comprehensive description and analysis of the events, institutions, and issues that have dominated the relations of Latin America with the United States throughout the years." Gil emphasizes the theme of U.S. policies designed to prevent the influence of extrahemispheric powers in the Americas and Latin American acquiescence. British historian Gordon Connell-Smith, *The United States and Latin America: An Historical Analysis of Inter-American Relations* (1974), examines the broad expanse of inter-

American relations from the late eighteenth century until the 1970s. He employs, with mixed results, what he calls a "contemporary history" approach. It views 1960s and early 1970s phenomena "in a wider historical perspective," and "earlier events in the light of the new perspectives which more recent events have induced." He is critical of the earlier histories by U.S. scholars who presumed mutual inter-American interests and benign U.S. purposes. This theme was not as revisionist as the author seemed to believe—a large number of U.S. writers at the time had also been finding fault with U.S. policies and actions. Harold Davis, John Finan, and Taylor Peck, *Latin American Diplomatic History: An Introduction* (1977), resolutely emphasize Latin American points of view (both collective and national). Against a background of "the origins and nature of Latin American foreign policies," the authors survey, in chronological order, the principal eras and themes from the colonial period until the 1970s. Demetrio Boersner, *Relaciones internacionales de América Latina: breve historia* (4 eds., 1982–1990), is an excellent, relatively brief survey by a Venezuelan historian, from the immediate postindependence period through the 1980s. Boersner dwells on the nineteenth and early twentieth centuries, with concise chapters on the international problems of the relatively weak new Latin American states, British commercial hegemony, and the rising power and subsequent imperialism of the United States. Also of interest is Robert N. Burr, *Our Troubled Hemisphere: Perspectives on United States–Latin American Relations* (1967), a brief insightful survey highlighting competing international and domestic U.S. and Latin American interests and objectives, with special attention to the post–World War II period.

Historians producing surveys over the past decade or so have tended to be more interdisciplinary than their forebears. Lester D. Langley, *America and the Americas: The United States in the Western Hemisphere* (1989), determinedly integrates concepts from the social sciences into his history writing. This lucid, interpretive, sometimes provocative synthesis addresses social and cultural phenomena as well as political and economic interactions. The book also serves as a thematic and conceptual point of departure as the "inaugural volume" of a series of books evaluating the relations of fourteen Latin American states (and of Canada) with the United States, for which Langley served as general editor. Peter H. Smith,

Talons of the Eagle: Dynamics of U.S.–Latin American Relations (2 eds., 1996, 1999), offers "a conceptual framework for the comprehension of changing patterns of inter-American relations over a span of nearly two centuries." Smith also describes his study as a "personal statement," as he interprets and synthesizes years of research and reflection on two centuries of inter-American relations. He considers structure, continuity, and change and identifies the defining characteristics and dynamics of each historical period. A relatively brief, well-conceived book by Don M. Coerver and Linda B. Hall, *The United States and Latin America* (1999), considers historical power and imperial relations. They address the Latin American movements for independence through the era of U.S. intervention; cover world power and regional concerns through World War II; analyze the cold war tensions paralleled by Latin American social revolution; and deal with recent transnational problems of foreign debt, migration of people, and the drug traffic.

International Politics

Latin American international politics, and particularly the systems mode of analysis that was a fundamental development in the study of IR, gained increasing prominence. As indicated in Chapter 1, a systems approach ideally takes into account the broad array of elements in international structures and processes having to do with interstate power relationships and institutions, state action, and transnational phenomena. Norman Bailey, *Latin America in World Politics* (1967), was an effort to integrate the panorama of Latin American international politics within a systemic analytic framework. This relatively brief, well-organized study was approached within the realist paradigm, and thus by design was primarily concerned with interstate power relationships and only peripherally with foreign policy analysis and transnational processes. Bailey posited a "quasi-anarchic" international system governed by a hierarchical global and regional balance of power structure made up of state actors designated, depending on their capabilities, as "paramounts," "clients," or "floaters." G. Pope Atkins, *Latin America and the Caribbean in the International System* (4 eds., 1977–1998), is a comprehensive effort concerned with overall Latin American international relations in overtly systemic terms, viewing the Latin American and Caribbean region as a separate subsystem with its own characteristics within the global system. The conceptual framework moved over the years from a qualified realist framework in the first edition to adoption of the pluralist concept of a combined interstate-transnational system (indicated by the change of title in the 1998 fourth edition from the original *Latin America in the International Political System*). The book includes analysis of the characteristics and evolution of the Latin American–Caribbean subsystem, policies of regional and extraregional state actors, interstate institutions, transnational actors, and the political, economic, military, social, and cultural relations among them. Peter Calvert, *The International Politics of Latin America* (1994), also contributes a broad-ranging analysis. Employing a political system framework, he addresses the nature of the state actors, the physical, economic, and intellectual environments in which they function, the formal Inter-American System of intergovernmental organizations, and Latin American relations with the rest of the external world. Calvert says the analysis is written from a neorealist perspective, which, unlike traditional realism emphasizing power politics in a state-centric system, incorporates "functionalist, structuralist, and pluralist perspectives" and the concept of globalization. Important works by two leading Latin American scholars emphasize a broad range of phenomena in the international system and Latin America's position in it: Gustavo Lagos Matus, ed., *Las relaciones entre América Latina, Estados Unidos y Europa Occidental* (1979); and Luciano Tomassini, ed., *Las relaciones internacionales de América Latina* (1981).

International Political Economy

Works on Latin America's international political economy that appeared in the nineteenth century leaned toward particular rather than general inquiries. Studies published over the past three decades, part of the revival of international political economy as a subfield of international relations, have tended to deal with specific themes and occurrences (some are recorded below). Among the more general appraisals are the following: Sistema Económico Latinoamericano (SELA), *Relaciones económicas internacionales de América Latina* (1987), issued by an important Latin

American interstate intergovernmental organization, asserts that although interdependence is the essential characteristic of the international system, bilateralism and concentration of world power and wealth persists. It analyzes the evolution of Latin American development within the world economy and the region's external and intraregional relations, and evaluates Latin American and Caribbean cooperation and integration as ways to redress the economic balance more in the region's favor. SELA followed with *La economía mundial y el desarrollo de América Latina y el Caribe* (1988), which analyzed aspects of the world economy that had major importance for the Latin American states: international commerce, foreign finance and investment, debt capitalization, new technology, and intellectual property. The study identified alternative scenarios of concerted joint regional action.

Colin Lewis, *Latin America in the World Economy* (1990), identifies and analyzes three principal sequences over the past century: Latin America's expansion from 1880 to 1920 into global commerce and finance and its economic and social consequences; the economic and political unrest through the 1960s and the search for alternative guiding principles; and the region's subsequent reintegration into the international economic system. See also the earlier collection of essays in Christopher Abel and Colin M. Lewis, eds., *Latin America, Economic Imperialism and the State: The Political Economy of the External Connection from Independence to the Present* (1985). A comprehensive, exemplary international economic history, Victor Bulmer-Thomas, *The Economic History of Latin America Since Independence* (1994), traces Latin American economic development from the end of the colonial era to the mid-1980s. The author analyzes the various Latin American economic sectors and development strategies in terms of the changing world economy and diverse national economies: nineteenth-century export-led growth, import-substation industrialization beginning in the 1930s, debt-led growth in the 1980s, and a return to export-led growth as of the late 1980s. Roberto Patricio Korzeniewicz and William C. Smith, eds., *Latin America in the World Economy* (1996), provides broad, sophisticated analyses from contemporary perspectives. Noted experts contributing to Laura Randall, ed., *The Political Economy of Latin America in the Postwar Period* (1997), cast the analysis in the context of long-standing and increasing interdependence of the Latin American and

U.S. economies. They evaluate post–World War II import substitution policies that led to increased deficits, inflation, and debt and survey the measures taken from the late 1980s to increase trade and investment. Jeffrey A. Frieden, Manuel Pastor Jr., and Michael Tomz, eds., *Modern Political Economy and Latin America: Theory and Policy* (2000), is a useful book of readings, with explanatory introductory and concluding chapters and brief introductions to each section. They highlight numerous contributions to the ongoing international political-economic debates in Latin America. Werner Baer and Donald V. Coes, eds., *United States Policies and the Latin American Economies* (1990), is a study in political economy to include international impacts on societal, regime, environmental, and other matters. Ten well-known U.S. and Latin American economists discuss the debt crisis and relationship to trade and growth, privatization and the state sector, public enterprises in Argentina and Brazil, labor sector, debt servicing, and prospects for economic integration.

THEORIES OF GENERAL APPLICATION

A considerable theoretical literature of general scope has been produced with direct reference to Latin America and the Caribbean. After presenting general treatments of these matters, four specific theories are addressed: Marxism-Leninism, structural dependency theory, neo-Marxist dependency theory, and world-system theory (see Chapter 1 for further discussion). Other theories and modes of foreign policy analysis identified in Chapter 1 are not taken up here but are referred to in the following chapters, to identify the approaches taken by specific authors or certain categories of works.

Marxism-Leninism

Karl Marx had little to say about Latin America, beyond a brief tract on Mexico.[3] After the establishment of the Soviet Union in 1917, Marxist-Leninist theorists were skeptical about the position of Latin America in their strategy for world revolution. They perceived the region as an atypical case of class struggle and proletarian revolution (see Chapter 1).

Post–World War II analyses, however, regularly included Latin America in Soviet studies. Although a significant portion of these writers tended toward polemics, simple ideologizing, or propaganda, serious interpretive efforts were also published. A noteworthy book is by three prominent Soviet analysts of Latin American affairs: Anatolii N. Glinkin, Boris F. Martynov, and Petr P. Yakovlev, *U.S. Policy in Latin America: Postwar to Present* (1989—a translation of a 1984 Spanish edition). The authors address inter-American relations from their perspective of a post–World War II world revolutionary process continuing from that begun by the Russian Revolution in 1917. They see U.S. regional policies, pursued in league with U.S. multinational corporations, as hegemonic and militarily aggressive, with periods of benign policies merely disguising imperialism. When Glinkin headed the Institute of Latin American Studies in the USSR Academy of Sciences, he published *Inter-American Relations from Bolívar to the Present* (1990). Applying anti-imperialist assumptions to the evolution of U.S.–Latin American relations from the 1820s into the 1980s, Glinkin devotes special attention to the struggle of progressive Latin American forces for independent foreign policies in regional and global affairs. Another Soviet writer, Ninaida Ivanova Romanova, *La expansión económica de Estados Unidos en América Latina* (1965), develops the specific theme of U.S economic imperialism in the region, with analyses of private investments, capital exports, commercial expansion, and Latin American economic integration. Abraham Guillén, *El imperialismo del dólar: América Latina, revolución o alienación* (1962), is a lengthy interpretation of U.S. imperialism in the Marxist-Leninist tradition by a well-known Latin American intellectual. Vivian Trias, *Historia del imperialismo norteamericano* (3 vols., 1975–1977), presents a comprehensive Marxist analysis of U.S. relations with Latin America.

Structural Economic Dependency

A form of international political economy, structural dependency theory was introduced by Latin American economists in the immediate post–World War II period. The theory was an explanation of the international economic structure and the Latin American position in it, with the explicit intent to serve as the basis for reformist policy actions on the part of

Latin American governments. It was partly a reaction to what structuralists saw as the ethnocentrism of theories of development and the paternalistic policies of outside states designed to "modernize" Latin American nations (see Chapter 1). It was also a dissent from orthodox monetarist policies, which structuralists thought a misguided prescription for the control of inflation and basis for economic growth (see Chapter 8). Structuralism was often at the center of debates about Latin American economic development, and had widespread influence on Latin American government policies until it fell out of favor. In the 1980s and 1990s, Latin Americans largely abandoned structuralism and the attendant policies as redemocratization was widely accompanied by economic neoliberalism.

Raúl Prebisch of Argentina founded the structural dependency school of theory. Prebisch was an economist and international official with considerable academic and government experience. In addition to holding several university posts over the years, he was (among other things) founder and first director of the Argentine Central Bank, executive secretary of the United Nations Economic Commission for Latin America (ECLA), and secretary general of the United Nations Commission for Trade and Development (UNCTAD). His theories served as the basis for ECLA's reformist approach and for UNCTAD's strategies at the center of the New International Economic Order movement. Among Prebisch's many works, *Capitalismo periférico: crisis y transformación* (1981), a collection of previously published articles, in particular explicates the international economic construct. Prebisch saw the world economy dominated by industrialized states at the center of the system and underdeveloped ones in a dependent position on the periphery. This center-periphery structure perpetuated underdevelopment of the nonindustrialized economies. Prebisch prescribed, as the way for Latin American governments to escape the dependency structure, numerous domestic economic, political, and social reforms, import substitution industrialization policies, intra–Latin American economic integration, and participation in commodities agreements of producers of raw materials around the world. His ideas had first gained widespread policy attention when the United Nations published *The Economic Development of Latin America and its Principal Problems* (1950; the Spanish version had appeared the previous year). It was known as the "ECLA Manifesto" during the initial

stages of the formation of Latin American economic integration organizations. From Prebisch's subsequent voluminous publications, the following
are indicative of his theoretical and policy thinking. *Nueva política comercial para el desarrollo* (1964) is the 148-page text of his statement at the
United Nations Conference on Trade and Development (UNCTAD). *Towards a Dynamic Development Policy for Latin America* (1963) was also
published by the United Nations. *Change and Development: Latin America's Great Task* (1971) is a report to the Inter-American Development
Bank that updated his prior assessments made over many years.

Prebisch gathered at ECLA a group of prominent development economists who made their own contributions within the structural dependency framework, among them the following: Mexican Víctor L.
Urquidi, *Free Trade and Economic Integration in Latin America* (1962),
and *The Challenge of Development in Latin America* (1964); Brazilian
Celso Furtado, *Development and Underdevelopment* (1964), *Obstacles to
Development in Latin America* (1970), and *Economic Development of Latin
America: Historical Background and Contemporary Problems* (2 eds., 1970,
1976); Peruvian Aníbal Pinto, *Hacia nuestra independencia económia*
(1953); Argentine Aldo Ferrer, *Economía internacional contemporánáo:
rexto para latinoamericanos* (1976); and Chilean Osvaldo Sunkel, *El subdesarrollo latinoamericano y la tería del desallollo* (1970; with the collaboration of Pedro Paz). In 1993 Sunkel edited a set of essays offering an updated version of structuralism as an alternative to neoliberalism:
*Development from Within: Toward a Neostructuralist Approach for Latin
America* (1993). See Chapter 8 for further commentary on structuralism
as theory in practice.

Neo-Marxist Dependency Theory.   Dependency theorists writing in
the Marxist tradition embraced structuralism's idea of a core-periphery
structure of the international economic system. But they expanded the
sociopolitical elements beyond structuralist limits and rejected reformist
public policies in favor of socialist revolution. They were neo-Marxist in
the sense that they assumed Latin America's domestic and international
problems to be a function of the international capitalist system, dominated by the United States–led capitalist states and multinational corporations, and in which Latin American states had little recourse.

Neo-Marxist dependency theory thrived particularly in the 1960s. Andre Gunder Frank, a highly militant pioneer neo-Marxist dependency theorist, was the first to extend structuralist theory to include sociopolitical outcomes. His principal works with direct reference to Latin America are *Capitalism and Underdevelopment in Latin America: Historical Studies of Chile and Brazil* (1967), *Latin America: Underdevelopment or Revolution; Essays on the Development of Underdevelopment and the Immediate Enemy* (1969), and *Lumpenbourgeoise-Lumpendevelopment: Dependence, Class, and Politics in Latin America* (1972). Frank argues that the bourgeoisie associated with international sectors of dependent economies are powerful because they control the most dynamic industries in the economy in league with international capital. The large lower classes live in extreme poverty with no political power. The internationalized bourgeoisie view authoritarian rule as necessary to repress dissent.

Probably the most influential single work on the subject, and one of the most subtly expressed, was by Fernando Henrique Cardoso and Enzo Faletto, *Dependency and Development in Latin America*. The book appeared in Spanish in 1969 but was not translated into English until 1979. The sophisticated analysis distinguishes dependent societies and economies from those where a viable domestic market exists, the former conforming along the lines that Frank asserted, but the latter amenable to authoritarian populism (as in Argentina and Brazil) until economic crisis allows reintroduction of more traditional authoritarian control. In two significant works by Theotonio Dos Santos—*Dependencia económica y cambio revolucionario en América Latina* (1970), and *La crisis norteamericana y América Latina* (1972)—the author expressed considerable skepticism about reform and stressed the need for socialist revolutions. But their success depended on a favorable balance of revolutionary and reactionary forces in individual Latin American societies.

In the United States, a number of young neo-Marxist dependency theorists were productive. James Petras was among the most prolific and articulate. His *Politics and Social Structure in Latin America* (1970) established him as a forceful analyst. The book is a somewhat randomly organized collection of his and coauthored papers, previously published articles, and fragments. He discusses Latin American political movements and social classes and U.S. policy and sharply criticizes many of his academic colleagues in the United States. Petras had earlier joined with Maurice Zeitlin. *Latin America: Reform or Revolution?* (1968) is a compilation of twenty-three papers by U.S. and Latin American writers. The collection indicates the variety of convictions, assumptions, prescriptions, and quality of analysis of the radical dependency school. The underlying theme is the contradiction between U.S. capitalist interests and the development of just and equitable Latin American economic, political, and social systems. Petras later edited *Latin America: From Dependence to Revolution* (1973), a collection of eight articles in which he figures prominently as author and coauthor. They deal with Chile, Brazil, and Argentina, alternative developmental models for Latin America, and U.S. actions in the region.

James D. Cockcroft, Andre Gunder Frank, and Dale L. Johnson, *Dependence and Underdevelopment: Latin America's Political Economy* (1972), present, in terms of the title's concepts, their ideas about class and politics and of social science and strategies of development. They, too, are highly critical of the existing academic scene. Ronald H. Chilcote and Joel Edelstein, eds., *Latin America: The Struggle with Dependency and Beyond* (1974), is a lengthy collection of papers by leading theorists, designed to indicate alternative perspectives of development and underdevelopment in the region. Among them are Susanne Jonas writing on Guatemala; James Cockcroft on Mexico; Juan E. Corradi on Argentina, Theotonio Dos Santos on Brazil, James Petras and Marcelo Cararozzi on Chile, and Donald Bray and Timothy Harding on Cuba. A. Szymanski, *The Logic of Imperialism* (1981), addresses Latin American foreign-policy making as closely interrelated with economic dependence, reflected in orientations of promoting the interests of the domestic bourgeoisie.

Reiterations of the theory persisted after its general decline. Frank Niess, *A Hemisphere to Itself: A History of U.S.–Latin American Relations* (1990), essentially repeated well-known dependency positions about U.S. exploitation of Latin America. He neither replies to objections to the theory nor adequately confronts recent phenomena in his explanations. The bibliographic essay on dependency literature is a very good survey. Sandor Halebsky and Richard L. Harris, eds., *Capital, Power and Inequality in Latin America* (1995), is a defense of old socialist dependency theory as the solution to Latin America's social and economic injustice. Robert A.

Packenham, *The Dependency Movement: Scholarship and Politics in Development Studies* (1992), in an extensively documented study, says, and laments, that Marxist dependency theory remains alive in the U.S. academic community primarily in the way it has politicized the social sciences in the long term.

In time, neo-Marxist theory was disavowed by a number of its leading creators and advocates. Fernando Henrique Cardoso himself, the most influential among Latin American theorists, after becoming president of Brazil in January 1995 adopted neoliberal economic policies to which he had subscribed some time before. In the meantime, Andre Gunder Frank had abandoned dependency theory and become a prominent advocate of world-system theory.

World-System Theory.   Employing its own neo-Marxist frame of reference, world-system theory gained notice in the 1970s and continued to develop thereafter. Immanuel Wallerstein, a sociologist and Africanist, was the most prominent theorist; his pioneer work is *The Modern World System* (3 vols., 1974–1989). His comprehensive framework of world history fundamentally revised and expanded neo-Marxist dependency theory. Wallerstein was joined by certain other dissatisfied dependency theorists, both structuralists and neo-Marxists, and by a new generation of adherents.

Wallerstein and his colleagues defined the world-system as the global capitalist order that had developed after about 1500 and eventually embraced the entire world, and which was characterized by the Marxian concept of historical materialism. The world-system and the Americas (with Latin America emerging as a separate region) were simultaneously born in the sixteenth century as "geosocial constructs." The European discovery and colonization of the Americas were the "constitutive act" of the world-system; after the sixteenth century, they were the prime testing ground for labor control methods and the model for the entire evolving world-system. For the first three centuries, all of the Americas were subordinated as formal colonies to a few European states. Then the United States moved from peripheral to semiperipheral to core status and after World War II to world-system hegemony. Latin America remained on the periphery.[4]

Andre Gunder Frank contributed *World Accumulation, 1492–1789* (1978), a general statement that did not focus on Latin America but included it as a prominent and critical part of the world-system. Frank is among those revisionist world-system theorists who argue that all of the elements associated with the current 500-year-old world system had their counterparts as long as 5,000 years ago (some revisionists claim as much as 8,000 years). As a contributor to Andre Gunder Frank and Barry Gills, eds., *The World System: Five Hundred or Five Thousand Years?* (1996), Wallerstein maintains that fragmented ancient and medieval relationships hardly made up a world-system; thus the Americas were not merely assimilated into a preexisting capital-accumulating economy—which, in fact, would not have developed without the Americas.

General Commentary

For good descriptions, explanations, and critiques of the above theories and related concepts in the Latin American context, see the following studies: Ronald H. Chilcote and Joel C. Edelstein, *Latin America: Capitalist and Socialist Perspectives on Development and Underdevelopment* (1986); Heraldo Muñoz, ed., *From Dependency to Development* (1981); James L. Dietz and James H. Street, eds., *Latin America's Economic Development: Institutionalist and Structuralist Perspectives* (1987); Julio Cole Harold, *Latin American Inflation: Theoretical Interpretations and Empirical Results* (1987); Heinz Rudolf Sonntag, *Duda/certeza, crisis: la evolución de las ciencias sociales de América Latina* (1988); Cristóbal Kay, *Latin American Theories of Development and Underdevelopment* (1989); James L. Dietz and Dilmus D. James, eds., *Progress toward Development in Latin America: From Prebisch to Technological Autonomy* (1990); Patricio Meller, ed., *The Latin American Development Debate: Neostructuralism, Neomonetarism, and Adjustment Processes* (1991); and James W. Parker, *Latin American Underdevelopment: A History of Perspectives in the United States, 1877–1965* (1995).

A widely read book by preeminent Latin American theorist Brazilian Hélio Jaguaribe, *Economic and Political Development: A General Theory and a Latin American Case Study* (1973), offered another alternative to developmentalism. After a thorough review and critique of extant models of development, Jaguaribe carefully constructs one that adheres to a realistic "historico-social process" under the sponsorship of state authority.

COLONIES AND DEPENDENCIES

Among the requirements for a general understanding of the international relations of Latin America and the Caribbean is a comprehension of the region's colonial subordination to European powers, from the late fifteenth to the early nineteenth centuries, and with the colonial vestiges remaining to the present day. Thus our review of the literature includes the Latin American colonial era from 1492 until 1824 and the elements that continued thereafter. The literature dealing with post-1824 developments, including today's situations, is included in this section so as to make a coherent sequential presentation of the theme of regional colonies and dependencies. The early nineteenth-century movements for independence are taken up in Chapter 7.

What came to be known as Latin America was initially part of the European imperial systems extended to the Americas. The process began with Christopher Columbus' voyages of discovery, sponsored by the Spanish Crown. The vast portion of the region was in the Spanish and Portuguese domains, with France, Britain, and the Netherlands challenging them. Up to the beginning of the successful Spanish American and Brazilian movements for independence in the first quarter of the nineteenth century, the Spanish and Portuguese empires were largely intact. The exception was the relatively small but not insignificant British, French, Netherlands, and Danish West Indies. Most of Spanish America achieved its independence from Spain between 1810 and 1824, and Brazil separated from Portugal in 1822. The first Latin American state to gain independence was Haiti in 1804, after an African slave revolt against France. Cuba separated from Spain in 1898 as a result of the United States' military defeat of Spain, but was not technically independent until the end of U.S. military occupation in 1902. The United States became an imperial power in the Caribbean, absorbing Puerto Rico and part of the Virgin Islands under its sovereignty. Various British, French, and Dutch arrangements have been made, most profoundly since World War II. Twelve former British colonies gained their independence between

1962 and 1984, which they have designated Commonwealth Caribbean Countries (to include the remaining British Caribbean dependencies). Suriname, a former colony of the Netherlands, became independent in 1975. The British Falklands colony in the South Atlantic was established in 1833, over Argentine protests; Argentina has continued to claim the territory, which it calls the Islas Malvinas, to the present day (the Falklands/Malvinas problem is treated in Chapter 7). It may be noted that the Dominican Republic became independent of Spain in 1822 but was occupied by Haiti and did not regain its independence until 1844. Panama, a province of Colombia, seceded in 1903, with U.S. assistance, to become formally independent.

General Works

Two compendiums are thorough and authoritative general sources. Silvio Zavala, *Programa de historia de América en la época colonial* (2 vols., 1961), is a narrative history of the more than three-century period of European colonialism in the New World. The work is a product of a lengthy project on the history of the western hemisphere sponsored by the Pan American Institute of Geography and History. A one-volume abridgment in English, prepared by Max Sevelle, was also issued: *The Colonial Period in the History of the New World* (1961). Zavala compares and contrasts Spanish, Portuguese, British, French, Dutch, and other colonial efforts; and assesses their respective principal characteristics, accomplishments, and problems. Leslie Bethel, ed., *Colonial Latin America* (2 vols., 1984), part of *The Cambridge History of Latin America* series, contains expert contributions that address a wide range of key elements of the three-century Hispanic and Luso-American colonial history. They cover the conquest and early settlement; imperial political, economic, and social systems; and cultural and intellectual life. Selections of chapters are brought together to provide continuous histories of the two principal empires in *Colonial Spanish America* (1987) and *Colonial Brazil* (1987).

On a more concise scale, Mark A. Burkholder and Lyman L. Johnson, *Colonial Latin America* (3 eds., 1990–1997), is a thorough textbook and good guide to the secondary literature. Stanley J. Stein and Barbara H. Stein, *The Colonial Heritage of Latin America: Essays on Economic Develop-

ment in Perspective (1970) is a set of essays astutely analyzing, in economic and social terms, "those features of Latin America's colonial origins and development and their projection into the nineteenth century." In sum, Spanish America and Brazil's "sustained backwardness" of dependence and underdevelopment relative to the North Atlantic world was "the principle heritage of three centuries of subordination to Spain and Portugal." A recent treatment of this general subject, from a variety of perspectives, is Jeremy Adelman, ed., *Colonial Legacies: The Problem of Persistence* (1999). Arthur P. Whitaker and others, *Latin America and the Enlightenment* (2 eds., 1942, 1961), contains six learned essays on the impact of the intellectual movement (especially the French elements) on Latin America, as well as the uneasy relationship of Spain with the Enlightenment. Harry Bernstein, *Origins of Inter-American Interest, 1700–1812* (1945), investigates a subject that otherwise has received little attention. He cogently summarizes "the contest for the New World" in terms of colonial Anglo-American and Spanish-American commercial, cultural, and political ties.

The Spanish–American Empire

Spain was the first and principal conqueror, colonizer, and developer of Latin America. A rich literature has addressed Spain's unprecedented problem of governing its vast empire, the Spanish imperial achievement, and the political, economic, and societal consequences (for good and ill) of Spanish rule. Only the more notable general items are included here; a few works on more specific topics are taken up elsewhere.

Among the earlier general works are four volumes by Bernard Moses. They are basic general treatments addressed to students and general readers that collectively contain a great deal of information. The first of them, *The Establishment of Spanish Rule in America* (1898), is an overall treatment of the Spanish-American colonial era that deals with the establishment of Spanish rule and the organizational and functional features of the political, economic, ecclesiastical, and military institutions that followed. This book was an influential one in the public debate over the hostile relations between Spain and the United States at the time. The other three books extend the narrative with reference to the southern continental portion of the empire. *The Spanish Dependencies in South America* (2 vols. 1914) analyzes the slow development of dependent South American societies and political entities during the middle period of Spanish rule in South America (from 1550 to 1730), and the increasing resentment of the creole and mestizo classes with Spanish restrictions placed on them. *South America on the Eve of Emancipation: The Southern Spanish Colonies in the Last Half-Century of their Dependence* (1908) deals with the societal and political characteristics during last part of the eighteenth into the early nineteenth centuries, the last half-century of Spanish control. *Spain's Declining Power in South America, 1730–1806* (1919) considers the complex elements that ultimately led to Spain's loss of almost all of its American empire.

Two classic works by leading U.S. historians are essential. Clarence H. Haring, *The Spanish Empire in America* (1947), is a broad-ranging institutional history, from 1492 to the Wars of Independence, focusing on the royal colonial government and commercial and inter-societal relations. J. H. Parry, *The Spanish Seaborne Empire* (1966), investigates the importance to Spain of oceanic trade in the conquest and then as it established and developed the overseas empire in the Americas and the Philippines. Within this theme, Parry deals objectively with the colonists' complex relations with Spain, problems of governance, and the challenges from other European powers. Also necessary is the immense, authoritative, multiauthored work compiled by eminent Spanish historian Jaime Vicens Vives, *Historia social y económica de España y América* (5 vols. 1957–1959). It was reissued as a second edition in 1971, with the new title *Historia de España y América*, but only the first volume was revised. The first four volumes are on the colonial period through the independence movements, and the fifth treats the nineteenth and twentieth centuries. Charles Gibson, *Spain in America* (1966), is an excellent summary account, from the conquest to establishment of the colonies and subsequent imperial adjustments. It deals with the institutions of the *encomienda* (the right to control Indian labor), church, and state; the relationship of Spaniards and Indians; and the borderlands. For a complete survey, see the volume edited by Victor Bulmer-Thomas, *Colonial Spanish America* (1987). University of Barcelona professor Xavier Rubert de Ventos, *The Hispanic Labyrinth: Spain's Encounter with Latin America*

(1990), offers a brilliant interpretive critique. A major element is a comparison of the colonial backgrounds and consequences of Spanish America and the United States, highlighting the indigenous populations, political organization and processes, legal systems, and religions.

Dealing with the early development of the empire, the noted Spanish intellectual and diplomat, Salvador de Madariaga, *The Rise of the Spanish American Empire* (1947), is a brilliant, idiosyncratic commentary on Spanish colonial rule in the Americas, criticizing its ruthless elements and complimenting its remarkable achievements. John Lynch, in *Spanish Colonial Administration, 1782–1810: The Intendant System in the Viceroyalty of the Rio de la Plata* (1958), deals with the latter years of the empire as the colonists themselves increased their revolutionary sentiments. Colin M. MacLachlan, *Spain's Empire in the New World: The Role of Ideas in Institutional and Social Change* (1988), discusses, among other things, Spain's imperial decision making and the bases for official appointments to colonial positions, with a particular focus on the eighteenth century. A remarkable scholarly book, Lothar Knauth, *Confrontación transpacífica: el Japón y el nuevo mundo hispánico, 1542–1639* (1972), analyzes Spain's unsuccessful attempt to at least partially Christianize Japan to counter Protestant activities in Asia, with Mexico forming an essential connection in the Spanish-Japanese encounter.

Portuguese Brazil

Deferring interest in America because of its prior extensive activities in Africa and Asia, Portugal in 1522 finally colonized Brazil. Like Spain, Portugal implanted its political, social, and economic system in the Americas, but with less strict control and different world perspectives and ambitions. For a complete survey, see the volume edited by Victor Bulmer-Thomas, *Colonial Brazil* (1987). Important works deal with specific time periods. Bailey W. Diffie, *A History of Colonial Brazil, 1500–1792* (1987), edited by Edwin J. Perkins for posthumous publication, is a thorough chronological treatment covering the important colonial internal and external elements. The dedicated editor, noting a serious problem of deciphering the author's notes on documentation, wisely decided nevertheless to publish this informative book. Kenneth R. Maxwell, *Conflicts and Conspiracies: Brazil and Portugal, 1750–1808* (1973), carefully researched archives in Brazil, Portugal, and Britain to produce an important study of Portugal's diplomatic attempts to block British commercial intrusion into Brazil without alienating Portugal's otherwise close relationship with Britain. The ironic outcome was to estrange Brazilian nationalists and push them closer to Britain. Charles R. Boxer, *The Dutch in Brazil, 1624–1654* (1957), a highly detailed and documented chronicle written by a professor of Portuguese at the University of London, centers on the expedition organized by the Dutch West India Company that for a time controlled most of northeastern Brazil.

The Circum-Caribbean

Caribbean colonialism has had special characteristics. A multiplicity of outside powers has asserted control over numerous entities, and dependent territories continue to the present, although in revised form and on a much reduced scale.

General Treatments.   In addition to attention in works cited in the "General Works" above, studies have been devoted to the subregion. J. H. Parry, P. M. Sherlock, and Anthony P. Maingot, *A Short History of the West Indies* (4 eds., 1956–1987), is a prominent introductory survey from European discovery to the mid-1980s. It devotes most attention (seventeen of twenty-one chapters) to colonial matters of governance, commerce, and war, primarily on the part of Spain, Britain, France, and the United States. Arthur P. Newton, *The European Nations in the West Indies, 1493–1688* (1933), is a good general history, with discussions of discovery, conquest, colonization, the slave trade, privateering, international rivalry, diplomacy, trade, and war. A. Curtis Wilgus, ed., *The Caribbean: British, Dutch, French, United States* (1958), is a collection of papers presented at the eighth annual Caribbean conference sponsored by the School of Inter-American Studies at the University of Florida, with the virtue of broad coverage of the dependent Caribbean entities and of the contributors' multinational perspectives. Eugene Revert, *Les Antilles* (1954), a survey of the entire area from a French perspective, considers the possibilities at the time for some sort of integration. Harold Mitchell,

Europe in the Caribbean (1963), is a broad treatment of European dependencies to the eve of independence and other self-governing arrangements. Annette Baker Fox, *Freedom and Welfare in the Caribbean: A Colonial Dilemma* (1949), is an early study by an international relations scholar who applies her skills to an analysis of the new ideas and dynamic political forces regarding the Caribbean dependencies. Another useful collection of essays is edited by Emanuel De Kadt, *Patterns of Foreign Influence in the Caribbean* (1972), in which nine participants at a Chatham House seminar expound geopolitical and international power considerations as background for studies on Jamaica, Guyana, the French Antilles, the Dutch Caribbean, Cuba, Guatemala, and U.S. policies. The emphasis is on foreign influences in local politics, economics, and societies. With reference to the British and U.S. territories, Mary Proudfoot, *Britain and the United States in the Caribbean: A Comparative Study in Methods of Development* (1954), is a data-rich study. It examines constitutional and economic relationships between the dependencies and the metropolitan states, political and social structures and processes, emigration, possibilities for federation of the British West Indies, and alternatives for Puerto Rico and the American Virgin Islands. Robert L. Paquette and Stanley L. Engerman, eds., *The Lesser Antilles in the Age of European Expansion* (1996), assesses the Lesser Antilles from time of discovery to the abolition of slavery, showing how they provided a base for expanding the slave-labor plantation system to other parts of the Americas. Richard Pares, *War and Trade in the West Indies, 1739–1763* (1936), is a detailed study of the complex period of war in the struggle for this portion of Spanish America by Great Britain, France, and the Netherlands.

Some formal intergovernmental organizations of Caribbean dependencies are of interest. Herbert Corkran, *Patterns of International Cooperation in the Caribbean, 1942–1969* (1972), describes four agencies as each evolved into a successor. The United Kingdom and the United States established the Anglo-American Caribbean Commission in 1942 to implement wartime measures in their Caribbean dependencies. It was reconstituted in 1946 as the Caribbean Commission to include France and the Netherlands. The Caribbean Council was organized in 1961 to include participation by the dependencies themselves (with the exception of the French overseas departments). The fourth iteration in 1965, the

Caribbean Economic Development Corporation, was actually under Puerto Rican leadership; it was dissolved in 1968. See also Bernard L. Poole, *The Caribbean Commission* (1951), which focuses on the commission's measures to deal with the serious economic and social problems in the Caribbean dependencies.

Puerto Rico.   A particularly large literature has accumulated on Puerto Rico. Until 1898, Spain administered the island as part of the Cuban colony, after which it fell under U.S. sovereignty. An excellent survey is Raymond Carr, *Puerto Rico: A Colonial Experiment* (1984), an objective, comprehensive analysis of Puerto Rico's relations with both Spain and the United States as imperial masters. It analyzes the constantly troubled relationships, from the beginnings of the Spanish Crown Colony to present Commonwealth status as a quasi-colonial possession of the United States (including political and social change). One of the most important early works was Salvador Brau, *Historia de Puerto Rico* (1904), a narrative history of Spanish colonial Puerto Rico from 1493 until its acquisition by the United States in 1898. The author, a poet, dramatist, journalist, and historian in the tradition of favoring some level of Puerto Rican autonomy, sought to rectify what he saw as numerous errors in the popular view of the history of his native country. He examined documents in the Archivo General de Indias in Spain, on which he based treatments of Spanish administration and defense, African slavery, corsairs and filibusterers, Dutch invasion, commerce, society, and other internal and external elements. Lidio Cruz Monclova, *Historia de Puerto Rico, siglo XIX* (3 vols.; 3 eds., 1952–1971), is a monumental work of scholarship for the period 1808–1898.

Leo Stanton Rowe, *The United States and Porto Rico* (1903), is an example of turn-of-the-century thinking about the political-cultural relationship (then a common theme in the writing on Latin America, as was the misspelling of "Puerto"). The author, at the time a professor of political science at the University of Pennsylvania, wrote the book while a member of the U.S. commission to rewrite the laws of Puerto Rico; he was later director of the Pan American Union (1920–1946). Rowe recognized the "clash of cultures"—the book's long title continues to say: "With Special Reference to the Problems Arising out of our Contact with the Spanish-American Civilization." In fact, he largely restricts the matter to competing perceptions of the nature of civil government.

One of the most significant studies is by long-time University of Puerto Rico political sociologist, Gordon K. Lewis, *Puerto Rico: Freedom and Power in the Caribbean* (1963). Polemical and without pretense of objectivity, the impressive scholarship on the island's social history is guided by Lewis' humane convictions and loosely Fabian socialist ideology. Lewis said that U.S. imperialism had been complex, changing, and not oppressive in the European imperial sense and in certain ways beneficial; yet its enduring character was a "distorting influence upon the local life." In contrast to Lewis, Henry Wells, *The Modernization of Puerto Rico* (1969), is understanding of U.S. endeavors to recast Puerto Rican political culture and society. The book is a systematic theory-based analysis, taking a broad view of the "Americanization process" and paying particular attention to the creation of the Commonwealth system. Another excellent work of broad scope dealing with the political-cultural equation is Arturo Morales Carrión, *Puerto Rico: A Political and Cultural History* (1983). Also in this realm is Nancy Morris, *Puerto Rico: Culture, Politics, and Identity* (1995). Effectively using survey research and interviews, she investigates the "elusive but pervasive" concept of national identity in the Puerto Rican context, with the U.S. presence looming large in the analysis.

Puerto Ricans generally did not see themselves as simply a Spanish administrative appendage of Cuba, and since 1898 they have debated the status of Puerto Rico as a dependency of the United States. The idea of national independence hesitantly emerged during Spanish rule, then reemerged during U.S. control but has not been realized. U.S.–Puerto Rican relations have revolved to a considerable extent around the "status question"—what is the appropriate political arrangement for the islanders: to continue as a Commonwealth within the U.S. system, to become a State in the Union, or to separate from the United States with sovereign independence?

Roberta Ann Johnson, *Puerto Rico: Commonwealth or Colony?* (1980), is a sympathetic and scholarly work on Puerto Rico as a submissive Spanish colony, when the rest of Spanish America was determinedly gaining its independence, and under U.S. rule, during which "building a mass movement for independence" was "almost an impossible task." Ronald Fernández, *The Disenchanted Island: Puerto Rico and the United States in the Twentieth Century* (1992), analyzes Puerto Ricans' aspirations since 1898, with particular attention to the independence movement. Edgardo Meléndez, *Puerto Rico's Statehood Movement* (1988), a professor at the University of Puerto Rico, offers a political history that traces and analyzes the movement in detail. It begins with "annexationism" in the nineteenth century and emphasizes political party organizations. José Trias Monge, *Puerto Rico: The Trials of the Oldest Colony in the World* (1997), is a thoughtful presentation by one of the implementers of the Commonwealth system. The author, chief legal adviser to Governor Luis Muñoz Marín (the central figure in the creation of the Commonwealth arrangement) and later Chief Justice of Puerto Rico (1974–85), briefly summarizes Spanish rule and then deals with the U.S. annexation and subsequent changing relationship. He emphasizes the status problem into the latter 1990s.

Other works deal with the status question in more specific contexts. Maria del Pilar Arguelles, *Morality and Power: The U.S. Colonial Experience in Puerto Rico from 1898–1948* (1995), sees hypocrisy in the United States ruling as a colonial power while avowing dedication in general to national self-determination and democratic rule. Alfredo Montalvo-Barbot, *Political Conflict and Constitutional Change in Puerto Rico, 1898–1952* (1997), views the conflict in terms of the competing perspectives of "political gradualism" and "classical colonialism." Pedro A. Cabán, *Constructing a Colonial People: Puerto Rico and the United States, 1898–1932* (1999), interprets how the United States attempted to "Americanize" Puerto Rico as an asset in its Caribbean imperial designs. Instead, it inspired a nationalist reaction and enduring cleavages among Puerto Ricans themselves. Truman R. Clark, *Puerto Rico and the United States, 1917–1933* (1975), is a fairly brief and solid history of a time period that has received relatively little attention, with sympathy for the dilemmas Puerto Ricans face in the status debate. Surendra Bhana, *The United States and the Development of the Puerto Rican Status Question, 1936–1968* (1975), focuses on U.S. policy in a detailed scholarly study of controversy and how to balance economic needs with political and national preferences. Bhana favors a revised commonwealth arrangement.

Some works grapple with the status dilemma along with related evolving problems. Jorge Heine, ed., *Time for Decision: The United States and*

Puerto Rico (1983), brings together eleven contributors to discuss important political and economic issues in the relationship, among them the implications of statehood and the links between Puerto Rican and national U.S. political parties. In Edwin Meléndez and Edgardo Meléndez, eds., *Colonial Dilemma* (1993), eighteen Puerto Rican writers articulate radical perspectives on a broad range of issues and themes involving Puerto Rico's internal life and the relationship with the United States in the 1990s.

The British West Indies.   The British West Indies forms a special category of Caribbean colonialism and dependency. A literature began to build in the nineteenth century, exemplified by British writer C. Salmon, *Caribbean Confederation* (1888) and *Depression in the West Indies* (1884). Frank Wesley Pitman, *The Development of the British West Indies, 1700–1763* (1917), deals with aspects of administration, white labor, the African slave trade, economic structure, and, especially, international trade (including illicit). Hume Wrong, *Government of the West Indies* (1923), is primarily a constitutional history of the British West Indies from the seventeenth century. Alan Burns, *History of the British West Indies* (2 eds., 1954, 1965), is a lengthy introductory history directed at general readers, with a great deal of information collected from secondary sources. Richard Pares, *Yankees and Creoles: The Trade between North America and the West Indies before the American Revolution*, traces the interaction between the British North American and Caribbean colonies during the eighteenth century. Pares includes a great deal of information about the trading companies and individual people involved.

Morley Ayearst, *The British West Indies: The Search for Self-Government* (1960), is a detailed political-legal-institutional history of colonial policies and administration. Beginning with the first settlements, it addresses the evolution of British governance, constitutional and political developments, local government and institutions, and the possibilities of federation. W. L. Burn, *The British West Indies* (1951), summarizes the impact of colonial policy on local British West Indian public institutions, with an emphasis on the recent past and from an essentially sympathetic view of British policies. A far different outlook is presented by Gordon K. Lewis, *The Growth of the Modern West Indies* (1966), which in fact is

THE LATIN AMERICAN AND CARIBBEAN REGION

about British imperialism in the Caribbean. Reflecting a combination of his non-dogmatic socialist convictions and impressive depth of scholarship and data gathering, the book analyzes the emergence of national societies out of British colonialism and pays much attention to the failed West Indies Federation (1958–1962). John Mordecai, *Federation of the West Indies* (1968), gives a detailed account of the ill-fated federation and concludes that those turbulent years left people wary of such efforts, although "the search for common identity continues." David Lowenthal, *The West Indies Federation* (1961), succinctly and cogently explains the factors that caused the federation's dissolution. Elizabeth W. Davies, *The Legal Status of British Territories: The West Indies and North Atlantic Region* (1995), is a thorough legal reference work.

The result of the British post–World War II decolonization process resulted in the independence of twelve states (see Chapter 2) and six entities with the constitutional status of "States in Association with Great Britain." The non-sovereign associated states—Anguilla, Bermuda, the British Virgin Islands, Montserrat, and the Turks and Caicos Islands—are internally self-governing but dependent on Britain for external affairs. The independent states had been associated states during their transition from colony to sovereignty.

The French and Netherlands Antilles.   France and the Netherlands had territorial and other interests in the area. Nellis Maynard Crouse, *The French Struggle for the West Indies, 1665–1713* (1943), chronicles the history of the struggle between France and Britain for supremacy of the West Indies, in which Spain and the Netherlands played minor roles. The result, in the author's view, was a draw. Arvin Murch, *Black Frenchmen: The Political Integration of the French Antilles* (1971), briefly summarizes elements of government, politics, and nationalism in the process of integrating the French Caribbean territories with the metropolis. France has converted its colonies to overseas departments (French Guiana, Guadeloupe, and Martinique), with coequal status with the metropolitan provinces.

Three lengthy companion volumes by Cornelis Ch. Goslinga together fully and authoritatively describe activities of the Netherlands in the circum-Caribbean from 1580–1942: *The Dutch in the Caribbean and on the*

Wild Coast, 1580–1680 (1971), *The Dutch in the Caribbean and in the Guianas, 1680–1791* (1985), and *The Dutch in the Caribbean and in Surinam, 1791/5–1942* (1990). See also Charles R. Boxer, *The Dutch in Brazil, 1624–1654* (1957, cited above). Betty Sedoc-Dahlberg, ed., *The Dutch Caribbean: Prospects for Democracy* (1990), analyzes the Dutch colonial experience and the decolonization process that led to the independence in 1975 of Suriname (formerly Dutch Guiana) and to the incorporation of the Netherlands Antilles and Aruba with coequal commonwealth status in the Kingdom of the Netherlands. It also has chapters on independent Suriname, including its foreign policies.

The Virgin Islands.   Spain had little interest in the Virgin Islands as it expanded Spanish rule throughout the circum-Caribbean. Dutch, French, and English buccaneers used the small island chain at the easternmost extension of the Greater Antilles as bases. France took possession of St. Croix in 1651. English planters took over Tortola in 1666 and the island came under British administration in 1672. Denmark occupied St. Thomas in 1666, claimed St. John in 1684, and purchased St. Croix from France in 1733. The United States purchased the three Danish islands in 1917. To the present day, the Virgin Islands have been divided between Britain and the United States, with forms of administration and dependency changing over the years.

Waldemar Westergaard, *The Danish West Indies under Company Rule (1671–1754)* (1917), is a narrative history, published on the eve of the transfer of the Danish Virgin Islands to the United States. The main part of the book deals with the activities of the Danish West India and Guinea Company (the author surveyed the company archives) during a time when "Sugar was King." Appended is a summary "supplementary chapter" on the years 1755–1917. Charles Callan Tansill, *The Purchase of the Danish West Indies* (1932), the Albert Shaw Lecture on Diplomacy for 1931 at Johns Hopkins University, is the standard, highly detailed narrative history on the subject. Luther Harris Evans, *The Virgin Islands from Naval Base to New Deal* (1945), is a study of U.S. administration of the islands from its acquisition in 1917 until 1935, emphasizing the U.S. Navy's "stewardship" role until 1931 and the subsequent civilian, constitutional, and institutional arrangements. Gordon K. Lewis, *The Virgin Is-*

lands: A Caribbean Lilliput (1972), is a scholarly, thoughtful, and humane book about a tiny territory with complex issues. After summarizing Danish and U.S. rule, Lewis focuses on post-1945 phenomena and presents a great deal of political, economic (notably tourism), social (including racial and demographic), and cultural information. He sees the islanders as having the strongest "dependency complex" in the Caribbean, and chastises the United States (especially the Congress) for the thoughtless nature of colonial administration toward the Virgin Islanders. Edward A. O'Neill, *Rape of the American Virgins* (1972), despite the journalistic title, contains useful descriptive material.

LATIN AMERICAN REGIONAL INTERNATIONAL RELATIONS

Many studies have dealt with specific time periods as the Latin American and Caribbean region and its subregional components have gone through successive periods of international history and stages of subsystem evolution. A large number of works focus on specific time frames in terms of general international phenomena and themes identified above, also from a variety of disciplinary perspectives. Historians, not surprisingly, have dominated the enterprise for the earlier eras. With reference to the post–World War II period, political scientists and economists have also been prominent.

An overall European regional dominance characterized nineteenth century Latin American international relations. The United States had a consistent interest and increasing power with regard to Mexico and the circum-Caribbean. Several of the general histories cited above provide information on this period. Certain thematic works are also of interest. Manuel Medina Castro, *Estados Unidos y América Latina: siglo XIX* (1968), is one of the better anti-imperialist treatments, taking on the inter-American relationship for the entire century from the perspective of a capitalist-imperialist United States exploiting the region. A revisionist diplomatic history by Joseph Smith, *Illusions of Conflict: Anglo-American Diplomacy toward Latin America, 1865–1896* (1979), thoroughly delves into the British-U.S. rivalry. He saw much of the conflict as an "illusion," inasmuch as, despite the genuine competition and clash of interests,

Britain perceived more important mutual interests that inspired its avoidance of serious conflict.

Mark T. Gilderhus, *The Second Century: U.S.–Latin American Relations since 1889* (1999), bridges the nineteenth and twentieth centuries. He takes up the "New Diplomacy" of the United States toward Latin America in last decade of the nineteenth century as it began its rise to world power, and continues to the end of the Cold War. This informative topical narrative history emphasizes U.S. goals and tactics, Latin American defiance of U.S. efforts to impose its democratic and capitalist values, and the limits to U.S. policy. Of interest is Dana G. Munro and others, *Latin America in World Affairs, 1914–1940* (1941), with contributions of four of the leading U.S. experts at the time. Leo S. Rowe provides a foreword, Clarence Haring describes Latin America's international "coming of age," Laurence Duggan deals with cultural relations, and Munro analyzes economic nationalism. No unifying idea is indicated and fundamental themes are ignored (notably the First World War and U.S. coercive interventions into the 1930s) but the individual chapters are worthy of consideration. Two comprehensive histories with different purposes and themes cover approximately the same time period. Donald Marquand Dozer, *Are We Good Neighbors? Three Decades of Inter-American Relations, 1930–1960* (1959), analyzes the impact of the ideas and purposes in what came to be known as the Good Neighbor Policy on Latin American attitudes toward the United States. The study relies extensively and effectively on statements by Latin American political leaders, journalists, intellectuals, and political activists.

Several works on Latin America in the cold war are of particular interest. The noted Spanish liberal Salvador de Madariaga, *Latin America between the Eagle and the Bear* (1962), makes an insightful polemical statement. He expresses his loathing of communism and fear of Soviet deceit in Latin America, but warns the United States that it forfeits moral leadership in the hemisphere by supporting brutal dictatorships and opposing all movements on the left for anticommunist reasons. F. Parkinson, *Latin America, the Cold War, and the World Powers, 1945–1973* (1974), seeks to overcome the prevailing scholarly overemphasis on the United States and the neglect of Latin American international positions. It deals with war, revolution, intervention, and crises—in Korea, Guatemala, Cuba (the

Revolution and the missile crisis), and Venezuela—and the rise and decline of insurgency. Two thoughtful books address comparative U.S. and Soviet power politics in their spheres of influence. Edy Kaufman, *The Superpowers and Their Spheres of Influence: The United States and the Soviet Union in Eastern Europe and Latin America* (1976), asserts the "unwritten understanding" between the superpowers to accept the other's sphere of influence. He analyzes how that reality was the major determinant of both regions' international relations within the global system. Jan F. Triska, ed., *Dominant Powers and Subordinate States: The United States in Latin America and the Soviet Union in Eastern Europe* (1986), is a comprehensive multiauthored study. The contributors find parallels in the spheres of influence in terms of geography, power asymmetries, and superpower competition as well as essential dissimilarities. The general conclusion is that the power political efforts had become counterproductive and served the interests of neither dominant power.

Particularly notable is a pioneering functional-empirical study, focusing on the decade 1961–1971, undertaken by Herbert Goldhamer, *The Foreign Powers in Latin America* (1972). He studies the interests and actions of a broad array of outside states, but organizes analysis along topical lines of the political, economic, and cultural instruments through which influence was exercised to realize state objectives.

Latin Americanists debated in the 1970s and 1980s whether cold war rigidities were being loosened to offer Latin America expanded autonomy or, to the contrary, if U.S. hegemony was being strengthened. Ronald G. Hellman and H. J. Rosenbaum, eds., *Latin America: The Search for a New International Role* (1975), includes scholars, government officials, and business people from the United States, Latin America, and elsewhere. They address developments related to the Latin American attempt to realize more independent foreign policies in inter-American and intra–Latin American relations and toward the rest of the world. Contributors to Roger W. Fontaine and James D. Theberge, eds., *Latin America's New Internationalism: The End of Hemispheric Isolation* (1976), "assess Latin America's current political and economic position in the world, and not simply the hemisphere alone." The collection emphasizes economic matters, with certain other issues also addressed, and reflects on the matter of Latin American solidarity. The ideas indicated in the title are implied only; most of the individual contributions are useful. A leading Brazilian analyst, Hélio Jaguaribe, *El nuevo escenario internacional* (1985), brings together several of his studies regarding international problems in the context of new international systemic characteristics. He emphasizes the distribution of U.S. and Soviet world hegemonic power, under which some Latin Americans were nevertheless capable of subsystem autonomy. Luis Maira, ed., *El sistema internacional y America Latina: una era de hegemonia norteamericana?* (1986), employs a group of expert analysts who ask if, in fact, a new era of U.S. hegemony was being structured. Guy Poitras, *The Ordeal of Hegemony: The United States and Latin America* (1990), is a scholarly international theory-based analysis. Poitras argues the incremental decline of U.S. domination of the region and identifies the factors in the reduction of hegemony—global power diffusion, competing adversarial strategic interests, Latin American defection, and lack of U.S. "political will." He examines the Central American crisis of the 1980s and U.S. attempts to contain it and the dynamics of the external debt problem, and offers advice to U.S. policymakers on how to move "beyond hegemony."

Two leading political scientists, John D. Martz and Lars Schoultz, edited an unusually high quality collection of essays, *Latin America, the United States, and the Inter-American System* (1980). A *festschrift* in honor of Professor Federico Gil by his former students and colleagues, the book addresses theoretical perspectives, dynamics of U.S. hegemonic policies and Latin American responses, and issues of human rights. Wolf Grabendorff and Riordan Roett, eds., *Latin America, Western Europe, and the U.S.: Reevaluating the Atlantic Triangle* (1985), is an important collection of original essays by fourteen European, Latin American, and U.S. specialists, emanating from a substantial research project. The central theme is complex triangular relationships resulting from European expansion of Latin American relations and the simultaneous decline of U.S. hemispheric dominance. The book explores specific topics of debt, defense and security, energy problems, and state policy perspectives (especially of Brazil, Argentina, France, Germany, the EC, and the United States). Kevin Middlebrook and Carlos Rico, eds., *The United States and Latin America in the 1980s: Contending Perspectives on a Decade of Crisis* (1986), is a set of excellent original essays and commentaries by twenty-four leading scholars from the United States, Latin America, and Europe, originally presented as conference papers. They offer "contending perspectives" on numerous contemporary issues in inter-American relations: political economy, external debt and capital flows, trade relations, democracy, human rights, migration, and security. Robert Wesson, ed., *U.S. Influence in Latin America in the 1980s* (1982) considers the declining U.S. influence in terms of its bilateral relations with ten countries.

International political economic studies also flourished. Adalbert Krieger Vasena, with Javier Pazos, *Latin America: A Broader World Role* (1973), look at international economic trends and the relationship of Latin America with the industrialized world and conclude that the latter does not take the former seriously enough, given its potential economic significance in global terms. Joseph Grunwald, ed., *Latin America and World Economy: A Changing International Order* (1978), is a collection of essays by established scholars who focus on general and national Latin American viewpoints. They discuss economic relations with industrial countries, regional integration and economic relations with the Third World, the issues of financing development and roles of multinational corporations, and the policies of Mexico and Brazil. Diana Tussie, ed., *Latin America in the World Economy: New Perspectives* (1983), brings together expert analysts of generally centrist persuasions to assess trends in the global economy and the impact on the Latin American states as they undertook to liberalize their political and economic systems. The contributors assess the balance of elements of Latin American dependency and autonomy in the evolving global capitalist system. Roberto Bouzas, ed., *De espaldas a la prosperidad: America y la econmia internacional a fines de los ochenta* (1989), assembles a group of Latin American experts who discuss the region's international economics as the region underwent political and economic transformation.

The latter part of the 1980s through the 1990s marked the beginning of the post–cold war era of the global international system. The evolving contours have been dealt with in broad terms by a number of analysts, listed in the order of their publication as the post–cold war world unfolded. Augusto Varas, ed., *Hemispheric Security and U.S. Policy in Latin America* (1989), has contributions by a diverse group of scholars on how U.S. and Latin American security assumptions were altered and the possibilities for policy convergence as their threat perceptions changed. Georges A. Fauriol, ed., *Security in the Americas* (1989), is based on symposium presentations at the National Defense University in Washington D.C. Seventeen experts analyze and speculate about the new and changing character of conflict and security in inter-American relations, to include not only the continuing concerns with warfare and drug trafficking but also the extensive new agenda of essentially domestic concerns extended to the international arena. Two multiauthored works by many well-known experts on Latin America and the Caribbean, part of an important scholarly annual series, deal broadly with the phenomena on regional, subregional, and country levels: Carlos Portales, ed., *El sistema internacional y America Latina: el mundo en transicion y America Latina* (1989); and Luciano Tomassini, ed., with Carlos J. Moneta y Augfusto Varas, *El sistema internacional y America Latina: la politica internacional en un mundo postmoderno* (1991). Henry Hamman, ed., *Setting the North-South Agenda: United States–Latin American Relations in the 1990s* (1991), is a debate by academics, journalists, and government officials about the probable and preferable direction of inter-American relations in the 1990s. They discuss the changing issues and state interests and the character of the post–cold war inter-American system. G. Pope Atkins, ed., *The United States and Latin America: Redefining U.S. Purposes in the Post–Cold War Era* (1992), is based on conference papers by fourteen experts. Within a framework of regional trends and the changing international system, the authors debate crucial issues and future prospects as they explore economic questions, democracy and human rights, immigration and refugees, drug traffic, and military problems. Jonathan Hartlyn, Lars Schoultz, and Augusto Varas, eds., *The United States and Latin America in the 1990s: Beyond the Cold War* (1992), includes excellent analyses by fifteen U.S. and Latin American authorities. They address various factors at work altering the substance of inter-American relations, and the international and domestic consequences for all state-parties and the tensions, problems, and opportunities faced in the inter-American system. Heraldo Muñoz, ed., *El fin del fantasma: las relaciones interamericanos después de la Guerra Fría* (1992), is a collection of papers based on an academic conference. Twenty contributors discuss several elements, including changing security concepts, the future of U.S. policy, continuing crisis situations, the drug traffic, and problems of the environment and movement of people. Abraham F. Lowenthal and Gregory F. Treverton, eds., *Latin America and the United States in a New World* (1994), deal insightfully with a large number of issues in terms of continuing global and regional phenomena consequent to the end of the cold war that are changing Latin American international roles and U.S. policies. Jorge I. Domínguez, ed., *International Security and Democracy: Latin America and the Caribbean in the Post–Cold War Era* (1998), has chapters authored by specialists in the field. They write on, among other things, the characteristics and challenges of the new era, the use of force in Latin American interstate relations, the United States and the future of inter-American security relations, and "why Latin America may miss the cold war." In Jorge I. Domínguez, ed., *The Future of Inter-American Relations* (1999), analysts from Latin America, the Caribbean, and the United States focus on the transnational phenomena of drug trafficking, immigration, and trade, and their policy, economic, and legal ramifications for the governments involved. Albert Fishlow and James Jones, eds., *The United States and the Americas: A Twenty-First Century View* (1999), is an exercise in forecasting. Fourteen senior Latin Americanists prepared sophisticated papers as background reading for participants at the 94th American Assembly at Columbia University in May 1998. They analyze various elements of the future of inter-American relations and U.S. interests in them.

An important university program in Chile for the study of international relations published a series of multiauthored works by leading scholars of many nationalities on subjects of contemporary interest. Programa de Seguimiento de las Políticas Exteriores Latinoamericanas (PROSPEL), *Anuario de Políticas Exteriores Latinoamericanas* (8 vols., 1984–1990, 1997; title varies), was established by Heraldo Muñoz, who compiled the first eight volumes (1984 to 1990). The series lapsed when Muñoz was appointed Chile's ambassador to the Organization of American States (he subsequently held other ambassadorial posts). Munoz's academic colleague, Alberto van Klaveren, revived it in 1997. He compiled a single volume, retitled *Anuario de Políticas Exteriores Latinoamericanas y del Caribe*, which covered the years 1993–1996. Each volume contains valuable expert analyses of several phenomena: the foreign policies of the Latin American and Caribbean states during the year or years indicated;

external relations such as intra-regional interactions and with the United States, Europe, Japan, and the Soviet Union or Russia; and functional themes such as participation in international governmental organizations, problems of drug trafficking, economic matters, conflict resolution, democratic development, and movement of people. Sundry principal documents and statistical and other data are appended.

THE SUBREGIONS

Writings on the different divisions within Latin America and the Caribbean are abundant. The major divisions, which overlap, are the circum-Caribbean and South America, with further subregions and subsystems identified within the two basic units. Mexico and Brazil, by the nature of their particular external relationships, have also constituted international subsystems; this element of their international relations is taken up in Chapter 3 in the circumstances of their respective foreign policies and external interactions. In the cases of all of the subregions in the following sections, see Chapter 6 for the subregional integration organizations, which further define the international characteristics of each area.

The Circum-Caribbean

The circum-Caribbean is a complex geographic and political region. It includes the islands of the Caribbean Sea and those nearby in the Atlantic Ocean, the entire Central American isthmus and the Yucatan peninsula of Mexico, and the north coast of South America extending into the Atlantic Ocean (thus including Colombia, Venezuela, and Suriname). It has its own further subregions, notably Central America and the Commonwealth Caribbean. From the immense literature delineating the subregion in general terms, the following listing is a representative sampling. As indicated and treated above, the Caribbean is also the site of continuing political dependencies of outside states.

The earlier general treatments included Chester Lloyd Jones, *Caribbean Interests of the United States* (1916), which at the time was the leading survey of U.S. political and economic actions in the region. Writing in the middle of the U.S. imperial period in the Caribbean, Jones employs a realist frame of reference. He addresses the Caribbean to U.S. national interests, its relations with regional states, economic matters, and the importance of naval bases. The works of Dana G. Munro over a long period of time is important because they are based on skillful historical scholarship and objective interpretation as well as on the author's notable diplomatic experience. He was a U.S. foreign service officer in the Caribbean area prior to becoming a professor of history at Princeton University. His efforts began in 1918 with the publication of *The Five Republics of Central America: Their Political and Economic Development and their Relations with the United States,* which became the standard work on the history of U.S. intervention and diplomacy. Munro continued with *The United States and the Caribbean Area* (1934), which was written during the period in which the United States had begun to liquidate its intervention and the Roosevelt administration was implementing the Good Neighbor Policy. Three and four decades later, respectively, Munro published two volumes that together detail the rise and fall of Caribbean imperialism in the first third of the twentieth century: *Intervention and Dollar Diplomacy in the Caribbean, 1900–1921* (1964), followed by *The United States and the Caribbean Republics, 1921–1933* (1974). They are enhanced by his access to a larger body of archival material not earlier available and by his further analytic reflection (he did not hesitate to point out the mistakes in U.S. policies and actions).

A number of long-term historical treatments provide informative surveys. Companion volumes by Lester D. Langley, *Struggle for the American Mediterranean: United States–European Rivalry in the Gulf-Caribbean, 1776–1904* (1976), and *The United States and the Caribbean in the Twentieth Century* (4 eds., 1980–1989), provide a thorough and thoughtful description and analysis of the critical elements of the roles of dominating outside powers over more than two centuries. Anthony P. Maingot, *The United States and the Caribbean: Challenges of an Asymmetrical Relationship* (1994), ranges from 1823 to the end of the cold war. Seeing U.S. policies as based on geopolitics and perceptions, Maingot examines the realities of complex interdependence, U.S. responses to the Communist challenge, and recent problems of drug trafficking, offshore investing, and migration. He offers perceptive observations on the evolution of Caribbean studies. Richard L. Millett and W. Marvin Will, eds., *The Rest-*

less Caribbean: Changing Patterns in International Relations (1979), is made up of twenty-one essays written on the eve of the Nicaraguan revolution by U.S. and Caribbean scholars. They focus on both independent and dependent Caribbean island entities (Cuba, the Dominican Republic, Haiti, Commonwealth Caribbean countries, Puerto Rico, and the French and Dutch dependencies). They address the historical context of intervention and exploitation, from 1492 to 1978; external and domestic constraints on Caribbean international politics; numerous contemporary issues; and certain national policies of the United States, the Soviet Union, Cuba, and other local states. Stephen J. Randall and Graeme S. Mount, *The Caribbean Basin: An International History* (1998), deals with the entire circum-Caribbean, with analyses of interactions among world powers in the area, the Caribbean's emergence from colonialism during the course of the twentieth century, and diplomatic, political, military, economic, and social matters.

Robert Freeman Smith, ed., *The United States and the Latin American Sphere of Influence* (2 vols., 1981–1983), focuses on U.S. domination of the Caribbean region since 1898. The first volume, *The Era of Caribbean Intervention, 1898–1930*, covers the era of U.S. imperialism, from the war with Spain to the early decisions to begin dismantling overt imperial policies. The second volume, *Era of Good Neighbors, Cold Warriors, and Hairshirts, 1930–1982*, ranges from the first elements of what came to be known as the Good Neighbor Policy, through post–World War II anticommunist calculations, to the end of the Carter administration's ambivalent approach. David Healy, *Drive to Hegemony: The United States and the Caribbean, 1898–1917* (1988), delves expertly into the first phase of U.S. Caribbean imperialism, from the aftermath of the U.S. war with Spain to its entry in World War I. Ransford W. Palmer, *Caribbean Dependence on the United States Economy* (1979), states that "a common characteristic of all Caribbean economies is their economic and financial dependence on one metropolitan country or another." Palmer then succinctly analyzes the theme in terms of trade, capital, human resources, tourism, and economic stability and development.

A number of books based on revised conference papers are of value. Three volumes resulting from the long series of annual conferences on the Caribbean (the first convened in 1951) held at the University of

Florida, edited by conference director A. Curtis Wilgus, deals with the region's international relations. The contributions vary in quality but the large numbers are expert and instructive. The product of the seventh annual conference, *The Caribbean: Contemporary International Relations* (1957), deals primarily with the transnational issues of trade and commerce, migration and travel, and cultural interchange, with some attention to the future of the British and Netherlands dependencies. Issued after the sixteenth gathering, *The Caribbean: Current United States Relations* (1966) addresses subjects having to do with monetary, business, trade, cultural, and diplomatic relations. The seventeenth conference yielded *The Caribbean: Its Hemispheric Role* (1967), a series of essays divided into four sections—on political capacity, economic potential, social patterns, and cultural influences. H. Michael Erisman and John D. Martz, eds., *Colossus Challenged: The Struggle for Caribbean Influence* (1982), is a set of particularly good essays analyzing the various factors relating to the Caribbean policies of the United States, the Soviet Union, Cuba, Venezuela, and Mexico; Central American perceptions; and U.S.-microstate relations. Alan Adelman and Reid Reiding, eds., *Confrontation in the Caribbean Basin: International Perspectives on Security, Sovereignty and Survival* (1984), focus on current Caribbean problems, but present them in a broad context. Contributors acknowledge the absence of pan-Caribbean culture and debate the conditions influencing the policies of local small and mid-sized powers and of the United States, Europe, and the Soviet Union. Economists contributing to Michael B. Connolly and John McDermott, eds., *The Economics of the Caribbean Basin* (1985), discuss a wide range of issues and problems.

Informative works appearing since the latter 1980s and identifying the rapidly and dramatically changing context of Caribbean international relations follow. Anthony P. Maingot, *U.S. Power and Caribbean Sovereignty: Geopolitics in a Sphere of Influence* (1988), uses the term "geopolitical" in the sense that the Caribbean is unambiguously a sphere of U.S. influence. But he sees nothing simple about the consequent relationships within that reality, and emphasizes their complexity and dynamism—including Caribbean motivations, perceptions, and bargaining resources. The book is theoretical throughout, and approached on a regional rather than individual country level. Anthony T. Bryan, J. Edward Greene, and Timothy

M. Shaw, eds., *Peace, Development, and Security in the Caribbean* (1990), is a substantial study by eighteen contributors from Caribbean countries, Canada, and Britain. They address Caribbean Basin issues and political geography; the roles of the United States, Canada, Europe, and the rest of Latin America; and, on comparative bases, the national environment, threats to nationhood, and small state responses. Paul Sutton, ed., *Europe and the Caribbean* (1991), contains contributions by established scholars on the Caribbean relations of Britain, France, the Netherlands, European Community, Spain, Soviet Union; the non-Hispanic Caribbean's European connection; U.S. perceptions; and the future of Europe in the region. Hilbourne A. Watson, ed., *The Caribbean in the Global Political Economy* (1994), and twelve colleagues analyze the dynamics of globalization and regionalism as they impact the political economy of the Commonwealth countries, Cuba, Haiti, and Puerto Rico. The numerous elements "are connected by a theory of global capitalism that reexamines the historical tendency of capitalist accumulation under conditions of radical scientific and technological change." Jean Grugel, *Politics and Development in the Caribbean Basin: Central America and the Caribbean in the New World Order* (1995), is a study in political economy. Grugel assesses the Caribbean position in the emerging global order and the unsuccessful attempts by revolutionary regimes to create alternative developmental models. Thomas Klak, ed., *Globalization and Neoliberalism: The Caribbean Context* (1997), is a solid analysis of the impact of recent global economic tendencies, with attention to "the micro and macro-consequences of unfettered economic globalization."

Jorge Rodríguez Beruff and Humberto García Muñiz, eds., *Security Problems and Policies in the Post–Cold War Caribbean* (1996), is more thematically limited than the title might imply. The ten contributors, however, offer good essays on their particular topics. They address specific roles of the United States, France, Britain, and Canada, Haiti, and Cuba; the question of Puerto Rican self-determination; and the problems of drugs and migration. Joseph S. Tulchin, Andrés Serbín, and Rafael Hernández, eds., *Cuba and the Caribbean: Regional Issues and Trends in the Post–Cold War Era* (1997), is made up of thirteen insightful essays about current international trends in the Caribbean, with attention to the dynamics of globalization, economic integration, geopolitics, international crime, and the issue of Cuban reinsertion into the international system. Six senior scholars in Michael Desch, Jorge Domínguez, and Andrés Serbin, eds., *From Pirates to Drug Lords: The Post–Cold War Caribbean Security Environment* (1998), analyze the state of the region in a turbulent era of simultaneous globalization and regionalization. They address international norms and institutions, possible roles for collective security mechanisms, and the national security issues of drug trafficking, environment, migration, and democratic stability. Joseph S. Tulchin, and Ralph H. Espach, eds., *Security in the Caribbean Basin: The Challenge of Regional Cooperation* (2000), is a post–cold war "redefinition of sovereignty" exercise, in which contributors examine transnational threats of drug trafficking, migratory flows, economic crises, and natural disasters. They demand cooperative multilateral policies, which in turn, the contributors argue, calls for a redefinition of such basic concepts as sovereignty and the nature of national and regional security interests.

Central America

The original five Central American states (Costa Rica, El Salvador, Guatemala, Honduras, and Nicaragua) have, since independence, perceived themselves a special international unit. They have not considered Panama (a province of Colombia until it became independent in 1903) or Belize (a British colony before its independence in 1991, and then part of the Commonwealth Caribbean) as part of their definition of Central America. In recent years, however, those two states have been increasingly involved in Central American affairs.

One of the few genuinely scholarly works written before post–World War II by a Central American about isthmian international relations is Laudelino Moreno, *Historia de las relaciones interestatuales de Centroamérica* (1928). A detailed descriptive survey from independence into the 1920s, the book emphasizes continuing Central American efforts and frustrations to form and sustain an isthmian federal state. It deals with structures of the federated state, civil wars, filibusterers, unionist-liberal advocates, nationalist dissolutionists, and the extensive U.S. patron-role.

John H. Coatsworth, *Central America and the United States: The Clients and the Colossus* (1994), is an exceptional revisionist survey history, concisely written and analytic throughout. Coatsworth asks "why a region so closely tied to the United States should have become the site of so much bloodshed and brutality," and finds the answer in those very ties, which make Central Americans too close and too subordinate to "the colossus." John E. Findling, *Close Neighbors, Distant Friends: United States–Central American Relations* (1987), is a broad chronological narrative history of the major eras and themes in relations from the nineteenth-century independence movements to the mid-1980s. Findling employs a straightforward geopolitical approach. Thomas M. Leonard, *Central America and the United States: The Search for Stability* (1991), is an excellent appraisal of the complex history of conflicting foreign policy goals in Central American–U.S. relationships. It ranges from the former's independence in the early nineteenth century, when the outside world began to impinge on Central America, through the Reagan administration and the crises of the 1980s. Victor Bulmer-Thomas, *The Political Economy of Central America Since 1920* (1987), is an ambitious, substantial, and instructive economic history, emphasizing the processes and consequences attendant to Central America's integration into the world economy. It may be supplemented with Bulmer-Thomas's treatment of more specific themes in his *Studies in the Economics of Central America* (1988). H. Rodrigo Jauberth, Gilberto Casteñeda, Jesús Hernández, and Pedro Vúskovic, *The Difficult Triangle: Mexico, the United States, and Central America* (1992), undertake a special and important topic. The three researchers, who reside in Costa Rica, Guatemala, Chile, and Mexico, respectively, examine the complex and troubled relationships in terms of historical roles and implications of recent phenomena such as economic integration and the Central American peace processes. Ralph Lee Woodward, ed., *Central America: Historical Perspectives on the Contemporary Crisis* (1988), provides an excellent survey of persistent internal and external problems plaguing the region since its independence and their impact on the continuing post–World War II domestic and international violence. See Chapter 7 for the extensive literature on Central American civil and international war in the 1980s. Walter LaFeber, *Inevitable Revolutions: The United States in Central America* (2 eds., 1983, 1993), is a first-rate study that also provides historical background for the crisis of the 1980s. LaFeber traces the history of violence and revolution in the subregion, searches for its causes, and finds great fault with the U.S. officials' misperceptions and imperialist actions

The Commonwealth Caribbean

The Commonwealth Caribbean countries are the eighteen former British colonies in the circum-Caribbean, twelve of which have become independent states, and six of which are nonsovereign but self-governing "States in Association with Great Britain." The independent states are Antigua and Barbuda, Bahamas, Barbados, Belize, Dominica, Grenada, Guyana, Jamaica, St. Kitts–Nevis, St. Lucia, St. Vincent, and Trinidad and Tobago. One of them (Belize) is on the Central American isthmus, another (Guyana) is on the South American continent, with the remainder islands in the Caribbean Sea. Certain of them also felt they had special mutual interests and created another level of subsystem within that community—the Organization of the Eastern Caribbean States—which forms another subsystem. For comparative foreign policy treatments of the Commonwealth Caribbean states, see Chapter 3; and for their attempts to join in political-economic union, their primary foreign policy effort, see Chapter 6.

Basil A. Ince, ed., *Contemporary International Relations of the Caribbean* (1979), deals with the Commonwealth Caribbean and the Third World, British ties and influences, political processes and foreign policies, and economic development and integration. Jorge Heine and Leslie F. Manigat, eds., *The Caribbean and World Politics: Cross-Currents and Cleavages* (1987), is restricted to the Commonwealth Caribbean countries and French Martinique and Guadeloupe, and is concerned primarily with international political economy. Based on symposium papers, thirteen contributors (mostly from the subject countries) consider the continuing decolonization process, economic dependency, and the gross economic asymmetries between the Caribbean entities and the United States. It pays considerable attention to Caribbean foreign policies, the roles of regional middle powers, and U.S. policies and the Caribbean. Andrés Serbin, *Sunset Over the Islands: The Caribbean in an Age of Global and Regional Challenges* (1998), argues that "no region of the world is so affected as the [Commonwealth] Caribbean by geopolitical and economic changes caused by the end of the Cold War and the impact of globalization." Contributors to Anthony T. Bryan and Andrés Serbín, eds., *Distant Cousins: The Caribbean–Latin American Relationship* (1994), find profound cultural and political differences between the English-speaking Caribbean and Latin America, but that recent developments are creating a changing and closer relationship. Jacqueline Anne Braveboy-Wagner, with W. Marvin Will, Dennis J. Gayle, and Ivelaw L. Griffith, *The Caribbean in the Pacific Century: Prospects for Caribbean-Pacific Cooperation* (1993), argue that the next century will be a Pacific, not a European one, especially in terms of trade. The English-speaking Caribbean is moving to diversify its traditional focus on Europe and North America.

South America

Scholars have dealt with the collection of states on the South American continent as an analytic entity. More often, however, they have studied South America beyond the Caribbean—especially the Southern Cone (which includes Argentina, Bolivia, Brazil, Chile, Paraguay, Peru, and Uruguay). South America contains further overlapping subregions—the Andean, Amazonian, and Platine countries, the first two of which also extend into the Caribbean zone. The South American international relations literature, despite the presence of much larger and autonomous states, is less extensive than that on the circum-Caribbean. This is probably because of the intense interest on the part of the United States in the Caribbean area and less concern for the more southerly zones (most of the literature regarding the former has to do with U.S. policies and relations). South America beyond the Caribbean, as a general matter, has historically been relatively isolated from the mainstream of international politics, and is populated by important countries that have developed intense regularized relationships among themselves. For evocations of the formal organizational expressions of these international subregions and subsystems, see Chapter 6; for the related informal conflict among them, which also defines their relationships, see Chapter 7.

An important historical study by Vicente G. Quesada, *Historia diplomática hispanoamericana* (3 vols., 1918–1920), deals with South

America. The author, formerly the Argentine minister to the United States (1885–1892), focuses on South American border disputes within a broad framework of international law and diplomacy. Volume 1 deals with Latin American international law and the Argentine-Bolivian boundaries; volume 2, with Brazil's policies toward the Platine states; and volume 3, with Brazil's imperialist policy and its boundaries with other South American states (all South American states but Chile bounded Brazil, often with vague borders inherited from the colonial layout).

Robert N. Burr, *By Reason or Force: Chile and the Balancing of Power in South America, 1830–1905* (1967), centers on Chile but gives the general picture (and provides the most authoritative analysis) of the Southern Cone balance-of-power system. In a conceptually related book (and an authoritative one as well), Jack Child, *Geopolitics and Conflict in South America: Quarrels Among Neighbors* (1985), defines geopolitics as geography applied to power politics and includes all the South American states. He provides informative background information on the South American setting and on classical geopolitical theory; explains the nature and impact of geopolitical thinking in South America, on both country and regional bases; and analyzes, in a series of case studies, the role of geopolitics in South American conflicts. Glen St. John Barclay, *Struggle for a Continent: The Diplomatic History of South America, 1917–1945* (1971), undertakes to include the entire continent in little more than 200 pages of narrative. Despite some factual errors and journalistic embellishments, the book provides a useful outline of the period. The author's treatment of Argentina (the most focused subject) has insights worth considering. Also investigating diplomatic elements, Samuel L. Baily, *The United States and the Development of South America, 1945–1975* (1976), finds that U.S. and South American interests, as well as those of the South Americans, are not necessarily congruous. He is critical of U.S. actions and sees the necessity for major revisions. Nine contributors to G. Pope Atkins, *South America into the 1990s: Evolving International Relationships in a New Era* (1990), investigate the Southern Cone (with Ecuador sometimes drawn in) in terms of the rapid pace of regional transformation evident at the end of the 1980s and projected into the 1990s. They define South America in systemic terms; analyze the impact of domestic politics on the foreign policies of the subregional states and the status of their geopolitical thinking; and examine extrahemispheric interests, actions, and perspectives (especially of the United States and of Europe).

Extrahemispheric Subsystems

Latin American and Caribbean states participate in extraregional international subsystems, both as objects of the actions of outsiders and as active participants in their own right. For example, most of them identified with the Third World—the Nonaligned Movement and the New International Economic Order, which was pursued especially in the United Nations Conference on Trade and Development and in the General Assembly. The twelve Commonwealth Caribbean states are, as former British colonies, members of the Commonwealth. Spain has taken the lead during the twentieth century in fostering pan-Hispanic connections and sometimes pan-Iberian ones to include Portugal and Brazil. Some governments posit certain Latin American states as part of an emerging Pacific Basin or Pacific Rim subsystem. See Chapters 4 and 6 for treatments of some of these matters.

—————— ■ ——————

CHAPTER 3

Latin American and Caribbean States

This chapter deals with the foreign policies and certain international interactions of the Latin American and Caribbean states. It first appraises the significant body of comparative and general regional and subregional literature, and then considers the states individually. The subject matter is complex, and elements are also found in other chapters. The present essay includes works on those general topics explored in Chapter 2 as they are applied to and focus on the regional states themselves (i.e., historical surveys, foreign policy analyses, and political economic investigations). It also incorporates studies of the individual Latin American and Caribbean states' relations with other states, within and outside the region, including those that deal primarily with the external states' policies and individual state participation in intergovernmental organizations. Other chapters in this book should be consulted for other matters. See Chapter 7 for international and internal warfare (including the wars for independence and the social revolutions in Mexico, Cuba, Bolivia, and Nicaragua); and Chapter 8 for several forms of interstate and intersocietal phenomena.[1]

GENERAL AND
COMPARATIVE STUDIES

Studies of Latin America's external interactions generally emerged with the end of World War I. Detailed histories initially dominated the literature; they were concerned primarily with policies after they had been adopted and put into action. In addition, legal expositions were produced that emphasized formal aspects of relations or advocated policy actions based on legal-institutional considerations. Scholars seldom focused on factors underlying policy formulation. Even with the advent of foreign policy analysis in the 1950s in the general study of international relations, Latin American foreign policies remained largely unexplored territory. The analytic situation changed, however, as occurrences with broad and significant international implications indicated the complexity of Latin Americans' foreign policy decisions and stimulated interest in knowing more about them. Outside governments increasingly recognized the international political and economic importance of the region, in particular of the large and middle-size states. Latin Americans increased their efforts to adopt more independent foreign policies, often in concert with one another and with some success. Foreign policy analysis became an important research effort, using concepts from general decisional theories and from the comparative study of political systems. Specialists on Latin America adopted extant methods of foreign policy analysis, but also amended them. Corrections were necessary since the theories tended to focus on great-power orientations and global phenomena and to neglect the behavior of smaller states within international regions.

The literature continued to include historical descriptions and interpretations of policy outcomes, but research was increasingly analytical and interdisciplinary in nature. Furthermore, in the writing of diplomatic history, social and cultural considerations competed with and then joined the traditional ones of diplomacy, politics, economics, and war. Latin Americanist foreign policy analysts often included historical elements among the factors considered.

SURVEY ANALYSES

Three broadly conceived international histories that emphasize Latin American interests and actions are noted. A lengthy study by Uruguayan historian Aureliano Rodríguez Larreta, *Orientación de la política internacional en América Latina* (2 vols., 1938), covers numerous themes with an emphasis on the nineteenth century. Harold Eugene Davis, John J. Finan, and F. Taylor Peck, *Latin American Diplomatic History: An Introduction* (1977), all U.S. historians, and Demetrio Boersner, *Relaciones internacionales de América Latina: breve historia* (4 eds., 1982–1990), a Venezuelan scholar, carefully adhere to their purposes of presenting their analyses from Latin American points of view. Contributors to Carlos Astiz, ed., *Latin American International Politics: Ambitions, Capabilities, and the National Interest of Mexico, Brazil, and Argentina* (1969), undertook a limited effort at systematic political analysis. Astiz accurately points out the long-standing need for more rigorous investigation of important themes, but the sixteen contributions are of varying quality and their provocative generalizations are not empirically supported. Parts of a study by historian Robert N. Burr, *Our Troubled Hemisphere: Perspectives on United States–Latin American Relations* (1967; especially chapters 1, 4, 5, and 7), make up a brief but insightful comparative Latin American foreign policy analysis.

Beginning in the mid-1970s, a number of multiauthored investigations appeared with theoretical, conceptual, empirical, and comparative purposes. A common problem to them all is the varying fidelity of authors to integrating the prescribed conceptual frameworks into their individual contributions. Nevertheless, they represent important advances in Latin American foreign policy analysis. The first comprehensive attempt was by Harold Davis, Larman Wilson, and others, *Latin American Foreign Policies* (1975), designed as a textbook for upper-level undergraduates and first-year graduate students. Authored by U.S. and Latin American scholars, the book contains chapters on general foreign policy processes and on those of almost all of the regional states (and presented from their perspectives). Davis provides an organizing framework focusing on how foreign policy formulation and orientations were influenced by historical tradition, domestic politics, international problems, and relations with other states, regions, and international organizations. Some of the individual contributors also include their own thematic emphases and conceptual preferences. A number of other analyses followed. Elizabeth Ferris and Jenny Lincoln edited two good anthologies, *Latin American Foreign Policies: Global and Regional Dimensions* (1981) and *The Dynamics of Latin American Foreign Policies* (1984—with the editors' names reversed). Authors from the United States, Latin America, and Europe contributed to both books. The former volume begins with an assessment of research in the field and a comparative overview of Latin American foreign policies. Subsequent chapters analyze global and regional elements in the policies of Argentina, Bolivia, Brazil, Chile, Cuba, Mexico, Peru, Venezuela, and the Commonwealth Caribbean states, emphasizing the changed internal and external settings that allow them more independent policy action. The second book criticizes the tendency of scholars to analyze regional states as objects of U.S. policy and, like the Davis and Wilson collection, insists on evaluating how they formulate and implement their own policies. Contributors analyze the increasingly independent policies of Argentina, Brazil, Chile, Colombia, Cuba, Mexico, Nicaragua, Peru, and Venezuela, and the Caribbean and South American subregions. The last chapter proposes directions of research toward a theory of comparative Latin American foreign policy analysis. Gerhard Drekonja Kornat and Juan Tokatlian, eds., *Teoría y práctica de la política exterior latinoamericana* (1983), is intended to serve as a university textbook. It is a broadly conceived set of twenty essays, about evenly divided between theoretical-topical concerns and state policies (of Argentina, Brazil, Colombia, Chile, Cuba, Mexico, Peru, and the Dominican Republic, plus a chapter on the internationalization of the Caribbean Basin). Juan Carlos Puig, ed., *América Latina: políticas exteriores comparadas* (1984), is a compilation of articles and commentaries by fifteen distinguished Latin American scholars. They explore economic and political aspects of the foreign policies of most Latin American states. The collection of essays on contemporary foreign policies edited by Heraldo Muñoz and Joseph Tulchin, *Latin American Nations in World Politics* (2 eds., 1984, 1996), was initially the result of a conference of scholars from the Universidad de Chile and the University of North Carolina at Chapel Hill. Both editions have introductory chapters of theoretical criticism and clarification. They include empirical studies of most Latin American states and analyses of regional themes and explorations of competing approaches to foreign policy analysis. The second edition includes an incongruous but otherwise good chapter on the Soviet Union.

Two works applying international systemic frameworks have considerable reference to Latin American and Caribbean policies. Luciano Tomassini, ed., *Las relaciones internacionales de la América Latina* (1981), is a broadly thematic, theory-based work by one of the prime movers of the modern study of Latin American IR. Peter Calvert, *The International Politics of Latin America* (1994), focuses closely throughout on the regional states. In addition, senior Brazilian analyst Hélio Jaguaribe, *El nuevo escenario internacional* (1985), brings together a number of his past studies that enlighten Latin American contemporary problems in a broad global context. In the international economic sphere, William P. Glade, *The Latin American Economies: A Study of Their Institutional Evolution* (1969), is an essential classic. A detailed analytic study of Latin American economic development and domestic and external variables are linked throughout in this history of the institutional foundations of Latin American economic growth from the colonial period to the present. Substantial reference is made to individual Latin American countries in various thematic contexts. Contributors to Laura Randall, ed., *The Political Economy of Latin America in the Postwar Period* (1997), follow a comparative analysis of the region's experience with changing postwar international economic strategies by parallel studies of developments in Argentina, Brazil, Chile, Cuba, Ecuador, Mexico, and Peru.

A serial publication cited and commented on in Chapter 2 is important for the matters taken up in this chapter. Each volume of Programa de Seguimiento de las Políticas Exteriores Latinoamericanas (PROSPEL), *Anuario de Políticas Exteriores Latinoamericanas* (8 vols., 1984–1990, 1997), retitled *Anuario de Políticas Exteriores Latinoamericanas y del Caribe* in 1997, includes expert analyses on the foreign policies of the Latin American and Caribbean states and their interstate relations. See also Roberto Russell, ed., *El Sistema Internacional y América Latina: La agenda internacional en los años '90* (1990).

The External Environment

Chapter 2, in defining the general characteristics of the region with respect to the international system, also provides the policy-making environment for the regional states. Various categories of works provide sharply differing perspectives of external factors and variables. Realist principles emphasize power politics and interstate balances of power; liberal and idealist perspectives seek to reform the power-based system and the state policies underlying it; and dependency and world-system theories challenge the world capitalist system and its negative consequences for Latin America and the Caribbean. Despite their differences, they commonly focus on external factors as the principal influence on or even the determinants of Latin American and Caribbean foreign policy decisions.

Most foreign policy analysts tend to focus on the domestic factors behind Latin American and Caribbean decision making and to emphasize the primacy of domestic politics. They do not deny the importance of the external environment within which the regional states operate, and in the instance of small states acknowledging that external factors may be determining. But analysts see their foreign policies as essentially the projection of domestic politics. External actions are considered to be means for protecting individual or group interests, furthering goals such as internal economic development and political stability, or satisfying nationalist causes. This was increasingly the case from the mid-1960s, and was even more evident with the end of the cold war, when critical transnational phenomena were clearly extensions of essentially domestic concerns (such as complex economic interactions, furtherance of democracy and human rights, movement of peoples, and drug trafficking). None of this is to deny, nor does it contradict, the Latin American and Caribbean desire to maximize state and regional autonomy or "the decisive importance of the United States for all the countries of the region."[2]

Decision Making

Three important books explicitly and critically apply decision theory to the analysis of Latin American foreign policymaking: Juan G. Tokatlian, ed., *Teoría y práctica de la política exterior latinoamericana* (1983); Carlos Eduardo Mena, *Toma de decisiones y políticas: algunas aplicaciones a la política exterior* (1989); and Roberto Russell, ed., *Política exterior y toma de decisiones en América Latina* (1990). The first two books are multiauthored. All of them are sophisticated critiques of competing foreign policy decision theories, with their application to Latin American processes.[3] With respect to economic elements in decision making, Albert O. Hirschman, *Journeys Toward Progress: Studies of Economic Policy Making in Latin America* (1963), is a classic treatment of the subject. The contributors to J. Buxton and N. Phillips, eds., *Case Studies in Latin American Political Economy* (1999), analyze factors behind the difficult reorientation of economic policy in the 1980s and 1990s to free market principles—by Argentina, Brazil, Uruguay, Colombia, Venezuela, and Mexico—and the external and internal consequences of their application. The authors in Jorge I. Domínguez, ed., *Latin America's International Relations and Their Domestic Consequences: War and Peace, Dependency and Autonomy, Integration and Disintegration* (1994), investigate the linkages between interstate and transnational operations and internal state and societal processes and their repercussions.

Two excellent books appeared on the concept of multilateral policy coordination and harmonization *(concertación)* and related aspects of Latin American foreign policies: Alicia Frohman, *Puentes sobre la turbulencia: la concertación política latinoamericana en los ochenta* (1990), and Luciano Tomassini, ed., *El sistema internacional y América Latina: nuevas formas de concertación regional en América Latina* (1990). Frohman and the contributors to Tomassini's collection emphasize changes in Latin American diplomacy from the old formality of protocol to intraregional consultation and collaboration. They emphasize personal contacts and the array of inter–Latin American consultative mechanisms. A related aspect is the influence of Latin American views about cooperative regionalism. Two Canadian professors, Gordon Mace and Jean-Philippe Thérien, eds., *Foreign Policy and Regionalism in the Americas* (1999), assemble fourteen expert contributors for a comparative analysis of the "emerging trend toward regionalism." Chapters are devoted to state strategies in the cases of Mexico, Jamaica, Venezuela, Colombia, Peru, Brazil, Argentina, and Chile. The authors define regionalism primarily in institutional terms—inter–Latin American and Caribbean integration arrangements and other international organizations at various international levels.

Nationalism

The most thorough general work on Latin American nationalism is Arthur P. Whitaker and David C. Jordan, eds., *Nationalism in Contemporary Latin America* (1966). The authors contribute thoughtful historical-conceptual studies of the evolution and implications of the principal varieties of nationalism, with ten country studies providing illustrations. They perhaps assign too many foreign policy goals and orientations to a nationalist source. This book should be read with Whitaker's earlier work, *Nationalism in Latin America* (1962). Victor Alba, *Nationalists Without Nations: The Oligarchy Versus the People in Latin America* (1968), is a subjective and provocative debunking of "pseudonationalist" Latin American oligarchies espousing nationalism to further their own interests. As a result, Alba says, Latin Americans are losing "the race for prosperity and well-being" and should, in addition to abolishing oligarchies, pursue transnational political and economic union. An instructive treatment by Gerhard Masur, *Nationalism in Latin America* (1966), aspires to be an inclusive study of the "complex evolution of Latin American countries toward realization of national aspirations, from the Spanish conquest to the present day." The paramount Latin American problem is to determine a "satisfactory basis for harmonious existence throughout the hemisphere." The book includes treatments of Mexico, Bolivia, Brazil, Argentina, and Cuba. Gustavo Adolfo Otero, *Sociología del nacionalismo en Hispano-América* (1947), applies sociological concepts in an informative analysis of the origins and evolution of the phenomenon. Shoshana Baron Tancer, *Economic Nationalism in Latin America: The Quest for Economic Independence* (1976), focuses on Latin American perceptions and policies in international commerce and analyzes the impact of economic nationalism in recent negotiations on commodity agreements, industrialization, regional integration, and foreign investment. Michael L. Krenn, *U.S. Policy Toward Economic Nationalism in Latin America, 1917–1929* (1990), notes that World War I temporarily removed European commercial interests and provided an opening for U.S. business and the U.S. government to seize the initiative. Krenn discovers the origin of many of today's problems in the 1917–1929 period and argues that the experience continued to influence U.S. inter-American policies to the present.

Certain Latin American statements of anti-imperialism and anti-Americanism have been an important part of the literature on regional nationalism. Of particular influence was Manuel Ugarte, *The Destiny of a Continent* (1925), by the celebrated Argentine thinker who feared Latin American political-social absorption by the United States. Other widely circulated polemics argue parallel themes related to historical U.S. exploitation of Latin America, with economic and legal-moral ramifications of intervention often emphasized. Among them are Juan José Arévalo, *The Shark and the Sardines* (1961); Genaro Carnero Checo, *El Aguila Rampante: El imperialism yanqui sobre América Latina* (1956); Ramón Oliveres, *El imperialismo yanqui en América: la dominación política y económica del continente* (1952); two books by Isidro Fabela, *Buena y mala vecinidad* (1958), and *Intervención* (1959); and Alonso Aguilar, *Pan-Americanism from Monroe to the Present: A View from the Other Side* (1968). A widely read example of impassioned xenophobia, Eduardo Galeano, *Open Veins of Latin America: Five Centuries of the Pillage of a Continent* (1973), says that for 500 years European and North American imperialism exploited Latin Americans and denied them their rightful destiny.

Geopolitical Formulations

Dating from the nineteenth century, Latin Americans have adopted and developed geopolitical strategic perspectives. Military men and their civilian associates dominated the field until recent years, when it opened to less traditional and more progressive geopolitical orientations. The original and long-lasting direction was based on the organic theory of the state. This led to a version of power politics that viewed conflict as natural, inevitable, and necessary, if a state was to survive and achieve its national "destiny." The most extensive geopolitical writing has been in the Southern Cone, most notably in Brazil, Argentina, and Chile. Critics said this kind of thinking facilitated conflict and arms races in the Southern Cone. Military regimes also used organic state theory to justify domestic repression from the 1960s into the 1980s.

Geopolitical writings by Latin Americans are massive in volume and extensive in scope. Two studies by Jack Child provide authoritative analyses of Latin American geopolitical thinking, which the reader should consult for references to the significant Latin American writers. *Geopolitics and Conflict in South America: Quarrels Among Neighbors* (1985), provides valuable background instruction on the South American setting and the classic schools of geopolitics. The book compares and contrasts geopolitical thinking in Brazil, the nine Spanish-American states, and the

Guianas, and links that thinking to the concept of the "national security state" prevalent in the 1970s into the 1980s. Child then deals in detail with the major South American conflicts and the geopolitical bases of intra–South American tensions and conflicts. A companion volume, *Antarctica and South American Geopolitics: Frozen Lebensraum* (1988), examines the considerable impact of the same geopolitical considerations on the states' policies toward Antarctica, especially on the part of the military regimes. This book also provides a good introduction to general South American geopolitical thought. A collection of essays in Philip L. Kelly and Jack Child, eds., *Geopolitics of the Southern Cone and Antarctica* (1988), provides various national and analytic perspectives to the same subjects as above, as well as discerns and cites a new (postmilitary regime) optimistic direction in the geopolitical literature. This strain provides bases for more cooperative and harmonious—or less competitive and conflictual—interstate relationships. Fifteen authorities discuss geopolitical doctrines; the impact of democratization on conflict and cooperation; the geopolitics of the South Atlantic, Antarctica, and La Plata Basin; and geopolitical thinking in Argentina, Brazil, Chile, and Bolivia. Philip L. Kelly, *Checkerboards and Shatterbelts: The Geopolitics of South America* (1997), deals with the complex geographic scope of the entire South American continent and its strategic relationship with the United States. An especially valuable chapter summarizes the thinking of sixteen individual South American geopolitical writers. Kelly skillfully examines the geopolitical school that emphasizes the impact of geographic features on foreign security policies (locations, distances, terrain, climate, and resources). He also analyzes the recent element of "accommodative regionalism," which he favors as the most productive. Howard T. Pittman, *Geopolitics in the ABC Countries: A Comparison* (1981), is an exceptionally thorough presentation of Latin American geopolitical writings and a remarkable feat of translation. Of particular value is the breadth of coverage of Latin American writers on the subject.

Related to geopolitics is the matter of boundary and territorial disputes (often bilateral) and competition for subregional influence. Inasmuch as they have threatened or resulted in interstate violence, works on these phenomena are included in Chapter 7. In more general terms, Alberto Cisneros Lavaller, *América Latina: conflicto o cooperación* (1986), studies both conflictual and cooperative patterns of behavior by Latin American states in their extra- and intraregional interactions over a two-decade period beginning in the mid-1960s. He applies quantitative analysis to the attributes, capabilities, and transactions of various parties, and constructs a theoretical model of regional interactions. Benigno Checa Drouet, *La doctrina americans del uti possidetis de 1810* (1936), is a concise study of the legal principle often cited by Latin American states in their claims regarding border disputes. Lawrence A. Herzog, ed., *Changing Boundaries in the Americas: New Perspectives on the U.S.-Mexican, Central American, and South American Borders* (1992), provides an overview of the title subject and an essay on "historical frontier imagery in the Americas." He then treats in detail the United States–Mexico border, Central America, and South America.

Geographic Levels of Policy and Relations

Latin American states have formulated policies and carried on interstate relations on several geographic levels: the overall Latin American–Caribbean region; the several subregions; the Western Hemisphere, to include especially the United States; and the extrahemispheric world. The many formal intergovernmental organizations on all four levels are addressed in Chapter 6, and other transnational actors are dealt with in Chapter 8.

The Circum-Caribbean.[4] The following works of a general nature, which are cited in Chapter 2 with further commentary, are relevant to the policies and relations of the circum-Caribbean states. Dana G. Munro, a former U.S. diplomat with much experience in the Caribbean area and later a distinguished historian, published important books over a span of almost a half-century. They are *The Five Republics of Central America: Their Political and Economic Development and Their Relation with the United States* (1918); *The United States and the Caribbean Area* (1934); *Intervention and Dollar Diplomacy in the Caribbean, 1900–1921* (1964); and *The United States and the Caribbean Republics, 1921–1933* (1974). From a series of books based on presentations at annual conferences on the Caribbean held at the University of Florida, three of them, edited by A. Curtis Wilgus, cover a wide range of subjects. They are *The Caribbean: Contemporary International Relations* (1957); *The Caribbean: Current United States Relations* (1966); and *The Caribbean: Its Hemispheric Role* (1967). More recent works are Richard L. Millett and W. Marvin Will, eds., *The Restless Caribbean: Changing Patterns in International Relations* (1979); H. Michael Erisman and John D. Martz, eds., *Colossus Challenged: The Struggle for Caribbean Influence* (1982), which includes studies of the Caribbean policies of Cuba, Venezuela, and Mexico, and of Central American perceptions; Jorge Heine and Leslie F. Manigat, eds., *The Caribbean and World Politics: Cross-Currents and Cleavages* (1987); Lester D. Langley, *The United States and the Caribbean in the Twentieth Century* (4 eds., 1980–1989); Jorge Rodríguez Beruff and Humberto García Muñiz, eds., *Security Problems and Policies in the Post–Cold War Caribbean* (1996); and Stephen J. Randall and Graeme S. Mount, *The Caribbean Basin: An International History* (1998). Michael A. Morris, *Caribbean Maritime Security* (1994), examines Caribbean coast guards and navies, traditional maritime issues, concerns with "boat people" and drug traffickers, and post–cold war security considerations.

Franklin W. Knight, *The Caribbean: The Genesis of a Fragmented Nationalism* (2 eds., 1978, 1990), is a brilliant and unorthodox socioeconomic political history of the Caribbean from pre-Columbian days to the date of publication. Knight argues that the regional processes in the rise and subsequent fragmentation of nationalism, nation building, and dependency on the outside world were determined by the creation of two uniquely Caribbean types of societies, which he calls "settler" and "exploitative." Roland H. Ebel, Raymond Taras, and James D. Cochrane, *Political Culture and Foreign Policy in Latin America: Case Studies from the Circum-Caribbean* (1991), is an innovative study of the linkages between societal variables and international behavior. The authors take on the difficult analysis of the effect of Spanish-American Caribbean political culture on foreign policies and subregional interactions, in an area of primary U.S. influence.

Central America.   Walter LaFeber, *Inevitable Revolutions: The United States in Central America* (2 eds., 1983, 1993), is an outstanding, detailed analytic history viewing Central America as a discrete international system. It surveys the entire period from independence in the 1820s to the early 1990s. LaFeber emphasizes the U.S. role in the region's turbulent history, as the United States sought simultaneously to transform the local states into representative democracies and to maintain U.S. economic and security dominance. A well-known Central American public figure on the democratic left, Vicente Sáenz, *Rompiendo cadenas, las del imperialismo en Central América y en otros repúblicas del continente* (3 eds., 1933–1961), surveys the entire history of imperialism in the Americas. In the instance of Central America, he argues the necessity to break the chains of U.S. political and economic dominance, which, among other things, helped dictators gain and maintain control of the state.

Several books deal with Central American turmoil in the 1980s in broad historical and analytic terms. See Chapter 7 for works that specifically address the conflict and subsequent settlement. The multidisciplinary collection of twelve essays edited by Ralph Lee Woodward, *Central America: Historical Perspectives on the Contemporary Crisis* (1988), deals mostly with the individual states. The authors collectively explore the historical bases for domestic and international turmoil in the 1980s. Rejecting the simplistic notion of the predicament as a clash between communism and democracy, they investigate the impact of political, economic, and cultural diversity and competing domestic interests in the continuous failure to achieve viable Central American political union or economic integration. They stress the negative roles of the external great powers and internal class rigidities. The contributors to Peter Calvert, ed., *The Central American Security System: North-South or East-West?* (1989), examine subregional security thinking and action in terms of local perceptions of regional rivalries and stability, economic interests, and national security. Alan Adelman and Reid Reiding, *Confrontation in the Caribbean Basin: International Perspectives on Security, Sovereignty and Survival* (1984), divide the state actors into three groups for analytic purposes: the local "embattled countries" (El Salvador, Guatemala, Nicaragua, and the English-speaking Caribbean); the regional powers (Mexico, Venezuela, and Cuba); and the global powers (the United States, the Soviet Union, and Western Europe). Also of interest for Central American policies is Thomas M. Leonard,

Central America and the United States: The Search for Stability (1991) (see Chapter 2 for commentary).

Commonwealth Caribbean States.   Jacqueline Anne Braveboy-Wagner provides a thorough comparative foreign policy analysis of the twelve Commonwealth Caribbean states, the first such study by a single author: *The Caribbean in World Affairs: The Foreign Policies of the English-Speaking States* (2 eds., 1989, 1999). She analyzes foreign policy processes—especially regarding security, economic development, and regional influence; and the bureaucratic and resource limitations that constrain both crisis responses and the effort to diversify external relations. She highlights the necessity for the small states to act, so far as possible, as a bloc, and describes the subregional interstate institutions created to do so. Contributors to Braveboy-Wagner and Dennis J. Gayle, eds., *Caribbean Public Policy: Regional, Cultural, and Socioeconomic Issues for the 21st Century* (1997), discuss the post–cold war issues of regionalism and integration, environment, labor and migration, gender, technology, and drug trafficking.

Scholars have explored the sovereignty, nation building, and security problems of the small English-speaking Caribbean states. Paget Henry and Carl Stone, eds., *The Newer Caribbean: Decolonization, Democracy, and Development* (1983), bring together sixteen well-researched studies that explore the early years (until the late 1970s) of postindependence nation building, after four centuries of first colonialism and slavery and then dependency and racism. The authors address the phenomena on both domestic and international levels. Neither Barbados (a key local state) nor the United States receive real attention, and chapters on Puerto Rico and the Dominican Republic do not fit well into the overall scheme. H. Michael Erisman, *Pursuing Postdependency Politics: South-South Relations in the Caribbean* (1992), argues, from a strong theoretical base, that cultivation of interregional South-South relations might generate sufficient bargaining leverage to provide an escape from the dependency inherent in the structure of extant North-South relations, or at least to diversify dependency enough to avoid overweening influence by a single external source. Anthony P. Maingot, *U.S. Power and Caribbean Sovereignty: Geopolitics in a Sphere of Influence* (1988), explores, on a comparative basis and in geopolitical terms, the motivations, perceptions, and bargaining postures of the small Caribbean states within the U.S. sphere of influence (which Maingot illustrates is no simple matter). Andrés Serbin, *Caribbean Geopolitics: Toward Security Through Peace?* (1990), examines, with theoretical insight, the confluence of external and internal factors in the geopolitical configuration of the anglophone Caribbean. He emphasizes the goals of subregional integration, the difficult relations with Latin America, and the possibilities of establishing a Commonwealth Caribbean zone of peace to supersede the historical colonial and sphere of influence dependency on outsiders. Ivelaw Lloyd Griffith, *The Quest for Security in the Caribbean: Problems and Promises in Subordinate States* (1993), is the most comprehensive investigation of Commonwealth Caribbean security policies. Seeing the states as forming a "security unit," Griffith explores the history, politics, economics, and geography of security and emphasizes Commonwealth Caribbean perceptions, ideology, capabilities, and individual and collective security measures. He also deals with systemic subregional geopolitics and drugs and suggests policies that the local states might adopt in the post–cold war era. Also of interest is Lambros Comitas and David Lowenthal, eds., *The Aftermath of Sovereignty: West Indian Perspectives* (1973). Jorge Heine and Leslie F. Manigat, eds., *The Caribbean and World Politics: Cross-Currents and Cleavages* (1986), present top-quality essays that pay considerable attention to Caribbean foreign policies, the roles of Latin American regional middle powers, and U.S. policies (see Chapter 2 for further commentary). Anthony T. Bryan and Andrés Serbín, eds., *Distant Cousins: The Caribbean–Latin American Relationship* (1994), has policy implications for the Commonwealth Caribbean states (see Chapter 2 for commentary). Other citations and commentaries on the Commonwealth Caribbean subregion, concerned more with interactions than state foreign policy processes, are found in Chapters 2, 4, 6, and 8.

South America.[5]   A survey history by Argentine scholar Vicente G. Quesada, *Historia diplomática hispanoamericana* (3 vols., 1918–1920), was one of the earliest studies of Latin American foreign policies. The book was a collection of papers, most of them previously published articles up to 1884. Despite the title, the posthumously published work focused on South American boundary and territorial questions (the principal intraregional concern). It emphasized Brazil's imperialist policies, boundaries, and certain other relations with the rest of South America and devoted significant attention to Chile and Argentina in similar terms. Two books by Arthur P. Whitaker together examine U.S. relations with eight South American states. *The United States and South America: The Northern Republics* (1948) studies Bolivia, Peru, Ecuador, Colombia, Venezuela; and *The United States and the Southern Cone* (1976) examines Argentina, Chile, and Uruguay. They are penetrating analyses that do not hesitate to criticize U.S. policies. Fredrick B. Pike, *The United States and the Andean Republics: Peru, Bolivia, and Ecuador* (1977), is an excellent, imaginative, broadly analytic comparative history since independence. He identifies the values in the political culture of each state as a base for analyzing the deeply diverging interests in their relationships with the United States. As with all of Pike's work, this is a thoroughly researched and deeply insightful work. G. Pope Atkins, ed., *South America into the 1990s: Evolving International Relationships in a New Era* (1990), contains considerable reference to the policies of individual South American states, particularly Brazil and Argentina. The superb diplomatic history by Robert N. Burr, *By Reason or Force: Chile and the Balancing of Power in South America, 1830–1905* (1967), is one of the few systematic analyses of balance of power policies and interactions having to do with Latin America. It centers on Chile but provides a broad description and analysis of the workings of the Southern Cone balance-of-power system.

Relations with the United States.   Graham H. Stuart and James L. Tigner, *Latin America and the United States* (6 eds., 1922–1975), has chapters dealing with U.S. relations with Colombia, Mexico, Cuba, Haiti, Dominican Republic, Argentina, Chile, Brazil, and, grouped together, the Central American states. J. Lloyd Mecham, *A Survey of United States–Latin American Relations* (1965), has six chapters that chronicle the history of U.S. policies toward nine individual Latin American states: Argentina, Brazil, Chile, Cuba, the Dominican Republic, Haiti, Mexico, Nicaragua, and Panama, and a chapter treating the Central American states. Published as companion volumes, T. Ray Shurbutt, ed., *United States–Latin American Relations, 1800–1850: The Formative Generations*

(1991), and Thomas M. Leonard, ed., *United StatesLatin American Relations, 1850–1903: Establishing a Relationship* (1999), make up a comprehensive survey. Chapters on individual states, written by experts on Mexico, Colombia, the Central American states, Peru, Argentina, Brazil, Uruguay, and Paraguay, are attentive to U.S. and Latin American perspectives. Mark T. Gilderhus, *The Second Century: U.S.–Latin American Relations Since 1889* (1999), pursues as a basic theme Latin American resistance to U.S. attempts to assert its power and impose its values from the late nineteenth century to the end of the cold war. A history by Donald Marquand Dozer, *Are We Good Neighbors? Three Decades of Inter-American Relations, 1930–1960* (1959), is particularly relevant for its treatment of Latin American attitudes in important opinion sectors: government and political leaders, journalists, intellectuals, and others. James D. Cockcroft, *Latin America: History, Politics, and U.S. Policy* (2 eds., 1989, 1996), is a thorough, multidisciplinary, polemical, fact-filled, state-by-state "analytic text-book," authored by a prominent dependency theorist. Frida Modak, ed., *25 años de relaciones América Latina–Estados Unidos* (1988), includes twenty-two contributors who interpret from generally leftist perspectives (some brilliantly, others shrilly) on an uncoordinated range of topics. They include the Cuban Revolution, insurgency, development, world economy, integration, democracy, Liberation Theology, national security doctrine, militarism, dictatorship, and events in several countries. Venezuelan writer and former diplomat Carlos Rangel, *The Latin Americans: Their Love-Hate Relationship with the United States* (2 eds., 1977, 1987), in sharp contrast to dependency theory but without absolving the United States of responsibility, concludes that the sources of most of Latin America's problems are internal rather than external. Robert Wesson and Heraldo Muñoz, eds., *Latin American Views of U.S. Policy* (1986), assemble leading scholars from Argentina, Brazil, Chile, and Mexico for their perspectives on the Reagan administration's policies toward the Inter-American System, Central America, Mexico, Brazil, Chile, and inter-American commerce. They are balanced, judicious, and insightful. The authors in Robert E. Biles, ed., *Inter-American Relations: The Latin American Perspective* (1988), admirably present Latin American points of view on Central American conflict, external debt, and problems confronting Mexico and Brazil. Other works on

Latin American–Caribbean relations with the United States, which do not deal substantially with Latin American state foreign policies, are cited and commented on in Chapters 2 and 5.

ARGENTINA

An early detailed narrative diplomatic history, published in France, was by the prolific Argentine author, Daniel Antokoletz, *Histoire de la diplomatie argentine* (2 vols., 1914). He was followed by the landmark work by Norberto Piñero, *La política internacional argentina* (1924). It is a series of essays covering a variety of themes from the movement for independence to the 1920s. They deal with British and U.S. activities during the revolution against Spain; subsequent sovereignty and border questions; relations with Britain and Germany; participation in The Hague conferences and the Pan American movement; and Argentina's position toward World War I and the League of Nations, and postwar Pan Americanism. Sergio Bagú, *Argentina en el mundo* (1961), by a professor of history at the National University of Buenos Aires, provides a conceptual treatment of Argentina's international history and educated speculation about its future in a world of mass society and international order. He concludes that if Argentina is to recover from the economic stagnation suffered since 1930, it must avoid participation in regional organizations that limit its "autonomy of decision." Isidro Ruíz Moreno, *Historia del las relaciones exteriores argentinas, 1810–1955* (1961), has value for its factual summary of a broad historical period. Well-known Argentine historian Roberto Etcheparaborda, *Historia de las relaciones internacionales argentinas* (1978), analyzes key circumstances and occurences in Argentina's diplomatic history and emphasizes its relations with neighbors Brazil, Chile, Peru, Uruguay, Paraguay, and Bolivia. His documentation and bibliography are excellent. Guillermo Miguel Figari, *Pasado, presente y futuro de la política exterior argentina* (1993), provides a sociological-historical dependency theory of Argentina's foreign policies since the mid-nineteenth century. It ranges from paradigms associated with national consolidation, the two world wars and the interbellum period, and the cold war transition from Juan Perón's "Third Position" to alignment with the West. Mario Rapaport, *El labertino argentino política internacional en un mundo con-*

flictivo (1997), offers an excellent survey of Argentina's foreign relations throughout much of the twentieth century. Alberto A. Conil Paz and Gustavo E. Ferrari, *Argentina's Foreign Policy, 1930–1962* (1996), identifies causes and effects in Argentina's policies toward the Inter-American System, neutrality in World War II, and orientations toward the United Nations, the United States, Great Britain, and South American neighbors. A massive undertaking, directed by Argentine scholars Andrés Cisneros and Carlos Escudé, has recently been concluded: *Historia general de las relaciones exteriores República Argentina* (14 vols., 1998–2000). The work assembles a large number of experts who provide extensive coverage, with themes organized within chronological historical periods.

A good general foreign policy analysis is found in Edward S. Milenky, *Argentina's Foreign Policies* (1978). He deals with policy-making processes and the substance of Argentina's policies, utilizing a political system framework. Milenky addresses Argentina's position in the international system; its capabilities, instrumentalities, and policymaking process; relations with the United States and extrahemispheric states; and its use of multilateral diplomacy. Sonia Camargo y José María Vásquez Ocampo, *Autoritanismo e democracia na Argentina e Brasil (uma década de política exterior, 1973–1984)* (1988), is a well-organized theoretical effort to analyze the relationship of foreign policy orientations to regime type. It devotes six chapters to the case of Argentina, focusing on the return of Juan Perón to the presidency and the new peronism. A final chapter compares the Argentine and Brazilian experiences. Argentine policy analysts Monica Hirst and Roberto Russell, *Democracia y política exterior: los casos de Argentina y Brazil* (1987), execute a tight analysis of the complex and far from obvious relationship between democracy and foreign policy in the two cases. Carlos Escudé, *Foreign Policy Theory in Menem's Argentina* (1997), is a theoretical discussion of the bases on which governing democratic elites sustain effective and development-oriented foreign policies. Rubén M. Perina and Roberto Russell, eds., *Argentina en el mundo (1973–1987)* (1988), bring together analysts who paint a comprehensive picture of Argentina's foreign policies during the dates indicated. After a conceptual treatment of the study of international relations and Argentina's foreign policies, chapters deal with the nature and content of Perónist policies (1973–1976), those of the military regime (1976–1983), and President Alfonsin's decisions during his first year in office. Others address relations with the Soviet Union, inter–Latin American cooperation, nuclear policies and non-proliferation, the impact of nationalism on policy, and Argentina's post-authoritarian role in the international system. Andrés Cisneros, ed., *Política exterior argentina, 1989–1999: historia de un éxito* (1998), addresses Argentina's policies for the decade beginning with the end of the cold war. Contributors to Alfredo Eric Calcagno, ed., *Argentina hacia el 2000: desafíos y opciones* (1989), analyze the future of Argentina's international role in terms of macroeconomic and demographic factors and the competition of international economic and technological development. Juan Carlos González Hernández and Enrique Alvarez Conde, *Argentina en el sistema internacional* (1984), is a well-informed discussion of Argentina's foreign policy goals and options. Of interest with reference to foreign economic relations is a book by Luis Maria Kreckler, *La diplomacia empresarial: una nueva forma de política exterior* (1997).

On the subregional level, Víctor Lascano, *Argentine Foreign Policy in Latin America* (1941), within the time frame 1808–1923, deals primarily with Argentina's relations with its South American neighbors, with some attention to the Monroe Doctrine, Pan Americanism, and Europe. Alberto Emilio Asseff, *Proyección continental de la Argentina de la geohistoria a la geopolitica nacional* (1980), is a thorough and perceptive evaluation of the implications of geopolitical doctrines. He focuses on the way they influenced the decisions and behavior of the military regime (1976–1983) toward its neighbors and during the Malvinas/Falklands War with Great Britain. See the general treatments of geopolitics (above) for Argentina's schools of thought. For a recent explication, see Adolfo Koutoudjian, *Geopolítica tridimensional Argentina: reflexiones para el siglo XXI* (1999).

Historians have produced several good surveys of Argentina's relations with the United States. Harold F. Peterson, *Argentina and the United States, 1810–1960* (1964), addresses social and historical elements that formed Argentina's perceptions of and policies toward the United States. He addresses the revolution for independence from Spain, the subsequent seeking of recognition from the outside world, the Malvinas/Falklands issue, international trade and investment, the two world wars, the cold war, and rivalry for hemispheric leadership. Joseph S. Tulchin, *Argentina and the United States: A Conflicted Relationship* (1990), sees relations as a history of repeated mutual misperceptions, misunderstandings, and lack of cooperation. The reasons, Tulchin says, stem from different historical experiences, national interests, and capabilities. He provides an abundance of information and expert interpretation. Arthur P. Whitaker, *The United States and Argentina* (1954), is a highly informative but oddly balanced treatment. It devotes considerable space to a description of Argentina's land, people, economics, and society; briefly summarizes the history of Argentina's relations with the United States to World War II; and devotes more than half of the book to relations during the era of Juan Perón (1943–1955). Nevertheless, the book constitutes an erudite introduction to an important country by a leading student of its history. See also Arthur P. Whitaker, *The United States and the Southern Cone* (1976), in which Argentina is one of the states studied. Thomas Francis McGann, *Argentina, the United States, and the Inter-American System, 1880–1914* (1957), is an excellent analysis of this particular element of the two states' relations.

Argentina's relations with the extrahemispheric world have always been important. Henry Stanley Ferns, *Britain and Argentina in the Nineteenth Century* (1960), is a long, attentive appraisal of relations from the beginning of the movement for independence from Spain in 1806 to the Baring banking emergency and the economic crisis of the 1890s. Ferns challenges arguments about "British imperialism" as accounting for Argentina's economic and other problems and assigns responsibility to Argentina itself, especially maneuvers by the large landholders to protect their interests. Alvaro Resio Trejo, *Historia de las relaciones ruso-argentinas* (1946), is a chronicle of Argentine relations with Russia to the Bolshevik Revolution of 1917. Aldo César Vacs, *Discreet Partners: Argentina and the USSR Since 1917* (1984), is a relatively brief, well-organized analysis, largely from an Argentine perspective. Vacs argues that relations hinged on economic complementarity, with diplomatic ties and military exchanges coming as adjunct elements.

BOLIVIA

The principal work on Bolivia's international relations is the recently published survey history by Kehman D. Lehman, *Bolivia and the United*

States: A Limited Partnership (1999), which emphasizes twentieth-century phenomena. Although acknowledging Bolivia's relative remoteness and U.S. dominance in the relationship, Lehman gives full play to Bolivia's perspectives, interests, and tactics. An interesting theme is how factors of both power and culture have complicated the relationship and the impact of mutual myth making about each other on policymaking by both states. Carlos Alberto Salinas Baldivieso, *Historia diplomática de Bolivia* (1938), is a brief but satisfactory early survey. Two books emphasize Bolivia's relations with neighboring states (Peru, Paraguay, Chile, Argentina, and Brazil) and their boundary and territorial problems: Valentín Abecia Baldivieso, *Las relaciones internacionales en la historia de Bolivia* (3 vols., 2 eds., 1978, 1986); and Jorge Escobari Cusicanqui, *Historia diplomática de Bolivia: política internacional* (4 eds., 1975–1982). Escobari Cusicanqui, *El derecho al mar* (1964), presents a thoughtful case for Bolivia's pursuit of access to the sea—its coastal territory had been lost to Chile as a result of the War of the Pacific (1879–1883). Also of interest are Eduardo Arze Quiroga, *Las relaciones internacionales de Bolivia, 1825–1990* (1991), by a prominent Bolivian historian; a lengthy treatment by Edgar Camacho Omiste, *Política exterior independiente* (1989); and a substantial multiauthored work, Raúl Barrios Morón and others, *Política exterior boliviano: tendencias y desafíos* (1995). Fredrick B. Pike, *The United States and the Andean Republics: Peru, Bolivia, and Ecuador* (1977), includes Bolivia as one of the states analyzed.

BRAZIL

Brazilian historian Manuel de Oliveira Lima, *Historia diplomática do Brasil: reconhecimento do imperio* (2 eds., 1901, 1902), surveyed Brazil's diplomatic history, highlighting the movement for independence and its aftermath and focusing and summarizing the rest of the nineteenth century. Hélio Vianna, *Historia diplomática do Brazil* (2 eds., 1958, 1961), is a satisfactory survey—but, curiously, makes no effort to address the two decades between the world wars. Noted Brazilian historian José Honorio Rodrígues produced companion works, *Aspiracoes nacionais: interpreteco historico-politico* (1965), and *Interesse nacional e política externa* (1966), in which he admirably and broadly analyzes continuing themes in Brazil's foreign policies and international relations to the time of publication. He strongly and personally condemns the military *golpe* of April 1964 and its aftermath. A monograph by Richard Graham, ed., *Brazil and the World System* (1991), analyzes the proposition that Brazil's history is understood in terms of its inclusion after independence into the world system. Amado Luiz Cervo and Clodoaldo Bueno, *Historia da política exterior do Brasil* (1992), survey Brazil's foreign policies from independence in 1822 until about 1990, largely in terms of its search for autonomous foreign policies and national development. The method is a mixture of much description in a theoretical framework. José Honorio Rodrígues and Ricardo A. S. Seitenfus, *Uma historia diplomática do Brasil, 1531–1945* (1995), is a good university textbook surveying numerous themes in Brazil's international history, from the colonial era to the end of World War II.

João Calogeras Pandía, *A política exterior do imperio* (3 vols., 1927–1928) covers in detail the history of Brazil's colonial origins and movement for independence, and the diplomacy of the first and second monarchs and the interim regency. Ron Seckinger, *The Brazilian Monarchy and the South American Republics, 1822–1831: Diplomacy and State Building* (1984), analyzes, in solid theoretical terms, Brazil and the rest of South America during the movements for independence and the immediate aftermath. Five chapters deal directly with Brazil in terms of the international environment; ideology, internationalism, and self-interest; territory and trade; and power politics. Seckinger highlights the Cisplatine War between Brazil and Argentina for control of Uruguay. Helio Lobo, *O Panamericanismo e o Brasil* (1939), is by a prominent Brazilian international legal expert and diplomat. It is a precise history of the Pan American movement from the Panama Congress of 1826 to the Lima conference in 1938, highlighting the meaning for and participation of Brazil.

Stanley E. Hilton, *Brazil and the Great Powers, 1930–1939: The Politics of Trade Rivalry* (1975), interprets economic policy as Brazil's response to great power competition among Germany, the United Kingdom, and the United States for overseas markets and raw materials. He discusses the motives and roles of President Getulio Vargas, other individuals, the armed forces, and interest groups involved in the policymaking process, and Brazil's commercial and military demands. Francisco Clementino de

San Tiago Dantas, *Política externa independente* (1962), is an informative interpretation of Brazil's post–World War II quest for an "independent foreign policy." Diplomat-historian Alvaro Teixeira Soares, *O Brasil no conflicto ideologico global, 1937–1979* (1980), provides many facts and solid interpretations, with less attention paid to the post–world war period than the earlier years. Dealing with recent years is Paulo Roberto Almeida, *Relaçoes internacionais e política externa do Brasil* (1998).

Ronald M. Schneider, *Brazil: Foreign Relations of a Future World Power* (1976), applies a political system approach, examining the external environment, governmental and nongovernmental actors, critical continuing issues, and the outlook for Brazil's foreign policy. Schneider sees Brazil close to realizing its long-held ambition to be a great power in the international system. In a similar vein, William Perry, *Contemporary Brazilian Foreign Policy: The International Strategy of an Emerging Power* (1976), makes the case that Brazil has the "unquestionable potential to play a significant role on the international stage," and speculates on the consequences for the United States and other Latin American states. Wayne A. Selcher, *Brazil's Multilateral Relations: Between First and Third Worlds* (1978), argues in conceptual terms that the way Brazil deals with different issues in different ways indicates it belongs completely to neither the First nor the Third World. He offers an interpretation of Brazil's "upward mobility" images and strategies and devotes chapters to its membership in several intergovernmental organizations—commodities agreements, international financial institutions, the United Nations, and the Inter-American System—and to its special relationships in southern Africa. Selcher edited a volume of essays, *Brazil in the International System: The Rise of a Middle Power* (1981), which begins with an excellent "coordinating foreword." Nine contributors provide a multinational, fact-filled evaluation of Brazil's capabilities, achievements, and interests. Several of them see Brazil as a prospective significant global middle power. They also address foreign policy decisions made by the authoritarian military regime, and specific policies toward the rest of Latin America, Germany, and sub-Saharan Africa. Celso Lafer, *O Brasil e a crise mundial: paz, poder e política externa* (1984), ponders Brazil's contemporary foreign policy problems. Sonia de Camargo and José María Vásquez Ocampo, *Autoritanismo e democracia na Argentina e Brasil (uma década de política exterior,*

1973–1984) (1988), analyze the relationship of foreign policy orientations to regime type. They devote eight chapters to Brazil, focusing on
the foreign policies of two of the presidents of the military regime from
1973 to 1983, and the interactions of military officers, diplomats, and
technocrats. A final chapter compares the experiences of Brazil and Argentina. Gesner Oliveira, *Brasil-FMI: frustraces e perspectivas* (1993), discusses relations with the International Monetary Fund (IMF) regarding
the debt crisis and economic stabilization.

E. Bradford Burns, *Nationalism in Brazil: A Historical Survey* (1968), is
the standard work on the subject. A concise and insightful interpretation,
it discusses three stages of evolution: origins in sixteenth-century colonial
nativism, the defensive nature after independence through the nineteenth
century, and, in the twentieth century, its increasing usefulness in promoting self-identification and modernization. Flávio Mendes de Oliveira
Castro, *História da organizaçao do Ministério das Relaçoes Exteriores*
(1983), provides considerable detail about the development and organization of Brazil's foreign ministry. Monica Hirst and Roberto Russell,
Democracia y política exterior: los casos de Argentina y Brazil (1987), is an
insightful comparative analysis of the relationship between democracy
and foreign policy.

A comprehensive international political economic study by Bertha K.
Becker and Claudio A. G. Egler, *Brazil: A New Regional Power in the
World Economy* (1992), is an admirably multidisciplinary textbook. It explores the dilemmas of the unbalanced yet impressive Brazilian economy—the majority of its population lives in poverty within the world's
eighth largest and heavily industrialized economy. The authors trace the
evolution of Brazil's socioeconomic system from the colonial period
through its rise to regional and even world economic power. They con-
template how the current world capitalist system might affect Brazil's future structure. Winston Fritsch, *External Constraints on Economic Policy
in Brazil, 1889–1930* (1988), is a revisionist study challenging the theory
that the nature of the First Republic's export economy was determined by
Brazilian coffee growers. Fritsch says that the principal influences were
foreign bankers supported by their governments.

As the giant of Latin America, and bordering on all other South American states except Chile, Brazil's regional policies and relations have al-

ways been important. Gino F. Costa, *Brazil's Foreign Policy: Toward Regional Dominance* (1989), by a professor of history at the Catholic University in Lima, still sees Brazil as a middle power capable of achieving great power. See the general section above on geopolitics, which refers extensively to Brazil. See also Renato de Mendonça, *Fronteira em marcha: ensaio de uma geopolítica brasileira* (1956). Michael A. Morris, *International Politics and the Sea: The Case of Brazil* (1979), deals with Brazil's emergence as a major ocean power and its importance for Brazilian foreign policy. Morris says the concern occupies a distinct position in Brazil's bilateral, regional, and global negotiations for a new ocean order.

The standard historical survey of Brazil's relations with the United States for many years after its publication was Lawrence F. Hill, *Diplomatic Relations Between the United States and Brazil* (1932), an authoritative scholarly survey. Moniz Bandeira, *Presença dos Estados Unidos no Brasil: dois séculos de historia* (1973), is a good, detailed narrative history of Brazil's U.S. relations, with useful references to other states. About half of the book addresses the period from 1930 to 1964. Specific time periods of Brazilian–United States relations are well covered. The survey by Joseph Smith, *Unequal Giants: Diplomatic Relations Between the United States and Brazil, 1889–1930* (1991), emphasizes disparities in power between the two states as they deal with political, economic, and military issues and events. Smith also highlights linkages between internal and external factors. Steven C. Topic, *Trade and Gunboats: The United States and Brazil in the Age of Empire* (1998), is a study in international political economic history. Like McCann, Topic pays close attention to the interaction of domestic and international variables in both states. E. Bradford Burns, *The Unwritten Alliance: Rio-Branco and Brazilian-American Relations* (1966), narrates Brazil's skillful diplomacy led by its celebrated foreign minister, who turned attention from Europe and Britain's long-standing primacy toward the Americas by creating an "unwritten alliance" with the United States and supporting the Pan American movement. Frank D. McCann Jr., *The Brazilian-American Alliance, 1937–1945* (1973), in a comprehensive, impressively researched study, tells how strategic demands in World War II pushed Brazil and the United States into alliance. It involved raw materials and military and naval bases supplied by Brazil, financial and technical assistance on the part of the United States, and direct wartime participation by the Brazilian army and navy. W. Michael Weis, *Cold Warriors and Coups d'Etat: Brazilian-American Relations, 1945–1964* (1993), picks up at the end of World War II and analyzes the following two-decade period. During that time, relations deteriorated to the point that the United States supported a coup d'état that overthrew an elected president and began a long period of military government. Weis faults the United States for judging Brazil's governments by their anticommunist commitment, thus misjudging their thrust to pursue more autonomous foreign policies. Gerald K. Haines, *The Americanization of Brazil: A Study of U.S. Cold War Diplomacy in the Third World, 1945–1954* (1989), is a solid, insightful study. Haines sees policy continuity in the Truman and Eisenhower presidencies founded on anticommunism, within which the U.S. ideology of democratic capitalism and developmentalist policies were subsumed. Haines asserts this was the first U.S. attempt "to deal with emerging Third World nationalism and the Third World's political and economic problems," ignoring the precedence of previous U.S. efforts in Latin America before the Third World concept had became fashionable and long after Latin America had "emerged." Ruth Leacock, *Requiem for Revolution: The United States and Brazil, 1961–1969* (1990), looks at how the Kennedy and Johnson administrations dealt with Brazilian politics as they moved from the left to the military authoritarian right. They shifted from calling for reform and counterinsurgency through the Alliance for Progress to supporting a Brazilian coup and getting along with the resulting military regime. Leacock criticizes both Brazil's sociopolitical structure and the U.S. exaggeration of the Communist threat. Jan Knippers Black, *United States Penetration in Brazil* (1977), also sharply criticizes the behavior of the U.S. government in Brazil, in concert with U.S. private interests, from 1960 to the mid-1970s. She argues that the influence they brought to bear on the Brazilian armed forces and police, corporations, political parties, news media, and development agencies helped to "divide, discredit, and destroy" popular movements seen to pose a threat to foreign capital. They also strengthened Brazilian authoritarian tendencies (dramatically demonstrated by the military regime that took power in 1964). Robert G. Wesson, *The United States and Brazil: Limits of Influence* (1981), sees Brazil as having "evolved from a subordinate U.S. ally to a self-confident entity with the potential to become a great power in the near future." He analyzes the U.S. role in Brazil's military, political, and cultural affairs; the effects of U.S. business investment on its economy and politics; and tensions over the issues of nuclear energy and human rights. Wesson concludes that the ability of the United States to influence Brazil, despite the power disparities, is limited to a narrow range of complementary interests.

Alan K. Manchester, *British Preeminence in Brazil, Its Rise and Decline* (1933), analyzes Brazil's special relationship with Great Britain in a scholarly history. Richard Graham, *Britain and the Onset of Modernization in Brazil, 1850–1914* (1968), was the distinguished historian's first (and impressively researched and written) book on Brazil. He says that Britain's actions were important catalysts for Brazil's modernization in the nineteenth century. With financial and technical assistance and political and social ideas, Britain helped build Brazil's infrastructure, develop coffee cultivation, and end the slave trade and then abolish slavery.

Brazil's special attitude toward Africa is explored in a scholarly, normative, and controversial study beginning with the Atlantic slave trade by Brazilian historian José Honorio Rodrígues, *Brazil and Africa* (1965). He argues that Brazil is essentially more African than Iberian and has had qualitatively different relations with southern Africa than with Spanish America. He discusses future relationships in terms of this assertion. Wayne A. Selcher, *The Afro-Asian Dimension of Brazilian Foreign Policy, 1956–1972* (1974), discusses Brazil's relations with Africa, the Middle East, and non-Communist Asia, with special attention to South Africa, Portuguese Africa, and Japan. He surveys the complex history of relationships, applies certain quantitative measures, and finds the Afro-Asian dimension to be relatively unimportant in the total scheme of Brazil's external relationships. Leon Hollerman, *Japan's Economic Strategy in Brazil: Challenge for the United States* (1988), concluded that "Japan will be increasingly competitive with the United States in matters concerning Brazil." Stanley E. Hilton, *Brazil and the Soviet Challenge, 1917–1947* (1991), argues that Brazil's political elites (civilian and military) who controlled domestic politics and foreign policy decisions held extreme anticommunist attitudes. Soviet subversive activities further inspired Brazil's continuing refusal to recognize the Soviet Union, the authoritarianism of the Duarte government from 1930 to 1945, and Brazil's espionage activities in the Southern Cone of South America.

CHILE

Scholarly surveys of Chile's relations with the United States date from the 1920s with two narratives by U.S. historians: William Roderick Sherman, *The Diplomatic and Commercial Relations of the United States and Chile, 1820–1914* (1926), and Henry Clay Evans, *Chile and Its Relations with the United States* (1927). Both focus on the nineteenth century and provide fact-filled, pedestrian chronicles based largely on U.S. sources. Frederick B. Pike, *Chile and the United States, 1880–1962* (1963), is a superb, carefully researched analysis of Chile's political, social, and economic developments related to relations with the United States. Pike argues that even though Chile's historical distrust of the United States results from distorted images, if the United States wishes to have Chile's friendship it must comprehend that viewpoint. Two prominent Chilean political scientists, Heraldo Muñoz and Carlos Portales, in *Elusive Friendship: A Survey of U.S.-Chilean Relations* (1991), trace relations from Chilean independence to 1990. They take a convincing revisionist position with their definition of the "elusive friendship" as one in which conflict has been more frequent than cooperation. William F. Sater, *Chile and the United States: Empires in Conflict* (1990), an excellent general survey, also emphasizes "the often stormy course of U.S.-Chilean relations." Sater integrates social and cultural phenomena with diplomatic, political, and economic matters; he provides a solid bibliographic essay. See also Arthur P. Whitaker, *The United States and the Southern Cone: Argentina, Chile, and Uruguay* (1976).

The leftist coalition government led by Salvador Allende (1970–1973) generated much academic interest, with the U.S. hostility toward it, the friendly relationship with Castro's Cuba, and its overthrow by the Chilean armed forces. Joaquín Fermandois H., *Chile y el mundo, 1970–1973: la política exterior del gobierno de la Unidad Popular y el sistema internacional* (1985), is a thorough, systematic foreign policy analysis. It addresses the competing foreign policy influences in Allende's Popular Unity coalition and other government actors and the armed forces;

relations with the United States in terms of "anti-imperialist principles" versus "hegemonic reaction"; relations with Argentina, Brazil, Mexico, Cuba, the Soviet Union, and Europe; and international economic relations. Jorge Vera Castillo, *La política exterior chilena durante el gobeirno del Presidente Salvador Allende, 1970–1973* (1987) is based on a conference (held before the departure of the military regime) that included academics as well as members of Allende's government. Edy Kaufman, *Crisis in Allende's Chile: New Perspectives* (1988), is a well-researched and somewhat speculative explanation of the nature of Allende's coalition government and the reasons for the military coup, including the role of the United States. Miles D. Wolpin, *Cuban Foreign Policy and Chilean Politics* (1972), is a major work. Wolpin analyzes both Cuban and U.S. efforts to influence Chilean party alignments and policies. It evaluates the "structural features of Chile's political system" that "effectively limited the transnational appeal of the Cuban Revolution." Heraldo Muñoz, *Las relaciones exteriores del gobierno militar chileno* (1986), analyzes the military regime that overthrew Allende (it stayed in power until 1989).

Alejandro Alvarez, *Chile ante la segunda conferencia de la Haya* (1907), is a scholarly treatment of Chile's participation in The Hague Conference of 1907. Walter Sánchez G. and Teresa Pereira L., eds., *Cientocincuenta años de política exterior chilena* (1977), is a well-researched, insightful narrative of the first post–World War II quarter-century. Oscar Pinochet de la Barra, *La antártica chilena* (4 eds., 1948–1976), is an important study of Chile's claim to a substantial sector of Antarctica. For a good analysis of Chile's important growing relations with Pacific countries, see Juan Salazar Sparks and others, *Chile y la comunidad del Pacífico* (1999).

COLOMBIA

The most significant of the early works was Colombian historian Antonio José Uribe, *Anales diplomáticos y consulares de Colombia* (6 vols., 1900–1920). Raimundo Rivas produced two notable early studies: *Relaciones internacionales entre Colombia y los Estados Unidos, 1810–1850* (1915), for which he took advantage of relatively recent access to a significant portion of Colombian archives; and *Historia diplomática de Colombia, 1810–1934*, written in the late 1930s but not published until 1961, fifteen years after his death. The latter work was still useful because of its broad topical coverage and further research in Colombian archives. Another Colombian historian, Germán Cavelier, produced an essential study, *La política internacional de Colombia* (4 vols., 1949–1959). A thoroughly researched chronological narrative, the coverage includes many commercial, political, and economic questions, as well as more specific topics related to such matters as boundary and territorial problems and questions of diplomatic asylum.

A number of foreign policy analyses have appeared. Ester Lozano de Rey and Pilar Marulanda de Galofre, *Como se hace la política exterior en Colombia* (1982), is a brief, serviceable study of the formulation and content of Colombian foreign policy. Essays by Colombian sociologists, in Rodrigo Parra Sandoval, ed., *Dependencia externa y desarrollo político en Colombia* (1970), conclude that the dependency theories of their U.S. and European colleagues are insufficient to explain linkages between the external world and Colombia's social structures and processes. Colombia's post–World War II foreign policy is well analyzed by Gerhard Drekonja Kornat, *Colombia política exterior* (1982), and by Rodrigo Pardo and Juan G. Tokatlian, *Política exterior colombiana: de la subordinación a la autonomía?* (1988). On the post–cold war period, see Socorro Ramírez, Luis Alberto Restrepo, and Maria Emma Mejía, eds., *Colombia entre la inserción y el aislamiento: la política exterior colombiana en los años noventa* (1997).

E. Taylor Parks, *Colombia and the United States, 1765–1934* (1935), by a U.S. diplomatic historian, was for many years the only survey in English of the relationship. It is stronger on the nineteenth century than later years. Canadian professor Stephen J. Randall contributes the best current general survey (with a good bibliographic essay), *Colombia and the United States: Hegemony and Interdependence* (1992). He emphasizes the tension attendant to the power disparities in the interstate relationship, evolving in the twentieth century to one of Colombia as a regional middle-power within the sphere of the superpower United States. In contrast, the outcome of intersocietal relations is one of considerable interdependence. In an earlier book, Randall, *The Diplomacy of Modernization: Colombian-American Relations, 1920–1940* (1977), examined the continued evolution of relations from the end of one world war to the beginning of another, when Presidents Hoover and Roosevelt sought to undo the Caribbean imperialism of the previous two decades. See also Arthur P. Whitaker, *The United States and South America: The Northern Republics* (1948), which includes Colombia among the five states studied; see above for commentary. With reference to the first part of the twentieth century, Richard L. Lael, *Arrogant Diplomacy: U.S. Policy Toward Colombia, 1903–1922* (1987), focuses on the Panama dispute between the two countries. He analyzes U.S. support for the Panamanian revolution for separation from Colombia and traces its effect on relations until it was resolved some two decades later. Lael sharply criticizes the United States for its irresponsible imperialism and unwillingness to acknowledge Colombia's interests.

A good survey of Colombian industry and tariff protection issues is presented in a major work by Luis Ospina Vásquez, *Industria y protección en Colombia, 1810–1930* (1955). In an economic study by Albrecht von Gleich and Diego Pizano Salazar, eds., *Colombia en la economía mundial* (1982), the coffee trade looms large. Two important studies deal directly with that commodity. Marco Palacios, *El café en Colombia (1850–1970): Una historia económica, social y política* (2 eds., 1980, 1983), is a landmark scholarly work. Applying an interdisciplinary, multimethod approach, Palacios investigates Colombia's emergence as a coffee-exporting country in the nineteenth century. He focuses on the societal effects of joining the economy with the world market. In a related approach, Charles W. Berquist, *Coffee and Conflict in Colombia, 1886–1910* (1978), addresses the political and economic consequences of Colombia's increasing integration with its coffee trade into the evolving world capitalist economy and inquires into the oligarchy's political and economic interests. Juan José Echavarría and Alfredo L. Fuentes, *Relaciones económicas de Colombia con los países del Caribe insular* (1981), closely analyze Colombia's economic relations with its Caribbean neighbors. They detail economic relations with the Caribbean Common Market, the Dutch Antilles, Puerto Rico, and the Dominican Republic.

· COSTA RICA

Francisco Rojas Aravena, ed., *Costa Rica y el sistema internacional* (1990), is a collection of essays in which Costa Rican scholars and officials analyze numerous elements of the small country's role in the international system. Rojas Aravena also wrote *Costa Rica: política exterior y crisis centroamericana* (1990), a thorough investigation of Costa Rica's policies toward and relations with its isthmian neighbors. Kyle Longley, *The Sparrow and the Hawk: Costa Rica and the United States During the Rise of José Figueres* (1997), theorizes about small state strategies in the case of Costa Rica, faced with choosing resistance or accommodation to seemingly overwhelming U.S. power. An excellent book by Martha Honey, *Hostile Acts: U.S. Policy in Costa Rica in the 1980s* (1994), is a thorough "study in contemporary imperialism." The subject is the Reagan and Bush administrations' willingness to subvert Costa Rica's democratic system in its determination to overthrow the Sandinista government in Nicaragua by way of sponsoring insurgency.

CUBA

Only a few general survey histories of Cuba's foreign policies and international relations have appeared. Until the Castro revolution of 1959, writers focused on Cuba's relations with the United States and its dominating presence. Russell H. Fitzgibbon, *Cuba and the United States, 1900–1935* (1935), is a survey of postindependent Cuba by a U.S. political scientist. He sought "a unified, objective, and scientific study of the whole of Cuban-American relations," and was one of the few to have achieved that standard of scholarship. Another impressive early effort by a prestigious Cuban historian, Herminio Portell-Vilá, *Historia de Cuba en sus relaciones con los Estados Unidos y España* (4 vols., 1938–1939), is a meticulously researched comprehensive history. It is judicious in tone and objective in both its criticism and accolades. Lester D. Langley, *The Cuban Policy of the United States: A Brief History* (1968), is an introductory-summary chronological history of the Cuban policy of the United States, more than half devoted to nineteenth-century U.S. interests in the Spanish colony. Two chapters deal, respectively, with the period 1898–1933 ("the years of paternalism"), and Batista and Castro. Analyst Pamela S. Falk, *Cuban Foreign Policy: Caribbean Tempest* (1986), is an introduction to the evolution of Cuban foreign policy for a general audience, useful primarily for the information it provides. The book is broadly topical but thin on analysis. Falk emphasizes the complexities of Cuba's actions since 1959 beyond the simplistic anti-Castro rhetoric that Cuba is simply a surrogate for the Soviet Union. The history by senior Cuban expert Louis A. Pérez Jr., *Cuba and the United States: Ties of Singular Intimacy* (1990), which begins in the eighteenth century and runs to the late 1980s, is a comprehensive analytic study. The general proposition is that "relations between Cuba and the United States seemed destined from the beginning to be close and complicated." Pérez argues that Cuba learned how to resist, manipulate, and accommodate, as well as accede to, U.S. power. He contributes a superb bibliographical essay. British historian Hugh Thomas, *Cuba: The Pursuit of Freedom* (1971), is a massive (1,696 pages), idiosyncratic, heavily detailed history with much information and interpretation about Cuba's international relations. The unbalanced two-part division of the study—the first a coverage of the years from 1762 to 1959, and the second on the Castro regime—is because "so much that seems obscure in the present Cuban scene became comprehensible if set against the experiences of the previous four or five generations.

A number of excellent foreign policy analyses have been produced but none within a broad overall scheme. They are cast in terms of particular phenomena or time periods, and are included in the following commentary along with similarly framed histories. Leland Hamilton Jenks, *Our Cuban Colony: A Study in Sugar* (1928), is a study in economic imperialism, a leading phase of contemporary modern commerce and investment, with strong domestic political implications for both Cuba and the United States. Irwin F. Gellman, *Roosevelt and Batista: Good Neighbor Diplomacy in Cuba, 1933–45* (1973), says that the Cuban case suggests closer scrutiny of the Good Neighbor Policy's commitment to nonintervention in the internal affairs of others. Gellman credits the Roosevelt administration for abrogating the Platt amendment, but faults it for allowing Sergeant Fulgencio Batista to take power and then supporting him so as to ensure stability and protect U.S. economic interests. Thus the United States continued to participate significantly in Cuba's internal affairs. Luis E. Aguilar, *Cuba 1933, Prologue to Revolution* (1972), produced a work of broader scope than the title implies. It is a perceptive analysis of events after independence as well as the revolutionary events of 1933, dictator Machado's downfall, and Batista's rise. It gives a full account of Sumner

LATIN AMERICAN AND CARIBBEAN STATES   121

Welle's mediation, his constant intrusion in Cuban politics, and distorted reports to President Roosevelt.

The era of the Cuban Revolution of 1959 has, as would be expected, received considerable attention. K. S. Karol, *Guerrillas in Power: The Course of the Cuban Revolution* (1970), is a thorough, subtle treatment by a Marxist journalist. Against a background of the revolution's overthrow of Batista and its path to an alliance with the Soviet Union in 1961, Karol interprets Cuba's subsequent complex and uneven relations with Moscow. Contributors to Jaime Suchlicki, ed., *Cuba, Castro, and Revolution* (1972), address trends in matters related to Cuba's foreign policy, its nationalism, relations with the Soviet Union, and the Cuban challenge to Latin American communism. Cole Blasier and Carmelo Mesa-Lago, eds., *Cuba in the World* (1979), includes the high-quality essays of thirteen expert contributors on important questions concerning Cuba's expanded participation in world affairs since the early 1970s and a broad range of thematic, regional, and bilateral issues. Martin Weinstein, ed., *Revolutionary Cuba in the World Arena* (1979), concisely examines Cuba's export of it political and economic values and practices in terms of foreign policy objectives, ideology, nationalism, security, sugar exports, and relations with the Soviet Union and the United States. H. Michael Erisman, *Cuba's International Relations: The Anatomy of a Nationalistic Foreign Policy* (1985), provides a good, compact introduction to Cuban foreign policy, primarily since the early 1970s, within a logical conceptual framework. Erisman highlights Cuba's emphasis on its role in the Third World and its relations with the United States and the Soviet Union (stressing Cuba's refusal to be a mere surrogate). His principal theme is the primacy of Cuba's nationalism, tempered by pragmatism and globalism rather than Marxism-Leninism. Philip Brenner, *From Confrontation to Negotiation: U.S. Relations with Cuba* (1988), summarizes the relationship and sharply criticizes the bases for three decades of U.S. policies, which had been anachronistic for at least the last ten years. He calls (intelligently and logically but politically before its time) for the "normalization" of the relationship. Two superb inquiries provide broad overviews and analyses of the subject. Jorge I. Domínguez, *To Make a World Safe for Revolution: Cuba's Foreign Policy* (1989), is a classic study, exceptionally informative, insightful, and well written. Domínguez argues that Cuba has "a specific foreign policy" resulting from internal and external variables and Fidel Castro's ideas and strategies. He fully recognizes the role of the Soviet Union, but without Castro, he says, the outcomes would have been quite different. Morris H. Morley, *Imperial State and Revolution: The United States and Cuba, 1952–1986* (1988), covers in detail the Cuban policies of six U.S. presidents. Morley's argument is in the world-system theoretical mold, saying that as an imperial state the United States worked to maintain Cuba on the periphery of the global system of capital accumulation. H. Michael Erisman and John M. Kirk, eds., *Cuban Foreign Policy Confronts a New International Order* (1991), bring together Cuban and U.S. scholars in a discourse on the relationships of Cuba and the Soviet Union–Eastern Europe; Cuba as mediator in international conflicts and supplier of development aid in the Third World; and Cuban policies toward Europe and Canada.

With the end of the cold war, the context for Cuba's policies and international relations changed dramatically. An excellent survey of the Castro years by David C. Jordan, *Revolutionary Cuba and the End of the Cold War* (1993), extends into the post–cold war era. Jordan evaluates the factors explaining Castro's seizure and long maintenance of political power, Cuba's problems of nationalism and dependency, the role of Castro's personality, Soviet strategy and U.S. policy reactions, and the end of the cold war and the removal of Soviet support. Carmelo Mesa-Lago, ed., *Cuba After the Cold War* (1993), is based on conference papers presented by prominent scholars who address the impact of the end of the cold war on Cuba and the critical international problems it had created. Economic matters are prominent. Donna Rich Kaplowitz, ed., *Cuba's New Ties to a Changing World* (1993), concentrates on Cuba's bilateral relations and the impact of the dissolution of the Soviet Union and major changes in Eastern Europe. She addresses Cuba's ties with China, Japan, Britain, the European Community, Canada, Mexico, Brazil, and Central American, Caribbean, and Middle Eastern states. Archibald R. M. Ritter and John M. Kirk, eds., *Cuba in the International System: Normalization and Integration* (1995), is a collection of sixteen significant essays by Cuban specialists (including Cubans). They address strategies of survival pursued by Cuban officials after the dissolution of the Soviet Union. Castro survived largely because of his ability to strengthen existing international relationships and to create new ones, despite continuing U.S. hostility. H. Michael Erisman provides a much-needed expert analysis of the full decade of the post–cold war period in *Cuba's Foreign Relations in a Post-Soviet World* (2000).

Cuban relations with the Soviet Union were an essential element of Cuba's international relations and for scholarly analysis. A general treatment of most of the postrevolutionary period, W. Raymond Duncan, *The Soviet Union and Cuba: Interests and Influence* (1985), argues, with compelling supporting evidence, that the concept of convergence of interests best defined the balance of influence between the two states after 1959. He says that despite the Soviet Union's obviously commanding power, Cuba manipulated the Soviets by combining acquiescence and resistance, depending on the issues and interests involved. A Soviet insider's knowledge and perspective adds to our understanding of Soviet interests. Yuri Pavlov, *Soviet-Cuban Alliance: 1959–1991* (1996), who had directed the Soviet foreign ministry's Latin American bureau during the last part of Gorbachev's premiership, interprets the Soviet decision to cooperate with the Central American peace process and describes Castro's deft maneuvering of Soviet officials. French Canadian professor Jacques Lévesque, *The USSR and the Cuban Revolution: Soviet Ideological and Strategical Perspectives, 1959–77* (1979), surveyed a very large number of Soviet writings and documents over almost two decades on the Cuban Revolution. The titles of the three parts of the book are indicative: from prudence to enthusiasm (1959–1963); from enthusiasm to disillusionment (1962–1968); and from disillusionment to accommodation (1969–1975). Lévesque argues the Cuban Revolution's profound impact on the outside world, especially on other revolutionaries and on the Soviet-U.S. relationship. Blanca Torres Ramírez, *Las relaciones cubano-sovieticas, 1959–1968* (1971), is a useful chronicle of Cuban-Soviet relations during the 1960s based on primary sources. Richard J. Payne, in *Opportunities and Dangers of Soviet-Cuban Expansion: Toward a Pragmatic U.S. Policy* (1988), adopts the role of "responsible academic critic" and examines Soviet-Cuban activities and the U.S. response to them in southern Africa, Afghanistan, Nicaragua, and the Commonwealth Caribbean. He calls for less ideology, emotion, and confrontation and more negotiation.

Cuba's remarkable activities in southern Africa and parts of the Middle East are the subject of two informative studies. Damián J. Fernández,

Cuba's Foreign Policy in the Middle East (1988), noting that Cuban activism had focused on Latin America and southern Africa, documents its serious involvement in the Middle East beginning in the 1970s. Factors behind Castro's decision to commit resources to that part of the world included the desire to export ideology and to increase leverage with the Soviet Union. Carlos Moore, *Castro, the Blacks, and Africa* (1993), asserts that race was a key factor in Castro's foreign policies, as he emphasized the racial bonds of blacks in Cuba, Africa, and the United States. Moore ascribes Castro's motives to a desire to embarrass the United States, solidify associations in Africa, and deflect Cuban's attention from domestic problems. Canadian scholars John M. Kirk and Peter McKenna, *Canada-Cuba Relations: The Other Good Neighbor Policy* (1997), provide a good treatment of the important but underresearched relationship since Castro came to power. They underscore Canada's "effective and principled policy." See also Miles D. Wolpin, *Cuban Foreign Policy and Chilean Politics* (1972) (cited above).

DOMINICAN REPUBLIC

A number of general works—survey histories and foreign policy analyses—have appeared that deal with various broad themes and time periods. For many years, Sumner Welles, *Naboth's Vineyard: The Dominican Republic, 1844–1924* (2 vols., 1928) constituted the most comprehensive and authoritative work. The author was a U.S. diplomat, and later a key figure in establishing President Franklin Roosevelt's Good Neighbor Policy. President Warren Harding in 1922 had sent Welles to the Dominican Republic to arrange elections and U.S. troop withdrawal. A gold mine of personal and State Department archival information, by present day standards the study seems a curious mix of sensitivity to another political culture and personal racial biases. At the same time, Melvin M. Knight published *The Americans in Santo Domingo* (1928) from the perspective of the U.S. anti-imperialist school. Charles Callan Tansill, *The United States and Santo Domingo, 1798–1873: A Chapter in Caribbean Diplomacy* (1938) is a highly detailed and heavily documented study with many references to papers from the foreign offices of France, Germany, and the United Kingdom. Tansill describes and assesses important aspects of U.S.

relations with both the Dominican Republic and Haiti, with treatments of their relations and an emphasis on the former state.

A more recent general work is by Michael J. Kryzanek and Howard J. Wiarda, *The Politics of External Influence in the Dominican Republic* (1988). A relatively brief thematic treatment within a broad time frame, the book is a provocative application of the concepts of dependence, independence, and interdependence of domestic and international systems. G. Pope Atkins and Larman C. Wilson, *The Dominican Republic and the United States: From Imperialism to Transnationalism* (1998), is a historical analysis, by two U.S. political scientists, of Dominican-U.S. relations from their beginning to date of publication. They include social and cultural as well as political and economic phenomena. The major theme is the long, tortuous movement from overt classic U.S. imperialism, with its military, political, economic, and cultural elements, through ambiguous relations in the long dictatorship of Rafael Trujillo and the following period dominated by President Joaquin Balaguer, to a post–cold war situation characterized by transnational phenomena. Atkins and Wilson earlier coauthored *The United States and the Trujillo Regime* (1972), a case study of U.S. policy problems with a Latin American dictatorship. The book addresses numerous elements of the relationship, including an assessment of U.S. responsibility for Trujillo's rise to and maintenance of power, and the role of the Inter-American System. Eric Paul Roorda, *The Dictator Next Door: The Good Neighbor Policy and the Trujillo Regime in the Dominican Republic, 1930–1945* (2000), is a deeply researched and tightly analyzed scholarly study of the vagaries of nonintervention policies when dealing with a brutal and clever dictator. Bernardo Vega contributes *Kennedy y los Trujillo* (1991) and *Trujillo y las fuerzas armadas norteamericanos* (1992), which are massive chronicles, particularly condemnatory of the roles played by certain U.S. officials and their effect on policies and relations. Vega, a Dominican economist and historian, former governor of the Dominican Central Bank, former Dominican ambassador to the United States, and director of the Fundación Cultural Dominicana, has edited and analyzed an indispensable series of documents on Dominican internal and foreign affairs, of which these are a part.

Dominican relations with Haiti and attitudes toward Haitians form a discrete category of analysis, a complex mixture of elements related to economics, politics, nationalism, society, culture, and race relations. Two classic works are highlighted: Rayford W. Logan, *Haiti and the Dominican Republic* (1968), by the noted African-American scholar; and Frank Moya Pons, *La dominación haitiana, 1822–1844* (1972), by a leading Dominican historian and social scientist. Important analyses of the unconscionable situation of Haitian laborers in the Dominican Republic are recommended. They are Frank Báez Evertsz, *Braceros haitianos en República Dominicana* (1986); Martin F. Murphy, *Dominican Sugar Plantations: Production and Foreign Labor Integration* (1991); and Saskia K. S. Wilhelms, *Haitian and Dominican Sugarcane Workers in Dominican Batayes: Patterns and Effects of Prejudice, Stereotypes, and Discrimination* (1995).

ECUADOR

Francisco Carrión Mena, *Política exterior del Ecuador: evolución, teoría y práctica* (1986) is a useful, conceptual general survey. A thorough multi-authored work sponsored by Universidad Central del Ecuador, Escuela de Ciencias Internacionales, *El Ecuador y los problemas internacionales* (1989), evaluates Ecuador's governmental agencies related to foreign policies, its participation in numerous intergovernmental organizations, and the external debt problem. In a brief empirical study testing the dependency theses of dependent foreign policy behavior, Jeanne A. K. Hey, *Theories of Dependent Foreign Policy and the Case of Ecuador in the 1980s* (1995), analyzes decisions made by two Ecuadorian presidents from 1981 to 1988. Charles Robert Gibson, *Foreign Trade in the Economic Development of Small Nations: The Case of Ecuador* (1971), argues that Ecuador's inability to realize economic growth with foreign trade is a consequence of internal constraints imposed by economic and policymaking structures, not the structure of trade or the world capitalist system. Two books by noted U.S. historians deal with Ecuador, among the states analyzed, in its relations with the United States: Fredrick B. Pike, *The United States and the Andean Republics: Peru, Bolivia, and Ecuador* (1977); and Arthur P. Whitaker, *The United States and South America: The Northern Republics* (1948). Two books by the well-known Ecuadorian jurist Teodoro Alvarado Garaicoa, *El Dominio del Mar* (1968) and *El mar territorial y el mar patrimonial* (1973), discuss the law of the sea and Ecuador's territorial waters position—the author justifies the 200-mile limit. Germánico Salgado, *Ecuador y la integración económica de América Latina* (1970), is a valuable examination of a small state's role and interest in economic integration.

HAITI

Jacques Nicholas Léger, *Haiti, Her History and Her Detractors* (1907), is a highly detailed chronological description of Haiti in the international system, from Columbus' first voyage to 1902. Appended is a complaint of the foreign powers' unsympathetic attitudes. At the time of publication, Léger was Haitian Envoy Extraordinary and Minister Plenipotentiary in the United States. Ludwell Lee Montague, *Haiti and the United States, 1714–1938* (1940), is a major work surveying Haiti's relations with the United States, with insightful appraisals of the country's economy and society. A very good survey history by Brenda Gayle Plummer, *Haiti and the United States: The Psychological Moment* (1992), is the most thorough study available. It is cast in the framework of contemporary social and cultural history writing. Much of the relationship, Plummer says, "has turned on matters of consciousness," with perceptions of race reflecting "psychic tensions deeply embedded in U.S. culture and society." Haitians, isolated much of the time from the rest of the world, suffer from their own violent and authoritarian politics. They perceive the United States as threatening, with its history of slavery, racism, and imperialism. Plummer includes a useful bibliographical essay. See also Plummer, *Haiti and the Great Powers, 1902–1915* (1988), and Alfred N. Hunt, *Haiti's Influence on Antebellum America* (1988). The distinguished longtime professor of history at Howard University in Washington, D.C., Rayford W. Logan, in his *The Diplomatic Relations of the United States with Haiti, 1776–1891* (1941), gives detailed coverage of the period under study. Logan notes: "The relations of the United States with Haiti have been different from those with any other nation. Haiti was the first nation in the Western world, after the United States, to win her independence. But Haiti was black, and her independence resulted from a slave insurrection. The relations between the two countries have therefore not

only been different—they have been vital, and at times even dramatic."
Alain Turnier, *Les Etats Unis et le marché haitien* (1955), expertly traces
the history of commercial trade relations from the early days of U.S. independence prior to the Haitian revolution against France (with commentary on French, British, and Spanish viewpoints). Sociologist and
professor of Afro-American studies Alex Dupuy contributes two thorough studies. *Haiti in the World Economy: Class, Race, and Underdevelopment Since 1700* (1989), based on neo-Marxist dependency and world-
system theories, argues that the French slave-labor plantation system and
U.S. capitalist imperialism, with their underlying class and racial constructs, kept Haiti undeveloped and on the periphery of the world capital-accumulating economy. In *Haiti in the New World Order: The Limits
of the Democratic Revolution* (1997), Dupuy continues the analysis with
reference to Haiti's place in the post–cold war world and the severe constraints placed on the country by the New World Order. J. Michael Dash,
*Haiti and the United States: National Stereotypes and the Literary Imagina-
tion* (2 eds., 1988, 1997), is a well-conceived cultural history investigating the imaginative literature in both countries. In the United States,
Haiti has been "invented" as a savage, evil, and mysterious land that must
be either isolated or dominated, and Haitians have resisted the stereotypes by "rewriting" themselves. The strength of these images continues
"to shape official policy and popular attitudes."

MEXICO

Mexico's foreign policies and international relations have generated an exceptionally large body of literature.[6] They include a large number of histories dealing with broad themes and time periods, but few works have
appeared surveying the entire breadth of foreign policies and international relations. The expansive treatments of Mexico's relations with the
United States form a large part of the literature. Nevertheless, a significant body of thematically and topically more specific works, not framed
directly to U.S. relations, has also been produced.

Several of the early survey histories are notable. Miguel Rebolledo,
México y los Estados Unidos (1917), deals with U.S. territorial formation
at the expense of Mexico, Mexican foreign policies as it faced the United

States, and relations during World War I (including Mexico's defenses). James Morton Callahan, *American Foreign Policy in Mexican Relations* (1932), incorporates the well-known U.S. historian's work going back to 1909. It surveys in detail the continuously problematic relationship from the time of U.S. independence to 1931. J. Fred Rippy, *The United States and Mexico* (2 eds., 1926, 1931), a narrative history of diplomatic relations addressed to university students and general readers, focuses on factors producing the many bilateral difficulties and how each state had dealt with them.

Historical surveys later appeared taking advantage of documentation and concepts not earlier available. Two of them became classic, standard works in their respective languages. Luis G. Zorrilla, *Historia de las relaciones entre México y los Estados Unidos de América, 1800–1958* (2 vols., 1965–1966), is a detailed and well-documented work by a noted Mexican scholar that deals with key historical themes. Karl M. Schmitt, *Mexico and the United States, 1821–1973: Conflict and Coexistence* (1974), stands as the best general survey by a U.S. author. A fact-filled analytic work, and empathetic to Mexican situations and perspectives, it examines the major issues from first contacts to about 1970. An interesting theme is Mexico's strategy of courting European states in an effort to counterbalance the U.S. presence. Alberto Maria Carreño, *La diplomacia extraordinaria entre México y los Estados Unidos, 1789–1947* (2 vols., 1951), is highly critical of the United States, with much supporting evidence. Howard F. Cline, *The United States and Mexico* (2 eds., 1953, 1963), is a lengthy, elegantly written, highly descriptive study. It deals with the problematic relationship since 1910 in less than half of the book, with the rest devoted to internal Mexican developments.

Mexican and U.S. specialists subsequently produced more good survey histories. Two of Mexico's leading historians, Carlos Vásquez and Manuel García y Griego, *México frente a los Estados Unidos: un ensayo historico, 1776–1980* (1982), write from the Mexican perspective and emphasize Mexico's weak position in its defensive efforts to deal with the United States in political, economic, and military relationships. Vásquez and García y Griego also edited *Mexican-U.S. Relations: Conflict and Convergence* (1983), in which contributors sharply debate the assertion of interdependence in the relationship. They address both intergovernmental and transnational phenomena (such as energy and migration). Two more distinguished Mexican historians, Josefina Zoraida Vázquez and Lorenzo Meyer, *The United States and Mexico* (1985), divide the presentation of a relatively brief book by each taking one of the two parts—from 1821 to 1898 and 1904 to 1985. They analyze from Mexican perspectives in an objective manner. Gerardo M. Bueno and Lorenzo Meyer, eds., *México–Estados Unidos* (1987), covers a wide range of important topics.

More recently, leading U.S. Latin Americanist diplomatic historian Lester D. Langley, *Mexico and the United States: The Fragile Relationship* (1991), concisely and insightfully deals with the issue of state and societal interdependence. He sees the two countries as simultaneously integrated and separate. Langley highlights the expansive border region and increasing numbers and importance of Mexican-Americans. W. Dirk Raat, *Mexico and the United States: Ambivalent Vistas* (1992), is an excellent general survey, with its main analytic concern the bilateral relationship in the context of the world economy. "The emphasis," Raat says, "is on the manner in which the United States affected Mexican history, shaped its values, attitudes, and conditions, and vice versa." Jaime E. Rodríguez O. and Kathryn Vincent, eds., *Myths, Misdeeds, and Misunderstandings: The Roots of Conflict in U.S.-Mexican Relations* (1997), is a collaboration by a Mexican and U.S. historian interpreting the history of relations from Mexican independence to the present, emphasizing the many conflicts between them. Clint E. Smith, *Inevitable Partnership: Understanding Mexico-U.S. Relations* (2000), traces the relations from independence to the date of publication. He interprets the relationship as beginning with violence and war, shifting to a long period of tension, and moving to the present era of interrelationships creating the "inevitable partnership." Several chapters deal with current matters of trade, democratization, migration, drugs, labor, and the environment.

Political scientists have engaged in general foreign policy analyses, addressing various specific elements, with increasing frequency since the mid-1960s. *La política exterior de México*, presented in special issues of *Foro Internacional* (1965, 1966), was a pathbreaking contribution, issued to commemorate the twenty-fifth anniversary of the founding of El Colegio de Mexico. The authors, who became leading Mexican foreign policy analysts, wrote articles on Mexico in the international system, basic trends in Mexican foreign policy, Mexico in the Organization of American States and in the United Nations, the country's role in the denuclearization of Latin America, its planning for commercial policy, and participation in a world community. *La política exterior de México: la práctica de México en el derecho internacional* (1969), is a scholarly work that addresses key foreign policy problems and the governmental organization to deal with them. Manuel Tello, *México: una posición internacional* (1972), deals with Mexican policy orientations regarding issues, processes, and procedures. Mario Ojeda Gómez, *Alcances y límites de la política exterior de México* (1976), is a concise, systematic analysis of Mexico's international actions within the world and the hemisphere's power structures, other fundamentals and conditions of Mexico's international orientations, and the special problem of economic debilities. A chapter is devoted to the foreign policies of the Echeverría government.

Modesto Seara Vázquez, *Política exterior de México* (3 eds., 1968–1985), designed as a university textbook, applies foreign policy analysis highlighting national role conceptions. Seara includes a great deal of descriptive material. He argues that Mexico's foreign policy is largely shaped by domestic factors, in particular matters of politics, economics, and national self-image. George W. Grayson, *The United States and Mexico: Patterns of Influence* (1984), sees a relationship of mutual dependence. The obvious unequal power balance makes Mexico the more vulnerable partner, but Mexico employs its own influence with the United States—depending on the issue and intensity of state interests involved. Grayson also addresses the matter of mutual misunderstanding of the other's political system. Mario Ojeda Gómez, *México: El surgimiento de una política exterior activa* (1986), after summarizing the "general antecedents," analyzes foreign policymaking after 1970 by the Echeverría, López Portillo, and De la Madrid governments. Yoram Shapira, *Mexican Foreign Policy Under Echeverria* (1978), gives special attention to Echeverría's Third World ideology and orientation. The authors in Olga Pellicer, ed., *La política exterior de México: desafíos en los ochenta* (1983), contributed excellent essays analyzing Mexican foreign policy as it moved from economic prosperity into a "postboom" period of critical economic problems. They address a wide range of internal and external variables.

Frederick C. Turner, *The Dynamic of Mexican Nationalism* (1968), is the standard work on the subject. Turner argues that the Mexican Revolution of 1910 and the following civil war formed current nationalism. Mexicans had begun the nation-building process after the end of the French occupation in 1865, but the maturation of self-identity was delayed by the long dictatorship of Porfiro Díaz and its alliance with a narrowly based domestic elite and foreign economic interests. Xenophobia toward Spain, France, and the United States was a major factor in the development of Mexican attitudes. Robert Freeman Smith, *The United States and Revolutionary Nationalism in Mexico, 1916–1932* (1972), is an insightful historical analysis of the clash of the new nationalism of the Mexican revolutionaries with the perceived interests of the United States. Sergio Aguayo Quesada, *Myths and [Mis]Perceptions: Changing U.S. Elite Visions of Mexico* (1998), contemplates at length "how an implicit understanding" by both parties "dating from the 1920s has guided perceptions and enabled them to survive tension in the relations." He describes how and why that situation is changing. David Barkin's acrimonious critique of U.S. policy, *Las Relaciones México–Estados Unidos* (1980), is a good example of the polemical literature related to nationalism and identity.

A large number of works by diplomatic historians and foreign policy analysts have addressed specific time periods and themes in Mexican–United States relations. William R. Manning, *Early Diplomatic Relations Between the United States and Mexico* (1916), engaged in extensive archival research to produce this detailed survey of the difficult relations during the first decade of Mexico's independence (1821–1830), highlighting the overriding border issue. Carlos Bosch García also narrates early-nineteenth-century diplomatic relations in two books: *Problemas diplomáticos del México independiente* (1947), and *Historia de las relaciones entre México y los Estados Unidos, 1819–1848* (2 eds., 1961, 1974). Legal historian George Lockhart Rives, *The United States and Mexico, 1821–1848* (2 vols., 1913), wrote a comprehensive narrative, from Mexican independence to the end of the Mexican-U.S. war. Daniel Cosio Villegas, *The United States Versus Porfirio Díaz* (1964), provides the details of the troubled relationship during the lengthy and complex Díaz dictatorship (1867–1910). British expert Alan Knight, *U.S.-Mexican Relations 1910–1940: An Interpretation* (1987), offers a monograph analyzing "the congruence of Mexican and U.S. history during the violent and radical first three decades of the Mexican Revolution." Stephen R. Niblo, *War, Diplomacy, and Development: The United States and Mexico, 1938–1954* (1995), is a fine study of the Mexican Revolution's "turn to the right" on the heels of its most radical nationalist phase, and of the concomitant reassertion of U.S. influence, especially economic. Niblo analyzes the consequences of rapid Mexican industrialization, Mexican-U.S. cooperation during World War II, and postwar private U.S. business investment. Alonso Gómez-Robledo Verduzco, ed., *Relaciones México–Estados Unidos: una visión interdisciplinaria* (1981), is a comprehensive discussion by experts on a wide range of contemporary issues. Daniela Spenser, *The Impossible Triangle: Mexico, Soviet Russia, and the United States in the 1920s* (1999), is an excellent, welcome study.

A number of recent works have focused on Mexico's actions and relations from the end of the 1980s into the post–cold war period. Many of them are edited books bringing together experts to examine the principal current issues, sometimes with historical or conceptual background. Among the most useful are Susan Kaufman Purcell, ed., *Mexico in Transition: Implications for U.S. Policy—Essays from Both Sides of the Border* (1988), in which contributors offer a wide range of perspectives on the dynamics of contemporary Mexico and what they mean for U.S. policy. Rodolfo de la Garza and Jesús Velasco, eds., *Bridging the Border: Transforming Mexico-U.S. Relations* (1997), bring together prominent U.S. and Mexican scholars. They analyze Mexico's new foreign policy orientations; strategies to influence U.S. policy as well as U.S. "think tanks" and private financial institutions; the domestic consequences of expatriate Mexicans; and discord in U.S.-Mexican labor relations since the ratification of the North American Free Trade Agreement (NAFTA).

Bruce Michael Bagley and Sergio Aguayo Quezada, eds., *Mexico: In Search of Security* (1993), is a multiauthored work addressing Mexico's redefinition of national security in the post–cold war world. Julie A. Erfani, *The Paradox of the Mexican State: Rereading Sovereignty from Independence to NAFTA* (1995), argues that the legal status-political myth concept of sovereignty, sustained by Mexican elites from the 1940s through the 1970s in order to make "a weak national state the symbol of domestic strength," had failed. This led proponents of NAFTA to adopt the notion of private sector authority within a strong private economy. James F. Rochlin, *Redefining Mexican "Security": Society, State, and Region Under NAFTA* (1997), is an innovative examination of elements of Mexican foreign policy as dimensions of the changing meaning of security since NAFTA went into effect (which coincides with the beginning of the post–cold war period). They include the evolution of democracy, human rights, civil-military relations, economic elements, environmental issues, migration of people, the drug traffic, and criminal activities. Rochlin perhaps assigns too much explanatory power to the single concept of security.

Robert A. Pastor and Jorge Castañeda, *Limits to Friendship: The United States and Mexico* (1988), is an unusual and effective book in which two accomplished and thoughtful U.S. and Mexican policy analysts and advisers debate, agree, and disagree. They engage specific themes—perceptions, intervention, frictions, intergovernmental and foreign policy orientations, economic integration, drug trafficking, the border, and cross-cultural fears—and make recommendations about how to deal with them.

Mexico's economic relations and external relations have loomed large in policy calculations—especially with the United States, which has long been Mexico's dominant trading partner. William O. Freithaler, *Mexico's Foreign Trade and Economic Development* (1968), is a brief factual, statistical study, which concludes that despite external trade difficulties Mexico will continue sustained economic growth. Three prominent economists representing both countries, Barry W. Poulson, T. Noel Osborn, and Hugo B. Margáin, eds., *U.S.-Mexico Economic Relations* (1979), offer their ideas as they debate the issues and reveal both differing and congruent perspectives. Contributors to Jorge I. Domínguez, ed., *Mexico's Political Economy: Challenges at Home and Abroad* (1982), link Mexico's internal politics and external relations and analyze the political economy of petroleum, agriculture, labor relations, membership in the General Agreement of Tariffs and Trade (GATT), and specific components of trade. Instituto Mexicana de Comercio Exterior, *El comercio exterior de México* (3 vols., 1982), is an exhaustive reference source. Clark W. Reynolds and Carlos Tello, eds., *U.S.-Mexico Relations: Economic and Social Aspects* (1983), an important work written just as the Mexican debt emerged, includes contributions on economic and social interdependence, trade, energy, security, migration, rural development, and the future of the bilateral relationship. Subsequent thoughtful and informative multinational-multiauthored works were written in the context of the Mexican postboom economic crisis in external debt, foreign investment, and trade: Peggy Musgrove, ed., *Mexico and the United States: Studies in Economic Interaction* (1985); Cathryn L. Thorup, ed., *The United States and Mexico: Face to Face with New Technology* (1987); Khosrow Fatemi, ed., *U.S.-Mexican Economic Relations: Problems and Prospects* (1988); and Riordan Roett, ed., *Mexico and the United States: Managing the Relationship* (1988). Ricardo Campos, *El Fondo Monetario Internacional y la deuda externa mexicana: estabilización y crisis* (3 eds., 1991–1995), is an important analysis of the difficult Mexican-IMF relationship during and after the severe debt crisis of the 1980s.

The Mexican–United States borderlands form a special region along the 2,000-mile international boundary, where intense long-term interstate and intersocietal interactions have formed a semiautonomous economic, social, and cultural zone. The scholarly interest has also been intense and produced an immense literature on the subject. Its breadth overlaps with subjects included in numerous works cited above and in Chapters 6, 7, and 8. The following is a sampling of major works.

Herbert E. Bolton, *The Spanish Borderlands: A Chronicle of Old Florida and the Southwest* (1921), is credited with creating, naming, and popularizing the field of "borderlands studies." Bolton, convinced that comprehending the area required understanding the deep Spanish influence, wrote the book "to tell of Spanish pathfinders and pioneers in the regions between Florida and California, now belonging to the United States, over which Spain held sway for centuries." Although criticized for ignoring the brutality of the Spanish conquest and his narrow time frame, Bolton stimulated a scholarly interest that has persisted to the present day. The process has dramatically extended the definition (to include northern Mexico), the time parameters, and thematic scope of borderlands studies. Oscar J. Martínez, *Troublesome Border* (1988), is a general history of the nineteenth and twentieth centuries that emphasizes the conflictual nature of the border area. Martínez also brings together twenty-six scholars and serves as editor of the contributions in *U.S.-Mexican Borderlands: Historical and Contemporary Perspectives* (1996). Divided into seven parts, the book investigates such phenomena as the long and tortuous history of making the border, the course of the Mexican Revolution and the border, and social and cultural incongruities. David E. Lorey, *The U.S.-Mexico Border in the Twentieth Century* (1999), is also a general treatment, emphasizing the evolution and the unique economic, social, and cultural borderlands characteristics, distinct from either Mexico or the United States. John House, *Frontier on the Rio Grande: A Political Geography of Development and Social Deprivation* (1982), is authoritative regarding the subject matter. Stanley R. Ross, ed., *Views Across the Border: The United States and Mexico* (1978), is based on seventeen papers presented at an academic conference, which are divided into seven border issue areas: international and intranational culture, politics, economics, migrants, health, psychology, and ecology. In a gloomy assessment, Raúl A. Fernández, *The U.S.-Mexico Border: A Politico-Economic Profile* (1977), focuses on the issues from an economic perspective. Fernández offers a further assessment, *The Mexican-American Border Region: Issues and Trends* (1989), which delineates the increasingly dense population, rising economic activity and problems, and the continuing importance of the border zone to both countries. Jesús Tamayo, *Zonas fronterizas* (1983), is a detailed analysis of bilateral border relations from a Mexican perspective. Contributors to Lay James Gibson and Alfonso Corona Renteria, eds., *The U.S. and Mexico: Borderland Development and the National Economies* (1984), examine the structure of the border region in terms of the flow of goods, services, capital, and people, and the specific issues of pollution, migration, and industry. David Spener and Kathleen Staudt, eds., *The U.S.-Mexico Border: Transcending Divisions, Contesting Identities* (1998), delineates the border "as a site from which to survey both the social and economic networks and the issues of identity and symbolism that surround borders." The book has interesting chapters on both theoretical and empirical matters.

A good survey of Mexico's Central American policies and relations during a significant historical period is provided by Jurgen Buchenau, *In the Shadow of the Giant: The Making of Mexico's Central American Policy, 1876–1930* (1996). He examines Mexican initiatives during the dictatorship of Porfirio Díaz (1876–1910) and the first two decades of the Mexican Revolution. U.S. actions often frustrated Mexico in the area, especially after the turn of the century. Olga Pellicer de Brody, *México y la revolución cubana* (1972), briefly and cogently argues that official Mexican revolutionary rhetoric applauded the Cuban Revolution of 1959 whereas in terms of action the government compromised with conservative Mexican sectors and the United States. Jaime Delgado, *España y México en el siglo diecinueve* (2 vols., 1950–1954), is a thorough survey. Alfred Paul Tischendorf, *Great Britain and Mexico in the Era of Porfiro Díaz* (1961), analyzes the considerable British public and private interests in Mexico, a fact often overshadowed by attention paid to those of the United States. Zbigniew Anthony Kruszewski and William Richardson, *Mexico and the Soviet Bloc: The Foreign Policy of a Middle Power* (1990), is a concise survey of the checkered relations from the end of Czarist rule through the 1980s, including Mexican–East European relations. Institute for European–Latin American Relations, *La UE y México: una nueva relación política y económica* (1997), is an exceptionally thorough treatment. It emphasizes Mexico's strategic importance to the European Union as a link between North American and Latin American markets, a significant source of energy, and an important market for European exports and direct investments. Hal P. Klepak, ed., *Natural Allies? Canadian and Mexican Perspectives on International Security* (1996), offers essays examining the historical and economic factors behind security thinking and the alternatives for cooperative security relations in the changing post–cold war hemispheric security environment. Jorge Castañeda, *Mexico and the United Nations* (1958), is an important survey of the subject as well as of the relationship to the Inter-American System.

NICARAGUA

Nicaragua was largely ignored in terms of foreign policy analysis until the advent of the revolutionary Sandinista government in 1979. Mary B. Vanderlaan, *Revolution and Foreign Policy in Nicaragua* (1986), is an excellent general treatment of the domestic and international constraints on Sandinista foreign policymaking. She identifies foreign policy purposes and goals and the patterns of foreign policy orientations. Vanderlaan finds that the Sandinistas were less motivated by revolutionary ideology than by the same things as the other small states trying to survive the determined hostility of the United States. Michael D. Gambone, *Eisenhower, Somoza, and the Cold War in Nicaragua, 1953–1961* (1997), is a well-documented analysis of uninspiring U.S. cold war thinking.

PANAMA

Lawrence O. Ealy, *The Republic of Panama in World Affairs, 1903–1950* (1951), stood for years as the primary scholarly historical survey of Panama's international relations. Ealy had responded to the dearth of literature about Panama as opposed to the Panama Canal and the Canal Zone, and sought to partially close the gap with this study of the small but strategically important state. Michael L. Conniff, *Panama and the United States: The Forced Alliance* (1992), is a thorough survey focusing on relations with the United States as Panama's fundamental foreign policy consideration and controller of its primary resource, the Panama Canal. The book is broadly conceived to include coverage of other political and economic as well as social and cultural phenomena. Conniff highlights Panamanians' constant love-hate perceptions of the United States. Also of interest is a good survey by Panamanian author Ernesto Castillero Pimentel, *Política Exterior de Panamá* (1961). Margaret E. Scranton, *The Noriega Years: U.S.-Panamanian Relations, 1981–1990* (1991), analyzes a decade of relations in terms of developments within Panama and decisional processes by the two governments. She addresses U.S. willingness to disregard Panamanian repression, electoral fraud, and drug trafficking overseen by military commander and de facto president Manuel Noriega, and why it decided in December 1989 to remove him from power with a military invasion. See also Chapter 6 for the considerable literature on the Panama Canal, the key element of Panamanian international life.

PARAGUAY

Solid surveys are provided by Cecilio Báez, *História diplomática del Paraguay* (2 vols., 1931–1932), a thorough description and appraisal; and by Antonio Salum-Flecha, *Historia diplomática del Paraguay de 1869–1938* (1972), a more concise treatment. Michael Grow, *The Good Neighbor Policy and Authoritarianism in Paraguay: United States Economic*

Expansion and Great Power Rivalry in Latin America During World War II
(1981), is a solid study of U.S. concern with Nazi influence in Paraguay
and its successful effort to bring its nationalist dictator to the U.S. side
with economic and military aid. The economic consequences of U.S. actions were an important factor in stimulating the civil war that ended the
old order in 1944. Antonio Salum-Flecha and others, *Política internacional, economía e integración* (1985), analyzes Paraguay's small-state position in economic integration organizations.

PERU

Arturo García Salazar, *História diplomática del Perú* (1930), is a useful
survey, especially of nineteenth-century relations. Víctor Andrés Belaunde, *La vida international de Perú* (1942), is a fact-filled historical review, organized around Peru's relations with its neighbors—Ecuador, Bolivia, Brazil, Chile, Colombia—with heavy emphasis on boundary and
territorial problems; it also deals with Peru's participation in international
conferences. The author was a prominent Peruvian figure—diplomat,
legislator, essayist, and scholar. Alberto Wagner de Reyna, *Historia
diplomática del Perú, 1900–1945* (1964), is well researched and particularly good on the twentieth century. It is organized by issues and themes.
James C. Carey, *Peru and the United States, 1900–1962* (1964), is a scholarly survey and evaluation of various aspects of the bilateral interstate relations. Carey also addresses the role of private U.S. interests (especially
investors). Ronald Bruce St. John, *The Foreign Policy of Peru* (1992), is a
complete historical overview since Peru's independence in 1824. St. John
posits the strong link between domestic and external demands in shaping
Peru's international orientations—and of internal conflict often interfer-
ing with foreign policy. See also the excellent histories by Arthur P.
Whitaker, *The United States and South America: The Northern Republics*
(1948), which includes Peru among the five states studied; and Fredrick
B. Pike, *The United States and the Andean Republics: Peru, Bolivia, and
Ecuador* (1977). Contributors to Eduardo Ferrero Costa, ed., *Relaciones
internacionales de Perú* (1986), engage in serious foreign policy analysis.
Based on a seminar of experts on national defense and international rela-
tions, the chapters deal with the changing nature of security issues that

Peru faces in the post–cold war world and with the country's orientations toward the Inter-American System, arms control, insurgency, the drug traffic, and environmental problems. Daniel M. Masterson, *Militarism and Politics in Latin America: Peru from Sánchez Cerro to Sendero Luminoso* (1991), includes assessments of the impact of U.S. military programs on the Peruvian armed forces. Bobbie B. Smetherman and Robert M. Smetherman, *Territorial Seas and Inter-American Relations: With Case Studies of the Peruvian and U.S. Fishing Industries* (1974), explains the Peruvian case for a 200-mile territorial sea limit and fully describes and analyzes the binational conflict. Thomas Scheetz, *Peru and the International Monetary Fund* (1986), says that the IMF's "monetarist approach in Peru has not addressed the roots of debt and financial crisis but has instead resulted in damaging stopgap policies" in favor of foreign bankers.

URUGUAY

Arthur P. Whitaker, *The United States and the Southern Cone* (1976), includes Uruguay among the three states studied. Roberto Russell and others, *Temas de política exterior latinoamericana: el caso uruguayo* (1986), is made up of revised papers presented at a 1985 conference on Uruguay's foreign policies, with an emphasis on the options open to a small state. Uruguayan Institute of International Law, *Uruguay and the United Nations* (1958), is a carefully prepared largely legal study. Aldo E. Solari, *El tercerismo en el Uruguay* (1965), written by a prominent Uruguayan sociologist, assesses the Uruguayan movement for a "third position" in international politics. Elizabeth A. Finch, *The Politics of Regional Integration: A Study of Uruguay's Decision to Join LAFTA* (1973), is a comprehensive analysis of the internal political debate in Uruguay about joining the Latin American Free Trade Association.

VENEZUELA

The analysis by U.S. historian Sheldon B. Liss, *Diplomacy and Dependency: Venezuela, the United States, and the Americas* (1978), is the most inclusive survey of Venezuela's international relations, from Venezuela's independence to its leadership in forming the Organization of Petroleum

Exporting Countries (OPEC). Venezuelan historian Armando Rojas, *Historia de las relaciones diplomaticas entre Venezuela y los Estados Unidos, 1810–1899* (2 vols., 1979), provides much information on the nineteenth century in the context of inter-American relations. It is highly informative, strong on description, but less so on analysis and interpretation. Arthur P. Whitaker, *The United States and South America: The Northern Republics* (1948), includes Venezuela among the five states studied. Judith Ewell, *Venezuela and the United States* (1996) has superseded past efforts and stands as the best general historical survey. She argues that the United States had recognized the potential importance of Venezuela in the Caribbean before it was confirmed by its location near the Panama Canal and its discovery of enormous petroleum reserves. Ewell approaches the 200-year history of relations from the perspectives of both sides, highlighting popular perceptions as well as official ones. Her bibliographical essay is excellent.

Charles Carreras, *United States Penetration of Venezuela and Its Effects on Diplomacy, 1895–1906* (1987), analyzes how aggressive investors behaved in Venezuela, with highly limited success, while the country was still a backwater prior to the discovery of oil reserves in that country. Carreras narrates the entrepreneurs' squabbles over mining and asphalt concessions and resultant diplomatic incidents. Benjamin A. Frankel, *Venezuela y los Estados Unidos (1810–1888)* (1997), is a thorough study of how economic and cultural variables influenced Venezuela's relations during much of the nineteenth century. Robert D. Bond, ed., *Contemporary Venezuela and Its Role in International Affairs* (1977), contains seven essays from several political and analytic viewpoints that together provide a thorough treatment of Venezuela's contemporary foreign policies (with adequate background information). Douglas Carlisle, *Venezuelan Foreign Policy: Its Organization and Beginning* (1978), after providing a summary historical background, examines in detail the development and organization of Venezuela's foreign ministry during the dictatorial government of Juan Vicente Gómez (1908–1935). Alfredo Toro Hardy, *Venezuela, Democracia y Política Exterior* (1986), is a thoughtful theoretical study of the influence of Venezuela's democratic political system on foreign policy orientations. Rubén Carpio Castillo, *Geopolítica de Venezuela* (1981), is useful as a summary of the subject, not a common research topic in the case of Venezuela. José Egidio Rodriguez, *Imagen y política international* (1987), is an interesting analysis of the role of Venezuelan self-images to national role perceptions in foreign policy formulation. Venezuelan historian Demetrio Boersner, *Venezuela y el Caribe: presencia cambiante* (1978), presents the contours of the country's important role in its immediate neighborhood. Freddy Vivas Gallardo, *Venezuela en la sociediad de las naciones, 1920–1939* (1981), analyzes the Venezuelan experience with the League of Nations, which provided it with an opening to the world.

CHAPTER 4

■

Nonhemispheric
States and Canada

This chapter addresses extrahemispheric states' and Canada's policies and relationships with Latin America and the Caribbean. Writers on the region's international relations have long had an interest in the European presence. They have addressed multitudinous themes, given the long history of relations and the diverse nature of interests and activities on the part of the numerous individual states involved. Research on the policies and interactions of the Soviet Union has also been significant, with the bulk of it conducted after the Soviet attachment to the Cuban Revolution of 1959 and other activities until the end of the cold war and the breakup of the Soviet Union. Studies of the relationships of other extrahemispheric states—China, Japan, and Israel—have not been extensive because of the episodic nature of those states' policies. Research on Canada's inter-American relations was slight until that country began to increase its activity, with a subsequent rapid growth of the literature. As a general matter, little effort has been devoted to foreign policy formulation or variables in the decision processes, other than to identify motives, interests, instruments, and capabilities.[1]

STUDIES OF A GENERAL NATURE

The pioneering effort by Herbert Goldhamer, *The Foreign Powers in Latin America* (1972), was the first notable comparative study of the Latin

American policies of the extrahemispheric states (and certain other external states). The analysis is organized by categories of interaction processes since World War II, within which the interests and actions of individual external states receive attention. William Perry and Peter Wehner, eds., *The Latin American Policies of U.S. Allies: Balancing Global Interests and Regional Concerns* (1985), is a collection of concise, realistic expert essays identifying the Latin American interests and actions of eight U.S. allies. Separate chapters are devoted to the Federal Republic of Germany, the United Kingdom, France, Spain, the Netherlands, Japan, Israel, and Canada. The authors identify fundamental variables underlying the respective states' regional involvement.

Some works cited and commented upon in Chapter 2 make significant reference to the policies and interactions of the extrahemispheric states and Canada: F. Parkinson, *Latin America, the Cold War, and the World Powers, 1945–1973* (1974); Roger W. Fontaine and James D. Theberge, eds., *Latin America's New Internationalism: The End of Hemispheric Isolation* (1976); and contributors to G. Pope Atkins, ed., *South America into the 1990s: Evolving International Relationships in a New Era* (1990).

EUROPE

After Latin American independence in the nineteenth century until the outbreak of World War I, certain European states in certain places played important roles. They were important or dominant traders and investors, cultural models, and military interveners; some had continuing imperial ambitions in the region. The European presence generally declined during the interbellum period and activities remained at relatively low levels into the post–World War II period. In the early 1970s, Europeans revived their economic and political relations, with the result that research increased in several quarters—U.S. scholars joined with European and Latin American colleagues to revive the long tradition of such attention. European endeavors were accelerated in the post–cold war period and the accompanying academic activity has been sustained to the present day.

Much of the writing on the European presence in Latin America and the Caribbean involves phenomena addressed in other chapters. The colonial era following European discovery of the New World and its continuing vestiges are addressed in Chapter 2. Chapter 7 includes studies on European roles in the Latin American movements for independence; their nineteenth- and early-twentieth-century military interventions and economic and cultural interactions; and their more recent actions toward Central American conflict and the search for peace. Citations on the external debt and redemocratization are in Chapter 8.

A number of works have addressed European relations in general terms, including the policies of the European Community/European Union. Wolf Grabendorff and Riordan Roett, *Latin America, Western Europe, and the United States* (1985), coedited an important set of contributions by fourteen U.S., Latin American, and European specialists. The central theme is the expansion of Latin American relations with Europe and the latter's growing economic and political influence that, with the simultaneous decline of U.S. hemispheric dominance, had formed a complex triangular set of new relationships. Chapters discuss the policy perspectives of France, Germany, and the European Community. Esperanza Duran, *European Interests in Latin America* (1985), is a concise, insightful treatment by a Mexican analyst who has academic experience in Great Britain and the United States. She notes the "strikingly limited" European interest in the region, indicated by the significant postwar decline in trade and their high priority interests in former Caribbean colonies. Programa de Relaciones Politicas y de Cooperacion al Desarrollo Europa/América Latina, *Europa–América Latina, el desafío de la cooperación* (1988), is based on seminar papers presented by thirteen Latin American and European participants, among them academics and representatives of intergovernmental organizations and nongovernmental organizations. They deal with a wide range of topics relating to Latin American images of Europe and interregional cooperation. Paul Sutton, ed., *Europe and the Caribbean* (1991), brings together established scholars who write on a variety of subjects. They address the Caribbean relations of Britain, France, the Netherlands, the European Community, Spain, and the Soviet Union; the European connection with the non-Hispanic Caribbean; U.S. perceptions; and the future of Europe in the region. Two good books deal with Europe in the context of Central American conflict in the 1980s and its aftermath: Eusebio M. Mujal-León, *European Socialism and the Conflict in Central America* (1989); and Joaquín Roy, ed., *The Reconstruction of Central America: The Role of the European Community* (1992). (See Chapter 7 for commentary on both.)

British scholar Alfred Glenn Mower Jr., *The European Community and Latin America: A Case Study in Global Role Expansion* (1982), studies European Community (EC) policies from an international political economy perspective—as well as from the EC perspective. He emphasizes the EC view of Latin America as part of the Third World. Mower provided a much-needed synthesis of a great deal of historical, political, and economic information and identification of the important variables that shape interregional relations. There is little analysis of connections with individual Latin American states. In Germán Granda Alva, Víctor Mate, and Mario Moreno, *La cooperación entre América y Europa* (1988), a Belgian (Granda) and two Spanish scholars cogently explore EC relations with Latin America in political, economic, and technical assistance areas. They devote a chapter to Central America and the Andean Group. Contributors to Susan Kaufman Purcell and Françoise Simon, eds., *Europe and Latin America in the World Economy* (1995), update the relationship with positive assessments, and those to Peter H. Smith, ed., *The Challenge of Integration: Europe and the Americas* (1993), focus on the increased connections in terms of the integration institutions in both regions (see Chapter 6 for commentary).

Special attention has been paid to Spanish policies and relations reflecting competing perceptions (and ideologies) of a special cultural relationship with Spanish America, as the former colonial mother country. Frederick B. Pike, *Hispanismo, 1898–1936: Spanish Conservatives and Liberals and Their Relations with Spanish America* (1971), is the prime scholarly work on these matters. Pike points out that in the 1890s, advocates of *hispanismo,* asserting that a distinct Spanish culture had been transplanted to the New World, believed that Spain must protect its former colonies from other external influences (especially from the United States). Although liberals and conservatives each proposed how best to preserve Hispanic civilization, Pike says that both were devoted to hierarchical corporatist structures and opposition to social revolution. Rafael Altamira, who in the 1890s had been a member of the Pan-Hispanic cultural movement of Spanish intellectuals, wrote *España y el programa americanista* (1917). It was an attempt to persuade the Spanish government to institutionalize the international cultural community of Spanish-speaking peoples with research institutes, student and professorial exchanges, and Pan-Hispanic political and commercial organizations. Altamira and his colleagues were partly motivated by concern over the Pan-American movement being sponsored by the United States. In the late 1930s, dictator General Francisco Franco converted benign *hispanismo* to aggressive falangist *hispanidad,* which had been widely popularized by Ramiro de Maeztu in *Defensa de la Hispanidad* (4 eds., 1934–1941). The book, by an anarchist turned falangist, was the primary source for the "theory" of the Pan-Hispanic elements of falangism. Julio Ycaza Tigerino, *Originalidad de Hispanoamérica* (1952), is a later philosophical discourse. Pedro Pérez Herrero and Nuria Tabanera, eds., *España/América Latina: un siglo de políticas culturales* (1993), presents six insightful essays by eight Spanish and two Latin American historians, who analyze official Spanish cultural policy toward Latin America from 1898 to 1992.

On a more general level regarding the Spanish presence in Latin America, the massive study directed by Jaime Vicens Vives, ed., *Historia de España y America* (5 vols., 2 eds., 1957–1959, 1971), cited and commented on in Chapter 2, devotes the 718-page volume 5 to Spanish relations with independent Latin America in the nineteenth and twentieth centuries. It provides a wealth of information. Montserrat Huguet Santos, Antonio Niño Rodríguez, and Pedro Pérez Herrero, eds., *La formación de la imagen de América Latina en España, 1898–1989* (1992), is a collection of sharply focused essays that add up to a thorough, original, longitudinal analysis of image formation and perception and the impact on Spanish ideology and policy within government entities. Silvia Enrich, *Historia diplomática entre España e Iberoamerica en el contexto de las relaciones internacionales (1955–1985),* deals insightfully with themes of Spain's Latin American relations during the Franco era and the following "new Spain and multipolarity." Celestino del Arenal, *La política exterior de España hacia Iberoamérica* (1994), is a solid historical and policy analysis of Spanish purposes in Latin America, emphasizing democratic Spain's orientation from 1976 to 1992 and the formation of an Ibero-American community. Howard Wiarda directed an exceptionally thorough multiauthored effort, *The Iberian–Latin American Connection: Implications for U.S. Foreign Pol-*

icy (1986), in which fourteen contributors explore a broad range of aspects about Spanish and, to a lesser extent, Portuguese policies toward Latin America, with due attention to implications for the United States. Chapters are devoted to the triangular relations among Spain, Latin America, and the United States; the economic, diplomatic, military, and intellectual dimensions of Iberian–Latin American relations; and Latin American country and subregional studies. Wiarda followed with *Iberia and Latin America: New Democracies, New Policies, New Models* (1996), a good concise treatment of the complex connection of Spain and Portugal's histories, cultures, and policies with Latin America over the previous two decades. He emphasizes the importance of democracy and mutual democratic transitions and raises important questions about the viability of an external democratic experience as a model for development. Joaquín Roy and Albert Galinsoga Jordá, eds., *The Ibero-American Space: Dimensions and Perceptions of the Special Relationship Between Spain and Latin America* (1997), stems from a conference in which thirteen authors (all from Spain except for one from Latin America and one from the United States) deal with the subject from several perspectives: conceptual, international legal, governmental, ethnohistorical, political, and economic. A separate chapter is devoted to the Cuban relationship. Robin L. Rosenberg, *Spain and Central America: Democracy and Foreign Policy* (1992), addresses the Spanish effort to influence political with its example and influence.

The United Kingdom had a highly significant presence in Latin America and the Caribbean until the 1930s. It was not sustained in the face of the global depression and World War II. Rory Miller, *Britain and Latin America in the Nineteenth and Twentieth Centuries* (1993), emphasizes British interests. He explores them chronologically in the contexts of the colonial and independence eras and the subsequent decades until the outbreak of World War I (commerce and investment are emphasized). Miller deals with Argentine, Brazilian, and Chilean perspectives; the First World War and the subsequent decline of British influence; and the Second World War and its consequences. Victor Bulmer-Thomas, ed., *Britain and Latin America: A Changing Relationship* (1989), provides a complete survey of the relationship of the post–World War II history of relations in thirteen clear and concise chapters. They deal with political, economic, and cultural relations; analyze Britain's sharply reduced role in and deteriorated relations with the region; and prescribe new policies for the 1990s.

With regard to French relations with Latin America, Thomas Schoonover, *The French in Central America: Culture and Commerce, 1820–1930* (1999), is an exhaustively researched study. Seeing the French role in Central America largely ignored in favor of the presence of other outside powers, Schoonover sought to fill the gap with this examination of France's attempts to establish its own sphere of influence. The French competed with British, German, and U.S. efforts for Central American trade, control of transisthmian rail and canal routes, leverage with local military forces, and influence by way of cultural development. In a companion volume, *Germany in Central America: Competitive Imperialism, 1821–1929* (1998), Schoonover investigates the course of Germany's interest in commercial expansion into the isthmus with its rapidly growing industry and the expanding world market. Central Americans saw the possibilities of developing their limited economic and human resources. Schoonover concludes that the consequences, however, were to transfer elements of German economic and social disorder to Central America. Alton Frye, *Nazi Germany and the American Hemisphere, 1933–1941* (1967), provides considerable information and insight about Nazi attempts to subvert Latin American political systems. He applauds the multilateral inter-American counterefforts. Weine Karlsson, Ake Magnusson, and Carlos Vidales, eds., *Suecia-Latinoamérica: relaciones y cooperación* (1993), is a comprehensive treatment of a relatively little-known subject. Chapters are devoted to the historical background from 1600, political contacts, international cooperation, nongovernment organizations, and cultural and economic relations.

THE SOVIET UNION

The policies of the Soviet Union and its various activities generated a substantial scholarly literature, its growing volume matching the increasing importance of occurrences after 1960. After the Cuban Revolution of 1959, Soviet relations with Cuba, as well as with other states and non-state actors in other parts of the hemisphere, were of continuing interest. That interest was further stimulated by the Soviet presence in the Central

American crises after 1979 and its reorientation to policies that actually cooperated with the Central American peace process. Academic attention dropped off dramatically with the end of the cold war and the dissolution of the Soviet Union, as the new Russia's Latin American relations were slight. It should be noted that Soviet international relations researchers shed little light on official perceptions and decision making toward Latin America, often asserting the benign intent of Soviet policies. They frequently surveyed or addressed U.S. policies and actions or Latin American responses to those actions and those of certain other states. The extensive research on two important areas of the Soviet presence is treated elsewhere in this book: The three-decade Soviet connection to the Cuban Revolution is addressed in Chapter 3; and Soviet participation in the Central American crises of the 1980s and related phenomena in the circum-Caribbean is included in Chapter 7.

Earlier works on the Soviet Union and Latin America were useful but unexceptional. J. Gregory Oswald and Anthony J. Strover, eds., *The Soviet Union and Latin America* (1970), is a collection of fifteen contributions based on a symposium sponsored by the Institute for the Study of the USSR in Munich. Notable Soviet experts from Europe and Latin America deal with the ideological, political, economic, and cultural factors in Soviet relations with several Latin American states, with the Soviet-Cuban relationship highlighted. They reveal an underlying anxiety about Communist expansion in Latin America and apprehension about all revolutionary movements in the region. James D. Theberge, *The Soviet Presence in Latin America* (1974), is a very brief but informative discourse on the Soviet's relations with Cuba and its other activities around Latin America. Leon Gouré and Morris Rothenberg, *Soviet Penetration of Latin America* (1975), reveal their concern in the book's title. The authors scrutinized official Soviet declarations in order to "shed light on Soviet perceptions, policies, and activities in Latin America."

Certain later works offered more subtle and satisfactory analysis, based on more complex considerations of Soviet motivations. Cole Blasier's book, *The Giant's Rival: The USSR and Latin America* (2 eds., 1983, 1988), is singled out for its excellence. Although acknowledging a steadily increased Soviet presence in Latin America—increased diplomatic contacts, trade, military assistance, and naval visits—Blasier argues that the export of revolution is not a high Soviet priority. He notes the Soviet emphasis on regular state-to-state diplomatic and trade relations with regional governments of all types, even military regimes. This reality makes overt subversion less likely. Blasier says Soviet officials see their Cuban alliance as politically useful but an economic burden, a commitment they are not likely to make to others. He criticizes U.S. assumptions that the Soviet Union can create or control revolutions and that the United States is able to prevent them. He also addresses Soviet relations with Argentina, Chile, Brazil, El Salvador, and Costa Rica as presenting different challenges. Nicola Miller also produced an excellent study, *Soviet Relations with Latin America, 1959–1987* (1989). She persuasively argues that Soviet policies were based on cautious low-risk self-interests (especially economic) rather than either revolutionary ideology or strategic expansionism. The Soviets had learned lessons, she says, from the politically and financially expensive Cuban experience that loomed large in their calculations. Eusebio M. Mujal-León, ed., *The USSR and Latin America: A Developing Relationship* (1988), includes twelve essays by fourteen leading Latin American and U.S. scholars. They differ in their viewpoints but agree that U.S. officials have consistently exaggerated the Soviet threat and that the Soviets tended, with some exceptions, to be cautious and pragmatic in their decisions and actions. They discuss the role of Latin America in Soviet Third World strategy; Soviet perspectives on the Latin American Communist movement and the Cuban connection; their economic (especially trade) relations in the region; and Soviet policies toward Central America, Mexico, Argentina, Brazil, and the Andean states. Augusto Varas, a Chilean scholar associated with the Latin American School of Social Sciences (FLACSO) in Santiago de Chile, edited *Soviet–Latin American Relations in the 1980s* (1987). It is an important collection of analytic contributions by ten Latin American scholars who focus on then-mutual perceptions that the Soviets and Latin Americans had of one another. After setting the stage with general overviews of elements of Latin America–Soviet relations, the chapters examine in detail the Soviet relationships with Cuba and Nicaragua, and, less extensively, those with Argentina, Brazil, Mexico, Peru, and Costa Rica. The authors tend to disagree with U.S. official assumptions about Soviet expansionism, seeing the Soviet Union more as a competitor on the inter-American scene. One of the few scholarly analyses supporting the Reagan administration's estimation of Soviet activities is edited by Dennis Bark, *The Red Orchestra: Instruments of Soviet Policy in Latin America and the Caribbean* (1986). This slim volume of essays deals with Soviet "proxies" (state and nonstate) in the region that serve to support an expanding Soviet presence and influence. Bark pays special attention to Cuba, Central America, and Grenada.

Ilya Prizel, *Latin America Through Soviet Eyes: The Evolution of Soviet Perceptions During the Brezhnev Era 1964–1982* (1990), is a survey analysis of changing perceptions of many elements of Latin American institutions and external relations held by Soviet academics, journalists, and politicians during the Brezhnev years. Prizel found a significantly increased level of sophisticated understanding not evident in the past. An epilogue comments on further changes under Gorbachev. Fundación Simón Bolívar, Centro de Estudios Internacionales, Foro Interamericano, *La perestroika y la America Latina* (1989), is based on conference discussions by participants from ten Latin American countries and the United States. The contributors are mostly political leaders and their associates with a broad range of viewpoints, who discuss the impact of *perestroika* on international politics and life and how Latin American democratic parties should respond. Roberto Russell, ed., *Nuevos rumbos en la relación Unión Soviética–América Latina* (1990), is an excellent multinational, multiauthored (seventeen contributors) analysis of changes in the Soviet political system and the consequent new focuses in Soviet–Latin American relations. It has chapters on Argentina, Brazil, and Uruguay. Wayne S. Smith, ed., *The Russians Aren't Coming: New Soviet Policy in Latin America* (1992), brought together fifteen authorities from the United States, Soviet Union, and Latin America. They cogently analyze post–cold war Soviet policies in Latin America, with appropriate historical background. The papers in the last two books were written on the eve of the dissolution of the Soviet Union.

OTHER EXTRAHEMISPHERIC STATES

Two books by policy analysts deal with Japan's post–cold war relations with Latin America. Susan Kaufman Purcell and Robert M. Immerman, eds., *Japan and Latin America in the New Global Order* (1992), is made up of five contributions in this brief but informative book on Japan's economic connections with Latin America. Chapters deal with the subject in general regional terms, bilateral relations with Mexico and Brazil, and the role of the United States in the processes. The analysis is cast in the context of Latin America emerging from the "lost decade" of the 1980s into a "growth decade" in the 1990s, in which Japan is reassessing relationships in the region. Barbara Stallings and Gabriel Székely, eds., *Japan, the United States, and Latin America: Toward a Trilateral Relationship in the Western Hemisphere* (1993), strongly emphasizes the Japanese role. Only the introductory chapter interprets the "new trilateralism" that includes the United States. The rest of the book is devoted to chapters on "Perspectives from Japan" and Japanese relations with Brazil, Mexico, Peru, Chile, and Panama—all of which are solid and informative analyses.

The best treatment on Israel and Latin America is a systematic foreign policy analysis by three Israeli scholars, Edy Kaufman, Yoram Shapira, and Joel Barromi, *Israeli–Latin American Relations* (1979). Dealing with the period from 1948 to 1973, the authors succeed in their purpose of examining "the attitudes of Latin American decision makers toward Israel (by studying) patterns of behavior, the grouping of nations according to levels of support of Israel, and an analysis of the influence of different variables on the policymaking process." They address the external and internal settings of Israeli policymaking and policy instruments, Latin American decision makers and their psychological environment, Latin American voting in the UN General Assembly, and the bilateral diplomatic relations. Edward B. Glick, *Latin America and the Palestine Problem* (1958), is tightly focused on the issue as addressed in the United Nations. Glick discusses Zionist and Israeli efforts to influence Latin America, paying close attention to the Palestine partition resolution. He discusses Israel's membership in the UN, and includes a chapter on "The Vatican, Latin America, and the Internationalization of Jerusalem." Also of interest is Bishara Bahbah, *Israel and Latin America: The Military Connection* (1986) (see Chapter 8 for commentary).

In a related work, Damián Fernández, ed., *Central America and the Middle East: The Internationalization of the Crisis* (1988), is a good collection by scholars who inquire into the connections between state and nonstate actors (including insurgents) in the Middle East and their Central American counterparts. They also examine how "Central America has become a battleground for the two sides in the Arab-Israeli confrontation."

A good survey of China and Latin America is Marisela Connelly and Romer Cornejo Bustamante, *China–América Latina: génesis y desarollo de sus relaciones* (1992). The authors describe those relations from the first commercial contacts and continue through those and political considerations into the 1980s. Three books focus on the People's Republic of China (PRC). Cecil Johnson, *Communist China and Latin America, 1959–1967* (1970), is an excellent, thorough examination of China's regional activities, highlighting the ideological dimension. It includes chapters on Sino-Cuban relations and on the PRC-oriented parties in Brazil, Peru, Bolivia, and Colombia. Johnson notes Chinese recognition of the various difficulties inhibiting the development of substantial relations. Leonardo Ruilova, *China Popular en América Latina* (1978), is a study by an Ecuadorian scholar specializing in sinology, done under the auspices of the Friedrich Ebert Foundation. The author chronicles at great length events from 1970 to 1978, and explores the Chinese ideological factor. He Li, *Sino–Latin American Economic Relations* (1991), is a thorough, tightly written analysis of the political economy of PRC relations with the region. Li traces developments from 1949 to 1990 and analyzes specific processes, problems, issues, and prospects.

CANADA

On the evolution of Canada's relations with Latin America, the classic work on the subject is by Canadian scholar J.C.M. Ogelsby, *Gringos from the Far North: Essays in the History of Canadian–Latin American Relations, 1866–1968* (1976). Ogelsby evaluates the evolution of Canada's relations with Latin America, at the time a relatively unexplored area of research. He stresses the dominant Canadian diplomatic, commercial, and investment interests, beyond which, Ogelsby says, Canada had no consistent policy. A later survey by another Canadian professor, James F. Rochlin, *Discovering the Americas: The Evolution of Canadian Foreign Policy Towards Latin America* (1994), highlights the period of increased involvement after 1959. Rochlin had earlier written *Canada as a Hemisphere Ac-*

tor (1992), which emphasizes the revitalization and extension of Canada's inter-American activities since the late 1980s. Also covering the period from about 1989 forward, Jerry Haar and Edgar Dosman, eds., *A Dynamic Partnership: Canada's Changing Role in the Americas* (1993), brought together thirteen experts who thoroughly explore the institutions, policies, and issues involved. They see a reorientation of Canada's regional policies to a long-term high priority position. Also of interest as an earlier effort is Norman L. Nicholson, *Canada in the American Community* (1963).

Contributing authors to Hal P. Klepak, ed., *Canada and Latin American Security* (1994) assess Canada's rapid and deep involvement in the latter 1980s in hemispheric security affairs. They analyze the nature of the inter-American security system, Canadian security interests in Latin America, and Canada's recent experience in peacekeeping and verification. Two books address Canada's earlier role in the Inter-American System: Marcel Roussin, *Le Canada et le Systéme Interaméricain* (1959); and John D. Harbron, *Canada and the Organization of American States* (1963). (See Chapter 6 for commentary on both.) Reflecting Canada's long-term particular interest in trade and investment in the English-speaking Caribbean, contributors to Jerry Haar and Anthony T. Bryan, eds., *Canadian-Caribbean Relations in Transition: Trade, Sustainable Development and Security* (1999), assess the dynamically evolving relationship in the post–cold war era.

CHAPTER 5

■

The United States

As in the treatments of the Latin American states and the extrahemispheric states and Canada, this chapter deals with the more general analytic and thematic research on United States policies toward relations with Latin America and the Caribbean. It begins with historical surveys and follows with foreign policy analyses. In both instances they are works with an overall regional focus, but include those with broad and more specific time periods and analytic purposes. Special attention is devoted to the Monroe Doctrine and related policy principles, and to the matter of policy perceptions. Studies devoted to the analysis of U.S. subregional policies are taken up separately.

Other chapters also deal with U.S policy–related phenomena. See Chapter 2 for treatments of Puerto Rico and the Virgin Islands; and Chapter 3 for policies toward and relations with individual Latin American and Caribbean states, and for Latin American anti-imperialist and other anti-American writing. Chapter 6 addresses U.S. participation in formal interstate organizations. Chapter 7 deals with U.S. involvement in various forms of Latin American–related warfare and the search for peace. Chapter 8 includes U.S. activities having to do with development, economic interactions, types of Latin American regimes, military cooperation, immigration, the drug traffic, and certain other interstate and transnational phenomena.[1]

HISTORICAL SURVEYS

A number of general historical surveys of U.S. relations with and policies toward Latin America have appeared. All but a few are also cited in Chapter 2, in the context of inter-American relations, and may be consulted for further commentary. The earliest general treatments were narrative diplomatic histories, focusing on regional, subregional, and bilateral interactions. They typically interpreted events and presented them in great detail. The earliest survey of the substance of U.S. policies toward Latin America was by U.S. historian John Holladay Latané, *The Diplomatic Relations of the United States and Spanish America* (1900); a revised edition appeared in 1920, titled *The United States and Latin America*. Cuban historian Raúl Cárdenas y Echarte, *La política de los Estados Unidos en el continente americano* (1921), was one of the earliest studies from Latin America that took a detached stance—he was writing at the height of U.S. Caribbean imperialism. He concludes that strategic rather than economic factors had the primary influence on U.S. policies. William Spence Robertson, *Hispanic-American Relations with the United States* (1923), surveys the period from 1830 to 1919.

Scholarship continued in the tradition of the earlier works. Graham Stuart produced six editions of *Latin America and the United States* beginning in 1922; the last edition, coauthored with James Tigner, appeared in 1975. Highly detailed and heavily documented, the book was a standard historical reference during its long life. Nicholas J. Spykman, *America's Strategy in World Politics* (1942), is a geopolitical balance-of-power analysis that concentrates on the position of Latin America in U.S. calculations. After discussing the general subjects of the United States in the interstate balance of power system, and power politics and war, Spykman addresses the Western Hemisphere and the Monroe Doctrine. He then devotes considerable attention to the "struggle for South America," in terms of propaganda, economic matters, politics, and military threats and defense. Samuel Flagg Bemis, *The Latin American Policy of the United States* (1943), is considered a classic work of the first order. Critics admire Bemis's scholarship and erudition even as they challenge his persistently confident defense of U.S. policy motivations, which he joined with sharp criticism of Latin Americans. J. Lloyd Mecham, *A Survey of United*

States–Latin American Relations (1965), deals with the history of U.S. policies of a general nature, as applied to Caribbean relations and as pursued with nine individual Latin American states. Mecham is critical of specific policies but applauds the underlying security orientations. British scholar Gordon Connell-Smith, *The United States and Latin America: An Historical Analysis of Inter-American Relations* (1974), strongly criticizes both the fundamentals of policy and most of its proximate elements. Federico G. Gil, *Latin–American–United States Relations* (1971), provides a useful brief history of various themes in U.S. policy.

The more recent diplomatic historical surveys have been more interdisciplinary and analytical in nature. Two noted historians exemplify them. Lester D. Langley, *America and the Americas: The United States in the Western Hemisphere* (1989), interprets the substance of U.S. policies in various historical and thematic contexts. He skillfully integrates political, economic, social, and cultural concepts. Peter H. Smith, *Talons of the Eagle: Dynamics of U.S.–Latin American Relations* (1999), also utilizes social science concepts in his history writing. This work is largely a critique of U.S. policy and policymakers as it surveys inter-American relations over a span of nearly two centuries. Political scientist Harold Molineu, *U.S. Policy Toward Latin America: From Regionalism to Globalism* (2 eds., 1986, 1990), engages in a historical-conceptual analysis of U.S. policies with salutary results. He begins with the organizing idea of conflict and discontinuities between regional and global approaches to U.S. Latin American policies. Molineu then subsumes the themes of the Western Hemisphere Idea, spheres of influence, economic control, dependency relations, democratic mission, and cold war strategy. He critically evaluates each of them as an explanation of U.S. behavior in Latin America. Don M. Coerver and Linda Hall, *The United States and Latin America* (1999), craft a useful, concise synthesis of the relationship on the regional level. They survey events from the early nineteenth century to the late 1990s, but most of the book is devoted to the twentieth century. Mark T. Gilderhus, *The Second Century: U.S.–Latin American Relations Since 1889* (1999), emphasizes U.S. goals, tactics, and capabilities as the hemispheric hegemon from the late nineteenth century to the end of the cold war. David Shavit, *The United States in Latin America: A Historical Dictionary* (1992), is a comprehensive reference work that provides useful information on states, policies, institutions, events, and personalities.

Numerous works have been devoted to specific time periods and corresponding themes of U.S. policy. Two multiauthored books, commissioned as companion volumes, together cover the nineteenth century: T. Ray Shurbutt, ed., *United States–Latin American Relations, 1800–1850: The Formative Generations* (1991); and Thomas Leonard, ed., *United States–Latin American Relations, 1850–1903: Establishing a Relationship* (1999). Joseph S. Tulchin, *The Aftermath of War: World War I and U.S. Policy Toward Latin America* (1971), evaluates the decade after the war as the United States began to move toward abandonment of intervention in Latin America. Michael L. Krenn, *U.S. Policy Toward Economic Nationalism in Latin America, 1917–1929* (1990), is a concise treatment of the U.S. post–World War I economic presence in Latin America. It deals with various forms of Latin American nationalism, from benign to xenophobic, and policy problems engendered by its own anticommunism and racism. Alexander DeConde, *Herbert Hoover's Latin American Policy* (1951), concludes that "in its main essentials, the good-neighbor policy has its roots in the Hoover administration." Three concisely written books are widely read descriptions and interpretations: Edward O. Guerrant, *Roosevelt's Good Neighbor Policy* (1950); Francisco M. Cuevas Cancino, *Roosevelt y la buena vecinidad* (1954); and Donald Marquand Dozer, *Are We Good Neighbors? Three Decades of Inter-American Relations, 1930–1960* (1959). Irwin F. Gellman, *Good Neighbor Diplomacy: United States Policies in Latin America, 1933–1945* (1979), sees a combination of self-interest and idealism in the policy, as well as shrewdness and misunderstanding of the region. He also addresses the serious differences of opinion among the high U.S. officials carrying out the policy. David Green, *The Containment of Latin America: A History of the Myths and Realities of the Good Neighbor Policy* (1971), is a highly detailed revisionist debunking of (and hostility toward) the policy, from its beginning to the end of the Truman presidency. Green says it was a concealment of the interests of U.S. military advisers and private business people to undermine Latin American revolutionary governments and movements. The policy failed because it sponsored creation of the Inter-American System in order to supervise security matters and take control of Latin American economies. More complex and credible is Bryce Wood, *The Making of the Good Neighbor Policy* (1961), a definitive reexamination of the concept from its piecemeal conception through its erratic maturation over the period from 1926 to 1943. He focuses on the challenges to good-neighborliness of events and realities of inter-American power asymmetries, especially from the inauguration of President Roosevelt to the middle of World War II. Wood pays much attention to the perspectives and influences of the strong personalities in the Roosevelt administration. Wood followed with his also excellent *The Dismantling of the Good Neighbor Policy* (1985). His scrupulous research underpins the assertion that the 1954 U.S. intervention in Guatemala signaled the end of the Good Neighbor Policy and with it the undermining of the political features of the Organization of American States. The consequence was in essence a unilateral abrogation of formal inter-American agreements prescribing nonintervention and multilateral consultation. Fredrick B. Pike, *FDR's Good Neighbor Policy: Sixty Years of Generally Gentle Chaos* (1995), is a thoughtful, thoroughly researched, balanced, and unorthodox analysis of the Good Neighbor Policy and its continuing implications. Pike concludes that the noninterventionist orientation was based on President Roosevelt's version of political realism—a rejection of pressuring Latin Americans to accept U.S. values because it would be counterproductive to achieving U.S. goals of hemispheric unity and stability.

Dick Steward, *Money, Marines, and Mission: Recent U.S.–Latin American Policy* (1980), surveys the period from 1933 to 1976. He seeks to "reinterpret economic, political, and intellectual aspects of inter-American history and understand decisions made" by U.S. presidents from Franklin Roosevelt to Gerald Ford. Stephen G. Rabe, *Eisenhower and Latin America: The Foreign Policy of Anticommunism* (1988), is a carefully researched and fully documented international history. The subtitle indicates the primary theme in this analysis of the evolution of U.S. cold war policies and related ideological thinking with reference to Latin America. It includes discussion of the intervention in Guatemala, free trade and investment policies, Vice President Nixon's unsettling trip to Latin America, and the hostility toward Fidel Castro in Cuba and Rafael Trujillo in the Dominican Republic. Edwin McCammon Martin, *Kennedy and*

Latin America (1994), is an authoritative insider's view of policies and events by President Kennedy's assistant secretary of state for inter-American affairs. He devotes more than half of the book to the Alliance for Progress, and includes a revealing chapter on the Cuban missile crisis. Chilean scholar Luis Maira, *América Latina y la crisis hegemonía norteamericana* (1982), brings together twelve Latin American experts who engage in considered analysis of the Reagan administration's reorientation of U.S. policy to seek the reestablishment of regional hegemony. Kevin Middlebrook and Carlos Rico, eds., *The United States and Latin America in the 1980s: Contending Perspectives on a Decade of Crisis* (1986), is an examination by leading U.S., Latin American, and European scholars of a wide range of issues as they debate U.S. policies on them.

THE MONROE AND OTHER DOCTRINES

Thousands of books and articles have been written on the Monroe Doctrine in the twentieth century alone, and until World War II it was possibly the most analyzed topic of U.S. foreign policy. This section deals only with major works on the doctrine—and even then it leaves out a large number of worthwhile studies.

Certain examinations of allied precursor doctrines further our understanding of Monroeism. Arthur P. Whitaker, *The Western Hemisphere Idea: Its Rise and Decline* (1954), is the essential source on the subject. Whitaker defines the concept as follows: "From its emergence in the late eighteenth and early nineteenth century to the present, the core of the Western Hemisphere Idea has been the proposition that the peoples of this Hemisphere stand in a special relationship to one another that sets them apart from the rest of the world." Another well-known historian of inter-American relations, Wilfrid Hardy Callcott, also addressed the Western Hemisphere Idea in *The Western Hemisphere: Its Influence on United States Policies to the End of World War II* (1968). It is also an excellent treatise, extended to include Canada. John A. Logan, *No Transfer: An American Security Principle* (1961), gives a scholarly account of the principle expressed in a congressional resolution of 1811 that anticipated the broader application by President Monroe. Logan says that the no-transfer warning to Europe "was power politics resorted to in order to banish power politics from America."

The Monroe Doctrine was always met with general disapproval in Europe and, after the turn of the twentieth century, hostility in Latin America. Among the early works was that of French writer Hector Petin, *Les Etats-Unis et la Doctrine de Monroe* (1900). He traced the history of the doctrine in terms of its beginnings as a declaration by the United States against European military intervention in Spanish America to a vindication for its own intervention there. More dispassionately, Horace Dominique de Barral-Montferrat, *De Monroe a Roosevelt, 1823–1905* (1905), chronicles U.S. expansionism, diplomatic and military intervention, and isthmian canal actions. He concludes that the doctrine was no longer credible once the United States engaged in its own extrahemispheric actions. Herbert Kraus, *Die Monroe-Doktrin, in ihren Beziehungen zur amerikanischen Diplomatie und zum Voelkerrecht* (1913), a masterful scholarly analysis, was the standard history for two decades after its publication. Mexican diplomat and historian Carlos Pereyra, *El mito de Monroe* (1914), an extension of the author's earlier work on the subject, is a lengthy condemnation of the doctrine as pretense for its imperialism in Latin America. He further asserts that the doctrine never benefited Latin America and that U.S. policy would have been the same with or without it. Alejandro Alvarez, *The Monroe Doctrine: Its Importance in the International Life of the States of the New World* (1924), is by the distinguished Chilean jurist. It is a classic Latin American interpretation and was long a leading work—although it contains only 110 pages of legal and case analysis and 449 pages of full-text documents. Alvarez emphasizes that the Monroe Doctrine is not a matter of international law but a unilateral proclamation of principle by the United States. Camilo Barcía Trelles, *La Doctrina de Monroe y la cooperación internacional* (1931), was another of the leading works from Latin America. The author traces the "American ideal" to the sixteenth-century writings of Spanish scholar Francisco Vitoria, whom Latin Americans consider the father of international law. He laments that after 1823 the United States did not accept Spanish American proposals to "Americanize" the doctrine as a multilateral security doctrine. Gaston Nerval, *Autopsy of the Monroe Doctrine: The Strange Story of Inter-American Relations* (1934), was widely circulated when published and reflected a broad sector of Latin American opinion. It is a lengthy complaint that the United States willfully misinterpreted and misused Monroe's statement as a justification for its imperialism in the Americas. British writer Albert B. Hart, *The Monroe Doctrine: An Interpretation* (1916), written in the midst of World War I, is encyclopedic in detail and a heavily documented multithematic interpretation. Another popular treatment was Charles H. Sherrill, *Modernizing the Monroe Doctrine* (1916). David Y. Thomas, *One Hundred Years of the Monroe Doctrine, 1823–1923* (1923), writing on the hundredth anniversary of the proclamation, recommended that if the doctrine was not extended to include Latin Americans then it should be abandoned. Jorge Roa, *Los Estados Unidos y Europa en Hispano America: interpretación política y económica de la Doctrina Monroe, 1823–1933* (1935), is an examination of the origins and evolution of the doctrine. Roa says that the declaration had no effect on events in the 1820s since British power actually protected Latin America from other Europeans' intervention, although the United States later deserved credit for deterring European aggression. The United States gained no economic advantages even as the doctrine supported mutual isolation of the Western Hemisphere.

All prior studies were superseded, in a scholarly sense, by the three-volume work of Dexter Perkins: *The Monroe Doctrine, 1823–1826* (1927), *The Monroe Doctrine, 1826–1867* (1933), and *The Monroe Doctrine, 1867–1907* (1937). These definitive diplomatic histories were the result of exhaustive archival research in all available relevant sites. Perkins became the single most recognized authority on the Monroe Doctrine. He later wrote *A History of the Monroe Doctrine* (1963), a summary of the three-volume study plus an appraisal of developments since 1903.

Alonso Aguilar Monteverde, *El panamericanismo de la Doctrina Monroe a la Doctrina Johnson* (1965), is hostile to the doctrine and skeptical of the motivations behind it—which always were, he said, aimed at "continental domination and plunder." Ernest R. May, *The Making of the Monroe Doctrine* (1975), reinterprets the origins of the doctrine and argues that Monroe made his statement with domestic political considerations in mind—especially the 1824 presidential election. He dismisses the influence of national interest calculations and special ideological or interest-group pressures, and concludes that "the whole process was governed by domestic politics, with policymakers' positions determined less by conviction than by ambition." Richard H. Collin, *Theodore Roosevelt's Caribbean: The Panama Canal, the Monroe Doctrine, and the Latin American Context* (1990), is a well-researched, lengthy, subtle diplomatic history of presidential power and U.S. imperialism. Collin argues that Roosevelt was the first president to make foreign policy coequal with domestic matters. Further, his imperialist pursuit was anything but simple, understandable in the context of the times rather than simply another phase of expanding U.S. domination of the hemisphere for either the accumulation of power or capital. Gaddis Smith, *The Last Years of the Monroe Doctrine, 1945–1993* (1994), is a provocative, and debatable, interpretation of how post–World War II U.S. presidents "resolved the policy contradiction of accepting a Soviet presence in the Caribbean while reaffirming the tenets of the Monroe Doctrine." David W. Dent, *The Legacy of the Monroe Doctrine: A Reference Guide to U.S. Involvement in Latin America and the Caribbean* (1998), is a substantial reference work. Dent provides chronologies of major events for all of the Latin American states and four of the Commonwealth Caribbean countries. Explanatory tables add to the value of the work.

FOREIGN POLICY ANALYSES

Political science research eventually produced good foreign policy analytic surveys and broad thematic collections. They tended to emphasize U.S. purposes in Latin America within relatively recent time frames, and a certain amount of contextual historical description or analysis tended to be included. A number of them addressed U.S. policy formulation in terms of decision models when they referred to rational choices, images and perceptions, or political-bureaucratic-organizational processes. A promising but limited debate about the formulation process declined. Writing on U.S. Latin American policies has often focused on shifting crises, events, issues, and orientations associated with changing presidential administrations.

Foreign policy surveys by political scientists and, to a lesser extent economists, proliferated after the late 1950s with the dramatically increased official and public interest in Latin America. The production has continued to the present day. George Wythe, *The United States and Inter-American Relations: A Contemporary Appraisal* (1964), are contemplations by an experienced economist. He criticizes as erroneous and counterproductive the U.S. assumption that its power can easily influence or remake Latin American states and societies. John D. Martz and Lars Schoultz, eds., *Latin America, the United States, and the Inter-American System* (1980), assembled a group of experts to analyze general U.S. policies, with a substantial treatment of the issues of human rights policies. Margaret Daly Hayes, *Latin America and the U.S. National Interest* (1984), is a dispassionate realist analysis with prescriptive purposes. She makes sensible, prudent policy recommendations based on prior evaluation and in terms of enlightened national interest. Hayes says that hemispheric unity and Latin American economic prosperity and stable domestic and international politics serve U.S. interests. She also analyzes the challenges posed by Brazil, the Caribbean Basin, and Mexico (Bruce Bagley authors the chapter on Mexico). Richard Newfarmer, ed., *From Gunboats to Diplomacy: New U.S. Policies for Latin America* (1984), has contributions from sixteen established analysts who are troubled by the U.S. policy reorientation that overemphasizes East-West conflict in Latin America and overshadows and ignores the internal origins of many regional problems. The result is an uneven application of democracy and human rights policies and ill-advised economic actions.

Lars Schoultz, *National Security and United States Policy Toward Latin America* (1987), is an important book. Schoultz concludes that "the core" of U.S. policy toward Latin America has been a concern with security and the causes and consequences of Latin American instability for U.S. security interests. Policymakers are deeply divided, however, over what constitutes a security threat, and here matters of variability and fragmentation came into play. Thus Schoultz also takes into account the values and perceptions of policymakers and the influences and constraints exercised by interest groups, bureaucratic processes, Congress, and public opinion. Michael Kryzanek, *U.S.–Latin American Relations* (3 eds., 1985–1996), intended to serve as a classroom text, discusses the evolution of U.S. policy, aspects of policy formulation, and a number of salient issues. Of particular value is the section on the policymaking process and the roles of government and nongovernment participants in decision making. Abraham Lowenthal, *Partners in Conflict: The United States and Latin America* (2 eds., 1987, 1990), in a relatively brief but wide-ranging study, focuses on the period from 1960 to the end of the 1980s. Included are chapters on Mexico, Brazil, and the Caribbean Basin. Lowenthal convincingly argues that inadequate understanding of Latin America's ongoing political and economic transformations flaws U.S. policy. He calls for a policy that moves from narrow security thinking to stress hemispheric cooperation for problem solving. John Martz edited two superb companion volumes of excellent essays that are indispensable for understanding U.S. policy, from the Kennedy administration into the Clinton presidency. The first, *United States Policy in Latin America: A Quarter Century of Crisis and Challenge, 1961–1986* (1988), includes the contributions of twelve experts who deal with policy objectives and perspectives and patterns of crisis management. They discuss policymaking from the Kennedy into the Reagan presidencies; crisis management during the Dominican intervention, the Allende presidency in Chile, Panama Canal treaty negotiations, and the Anglo-Argentine war; and the challenges of the debt crisis, Central American conflict, the Castro presence, and Latin American redemocratization. In the second book, *United States Policy in Latin America: A Decade of Crisis and Challenge* (1995), thirteen prominent scholars explore key bilateral relations and critical problems in the context of a dramatically changing Latin America and the evolving post–cold war period. Martz provides incisive introductions in both volumes to U.S. foreign policy formulation toward Latin America. Howard J. Wiarda, *Finding Our Way? Toward Maturity in U.S.–Latin American Relations* (1987), is a broad-ranging and provocative exploration of U.S. policies, including problems of development, democracy, ethnocentrism, population security, and paralyzed policymaking. Except for the introduction, all of the chapters are revised prior published articles and papers. Wiarda says that his outlook has changed from an earlier more skeptical and pessimistic view; the evidence presented, however, continues to support the original convictions. Dario Moreno, *U.S. Policy in Latin America: The Endless Debate* (1990), documents and contrasts President Carter's egalitarian, antiimperialist, pro-democratic policies with Reagan's imperialist, anticommunist, and covert ones. Guy Poitras, *The Ordeal of Hegemony: The United States and Latin America* (1990), is a solid theory-based analysis of the decline of U.S. hegemony in Latin America. Poitras emphasizes recent events related to foreign debt, Latin American assertiveness, and competition from external adversaries. He says that U.S. policymakers overemphasized the Soviet threat, and urges cooperation with Latin America in the "post-hegemonic" period.

Two books address the concept of "grand strategy" from different perspectives. Tom J. Farer, *The Grand Strategy of the United States in Latin America* (1988), is by a professor of international law and former member of the Inter-American Commission for Human Rights. He collects a number of his subtle, lively essays, many previously published, on strategy, morality, national interest, human rights, law and intervention, and the United States in Central America. The underlying themes throughout are the need for U.S. restraint and the idealist-realist tension in U.S. policy debates. Michael C. Desch, *When the Third World Matters: Latin America and the United States' Grand Strategy* (1993), examines U.S. strategy within four historical contexts. They are World War I and the preoccupation with Mexico; World War II and the response to perceived German threats; the Cuban missile crisis and the role of Cuba; and the cold war and its changing hemispheric situations. Desch says that in each instance the Latin American element appeared to have no inherent strategic content within the larger situation of vital importance, yet proved to be significant nonetheless. This insight is useful in its own terms, but is less compelling as the basis for a realist-rationalist theory of "grand strategy"—which itself does not integrate the obvious matter of regional spheres of influence in balance-of-power systems. A good historical inquiry is David G. Haglund, *Latin America and the Transformation of U.S. Strategic Thought, 1936–1940* (1984). See also Augusto Varas, ed., *Hemispheric Security and U.S. Policy in Latin America* (1989) (see Chapter 2 for commentary).

The end of the cold war generated scholarly analyses about the characteristics and the new era and the meaning for U.S. policies toward Latin America and the Caribbean. Robert A. Pastor, *Whirlpool: U.S. Foreign Policy Toward Latin America and the Caribbean* (1992), by a former national security adviser on Latin America to President Carter and subsequently a prolific scholar on regional affairs, is an important and thoughtful book. Pastor asks if the end of the cold war has liberated the United

States from its historical pattern of suddenly becoming obsessed with Latin America and the Caribbean and just as abruptly neglecting the region ("drawn into the whirlpool"). He provides a detailed overview of past U.S. behavior. Pastor maintains that the collapse of the Soviet Union and communism is less important than hemispheric trends of democracy and free trade, and offers far-reaching policy recommendations, which are partly based on a redefinition of sovereignty. Contributors to Lars Schoultz, William C. Smith, and Augusto C. Varas, eds., *Security, Democracy, and Development in U.S.–Latin American Relations* (1994), say that the states of the Western Hemisphere must adjust to the new strategic conditions that have transformed inter-American issues. They explore matters of U.S. security interests, threat perceptions, values, and military activities and declining military influence, as well as the issues of drugs, terrorism, arms production and arms races, and the roles of Latin American armed forces. The following volumes, which address the meaning of end of the cold war for U.S. purposes, interests, and policies, were cited and commented upon in Chapter 2. They also examine, to varying degrees, past elements of U.S. policy. They are: Henry Hamman, ed., *Setting the North-South Agenda: United States–Latin American Relations in the 1990s* (1991); G. Pope Atkins, ed., *The United States and Latin America: Redefining U.S. Purposes in the Post–Cold War Era* (1992); Jonathan Hartlyn, Lars Schoultz, and Augusto Varas, eds., *The United States and Latin America in the 1990s: Beyond the Cold War* (1992); Heraldo Muñoz, ed., *El fin del fantasma: las relaciones interamericanos después de la Guerra Fría* (1992); and Abraham F. Lowenthal and Gregory F. Treverton, eds., *Latin America and the United States in a New World* (1994). Several works published in the 1990s cited above contain substantial material on post–cold war U.S. policymaking.

David W. Dent, ed., *U.S.–Latin American Policymaking: A Reference Handbook* (1995), is a complete, well-conceived, highly useful reference work, with twenty-four experts contributing focused essays on the inter-American and U.S. domestic environments, policymaking structures and actors, and major policy issues. It includes discussions of the applicability of various decision models to U.S. policymaking toward Latin America. Those models are explored by contributors to Julio Cotler and Richard Fagen, eds., *Latin America and the United States: The Changing Political*

Realities (1974). C. Neale Ronning and Albert P. Vannucci, eds., *Ambassadors in Foreign Policy: The Influence on U.S.–Latin American Policy* (1987), is a concise collection of insightful and sometimes disturbing articles about the personal influence of six U.S. ambassadors on Latin American policies. The subjects are Dwight Morrow in Mexico (1927–1930), Sumner Welles and the Cuban uprising (1933), Spruille Braden in Argentina (1945), Adolph Berle in Brazil (1945–1946), Lincoln Gordon and Brazil's military revolution (1964), and Nathaniel Davis (author of the article) on the Allende years in Chile.

PERCEPTIONS

Researchers have been interested in the foundations and development of U.S. perceptions of Latin Americans, which they have found to be negative ones. Philip W. Powell, *Tree of Hate: Propaganda and Prejudices Affecting United States Relations with the Hispanic World* (1971), is an explication of the origins and assumptions of the propagandist Black Legend of things Spanish and its adoption in the U.S. mentality of Spanish America. John J. Johnson, *A Hemisphere Apart: The Foundations of United States Policy Toward Latin America* (1990), analyzes U.S. views of the nineteenth-century Spanish American movements for independence and the shift from support of them to limited interest and disdain for the people and their institutions. Johnson finds "more than mere glimmerings of why a cloud of misunderstanding, apprehension, and distrust has overhung hemispheric relations for more than two centuries." Fredrick B. Pike, *The United States and Latin America: Myths and Stereotypes of Civilization and Nature* (1992), argues that U.S. and Latin American stereotypes of each other began with the first colonial-period contacts and continue to impinge on relations. The U.S. perception derives from the view of Latin America's civilization as primitive because it accepts rather than dominates nature. Martha L. Cottam, *Images and Intervention: U.S. Policies in Latin America* (1994), applies political psychological concepts of image formation to U.S. policymakers toward Latin America (especially the circum-Caribbean). Cottam concludes that U.S. interventions will not cease in the post–cold war era if decisions continue to be shaped in the cold war pattern of negative, contemptuous, and paternalistic views of "dependent" (weak, inferior, childlike, inept, and corrupt) Latin American people and cultures. She investigates a broad range of cases for supporting data. Eldon Kenworthy, ed., *America/Américas: Myth in the Making of U.S. Policy Toward Latin America* (1995), is a complex, sweeping, provocative interpretation of negative U.S. perceptions of Latin America and their influence on regional actions. Kenworthy sees the mindset rooted in the myth of U.S. exceptionalism and fear of extrahemispheric rivals coupled with the view of Latin Americans as culturally and politically inferior. This results in both forceful and benign paternalism toward them. Lars Schoultz, *Beneath the United States: A History of U.S. Policy Toward Latin America* (1998), asserts as his general theme that "a belief in Latin American inferiority is the essential core of United States policy toward Latin America because it determines the precise steps the United States takes to protect its interests in the region."

SUBREGIONAL POLICIES

Robert May, *The Southern Dream of Caribbean Empire, 1854–1861* (1989), focuses primarily on expansionist sentiment in the southern slave states. The debate, which took place in the context of national partisanship and policies, centered on the matter of extending slavery rather than the U.S. sphere of political and economic influence. On Caribbean policies, three books by Dana G. Munro are of particular interest, not only for their thorough scholarship but also because he was an influential and keenly observant U.S. foreign service officer serving in the Caribbean and in the State Department's Latin American division after World War I. They are: *The Five Republics of Central America: Their Political and Economic Development and Their Relations with the United States* (1918); *The United States and the Caribbean Area* (1934); *Intervention and Dollar Diplomacy in the Caribbean, 1900–1921* (1964); and *The United States and the Caribbean Republics, 1921–1933* (1974). Munro defends some elements of U.S. imperial policy but criticizes others, especially the earlier phase of heavy-handed military interventions into World War I. He defends (but far from uncritically) the thrust of the postwar period as a transition phase of dismantling intervention and making possible the noninterventionism of the Good Neighbor Policy. The scholarship is thorough and sophisticated and the analysis is thoughtful and nuanced. Howard C. Hill, *Roosevelt and the Caribbean* (1927), was one of the best accounts when published because of its objectivity at the height of U.S. intervention in the Caribbean. He sees President Theodore Roosevelt's approach as a pragmatic one seeking security objectives and discounts economic and commercial considerations. Wilfrid Hardy Callcott, *The Caribbean Policy of the United States, 1890–1920* (1942), is the text of the Albert Shaw Lecture for 1942 at Johns Hopkins University. He sees Caribbean policy as prosecuted through four historical periods of U.S. foreign policy, each dominated by a central focus: mainland development (1776–1890), evolution of Caribbean policy (1890–1920), hemisphere policy (1920–1940); and worldwide policy (from 1940). For cogent radical dissenting views of U.S. policies, see Philip S. Foner, *The Spanish-Cuban-American War and the Birth of American Imperialism* (1972). Lloyd S. Etheredge, *Can Governments Learn? American Foreign Policy and Central American Revolutions* (1985), deals with recurring post–World War II U.S. policy problems in Central America. Etheridge examines the learning capacity of changing administrations with case studies of behavior when faced with persisting political situations. Cynthia Weber, *Faking It: U.S. Hegemony in a "Post-Phallic" Era* (1999), is analyzed from a determinedly feminist perspective. In a review of the book in the *American Political Science Review* (June 2000), Ann Sisson Runyan says:

> What happens when queer theory "takes on" U.S. foreign policy? Suddenly, the dry and all-too-familiar landscape of rational choice, power politics, military interventions, and regime building gives way to an iconoclastic phantasmagoria of castration, love-scorned melancholia, male hysteria, and cross-dressing. At the center of this passion play is the U.S. body politic, which loses "his" vital member at the hands of Castr(o's/ating) Cuba, denying "him" "straight" forward power projections and reflections in the Caribbean She/Sea. Ever since this dismemberment, which ushered in a "post-phallic" era, U.S. foreign relations in the Caribbean can be read as a series of compensatory strategies designed to "fake" phallic power.

Several studies on the circum-Caribbean with abundant treatment of U.S. policies are cited and commented upon in Chapter 2: Chester Lloyd

Jones, *Caribbean Interests of the United States* (1916), and Chester Lloyd Jones, Henry Kittredge Norton, and Peter Thomas Moon, *The United States and the Caribbean* (1929); A. Curtis Wilgus, ed., *The Caribbean: Current United States Relations* (1966); Lester D. Langley, *Struggle for the American Mediterranean: United States–European Rivalry in the Gulf-Caribbean, 1776–1904* (1976), and Langley, *The United States and the Caribbean in the Twentieth Century* (4 eds., 1980–1989); H. Michael Erisman and John D. Martz, eds., *Colossus Challenged: The Struggle for Caribbean Influence* (1982); John E. Findling, *Close Neighbors, Distant Friends: United States–Central American Relations* (1987); David Healy, *Drive to Hegemony: The United States and the Caribbean, 1898–1917* (1988); Anthony P. Maingot, *U.S. Power and Caribbean Sovereignty: Geopolitics in a Sphere of Influence* (1988), and Maingot, *The United States and the Caribbean: Challenges of an Asymmetrical Relationship* (1994); Thomas M. Leonard, *Central America and the United States: The Search for Stability* (1991); and Joseph S. Tulchin, Andrés Serbín, and Rafael Hernández, eds., *Cuba and the Caribbean: Regional Issues and Trends in the Post–Cold War Era* (1997).

On South America, see two works that were cited and commented upon in Chapter 2: G. Pope Atkins, ed., *South America into the 1990s: Evolving International Relationships in a New Era* (1990), and Samuel L. Baily, *The United States and the Development of South America, 1945–1975* (1976).

CHAPTER 6

■

Interstate Institutions

This chapter deals with a large number of interstate organizations in which the Latin American and Caribbean states have participated. They are divided into four categories: (1) regional and subregional organizations, the result of Latin American and Caribbean formation of political and economic integration and other interstate groupings among themselves; (2) the multipurpose Inter-American System, which eventually included all of the western hemispheric states as members; (3) other formal bilateral and multilateral arrangements (international regimes) within the Americas—Mexican-U.S. border agreements, the North American Free Trade Agreement, the effort to create a Western Hemisphere Free Trade Area, and the Panama Canal treaty arrangements; and (4) the global associations—the League of Nations and the United Nations. Subsumed under the United Nations are citations on the New International Economic Order and the Law of the Sea.[1] See Chapter 3 for the positions of individual Latin American and Caribbean states on participation in interstate institutions. In the instance of the extrahemispheric states and Canada, see Chapter 4; and of the United States, Chapter 5.

GENERAL WORKS

Two reference works offer information on a wide range of subjects related to the content of this chapter. Larman C. Wilson and David W. Dent,

Historical Dictionary of Inter-American Organizations (1997), is not restricted to history and is more than a dictionary. It provides a conceptual introduction and abundant information on inter-American organizations (mostly intergovernmental but with a section on nongovernmental ones), along with related events, trends, issues, and leaders. It contains some 400 subject entries, a thorough bibliography, a chronology of major events, and appendices of useful data. G. Pope Atkins, *Encyclopedia of the Inter-American System* (1997), focuses on the Inter-American System but has major entries on related institutions—inter–Latin American and Caribbean organizations, The Hague System, the League of Nations, the United Nations, and more. It is a comprehensive multidisciplinary treatment, with bibliographic commentary following each of almost 200 entries. Several appendices present relevant documents, organizational charts, and tables of data. In addition, Gordon Mace and Louis Bélanger, eds., *The Americas in Transition: The Contours of Regionalism* (1999), assemble fourteen experts to explore post–cold war concepts of regionalism. They highlight the policy strategies of the Latin American states, the United States, and Canada with regard to an array of formal interstate institutions in the Americas. Among them are the Organization of American States, the Inter-American Development Bank, the North American Free Trade Agreement, and the Common Market of the South.

LATIN AMERICAN AND
CARIBBEAN INTEGRATION AND ASSOCIATION

Nineteenth-Century Spanish-American Congresses

Latin American initiatives for integration and association date from the end of the nineteenth-century movements for independence. Spanish-American attempts to create political union and mutual security agreements were pursued in four interstate congresses between 1826 and 1865. Central American efforts at federation began with independence from Spain in the 1830s and in a real sense have continued to the present day (they are discussed in a later section below). Simón Bolívar, a revered Spanish-American revolutionary leader, envisioned the establishment of some sort of international Spanish-American federation, with a major purpose of mutual security against outside threats. He organized and called the first congress at Panama in 1826. Over the next four decades, three more assemblies were organized: the American Congress at Lima (1847–1848), the Continental Congress at Santiago de Chile (1856), and the Second Lima Conference (1864–1865). Agreements were signed at each meeting regarding various matters, chief among them proposals for union and alliance. But once external threats receded the treaties were forgotten (only one of them went into effect). The movement finally ended in disillusionment, but several broad principles of international cooperation developed that were later adopted as primary purposes by the Inter-American System—the legal principle of nonintervention, the concept of regional collective security, and the peaceful settlement of disputes. Furthermore, the post–World War II economic and political integration and cooperation associations may be seen as a continuing manifestation of the nineteenth-century desire for some sort of inter–Latin American union.

A number of Latin American writers have written institutional and philosophical histories assuming the linkage between the "old" Pan-Americanism of Spanish-American states and the "new" United States–initiated Pan-Americanism dating from the 1880s. Octavio Méndez Pereira, *Bolívar y las relaciones interamericanas* (1960), interprets the early period in terms of the impact of the ideas of the celebrated leader. Alejandro Magnet, *Origines y antecedentes del panamericanismo* (1945), is a significant historical survey of the Spanish-American movement from its beginnings. He sees it as transformed in 1889 into a United States–led hegemonic institutional arrangement institutionalized in the Inter-American System, and attributes the conversion to the weaknesses of the Spanish-American states and their awe of U.S. power. Thoughtful lengthy histories resulted from an international competition sponsored by the Venezuelan government as part of its preparation to host the Tenth Inter-American Conference in 1954 in Caracas. The titles of all forty-three works submitted were the same, as the specified theme of the contest. The first prize winner was Jesús María Yepes, *Del Congreso de Panamá a la Conferencia de Caracas, 1826–1954: El genio de Bolívar a través de la historia de las relaciones interamericanas* (2 vols., 1955). Yepes took a traditional historical approach with heavy concentration on Latin American perspectives and influences on the evolution of Panamericanism. Recipient of the second prize, Francisco M. Cuevas Cancino, *Del Congreso de Panamá a la Conferencia de Caracas, 1826–1954: El genio de Bolívar a través de la historia de las relaciones interamericanas* (2 vols., 1955), also produced a detailed scholarly account. Rather than a straight chronological approach, the author emphasizes Bolivar's long-term influence on Spanish-Americanism (hispanoamericanismo), U.S.-led Pan-Americanism, and the consolidation of the Organization of American States.

Enrique Ventura Corominas, *Historia de las conferencias interamericanas* (1959), is a narrative account of inter-American conferences from the Congress of Panama in 1926 to the Caracas conference of 1954. Essentially an institutional history, it also provides interesting analytic and thematic commentary. The author was formerly president of the Council of the Organization of American States. Segundo F. Ayala, *Bolívar y el sistema interamericano: el ideal panamericano a través de la historia de las conferencias interamericanas, desde el Congreso de Panamá hasta la unidécima conferencia interamericana, 1826–1964* (3 vols., 1962–1964), is a prominent and voluminous example of Latin American Bolivarian idealism and the links of Spanish-Americanism to Pan-Americanism. Ismael Moreno Pino, *Orígines y evolución del Sistema Interamericano* (1977), is a solid work tracing the history from 1826 until the date of publication from a Mexican perspective.

U.S. scholars contributed studies asserting the long-term historical continuity of inter-American ideas and conferences. Two meticulously prepared books by Joseph Byrne Lockey, *Pan Americanism: Its Beginnings* (1920), and *Essays in Pan Americanism* (1939), include articles and papers written by a leading authority on the subject. Samuel Guy Inman, *Inter-American Conferences, 1826–1954: History and Problems* (1965), published posthumously, is a somewhat utopian view of the evolution of Pan-Americanism over the period indicated. Of particular interest are insights based on the author's long career and personal experiences in the region.

Three forceful Latin American polemics are of interest. José Vasconcelos, *Bolivarismo y Monroeismo* (1937), by the great Spanish-Mexican exile, public figure, and intellectual, distinguishes Bolivarian ideas of Spanish-American federation and U.S. hemispheric hegemony based on Monroeism (i.e., the principles of the Monroe Doctrine). He points out that the competing doctrines originated simultaneously in the 1820s. Alonso Aguilar, *Pan-Americanism from Monroe to the Present: A View from the Other Side* (1968), is a strong anti-imperialist statement, with research based on primary sources. It articulates a Latin American view of the hemisphere-dominating purposes to which the United States has put the Pan-American idea. Ricardo A. Martínez, *De Bolívar a Dulles: El Panamericanismo, doctrina y practica imperialista* (1959), is another survey history arguing that Pan-Americanism under U.S. imperialist tutelage has been contrary to Bolivar's earlier vision of Spanish-Americanism. Indalecio Liévano Aguirre, *Bolivarismo y Monroismo* (1987), also takes a Bolivarian position drawing negative comparisons with Monroeism.

Post–World War II Latin American– Caribbean Institutions

Researchers have produced an imposing literature on the complex set of post–World War II Latin American economic-political integration organizations. The institutions have been organized to include different but overlapping memberships on transregional, intra–South American, Central American, Caribbean Commonwealth, and inter-Caribbean bases. In addition, beginning in the 1960s, Latin American states in various combinations organized other transregional special-purpose associations as ways to coordinate their foreign policies in order to present, so far as possible, a united front to the outside world, as well as to facilitate their own developmental efforts. All of these interstate groupings are included here except for Central American phenomena, which are addressed separately in the following section. Central American efforts have a continuous complex history dating from independence in the 1820s to the present.

Heraldo Muñoz and Francisco Orrego Vicuña, eds., *La cooperación regional en América Latina: diagnostico y proyección futuras* (1987), includes contributions that make up a broad analysis of both the Latin American Integration Association (LAIA or ALADI) and other associations for inter–Latin American cooperation—the Special Latin American Coordinating Committee (CECLA), the Latin American Economic Association (SELA), the Cartagena consensus to coordinate Latin American positions in external debt negotiations, and the Contadora Groups coordinating responses to Central American conflict. The analysts indicate impediments to regional cooperation, such as nationalist viewpoints, ideological differences, long-standing rivalries and conflicts, domestic interest opposition, and changing international conditions. They tend to agree that Latin American democracy is a necessary prerequisite for beneficial cooperation but must be joined with a convergence of interests. The following studies are among the more useful of many on the general subject of post–World War II integration efforts. Mexican economist Víctor L. Urquidi, *Free Trade and Economic Integration in Latin America* (1962), a leading structuralist dependency theorist, presents in detail his policy argument for Latin American economic integration as a means of escaping regional dependence on outside economic powers. At the time, Urquidi was director of the Mexican office of the UN Economic Commission on Latin America, the leading institutional advocate of the position he articulates. Miguel S. Wionczek, ed., *Latin American Economic Integration: Experiences and Prospects* (1966), is a revised version of a 1964 Spanish edition. It contains a great deal of information on the Latin American Free Trade Association (LAFTA) and Central American integration institutions, as well as extended discussion of the problems they face. Sidney Dell, *A Latin American Common Market?* (1966), is an analysis of the problems and possibilities of a Latin American–wide common market, which he favors as a stimulus to economic development. Dell further argues that domestic reforms—of tax structures, income distribution, and land tenure—are required for a viable common market. He also advocates special measures favoring less developed economies within the market so as to avoid the stronger ones extracting resources from them and the resulting debilitating intramarket political polarization. Chilean economist and Inter-American Development Bank president Felipe Herrera, *Nacionalismo latinoamericano* (1967), addresses the domestic and external problems that Latin Americans must resolve before workable economic integration can be achieved. Despite the title, Latin American integration is the principal subject. Herrera revisited the problems in 1986 in his *Desarrollo e integración* (1986). Joseph Grunwald, Miguel S. Wionczek, and Martin Carnoy, *Latin American Economic Integration and U.S. Policy* (1972), are concerned about the serious problems hindering the integration efforts, which had reached crisis proportions in LAFTA and the Central American Common Market (CACM). They address comments about obstacles to be overcome to regional governing elites, whom they urge to revive integration efforts. Altaf Gauhar, ed., *Regional Integration: The Latin American Challenge* (1985), is a collection of revised conference papers advising reconceptualization of regional integration so as to adjust to the economic crisis and social instability of the 1980s. They counsel Latin Americans to depart from development models designed by outsiders and adopt their own formulations. Among the contributors are some of the most prominent Latin American writers on these matters: Osvaldo Sunkel, Enrique Iglesias, Celso Furtado, Aldo Ferrer, Juan Somavía, José Ocampo, Gert Rosenthal, and Luciano Tomassini. Simón Alberto Consalvi, *Un momento histórico de América Latina: Acapulco, 1987* (1988), is a concise and useful book by a noted Venezuelan writer and public figure, who enthusiastically traces the early evolution of the Rio Group (Permanent Mechanism of Consultation and Policy Coordination).

Studies have been devoted to Latin American relations with other world regions. Analysts have paid adequate attention to the Latin American–European interregional connections. Willy J. Stevens, ed., *América Latina se ha quedado sola* (1989), involves twelve authors who contribute ten essays on Latin America's political and economic integration and relations with Europe (to include the issues of the arms market and transatlantic terrorism). Special attention is paid to Colombia. Sistema Económico Latinoamericano (SELA), *América Latina y el Caribe ante el nuevo escenario europeo* (1993), is an analysis by SELA for its member states regarding the relations of Latin American and Caribbean states and integration organizations with the increasingly integrated European Community. Peter H. Smith, ed., *The Challenge of Integration: Europe and the Americas* (1993), is a useful collection of essays with due attention to both Latin American and European points of views. Susan Kaufman Purcell and Françoise Simon, eds., *Europe and Latin America in the World Economy* (1995), is a discussion by eight experts about post–cold war interregional economic relationships in the context of accelerated economic integration in both regions. They include assessments of the roles of Germany, Spain, and Eastern Europe, and trilateral connections involving the United States.

Certain Latin American states pursued their economic interests in an evolving Pacific Rim trading system. Shoji Nishijima and Peter H. Smith, eds., *Cooperation or Rivalry? Regional Integration in the Americas and the Pacific Rim* (1996), with a multinational group of eleven more contributors, examine issues of cooperation and rivalry in integration theory and practice. They include evaluations of the North American Free Trade Agreement (NAFTA) and its possible expansion into a Western Hemisphere Free Trade Agreement (WHFTA), and the meaning for Latin America and the Pacific Rim. Manfred Mols, Manfred Wilhelmy, and Hernán Gutiírres, eds., *América Latina y el sudeste asia: perfiles de cooperación regional* (1995), bring together seven German and Chilean analysts who insightfully appraise a little-researched topic in cross-regional interactions. The essays compare and contrast the concepts and practices of integration in Latin America and regionalism in Southeast Asia. They address the degree of institutional cooperation and separation between the two.

With reference to LAFTA, Martin Carnoy, *Industrialization in a Latin American Common Market* (1972), takes on the thorny issues in an excellent analysis. Edward S. Milenky, *The Politics of Regional Organization in Latin America: The Latin American Free Trade Association* (1973), highlights the politics of economic integration between 1960 and 1972 in this solid treatment of various specific issues—trade, international payments, regional planning, and institutional development. Juan Mario Vacchino, *Integración latinoamericana de la ALALC a la ALADI: una salida para los problemas de su desarrollo* (1983), is a historical assessment of the problems of LAFTA and its general failure, and of the prospects of the successor Latin American Integration Association (ALADI). ALADI is insightfully discussed in Heraldo Muñoz and Francisco Orrego Vicuña, eds., *La cooperación regional en América Latina: diagnostico y proyección futuras* (1987).

David Morawetz, *The Andean Group: A Case Study in Economic Integration Among Developing Countries* (1974), is a policy analysis that addresses crucial problems facing the organization regarding communications, economic policy harmonization, the common external tariff, and equitable distribution of benefits among the members. Edgar Camacho Omiste, a Bolivian analyst, *Integración Andina* (1975), engages in a neo-Marxist analysis. He contends that the lack of Andean unity and commercial integration is a function of the international capitalist system and world division of labor, which create conditions favoring the dominant social classes in the member states. Alicia Puyana De Palacios, *Economic Integration Among Unequal Partners: The Case of the Andean Group* (1982), is a study in political economy. It addresses the politics of harmonizing national economic policies with common policies toward foreign capital, a common external tariff, and sectoral industrial planning. The author concludes that the organization has limited success in expanding trade and investment and in economic development.

On the Common Market of the South (MERCOSUR), Belter Garré Copello, *El Tratado de Asunción y el Mercado Comun del Sur (MERCOSUR): los Megabloques económicos y América Austral* (1991) is a straightforward description and analysis, with numerous relevant documents. Augusto Mario Morello, ed., *El MERCOSUR: aspectos institucionales y económicos* (1993), is a set of essays addressing the enabling Asunción treaty; the applicable laws of the individual member states; their labor markets, environmental legislation, and educational systems; the compatibility of MERCOSUR's provision with other organizations to which the member states belong (such as ALADI); and conflict settlement mechanisms. Riordan Roett, ed., *Mercosur: Regional Integration, World Markets* (1998), is a brief but helpful description of MERCOSUR's origins and the prospects for its membership expansion, the difficulties of evolving from a customs union to a common market, and relations with Europe and the United States.

Commonwealth Caribbean integration is a reflection of the desire of the English-speaking Caribbean states, since their independence beginning in the mid-1960s, to pursue much of their development and external relations on a formally organized basis. (See Chapter 2 regarding their unsuccessful pre-independence attempt to form the West Indies Federation in association with Great Britain.) Fuat Andic, Stephen Andic, and Douglas Dosser, *A Theory of Economic Integration for Developing Countries, Illustrated by Caribbean Countries* (1971), is a general theoretical treatment, which within that context provides substantial information on Commonwealth Caribbean integration. W. Andrew Axline, *Caribbean Integration: The Politics of Regionalism* (1979), provides a helpful review of regional integration theory and the politics of development, and applies the concepts to the Commonwealth Caribbean. Axline supplies information on the states of the region, the creation of the Caribbean Free Trade Association (CARIFTA) and the Caribbean Community (CARICOM), and the problems in specific elements during the integration process. He highlights interstate negotiations on key decisions. Anthony J. Payne, *The Politics of the Caribbean Community, 1961–1979: Regional Integration Among New States* (1980), is a thorough study of the process of integrating the Commonwealth Caribbean states. Payne traces the history of intracommunity relations and events culminating in the formation of CARICOM. He applauds the community for applying their own concepts rather than conforming to extant conventional integration theories. H. Michael Erisman, *Pursuing Postdependency Politics: South-South Relations in the Caribbean* (1992), addresses CARICOM in a concise analysis and advocacy of the potential for stronger South-South interregional relations to reduce the CARICOM countries' dependency on industrialized economies. Chandra Hardy, *The Caribbean Development Bank* (1995), examines the policies and projects of the CARICOM institution. Hardy critically evaluates the bank's effectiveness as an instrument of development. Don D. Marshall, *Caribbean Political Economy at the Crossroads: NAFTA and Regional Developmentalism* (1998), submits that the expanding North American Free Trade Agreement or the hemispheric turn toward bloc formation may "offer a way out" for the Commonwealth Caribbean economies that are increasingly "obsolete." Marshall warns, however, that politics "must be brought back into the regionalization process, for each island government is witnessing the narrowing of the range of its state power by powerful transnational corporations, international financial institutions, U.S. interests, and corporate-backed World Trade Organization commissions."

Central American Federation and Integration

This section evaluates works directly addressing Central American federation after the states' independence in the nineteenth century as well as post–World War II Central American political and economic integration efforts.

A classic work on Central American federation by a Central American scholar is by Laudelino Moreno, *Historia de las relaciones interestatuales de*

Centroamérica (1928), long the leading study. The objective scholarly narrative deals with the movement for a Central American Union from the first postindependence initiatives to the time of publication. Alberto Herrarte, *La unión de Centroamérica: tragedia y esperanza: ensayo político-social sobre la realidad de Centro América* (2 eds., 1955, 1964), by a professor of law, is a serious inquiry into why Central Americans were unable to sustain the union movement. He says the major impediment was the intransigence of domestic interests and downplays nationalist and exogenous factors. Thomas L. Karnes, *The Failure of Union: Central America, 1824–1975* (2 eds., 1961, 1976), is a scholarly investigation of the long history of failures of both interstate agreement and aggressive unilateral military attempts to bring about unification. Karnes is pessimistic about any kind of federation, including the post–World War II political-economic integration efforts (he sees them as the latest phase in the history of attempts at union). Pedro Joaquín Chamorro Zelaya, *Historia de la federación de la América Central, 1823–1840* (1951), is an admirable survey of the organization, travails, and subsequent dissolution of the Central American Federation. It includes an appendix of the full text of several key documents.

On the post–World War II period of Central American unification, Sidney Dell, *The Central American Integration Programme* (1966), is one of the earlier expert analyses. James D. Cochrane, *The Politics of Regional Integration: The Central American Case* (1969), evaluates the evolution of the Central American Common Market (CACM) and the reasons for its moderate success at the time of writing. He is skeptical of economic integration theories because they do not take into account specific regional characteristics and realities. Guatemalan economist Isaac Cohen Orantes, *Regional Integration in Central America* (1972), seeks to evaluate "the political consequences of regional economic integration" in Central America from 1950 to 1960 by examining expectations of both "theoreticians" and "practitioners" with what in fact transpired. The author has been an official of the Economic Commission for Latin America and the Caribbean. Félix Guillermo Fernández-Shaw y Baldasano, *La integración de Centroamérica* (1965), is a valuable reference work by a Spanish diplomat and scholar with professional experience in the isthmus. The book highlights political, economic, and cultural integration efforts, and includes voluminous appendices of charts, tables, and documents. Roger D. Hansen, *Central America: Regional Integration and Economic Development* (1967), is a policy study well worth attention despite its brevity. Two prominent scholars make important empirically supported theoretical analyses: Joseph A. Nye, *Central American Integration* (1967); and Jeffrey B. Nugent, *Economic Integration in Central America* (1974). William R. Cline and Enrique Delgado, eds., *Economic Integration in Central America* (1978), is a lengthy and important collection of contributions by leading economic policy analysts. They stress cost-benefit analysis in domestic matters (such as employment and incomes) and comparative advantage in trade and development. Royce Q. Shaw, *Central America: Regional Integration and National Political Development* (1979), says that understanding the failures of Central American integration "lies in neither advanced economic nor regional integration theory but in the domestic politics of the regional states." And in that arena, "political elites played more important roles than technocrats." George Irvin and Stuart Holland, eds., *Central America: The Future of Economic Integration* (1989), is a useful collection of broad ranging analyses written as the Central American peace process was gaining momentum but still fraught with difficulties. Irma Tirado de Alonso, ed., *Trade, Industrialization, and Integration in Twentieth-Century Central America* (1994), begins with an introduction to the challenges to Central Americans of the titled phenomena, and a macroeconomic evaluation of the countries and the subregion. Fourteen contributors subsequently address the structures, problems, and issues with respect to trade, industrialization, and integration. Comisión Económica para América Latina y el Caribe; Banco Interamericano de Desarrollo, *La integración centroamericana y la institucionalidad regional* (1998), is a valuable source of a great deal of information, much of which is difficult to find elsewhere.

THE INTER-AMERICAN SYSTEM

The formal Inter-American System refers to multipurpose organizations among most or all of the American states that originated in 1889 and evolved thereafter to the present day. Some scholars, as indicated above, argue that the system had its beginnings in the 1820s with the Spanish

American initiatives to form some sort of federation, a position disputed by other analysts. In any event, this section deals with the post-1889 hemispherewide Inter-American System. The designation denotes not a centralized institution but an "umbrella" concept covering an uninterrupted history and current network of institutional principles, policies, procedures, and structures. Today the system consists largely (but not exclusively) of the separate but coordinated Organization of American States (OAS) and Inter-American Development Bank (IDB). Other post–World War II elements have included a scattered system for the peaceful settlement of disputes and the Inter-American Treaty of Reciprocal Assistance (Rio Treaty) regime, both of which are presently moribund. In 1991 the OAS achieved universal membership of all thirty-five sovereign states in the Americas—the thirty-three Latin American and Caribbean states, the United States, and Canada. (Cuba has been a "nonparticipating" member since 1962.) The OAS has also conferred observer status on thirty extrahemispheric states and the United Nations. The IDB, founded in 1960, has evolved a membership of forty-four states, including sixteen from outside the hemisphere. The Inter-American System's activities have evolved to promote (1) nonintervention and sovereign equality; (2) codification of international law; (3) economic, social, and cultural cooperation; (4) peace and security; (5) representative democracy and human rights; (6) measures against the drug traffic; and (7) protection of the environment.[2] See Chapter 7 for the Inter-American System's actions in specific cases of inter-American disputes and threats from outsiders; and Chapter 8 for works dealing with democracy and human rights; economic, social, and cultural cooperation; the drug traffic; and the environment.

General Treatments

Comprehensive general works on the Inter-American System, and of the Organization of American States that include historical antecedents, traditionally employed an institutional-legal approach (sometimes with a philosophical overlay). They are dated but a number are still useful for the information they provide. A majority of the studies cited above, on the nineteenth-century Spanish-American congresses, include substantial material relevant to the Inter-American System and Pan-Americanism. Five authoritative studies are essential reference works—although dated, they remain useful sources. Charles G. Fenwick, *The Organization of American States: The Inter-American Regional System* (1963), is a comprehensive legal-historical treatment by a scholar and longtime official of the Pan American Union. Ann Van Wynen Thomas and A. J. Thomas, Jr. *The Organization of American States* (1963), by two legal scholars, provides historical background on the organization and explains its institutional structures, principles, and functions. Three U.S. political scientists offer books that focus on but go beyond the titled subjects to constitute general works. J. Lloyd Mecham, *The United States and Inter-American Security, 1889–1960* (1961), is a detailed, chronological, interpretive (often subjectively) treatment that filled a long-existing gap. Mecham deals with historical precedents beginning with the Spanish-American congress of 1826; the stages of development of the inter-American security system, calling attention to the linkages with other organizational principles and activities; and the juridical and structural formalization of inter-American security procedures. He discusses the competing interests of the member states and asserts that the strength of the alliance depends on the solidarity between the United States and its Latin American associates. Jerome Slater, *The OAS and United States Foreign Policy* (1967), provides thorough descriptions and realistic assessments of the overall inter-American organization, mostly since the establishment of the OAS in 1948. He astutely analyzes the OAS from certain often-asserted standpoints: as a collective security system, an anticommunist alliance, an antidictatorial alliance, and a pro-democracy alliance. He undertakes several empirical case studies. The analysis in the final chapter of integrative and disintegrative tendencies in the organization is insightful. M. Margaret Ball, *The OAS in Transition* (1969), considers the OAS as a complex organization in the midst of a period of fundamental transformation. She deals in detail with its evolution, principles, structures, and activities. Her commentary is realistic and astute.

Jesús María Yepes, *Le Panamericanisme au point de vue historique, juridique et politique* (1936), is a collection of lectures given in his course at the Institute of Advanced International Studies, University of Paris. Yepes examines the arguments for and against the Pan-American movement, the achievements of Pan-Americanism, and the changes in the Latin American policies of the United States under the Good Neighbor Policy. Teodoro Alvarado Garaicoa, *La Trascendencia de las Reuniones Interamericanos* (1949), by a distinguished Ecuadorian jurist, is a legal history of the International Conferences of American States through the ninth (1948), with brief mention of the first three Meetings of Consultation of Ministers of Foreign Affairs. Félix Guillermo Fernández-Shaw y Baldasano, *La Organización de los Estados Americanos (O.E.A.): una nueva visión de América* (2 eds., 1959, 1963), is a useful, lengthy, and factually detailed institutional history and useful reference work. He surveys the Inter-American System from 1889 and the OAS and its various elements after its establishment in 1948. He also deals with the antecedent Spanish-American congresses beginning in 1826. José Joaquín Caicedo Castilla, *El Panamericanismo* (1961), is an institutional history by a Colombian jurist and public official. Samuel Guy Inman, *Inter-American Conferences, 1826–1954: History and Problems* (1965), deals in chronological order with inter-American conferences from 1889 to 1954 (and the Spanish-American precursors from 1826–1865). Inman offers personal insights based on his long career in religious missionary efforts in Latin America. More than four decades previously, Inman had published *Problems in Pan Americanism* (1925), interesting as an early work by an earnest advocate. Inter-American Institute of International Legal Studies, *The Inter-American System: Its Development and Strengthening* (1966), is a highly detailed treatment of institutions and their functions and major themes. It devotes significant space to the reproduction of documents. British historian Gordon Connell-Smith, *The Inter-American System* (1966), is a comprehensive treatment, valuable because it brings together a great deal of scattered material. He sees the organization in simple terms as an artificial association of one powerful state member and twenty weak ones, serving the interests of the former by helping it to maintain its hemispheric hegemony—although he acknowledges that Latin Americans have had some success in restraining U.S. power. Minerva M. Etzioni, *The Majority of One: Towards a Theory of Regional Compatibility* (1970), claims to offer "a new theory of international organizations," but in fact interprets details (which is useful) about the overwhelming U.S. predominance in the OAS as it seeks to achieve its political interests. César Sepúlveda, *El Sistema In-*

teramericano: genesis, integración, decadencia (1974), is by a Mexican scholar who also applies a legal-institutional approach. He takes a minority Latin American viewpoint at the time by being "moderately optimistic" about the future of the system, despite its serious deterioration following the Dominican Republic crisis of 1965. Rodrigo Díaz Albonico, ed., *Antecedentes, balance y perspectivas del Sistema Interamericano* (1977), is a multiauthored work by Latin American specialists. Three German scholars produced solid studies. Gerhard Kutzner, *Die Organisation der Amerikanischen Staaten (OAS)* (1970), focuses on the legal-institutional framework and certain organizational problems (including those of a political nature). Niels Brandt, *Das Interamerikanische Friedensystem: Idee und Wirklichkeit* (1971), is particularly thorough. Lothar Brock, *Entwicklungsnationalismus und Kompradorenpolitik: Die Gründug de OAS und die Entwicklung der Abhangigkeit Lateinamerikas von den USA* (1975), is the most analytical in terms of principles and practices.

O. Carlos Stoetzer, *The Organization of American States* (2 eds., 1965, 1993), is a chronological-thematic compendium in the institutional-legal tradition that provides a thorough and valuable reference work. In organizational administrative terms, Ruth D. Masters, ed., *Handbook of International Organizations in the Americas* (1945), contains synopses of 109 organizations and is still useful for the information provided. Key-Sung Cho, *Organismos interamericanos: sus antecedentes, estructuras, funciones, y perspectivas* (1984), is by an experienced diplomat who provides useful descriptive organizational information.

Three works provide needed political frames of reference and more current assessments. Tom J. Farer, ed., *The Future of the Inter-American System* (1988), is a reevaluation by experts who see the Inter-American System as an anachronism as presently constituted and recommend reforms that take into account prevailing hemispheric political and economic realities. L. Ronald Scheman, *The Inter-American Dilemma: The Search for Inter-American Cooperation at the Centennial of the Inter-American System* (1988), also sees the system in need of basic revision. Scheman, a former OAS assistant secretary-general for management, calls for reforms in the OAS, IDB, and other regional organizations that accommodate the diverging interests of the United States and the Latin American and Caribbean states. Viron P. Vaky and Heraldo Muñoz, *The Future of the*

Organization of American States (1993), is by a former U.S. diplomat who was assistant secretary of state for inter-American affairs and a Chilean scholar who served as his country's ambassador to the OAS. They realistically assess requirements for success in the post–cold war era.

Inter-American Development Bank

Sidney Dell, *The Inter-Development Bank: A Study in Development Financing* (1972), is a thorough study of the IDB as an autonomous institution and a case study in development financing and the problems encountered. At the time of writing Dell was director of the Financing Division of the United Nations Commission on Trade and Development (UNCTAD). Peter R. Dewitt Jr., *The Inter-American Development Bank and Political Influence: With Special Reference to Costa Rica* (1977), analyzes the role of the IDB on Latin American development, highlighting the case of Costa Rica. He says that the United States sways the bank's decisions to choose development projects that serve the interests of foreign private investment, which often do not rationalize the recipients' sustained economic development. He makes specific recommendations for IDB trade and investment projects. Diana Tussie, *The Inter-American Development Bank* (1994), is a brief and informative description, analysis, and critique of the bank's functions and operations. The book is divided into two parts, titled "Historical Setting and Record of Performance" and "Development Agenda," with the last chapter on "looming development challenges."

Principles and Practices

Codification of International Law.   Mario A. Gómez de la Torre, *Derecho constitucional interamericano* (2 vols., 1964), is a juridical treatment of the history from 1826 to the 1960s. Alejandro Alvarez, *International Law and Related Subjects from the Point of View of the American Continent* (1922), is a very concise but important statement by the eminent Chilean jurist and leader of the movement to codify a distinctly American international law. Alvarez had earlier published pathbreaking works in French articulating his views about the long-standing Latin

American aspiration for such a body of law, including *Le droit international américain* (1902). It was published the first year that the Inter-American System addressed the matter as a possible institutional principle. Francisco José Urrutia, *Le continent américain et le droit internacional* (1928), is by a strong advocate of a distinct American international legal system. He surveys the origins of such principles in both Latin America and the United States following their revolutions for independence and in the six International Conferences of American States from 1889 to 1928. It was published at the time the Sixth International Conference of American States received for consideration several important draft conventions from the International Commission of Jurists headed by Alejandro Alvarez. H. B. Jacobini, *A Study of the Philosophy of International Law as Seen in Works of Latin American Writers* (1954), begins with a survey of the development of international law since the fifteenth century, and proceeds to analyze the works of Latin American writers on the subject in the nineteenth and twentieth centuries. Jacobini highlights both European influences on Latin American views and the Latin American movement for codification of a distinct body of American international law, which he sees as a minority position. C. Neale Ronning, *Law and Politics in Inter-American Diplomacy* (1963), is a brief book that accomplishes its purpose to assess "today's battered rule of international law in the lights of the requirements of a hemisphere already quite different from the 'world community' in which those rules emerged." He sees the situation in such matters as recognition of new governments, treatment of aliens and their property, intervention in domestic affairs of sovereign states, diplomatic asylum, and territorial waters. Philip B. Taylor Jr., *Law and Politics in Inter-American Diplomacy* (1963), addresses the distinctions and tensions between general and inter-American international law. César Sepúlveda, *Las fuentes del derecho internacional americano: una encuesta sobre los métodos de creación de reglas internacionales en el Hemisferio Occidental* (2 eds., 1969, 1975), is a thoughtful contribution that approaches the question of American international law in terms of the accepted bases of international law. He examines the role of the Inter-American System as a legitimate source of a body of American law. José Joaquín Caicedo Castilla, *El derecho internacional en el Sistema Interamericano* (1970), is an important and informative supportive statement for American international law.

Nigel S. Rodley and C. Neale Ronning, eds., *International Law in the Western Hemisphere* (1974), is based on papers presented at an academic conference by highly qualified analysts and represents one of the few scholarly efforts on the subject at the time. Although limited in scope and dated by subsequent international legal developments, the book remains useful with respect to the development of elements of inter-American law regarding water resources, military and economic intervention, and human rights.

Nonintervention.   In the early years of the development of the Inter-American System, Latin Americans urged the adoption on a juridical multilateral basis of two noninterventionist doctrines. The earliest was the Calvo Doctrine, which maintained that, as a matter of American international law, no state has the right to collect private debts owed to its citizens. Donald R. Shea, *The Calvo Clause: A Problem of Inter-American and International Law and Diplomacy* (1955), is an excellent historical analysis of the Calvo proposition in terms of inter-American politics, economics, and law. Shea concludes that it has in fact achieved a limited validity despite the position of most jurists to the contrary. The second precept was the Drago Doctrine, proposed in 1902 by Argentine foreign minister Luis María Drago. It complemented the Calvo Doctrine by seeking to make illegal armed intervention to force payment of foreign governmental debts. Alfredo N. Vivot, *La doctrina Drago* (1911), is a contemporary legal analysis of the doctrine, focusing on its first expression in 1902 and its acceptance with debilitating reservations in The Hague Convention of 1907. Vivot considers the doctrine a policy rather than a legal proposition. Ann Van Wynen Thomas and A. J. Thomas Jr., *Non-Intervention: The Law and Its Import in the Americas* (1956), is an encyclopedic and orderly historical survey and analysis of the subject. The book is divided into three parts, the first an examination of the development of the doctrine of nonintervention; the second a discussion of the doctrine as a legal principle; and the third an attempt, not entirely successful, to sort the various categories of intervention susceptible to legal jurisdiction.

Peace and Security.   Herman Meyer-Lindenberg, *El procedimiento interamericano para consolidar la paz* (1941), is a scholarly treatment of the inter-American structure for the peaceful settlement of disputes, which he aptly criticizes as unnecessarily complicated. About a third of the book is devoted to documents. Antonio Gómez Robledo, *La seguridad colectiva en el continente americano* (1959), is an incisive historical survey of the concept of collective security and its application by the Inter-American System (of which he approves). The author goes into the details of inter-American institutional arrangements for regional mutual security. Rodolfo Garrié Faget, *Organismos militares interamericanos* (1968), is a brief, useful description of inter-American security-related agencies: the Inter-American Defense Committee, the Central American Defense Council, the Consultative Defense Committee of the OAS, and the informal but regular Meetings of the Commanders of the American Armed Forces. Relevant documents are appended. James R. Jose, *An Inter-American Peace Force Within the Framework of the Organization of American States: Advantages, Impediments, Implications* (1970), is a solid conceptual analysis of the subject. Jose concludes that an Inter-American Peace Force would not "make a positive contribution to the peace-keeping machinery of the inter-American system." Jerome Slater, *A Reevaluation of Collective Security: The OAS in Action* (1965), is a realistic conceptual and policy assessment, which also provides useful institutional information.

OTHER INTER-AMERICAN REGIMES

This section addresses bilateral and multilateral treaty arrangements involving American states in the governance of particular matters. They are the several Mexican–United States border accords, the North American Free Trade Agreement, the evolving process seeking a Western Hemisphere Free Trade Association, and U.S.-Panamanian terms for regulating the Panama Canal.

Mexico–United States Border Agreements

Riverine and Related Arrangements.   Norris Hundley, *Dividing the Waters: A Century of Controversy Between the United States and Mexico* (1966), is a detailed scholarly study, dealing with the Colorado River, the Rio Grande, and the Tijuana River. Hundley surveys the process from the

Treaty of La Mesilla in 1853 to the Treaty on International Waters in 1944. Addressing the same set of problems, Ernesto Enríquez Coyro, *El tratado entre México y los Estados Unidos de América sobre ríos internacionales: una lucha nacional de noventa años* (2 vols., 1975–1976), is an important and authoritative contribution by the author of the legal study on which the Mexican position was based during the 1944 negotiations for a settlement of the long-standing dispute with the United States over river rights. Based on further exhaustive research, the author also surveys the 1853–1944 time span. Charles A. Timm, *The International Boundary Commission, United States and Mexico* (1941), is a carefully researched legal-institutional study of the bilateral commission that was created by an 1824 treaty to exercise exclusive jurisdiction over questions arising concerning the mutual boundary. The commission was still active at the time of publication. Sheldon B. Liss had written *A Century of Disagreement: The Chamizal Conflict, 1864–1964* (1965), a concise scholarly review of a pivotal territorial dispute, which was finally resolved in 1963 after fifty-two years of negotiations. Liss provides a solid evaluation of the resolution of the controversy in 1963. Alan C. Lamborn and Stephen P. Mumme, *Statecraft, Domestic Politics, and Foreign Policy Making: The El Chamizal Dispute* (1988), addresses the Chamizal matter as a case study within a theoretical decision-making framework. The authors broaden their essentially realist-rationalist assumption of the linking of foreign policymaking to the strategic context by factoring in domestic politics. See Chapter 3 on the Mexican-U.S. borderlands, and Chapter 7 on the Mexican–United States war and its settlement.

Maquiladora Arrangement. Donald Baerrensen, *The Border Industrialization Program* (1971), provides much background information and analysis. Baerrensen is supportive of the maquiladora program. Khosrow Fatemi, ed., *The Maquiladora Industry: Economic Solution or Problem?* (1990), contains helpful appraisals by leading specialists. They address the subject not only with reference to such matters as production sharing and the question of mutual benefits versus exploitation, but also the relationship to Mexico's external debt, transborder movement of people and drug trafficking, transfer of technology, and energy sources. Leslie Sklair, *Assembling for Development: The Maquila Industry in Mexico and the*

United States (1989), is authored by a sociologist at the London School of Economics and Political Science. Sklair also takes a global viewpoint in an examination of "the emergence of production-sharing as a strategy for economic and social development using low-cost labor in Third World countries to assemble components produced in developed countries." He analyzes the Mexican case as a primary center for such production sharing. Altha J. Cravey, *Women and Work in Mexico's Maquiladoras* (1998), also places the maquilas in a global context, in this instance the phenomenon of assembly plants and their large female labor forces. Since the Mexican plants have employed predominantly female labor, the question of "gender restructuring in the workplace is a crucial element in the reorientation of Mexican development."

North American Free Trade Agreement

Sidney Weintraub, *Free Trade Between Mexico and the United States?* (1984), is the prescient analysis of a leading expert, who discusses the subject at a time when such an eventuality was considered virtually impossible. Weintraub followed with *A Marriage of Convenience: Relations Between Mexico and the United States* (1990), written in the early stages of the North American Free Trade Agreement process. He emphasizes the growing economic interdependence of the two partners and urges adoption of "a model of managed integration." Gary Clyde Hufbauer and Jeffrey J. Schott provide valuable information and analysis in two studies. In *North American Free Trade: Issues and Recommendations* (1992), they address the major issues in the complex and intense NAFTA negotiations and make rational recommendations. They followed with *NAFTA: An Assessment* (1993), which evaluates the final agreement. They appraise each signatory state's negotiating objectives; the implications of the agreement for trade, investment, employment, labor, and the environment; and the principal issues of rules of origin, intellectual property, energy, steel, textiles, agricultural, and financial services. H. Rodrigo Jauberth, Gilberto Casteñeda, Jesús Hernández, and Pedro Vúskovic, *The Difficult Triangle: Mexico, the United States, and Central America* (1992), includes as an important element an assessment of the probable impact of NAFTA on Central America. Ricardo Grinspun and Maxwell A. Cameron, *The Political Economy of*

North American Free Trade (1993), is a good analysis of the negotiation process, particularly as the authors address the social, political, and environmental factors underlying the initiation of negotiations. William A. Orme Jr., *Understanding NAFTA: Mexico, Free Trade, and the New North America* (2 eds., 1993, 1996), is a clearly written explication of NAFTA issues and the consequences of the treaty for Mexico and the United States. The first volume was written in the midst of the NAFTA debate, an uncertainty not burdening the second (retitled) edition. George W. Grayson, *The North American Free Trade Agreement: Regional Community and the New World Order* (1994), addresses the acrimonious U.S. process of congressional approval of the agreement and the complex network of party and ideological positions. Grayson ponders the significance of NAFTA for the U.S. role in inter-American relations. Charles F. Doran and Gregory P. Marchildon, eds., *The NAFTA Puzzle: Political Parties and Trade in North America* (1994), is a multiauthored comparative analysis of trade and political party orientations in the three North American states. The authors focus on the political parties themselves and party politics, free trade policies, and economic development. Included is particular reference to the NAFTA vote in the legislatures. M. Delal Baer, Joseph T. Jockel, and Sidney Weintraub, eds., *NAFTA and Sovereignty: Trade-Offs for Canada, Mexico, and the United States* (1996), along with three more contributors, emphasize how thoroughly domestic and foreign policies have become indistinguishable. This reality compels a redefinition of sovereignty in theory and practice. Emile G. McAnany and Kenton T. Wilkinson, eds., *Mass Media and Free Trade: NAFTA and the Cultural Industries* (1997), allows economists, sociologists, anthropologists, and humanities and communications scholars to speculate about NAFTA's effects on the transborder flows of cultural products. Stephen Blank and Jerry Haar, *Making NAFTA Work: U.S. Firms and the New North American Business Environment* (1997), investigate how NAFTA accelerated changes in the North American business environment as well as "transformed corporate strategies and structures and affected patterns of U.S. investment." They base their analysis on survey questionnaires and interviews with executives of multinational corporations with Mexican subsidiaries. Frederick W. Mayer, *Interpreting NAFTA: The Science and Art of Political Analysis* (1998), is a careful treatment of the domestic U.S. political debate and process accompanying the NAFTA negotiations, from congressional approval of a "fast-track" process in 1991 through its approval of the agreement in 1993. Mayer manages to apply formal modeling and provide a readable narrative. Joseph A. McKinney, *Created from NAFTA: The Structure, Function, and Significance of the Treaty's Related Institutions* (2000), investigates the NAFTA institutions mandated by the agreement and legislation with respect to labor and the environment, as agreed to by the participants as a result of their experience.

Western Hemisphere Free Trade

President George Bush proposed hemispheric free trade in June 1990 when he presented the Enterprise for the Americas Initiative (EAI). The United States eventually signed "framework agreements" with almost all of the Latin American and Caribbean states, including certain of the subregional economic integration organizations, as the foundation for negotiation of free trade. Later, leaders of the American states, under the aegis of the Organization of American States, declared the goal of creating a Hemispheric Free Trade Area (HFTA) by the year 2005. A rudimentary structure evolved but the HFTA's overall organization and its relationship to the Inter-American System are yet to be decided.

Sylvia Saborio, ed., *The Premise and Promise: Free Trade in the Americas* (1992), contains chapters by ten specialists from the United States, Mexico, and Canada. They deal with different national perspectives on free trade in the Americas and the negotiating path to a WHFTA, as well as "examine the rationale, feasibility, and implications" of the U.S.–Latin American free trade agreements and the complex situation among the United States, NAFTA, Chile, Central America, CARICOM, ANCOM, and MERCOSUR. Roy Green, ed., *The Enterprise for the Americas Initiative: Issues and Prospects for a Free Trade Agreement in the Western Hemisphere* (1993), has wide-ranging essays of a fairly technical nature on issues attendant to creating a WHFTA, with much attention to the elements of the EAI and the evolving decisions about NAFTA. *Free Trade in the Western Hemisphere*, the entire issue of *Annals of the American Academy of Political and Social Science* (March 1993), and *Integrating the Americas: Shaping Future Trade Policy* (1994), are edited by Sidney Weintraub, a leading expert and advocate of hemispheric free trade. Weintraub assembles nine other specialists to focus on new ideas about regional integration and implications for inter-American relations. They offer suggestions "for strengthening the separate integration arrangements and analyze proposals for consolidating them into" a Western Hemisphere free trade area. Gary Clyde Hufbauer and Jeffrey J. Schott, *Western Hemisphere Economic Integration* (1994), is a thorough analysis of processes and consequences of proposals for extending NAFTA throughout the Western Hemisphere. They assess both the economics and politics of several avenues that might be followed, as well as the impact on the global trading system. Richard G. Lipsey and Patricio Meller, *Western Hemisphere Trade Integration: A Canadian–Latin American Dialogue* (1997), is a wide-ranging treatment by fifteen contributors. They address NAFTA in the world economy and comment on MERCOSUR and the Group of 3 (a trade agreement among Colombia, Mexico, and Venezuela). They take up the cases of Chile's trade strategy as a small country, Bolivia's border trade, and Paraguay's small-country perspective as a member of MERCOSUR. They examine social and labor issues in the Canada-U.S. experience with integration and their trade dispute settlement mechanism and analyze the trade and investment between Canada and the Latin American Integration Association.

Transisthmian Canal

Ira Dudley Travis, *The History of the Clayton-Bulwer Treaty* (1900), is mentioned as an early objective and solid diplomatic history, well researched in terms of the sources available at the time. Travis narrates events leading to adoption of the treaty in 1850, and evaluates the way U.S. officials reinterpreted its provisions over the following half-century.

Many good general studies regarding the Panama Canal have been provided over the years. Mary Wilhelmine Williams, *Anglo-American Isthmian Diplomacy, 1815-1915* (1916), published two years after the canal opened, represents an early scholarly work on the subject and the standard source for years after its publication. Lincoln Hutchinson, *The Panama Canal and International Trade Competition* (1915), also writing as the Panama Canal opened for operations, deals with political-commercial considerations in canal diplomacy, particularly on the part of the United States. Antonio José Uribe, *Colombia y los Estados Unidos de América: El canal interoceanico* (1925), is an objective scholarly rendering by a Colombian historian. Hugh Gordon Miller, *The Isthmian Highway: A Review of the Problems of the Caribbean* (1929), is a highly detailed and heavily documented treatise by a lawyer and former U.S. official, widely read at the time. Although sympathetic to U.S. interests, Miller is relatively unbiased in his evaluations. Of interest is the discussion of the Monroe Doctrine's application to the protection and operation of the canal. Alvaro Rebolledo, *Reseña histórico-política de la comunicación interoceánica, con especial referencia a la separación de Panamá y a los arreglos entre los Estados Unidos y Colombia* (1930), is by a Colombian historian who seeks to correct (and not without reason) diplomatic histories of Panama and the canal that overlook Colombia's importance in the story. Dwight C. Miner, *The Fight for the Panama Route: The Story of the Spooner Act and the Hay-Herrán Treaty* (1940), examines all sides in the conflict, between and within Colombia and the United States, during the complex and controversial diplomacy and power politics leading up to the Panamanian rebellion against Colombia in 1903. Miles Percy DuVal, *Cadiz to Cathay: The Story of the Long Diplomatic Struggle for the Panama Canal* (2 eds., 1940, 1947), is a remarkably inclusive examination of the evolution of plans to build a Central American interoceanic canal. The narrative begins with the first Spanish proposal in 1502 and proceeds through post–Latin American independence, U.S.-British competition, the French presence and initiation of canal construction, and the U.S. acquisition of construction rights and completion of the project. Gerstle Mack, *The Land Divided: A History of Panama and Other Isthmian Canal Projects* (1944), is a remarkable history by an author trained as an architect. He examines the various Panama Canal projects, particularly those undertaken by French and U.S. officials and engineers. Mack addresses an array of themes: high strategy, diplomacy, politics, economics, engineering, and medicine. Ernesto Castillero Pimental, *Panamá y los Estados Unidos* (1953), is a thorough legal historical examination of problems regarding the canal and the possibilities for their resolution. Lyman M. Tondel Jr., ed., *The Panama Canal* (1965), is a useful descriptive-documentary history. Lawrence O. Ealy, *Yanqui Pol-*

itics and the Isthmian Canal (1971), an expert on Panama's international relations, adds a concise diplomatic history; and Walter LaFeber, *The Panama Canal: The Crisis in Historical Perspective* (2 eds., 1978, 1989), a noted scholar of Central American affairs, does the same. David McCullough, *The Path Between the Seas: The Creation of the Panama Canal, 1870–1914* (1977), is a comprehensive account of the building of the Panama Canal, from the initial French efforts to its completion by the United States. McCullough documents the feat as both an engineering marvel and vast historical phenomenon—"involving financial collapse and scandal, a revolution, a new Central American republic, and an entire chain of events." He pays due attention to the dominant personalities who appeared on the scene. David Farnsworth and James McKenney, *U.S.-Panama Relations, 1903–1978: A Study in Linkage Politics* (1983), survey the canal dispute from its origins until the adoption of the 1997 treaties. The authors focus on "the extent to which domestic politics in each country influenced decisions about foreign policy and about the treaty negotiations, and how these decisions in turn affected internal political circumstances." They also examine an array of ancillary issues. John Major, *Prize Possession: The United States and the Panama Canal: 1903–1979* (1993), is a well-researched, thorough history that emphasizes four topics: the place in U.S. global strategy of the defense of the Panama Canal; the regimented governance of the Canal Zone; the strictly segregated labor force and the commercial development at Panama's expense; and U.S. intervention into Panama's politics. Major clearly is not sympathetic to U.S. policies and actions.

Analysts have studied the uninspiring U.S. ratification process. William L. Furlong and Margaret E. Scranton, *The Dynamics of Foreign Policymaking: The President, the Congress, and the Panama Canal Treaties* (1984), investigate the politics of negotiating, ratifying, and implementing the 1997 Panama Canal treaties. The authors do so within a framework for analysis devised in terms of the U.S. foreign policymaking system. They provide a summary of the historical background, and do not disguise their pro-treaties biases. George D. Moffett III, *The Limits of Victory: Ratification of the Panama Canal Treaties* (1985), is by a former assistant to the chief of President Carter's White House staff and based on interviews with participants and oral histories. He evaluates how, and why at such a high political price, the president finally won a very difficult political contest with the U.S. Senate to advise and consent to the treaty. Moffett sees the process as an "object lesson in the limits of public education," and concludes, "it proved easier to arouse opinion than to direct it." William J. Jorden, *Panama Odyssey* (1984), and William Hogan, *The Panama Canal in American Politics: Domestic Advocacy and the Evolution of Policy* (1986), also contributes to our understanding of the 1977 U.S. treaty ratification process.

GLOBAL AND
EXTRAHEMISPHERIC ORGANIZATIONS

This section deals with the global and extrahemispheric institutions—intergovernmental organizations and international regimes—in which the Latin American states have participated. The book-length literature on these subjects is remarkably limited, so that a limited scope of the phenomena is addressed. Studies are cited concerning the League of Nations and the United Nations (UN), the New International Economic Order (NIEO), and the Antarctic Treaty and the Law of the Sea. The participation of the Latin American states has reflected their desire to participate in international affairs beyond the Western Hemisphere and to present a united front to the outside world. The Commonwealth Caribbean countries, sovereign states only beginning in the 1960s, have largely limited their activities to the UN and NIEO.

During the life of the League of Nations (1920–1945), all Latin American states were members at some time or another, although never were all of them participants at the same time and they generally were frustrated in the pursuit of their international purposes and interests. Augustín Edwards, *La América Latina y la Liga de las Naciones* (1937), is a scholarly effort by a Chilean author. He describes in detail the history of the Latin American association with the League of Nations and includes treatments of individual states. Francisco José Urrutia, *La evolución del principio de arbitraje en América: La Sociedad de Naciones* (1920), is a legal-historical treatment by a prominent Colombian scholar of the Latin American effort to extend inter-American arbitration principles beyond the inter-American conferences and gain approval of the world community. See Chapter 7 for works that refer to the role of the League of Nations in attempts to settle the Chaco War.

Latin American participation in the United Nations contrasted sharply with that of the League of Nations. They were instrumental in shaping the organization at the end of World War II and have remained active participants ever since, playing important leadership roles in certain areas of activity. The UN itself has been active in the region in several of its functional roles.

John A. Houston, *Latin America in the United Nations* (1956), is a statistical and interpretive analysis of Latin American voting in the UN, with special reference to the General Assembly, on issues relating to peace and security, dependent peoples, standards of living, and human rights. Houston gives extended attention to the matter of bloc voting and the relationship between Latin American voting and U.S. preferences. Gastón de Prat Guy, *Política internacional del grupo latinoamericano* (1967), is a brief treatment of the important element of Latin American diplomacy in the UN of holding regular informal meetings in order to coordinate, so far as possible, a common stance on the issues. Antonio Gómez Robledo, *Las Naciones Unidas y el Sistema Interamericano: conflictos jurisdiccionales* (1974), is a brief but solid examination of the competing jurisdictions and informal interorganizational agreements made about them by a prolific Mexican international relations scholar.

Manuel Pastor Jr., *The International Monetary Fund and Latin America: Economic Stabilization and Class Conflict* (1987), agrees with the critics of the IMF who oppose the organization's economic liberalization and austerity requirements for standby agreements with Latin American governments. He sees IMF actions bringing "hardship to the majority of people in the region," as well as "class biases and erroneous arguments underpinning the IMF positions." Pastor's conclusions are based on analysis of IMF programs in eighteen of the Latin American countries between 1965 and 1981 (that is, during the pre-crisis years).

The Third World Association that came to be called the New International Economic Order (NIEO) has been centered in the United Nations Conference on Trade and Development (UNCTAD). Raúl Prebisch of Argentina, the founder of structural dependency theory, organized the conference. The first UNCTAD meeting was held in 1961 and almost all

Latin American states became members. Three works by noted scholars deal generally with the Latin American role in NIEO: Jorge Lozoya and Jaime Estévez, eds., *Latin America and the New International Economic Order* (1980); Eduardo Hill and Luciano Tomassini, eds., *América Latina y el nuevo orden economico internacional* (1979); and Ricardo Ffrench-Davis and Ernesto Tironi, eds., *Latin America and the New International Economic Order* (1982), which employs technical economic analysis. Luis Jorge Garay Salamanca, *América Latina ante el reordenamiento económico internacional* (1994), analyzes the subject in terms of the process of configuring NIEO, the resurgence of regionalism, and the relationship to Latin American economic integration, with a case study of Colombia's foreign commercial policy. Barry B. Levine, ed., *El desafío neoliberal: el fin del tercermundismo en América Latina* (1992), analyzes the challenges to Third World thinking of the end of the cold war and the rise of neoliberalism. He focuses on country studies—of Chile, Mexico, Colombia, Brazil, Venezuela, Peru, and in the Caribbean area.

The Law of the Sea negotiations progressed under United Nations leadership, beginning in 1958 with the First United Nations Conference on the Law of the Sea at Geneva called by the UN General Assembly. Most Latin American states were highly interested in the outcome, actively participated in the deliberations, and signed the Law of the Sea Convention in 1982 (it went into effect in 1994). Edmundo Vargas Carreño, *América Latina y los problemas contemporáneos del derecho del mar* (1973) is a succinct analysis by a Chilean jurist and scholar of the contemporary issues being debated in the law of the sea negotiations. A valuable appendix includes, among other things, a summary of each Latin American state's claims and positions regarding various conference resolutions.

——————— ■ ———————

CHAPTER 7

Warfare, Intervention, and Diplomacy for Peace

Warfare, its approximations, and the search for peace are the general themes addressed in this chapter. They incorporate political, ideological, diplomatic, and other elements. The presentation is organized by categories of warfare, which often have overlapping elements. Citations on individual Latin American states are included. The sequence of presentation is as follows: (1) the nineteenth-century movements for independence by Spanish Americans from Spain and Brazilians from Portugal; (2) inter–Latin American conflicts—boundary and territorial disputes and interstate warfare, in which extraregional states were sometimes involved; (3) external state interventions—European and U.S. intrusions in Mexico, European actions in South America, and U.S. imperialist and sphere of influence involvement in the circum-Caribbean; (4) world events—the Spanish-American War, the two world wars, the Cuban missile crisis, Cuba in Africa, and Argentine-British conflict in the South Atlantic; (5) Latin American internal war—social revolutions and insurgency; and (6) the Central American conflict after 1979 and the peace process.[1]

LATIN AMERICAN REVOLUTIONS
FOR INDEPENDENCE

During the first quarter of the nineteenth century, after three centuries of colonial rule, the vast Spanish Empire in the Americas was reduced to the colony of Cuba. At the same time, Brazilians ejected Portugal as their colonial master. Cuba later separated from Spain in 1898 as the immediate result of the Spanish-American War. The Caribbean holdings of other European states did not undertake such movements.

General Treatments

R. A. Humphreys and John Lynch, eds., *The Origins of the Latin American Revolutions, 1808–1826* (1965), compiled by two distinguished British historians, was later revised and updated by Lynch and retitled *Latin American Revolutions, 1808–1826: Old and New World Origins* (1994). In both instances they include treatments of the roles of Britain, France, and the United States in the revolutions, as well as the development of Latin American nationalism. The two editions are different enough to be considered separate volumes. Richard Graham, *Independence in Latin America: A Comparative Approach* (2 eds., 1972, 1994), is a brief, stimulating, and instructive history of the diverse Latin American experiences during the wars for independence. Graham focuses on the causative factors that shaped events, and treats individual countries as cases for comparative analysis. Jay Kinsbruner, *Independence in Spanish America: Civil Wars, Revolutions, and Underdevelopment* (3 eds., 1973–2000), is a concise but thorough and well-organized interpretive survey of Spanish-American independence, with information on the colonial background and postindependence problems. Kinsbruner argues that the several movements for independence demonstrated a significant variety of phenomena, including attempts at fundamental social revolutions as well as political revolutions in favor of the Spanish-American governing elites. Leslie Bethell, ed., *The Independence of Latin America* (1987), includes chapters covering a full range of description and interpretation. They address the origins of the independence movement from Spain in Mexico, Central America, and Spanish South America, and Brazilian independence from Portugal. Political scientist Jorge I. Domínguez, *Insurrection or Loyalty: The Breakdown of the Spanish American Empire* (1980), engages in a provocative historical analysis from a "social science perspective" of modernization. He investigates comparatively the Mexican, Venezuelan, and Chilean insurrections against Spain and the contrasting loyalty in Cuba. Timothy E. Anna, *Spain and the Loss of America* (1983), is a revisionist interpretation of the independence movements in Mexico, Peru, and elsewhere. The celebrated Spanish intellectual, Salvador de Madariaga, *The Fall of the Spanish-American Empire* (1947), gives his provocative interpretation. It is a companion volume to *The Rise of the Spanish American Empire* (see Chapter 2). Jaime E. Rodriguez O., *The Independence of Spanish America* (1998), provides a good survey.

Scholarly investigations focus on the roles of outside great powers. John Rydjord, *Foreign Interest in the Independence of New Spain: An Introduction to the Wars for Independence* (1935), is a survey of the British, French, and U.S. presence in the revolutionary setting. The author emphasizes the importance of the ideological examples of the American and French Revolutions, and British and U.S. interests in helping to end the Spanish-American empire. William W. Kaufmann, *British Policy and the Independence of Latin America, 1804–1828* (1951), is a thorough survey of British interests and diplomacy. William Spence Robertson, *France and Latin American Independence* (1939), the Albert Shaw Lecture on Diplomatic History in 1939 at Johns Hopkins University, is a highly detailed narrative. Charles Caroll Griffin, *The United States and the Disruption of the Spanish American Empire: A Study on the Relations of the United States with Spain and the Rebel Spanish Colonies* (1937), emphasizes U.S. diplomatic and economic relations with Spain and the Spanish-American revolutionaries, as well as the tension between its political interests and republican and free-trade values. Arthur P. Whitaker, *The United States and the Independence of Latin America, 1800–1830* (1941), is a classic examination focusing on U.S. national interests. He pays significant attention to the roles of individuals and intersocietal connections. Boleslav Levin, *Los movimientos de emancipación en Hispanoamerica y independencia de los Estados Unidos* (1952), is a relatively brief treatment that concludes Spain was more apprehensive of possible U.S. territorial expansion than its revolutionary and republican example for Spanish Americans. Frederic L. Paxson, *The Independence of the South American Republics: A Study in Recognition and Foreign Policy* (1903), is a factually detailed analysis of the complex mixture of international politics and the U.S. doctrine of recognition with respect to the newly independent-by-revolution South American states. Russell H. Bartley, *Imperial Russia and the Struggle for Latin American Independence, 1808–1828* (1978), includes a survey of efforts by Russian researchers. Bartley's is one of the few works that sheds light on Russian interests and actions during the Latin American movements for independence—which he sees as a function of its own imperial expansion. Dealing with nonstate mercenaries, Alfred Hasbrouk, *Foreign Legionaries in the Liberation of Spanish South America* (1969), examines the roles of foreign private armies in the Spanish-American revolutions. He addresses the smuggling in arms and military supplies. Hasbrouk sees this foreign presence as an important element in the revolutionary success.

Bernard Moses (1846–1930), *The Intellectual Background of the Revolution in South America, 1810–1824* (1926), is a history of the emancipatory ideas held by the leaders for independence. Peruvian scholar and diplomat Víctor Andrés Belaunde, *Bolívar and the Political Thought of the Spanish American Revolution* (1938), is among the best treatments of Bolivarian thought. Belaunde synthesizes the early-nineteenth-century Spanish-American political and constitutional philosophy that influenced the Liberator and provided the intellectual context of the revolution.

Three of the general treatments cited above include Brazil's movement for independence from Portugal in their discussions—Leslie Bethel, ed., *The Independence of Latin America*; Richard Graham, *Independence in Latin America: A Comparative Approach*; and Arthur P. Whitaker, *The United States and the Independence of Latin America, 1800–1830*. Whitaker addresses Brazilian representations in Lisbon, military events, the Cisplatine question, and the role of the heir to the Portuguese throne and the declaration of independence by him. See also Manuel de Oliveira Lima, *O movimento da independencia, 1821–1822* (1922), by a prominent Brazilian historian. He focuses narrowly and in detail on the critical two-year period of Brazilian's movement for independence. It begins with the return of Portugal's king to Lisbon in 1820 and then considers Portuguese domestic matters and overseas policies. A.J.R. Russell-Wood, ed., *From Colony to Nation: Essays on the Independence of Brazil* (1978), provides excellent analyses of numerous topics.

Spanish-American Country Studies

Harris Gaylord Warren, *The Sword Was Their Passport: A History of American Filibustering in the Mexican Revolution* (1943), is a solid treatment of irregular military expeditions during the Mexican war for independence from Spain, organized between 1812 and 1821 primarily in the United States but also in England.

On Chile, Alejandro Alvarez, *La diplomacia de Chile durante la emancipación* (1916), is a brilliant discursive treatment of the country's movement for independence as a manifestation of a common American hemispheric doctrine of emancipation and its particular development by Spanish Americans. Alvarez also considers the juridical aspects of Chile's war for independence. Ricardo Montaner y Bello, *Historia diplomática de la independencia de Chile* (1941), is a classic work by a prominent Chilean historian. He highlights Chile's diplomacy with European states as it sought recognition for the new Chilean state. Agustín Bianchi Barros, *Bosquejo historico de las relaciones chileno-norteamericanas durante la independencia* (1946), is another salient work by a noted Chilean historian, dealing with Chile's negotiations with the United States. British scholar Simon Collier, *Ideas and Politics of Chilean Independence, 1808–1833* (1967), examines political concepts based on French, British, and U.S. philosophical sources that were behind the Chilean movement for independence and during the formative years of the new nation-state. It focuses primarily on the relationship of ideas to political action and less so to the military struggle. Donald E. Worcester, *Sea Power and Chilean Independence* (1962), analyzes a significant element of that struggle.

Studies of Paraguay have emphasized the country's determination to separate from both Spain and Argentina. Solid treatments are offered by Julio César Chaves, *Historia de las relaciones entre Buenos Aires y el Paraguay, 1810–1813* (2d ed., 1959), and his briefer and more narrowly focused study, *La revolución paraguaya de la independencia* (1961); and by Richard Alan White, *Paraguay's Autonomous Revolution, 1810–1840* (1978). On Argentina, see Armando Alonso Pineiro, *La trama de los 5000 dias: origines de las relaciones argentino-americanas* (1986), which narrates Argentina's diplomatic contacts with the United States during its movement for independence from Spain. Peru is dealt with by Heraclio Bonilla and others, *La independencia en el Perú* (1972). John Street, *Artigas and the Emancipation of Uruguay* (1959), focuses on the national caudillo-hero.

The Case of Cuba

Cuba stands apart as Spain's last colonial and military bastion in the Americas and as the last to gain its independence (in 1898). Surveys are numerous of the long historical period during which the concern with Cuban independence was paramount. James Morton Callahan, *Cuba and International Relations: A Historical Study in American Diplomacy* (1899), is a lengthy diplomatic historical narrative survey, from 1783 to its publication as the Spanish-American War ended. Callahan wrote the following in the preface:

> There are hundreds of books concerning Cuba but none treats the subject from the standpoint of the part it has played in American history and international relations. Recent significant events in the West Indies induced me to undertake this study. The nature of the subject has led to an extensive consideration of the U.S. policy of expansion.

Willis Fletcher Johnson, *The History of Cuba* (5 vols., 1920), is a massive, highly detailed, broadly thematic work. The time frame is from European discovery forward, with considerable attention to the international relations of the nineteenth century and the separation of Cuba from Spain in 1898. Eminent Cuban historian Emilio Roig de Leuchsenring, *Cuba y los Estados Unidos, 1805–1898* (1949), presents an excellent diplomatic history of nineteenth-century relations, accenting the Cuban struggle for autonomy. Philip S. Foner, *A History of Cuba and Its Relations with the United States* (2 vols., 1962), is an anti-imperialist analysis by a prolific U.S. Marxist writer who carefully researched the primary sources. The first volume is devoted to the years 1492–1845, which includes the emergence of U.S. interest beginning in about 1800 and the independence movements of 1820–1830. The second volume deals with the period from 1845 to 1895. Major topics addressed are the unsuccessful U.S. efforts to annex Cuba, filibustering movements from the United States in the 1850s (including southern slaveholders seeking to expand slavery), the revolutionary movement of 1868, and the Second War for Independence up to 1895. Ramiro Guerra y Sánchez, *La guerra de los diez años, 1868–1878* (2 vols., 2 eds., 1950, 1952), is an

outstanding history of the Ten Year's War—the first major Cuban struggle for independence from Spain. It is a multifaceted study of the social
and economic elements as well as the political maneuverings and military operations. Louis A. Pérez Jr., *Cuba Between Empires, 1878–1902*
(1983), by a distinguished U.S. historian of his native Cuba, is an excellent analysis of Cuba from the First War for Independence to the establishment of the Cuban republic. José Ignacio Rodríguez, *Estudio historico
sobre el origin, desenvolvimiento y manisfestaciones practicas de la idea de la
anexión de la Isla de Cuba a los Estados Unidos* (1900), is a lengthy analytical inquiry into the matter of Cubans themselves (especially slaveown-
ers) favoring annexation to the United States. Philip S. Foner edited two
volumes of the works of José Martí, the great Cuban patriot and revolutionary theorist: *Inside the Monster: Writings on the United States and
American Imperialism* (1975) and *Our America: Writings on Latin America and the Struggle for Cuban Independence* (1977). John M. Kirk, *José
Martí: Mentor of the Cuban Nation* (1983), is a concise review of the
massive body of Martí's work and reappraisal of his thought. Kirk sees
Martí as a coherent revolutionary theorist who envisioned Cuban independence in social, economic, and moral terms. See also the section below on the Spanish-American War.

The Case of Haiti

The Haitian revolution for independence of 1804 is a unique situation. It
was the first successful revolution in Latin America, the first African slave
revolt that established a sovereign state, and the only former French
colony in the Americas to gain independence. Beaurbrun Ardouin, *Etudes
sur l'histoire d'Haiti* (1924–1930), is a comprehensive investigation.
C.L.R. James, *The Black Jacobeans* (2 eds., 1938, 1963), is a classic and
provocative treatment. Etienne D. Charlier, *Aperçu sur la formation historique de la nation haitienne* (1954), is a thorough analysis of the reasons
why Haitians revolted against French rule—it was not a simple matter.
Thomas O. Ott, *The Haitian Revolution, 1789–1801* (1973), looks at the
revolution as a long socio-economic convulsion. Ott relates ideas to
events but concludes that more important were two men, the revolutionary hero Touissaint Louverture and his successor, Jean Jacques Dessalines.

Carolyn E. Fick, *The Making of Haiti: The Saint Domingue Revolution from Below* (1990), is a recent and well-researched social history.

INTER–LATIN AMERICAN CONFLICTS

General Works

Michael A. Morris and Victor Millán, eds., *Controlling Latin American Conflicts: Ten Approaches* (1983), brings together nine U.S. and Latin American contributors who offer ten strategies for the containment and resolution of intraregional conflict. Although their concern was with the sharp increase in violence and the moribund state of inter-American collective security agreements, the studies remain of interest for their thoughtful concepts and useful historical data. Following an introductory typology of conflict in the region, the essays deal with the strengths and weaknesses of peaceful settlement procedures, confidence-building measures, Latin American initiated peace processes, and identifying shared values and interests among disputants. An interesting kind of political economy is advanced in three books edited by José A. Silva-Michelena, which have overlapping content and make up an impressive multinational and multidisciplinary collection: *Paz, seguridad y desarrollo en América Latina* (1987), *Los factores de la paz* (1987), and *Latin America: Peace, Democratization, and Economic Crisis* (1988). The contributors apply objective systematic methods to investigations of processes of social change, with the normative purpose of discovering possibilities for more humane societies. They investigate the impact of world economic crisis on peace and security, pointing out the underlying politico-economic realities that characterize regional conflicts that must be taken into account when constructing a system for peace and security.

Boundary and Territorial Disputes

Latin American boundary and territorial disputes, sometimes related to interstate competition for subregional influence, have occurred between all of the regional states with a common land frontier. Only the Caribbean island states have escaped such conflict, except for the Dominican Republic and Haiti who share the island of Hispaniola. Two volumes by Gordon Ireland—*Boundaries, Possessions, and Conflicts in South America* (1938) and *Boundaries, Possessions, and Conflicts in Central and North America, and the Caribbean* (1941)—contain a great deal of geographic, historical, and legal information and continue to be useful, exhaustive references to conflicts from the early nineteenth century into the 1930s.

With reference to the Gulf of Venezuela dispute between Colombia and Venezuela on the northern South American coast, Colombian analyst Daniel Valois Arce, *Reseña historica sobre los limites de Colombia y Venezuela* (1970), provides a historical survey of the negotiations and settlements entered into by the two states. He carefully avoids prescribing solutions. Alfredo Vázquez Carrizosa, *Las relaciones de Colombia y Venezuela: la historia atormentada de dos naciones* (1983), also makes the Colombian case in a thoughtful manner. He urges peaceful settlement through international third-party procedures.

Venezuela also had a territorial dispute with Great Britain over British Guiana, later to include independent Guyana. An early legal study by Georges Pariset, *Historique sommaire du conflit anglo-vénézuélien en Guyane; des origines au traité d'arbitrage, 1493–1897* (1898), analyzes the utility of the papal award of 1493 and of the Monroe Doctrine as bases for settlement, with skeptical conclusions in both instances. Simón Alberto Consalvi, *Grover Cleveland y la controversia Venezuela–Gran Bretaña* (1992), deals with the U.S. third-party settlement efforts. Jacqueline Anne Braveboy-Wagner, *The Venezuelan-Guyana Border Dispute: Britain's Colonial Legacy in Latin America* (1984), is a solid analysis of Venezuela's historical claim to some two-thirds of Guyana's territory and the diplomatic and legal elements of the dispute. She emphasizes the interests of the actors involved, the roles of outsiders, and the possibilities for alternative solutions.

Aspects of the tragic Haitian–Dominican Republic relations, in which the border and territorial matters loom large, is analyzed by two distinguished scholars, one from each country. Jean Price-Mars, *La République d'Haití et la République Dominicaine* (1953), a noted Haitian intellectual, anthropologist, sociologist, and public official, traces the complex history of the divisive relations in terms of historical, geographic, ethnological, and other factors. With reference to a critical historical period, Frank Moya Pons, *La dominación haitiana, 1822–1844* (1978), a leading Dominican historian, provides an excellent (and the first) scholarly study of Haiti's invasion and occupation of Spanish Santo Domingo in 1822 and its forced political unification of the island until 1844.

Great Britain also had a dispute with Guatemala over British Guiana, later to involve independent Belize. Canadian lawyer Louis M. Bloomfield, *The British Honduras-Guatemala Dispute* (1953), presents a full and impartial legal-historical review. Guatemalan international lawyer and diplomat Carlos García Bauer, *La controversia sobre el territorio de Belice y el procedimiento ex-aequeo* (1958), is a scholarly analysis with a view to determining how the controversy might be equitably and juridically settled through third-party peaceful settlement procedures. U.S. attorney William J. Bianchi, *Belize: The Controversy Between Guatemala and Great Britain over the Territory of British Honduras in Central America* (1959), concisely analyzes the matter and concludes that "Guatemala has a legally desperate case."

South American geopolitical literature, oriented toward subregional interstate politics, is closely related to boundary and territorial matters. See in particular Jack Child, *Geopolitics and Conflict in South America: Quarrels Among Neighbors* (1985), an empirical analysis of conflict among South American states and the geopolitical (geography married to power politics in terms of organic state theory) bases for them. See also the general discussion on geopolitics in Chapter 3.

The border and territorial problems among states in the Southern Cone have been a major source of writing. Argentina has been at the center of many of the disputes. Argentine historian César Díaz Cisneros, *Límites de la República Argentina: fundamentos histórico-juridicos* (1944), explores the formation of Argentina's territory and frontiers and the state of frontier questions and their resolution with Chile, Bolivia, Paraguay, Brazil, and Uruguay. He also discusses Argentine sovereignty in the territorial sea, Malvinas Islands, Antarctic regions, and airspace. Domingo Sabaté Lichtschein, *Problemas argentinos de soberanía territorial* (3 eds., 1976–1985), is a tightly argued legal analysis of Argentina's boundary problems, the Beagle Channel dispute with Chile, and Argentina's claims in Antarctica and the South Atlantic. Argentine historian Miguel Angel

Scenna, *Argentina-Brazil: cuatro siglos de rivalidad* (1975), in a lengthy, fact-filled, chronological narrative summarizes the long territorial and power rivalry between the two states, from the Treaty of Tordesillas until the death of Argentine president Juan Perón. Ricardo R. Caillet-Bois, *Cuestiones internacionales (1852–1966)* (1970), is a brief but informative history of Argentina's boundary and related international disputes. He deals mostly with Chilean relations but also with the "carrot and stick" diplomacy with Bolivia, Paraguay, and Uruguay. Luis Antonio Morzone, *Soberania territorial argentino* (2 eds., 1978, 1982), is a geopolitical treatment by an Argentine scholar. He addresses problems related to the Beagle Channel, Antarctica, the continental shelf, airspace, and river boundaries with Paraguay. Armando Amuchástegui Astrada, *Argentina-Chile: controversia y mediación* (1980), is an exhaustive legal historical analysis, beginning with the Spanish colonial period and favoring the Chilean position. Carlos M. Goñi Garrido, *Crónica del conflicto chileno-argentino* (1984), provides historical background on the Beagle Channel conflict; it was published prior to the papal settlement. Chilean writer Oscar Espinosa Moraga, *El precio de la paz chileno-argentina, 1810–1869* (3 vols., 1969), is a treatment of the colonial background and, in considerable descriptive detail, the nineteenth century. The author deals with diplomacy and agreements regarding conflicts over Patagonia, the expansion of Argentina to the Pacific, and the Puna de Atacama dispute. Gustavo Ferrari, *Conflicto y paz con Chile, 1898–1903* (1968), is a thorough and sophisticated diplomatic history by a leading Argentine historian dealing with events surrounding a boundary conflict that seriously threatened all-out war but was avoided for a number of reasons. José Guillermo Guerra, *La soberania de Chile en las islas al sud del Canal Beagle* (1917), is a presentation of the Chilean case. Guerra, a professor of international law at the National University of Chile, discusses geographic, juridical, and other questions with regard to the dispute. Sergio Villalobos R., *El Beagle, historia de una controversia* (1979), by a noted Chilean historian, is a brief and well-documented historical defense of Chilean claims.

Julio A. Barberis, *Régimen juridico del Río de la Plata* (1970), is a juridical study of the claims of Argentina and Uruguay of their riparian rights. Oscar Espinosa Moraga, *Bolivia y el mar, 1810–1864* (1965), articulates the Chilean author's view that Argentina gave inordinate support to Bolivia in the latter's quest to regain an outlet to the Pacific Ocean. Robert Talbot, *A History of Chilean Boundaries* (1974), noting that boundary disputes have constituted a great deal of Chilean foreign policy attention, describes and interprets those disputes and how they have been settled— by direct diplomacy, third-party peaceful settlement procedures, and warfare. The history by Efraim Cardozo, *Los derechos del Paraguay sobre los saltos del Guairá* (1965), deals with the border controversy between Paraguay and Brazil for control of the Guairá Falls, of great hydroelectric potential. Cardozo claims that the falls had always belonged to Paraguay and were illegally taken by Brazil through its redefinition of the boundary with Paraguay following the War of the Triple Alliance. On the hopeful and cooperative side, see Luis Moreno Guerra, *Integración fronteriza: el ejemplo del Ecuador y Colombia* (1996); and Raúl Barrios Morón, ed., *Bolivia, Chile y Perú: una opción cooperativa* (1997).

The literature on the Mexico–United States "borderlands" is included in the section below on Mexico and international violence.

Interstate Warfare

Bryce Wood, *The United States and Latin American Wars, 1932–1942* (1966), with the meticulous research and elegant presentation for which the author was noted, deals in detail with three conflicts. They are the horrendous Chaco War between Bolivia and Paraguay and the subsequent byzantine multilateral third-party peace process; the Leticia dispute between Colombia and Peru; and the Marañon conflict between Ecuador and Peru in their Amazonian zones.

Cisplatine War (1825–1828).   The postindependence war between Argentina and Brazil for control of Uruguay (which had been Portuguese Brazil's Cisplatine province) in fact resulted in Uruguay's independence. Uruguayan historian Carlos Carbajal, *La penetración luso-brasileña en el Uruguay: ensayo histórico-sociológico* (1948), examines the colonial elements that led to the Argentine-Brazilian rivalry. Juan Beverina, *La guerra contra el imperio del Brasil: contribución al estudio de sus antecedentes y de las operaciones hasta Ituzaingo* (1927), written by a retired Argentine army colonel, is a well-researched and detailed description of the military operations. David Carneiro, *Historia da Guerra Cisplatina* (1946), is also a military history from a Brazilian point of view that rejects Argentine claims of victory, inasmuch as Uruguay gained its independence.

Paraguayan War/War of the Triple Alliance (1865–1870).   The war ensued because of the expansionist ambitions of the Paraguayan dictator and resistance to them by the alliance of a faction in Uruguay and Argentina and Brazil. Juan Beverina, *La guerra del Paraguay* (7 vols., 1921–1933), is a highly detailed operational military history by a retired Argentine army officer and writer on military affairs. Pelham H. Box, *The Origins of the Paraguayan War* (1930), reviews the boundary questions of Paraguay with Argentina and Brazil; the complex relations among groups and personalities in Argentina, Brazil, and Uruguay with each other; the ambitions of Francisco Solano López of Paraguay; and the catastrophic war itself. Ramón J. Cárcano, *Guerra del Paraguay* (2 vols., 1939–1942), is an engrossing popular history that reveals British and French interests in the area. Santiago Dallegri, *El Paraguay y la guerra de la Triple Alianza* (1964), is well written in a popular vein. In addition to defending the Paraguayan side of the story, Dallegri introduces literary depictions in an interesting manner. Charles J. Kolinski, *Independence or Death! The Story of the Paraguayan War* (1965), rejects academic paraphernalia but objectively and clearly presents the complex events.

War of the Pacific (1879–1883).   The war had complex origins in interstate competition over nitrate resources in the Atacama Desert fueled by nationalist resentments. The result was a serious military struggle between Chile and the alliance of Peru and Bolivia and territorial losses by both of the allied states to victorious Chile. Gonzalo Bulnes, *La Guerra del Pacifico* (3 vols., 1912–1919), is a massive, detailed, heavily documented history by a prominent Chilean historian. It was long the standard work on the war and the Chilean occupation of Peru. Bulnes also provided a brief summary chronicle of events, with minimal interpretation, in *Chile and Peru: The Causes of the War of 1879* (1920). William F. Sater, *Chile and the War of the Pacific* (1986), is a full treatment of the warfare itself and the "politics of war"; the roles of military men, journalists, and private foreign interests; "life on the home front"; the search for peace; and the war's economic consequences. Roberto Quere-jazu Calvo, *La Guerra del Pacífico* (1983), by a Bolivian scholar, helps fill the gap in the literature on Bolivia's role. Nelson Manrique, *Campesinado y nación: las guerrillas indíginas en la guerra con Chile* (1981), is a detailed and tightly analyzed study of the role of Peruvian peasant guerrilla forces who took advantage of the warfare to prosecute grievances against their landowner masters—who in turn collaborated with invading Chilean forces to protect their property. Robert N. Burr, *The Stillborn Panama Congress: Power, Politics and Chilean-Colombian Relations During the War of the Pacific* (1962), is a superbly researched analytical study that focuses on the evolving interstate balance of power system among Chile, Colombia, Peru, and Venezuela and its relationship to the War of the Pacific.

Former Chilean minister of foreign relations Luis Barros Borgoño, *The Problem of the Pacific and the New Policies of Bolivia* (1924), writes on the Tacna-Arica question consequent to Chile's military victory. The book is a detailed legal history from 1873 to the early 1920s in the context of international law and Bolivia's appeal to the League of Nations. Appended are two "juridical reports" by John W. Davis, president of the American Bar Association and former U.S. ambassador to Great Britain, on the requests submitted by Peru and Bolivia to the League; they are favorable to Chile. Herbert Millington, *American Diplomacy and the War of the Pacific* (1948), says that despite the "meddling and muddling" of the U.S. "clumsy involvement in the war," the diplomatic record also "had its constructive side." Millington discusses, with much more description than analysis, the unofficial mediation, the Arica conference, and economic diplomacy. William Jefferson Dennis, *Tacna and Arica: An Account of the Chile-Peru Boundary Dispute and the Arbitration by the United States* (1931), is a detailed history focusing on the evolution of the dispute from the War of the Pacific and the Ancón Treaty settlement (with mediation by Presidents Harding and Coolidge). It deals with the failed 1925–1926 plebiscite and the final settlement by direct negotiations. Joe F. Wilson, *The United States, Chile and Peru in the Tacna and Arica Plebiscite* (1979), also provides considerable detail in a well-documented history of the Tacna-Arica question. Wilson highlights "the only plebiscite attempted in the Western Hemisphere."

The Chaco War and the Peace Process (1932–1939).   The especially violent and bloody war between Bolivia and Paraguay from 1932 to 1935 was the culmination of a century of disputes over undetermined state frontiers. After a cease-fire was agreed to in 1935, a peace process dragged on until 1939. Various groups of outside states, often in competition with each other, sought to facilitate a settlement—with their own interests very much in mind. Three works deal with the conduct of the war itself from 1932 to 1935. They pay close attention to military affairs but take adequate account of the diplomatic efforts. David H. Zook, *The Conduct of the Chaco War* (1960), devotes the least space to diplomacy; Roberto Querejazu Calvo, *Masamaclay: historia política, diplomática y militar de la guerra del Chaco* (2 eds., 1965, 1975), is the most comprehensive work, with increased attention to diplomatic affairs in the second edition; and Bruce W. Farcau, *The Chaco War: Bolivia and Paraguay, 1932–1935* (1996). Carlos José Fernández, *La guerra del Chaco* (4 vols., 1955–1967), is an exceptionally complete and innovative documentary history. Leslie B. Rout, *Politics of the Chaco Peace Conference, 1935–39* (1970), is a significant scholarly study of the various international groups that weighed in during the prolonged effort to come to a final settlement following the cease-fire of 1935—the League of Nations, the Inter-American System, the regional ABCP Group (neighbors Argentina, Brazil, Chile, and Peru), and the Washington Group of Neutrals. William R. Garner, *The Chaco Dispute: A Study of Prestige Diplomacy* (1966), is a relatively brief study within a conceptual analytic framework and relying entirely on secondary sources. Garner's assertion that the tension between Argentina and the United States during the long third-party Buenos Aires conference was essentially a matter of "prestige diplomacy" has merit, but it does not stand alone as a satisfactory explanation.

Ecuador-Peru Conflict.   The two states had a serious long-standing territorial dispute centering on the Marañon River, which in 1941–1942 verged on warfare. The Inter-American System, led by the United States (which had just entered World War II), forced a settlement of the dispute. But the matter remained unresolved and violence periodically ensued, the latest serious incident occurring in 1995. In each instance the "guarantor states" named in the 1942 agreement (the United States, Argentina,

Brazil, and Chile) undertook their roles and at least temporarily relieved the international tensions. Jorge Pérez Concha, *Ensayo histórico-crítico de las relaciones diplomáticas del Ecuador con los estados limítrofes* (2 vols., 2 eds., 1961, 1964), is an extensively researched and comprehensive study that devotes the entire second volume to the Rio Protocol of 1942 and the events that followed. Rafael Euclides Silva, *Derecho territorial ecuatoriano* (1962), is a comprehensive statement of Ecuador's case, with extensive useful historical information and a full bibliography. David H. Zook, *Zarumilla-Marañón: The Ecuador-Peru Dispute* (1964), became the primary reference on the dispute as the situation stood at the time of publication. Zook dealt well with the intricate inter-American diplomacy periodically called upon to deal with the problems. Bryce Wood, *Aggression and History: The Case of Ecuador and Peru* (1978), discusses the military operations and diplomacy of the 1941 war. He pursues three principal themes: the nature of aggression, the writing of nationalistic history, and the nature of interstate power politics. The volume is an outgrowth of Part 2 of Wood's *The United States and Latin American Wars, 1932–1942* (see above). Woods called on additional archival sources in the United States and the United Kingdom and secondary sources (including children's textbooks, polemical literature, and government publications), and took a different thematic approach. William L. Krieg, *Ecuadorian-Peruvian Rivalry in the Upper Amazon* (2 eds., 1979, 1986), is a comprehensive and reliable study done for the U.S. Department of State. Gustavo Pons Muzzo, *Estudio historico sobre el Protocolo de Río de Janeiro: el Ecuador, país amazónica* (1994), is a descriptive documentary history of the Rio Protocol, from its signing in 1942 through the continuing conflict to the date of publication. Gabriel Marcella and Richard Downes, eds., *Security Cooperation in the Western Hemisphere: Resolving the Ecuador-Peru Conflict* (1998), brings together eleven U.S. and South American experts after the 1995 events for a thorough examination of the historical, political, diplomatic, military, and international elements in the diplomacy for peace.

Caribbean Conflict.   With reference to the widespread post–World War II transnational Caribbean conflict, two concise studies by Charles D. Ameringer are essential—*The Democratic Left in Exile: The Anti-Dictatorial*

Struggle in the Caribbean, 1945–1959 (1974), and *The Caribbean Legion: Patriots, Politicians, Soldiers of Fortune, 1946–1950* (1996). The first reports on the politics of the exiles, who were loosely grouped together as the "Democratic Left." The focus is on their activities and other events in Cuba, Costa Rica, the Dominican Republic, Guatemala, Honduras, Nicaragua, Puerto Rico, and Venezuela. Ameringer interviewed many of the prominent personages involved. The second volume, also carefully researched and utilizing interviews, continues the earlier analysis with a careful examination of the Caribbean Legion that worked to overthrow Caribbean dictators. Ameringer pictures the legion as an undefined and passing phenomenon, a complex mixture of idealists, adventurers, and mercenaries with various personal, political, and ideological motivations.

The war between El Salvador and Honduras in 1961 is well described and analyzed by Thomas P. Anderson, *The War of the Dispossessed: Honduras and El Salvador, 1969* (1981). Although the fighting lasted only four days, it was the culmination of many years of binational hostility and resulted in 2,000 deaths and 100,000 refugees. It badly disrupted Central American integration efforts. Anderson emphasizes as causal factors overpopulation, poverty, dependent economics, and the governments' desires to conceal internal problems.

EXTERNAL INTERVENTIONS

Mexico and International Conflict

The Texas Question and War with the United States. Mexican and U.S. researchers have paid a great deal of attention to the Texas revolution and the Mexican–United States war. Two general works are of interest. Alberto Maria Carreño, *México y los Estados Unidos de América* (1922), is a detailed history by a prolific Mexican historian of U.S. territorial expansion at the expense of Mexico. Gaston García Cantú, *Las invasiones norteamericanos en México* (3 eds., 1971–1980), deals with the history of U.S. interventions begining in 1800.

David J. Weber, *The Mexican Frontier, 1821–1846: The American Southwest Under Mexico* (1982), is an excellent treatment of the region under Mexican jurisdiction from its own revolution until the war with the United States. David M. Pletcher, *The Diplomacy of Annexation: Texas, Oregon, and the Mexican War* (1973), is a well-researched, judicious, and comprehensive history of U.S. territorial expansionism from 1815 to 1848 at the expense especially of Mexico and of Great Britain. Pletcher also addresses France's lively role. Gene M. Brack, *Mexico Views Manifest Destiny, 1821–1846: An Essay on the Origins of the Mexican War* (1975), addresses misconceptions about the origins of the war in 1846 following two decades of difficult bilateral relations involving an array of issues. Most important was U.S. expansion toward northern Mexico combined with ethnocentric and racist elements in the United States. Justin Harvey Smith, *The War with Mexico* (2 vols., 1919), is the early definitive, classic work on the subject by a leading U.S. scholar, who engaged in careful and exhaustive research. Smith lays responsibility for the war primarily on President Polk's policy, not on Mexico. Frederick Merk, with Lois Bannister Merk, *The Monroe Doctrine and American Expansionism: 1843–1849* (1966), argues that by the end of the Polk administration the assertion of the Monroe Doctrine based on fears of British influence in the U.S. annexation of Texas and war with Mexico had been subverted—by the doctrine of Manifest Destiny and by southerners seeking to extend slavery. Humberto Escoto Ochoa, *Integración y desintegración de nuestra frontera norte* (1949), is a useful evaluation of the treaties that formally settled the numerous Mexican territorial losses to the United States. Otis A. Singletary, *The Mexican War* (1960), is a multifaceted study of the political and economic as well as military and diplomatic factors in the war. Singletary is especially interested in the motivations and thinking of U.S. officials—whom he sees at best animated by the spirit of Manifest Destiny and at worst by land-grabbing from a weak neighbor. They were careless in their cost-risk-benefit calculations of entry into the war and of winning it, which was also undermined by "hidden warfare" in Washington. Glen W. Price, *Origins of the War with Mexico: The Polk-Stockton Intrigue* (1967), sees the acquisition of California as President Polk's principal objective. Price examines his intrigues with ambitious Commodore Robert F. Stockton. Political rhetoric that the United States had entered the war because Mexico had invaded U.S. territory veiled the desire to increase the number of slave states. K. Jack Bauer, *The Mexican War 1846–1848* (1974), writes the history of what he sees as a clearly "unavoidable war." He focuses on the ill-conceived U.S. application of "graduated force," military operations, and the leading military and civilian personalities on both sides.

For Mexican viewpoints of the war, see Cecil Robinson (translator and editor), *The View from Chapultepec: Mexican Writers on the Mexican-American War* (1989); and Robert W. Johannsen, *To the Halls of Montezuma: The Mexican View in the American Imagination* (1985). Richard Griswold del Castillo, *The Treaty of Guadalupe Hidalgo: A Legacy of Conflict* (1992), is an excellent study of the treaty signed in 1848 ending the war. Paul N. Garber, *The Gadsden Treaty* (1923), is a detailed treatment of the U.S. purchase of border territory in 1853 that gave final shape to the boundary.

French Occupation.   French intervention in and occupation of Mexico from 1861 to 1867 grew out of an allied European intervention ostensibly to collect debts. But when Spain and Britain came to agreements with Mexico and withdrew, the larger French imperial ambitions became evident. French troops occupied the capital and France formed the Empire of Mexico headed by Archduke Maximilian of Austria. For a variety of international and French domestic reasons combined with continuing Mexican military resistance, France withdrew its forces and Maximilian was executed. Percy F. Martin, *Maximilian in Mexico: The Story of the French Intervention, 1861–1867* (1914), is a highly detailed study. Martin presents detailed biographies of the leading personalities and deals with allied ambitions and attitudes and their military actions in Mexico. He addresses, among numerous other things, the problems of finance and continuing military operations, the Mexican Liberal, and the French withdrawal. Some attention is also paid to U.S. reactions. Alfred Jackson Hanna and Kathryn Abbey Hanna, *Napoleon III and Mexico: American Triumph over Monarchy* (1971), is cast in terms of Napoleon III's "grand design for the Americas" to substitute "enlightened monarchies" for weak Spanish American "republics," and to enhance the power and prestige of the Second French Empire. Jack Aubrey Dabbs, *The French Army in Mexico, 1861–1867: A Study in Military Government* (1963), addresses France's military government in Mexico as a case study of problems faced by an army of occupation. In addition to governing a foreign country, the armed forces engaged in continuing combat with the local opposition as it prepared to turn over governmental powers to imperial civilian authorities.

European Actions in South America

Military interventions by European states during the nineteenth century in the Southern Cone have been the subject of numerous histories. Juan Beverina, *Las invasiones inglesas al río de la plata (1806–1807)* (2 vols., 1939), is a massively detailed and heavily documented military history by the then-long-retired Argentine army colonel, experienced at such historical research. John Frank Cady, *Foreign Intervention in the Rio de la Plata, 1838–1850: A Study of French, British and American Policy in Relation to the Dictator Juan Manuel Rosas* (1929), was the leading work on both European and U.S. military actions. Most notable were the Anglo-French blockade of the Río de la Plata, and the U.S. naval attacks on the Malvinas (Falkland) Islands in the South Atlantic. With reference to the former events, prolific Spanish historian Carlos Pereyra, *Rosas y Thiers: la diplomacia europea en el Río de la Plata, 1838–1850* (1919), is a highly detailed narrative history of the events, with close attention to the individuals involved. Two Argentine historians provide largely objective scholarly treatments: Néstor S. Colli, *Rosas y el bloqueo anglo-francés* (2 eds., 1963, 1978); and Mariano José Drago, *El bloque francés de 1838 en el Río de La Plata* (1948). William Columbus Davis, *The Last Conquistadores: The Spanish Intervention in Peru and Chile, 1863–1866* (1950), is a classic study, with analysis of the impact of Spanish domestic factors. Gabriel A. Puentes, *La intervención francesa en el Río de la Plata: federales, unitarios y románticos* (1958), presents a thorough account of the problems between Argentine dictator Juan Manuel Rosas and the French government that led to the Anglo-French blockade. Puentes sees the intervention as a French ploy to deflect European attention from its imperial purposes in Africa.

Miriam Hood, *Gunboat Diplomacy, 1895–1905: Great Power Pressure in Venezuela* (2 eds., 1977, 1983), addresses the Anglo-German blockade to force payment of the Venezuelan government's debts to private bondholders who were citizens of the two great powers. Hood notes that the event was not "any notable departure from the normal and accepted principles of international law," a fact reflected in President Theodore Roosevelt's corollary to the Monroe Doctrine announced at the time.

U.S. Interventions

Caribbean Imperialism. Two important books by Dana G. Munro are essential reading. Munro was a U.S. diplomat dealing with the region during part of the time period he later wrote about as a distinguished historian. In *Intervention and Dollar Diplomacy in the Caribbean, 1900–1921* (1964), and *The United States and the Caribbean Republics, 1921–1933* (1974), Munro challenges the "common view that selfish interests of American business dominated American foreign policy." He argues that the "fundamental purpose of policy was to create political and economic stability . . . so that disorder and failure to meet foreign obligations would not imperil U.S. security." C. Neale Ronning, ed., *Intervention in Latin America* (1970), contains two dozen essays by scholars and political leaders who address elements of U.S. intervention in the Caribbean during the first third of the twentieth century, and U.S. nonintervention policies during the second third. Whitney T. Perkins, *Constraint of Empire: The United States and Caribbean Interventions* (1981), analyzes imperial relations with Cuba, the Dominican Republic, Haiti, and Nicaragua. Perkins expresses the U.S. dilemma: "Possessing dominant power and professing liberal values, the United States had to attempt to reconcile a capacity to control with a commitment to liberate." He sees the process not as one in which the United States simply imposed its will but as a complex mutual adaptation despite power disparities. Lester D. Langley, *The Banana Wars: United States Intervention in the Caribbean, 1898–1934* (1983), addresses U.S. occupation of and interventions in Cuba to the eve of World War I, the wartime interventions in Nicaragua and Mexico, the occupations of the Dominican Republic and Haiti during and after the war, and "the last banana war" in Nicaragua from 1921 to 1933. Langley argues that U.S. imperialism was distinguished from European empires by the strong role of U.S. private capital, the weakness of bureaucratic control, and the military influence in determining the course of the interventions. See also Chapter 5 for citations regarding the Caribbean policies of the United States.

Cuba. Three excellent works by Louis A. Pérez Jr. are essential reading on the subject of U.S. military and other interventions in Cuba during the U.S. imperial period. In *Cuba Between Empires, 1878–1902* (1983), Pérez investigates U.S. influence on Cuban events culminating in the Spanish-American War of 1898 and the subsequent U.S. military occupation. He follows with *Cuba Under the Platt Amendment, 1902–1934* (1986), and notes the following in the introduction:

> Cuba ceded territory for the establishment of a foreign naval station, acquiesced to limitations of national sovereignty, and authorized future U.S. intervention. These were the conditions of independence, forced on Cuba, appended directly into the Constitution of 1901, and negotiated later into the Permanent Treaty of 1903, loosely known as the Platt Amendment.

Pérez had earlier written *Intervention, Revolution, and Politics in Cuba, 1913–1921* (1978), which analyzes changes in U.S. policy centering on interpretations of the Platt Amendment (which he also addresses in the previously cited book). The provision itself allowed military intervention in order to protect "life, property and individual liberty" (the only occurrence was 1906–1909), whereas the new U.S. position emphasized "preventing disorder by intervention of a politico-diplomatic nature."

Luis Machado y Ortega, *La enmienda Platt* (1922), is a closely reasoned international legal study of the bases for the Platt Amendment and its applications. The Cuban author concludes that the amendment permits U.S. intervention only when requested by the Cuban government or an international tribunal when a threat exists to Cuban independence. Emilio Roig de Leuchsenring, *Historia de la enmienda Platt: una interpretación de la realidad cubana* (2 vols., 1935), is by a prolific Cuban writer on such matters. He emphasizes how Cubans centered on the Platt Amendment more than any other element of relations with the United States as the symbol of Cubans' alienation. Philip Green Wright, *The Cuban Situation and Our Treaty Relations* (1931), is a concise and clearly stated study of the Platt amendment that focuses almost entirely on the economic implications, especially in the sugar industry. Leland H. Jenks, a well-known anti-imperialist writer, charges in *Our Cuban Colony: A Study in Sugar* (1928) that U.S. intervention in Cuba served selfish business interests rather than the national interest.

José M. Hernández, *Cuba and the United States: Intervention and Militarism, 1868–1933* (1993), skillfully examines the effects of the first two U.S. interventions in Cuba (1898–1902 and 1906–1909). Hernández argues that the United States may have restrained certain excesses of Cuban government but did not deter them from "using violence as a method for transferring power in Cuba." David Healy, *The United States in Cuba, 1898–1902: Generals, Politicians and the Search for Policy* (1963), is a superb multifactor analysis of the history of U.S. policies during the four years of military occupation following victory in the war with Spain. It is revealing of the compromises made under the opposing annexationist and anti-imperialist pressures in the United States. David Alexander Lockmiller, *Magoon in Cuba: A History of the Second Intervention, 1906–1909* (1938), is a study of the U.S. intervention requested by the Cuban president during an uprising in 1906 and prolonged by economic crisis and labor unrest. The author recognizes the accomplishments of Charles E. Magoon, governor of the provisional government. Allan R. Millett, *The Politics of Intervention: The Military Occupation of Cuba 1906–1909* (1968), pays close attention to the debates among U.S. officials, including in the armed forces, about the efficacy of U.S. efforts to reform Cuban domestic institutions as well as to supervise elections prior to withdrawal.

Nicaragua.   William Kamman, *A Search for Stability: United States Diplomacy Toward Nicaragua, 1925–1933* (1968), is a detailed and revealing study of how various factors influenced U.S. diplomacy. Kamman deals with the events leading to the second U.S. intervention and the subsequent complex and chaotic events during the U.S. military occupation. Roscoe R. Hill, *Fiscal Intervention in Nicaragua* (1933), is authored by a member of the U.S. High Commission that administered important parts of Nicaragua's financial system. Hill writes an authoritative history of the financial and public debt elements of U.S. intervention. Lejeune Cummins, *Quijote on a Burro: Sandino and the Marines, a Study in the Formulation of Foreign Policy* (1958), is a well-documented study emphasizing clashes in the field between insurgents and U.S. Marines and the Nicaraguan National Guard during the U.S. military occupation of Nicaragua (1927–1933). Cummins paints a sympathetic portrait of Augusto César Sandino, seeking to correct the image of him as essentially a bandit. Neill Macauley, *The Sandino Affair* (1967), is a detailed chronicle, based largely on U.S. Marine Corps records, of the U.S. military campaign against guerrilla general Sandino and his forces. Sandino eluded the Marines and the National Guard and became a Caribbeanwide symbol of resistance to U.S. imperialism and intervention. Macauley focuses some attention to diplomatic and political aspects. Thomas J. Dodd, *Managing Democracy in Central America: A Case Study of United States Election Supervision in Nicaragua, 1927–1933* (1992), is a concise and well-researched historical narrative of U.S. attempts to promote democratic institutions in Nicaragua through electoral supervision as a part of its interventionist agenda. Dodd's work calls attention to U.S. intervention as more than exclusively military in nature and intent. In fact, Dodd says, in time U.S. electoral involvement replaced military intervention and financial management as the primary focus—and proved to be an ineffectual endeavor.

Haiti. Brenda Gayle Plummer, *Haiti and the Great Powers, 1902–1915* (1988), deals with international events after the United States joined the ranks of the great powers and how they treated Haiti as an object of their maneuvering. The "lessons" of that experience and the outbreak of the war led to U.S. military intervention and occupation in 1915. Plummer is sympathetic to Haitian sensibilities. Hans Schmidt, *The United States Occupation of Haiti, 1915–1934* (1971), surveys the complicated history of the nineteen-year U.S. military occupation of Haiti and its governance by the U.S. Navy. David Healy, *Gunboat Diplomacy in the Wilson Era: The U.S. Navy in Haiti, 1915–1916* (1976), focuses on the extraordinary role of Rear Admiral William B. Caperton, U.S. commander of the intervention and subsequent governor with broad authority in political decision making. Healy sees the operation as revealing the complex and special nature of Wilsonian Caribbean interventionist practices.

Dominican Republic. Bruce Calder, *The Impact of Intervention: The Dominican Republic During the U.S. Occupation of 1916–1924* (1984), is the best general description and analysis of the U.S. military intervention and occupation from 1916 to 1924. Calder is highly critical of U.S. policy thinking and actions. Stephen M. Fuller and Graham A. Cosmos, *Marines in the Dominican Republic 1916–1924* (1974), are generally objective in this official history and detailed chronicle of the Marines' military operations and administration. The authors view the United States as provoked into intervention and accept the official strategic rationale. Marvin Goldwert, *The Constabulary in the Dominican Republic and Nicaragua: Progeny and Legacy of United States Intervention* (1962), is a classic study that reveals how all recruitment for the constabulary was from the lower classes because the upper classes boycotted the service for nationalist reasons. They remained alienated from the military organization and U.S. policy for many years after. Two contemporary studies remain of value. Carl Kelsey, *The American Intervention in Haiti and the Dominican Republic* (1922), is a solid and objective summary by a professor at the University of Pennsylvania who made this investigation for the American Academy of Political and Social Science. Melvin M. Knight, *The Americans in Santo Domingo* (1928), is an anti-imperialist indictment of deceitful U.S. foreign policy and of private investors for their colonial ambitions reflected in the invasion and occupation of the country.

Cold War Interventions.   William E. Kane, *Civil Strife in Latin America: A Legal History of U.S. Involvement* (1972), is authored by an attorney writing under the auspices of the American Society of International Law. He argues that the myth of Soviet Communist subversion and its threat to U.S. security explains U.S. unilateral intervention in Latin America, which occurred despite the nonintervention provisions in the Charter of the Organization of American States. Kane says that a more thorough understanding of Latin American civil strife would support multilateral cooperation.

Guatemala.   The first cold war intervention took place in Guatemala in 1954. Its significance engendered an immediate and continuing scholarly interest. Ronald M. Schneider, *Communism in Guatemala, 1944–1954* (1958), is a valuable and well-documented work on the reality of Communist actions in Guatemala. Eduardo Galeano, *Guatemala: Occupied Country* (1969), is by an Uruguayan journalist, champion of leftist causes, and an informative, often dogmatic anti-imperialist. José M. Aybar de Soto, *Dependency and Intervention: The Case of Guatemala in 1954* (1978), views the intervention through the lens of dependency theory.

He sees a symbiotic relationship between the U.S. government and multinational corporations that inspired the action. Richard H. Immerman, *The CIA in Guatemala: The Foreign Policy of Intervention* (1982), is an empirically supported argument that the intervention was much more than a CIA covert operation to support the United Fruit Company—it revealed that cold war tensions blinded the United States from understanding Guatemalans. The events, Immerman says, may have subverted Guatemala's last hope for modernization. Piero Gleijeses, *Shattered Hope: The Guatemalan Revolution and the United States, 1944–1954* (1991), is a thoroughly researched and both passionate and analytic treatment of the rise and fall of the regime of Jacobo Arbenz. Gleijeses acknowledges that Communists did have influence with Arbenz but argues that they never posed a threat of taking power. He also sees U.S. policy, which he sharply criticizes, as a complex amalgam of several factors. Nick Cullather, *Secret History: The CIA's Classified Account of Its Operations in Guatemala, 1952–1954* (1999), is the declassified historical study the author wrote under contract with the CIA soon after the events and intended for internal dissemination. It is an objective and revealing account.

Cuba.   The U.S.-sponsored Cuban-exile invasion in 1961 at the Bay of Pigs in Cuba is the subject of Haynes B. Johnson and others, *The Bay of Pigs: The Leaders' Story of Brigade 2506* (1964). Johnson, a noted U.S. journalist, conducted extensive interviews with members of the brigade. Four of the commanders collaborated in the writing. The bulk of the presentation focuses on the operation itself and the defeat and later release of the invaders. It documents their disillusionment with U.S. ambivalence. Johnson castigates the CIA for its ineptitude and speculates that the failure influenced the Soviet decision to station missiles in Cuba. Trumbull Higgins, *The Perfect Failure: Kennedy, Eisenhower, and the CIA at the Bay of Pigs* (1987), is a retrospective examination at a distance from the events that sharply criticizes U.S. decision makers for their total conceptual and operational irresponsibility. James G. Blight and Peter Kornbluh, eds., *Politics of Illusion: The Bay of Pigs Reexamined* (1999), is an oral history based on a series of meetings of U.S. officials, a Soviet official, and Cubans involved in the events, and cites recently released documentation. The account "demonstrates that all anti-Castro parties were guilty of illusions to some degree and that delusion, not betrayal, was the fundamental cause of the disaster."

Dominican Republic.   The Dominican civil war of 1965, the U.S. intervention, and subsequent inter-American actions have been well researched and analyzed. On the background to the civil war, see Theodore Draper, *The Dominican Revolt: A Case Study in American Policy* (1968). This is one of the major works on the subject by a skillful and perceptive journalist who sharply rejects President Johnson's policy. The book is based on Draper's journal articles published at the time, to be read with his follow-up commentary, "The Dominican Intervention Reconsidered," *Political Science Quarterly* 86:1 (March 1971), 1–36. John Bartlow Martin, *Overtaken by Events* (1966), offers many details from an insider's perspective and focuses on the personalities involved and the complexity of the issues. A journalist by profession, Martin had recently been President Kennedy's ambassador to the Dominican Republic and was later President Johnson's personal envoy during the intervention. Two concise collections expertly discuss and debate the international legal elements and implications: A. J. Thomas Jr. and Ann Van Wynen Thomas, eds., *The Dominican Republic Crisis 1965* (1967), edited by two legal scholars at Southern Methodist University; and John Carey, ed., *The Dominican Republic Crisis, 1965* (1967), edited by a professor of law at New York University. The leading scholarly works on the international politics of the intervention took several approaches. Jerome Slater, *Intervention and Negotiation: The U.S. and the Dominican Revolution* (1970), is a thorough and thoughtful examination of the complexities of the intervention that takes U.S. decision makers to task for thinking in narrow doctrinal anti-Communist terms. Abraham F. Lowenthal, *The Dominican Intervention* (1972), investigates the U.S. decision-making process that led to the intervention and assesses the value of explanations that have been framed in terms of competing theoretical perspectives. Piero Gleijeses, *The Dominican Crisis: The 1965 Constitutionalist Revolt and American Intervention* (1978), is valuable primarily for its thorough analysis of the Dominican left with documentation not available in other studies. Gleijeses is uncompromisingly critical of the United States. U. Shiv Kumar, *U. S. Interventionism in Latin America: Dominican Crisis and the OAS* (1987), is a general analysis by an Indian professor, faultfinding of U.S. actions. Bruce Palmer Jr., *Intervention in the Caribbean: The Dominican Crisis of 1965* (1989), by the commander of U.S. forces during the intervention, gives an insider's view of decision making and an authoritative account of military operations.

Chile.   James Petras and Morris Morley, *The United States and Chile: Imperialism and the Overthrow of the Allende Government* (1975), is a brief expression of anger over the deep U.S. involvement in the overthrow of democratically elected President Allende so as to protect U.S. corporate interests. The authors present evidence based on congressional hearings, their interviews, and other sources that validate their accusations. Poul Jensen, *The Garrotte: The United States and Chile, 1970–1973* (2 vols., 1989), is a well-documented study by a Danish scholar who also blames the United States for Allende's overthrow—as does Chilean writer Robinson Rojas Sandford, *El imperialismo yanqui en Chile* (1971). A leading U.S. scholar on Chile, Paul E. Sigmund, *The United States and Democracy in Chile* (1993), argues a relatively limited U.S. role in the overthrow of Allende and more multiple responsibilities for the well-known events.

Grenada.   The U.S. military invasion in 1983 of the Commonwealth Caribbean island-state was an adjunct of the Central American crisis (see below) but had its own dynamics (violent actions within the ruling radical government with certain links to the Soviet Union and Cuba). Robert J. Beck, *The Grenada Invasion: Politics, Law, and Foreign Policy Decisionmaking* (1993), is a solid conceptual analysis of how and why the Reagan administration decided to invade Grenada and of the role played by international law—it did not determine policy but both restrained U.S. actions and was used to justify them. Not sympathetic to U.S. rationales, Beck argues that without the unusual circumstances of the internecine political violence in Grenada, the United States probably would not have taken the military action. Reynold A. Burrowes, *Revolution and Rescue in Grenada: An Account of the U.S.-Caribbean Invasion* (1988), considers the politics in Grenada, details of the invasion, elements of U.S. decision making, the reaction of outsiders (including the British government), and the postinvasion situation. Two studies take opposite philosophical views. Anthony Payne, Paul Sutton, and Tony Thorndike, *Grenada: Revolution and Invasion* (1984), argue that the U.S. invasion was illegal and "seriously damaged the image of the morality of international relations." Gregory Sandford and Richard Vigilante, *Grenada: The Untold Story* (1984), make a case for the legality and morality of the invasion. Kai P. Schoenhals and Richard A. Melanson, *Revolution and Intervention in Grenada: The New Jewel Movement, the United States, and the Caribbean* (1985), is a thorough discursive treatment, critical of the United States; and Jorge Heine, ed., *A Revolution Aborted: The Lessons of Grenada* (1990), is a collection of analytical essays.

Post–Cold War Interventions.   Two U.S. invasions occurred after the end of the cold war. Both of them followed long periods of internal conflicts in small Caribbean states that culminated in the U.S. military actions. President George Bush in December 1989 ordered U.S. troops into Panama, an action that revolved around the machinations of Panamanian de facto head of government General Manuel Antonio Noriega. For details, see Bruce W. Watson and Peter G. Tsouras, eds., *Operation Just Cause: The U.S. Intervention in Panama* (1990); and Thomas Donnelly, Margaret Roth, and Caleb Baker, *Operation Just Cause: The Storming of Panama* (1992).

In Haiti, a military coup in 1991, led by General Raoul Cédras, overthrew the country's first democratically elected president, Jean-Bertrand Aristide. In September 1994, following considerable internal violence and intense international efforts at resolution, President Bill Clinton ordered a military landing, sanctioned by the United Nations Security Council. At the last moment, Haitian authorities agreed not to oppose the landing or the subsequent occupation and civil-military activities. Chetan Kumar, *Building Peace in Haiti* (1998), is a brief treatment by an Indian scholar who is highly critical of the intervention and what he sees as U.S. interference in Haiti's domestic affairs. He does not address the possible consequences of nonintervention. Roland I. Peruse, *Haitian Democracy Restored 1991–1995* (1995), is highly supportive of the intervention and credits it with restoring democracy to Haiti. He uses a procedural electoral definition of democracy rather than a substantive one.

WORLD EVENTS

Spanish-American War

Numerous historians have pointed out that the name of the war should be extended to acknowledge the participation of the Cuban and Philippine colonies in rebellion against Spain—and for whom the outcome had tremendous consequences. This section emphasizes works that substantially recognize the Cuban element. Elbert Jay Benton, *International Law and Diplomacy of the Spanish American War* (1908), the Albert Shaw Lecture on Diplomatic History for 1907 at Johns Hopkins University, is an early, thorough, and objective study. French Ensor Chadwick, *The Relations of the United States and Spain* (2 vols., 1909, 1911), deals with U.S.-Spanish diplomacy leading up to the war in the first volume, and with the war itself and the peace negotiations in the second volume. In consonance with much thinking at the time, Chadwick argues the racial and constitutional superiority of the United States over Spain. Bertha A. Reuter, *Anglo-American Relations During the Spanish-American War* (1924), was a pathbreaking study at the time of research and writing. Walter Millis, *The Martial Spirit: A Study of Our War with Spain* (1931), presents a U.S. anti-imperialist's interpretation. For Cuban viewpoints, see Rafael Martínez Ortiz, *Cuba: Los primeros años de independencia* (1929); and Cosme de la Torriente, *Fin de la dominación de España en Cuba* (1948). Philip S. Foner, *The Spanish-Cuban-American War and the Birth of American Imperialism* (2 vols., 1972), says that his revisionist renaming of the war is to correct the "bias of historians who relegated Cuba to a passive position of a prize in the struggle between the United States and Spain." The Cuban nation was a central protagonist until it was "subjected to neocolonial status by the United States." Foner succeeds in portraying the conflict as many Cubans saw it.

David F. Trask, *The War with Spain in 1898* (1981), established the scholarly standard in this exhaustively researched and analyzed study of political, diplomatic, military, cultural, and social factors. John L. Offner, *An Unwanted War: The Diplomacy of the United States and Spain over Cuba, 1895–1898* (1992), stresses the influences of domestic as well as international politics on U.S. and Spanish policies. The thesis is that "the

United States and Spain tried hard to find a peaceful resolution to the stalemated Cuban-Spanish war," but "Cuban nationalists were unyielding," and "powerful domestic forces propelled Washington and Madrid into a conflict." Louis A. Pérez Jr., *The War of 1898: The United States and Cuba in History and Historiography* (1999), is a relatively brief history that is "principally about one aspect of 1898: the complex relationship between Cuba and the United States." It also complains about what Pérez sees as the trend among U.S. historians not to recognize the important role of Cubans in defeating Spain, without whom the story would have been a very different one.

World War I

Although the United States wanted a united inter-American front during the war, eight of the twenty Latin American states declared war on Germany and five more severed relations with the Central powers. They cooperated with the Allied powers in various ways but none of them provided military forces. The remaining seven states maintained their neutrality throughout the war. F. A. Kirkpatrick, *South America and the War* (1918), addresses the political conditions in Latin America, the German outlook on the region, the economic and propaganda elements of the war in Latin America, and the situation of Pan-Americanism. The book is valuable primarily for the abundant information it brings together in a single volume. Percy Alvin Martin, *Latin America and the War* (1925), is devoted to treatments of the individual states. Martin describes in considerable detail the impact of the war on those states and the official attitudes toward it.

World War II

The Second World War involved considerable, but not universal, inter-American cooperation. After the outbreak of the war in September 1939, the United States and the Latin American states agreed within the Inter-American System on a common policy of neutrality. Following the Japanese attack on the United States on December 7, 1941, at Pearl Harbor, eighteen of the Latin American states broke relations with the Axis and thirteen of them declared war. Argentina and Chile remained neutral until the last part of the conflict when they, too, declared war. Robert Arthur Humphreys, *Latin America and the Second World War* (2 vols., 1982), offers two brief volumes that address the Latin American situation on the eve of the war, the period of neutrality, the Caribbean area as a "danger zone," and the experiences of Mexico, Brazil, Bolivia, and Argentina. The positions and roles of the major countries generated much scholarly interest. German activities in Latin America were matters of considerable inter-American concern. Leslie B. Rout and John F. Bratzel, *The Shadow War: German Espionage and United States Counterespionage in Latin America During World War II* (1986), is based on thorough research in the United States, Britain, Germany, Mexico, Argentina, Brazil, and Chile, as well as interviews with former FBI agents, German agents, and diplomats. The authors present a thorough picture of German spying activities and efforts at subversion, both of which were generally weak and ineffective. They also found Latin American counterefforts to be the same. Although supportive of the necessity for the U.S. role, Rout and Bratzel also acknowledge the precedents set for later CIA meddling in the region.

Scholars paid close attention to Argentina. Ronald C. Newton, *The "Nazi Menace" in Argentina, 1931–1947* (1992), examines in detail the long history of the titled phenomenon from Hitler's earliest machinations through the end of the war. O. Edmund Smith Jr., *Yankee Diplomacy: U.S. Intervention in Argentina* (1953), deals mainly with World War II and the first part of the Perón dictatorship. Smith concludes that the United States, in its resolve to preserve hemispheric solidarity on democratic principles, not only validated the prejudices of Argentine "supernationalists" but revived Latin American misgivings about U.S. intervention and suspicions regarding the sincerity of the Good Neighbor Policy. Michael Francis, *The Limits of Hegemony: United States Relations with Argentina During World War II* (1977), analyzes U.S. pressures on Argentina to declare war on the Axis powers, including in the Inter-American System where similar insistence was exerted on other members to present a united front. Randall Bennett Woods, *The Roosevelt Foreign-Policy Establishment and the "Good Neighbor": The United States and Argentina, 1941–1945* (1979), analyzes the tensions in relations during the war.

Woods concludes that they subverted the Good Neighbor Policy, especially Argentina's persistent neutrality and the bureaucratic and personal competition within the Roosevelt administration of how to respond. Mario Rapaport, *Gran Bretaña, Estados Unidos y las clases dirigentes argentinas: 1940–1945* (1981), takes a revisionist view. He sees a declining Britain trying to preserve its position of primacy with Argentina—for wartime access to products for its armed forces and protection of its significant investments—against challenges from both Germany and the United States. Guido Di Tella and D. Cameron Watt, eds., *Argentina Between the Great Powers, 1939–1946* (1990), includes ten thought-provoking revisionist essays by a dozen established scholars. They address the process in Argentina's decision to remain neutral throughout most of the war and in the problem of relations with their long-term patron, the United Kingdom. They also examine the flirtation with Nazi Germany as a possible counterweight to its long-term adversary, the United States. Isidro J. Ruíz Moreno, *La neutralidad Argentina en la Segunda Guerra* (1997), is a solid analysis of the phenomenon and the issue. On Chile, see Mario Barros Van Buren, *La diplomacia chilena en la Segunda Guerra Mundial* (1998), which is a thorough examination.

Brazil was the most important military contributor, with deployment of an expeditionary army unit into combat in Italy and naval units for submarine patrol in the Atlantic, as well as granting the United States critical base rights. Brazil was also a key state in the effort to break Axis espionage networks. Frank D. McCann Jr., *The Brazilian-American Alliance, 1937–1945* (1973), examines the evolution of the close alliance during the regime of Getúlio Vargas. McCann uses Brazil's decision to join the Allies as a way to assess the role U.S. economic and military aid, the military influence on U.S. policy, and the way the Vargas government functioned. Stanley E. Hilton, *Hitler's Secret War in South America, 1939–1945: German Military Espionage and Allied Counterespionage in Brazil* (1981), describes German intelligence operations and the agents who carried them out, their Brazilian collaborators, and Brazilian and external states' counterintelligence and counterespionage actions. The Mexican experience, which included dispatch of an air force squadron to the Philippines as well as important diplomatic activities, is analyzed by Blanca Torres, *México en la segunda guerra mundial* (1979); and by Friedrich E. Schuler, *Mexico Be-*

tween Hitler and Roosevelt: Mexican Foreign Relations in the Age of Lázaro Cárdenas, 1934–1940 (1998). An interesting treatment of a small state's perceptions and activities is Carlos Calvo Gamboa, *Costa Rica en la Segunda Guerra Mundial, 1939–1945* (1985).

Cuban Missile Crisis

The "October crisis" followed confirmation by the United States of the presence in Cuba of Soviet intercontinental ballistic missiles and nuclear missile bases. The confrontation that followed was essentially between the United States and the Soviet Union as superpower cold war antagonists. The scholarly literature dealing with the intense international developments has emphasized the global elements, although attention has also been paid to the role of Cuba and some to the Inter-American System. That attention is identified in this section.

Graham T. Allison, *Essence of Decision: Explaining the Cuban Missile Crisis* (1971), is included here as the premier treatment and its development of conceptual models for understanding government behavior—within which the Cuban and inter-American factors are subsumed. Lyman M. Tondel Jr., ed., *The Inter-American Security System and the Cuban Crisis* (1964), is a useful descriptive and documentary source of the careful way in which the United States consulted with its Latin American allies within the Inter-American System. Abram Chayes, *The Cuban Missile Crisis: International Crises and the Role of Law* (1974), is authored by a Harvard professor who was a principal adviser to the State Department during the crisis. He makes the case for the role of international law as a part of U.S. decision making and for approaching the Organization of American States for an authorizing resolution. Miguel José Garelli Farias, *La crisis internacional de 1962 y el bloqueo de Cuba* (1967), is a brief and informative discussion of the legal ramifications of the missile crisis by a Mexican scholar.

Herbert S. Dinerstein, *The Making of a Missile Crisis: October 1962* (1976), is authored by a Soviet specialist who concluded that in spite of the acclaimed rationality of the Kennedy administration's decision making and its access to secret data, policymakers were locked into "remembered experiences" not applicable to new situations. Dinerstein seeks to redress the imbalance by examining the interactions of all three parties, with due attention to the Soviet Union and Cuba (to which he devotes three of the six chapters). James A. Nathan, ed., *The Cuban Missile Crisis Revisited* (1992), has three contributions of particular relevance to Cuba: by Philip Brenner on Cuba's perspectives of the crisis; by Elizabeth Cohn on President Kennedy's decision to impose a blockade on Cuba; and by James G. Hershberg on the question of whether the president planned a military strike on the missile sites. James G. Blight, Bruce J. Allen, and David A. Welch, *Cuba on the Brink: Castro, the Missile Crisis, and the Soviet Collapse* (1993), contains the background, context, proceedings, and interpretations of a conference held in Havana. An impressive array of scholars and former officials from the United States, the Soviet Union, and Cuba (including Fidel Castro) gathered "to exchange views and to cross-examine one another on the causes, conduct, and consequences of the most dramatic and dangerous crisis of the nuclear age." Donna Rich Kaplowitz, *Anatomy of a Failed Embargo: U.S. Sanctions Against Cuba* (1998), is a comprehensive analysis of an important consequence of the crisis: one of the "most comprehensive and longest-lasting embargoes in the history of U.S. foreign policy." Kaplowitz focuses on why it failed in its purpose to overthrow Castro.

Cuba in Africa

Carmelo Mesa-Lago and June S. Belkin, eds., *Cuba in Africa* (1982), is a systematic foreign policy analysis by fourteen contributors of Cuba's role in Africa and its relations with the Soviet Union in that context. Four major essays are each preceded by an introduction and followed by commentaries and a conclusion. The general theme (although not all contributors entirely agree) is that Cuba's military involvement in wars in Angola and the Horn of Africa furthered its prestige with elements of the Third World Non-Aligned Movement and made it a world actor of some significance. Juan F. Benemelis, *Castro, subversión y terrorismo en África* (1988), is by a Cuban who served in Africa and South Yemen before going into exile in 1980. He examines in detail Cuba's presence in Africa and the Middle East. See also Sergio Díaz-Briquets, ed., *Cuban Internationalism in Sub-Saharan Africa* (1989).

Argentine-British South Atlantic Conflict

The persistent Argentine-British conflict over the South Atlantic Falklands or Malvinas Islands began with the British occupation in 1833 and continued through an all-out war in 1982 and its aftermath. Julius Goebel Jr., *The Struggle for the Falkland Islands: A Study in Legal and Diplomatic History* (1927), was the definitive treatment at the time of its publication. Goebel, a professor of law, examines the multilateral contest for sovereignty over the islands, from their discovery to British acquisition by force in 1833 through Argentina's subsequent efforts to reclaim them. Goebel concluded that Argentina had the stronger legal claim, but that the reality was sovereignty supported by power. Ricardo R. Caillet-Bois, *Una tierra argentina: las islas Malvinas* (1948), is a well-researched and clearly argued statement of the Argentine position. Ernesto J. Fitte, *La agresión norteamericano a las Islas Malvinas* (1966), is a detailed narrative by a noted Argentine historian of the U.S. naval attack against the Argentine settlement in 1833. Fitte also wrote *La disputa con Gran Bretaña por las islas del Atlántico sur* (1968), something of a polemic that includes commentary on Argentina's claims to the Georgia, Sandwich, and Orcada Islands. Alberto Coll and Anthony C. Arend, eds., *The Falklands War: Lessons for Strategy, Diplomacy, and International Law* (1985), is a collection of analyses by scholars and practitioners of the challenges to international law and to diplomacy of the war, with assessments of the strategic, military, and political implications. Virginia Gamba-Stonehouse, *The Falklands/Malvinas War: A Model for North-South Crisis Prevention* (1987), sees the war as the consequence of North-South problems of communication in terms of strategic language. She examines matters of balances of power, crisis prevention techniques, South American defense policies, and decision making and risk assessment in the war. Peter Beck, *The Falkland Islands as an International Problem* (1988), argues that a serious international problem exists even though the issues are artificially provoked by rhetoric on the part of both the Argentine and British governments. Lowell S. Gustafson, *The Sovereignty Dispute over the Falkland (Malvinas) Islands* (1988), addresses the factors involved in the lead-up to the war and the postwar problems. Gustafson points out the conceptual difficulties with definitions of sovereignty and related phenomena when applied to the Falklands-Malvinas case. He deals with the careless diplomacy by both states prior to the war, the effective role played by the "Falklands lobby" with the British parliament, and Argentine miscalculations about Third World support. Douglas Kinney, *National Interest/ National Honor: The Diplomacy of the Falklands Crisis* (1989), supplies a conceptual and historical background of colonization, interstate conflict, crisis management, and conflict resolution. Kinney then traces the origins and course of the war and the Argentine and British domestic politics involved; the third-party roles of the United States, Peru, and the United Nations; and the outcomes. G. M. Dillon, *The Falklands, Politics, and War* (1989), is a clear and detailed analysis that places a large share of responsibility for the war on Prime Minister Margaret Thatcher and other British officials for their prior indecision and inaction. Several sensible proposals to resolve the issues with Argentina had been proposed but not sufficiently supported by the political leadership. Nevertheless, the British military victory was a political success for the government. Lawrence Freedman and Virginia Gamba-Stonehouse, *Signals of War: The Falklands Conflict of 1982* (1991), is largely a chronicle, set in the context of perceptions and misperceptions on the part of both Argentine and British officials. The authors take into account the perspectives of both sides as they consider the origins and course of the war, and deal with U.S., Peruvian, and international organizational attempts first to deter and then to end warfare. Alex Danchev, ed., *International Perspectives on the Falklands Conflict: A Matter of Life and Death* (1992), brings together analysts to examine various aspects of the conflict and prospects for the future. Agustín M. Romero, *Malvinas: la política exterior de Alfonsín y Menem* (1999), is a concise treatment of postwar Argentine policies.

INTERNAL WAR

Social Revolutions

Mexican Revolution of 1910.   Alan Knight, *The Mexican Revolution* (2 vols., 1986), is a superb comprehensive study by a British historian based on extensive and original research. Knight emphasizes the fundamentally local, popular, and agrarian character of the revolution. He analyzes the complex regime of dictator Porfirio Díaz that was overthrown, the unsure combination of liberalism and populism among the revolutionaries, the violent events of the civil war among competing revolutionary ambitions and constituencies, and the victorious Caranza regime that prefigured postrevolutionary Mexico. Knight ends with an insightful appraisal of what the revolution actually changed. Isidro Fabela, *La historia diplomatica de la revolución mexicana* (1958), is by a noted Mexican intellectual, government official, strong advocate of the revolution, and outspoken critic of the United States. Berta Ulloa, *Revolución Mexicana, 1910–1920* (2 eds., 1963, 1985), is a culminating synthesis of the author's prolific pioneering research on the Mexican Revolution. Ulloa illuminates the linkage between domestic and foreign factors during the turbulent years of violence and intrigue, with the former at the forefront. Two works by Charles C. Cumberland—*Mexican Revolution: Genesis Under Madero* (1952), and the sequel, *Mexican Revolution: The Constitutionalist Years* (1972)—are major contributions to the history of the Mexican Revolution. The first volume deals with the revolution up to Madeiro's death in 1913, and examines his liberal ideas and brief government. The second and longer book, addressing events between 1913 and 1930, is about the civil war and the individuals competing for power, with Carranza finally winning out. Arnaldo Córdova, *La ideología de la Revolución Mexicana* (1973), disputes the notion that the Mexican Revolution was fundamentally the competition for power and not about ideology. He examines the thinking of political theorists and leaders during the period from 1895 to 1929 as the elements of revolutionary ideology formed and coalesced and were institutionalized. Córdova says that the ideas were not borrowed from the outside but were pragmatic expressions of grievances and needs of the major participants. Boris Timofeevich Rudenko, Nikolai Matveevich Lavrov, and Moisei Samuilovich Al'perovich, *Cuatro estudios sobre la Revolución Mexicana* (2 eds., 1960, 1984), is authored by well-known Soviet writers on the subject who view the Mexican events as a democratic-bourgeois revolution. They analyze post–World War II historiography in Mexico and the bourgeois literature in the United States.

Mark T. Gilderhus, *Diplomacy and Revolution: U.S. Mexican Relations Under Wilson and Carranza* (1977), is a relatively brief treatment based on solid research in Mexican and U.S. archives. Gilderhus addresses

President Woodrow Wilson's interventions and recognition policy, the question of petroleum, and the overthrow of Carranza. He sees Wilson's thinking as a complex amalgam of dogmatic liberalism, idealism, materialism, capitalism, and pragmatism. Linda B. Hall and Don M. Coerver, *Revolution on the Border: The United States and Mexico* (1988), deals with problems of the border (and sometimes beyond) from 1910 to 1920, including U.S. military actions, Mexican migration to the United States, and the issues of oil, mining, trade, and arms. For U.S. involvement in the Mexican countryside see Daniel Nugent, ed., *Rural Revolt in Mexico and U.S. Intervention* (1988). Robert E. Quirk, *An Affair of Honor: Woodrow Wilson and the Occupation of Vera Cruz* (1962), examines the factors leading President Wilson to occupy Vera Cruz in 1917, the subsequent Mexican hostility, and the consequences for U.S. relations with Latin America. Quirk points out the irony "that moral imperialism led idealistic Wilson to use the club of armed intervention more frequently than any other president." Alberto Salinas Carranza, *La expedición punitiva* (1936), is a comprehensive history of the diplomatic and military phases of the expeditionary intervention led by famed U.S. general John J. Pershing after Pancho Villa in 1916–1917. It is based on the Carranza papers, eyewitness accounts, and interviews with participants. Clarence Clemens Clendenen, *The United States and Pancho Villa: A Study in Unconventional Diplomacy* (1961), won the Beveridge Award of the American History Association. Clendenen, a retired U.S. Army colonel, seeks to correct the view of General Francisco Villa as "merely a colorful and romantic figure rather than a revolutionary leader whose actions affected the American people." Clendenen followed with *Blood on the Border: The United States Army and the Mexican Irregulars* (1969). The book spans the period from the end of the Mexican-U.S. war in 1848 to 1917 in the midst of the Mexican Revolution. Most of it, however, deals with the U.S. punitive expedition.

Friedrich Katz, *The Secret War in Mexico: Europe, the United States, and the Mexican Revolution* (1981), is an important, well-researched, comprehensive study. It incorporates and significantly expands and reinterprets the author's *Deutschland, Diaz und die Mexikanische Revolution: Die Deutsche Politik in Mexico, 1870–1920* (1964). The study is about international power struggles between Europe and the United States during

the Mexican Revolution from 1910 to 1920, complicated by the participation of private business interests. The complex interplay of overt and
covert actions by foreign governments and investors trying to influence
events in Mexico are linked to internal Mexican developments and the
revolutionary factions (which Katz examines in some detail). Peter
Calvert, *The Mexican Revolution, 1910–1914: The Diplomacy of Anglo-
American Conflict* (1968), takes a British view critical of U.S. policies and
actions during the early phase of the revolution, when the United States
occupied Vera Cruz and a weakened President General Victoriano Huerta
resigned. Calvert acknowledges the Anglo-American clash of political and
economic interests but emphasizes the impact of misinformation and
misperceptions on outcomes.

Cuban Revolution of 1959.   Ramón L. Bonachea and Marta San
Martín, *The Cuban Insurrection, 1952–1959* (1974), challenge the
proposition that the Cuban Revolution was a success of rural insurrection
and demonstrates in detail the importance of urban guerrilla warfare in
the victory. Bonachea had participated in the revolution and later left
Cuba in disillusionment with its course. Jules Robert Benjamin, *The
United States and the Origins of the Cuban Revolution: An Empire of Liberty in an Age of National Liberation* (1990), argues that the hostility between revolutionary Cuba and the United States is a product of the long
history of U.S. domination and Cuban resistance to it rather than cold
war factors. Benjamin criticizes the United States for its failure to understand the difficulties created for Cubans by the attempt to "Americanize"
the island and its impact on Cuban nationalism. Thomas G. Paterson,
*Contesting Castro: The United States and the Triumph of the Cuban Revolu-
tion* (1994), is a thorough and provocative analysis of U.S.-Cuban relations from the beginning of Castro's insurrection in 1956 into the early
years of his revolutionary regime. Paterson explores the reasons for U.S.
conflict with Castro and why the United States was unable to prevent
Castro's rise to power.

Nicaraguan Revolution of 1979.   Two early treatments by Central
American experts of the Nicaraguan Revolution remain authoritative
studies. Thomas W. Walker, ed., *Nicaragua in Revolution* (1982), deals

primarily with the complex and dynamic revolutionary process. An array of experts contribute twenty-one chapters that thoroughly address the historical context, the creation of a "revolutionary society," the principal revolutionary groupings, and the external influences on them and on events. John Booth, *The End and the Beginning: The Nicaraguan Revolution* (1982), addresses the factors (including the U.S. political, economic, and cultural presence) involved in the Sandinista-led victory in 1979 that overthrew Anastasio Somoza Debayle and ended forty-six years of Somoza family rule. Both studies deemphasize the role of Cuba and note the more important actions of Costa Rica and Panama in opposing the Somoza regime.

Further studies on the Nicaraguan Revolution are abundant. Robert A. Pastor, *Condemned to Repetition: The United States and Nicaragua* (1987), is a narrative of U.S. policymaking toward revolutionary Nicaragua by the Carter administration and, in more summary fashion, the early Reagan presidency (Pastor was Latin American adviser on President Carter's National Security Council staff). It is a balanced and critical study that addresses events leading to the revolution, the succession crisis from 1977 to 1979, and the U.S. approach to social revolution (Pastor emphasizes the mistakes). Dennis Gilbert, *Sandinistas: The Party and the Revolution* (1988), deals with the role of ideology in the revolution itself and its continuing impact on the actions of the Sandinista regime. Gilbert examines the Marxist and nationalist elements in the pragmatic world of exercising governing powers and assesses the regime's successes and failures. Donald C. Hodges, *Intellectual Foundations of the Nicaraguan Revolution* (1986), also investigates the Sandinista's ideological orientation. He finds it far from a Marxist-Leninist formulation but its explicit nature difficult to ascertain. Nevertheless, he skillfully identifies the various ideological currents and influences at work in the revolution. Shirley Christian, *Nicaragua: Revolution in the Family* (1988), stands out among many efforts by journalists. A reporter for the *New York Times,* Christian calls on her on-the-scene experiences and personal insights. She downplays the importance of Soviet intrusion and of societal grievances and emphasizes the wielding of political power by the revolutionaries. Christian supplies substantial background on the rise and fall of the Somoza dynasty and demonstrates the clear desire of most Nicaraguans to see it gone. She is unsympathetic to the Sandinistas and sees U.S. diplomacy as naive and inept. Morris H. Morley, *Washington, Somoza, and the Sandinistas: State and Regime in U.S. Policy Toward Nicaragua, 1969–1981* (1994), is an adroit case study within a conceptual framework, with references to related Latin American phenomena for comparative purposes. Morley argues that U.S. policy is understood not in terms of support for or opposition to particular regime types, but as a preference for strong central states in the Caribbean of any kind that the United States could deal with so as to preserve its regional hegemony.

Insurgents and Insurgency

General Treatments. Luis Mercier Vega, *Guerrillas in Latin America* (1969), is one of the early important general studies on the subject. Part 1 is a general comparative analysis, part 2 is devoted to eight country studies, and part 3 is a translation of guerrilla-related documents. Richard Gott, *Guerrilla Movements in Latin America* (1970), is a highly detailed chronicle by a Chilean author whose sympathy with the guerrillas is evident. He provides a great deal of useful but uncoordinated and unanalyzed information about Cuban-inspired rural insurgent movements in Bolivia, Colombia, Guatemala, Peru, and Venezuela. Abraham Guillén, *Philosophy of the Urban Guerrilla* (1973), is by a Spanish journalist who fled Franco's Spain and became an Uruguayan citizen. The book is a collection of his previously published writings on the Marxist and Anarchist concepts and tactics underlying urban guerrilla movements in Latin America. Donald C. Hodges, *The Latin American Revolution: Politics and Strategy from Afro-Marxism to Guevarism* (1974), is an excellent empirical-historical-theoretical-political analysis. Hodges had translated and edited the book by Abraham Guillén. James Kohl and John Litt, eds., *Urban Guerrilla Warfare in Latin America* (1974), reject what they see as the distorted characterization of Latin America urban revolutionaries simply as terrorists. They deal with the insurgents' origins, development, strategy, and tactics. The treatment is organized around long narratives of the phenomena in Argentina, Brazil, and Uruguay. Michael Radu and Vladimir Tismaneanu, *Latin American Revolutionaries: Groups, Goals, Methods* (1990), is a thorough description and comparative analysis of the important insurgency organizations that were on the scene after the Cuban Revolution (forty-four groups in thirteen Latin American states). The authors examine the formative social, ideological, and political factors; and describe each organization's origins, ideology, leadership, structure, membership, recruiting sources, tactics, performance, factional struggles, and international connections. Radu and Tismaneanu had earlier produced the encyclopedic *Revolutionary Organizations in Latin America: A Handbook* (1988). Timothy P. Wickham-Crowley, *Exploring Revolution: Essays on Latin American Insurgency and Revolutionary Theory* (1991), analyzes the processes of revolutionary and counterrevolutionary mobilization and demobilization, and the relevance of particular revolutionary theories to the Latin American experience. Focusing on events since 1956, he explores the rise and fall of guerrilla governments, terror and guerrilla warfare, consciousness-raising in the revolutionary struggles, what makes peasants insurrectionary, and the adaptation of revolutionary theories to Latin American reality. Wickham-Crowley followed with *Guerrillas and Revolution in Latin America: A Comparative Study of Insurgents and Regimes Since 1956* (1992), a comparative study of the origins and outcomes of rural insurgencies in Latin American countries after 1956. The analysis focuses on the personal backgrounds of guerrillas and on national social conditions. The author considers why insurgencies emerged in some countries and not others, and why only two had succeeded in seizing power (in Cuba and Nicaragua). Liza Gross, *Handbook of Leftist Groups in Latin America and the Caribbean* (1995), is by an Argentine journalist who provides a concise and informative reference work, organized by states. Daniel Castro, ed., *Revolution and Revolutionaries: Guerrilla Movements in Latin America* (1999), includes the writings of both academic analysts and guerrilla theorists, with emphases on social revolutionary phenomena. The collection is valuable for its long historical view, tracing guerrillas and their movements from the Great Andean Rebellion (1780–1783) against Spanish rule led by Inca Chief Tupac Amaru to the Zapatista uprising in Mexico in the 1990s.

In the case of Argentina, Marie José Moyano, *Argentina's Lost Patrol: Armed Struggle, 1969–1979* (1995), is a psychological diagnosis of why guerrillas in the 1970s abandoned political strategies and single-mindedly clung to military operations, thereby separating themselves from political and social reality. Moyano's analysis is based on interviews with former insurgents and military men.

With reference to Peru, the focus has been on the particularly violent and effective Shining Path organization. Solid descriptions and analyses are provided by R. Mercado, *El Partido Comunista del Perú: Sendero Luminoso* (1982); Gustavo Gorriti Ellenbogen, *Sendero: Historia de la guerra milenaria en el Perú* (1990); and Gabriela Tarazona-Sevillano, with John B. Reuter, *Sendero Luminoso and the Threat of Narcoterrorism* (1990). David Scott Palmer, ed., *The Shining Path of Peru* (1992), is a comprehensive examination by a Peruvian specialist and expert on the insurgency group. Steve J. Stern, ed., *Shining and Other Paths: War and Society in Peru, 1980–1995* (1998), is a significant collection that brings together fifteen scholars, journalists, and development officials from Peru, Europe, and the United States who deal from their professional perspectives with the Sendero phenomenon. Cynthia McClintock, *Revolutionary Movements in Latin America: El Salvador's FMLN and Peru's Shining Path* (1998), is a thorough examination of two very different insurgencies. McClintock asks why they were able to pose such serious challenges to their respective governments. She considers the interplay of political and economic variables, the nature of the insurgent organizations, and the roles of international actors.

The scholarly attention to Central American insurgents and insurgencies are dealt with below in the context of Central American civil and international wars and the related peace processes.

The Cuban Model.   Historians, social scientists, and journalists have created a huge body of literature on the Cuban Revolution. Much of that subject is dealt with in Chapter 3, and some items are cited above in the section on social revolutions. In a more theoretical vein, Régis Debray, *Revolution in the Revolution? Armed Struggle and Political Struggle in Latin America* (1967), is the widely read and concisely stated tract by the celebrated young French radical revolutionary philosopher. He theorizes and urges guerrilla warfare in Latin America based on a revolutionary strategy devised by Fidel Castro and Che Guevara as a major variant of Marxism-

Leninism. The Latin American situation is different from that of Russia and China, Debray says, and requires political leadership by an autonomous guerrilla force with the Communist Party an adjunct rather than the vanguard.

Of singular significance is the insurgency strategy for Latin America expounded by Cuban revolutionary Ernesto "Che" Guevara. (All of the edited collections of Guevara's works cited below are listed in the References under "Guevara, Ernesto Che.") Guevara's first book, *Che Guevara on Guerrilla Warfare* (1961), is a translation of the "officially sanctioned" version (it was published in several editions in several languages). An exceptionally thorough treatment is by Brian Loveman and Thomas M. Davies Jr., eds., *Guerrilla Warfare* (3 eds., 1985–1997). The book contains the text of the authorized version, two later essays by Guevara, and an excellent extended analysis by the editors. They write a helpful introduction and provide case studies of other guerrilla writings and movements (in Guatemala, Venezuela, Colombia, Peru, Bolivia, Nicaragua, and El Salvador) that influenced Guevara—along with a great deal more related information and analysis. Also of interest is Guevara's *Reminiscences of the Cuban Revolutionary War* (1968), which is based on his notes in the field from the time he landed with Castro's guerrilla group in the mountains of eastern Cuba until their march into Havana. Guevara expounds at length on the meaning of the experience for the Latin American revolution.

Numerous edited books about Guevara and edited collections of his works were produced, especially after his death in Bolivia in late 1967. Many of them were exaggerated eulogies or condemnations. The large number of compilations of Guevara's writings, speeches, and interviews varied in scope and, when in English, the quality of translation. Among the most accurate and useful in English are *Che: Selected Works of Ernesto Guevara* (1969), edited by Rolando E. Bonachea and Nelson P. Valdes; *"Che" Guevara on Revolution: A Documentary Overview* (1969), edited by Jay Mallin; *Che Guevara Speaks: Selected Speeches and Writings* (1970), edited by George Lavan; and *Venceremos! The Speeches and Writings of Che Guevara* (1968), edited by John Gerassi. A particularly thorough collection in Spanish is *Obras Completas* (5 vols., 1973–1974).

Of particular interest is Guevara's Bolivian diary, based on his personal handwritten diary kept from the time his band of Cubans arrived in November 1966 until they were overcome by Bolivian troops in October 1967. The diary, in addition to being a chronicle of events, is an exposition of revolutionary purpose, method, and practice and revealing of Guevara's pragmatic thinking not so evident in his earlier formal writings. Bolivians took the diary after capturing and executing Guevara and it found its way outside the country. A somewhat incomplete version (thirteen days of entries were missing) was surreptitiously sent to Cuba, which Fidel Castro ordered published (with his own introduction): *El diario del Ché in Bolivia: noviembre 7, 1966 a octubre 7, 1967* (1968). Castro disseminated this "official version" to publishers around the world. The diary was published in the United States by Bantam Books in English and Spanish under the title *The Diary of Ché Guevara—Bolivia: November 7, 1966–October 7, 1967* (1968), with Castro's introduction. (The English version had first been run in *Ramparts* magazine.) The English translation, however, is awkward. A useful account was published at the same time by Stein and Day under license from the Bolivian government: *The Complete Bolivian Diaries of Che Guevara and Other Captured Documents* (1968). It includes the thirteen pages missing in the Cuban transcription, as well as the diaries of three other guerrillas in Guevara's group. The translation is better than the above-mentioned version but still leaves much to be desired. The editor is Daniel James, a former journalist and freelance writer specializing in Latin America. James was aggressively anticommunist and hostile to Castro, which he does not disguise in his sixty-page introduction (or in an earlier work he had published on him). James also produced soon after the appearance of the diaries a highly subjective debunking biography of Guevara.

Régis Debray, *Che's Guerrilla War* (1976), who accompanied Guevara to Bolivia and was also captured but later released by the Bolivian government retrospectively ponders the matter. Debray is uncharacteristically less philosophical than technical. He blames situational factors (guerrilla isolation from Indian peasants, hunger, disease) and tactical errors (the broad Latin America strategy was astute). Henry Butterfield Ryan, *The Fall of Che Guevara: A Story of Soldiers, Spies, and Diplomats* (1998), deals with the matter of the U.S. operational intelligence presence in Bolivia to counter the Guevara-led Cuban guerrilla group. He highlights the roles played by two principal U.S. officials.

Latin American Peace Processes

Cynthia J. Arnson, ed., *Comparative Peace Processes in Latin America* (1999), is a comprehensive effort based on the Project on Comparative Peace Processes sponsored by the Woodrow Wilson Center, Instituto de Defensa Legal (Lima), and the Washington office of the Friedrich Ebert Foundation. Twenty-six contributors offer sophisticated analysis and commentary. They treat guerrilla conflict and peace processes in Nicaragua, El Salvador, Guatemala, Mexico (Chiapas), Colombia, and Peru; and essays on the lessons of Central America and for the international community, the "contributions of truth telling," the postconflict political economy of Central America, and the lessons learned in comparative perspective.

Tommie Sue Montgomery, ed., *Peacemaking and Democratization in the Western Hemisphere* (2000), presents wide-ranging and informative studies by academics and practitioners. They address the multilateral efforts of outside states, the Organization of American States, and the United Nations in peacemaking and peacebuilding missions in Latin America—with, variously, political, electoral, and military elements. Case studies are made of activities in the Dominican Republic, El Salvador, Haiti, Mexico, and Nicaragua, and along the Peru-Ecuador border.

CENTRAL AMERICAN CONFLICT
AND THE PEACE PROCESS

Scholarly interest in the intricate Central American conflicts after 1979 and the eventual settlements created something of an academic industry unto itself. The books alone on the international and civil wars, the peace processes, and the domestic implications for the actors involved reached the magnitude of about a thousand in number. The literature has inevitably included works widely varying in quality. The following highly selective list of citations is representative of the complexity of the phenomena.

Internal and Transnational Wars

Early works suffered the disadvantage of closeness to events and the rapid pace of profound change in situations. Some of the perspectives, however,

252 WARFARE, INTERVENTION, AND DIPLOMACY FOR PEACE

held up well. Donald E. Schulz and Douglas H. Graham, eds., *Revolution and Counterrevolution in Central America and the Caribbean* (1984), is a comprehensive multidisciplinary investigation. Schulz's introduction, titled "Theories in Search of Central American Reality," is an insightful survey and warning about the tendency to manipulate data to fit preconceived explanations. The first part of the book discusses the Central American context, the second deals with the individual states and societies, and the third addresses the international elements of the interstate and civil conflicts. Wolf Grabendorff, Heinrich-W. Krumwiede, and Jorge Todt, eds., *Political Change in Central America: Internal and External Dimensions* (1984), separately address the two dimensions. The first part of the book focuses on the individual countries of Nicaragua, El Salvador, and Guatemala. The second part deals with the interests and strategies of the outside states, with chapters on the United States, the socialist states, Venezuela, Mexico, and Europe. Another edited collection of a more normative nature, Robert S. Leiken, ed., *Central America: Anatomy of Conflict* (1984), was issued with some urgency about the evolving imbroglio and concern with misguided U.S. policies. Experts closely analyze a broad array of topics and make what by and large turned out to be perceptive policy recommendations.

Kenneth M. Coleman and George C. Herring, eds., *Understanding the Central American Crisis: Sources of Conflict, U.S. Policy, and Options for Peace* (2 eds., 1985, 1991), is a collection of provocative essays on the internal sources of Central American warfare and the failure of the United States to deal appropriately with that fundamental source of conflict. Morris J. Blachman, William M. Leogrande, and Kenneth E. Sharpe, eds., *Confronting Revolution: Security Through Diplomacy in Central America* (1986), is among the best of the unabashedly normative treatises. Fifteen scholars provide thoughtful and perhaps impatient critiques of U.S. policy calculations and actions. They also argue that the key to understanding and to good policies lies essentially in the societal conditions within Latin America, not in external Communist expansionism; and that the United States should substitute its futile "hegemonic strategic vision" with "principled realism." Nora Hamilton, Jeffry A. Frieden, Linda Fuller, and Manuel Pastor Jr., eds., *Crisis in Central America: Regional Dynamics and U.S. Policy in the 1980s* (1988), is a critique from the left that sees the roots of the Reagan administration's failures in its efforts to revive U.S. hegemony on the isthmus. It also focuses on Central American domestic factors as the source of deprivation, alienation, and violence. William M. LeoGrande, *Our Own Backyard: The United States in Central America, 1977–1992* (1998), is a superb comprehensive retrospective chronicle and analysis. Few actors come out unscathed—the United States, its unsavory state allies and private proxies, and their enemies in Nicaragua and El Salvador. His conclusions about causes and effects of many of the related phenomena are admirably unbiased.

Researchers focused on policymaking and domestic elements in the United States. Cynthia Arnson, *Crossroads: Congress, the President, and Central America, 1976–1993* (2 eds., 1989, 1993), is a detailed policy analysis. Arnson, formerly a legislative assistant in the U.S. House of Representatives and then associate director of Americas Watch, works deftly through the complex events as they unfolded (including the Iran-Contra affair). Richard Sobel, ed., *Public Opinion in U.S. Foreign Policy: The Controversy over Contra Aid* (1993), is a solid empirical investigation of the controversy by skillful analysts. They generally observe that negative public opinion did not deter the Reagan administration or his congressional supporters from aiding the contras—but it did push them into covertness that turned into scandal. Christian Smith, *Resisting Reagan: The U.S. Central American Peace Movement* (1996), is a detailed sociological analysis. Smith examines the Central American context, low-intensity conflict, and the U.S. role. He deals with the emergence of the peace movement (including the "social structure of moral outrage" and individual activists), its strategies, collective identity, policy battles, dealing with "harassment and repression," and demise. Smith assesses the movement's achievements and the meaning for social-movement theory. Walter F. Hahn, ed., *Central America and the Reagan Doctrine* (1987), supports the Reagan administration's approach to Central America. The book includes sixteen essays, some by contributors close to the administration, which had originally appeared in the journal *Strategic Review* between 1982 and 1986. They analyze, from a conservative-realist perspective, four categories of concerns: grand strategy, internal Nicaraguan politics, regional issues, and U.S. policy options. Their point of reference is the Reagan Doctrine of active U.S. assistance to forces fighting Communist regimes.

The overall argument is that the Central American crisis is a function of Soviet-Cuban ambitions in the region. John N. Moore, *The Secret War in Central America: Sandinista Assault on World Order* (1987), is a legal brief advocating the Reagan administration's approach. Moore was the U.S. legal counsel before the World Court in *Nicaragua v. The United States,* 1984.

The roles of other outsiders received attention. With regard to the Soviet Union, Timothy Ashley, *The Bear in the Back Yard: Moscow's Caribbean Strategy* (1987), asserts that the Soviet role in the Caribbean threatens to "destabilize" the U.S. position in the contiguous subregion. He advocates more U.S. use of surrogate counterinsurgents and increased coordination with other countries and military assistance to them. Ashley discusses Cuba, Nicaragua, Grenada, and, to a lesser extent, Jamaica, El Salvador, Honduras, Guyana, and Suriname. Jan S. Adams, *A Foreign Policy in Transition: Moscow's Retreat from Central America and the Caribbean, 1985–1992* (1993), is a well-documented analysis of the movement of Soviet policy from Brezhnev's contentiousness to Gorbachev's pereistroika and "new political thinking," which resulted in Soviet cooperation in the Central American peace process and deteriorated relations with Cuba.

H. Rodrigo Jauberth, Gilberto Castañeda, Jesús Hernández, and Pedro Vúscovic, *The Difficult Triangle* (1992), is a thorough exploration of the complex Mexican–U.S.-Central American triangle in the context of the regional crisis. Ariel C. Armony, *Argentina, the United States, and the Anti-Communist Crusade in Central America, 1977–1984* (1997), tells in detail the story of how the Argentine military regime, animated by anticommunist ideology and its counterinsurgency experience in the "dirty war" at home, helped organize the anti-Sandinista Nicaraguan Contra forces. They began the process independently of the United States and then served as U.S. surrogates to fund them. Jonathan Lemco, *Canada and the Crisis in Central America* (1991), is by a Canadian scholar who inquires into Canada's interest in the region and how its independent support of the peace process affects relations with the United States.

Joseph Cirincione, ed., *Central America and the Western Alliance* (1985), deals with the interest of European states and their secondary presence in the imbroglio. The book is based on a high-level conference of distinguished analysts. Eusebio M. Mujal-León, *European Socialism and the Conflict in Central America* (1989), is a brief, useful survey of the rationales for European Socialism's involvement. Distinctions are made of the country party-to-party differences, but generally the movement moved from early "unbridled optimism and involvement" to growing disenchantment with the Sandinistas and renewed "activism and intensified engagement" in support of the Central American peace initiative. Damián Fernández, ed., *Central America and the Middle East: The Internationalization of the Crisis* (1988), is set in a theoretical framework about conflict and its resolution. Fernández examines the linkages between the Middle Eastern actors (including insurgent groups) and their Central American counterparts.

The Search for Peace

Mexico, Colombia, and Panama in 1983 launched the hopeful initiative for the negotiation of Central American peace, which suffered from a lukewarm and sometimes contrary U.S. reception. The Central American peace process beginning in 1987 was initiated by the Central American states, led by President Oscar Arias of Costa Rica. Known as Esquipulus II, it involved critical participation of the United Nations and the Organization of American States, and overcoming initial opposition by the United States.

Fernando Cepeda Ulloa y Rodrigo Pardo García-Peña. *Contadora: Desafío a la Diplomácia Tradicional* (1985), focuses on the positions of Colombia, Mexico, the United States, and Europe toward Contadora and Central America. Luis Méndez Asensio, *Contadora* (1987), clearly recognizes the complexities involved. Bruce Michael Bagley, ed., *Contadora and the Diplomacy of Peace in Central America: The United States, Central America, and Contadora* (1989), is an examination by ten specialists of the evolution of U.S. policies toward Central America and the Contadora initiative. They explore the nature of the debate over the process and its potential contribution to regional peace. Jack Child, *The Central American Peace Process, 1983–1991: Sheathing Swords, Building Confidence* (1992), is a concise and authoritative treatment. Child defines the numerous peace-related concepts involved and traces the complex events in their terms. Child earlier edited *Conflict in Central America: Approaches to*

Peace and Security (1986), which is based on a series of workshops from 1983 to 1985 sponsored by the International Peace Academy in New York. A multinational group of contributors dealt with conflict resolution, the Contadora process, roles of peacekeeping and confidence-building measures, and the importance of economic development in peace seeking. Cristina Equizábel, ed., *América Latina y la crisis centroamericana: en busca de una solución regional,* brings together numerous leading experts in Latin America to thoroughly analyze the theme of the title. Joaquin Roy, ed., *The Reconstruction of Central America: The Role of the European Community* (1992), is a comprehensive description and analysis by twenty-six scholars. They address the subject in terms of general Latin American and Central American relations with the European Community, Central American Regionalism, and the region's economic and political situations.

Country Studies

El Salvador. Enrique Baloyra, *El Salvador in Transition* (1982), is an admirably objective analysis of factional disputes within the armed forces and important civilian groups—some promoting an end to the long period of military rule (since 1931) and others resisting such efforts. Baloyra characterizes U.S. policy as trying to force a union of military and civilian reactionary allies with centrist anticommunist reformers, an impossible task. Hugh Byrne, *El Salvador's Civil War: A Study of Revolution* (1996), says that the political strategies of insurgency and counterinsurgency explain the revolutionary outcomes in El Salvador's civil war in the 1980s. He also discusses conflict resolution through negotiations. Ian Johnstone, *Rights and Reconciliation: Strategies in El Salvador* (1995), is by an official in the office of the United Nations Secretary General. He argues that the case of the UN role in the Salvadoran peace process demonstrates that the twin goals of peace and justice are compatible and may be mutually reinforcing. Tommie Sue Montgomery, *Revolution in El Salvador: From Civil Strife to Civil Peace* (2 eds., 1982, 1995), is based on thorough research, including numerous visits and lengthy stays in the country to observe events and conduct some 200 interviews. Montgomery investigates the growth of revolutionary organizations, U.S.

counterinsurgency strategy (of which she is highly critical) and actions to promote democracy, the peace process, and the key mediation role of the Roman Catholic Church.

Nicaragua. E. Bradford Burns, *At War in Nicaragua: The Reagan Doctrine and the Politics of Nostalgia* (1987), is a forthright defense of the thesis that the United States had isolated itself internationally with its obsession to depose the Sandinista regime. Burns favors the Contadora initiative. Peter Kornbluh, *The Price of Intervention: Reagan's War Against the Sandinistas* (1987), is a well-documented and highly critical treatment of the Reagan administration's actions, with the themes expressed in the title. Thomas W. Walker, ed., *Reagan Versus the Sandinistas: The Undeclared War on Nicaragua* (1987), brings together sixteen authors for a comprehensive examination of the Reagan administration's effort to undo the Sandinista revolution. They look into Reagan's "low intensity war," attempts at economic destabilization, direct CIA sabotage, sponsorship of Contras, and other coercive tactics. The book concludes with consideration of the implications for international law, U.S. international interests and domestic politics, and the future of Nicaragua itself. Roy Gutman, *Banana Diplomacy: The Making of American Foreign Policy in Nicaragua, 1981–1987* (1988), is by the national security correspondent for *Newsday* who describes the book as "a case study of the perils of fighting strategic battles in secret, on the cheap, and by proxy." He offers a detailed narrative based on interviews with principal actors in the United States, Central America, Argentina, and elsewhere. Gutman criticizes the decreased role of professional foreign policymakers in the U.S. government and the increased influence of "ideologues and outsiders." William I. Robinson, *A Faustian Bargain: U.S. Intervention in the Nicaraguan Elections and American Foreign Policy in the Post–Cold War Era* (1992), is a good treatment of "war as politics and politics as war" during the administrations of Presidents Carter, Reagan, and Bush. David Ryan, *U.S.-Sandinista Diplomatic Relations: Voice of Intolerance* (1995), analyzes why no agreement was reached by the two parties during the Sandinista tenure (1979–1990). Ryan's answer lies primarily in the Reagan administration's application of the "traditional hegemonic approach" to a determined effort to remove the revolutionary government. The method included blocking reconciliatory diplomatic initiatives and rhetorically supporting them and engaging in numerous hostile acts. Gary Prevost and Harry Vanden, eds., *The Undermining of the Sandinista Revolution* (1997), investigates the reasons why the revolution failed. The authors find answers less in internal factors (which they carefully consider) than in external ones—primarily hostile U.S. policies under Reagan and Bush, especially the creation and support of the contras and the economic embargo, as well as the end of Soviet and Cuban assistance. See also the voluminous surveys and analyses by Robert Kagan, *A Twilight Struggle: American Power and Nicaragua, 1977–1990* (1996); and Augusto Zamora R., *El conflicto Estados Unidos–Nicaragua, 1979–1990* (1996).

Guatemala.   Susanne Jonas, *The Battle for Guatemala: Rebels, Death Squads, and U.S. Power* (1991), is by an experienced observer and analyst of Central America and of Guatemala in particular. Jonas presents a solid empirically based analysis of Guatemala's brutal thirty-year civil war, including the country's economic-social-political structure, the uninspiring role of the United States, and official violence and the persistence of revolutionary movements. Jonas followed with *Of Centaurs and Doves: Guatemala's Peace Process* (1998), an exceptionally well-researched treatment, beginning with an assessment of the Guatemalan peace accords finally signed in December 1996. She evaluates the process and the major players in it and addresses the broader significance for Central America.

Honduras.   Donald E. Schulz and Deborah Sundloff Schulz, *The United States, Honduras, and the Crisis in Central America* (1994), analyze the increased importance of Honduras for the United States in the 1980s after the Reagan administration made it a "launching pad" for contra operations against the Sandinistas in Nicaragua and counterinsurgency operations in El Salvador. Philip L. Shepherd, *The Honduran Crisis and Economic Assistance* (1989), examines the deterioration of the Honduran economy during the 1980s regional crisis. The problems were immense: declining terms of trade, reduced exports and foreign investment, rising external debt, and U.S.-induced militarization and ill-conceived U.S. economic assistance.

—————— ■ ——————

CHAPTER 8

Interstate and
Transnational Phenomena

This chapter deals with a complex assortment of subjects.[1] It is organized as a sequence of connected categories of interstate relations and transnational phenomena and the related state and transnational actors and their policies.[2] The progression begins with the strategies and actions of external states to help develop Latin American nations. Business enterprises and multinational corporations are then taken up, followed by economic policies and interactions concerning trade, investment, debt, and expropriations. International environmental concerns are addressed, including their connection to economic development ("sustainable development"). A shift is made to the subject of Latin American political regime types and related phenomena as matters of foreign policy and international interactions (democracy and human rights; Latin American armed forces, military rule, and foreign military assistance; revolutionary regimes and revolutionary change— including the matter of international communism). The category of transnational networks follows, which includes the Roman Catholic Church, Protestant churches, labor movements, and political party associations. The last part of the chapter deals with three categories of intersocietal relations: the movement of people, cultural relations, and the drug traffic.

DEVELOPMENT THEORY IN PRACTICE

Theories of development that have been advocated as bases for policy action may be thought of as development strategies. Heraldo Muñoz points out that the term "development" has several policy-theoretical definitions. It has been posited as (1) the equivalent of the "modernization" process identified with the historical development of Western Europe and the United States; (2) specific economic models; and (3) the combination of economic progress, social equality, increased personal and political freedom, and other nonmaterial factors.[3] Policies were almost strictly economic in nature until after World War II. After that a purely economic strategy of development became rare. Most constructs today, including those by economists, are multifaceted. They are some combination of economic, social, political ideological, military, and environmental elements. For the Latin American and Caribbean states, the desire for foreign policy independence and security concerns (which itself has undergone periodic redefinition) are also part of the policy purpose mix. See also in this book Chapter 2 on development (modernization) and structural dependency theories, and Chapter 6 on integration movements.

The Alliance for Progress was a major inter-American undertaking. The concept had been proposed in 1958 by the president of Brazil, advanced as a high priority by President John F. Kennedy in 1961, and soon after formally adopted as a high-priority multilateral program by the Inter-American System. The Alliance for Progress was based largely on liberal developmental theories of modernization and blended with specific interests of the Latin American states and the United States—which were both mutual and competing. Economic development was a key purpose, but it was accompanied by and blended with matters of hemispheric security, political and social stability, opposition to militarism and dictatorship and the advancement of democracy, and as an alternative to the Cuban revolutionary model and Communist-inspired insurgency.

Researchers widely addressed the Alliance for Progress and produced a voluminous scholarly literature. Brazilian president Juscelino Kubitschek's proposal for "Operation Pan America," which initiated the process that led to the Alliance for Progress, is analyzed by Licurgo Costa, *Uma nova política para las Américas: Doutrina Kubitschek e OPA* (1960). It is a thorough study that pays special attention to Latin America's economic problems—and calls for closer relations between Brazil and the United States. Sharp criticism of the alliance came early. Simon G. Hanson, *Five Years of the Alliance for Progress: An Appraisal* (1967), was by the editor of *Inter-American Economic Affairs*. A particularly disenchanted U.S. economist, Hanson conducted a thorough examination of the effort and concluded that in fact it had rewarded rather than discouraged "resistance to change." Hanson followed with *Dollar Diplomacy Modern Style: Chapters in the Failure of the Alliance for Progress* (1971), which is decidedly polemical but based on careful observation. Hanson had earlier written *Economic Development in Latin America* (1951), in which he focuses on economic factors but accents their connections with the political system. Herbert K. May, *Problems and Prospects of the Alliance for Progress* (1968), is a sound and serious expert critique. Jerome Levinson and Juan de Onís, *The Alliance that Lost Its Way: A Critical Report on the Alliance for Progress* (1970), is coauthored by a former official of the U.S. Agency for International Development and a correspondent for the *New York Times*. They provide a good summary description and critique. L. Ronald Scheman, ed., *The Alliance for Progress: A Retrospective* (1988), is based on a conference held at Georgetown University on the twenty-fifth anniversary of the formal beginning of Alliance for Progress. Among the thirty-one contributors are architects of the program and well-known analysts. They explore the alliance's historical successes, failures, and relevance to current policy.

In a related but more general fashion, the erudite observations and reflections of Albert O. Hirschman are brought together in *A Bias for Hope: Essays on Development and Latin America* (1971). A collection of sixteen previously published articles between 1954 and 1970, they reveal the evolution of Hirschman's philosophical optimism indicated in the title. Hirschman had earlier edited *Latin American Issues: Essays and Comments* (1961), a collection of chapters based on conference papers written mostly by economists. They had been "asked to repress the urge to judge or prescribe and to look into Latin American policy-making" with regard to development. This was an early and expert effort on the subject. Other works of interest are Roberto Alemann and others, *Economic Development Issues: Latin America* (1967), which cogently presents Latin American views, and Felipe Herrera, *Nacionalismo, Regionalismo, Internacionalismo: América Latina en el Contexto Internacional* (1970), by the Chilean lawyer and economist who was first president of the Inter-American Development Bank. Robert Packenham, *Liberal America and the Third World: Political Development Ideas in Foreign Aid and Social Science* (1973), is an exploration of "liberal" assumptions and their tendency to come to naught as policy.

After 1969 the United States in effect ended the Alliance for Progress. Latin Americans reacted in the Inter-American System by pressing the parallel ideas of "collective security for development" and "cooperation for integral development." Together they meant that economic and social problems would be taken as seriously as the political and military elements of mutual security, and self-sustained development that emphasized "ideological pluralism" and the human aspects of economic and social development. For thorough explanations and defenses of these ideas, see two official publications: Inter-American Economic and Social Council, *Hemispheric Cooperation and Integral Development: Report for the Secretary General* (1982); and Sistema Económico Latinoamericano, *Políticas de ajuste: financiamiento del desarrollo en América Latina* (1987). These concepts were institutionally formalized in 1992 with the creation of the Inter-American Council for Integral Development as a major organ of the Organization of American States. For further informed and thoughtful official commentary, see Enrique V. Iglesias, *Reflections on Economic Development: Toward a New Latin American Consensus* (1993), by the president of the Inter-American Development Bank. Iglesias is an economist and former foreign minister of Uruguay. Steven E. Sanderson, *The Politics of Trade in Latin American Development* (1992), examines the literature on international trade, economic development, regional economic history, and resource management to discover the historical differences of economic thought between Latin Americans and the industrialized world.

The developmentalism underpinning the Alliance for Progress was a major target of structural dependency theorists (see Chapter 2). They prescribed independent Latin American policies to reduce dependency on the outside world, which they saw being perpetuated by the alliance. Within Latin America, the structuralists also carried on a vigorous debate with monetarists over the appropriate bases for Latin American development. The encounter began after World War II, with the structuralists generally winning out as the primary influence on Latin American government policies.

International monetarism was a development strategy centered on economic stabilization. Monetarists sought inflation control through fiscal adjustments, export-led growth through free trade and integration into the global economy, and foreign capital investment. For the developmental views of an important monetarist, see the works of Brazilian political economist and former Brazilian minister of economic planning, Roberto de Oliveira Campos: *Economia, Planejamento e Nacionalismo* (1963), *Reflections on Latin American Development* (1967), and *O Mundo que Vejo e Nao Desejo* (1976). Campos addresses many aspects of economic development—relations with the United States, government policy and public and private administration, and, in particular, the connection of international trade and foreign assistance to economic development. He also discusses the purposes, accomplishments, and failures of the Alliance for Progress. Adalbert Krieger Vasena, with Javier Pazos, *Latin America: A Broader World Role* (1973), also represents traditionalism and monetarism.

By the mid-1980s, Latin Americans began to abandon structural theory and policies of state intervention in the economy, import substitution industrialization, and defensive economic integration, which were seen to have failed. After considerable political contention, most governments in the region adopted policies of what came to be called economic neoliberalism—reduced government controls, privatization of state-owned enterprises, assistance to private sectoral development, lowering of barriers to trade, and openness toward external investment. Economic integration for free trade was revived and reformed and parallel free trade arrangements were made with the United States and Europe (see Chapter 6). The concept of neoliberalism also embraced Latin American redemocratization. A general inter-American consensus emerged that democratic development and economic reform constituted the overarching norms in hemispheric relations.

The rise of neoliberalism has generated its own literature. James L. Dietz, ed., *Latin America's Economic Development: Confronting Crisis* (2 eds., 1987, 1995), contains twenty articles on a wide range of economic issues facing the region. Among the subjects addressed are economic history, inflation, balance of payments, transnational corporations, development strategies (such as import substitution versus export-led growth), income distribution, labor markets, and the role of women. Critics of neoliberalism are particularly worried about its socioeconomic consequences. They argue that even if neoliberalism has macroeconomic benefits and certain sectors prosper from it (usually those who already hold most of the wealth), too many other people remain poor and have only marginal opportunities for betterment. Contributors to William C. Smith, Carlos H. Acuña, and Eduardo A. Gamarra, eds., *Latin American Political Economy in the Age of Neoliberal Reform: Theoretical and Comparative Perspectives for the 1990s* (1994), point to increasing poverty and economic inequality under neoliberal policies. They advocate and engage in rethinking Latin American political economy. The authors in Richard Tardanico and Rafael Menjívar Larín, eds., *Global Restructuring Employment, and Social Inequality in Urban Latin America* (1997), argue that in the 1990s "Latin American states have become more vulnerable to transnational capital movements and market shifts." They focus on the negative consequences of internal economic restructuring in case studies of Argentina, Chile, Costa Rica, the Dominican Republic, Guatemala, Mexico, and Venezuela. Duncan Green, *Silent Revolution: The Rise of Market Economics in Latin America* (1995), emphasizes "what has become an economic model of enormous social and environmental cost and suggests popular alternatives." Green includes chapters on import substitution, the International Monetary Fund, economic transformations since 1982, the environmental costs of economic adjustment, Latin America in the changing world economy, export-led growth and regional trade, the politics of neoliberalism, and the search for alternatives (such as neostructuralism).

Victor Bulmer-Thomas, ed., *The New Economic Model in Latin America and Its Impact on Income Distribution and Poverty* (1996), is the result of two years of work by a study group of fourteen experts. They address the attempts by Latin Americans over the past two decades or so to fully integrate into a world economy that was becoming increasingly globalized. This continuing process in the post–debt crisis, post–import substitution, post–cold war period requires deep structural changes. The subject matter of the volume is the "new economic model" in Latin America—a gradual process in which countries go through different phases as they deal with income distribution and poverty. It includes case studies of Brazil, Chile, Honduras, and Mexico. Analysts in Luciano Tomassini, ed., *Transnacionalización y desarrollo nacional en América Latina* (1984), lay out the shortcomings of realism in ignoring or dealing inadequately with transnational phenomena and national development. They also point out that, in contrast to the rich literature on transnationalization in industrialized countries, the writing in Latin America has serious limitations. Well-known Latin American writers help fill this gap with insightful essays on various aspects of the subject in the Latin American context. For feminist perspectives of development in the transnational era, see Christine E. Bose and Edna Acosta-Belen, eds., *Women in the Latin American Development Process* (1995). The ten chapters by thirteen contributors have important transnational content, including women's social movements, the global economy and changing definitions of gender, gender and transnational corporations, and women in the world capitalist crisis. The editors hope the book "helps promote the international connections and comparative perspectives that will enhance research on women in the global economy and the formulation of development policies that could truly improve women's material conditions and perhaps even undermine the structures and ideologies that perpetuate their subordinate status."

Of interest to the student of Latin American development are the activities of private economic advisors to Latin American governments. Paul W. Drake, *The Money Doctor in the Andes: The Kemmerer Missions, 1923–1933* (1989), is the story of economic teams led by Princeton University economist Edwin Walter Kemmerer to five South American states at their urgent invitation. Determined to remain independent from the U.S. government, they analyzed the economies in terms of their new methodologies and made recommendations (virtually the same in all cases) for numerous economic, monetary, and fiscal reforms, which were adopted intact. Drake sees a kind of neodependency in the events. The world depression subverted all efforts. Drake followed with an edited volume of essays, *Money Doctors, Foreign Debts, and Economic Reforms in Latin America from the 1890s to the Present* (1994), in which the contributors focus on international advising, lending, and the links among Latin

American and external interest groups and international agencies. They indicate the increasing influence of foreign economic advisers (the "money doctors") on Latin American decision makers and on the political-economic outcomes, not in a particularly complimentary light.

BUSINESS ENTERPRISE AND MULTINATIONAL CORPORATIONS

Business enterprise in Latin America has been an important phenomenon since Latin Americans began to welcome foreign capital and expertise in the nineteenth century. Multinational corporations (MNCs) as we know them today began to evolve in the early twentieth century. They have been especially prominent in Latin America with accelerated growth after World War II.

General Studies

Early interest in the subject of the role of business enterprise in Latin America is manifested in several studies. Dudley Maynard Phelps, *Migration of Industry to South America* (1936), focuses on the first third of the twentieth century and the establishment by large corporations of subsidiaries in Argentina, Chile, Brazil, and Uruguay. Phelps explores the reasons for industrial migration and the problems confronted, largely from the corporate perspective. J. Fred Rippy, *Latin America and the Industrial Age* (2 eds., 1944, 1947), "deals with the salient aspects of a grand epic: the joint mastery by Latins and Anglo-Saxons of the Latin-American physical environment, the development of Latin American resources through science and technology." The essays deal with many industries: steamboat, railway, telegraph, telephone, rubber, mineral, petroleum, electrical, sanitation, medical, and airline. D.C.M. Platt, ed., *Business Imperialism: An Inquiry Based on British Experience in Latin America* (1977), includes five expert contributors who provide empirical studies on commercial banks, insurance companies, public utilities, and shipping, and on the trade in coffee, nitrates, and beef. Case studies on Peru and Argentina explore business-government relations. Thomas F. O'Brien contributed two books that form an excellent comprehensive history of U.S.

business in Latin America during the twentieth century. *The Revolutionary Mission: American Business in Latin America, 1900–1945* (1996) is an exploration of the U.S. corporate culture's "revolutionary mission" to spread American materialist values and consequent impact on Latin American societies; and the latter's reaction of it with a mix of acceptance and rejection. The second work employs a broader time frame and more summary treatment. *The Century of U.S. Capitalism in Latin America* (1999) surveys U.S.-based business enterprise around Latin America.

Analyses of MNCs reached a height in the 1970s. The interest subsequently declined along with external investment itself in the region, but revived as the economic predicament of the 1980s faded. Jack N. Behrman, *The Role of International Companies in Latin America* (1972), is a concise, fairly technical but clearly written business administration approach. Behrman examines the inadequacies of tariff reductions by Latin Americans, the automotive and petrochemical industries, trade-offs between efficiency and equity, and complementation agreements (he recommends multisector arrangements and international specialization). Richard S. Newfarmer, ed., *Profits, Progress and Poverty: Case Studies of International Industries in Latin America* (1985), is a collection of essays on multinational corporations and their impact on Latin American development. Contributors investigate the automobile, cigarette, electrical, food processing, iron and steel, pharmaceutical, tire, and tractor industries. Robert Grosse, *Multinationals in Latin America* (1989), applies bargaining theory to the analysis. Grosse views multinational enterprise "as a goal-oriented actor (seeking profits and growth), constrained by government policymakers and competing firms, each seeking somewhat conflicting goals." He traces the history of MNCs and recent trends in Latin America, and discusses the regulatory and economic environments, corporate strategies, and specific industries.

Certain dependency theorists have viewed MNCs as instruments of neoimperialism. They ally with local elites and distort development by hampering national acquisition of technology and capital. Theotonio Dos Santos, *Imperialismo y empresas Multinacionales* (1973), by a leading neo-Marxist dependency theorist, is a brief, complex, fault-finding analysis. He asserts that the MNC-created international division of labor has actually deepened the "final crisis" of capitalism. See citations in Chapter

2 on neo-Marxist dependency theory for numerous references to this favorite target.

Numerous studies address specific sectors of business enterprise and MNC activity. Charles Kepner and Jay Soothill, *The Banana Empire* (1935), is a treatment from a 1930s anti-imperialist position. Lester D. Langley and Thomas D. Schoonover, *The Banana Men: American Mercenaries and Entrepreneurs in Central America, 1880–1930* (1995), is sharply critical of the "sordid record" of the "banana men" and their "kingdoms," with much supporting evidence. The authors describe the foreigners' roles in Central American wars and in the transformation of Central American political culture, economy, and social values. Yhe book highlights the cases of Nicaragua and Honduras. D. Joslin, *A Century of Banking in Latin America* (1963), focuses mostly on British banks during the years 1862–1936, with an epilogue summarizing occurrences to 1960. Daniel Jay Baum, *The Banks of Canada in the Commonwealth Caribbean: Economic Nationalism and Multinational Enterprises of a Medium Power* (1974), is a good analytical reference on the subject. W.A.M. Burden, *The Struggle for Airways in Latin America* (1943), is a scholarly history of commercial airline rivalry and its rapid growth in Latin America, from the end of World War I to the outbreak of World War II. Wesley Phillips Newton, *The Perilous Sky: U.S. Aviation Diplomacy and Latin America, 1919–1931* (1978), provides a thorough description and interpretation of the subject. Rhys Jenkins, *Transnational Corporations and the Latin American Automobile Industry* (1986), deals with the origins of the Latin American automobile industry and its internationalization, technical matters such as market conditions, pricing, profitability, and the restructuring of the global industry. Jenkins had earlier written *Dependent Industrialization in Latin America: The Automotive Industry in Argentina, Chile, and Mexico* (1976).

For a general legal study of expropriation of foreign companies by Latin American states, see Andreas F. Lowenfeld, ed., *Expropriation in the Americas: A Comparative Law Study* (1971). Thirteen contributors present studies of Argentina, Brazil, Chile, Mexico, Peru, the United States, and Venezuela. The emphasis is on technical analyses with some attention to policies. Eric N. Baklanoff, *Expropriations of U.S. Investments in Cuba, Mexico, and Chile* (1975), provides country studies with historical background and an emphasis on the domestic and international politics of expropriation. Further case studies with reference to specific industries is provided by George M. Ingram, *Expropriation of U.S. Property in South America: Nationalization of Oil and Copper Companies in Peru, Bolivia and Chile* (1974). Paul E. Sigmund, *Multinationals in Latin America: The Politics of Nationalization* (1980), is a nuanced study of the complexities of the domestic and international politics of nationalization. On a related phenomenon, see the thorough study by Robert H. Swansbrough, *The Embattled Colossus: Economic Nationalism and United States Investors in Latin America* (1976).

The economics and politics of petroleum are a special category of the expropriation phenomena. Two authors provide comprehensive studies of the history and politics of the business strategies pursued by Latin American state oil companies—George Philip, *Oil and Politics in Latin America: Nationalist Movements and State Companies* (1982); and John Wirth, *Latin American Oil Companies and the Politics of Energy* (1985). Fehmy Saddy, ed., *Arab–Latin American Relations: Energy, Trade, and Investment* (1983), is a collection of analyses by ten Latin American and Middle Eastern experts who explore numerous elements of South-South interregional relations. They focus on the concept of global interdependence in the three areas indicated. Gerard Colby, with Charlotte Dennett, *Thy Will Be Done: The Conquest of the Amazon: Nelson Rockefeller and Evangelism in the Age of Oil* (1995), is a study in the spread of U.S. social, economic, and political values by way of corporate activity. For a dogmatic Marxist-Leninist view by a prominent Soviet Latin American analyst, see Victor Volski, *América Latina: petróleo e independencia* (1966).

Most of the research and writing on the politics of petroleum has been with reference to the major Latin American oil-producing countries, especially Mexico and Venezuela. Country citations are included in the following sections on general individual country experiences with international business enterprises and MNCs.

Country Studies

Mexico. Van R. Whiting Jr., *The Political Economy of Foreign Investment in Mexico: Nationalism, Liberalism, and Constraints on Choice* (1992), argues that theories of both dependency and statism fail to explain Mexico's policies toward foreign investment. Whiting thoroughly examines the factors that shape Mexican decisions, including the role of the state, nationalism versus liberalism, the industrial structure, and the "political economy of nationalism." Douglas C. Bennett and Kenneth E. Sharpe, *Transnational Corporations Versus the State: The Political Economy of the Mexican Auto Industry* (1985), is a case study in dependency theory, focusing on economic dislocations created by MNCs in Mexico's automotive sector. On MNCs in Mexico as actors and as issues, see Lorenzo Meyer, *Las empresas transnacionales de México* (1974); and Bernardo Sepúlveda and Antonio Chumacero, *La inversión extranjera en México* (1973). Harry K. Wright, *Foreign Enterprise in México: Laws and Policies* (1971), is a legal study of foreign capital investment and its relationship to economic development. José Luis Cecena, *México en la órbita imperial* (1970), is an examination of the impact of international business and the world capitalist system on Mexico's economy from 1821 to 1869. John Mason Hart, *Revolutionary Mexico: The Coming and Process of the Mexican Revolution* (1987), addresses the heavy presence of U.S. investors in Mexico during the "developmental dictatorship" of Porfirio Díaz.

Studies on petroleum and international politics in Mexico have been an important area of research. Wendell Chaffee Gordon, *The Expropriation of Foreign-Owned Property in Mexico* (1941), is a classic study focusing on the oil industry. Linda B. Hall, *Oil, Banks, and Politics: The United States and Postrevolutionary Mexico, 1917–1924* (1995), addresses how the Mexican government handled a major dilemma as it sought to establish a postrevolutionary political system. To gain U.S. recognition, it was required to begin to pay the international debt and make petroleum reserves available; at the same time, it had to satisfy manifest revolutionary nationalism at home. Roscoe B. Gaither, *Expropriation in Mexico: The Facts and the Law* (1940), is an informative analysis by a U.S. lawyer long resident in Mexico. He focuses on the Mexican seizure of U.S. and British oil company properties. George W. Grayson, *The Politics of Mexican Oil* (1981), is authored by a prominent Mexican specialist. Grayson provides an excellent survey of the history, politics, and economics of this major issue in Mexican politics and international relations (primarily with the United States). Grayson focuses directly on the international element in

Oil and Mexican Foreign Policy (1988). He engages in foreign policy analysis in terms of the Mexican political system and the linkage between exogenous factors and the domestic decision-making process. Lorenzo Meyer, *Mexico and the United States in the Oil Controversy, 1917–1942* (1977), is a scholarly study of the international politics of the matter that firmly presents Mexico's legitimate nationalist grievances toward foreign oil producers who extract a vital national resource and repatriate the profits. Robert Jones Shafer and Donald Mabry, *Neighbors—Mexico and the United States: Wetbacks and Oil* (1981), combines the old bilateral problem of human migration with the more recent issue of Mexico's emergence as a major oil producer and exporter. The United States hopes to benefit from the latter and regulate the former, whereas Mexico must deal with poverty and economic development. Jonathan C. Brown, *Oil and Revolution in Mexico* (1993), is a thoroughly researched history analyzed in terms of the relationship of the oil companies to Mexico's development (and ambivalent reaction), from the late nineteenth century to about 1920. Edward J. Williams, *The Rebirth of the Mexican Petroleum Industry: Developmental Directions and Policy Implications* (1979), concentrates on the key events in the development of Mexico's petroleum policy after 1975. In a similar vein, Enrique Ruiz Garcia, *La estrategia mundial del petróleo: una teoría del poder, una teoría de la dependencia* (1982), posited that Mexican petroleum development was following the classic pattern of capitalist exploitation of a finite resource.

Peru.   Charles T. Goodsell, *American Corporations and Peruvian Politics* (1974), places the analysis in a theoretical framework and an overview of the presence of U.S. business in Peru. Goodsell examines political attitudes in U.S. business, corporate political behavior, the conduct of U.S. governments, bargaining processes over investments, corporate relations with local governments in Peru, and the corporate role in the country's infrastructure integration. Anibal Quijano, *Nationalism and Capitalism in Peru: A Study of Neo-Imperialism* (1971), deals with the mixed policies of the reformist military regime in Peru—expropriating some U.S. companies but extending benefits to others—in the context of radical changes in Peru and in South America at large. At the time Quijano, an economist and sociologist, was a leading dependency theorist; he later joined the ranks of world-system theorists. He concludes that the Peruvian government is breaking up classic imperialism but dependency will continue as a form of neoimperialism. Alfonso W. Quiroz, *Domestic and Foreign Finance in Modern Peru, 1850–1950: Financing Visions of Development* (1993), is a well-researched study, particularly valuable for the earlier period, which has been neglected in the case of Peru. Adalberto J. Pinelo, *The Multinational Corporation as a Force in Latin American Politics: A Case Study of the International Petroleum Company in Peru* (1973), sympathizes with IPC in its long and turbulent relationship with Peruvian governments. Rosemary Thorp and Geoffrey Bertram, *Peru, 1880–1977: Growth and Policy in an Open Economy* (1968), is an expert political economic analysis of Peru's economy that highlights the roles of foreign business enterprise and other forms of foreign investment.

Venezuela.   Researchers have thoroughly explored international aspects of Venezuela's petroleum economy and its essential position during the twentieth century in the Venezuela-U.S. relationship. Rómulo Betancourt, *Venezuela: Oil and Politics* (1979), is by the former Venezuelan president and intellectual. It provides an authoritative and candid assessment about Venezuelan politics and foreign oil companies in the country. Edwin Lieuwen, *Petroleum in Venezuela: A History* (1954), is a classic, objective historical analysis. B. S. McBeth, *Juan Vicente Gómez and the Oil Companies in Venezuela, 1908–1935* (1983), is an excellent account of "petroleum diplomacy" in the first decades of Venezuela as an oil producing country. Aníbal Martínez, *Chronology of Venezuelan Oil* (1970), is a useful reference work. James F. Petras, Morris Morley, and Steven Smith, *The Nationalization of Venezuelan Oil* (1977), covers the 1976 process from a dependency theoretical perspective. Stephen G. Rabe, *The Road to OPEC: United States Relations with Venezuela, 1919–1976* (1982), deals with the years in which U.S. oil companies ran the Venezuelan oil industry, which produced the country's oil economy and profoundly changed its politics. It examines the numerous bilateral issues over the years, which culminated in Venezuela's nationalization of the oil industry and its leadership in forming the Organization of Petroleum Exporting Countries. Franklin Tugwell, *The Politics of Oil in Venezuela* (1975), assesses Venezuela's "petroleum diplomacy" as it bargained with the foreign oil companies and the U.S. government to acquire the entire industry.

Other Countries.   Luis V. Sommi, *Los capitales alemanes en la Argentina: historia de su expansión* (1945), is a detailed description of German investments and business enterprises in Argentina during the nineteenth century and the twentieth until the beginning of World War II. Winthrop R. Wright, *British-Owned Railways in Argentina: Their Effect on the Growth of Economic Nationalism, 1854–1948* (1974), is a solid analytic history of the subject that emphasizes the "convenient reference points" over time for Argentine nationalist groups provided by the British-owned railways.

Thomas Millington, *Debt Politics After Independence: The Funding Conflict in Bolivia* (1992), is a study of bonded foreign investment in Bolivia's earliest year of statehood. Margaret A. Marsh, *The Bankers in Bolivia: A Study of American Foreign Investment* (1928), is an accounting of the subject after World War I, not complimentary to U.S. investors.

Peter Evans, *Dependent Development: The Alliance of Multinational, State, and Local Capital in Brazil* (1979), is a good analysis of the complex functioning of Brazil's federal system and the presence of multinational corporations. Elizabeth A. Cobbs, *The Rich Neighbor Policy: Rockefeller and Kaiser in Brazil* (1992), focuses on two prominent entrepreneurs. Nelson Rockefeller saw a complementary relationship between the interests of foreign business enterprise and those of host governments seeking rational national development. Henry Kaiser believed good foreign business practices required sensitivity to the development aspirations of host countries. Cobbs sees Rockefeller and Kaiser as exemplifying "other aspects of the complex relationship of private Americans to Latin American development" than the narrow self-interests of many U.S. corporations in Latin America.

Juan Gabriel Valdés, *Pinochet's Economists: The Chicago School of Economics in Chile* (1995), is authored by an important public figure in Chile's redemocratization. He gives an enlightening accounting of the roles of young Chilean economists trained at the University of Chicago in the pre-Pinochet period who then put in place the neoliberal economic policies in the 1970s during the Pinochet dictatorship. Theodore H. Moran, *Multinational Corporations and the Politics of Dependence: Copper in Chile* (1975), is a thorough political-economic analysis of the critical Chilean commodity. J. Fred Rippy, *The Capitalists and Colombia* (1931), gives historical background of U.S. capital investment in Colombia and then focuses on its role in the U.S. "taking of Panama"—which cleared the way for Wall Street, the petroleum industry, bankers, and other capitalists to operate in Panama. He also deals with the contributions of U.S. capital investment.

Two books by Dominican writers critically examine the role of Gulf + Western in the Dominican Republic: José Israel Cuello H. and Julio E. Peynado, *La Gulf y Western en la reformismo* (1974); and José del Castillo and others, *La Gulf y Western en la Republica Dominicana* (1974).

John D. Martz, *Politics and Petroleum in Ecuador* (1987), addresses the subject during the period from 1972 to 1984 when Ecuador moved from a military regime to a more democratic government. Martz deals expertly with domestic, external state, and multinational corporate factors and the question of the relevance of regime types to public policy and international orientations.

Paul J. Dosal, *Doing Business with the Dictators: A Political History of United Fruit in Guatemala, 1899–1944* (1993), details the company's immense presence and influence in the country. Dosal was the first scholar to obtain access to the company's documents.

ECONOMIC POLICIES AND RELATIONS

See Chapters 3, 4, and 5 for studies related to the general economic policies of the Latin American and Caribbean states and of the external states.

Trade and Investment

Roberto Cortés-Conde and Shane J. Hunt, *The Latin American Economies: Growth and the Export Sector, 1880–1930* (1985), is an informative historical study of Latin Americans seeking to fully integrate into the global economy up to the beginning of the world depression. Set in approximately the same historical period is a study by Max Winkler, *Investments of United States Capital in Latin America* (1928), which provides a great deal of descriptive information. Winkler deals with Latin American economic life and the characteristics of the international investment, with the bulk devoted to foreign investments by countries. A large number of statistical tables are provided. Two classic histories survey British investments and trade, respectively: J. Fred Rippy, *British Investments in*

Latin America, 1822–1949: A Case Study in the Operations of Retarded Regions (1959); and D.C.M. Platt, *Latin America and the British Trade, 1806–1914* (1972). Also of interest is Benjamin Orlove, ed., *The Allure of the Foreign: Imported Goods in Postcolonial Latin America* (1997). Steven C. Topik and Allen Wells, eds., *The Second Conquest of Latin America: Coffee, Henequen, and Oil During the Export Boom, 1850–1930* (1998), focuses on three major commodities in this study of Latin Americans' strategy of export-led economic growth as they first integrated into the world economy. Manuel A. Machado Jr., *Aftosa: A Historical Survey of Foot-and-Mouth Disease and Inter-American Relations* (1969), is a study of the problem of foot-and-mouth disease as an inter-American problem from its origins in Argentina in the 1860s. Machado examines the impact on U.S. trading relationships with Argentina and Mexico and joint efforts to eradicate the disease. Dick Steward, *Trade and Hemisphere: The Good Neighbor Policy and Reciprocal Trade* (1975), deals with the early efforts of President Franklin Roosevelt's secretary of state Cordell Hull in the midst of the world depression.

Donald W. Baerresen, Martin Carnoy, and Joseph Grunwald, *Latin American Trade Patterns* (1965), is a useful statistical source book. The first part is a sixty-six-page descriptive and analytic historical survey of trade patterns and part 2 is 258 pages of trade statistics to 1963, with notes on sources. Mark B. Rosenberg, ed., *The Changing Hemispheric Trade Environment: Opportunities and Obstacles* (1991), analyzes the characteristics of the postcrisis 1980s as Latin Americans were undergoing political and economic transformations toward democracy and liberalized trade.

Manuel R. Agosin, ed., *Direct Foreign Investment in Latin America* (1995), has contributions from eight experts from Chile, Argentina, and Colombia who discuss foreign direct investment in the 1980s and 1990s in their respective countries. Institute for European–Latin American Relations and Inter-American Development Bank, *Foreign Direct Investment in Latin America: Perspectives of the Major Investors* (1998), notes that "the liberalization of investment norms and strengthening of regional integration have helped make Latin America and the Caribbean attractive for direct foreign investment." The study identifies the factors that have drawn investors to the region.

Anthony T. Bryan, ed., *The Caribbean: New Dynamics in Trade and Political Economy* (1994), is concerned with the implications of global changes for the Caribbean countries. Eleven well-known academics and other contributors from the Caribbean and the United States examine external debt and structural adjustment; benefits and risks of trade liberalization, privatization, and foreign investment; public-private sector relations; and the possibilities of the disappearance of trade preferences in Europe and North America. Also of interest are Eva Paus, ed., *Struggle Against Dependence: Nontraditional Export Growth in Central America and the Caribbean* (1988); and Irma Tirado de Alonso, ed., *Trade Issues in the Caribbean* (1992).

External Debt

The Latin American states have a long history of foreign debt accumulation and associated problems. Two sophisticated comprehensive studies deal with the origins and development of the Latin American foreign debt problem. Carlos Marichal, *A Century of Debt Crisis in Latin America: From Independence to the Great Depression, 1820–1930* (1989), is a political-economic history that traces the contracting and default of Latin American international debt and the complex relations between borrowers and lenders. Marichal finds the major causes of the problems to be cycles in international capital markets and Latin American diversion of resources from investment to consumption. Vinod K. Aggarwal, *Debt Games: Strategic Interaction in International Debt Rescheduling* (1996), examines Latin American external debt negotiations from the 1820s to the 1990s. Aggarwal constructs a "strategic interaction model" (a kind of "situational theory") to facilitate comparative empirical analysis of sixty-one case studies of the strategies employed by borrowers and lenders. He deals with decisions regarding economic and debt adjustments and interventions into the negotiating processes by governments and intergovernmental organizations. Frank Griffith Dawson, *The First Latin American Debt Crisis: The City of London and the 1822–25 Loan Bubble* (1990), addresses the investment boom in the earliest days of Latin American independence. British private investors funded large amounts of the new states' bonds, most of which were defaulted by 1830.

The external debt difficulties of the 1980s and the aftermath generated a very large literature. Academic interest in foreign debt issues waned considerably after the crisis years. A number of studies addressed the problems in broad terms. Antonio Jorge and Jorge Salazar-Carrillo, eds., *The Latin American Debt* (1992), include contributions by thirteen analysts on general issues of Latin American debt, foreign investment, and economic development; and proposals for and issues of debt relief. Ernest J. Oliveri, *Latin American Debt and the Politics of International Finance* (1992), discusses the origins and characteristics of the 1980s debt crisis, commercial banks as political actors, and attempts at regime building in international finance. Oliveri examines the cases of the three most indebted countries (Mexico, Brazil, and Argentina), and the matter of adjusting formal and informal management rules and techniques to the evolving systemic stresses produced by the crisis. Miguel S. Wionczek, ed., in collaboration with Luciano Tomassini, *Politics and Economics of External Debt Crisis: The Latin American Experience* (1985), is a collection of analyses from the borrowing countries' perspectives, which the contributors say are badly underrepresented in the literature. Special attention is devoted to Argentina, Brazil, Mexico, Venezuela, Chile, Peru, and Central America. Pedro-Pablo Kuczynski Godard, *Latin American Debt* (1988), is authored by an international investment banker and former Peruvian cabinet minister. He sees the debt problem as a function of the failures of the state and state-run enterprise. He advocates internal economic reforms and a strategy of attracting foreign investment over increased borrowing.

On Latin American economic adjustment policies and debt renegotiations with creditors, see Andres Bianchi, Robert Devlin, and Joseph Ramos, *External Debt in Latin America: Adjustment Policies and Renegotiation* (1985); two studies by the Economic Commission for Latin America and the Caribbean—*External Debt in Latin America: Adjustment Policies and Renegotiation* (1985); and *Debt, Adjustment, and Renegotiation in Latin America: Orthodox and Alternative Approaches* (1986); Rosemary Thorp and Laurence Whitehead, eds., *Latin American Debt and the Adjustment Crisis* (1987); Roberto Bouzas, ed., *Entre la heterodoxia y el ajuste: negociaciones financieras externas de América Latina (1982–1987)* (1988); Philip L. Brock, Michael B. Connolly, and Claudio González-

Vega, eds., *Latin American Debt and Adjustment: External Shocks and Macroeconomic Policies* (1989); and John Williamson, ed., *Latin American Adjustment: How Much Has Happened?* (1990).

Robert Grosse edited two books with fairly technical economic analyses of the debt problem. Contributors to *Private Sector Solutions to the Latin American Debt Problem* (1992) emphasize that "private firms and lending banks wanted simply to protect their capital, to benefit from reduced-value debt instruments, and to move borrowers into situations of renewed credit-worthiness." *Government Responses to the Latin American Debt Problem* (1995) has treatments of five Latin American borrowing countries (Chile, Brazil, Peru, Bolivia, and Mexico) and the Brady plans for commercial debt relief. It also compares the factors indicating the return to creditworthiness of ten borrowing countries. See also Robert Devlin, *Debt and Crisis in Latin America: The Supply Side of the Story* (1989).

A number of studies approached the phenomena in terms of developmental concepts. William L. Canak, ed., *Lost Promises: Debt, Austerity, and Development in Latin America* (1989), is a broad-ranging systematic comparative analysis of the political and social impact of economic austerity programs in the 1980s and the economic dislocations they generated. See also Richard E. Feinberg and Ricardo Ffrench-Davis, eds., *Development and External Debt in Latin America: Bases for a New Consensus* (1988); Jeffrey A. Frieden, *Debt, Development, and Democracy: Modern Political Economy and Latin America, 1965–1985* (1992); and August Blake Friscia and Charles J.L.T. Kovaks, *Beyond the Lost Decade: Debt and Development in Latin America* (1993). Barbara Stallings and Robert Kaufman, eds., *Debt and Democracy in Latin America* (1989), contains essays authored by prominent analysts who address the puzzle of Latin American democratization paralleling deeply adverse economic conditions. They describe and analyze the historical precedents, current economic and political variables, and present case studies of Mexico, Brazil, Costa Rica, Peru, Chile, Argentina, and Brazil. Scott MacDonald, Jane Hughes, and Uwe Bott, eds., *Latin American Debt in the 1990s: Lessons from the Past and Forecasts* (1991), has nine contributions that analyze the relationship of the problems of external debt to Latin American democratization. They highlight the roles of creditor and debtor governments, commercial banks, and international financial institutions.

ENVIRONMENTAL ISSUES

Sustainable development is the balance between economic growth and environmental protection. This book focuses on the sustainable development conundrum of the parallel need for economic growth and environmental protection and the problems with their compatibility. Joseph S. Tulchin, ed., with Andrew Rudman, *Economic Development and Environmental Protection in Latin America* (1991), is a collection of nineteen contributions that discuss clearly but too briefly environmental theory and practice. They emphasize the need to adopt principles of sustainable development and make specific proposals for state policies and for international institutional roles. Heraldo Munoz, ed., *Environment and Diplomacy in the Americas* (1992), is a useful and convenient reference work. It contains four brief essays on environmental aspects of inter-American relations and development policies, with 116 pages of official documents appended. Heraldo Muñoz and Robin L. Rosenberg, eds., *Difficult Liaison: Trade and Environment in the Americas* (1993), is a product of the Organization of American States Seminar on International Trade and the Environment. Seventeen participants analyze, in papers and commentaries, questions of international trade and environmental protection in contexts of interdependent global economy, problems of natural resources, certain Latin American structures and processes, and other institutional and juridical aspects. Gordon J. MacDonald, Daniel L. Nielson, and Marc A. Stern, eds., *Latin American Environmental Policy in International Perspective* (1996), present essays by fourteen experts from the United States, Latin America, Europe, and Africa who provide considerable information and realistic evaluations of inter-American environmental policy in terms of sustainable development. They assess the impact of Latin American democratization, free trade, multilateral development banks, and nongovernmental organizations.

From the left, Daniel Faber, *Environment Under Fire: Imperialism and the Ecological Crisis in Central America* (1993), sees the matter in terms of neoimperialist economic dependency. On the other hand, contributors to Michael Painter and William H. Durham, eds., *The Social Causes of Environmental Destruction in Latin America* (1994), emphasize origins of problems in domestic phenomena.

POLITICAL SYSTEMS AND
INTERNATIONAL PROCESSES

This section deals with regime types and their significance for regional and external state foreign policies and international processes. Democracy and human rights involve matters that raise questions about both efforts to achieve or maintain representative democracy and respect for human rights and the corollary matters of dealing with dictatorship, military regimes, military coups d'état, and violations of human rights. The latter consideration extends the subject to questions of international military relations, often understood in terms of regime types. A third area in the general category of regime types is that of social revolutionary political regimes, which also give rise to international issues and actions (as in Mexico after about 1910, Cuba after 1959, and Nicaragua from 1979 to 1990).

As a general matter, Michael J. Kryzanek, *Leaders, Leadership, and U.S. Policy in Latin America* (1992), is an innovative treatment of U.S. policy with several categories of Latin American leaders and political regimes. He provides good definitional and conceptual background and engages in case studies of individual leaders' and regimes' positions on the issues of drugs, debt, trade, development, and security.

Democracy and Human Rights

Two studies examine the Reagan administration's policies in the 1980s and come to similar conclusions. John A. Booth and Mitchell A. Seligson, eds., *Elections and Democracy in Central America* (1989), is an instructive evaluation by eight scholars of the official rhetoric about U.S. responsibility for bringing democracy to El Salvador, Guatemala, and Honduras, in contrast to Communist Nicaragua's "totalitarian dungeon." They conclude, to the contrary, that despite elections held under U.S. tutelage, those states "cannot by a reasonable standard be called democratic." Thomas H. Carothers, *In the Name of Democracy: U.S. Policy Toward Latin America in the Reagan Years* (1991), is a thoughtful assessment by a lawyer who served in several capacities in the Reagan administration. He is struck by the degree to which promoting democracy had penetrated

Reagan's policy, but startled by how little many U.S. officials knew about Latin American development and past U.S. efforts to influence it, resulting in simplistic formulas derived solely from U.S. experience. Carothers concludes that the resurgence of Latin American democracy in most cases is the result of internal factors rather than U.S. policy, which sometimes played positive roles but also caused harm. Pressures from Congress and other foreign policy agents concerned with human rights forced moderation of the administration's cold war instincts. Robert A. Pastor, ed., *Democracy in the Americas: Stopping the Pendulum* (1989), is a collection of analyses by prominent scholars on the definition and meaning of democracy and the endogenous and exogenous factors in its establishment, development, and maintenance. Juan Somavía, ed., *Cooperación política regional para la democracia* (1986), grew out of a seminar in Montevideo sponsored by the Instituto Latinoamericano de Estudios Transnacionales and the Uruguayan Ministry of Foreign Relations. Among the sixteen contributors are government officials, scholars, and analysts from international governmental organizations who address the question of what Latin Americans can jointly accomplish to strengthen democracy. They specifically address matters of security, peace, disarmament, and external debt. Frank Brodhead and Edward S. Herman, *Demonstration Elections: U.S.-Staged Elections in the Dominican Republic, Vietnam, and El Salvador* (1984), are critical of the process. A later examination of the same topic, Kevin J. Middlebrook, ed., *Electoral Observation and Democratic Transitions in Latin America* (1998), explores the impact of electoral observation on six Latin American democratic transitions and what future direction the technique should take. Howard J. Wiarda, *The Democratic Revolution in Latin America: History, Politics, and U.S. Policy* (1990), provides background on Latin American political traditions and makes numerous recommendations for the new democratic possibilities of U.S. policy toward Latin America. He sees Latin American and U.S. interests as harmonious on this matter. Augusto Varas, ed., *Jaque de la democracia: orden internacional y violencia política en América Latina* (1990), is an excellent multidisciplinary analyses by eighteen contributors. They investigate the international and domestic challenges to Latin American democracy posed by political violence on the part of narcotraffickers, terrorists, and government (especially military) repression. Juan

Carlos Zarate, *Forging Democracy: A Comparative Study of the Effects of U.S. Foreign Policy on Central American Democratization* (1994), says that "regional hegemons can and do determine the political evolutions of countries within their respective spheres of influence." Zarate analyzes U.S. influence on regime formation since the late 1940s in Costa Rica, Guatemala, and Nicaragua.

Writings in the post–cold war period have tended to take reflective long-term perspectives. Abraham F. Lowenthal, ed., *Exporting Democracy: The United States and Latin America* (1991), includes fifteen U.S., Latin American, and European scholars who examine U.S. motives behind attempts to promote Latin American democracy, and the instruments employed and the final consequences. They deal with periods of intense efforts (1912–1932, 1944–1954, the 1960s, and the 1980s); provide case studies of Argentina, Chile, the Dominican Republic, Mexico, and Nicaragua; and the roles of U.S. business and organized labor. The general conclusion is that the U.S. efforts to export democracy have had little enduring success and have often been counterproductive. Tom Farer, ed., *Beyond Sovereignty: Collectively Defending Democracy in the Americas* (1996), is an important book, with seventeen distinguished experts tackling profound and complex issues. Farer's lively introduction furnishes a clear and insightful framework, and subsequent chapters provide strong theoretical and empirical bases with high-quality scholarship. Laurence Whitehead, ed., *The International Dimensions of Democratization: Europe and the Americas* (1996), includes seven chapters dealing with the Americas and three more providing analytic context (four of them treat democratization in Europe). In the Americas-specific chapters, leading scholars address themes related to Caribbean democracy, U.S. human rights policy and "political development assistance," the activities of the international political parties association, and international dimensions of democratic development in Brazil and Chile. Felipe Aguero and Jeffrey Stark, eds., *Fault Lines of Democratic Governance in the Americas* (1997), includes chapters on globalization and democracy, security and organized force in the hemisphere, and civil-military relations. Jorge I. Domínguez, ed., *Democratic Politics in Latin America and the Caribbean* (1998), is a compilation of previously published chapters written by Domínguez for other books, which include substantial treatment of international matters.

Lars Schoultz, *Human Rights and United States Policy Toward Latin America* (1981), is a classic, essential work. Schoultz applies a political process model to the analysis of such empirical matters as integrating human rights considerations into policy action, public opinion, interest group activity, President Carter's policies, and bureaucratic politics within the State Department. He emphasizes U.S. policymakers' core concerns with the causes of Latin American instability and the consequences for U.S. security interests. Margaret E. Crahan, ed., *Human Rights and Basic Needs in the Americas* (1982), and Jesuit scholars Alfred Henelly and John Langan, eds., *Human Rights in the Americas: The Struggle for Consensus* (1982), are companion volumes growing out of a lengthy interdisciplinary project sponsored by Woodstock Theological Center at Georgetown University and involving nineteen prominent scholars. They broaden their perspective by examining "the larger picture of what such rights mean to people in different historical, cultural, economic circumstances" in various parts of the world. The Henelly and Langan collection also defines human rights to go beyond freedom from state torture and murder to include basic matters of existence, such as rights to food, health, and work—which, although insightful and humane, tends to fragment some of the analysis. Certain essays in the Crahan compilation represent the Roman Catholic, classic liberal, and Marxist traditions. Alfred Glenn Mower Jr., *Regional Human Rights: A Comparative Study of the West European and Inter-American Systems* (1991), presents a useful comparative conceptual-policy-institutional analysis. Edward L. Cleary, *The Struggle of Human Rights in Latin America* (1997), is a concise survey of the origins, evolution, and consequences of human rights movements in Latin America and their international implications.

On the protection of human rights as a principle and practice of the Inter-American System, see Cecilia Medina Quiroga, *The Battle of Human Rights: Gross, Systematic Violations and the Inter-American System* (1988); Thomas Buergenthal, Robert Norris, and Dinah Shelton, *Protecting Human Rights in the Americas: Selected Problems* (4 eds., 1973–1995); and Alfred Glenn Mower Jr., *Regional Human Rights: A Comparative Study of the West European and Inter-American Systems* (1991). Rafael Nieto-Navia, *Introducción al sistema interamericano de protección a los derechos humanos* (1993), is by a Colombian professor of international law and former president of Inter-American Court of Human Rights. The book is a good textbook presentation from a historical-institutional-juridical-philosophical perspective. When he was president of the court, Nieto-Navia edited *El corte y el sistema interamericanos de derechos humanos* (1994), a lengthy and useful reference work on the court's functions, structure, and procedures.

See also Chapter 7, the sections on Latin American peace processes and on Central American conflict and peace, including citations on peacemaking and democratization.

Armed Forces, Military Rule, and Military Assistance

Studies have addressed the relationship of Latin American armed forces and military regimes to international politics. Frederick M. Nunn has authored two important companion volumes—*Yesterday's Soldiers: European Military Professionalism in South America, 1890–1940* (1983) and *The Time of the Generals: Latin American Professional Militarism in World Perspective* (1992). The first surveys the period from when the armies of Argentina, Brazil, Chile, and Peru invited German or French missions to guide their professional modernization. The European officers inculcated their own professional ideals and values, and the South Americans transformed professionalism into militarism. The second book refers primarily to the military regimes in the same four South American states from 1964 to 1989, which Nunn says was "the most clearly defined era of military rule and influence in the history of Latin America." The South American officers retained their French and German professional legacy; by and large, they placed little value on U.S. military traditions or post–World War II experience. Edwin Lieuwen, *Arms and Politics in Latin America* (2 eds., 1960, 1961), is a classic, pioneering study. The first part examines Latin America's armed forces as such, and the second part addresses the military aspects of U.S. policies in the region. Lieuwen sees direct linkages between U.S. policies and the frequent role of the Latin American armed forces as governors or direct arbiters of domestic politics. See also Augusto Varas, *Militarization and the International Arms Race in Latin America* (1985).

Brian Loveman and Thomas M. Davies Jr., eds., *The Politics of Antipolitics: The Military in Latin America* (3 eds., 1978–1997), is a major collection by an impressive array of specialists. In twenty-eight chapters, the contributors examine the historical origins and persistence of military antipolitics (with and without military rule) and the relationship to outside military establishments. They highlight the period from 1965 to 1995 and what they tend to see as "illusory transitions to democracy." Six case studies are presented—of Argentina, Brazil, Chile, Peru, El Salvador, and Guatemala. National security and its changing definition is a reoccurring theme. Brian Loveman, *Por la patria: Politics and the Armed Forces in Latin America* (1999), is a comprehensive survey of the complex matter of civil-military relations in the different Latin American states. He addresses the history since colonial times of the influence of Spanish, German, French, and U.S. military men on the professional-political thinking of their Latin American counterparts. Loveman is skeptical of the depth of change within the armed forces in their relations with civilian authorities, as they undertake new roles in the post–cold war era. Richard L. Millett and Michael Gold-Biss, eds., *Beyond Praetorianism: The Latin American Military in Transition* (1996), deals with civil-military developments as the Latin American states in the 1980s moved away from military regimes and personalist dictatorships to more open constitutional governments. The authors present a mixed picture. Samuel Fitch, *The Armed Forces and Democracy in Latin America* (1998), is a thorough and nuanced investigation of the significant reduction of military influence in many Latin American states alongside their continuing influence, institutional autonomy, and resistance to subordination to democratic civilian authority. Fitch focuses on the revealing cases of Argentina, Ecuador, Brazil, Chile, Guatemala, Honduras, Peru, and Uruguay.

U.S. assistance programs and their motives and consequences have received due scholarly attention. Don L. Etchison, *The United States and Militarism in Central America* (1975), is a concise statement of how U.S. aid strengthens the armed forces relations to the civilian ruling classes. Horacio Luis Veneroni, *Estados Unidos y las fuerzas armadas de América Latina* (1971), deals critically with U.S. military policies and programs. Willard F. Barber and C. Neale Ronning, *Internal Security and Military Power: Counterinsurgency and Civic Action in Latin America* (1966), is an insightful work, highly critical of U.S. policy thinking and actions. Jan Knippers Black, *Sentinels of Empire: The United States and Latin American Militarism*, sees irony and tragedy in the professed U.S. policy goal of Latin American stability. That policy has always frustrated or subverted revolutionary movements in client states in favor of the illusory stability provided by militarism. Martha K. Huggins, *Political Policing: The United States and Latin America* (1998), surveys U.S. police training in Latin America from the efforts during U.S. Caribbean interventions by President Woodrow Wilson through cold war assistance for counterinsurgency measures. Huggins, writing with "patriotic outrage," sees a persistent history of U.S. tolerance for Latin American police torture and death squads. Lars Schoultz, William C. Smith, and Augusto Varas, eds., *Security, Democracy, and Development in U.S.–Latin American Relations* (1994), brings together twelve scholars from Latin America and the United States who examine various critical post–cold war issues in terms of the titled concepts. They emphasize broad aspects of inter-American military relations and arms control.

For a detailed conceptual-empirical treatment of inter-American military cooperation, see John Child, *Unequal Alliance: The Inter-American Military System 1938–1978* (1980). Stetson Conn and Byron Fairchild, *The Western Hemisphere: The Framework of Hemispheric Defense* and *Guarding the United States and Its Outposts* (1960), are authoritative and important official histories on the activities of the U.S. Army in Latin America during World War II. They document in detail and analyze general military relations with Latin America, paying special attention to Brazil and Mexico.

Bishara Bahbah, *Israel and Latin America: The Military Connection* (1986), provides a dispassionate analysis of Israel's extensive military connection with Latin America as a major provider of weapons and equipment in the 1970s and 1980s, and its importance for the Israeli economy and arms industry. At the same time Bahbah is highly critical of Israeli policy in terms of the moral-ethical dilemmas involved.

Revolutionary Movements

General Treatments.   Of particular interest is the superb contribution by Cole Blasier, *The Hovering Giant: U.S. Responses to Revolutionary*

Change in Latin America (2 eds., 1976, 1985). Blasier addresses U.S. responses to Latin American revolution in the twentieth century and provides some guidelines for U.S. policymakers in future situations. The first edition ranged from the Mexican Revolution of 1910 to the Dominican civil war in 1965, the Velasco reformist military regime in Peru, and the Marxist Allende government in Chile. The second edition (1985) extended the scope to include Carter's and Reagan's responses to situations in Cuba, Grenada, Nicaragua, El Salvador, and Guatemala. Blasier concludes that perceived threats (including ideological) from outsiders explains U.S. policy toward revolutionary movements and governments. He laments that U.S. policymakers have learned so little from their experience and continue patterns of action that do not serve U.S. interests. Martin C. Needler, *The United States and the Latin American Revolution* (1969), is a concise, insightful, and critical treatment of U.S. policies during the Kennedy and Johnson presidencies. He urges a dramatic change in U.S. policies from opposing revolutionary movements to working with them. Stephen G. Rabe, *The Most Dangerous Area in the World: John F. Kennedy Confronts Communist Revolution in Latin America* (1999), argues that Kennedy's "obsession with the Cold War mutilated his good intentions toward the southern hemisphere during the pivotal period of U.S. policies in the 1960s." Robert Wesson, ed., *Communism in Central America and the Caribbean* (1982), blames U.S. support for the status quo and unsavory governments for the almost inevitable anti-Americanism of Caribbean recruits of radical movements. Wesson examines the regional influence of Cuba and the Soviet Union, and provides case studies of Nicaragua, El Salvador, Guatemala, Costa Rica, Honduras, Panama, Jamaica, the island states of the Eastern Caribbean, and Guyana.

Jorge G. Castañeda, *Utopia Unarmed: The Latin American Left After the Cold War* (1993), is a normative evaluation of the condition of the Latin American left (including former insurgents) in the post–cold war world. Castañeda argues that with the failure of the Cuban model, the dissolution of the Soviet Union, and the sharp decline of world communism, the Latin American left has the opportunity to escape the Communist label—as well as move beyond simply blaming the United States for the region's problems. He urges adoption of a unified commitment to representative democracy and principles of human rights, as well as the nurture of their transnational networks.

International Communism.   Only certain general works on the subject are cited in this section. See also Chapter 3 on Cuba and Nicaragua; Chapter 4 on the Soviet Union; and Chapter 7 on Central American conflict and peace.

The Spanish-Mexican journalist and scholar, Víctor Alba, makes two provocative contributions. *Esquema histórico del communismo en Iberoamérica* (3 eds., 1954–1960), is about Latin American Communist parties and their linkages to both labor movements and to dictatorships that adopt anti–United States orientations. *Historia del frente popular: análisis de una táctica política* (1959), examines the Soviet attempt to use popular front coalition of parties of the left to further the activities of the international Communist movement. Manuel Caballero, *Latin America and the Comintern 1919–1943* (1986), is an important comparative analysis by a Venezuelan scholar on the historical and theoretical development and actions of the Leninist Third (Communist) International (1919–1943) and its affiliated Latin American Communist parties. Caballero says that Latin America was on the periphery of the world revolution and relegated to a supporting role. Donald L. Herman, *The Comintern in Mexico* (1974), is a solid examination of the activities of the Communist International (Comintern) in Mexico. Herman deals with the origins of the Mexican Communist Movement, the hesitant appearance of the Comintern in Latin America, and the evolution to the Popular Front era. Revolutionary Mexico would have seemed to provide favorable conditions for Communist advances, but the uninformed and inept Comintern agents were themselves major impediments. Two book by Robert J. Alexander, a careful scholar and "old Social Democrat," provide summary overviews that usefully fill information gaps. *Communism in Latin America* (1957) deals with the history of communism in Latin America and the conditions favoring its rise in the region; the roles of the Comintern and the Soviet Union; and Latin American Communist leaders and Communists in Latin American labor movements. Most of the states receive some individual attention. In *Trotskyism in Latin America* (1973), Alexander characterizes Trotskyism as "a small but persistent force in Latin American left-wing politics for more than forty years," which he presents as a significant movement in Chile, Cuba, Bolivia, and Mexico. Alexander recognizes that in general Trotskyism has played a minor role in Latin American politics. Rodney Arismendi, *Lenín, la revolución y América Latina* (1970), a well-known Uruguayan Communist, offers a philosophical discourse on the significance of Lenin's thought to the Latin American revolution. Donald L. Herman, ed., *The Communist Tide in Latin America* (1973), contains four essays that do not give evidence for a "tide" but do provide very good scholarly descriptions of the elements of Communist activities in Latin America.

Theodore Draper, *Castroism: Theory and Practice* (1965), is a serious analysis of the complex nature of Castroism and its special and somewhat unorthodox position in the international Communist movement. Draper argues that Castroism is more a matter of evolving pragmatic political tactics than of growing out of an ideological framework. Robert K. Furtak, *Kuba und der Weltkommunismus* (1967) is a careful study of the Castro Revolution. Furtak says the revolution made Cuba a center of world communism, along with the Soviet Union, China, and Yugoslavia, by offering a distinct revolutionary path. D. Bruce Jackson, *Castro, the Kremlin, and Communism in Latin America* (1969), is an authoritative analysis of Latin American communism in the 1960s. Jackson highlights the importance of the Tricontinental Conference of January 1966 and the subsequent tension between Castroites and old-line Communists. William Ratliff, *Castroism and Communism in Latin America, 1959–1976* (1976), defines international Marxism-Leninism in the Soviet Union, the People's Republic of China, and Cuba. Ratliff evaluates the Sino-Soviet dispute in the 1960s and the pro-Soviet and pro-Chinese organizations in Latin America. He also examines Castroism and its relation to rural and urban guerrilla warfare.

Karl M. Schmitt, *Communism in Mexico: A Study in Political Frustration* (1965), is one of the important sources for understanding the subject. It is a thorough history of the Mexican Communist movement, which involved several party organizations. Schmitt emphasizes Mexican organizations and politics but pays due attention to Communist front organizations and the role of the Comintern—as well as to U.S. misunderstanding of the Mexican dynamics involved. Manuel Márques Fuentes and Octavio Rodríguez Araujo, *El Partido Comunista Mexicana: en el periodo de la Internacional Comunista, 1919–1943* (2 eds., 1973, 1981).

SOME TRANSNATIONAL NETWORKS
The Roman Catholic Church

The Holy See, the central focus of Roman Catholic transnational activities, is itself a sovereign state in the international system. Numerous general works dealing with the Roman Catholic Church in Latin America include a great deal of transnational content. The more recent works tend to be cast in terms of the church in changing times, much of which involves transnational issues.

Pilar García Jordán, *Iglesia y poser en Perú contemporaneo, 1821–1919* (1991), provides information on and analysis of nineteenth-century postindependence Church-State turbulence and turn-of-the-century accommodations, all of which involved the Holy See. Three books are original in concept, thorough in coverage, and insightful in analysis— William V. D'Antonio and Frederick B. Pike, eds., *Religion, Revolution, and Reform: New Forces for Change in Latin America* (1964); Henry A. Lansberger, *Church and Social Change in Latin America* (1970); and Hugo Latorre Cabal, *The Revolution of the Latin American Church* (1978). Edward L. Cleary, *Crisis and Change: The Church in Latin America Today* (1985), is a concise and informative survey of the key elements of Latin American religious thought (which inherently are transnational in their nature and application), with a separate chapter on liberation theory (see below). Daniel H. Levine, ed., *Churches and Politics in Latin America* (1986), has contributions by scholars and clergy who focus on the idea of a church traditionally dedicated to the political and social status quo undergoing significant changes. It includes chapters on the Christian left, activist clergy, national security, the transregional Conference of Latin American Bishops (CELAM), human rights, and Marxism. Edward L. Cleary and Hannah Stewart-Gambino, eds., *Conflict and Competition: The Latin American Church in a Changing Environment* (1992) also address numerous transnational aspects of church life. Irish historian Dermot Keogh, ed., *Church and Politics in Latin America* (1990), brings together contributors for helpful analyses that provide (1) an overview of the contemporary church in transnational context, including relations with the Vatican; (2) an examination of the church's responses to political violence; (3) address the issue of politics and the Gospel; and (4) explore the church's stance on revolutionary and counter-revolutionary movements. Edward A. Lynch, *Religion and Politics in Latin America* (1991), addresses liberation theology and the Christian Democratic parties.

Liberation theology is a transnational issue, especially within the church itself. It is also related to matters of political ideology, dependency theory, and international politics. The literature of and on liberation theology is large. Gustavo Gutiérrez, *A Theology of Liberation: History, Politics, and Salvation* (1973), is the classic theological work, by a priest who was a leader among the earliest thinkers on the subject. For works by other prominent Latin American liberation theologians, see Leonardo Boff, Clodovis Boff, Enrique Dussell, Gustavo Gutiérrez, Juan Luis Segundo, and Jon Sobrino; Boff (1985) and Cardenal (1976–1982) are of particular interest. Clodovis Boff and Leonardo Boff, *Liberation Theology: From Confrontation to Dialogue* (1986), is a brief summary and defense by Brazilian brothers who are both priests and leaders of the movement. Enrique Dussell, *A History of the Church in Latin America: Colonialism to Liberation (1492–1979)* (1981), is by a prominent liberation theologian. Michael R. Candelaria, *Popular Religion and Liberation: The Dilemma of Liberation Theology* (1990), examines issues in the debate over whether the theology has an emancipatory or alienating character. The book focuses on two prominent Latin American theologians who take opposite positions. Juan Carlos Scannone of Argentina defends liberation theology, whereas Juan Luis Segundo of Uruguay looks forward to its demise.

Philip Berryman, *Liberation Theology: Essential Facts About the Revolutionary Religious Movement in Latin America and Beyond* (1987), is an informative and sympathetic treatment of liberation theology by a U.S. priest. Paul E. Sigmund, *Liberation Theology at the Crossroads: Democracy or Revolution?* (1990), detects changes in Liberation Theology over the past twenty years. He sees movement from an uncritical borrowing of Marxism and preoccupation with socialism to a recognition that "the poor will not be liberated by cataclysmic changes but by organizational efforts." Sigmund finds Marxism and dependency theory important elements but much more nuanced. As a result of experience with brutal military regimes, he sees more acceptance of the legitimacy of other possibilities. David Batstone, Eduardo Mendieta, Lois Ann Lorentzen, and Dwight N. Hopkins, eds., *Liberation Theologies, Postmodernity and the Americas* (1997), argues that liberation theologies over the past three decades had irrevocably altered religious thinking and practice throughout the Americas.

Richard L. Rubenstein and John K. Roth, eds., *The Politics of Latin American Liberation Theology: The Challenge to U.S. Public Policy* (1988), is one of the few studies to address liberation theology as a matter of U.S. foreign policy, inspired by the Reagan administration's hostile reaction to it. The contributors address the subject in the context of Latin America's economic and social problems and issues.

Protestant Churches

Latin American societies have since the 1960s experienced the phenomenal growth of Protestant, in particular Pentecostal, movements. David Martin, *Tongues of Fire: The Explosion of Protestantism in Latin America* (1990), is a sociological-historical study of the subject. It focuses on the rise of evangelical Protestantism as a major cultural and political phenomenon. Martin says it has taken root in Latin America, especially among the poor, because of the collapse of the linkages among faith, community, and politics, and because it provides an empowering religion for poor. Martin sees the possibility of the marginalization of both progressive Catholicism and mainstream Protestantism. David Stoll, *Is Latin America Turning Protestant? The Politics of Evangelical Growth* (1990), focuses on the three cases of Nicaragua, Guatemala, and Ecuador. Stoll is candid about the negative aspects of evangelical Protestantism. Virginia Garrard-Burnett and David Stoll, eds., *Rethinking Protestantism in Latin America* (1993), is edited by two leading experts on the subject. The contributors challenge certain assumptions and stereotypes about fundamentalist Protestantism in Latin America, without necessarily defending the movement. Pentecostalism receives the most attention. The analysis examines the religious, social, and political elements and consequences. Edward L. Cleary and Hannah Stewart-Gambino, eds., *Power, Politics, and Pentecostals in Latin America* (1997), is a collection of clearly stated and well-documented examinations of numerous issues related to the rapid growth of Pentecostalism in Latin America and the political and social as well as religious consequences. Included are case studies of Brazil, Chile, Guatemala, and Venezuela.

Subnational Associations

Transnational political parties and labor movements and other subnational actors in domestic political systems with transnational connections are important yet neglected as subjects of academic research. Transnational political parties—most prominently the European-based parties organized with their Latin American and other regional counterparts in the Socialist International and the Christian Democratic World Union—have quickened their operations since the mid-1970s and are especially active as of the late 1980s. A definitive work, however, remains to be written. The Comintern and certain Communist parties in Latin America and their relations to the Soviet Union are cited above as part of the international Communist movement.

Felicity Williams, *La Internacional Socialista y América Latina: Una Visión Crítica* (1984), is an informative treatment of the relationship of the Socialist International (SI) to Latin America. Williams is sympathetic to social democracy and its opposition to U.S. imperialism in Latin America. Carlos Morales Abarzua, *La Internacional Socialista: America Latina y el Caribe* (1986), analyzes the SI and its activities in Latin America and the Caribbean (with special attention to Chile). The author was a prominent member of the Chilean Unidad Popular during the government of Salvador Allende and was subsequently imprisoned by the military regime. He issues a call for action to support the struggle for socialism and democracy in the region.

The literature on the subject of international labor organizations in Latin America is sparse, despite their large number and importance. Philip S. Foner, *U.S. Labor Movement and Latin America: A History of Workers' Response to Intervention* (1962), is a thoroughly researched and documented Marxist analysis, primarily designed to be a documentary record. It begins with the Mexican–United States war, proceeds through the U.S. war with Spain and the Mexican Revolution, and ends with the founding of the Pan-American Foundation of Labor. Gregg Andrews,

"Shoulder to Shoulder?" The American Federation of Labor, the United States, and the Mexican Revolution, 1910–1924 (1991), investigates how U.S. labor reacted to the Mexican Revolution and with what effect. He concludes that Samuel Gompers and the American Federation of Labor helped shape U.S. policy toward the revolution.

Carrie A. Meyer, *The Economics and Politics of NGOs in Latin America* (1999), is a good, concise analysis of an important but underresearched subject. Meyer deals with the growth and evolution of nongovernmental organizations (NGOs), democratization, entrepreneurship, ecology, biodiversity, and sustainable development. She also analyzes NGO–public sector relations and inter-NGO relations. Mary A. Gardner, *The Inter-American Press Association: Its Fight for Freedom of the Press, 1926–1960* (1967), provides information about the founding, evolution, and activities of the Inter-American Press Association.

Alison Brysk, *From Tribal Village to Global Village: Indian Rights and International Relations in Latin America* (2000), is a remarkable book by an activist and scholar who engages in highly original documentary and field research, multidisciplinary analysis, and normative purpose. Brysk says it is a study of "how even the most marginalized groups in Latin American society can influence broader national and international institutions by projecting ethnic identities into the global stage," made possible by today's globalization (broadly defined beyond simply the economic arena). She integrates case studies from Ecuador (annual mass protests), Mexico (Zapatista guerrillas), Brazil (obstructing dam construction), Nicaragua (Miskito autonomist movement), and Bolivia (attacking armed forces eliminating coca crops).

INTERSOCIETAL PHENOMENA

Cultural Relations

Transnational cultural relations involve a broad array of phenomena having to do with the transmission and diffusion of cultural values. The themes range from amorphous intercivilization theories to more concrete elements, such as news and entertainment media, educational and professional connections, and public and private cultural exchange programs.

The subjects taken up in the following two sections—human migrations and the drug traffic—also involve cultural consequences. These phenomena tend to be analytically difficult, but they are real and important to our understanding of Latin American and Caribbean international relations.

On an abstract level are studies of comparative cultures or cross-cultural relations. Scholars in the United States and Latin America have undertaken such examinations throughout the twentieth century, but during the latter half their frequency declined in favor of more concrete political, economic, and historical subjects. Students were also less persuaded by the underlying concepts of cross-cultural studies and the dangers of speculation and stereotyping. Nevertheless, more recent interpretations have been offered. Samuel Shapiro, ed., *Cultural Factors in Inter-American Relations* (1968), includes twenty-four essays that examine a variety of elements and their importance to intersocietal relations in the Americas. Carlos Rangel, *The Latin Americans: Their Love-Hate Relationship with the United States* (1987), explores the intense and ambivalent psychological reaction of Latin Americans, largely rooted in cultural perceptions. In similar terms, Mariano Baptista Gumucio, *Latinoamericanos y norteamericanos: Cinco siglos de dos culturas* (1987), observes the differences in how Latin Americans and people in the United States tend to view each other through fundamentally different cultural lenses. In the United States, Lawrence Harrison has undertaken a revival of an old theme in two related works: *Underdevelopment Is a State of Mind: The Latin American Case* (1985), and *The Pan-American Dream: Do Latin America's Cultural Values Discourage True Partnership with the United States and Canada?* (1997). In both books Harrison asserts his provocative but hardly novel thesis that the most important factor explaining U.S. and Canadian "progress" and Latin American "underdevelopment" is "the contrast between Anglo-Protestant and Ibero-Catholic culture." Thus his answer to the subtitle question in the second volume is "not necessarily," but a successful process will be very difficult. Many analysts consider the once-common assertion that Latin American political culture is inherently nondemocratic and authoritarian as simplistic and anachronistic.

Harry Bernstein, *Making an Inter-American Mind* (1961), is a history of nineteenth-century intercultural developments. Although dealing specifically with the interaction of individual scientists and scholars from Latin America and the United States, Bernstein deals broadly and insightfully with the diffusion of ideas and knowledge. J. Manuel Espinosa, *Inter-American Beginnings of U.S. Cultural Diplomacy, 1936–1948* (1976), is an official history of the U.S. State Department's increasing "cultural diplomacy" from 1936 through World War II. It provides a great deal of information on policies and programs, with valuable background chapters on the Pan American Movement and on private inter-American cultural exchange activity.

Robert L. Earle and John D. Wirth, eds., *Identities in North America: The Search for Community* (1995), is based on several years of discussion by thirteen scholars from Mexico, the United States, and Canada. The general conclusion is that economic and social phenomena are reinforcing a common North American identity, the North American Free Trade Agreement (NAFTA) notwithstanding. Helen Delpar, *The Enormous Vogue of Things Mexican: Cultural Relations Between the United States and Mexico, 1920–1935* (1992), addresses the cultural side of expanded Mexican-U.S. relations between 1920 and 1935. They engendered increased attention in the United States to cultural "things Mexican," reflected in certain individual and institutional activities and themes. Jaime E. Rodríguez O. and Kathryn Vincent, eds., *Common Border, Uncommon Paths: Race and Culture in U.S.-Mexican Relations* (1997), "focuses on racism and nationalism in U.S.-Mexican relations and examines representations of Mexicans and Americans in literature, culture, and social expression." David J. Weber and Jane M. Rausch, eds., *Where Cultures Meet: Frontiers in Latin American History* (1994), is an interesting and thoughtful study of cultural clash and diffusion in inter–Latin American relations.

Ransford W. Palmer, ed., *U.S.-Caribbean Relations: Their Impact on Peoples and Culture* (1998), has contributions by nine authors on the cultural impacts of economic development, migration, immigration policy, Caribbean perceptions of culture and sovereignty, and religious imperatives in the region. Hopeton S. Dunn, *Globalization, Communications and Caribbean Identity* (1995), examines the global and regional transnational forces at work that are decreasing the importance of state and societal boundaries.

James Schwoch, *The American Radio Industry and Its Latin American Activities, 1900–1939* (1990), is a scholarly exploration from technological, political, social, economic, and cultural perspectives of the growth of radio during the first four decades of the twentieth century, as promoted by both private corporations and the public sector. Howard H. Frederick, *Cuban-American Radio Wars: Ideology in International Telecommunications* (1986), refers to the ideological "radio wars" between the Voice of America and Radio Havana, which had its origins in the early 1960s. Cuban officials were particularly outraged in 1983 with the establishment of Radio Marti within the Voice of America, aimed directly at Cuba. It both coopted the name of the revered nineteenth-century Cuban national hero (who was no admirer of the imperialist United States) and sought to demoralize the Cuban people. The consequence was the first electronic jamming in the hemisphere. Luís Ramiro Beltrán and Elizabeth Fox de Cardona, *Comunicación dominada: Estados Unidos en los medios de América Latina* (1980), condemns the cultural imperialism inherent to the U.S. news and entertainment media.

Movement of People

Movements of people into, out of, and between the countries of Latin America and the Caribbean have been fundamental matters of societal formation and national concern. Outside states have been senders to and recipients of populations, both of which have also been of considerable importance to them. Asian migrants, misnamed Indians by Christopher Columbus, were the first migrants, followed and subdued by Spanish and Portuguese conquerors and colonists. They formed the societies and polities that then received migrants from around the world. That migration, the subject of this section, began in the colonial period.

Black Africans in large numbers were shipped across the Atlantic in the three-century slave trade. Spain and Portugal introduced the largest numbers of slaves, although the British, French, and Dutch colonies also did so to support their plantation economies. The flow of African labor went to all European parts of the Western Hemisphere—to Spanish America, Portuguese Brazil, and the rest of the European Caribbean, as well as north of Florida (including the nonplantation regions of New England

and French Canada. The literature on this Americas-wide phenomenon is very large and increasing in volume. The following is a highly selective listing of recent treatments of a general inter-American nature, which provide several analytic and sometimes provocative perspectives: Robin Blackburn, *The Making of New World Slavery: From the Baroque to the Modern, 1492–1800* (1997), Johannes M. Postma, *The Dutch in the Atlantic Slave Trace, 1600–1815* (1990), Barbara L. Solow, ed., *Slavery and the Rise of the Atlantic System* (1991), Hugh Thomas, *The Slave Trade: The Story of the Atlantic Slave Trade: 1440–1870* (1997), and John Thornton, *Africa and the Africans in the Making of the Atlantic World, 1400–1680* (1992). With specific reference to Latin America, an informative collection of analyses is provided by Darién J. Davis, ed., *Slavery and Beyond: The African Impact on Latin America and the Caribbean* (1995). Benjamin Nuñez, *Dictionary of Afro–Latin American Civilization* (1980), is a comprehensive reference work.

Also of special interest is the Jewish Diaspora in Latin America, addressed in the following general treatments. Martin A. Cohen, ed., *The Jewish Experience in Latin America* (2 vols., 1971), compiled by a professor of Jewish history at the Hebrew Union College in New York, is a carefully selected collection of articles previously published by the American Jewish Historical Society between 1895 and 1966. All but two of them deal with the Spanish and Portuguese American colonial period. Cohen provides a lengthy and informative introduction about the considerable complexities involved. Judith Laikin Elkin and Gilbert W. Merkx, eds., *The Jewish Presence in Latin America* (1988), observes that, as a result of Latin American societies' assumption of adherence to Roman Catholic norms, the Jewish presence was a reticent one—although relatively assertive on issues directly affecting Jewish populations. This element, combined with their small size (in the early 1970s numbering about 1 million in all of Latin America), made Jewish communities nearly invisible. The authors analyze the communities and their intersocietal relations in detail.

Daniel M. Masterson, John F. Bratzel, and Sayaka Funada, *Japanese in Latin America, 1800 to the Present* (1998), is a groundbreaking history that explores the Japanese Diaspora in Latin America beginning in 1880. The authors pay particular attention to Japanese communities in Mexico,

Brazil, Peru, Argentina, Chile, Bolivia, and Paraguay. They examine conditions in Japan that uprooted farmers in the late nineteenth century and the cultural barriers they encountered in the host countries. They were economically well adapted by the beginning of World War II, but during the war suffered suspicion, mistrust, internment, and deportation. The post–World War II experience is summarized.

Researchers have provided studies with reference to general patterns of immigration to Latin American and inter-American immigration and emigration. Magnus Morner and Harold Sims, *Adventurers and Proletarians: The Story of Migrants in Latin America* (1985), is a study prepared for the United Nations Economic and Social Council (UNESCO). It is a brief but highly useful summary, organized chronologically, beginning with colonial antecedents, and analytic throughout. The authors examine the migration in terms of their origin, numbers, occupation, and distribution; the impact of immigration on host countries; and migration from and within Latin America. Max J. Castro edited two recent books that deal thoroughly with current trends and questions: *Trends in International Migration and Immigration Policy in the Americas* (1998), and *Free Markets, Open Societies, Closed Borders? International Migration and Immigration Policy in the Americas* (1998). The expert contributors in both are concerned generally with dramatic increases of immigration into the United States and, in lesser numbers but proportionally high, Canada. The sending countries rely on their emigrants' remittances home, whereas the receiving countries are tightening their immigration policies—at the same time they are promoting hemispheric free trade. The authors analyze this predicament for the individual states and for inter-American relations in terms of politics, economics, and sociology. Kenneth F. Johnson and Miles W. Williams, *Illegal Aliens in the Western Hemisphere: Political and Economic Factors* (1981), is a thorough investigation of strategies for handling illegal aliens in the Western Hemisphere. The authors analyze the matter with regard to Mexican and other migrants to North America, between Colombia and Venezuela, and into Argentina and within the rest of the Southern Cone. C. Neale Ronning, *Diplomatic Asylum: Legal Norms and Political Reality in Latin American Relations* (1957), is a good legal-political analysis of the granting of temporary refuge or protection by a state to political transgressors from another.

Keith W. Yundt, *Latin American States and Political Refugees* (1988), deals with the problem of people who flee a state for political reasons and enter another, for purposes of personal safety. Yundt is concerned with contemporary problems in Central America and the rest of the Caribbean, Mexico, and South America, that have caused mass migration of people seeking territorial asylum. He asks what general (not only legal) obligations outside states have to refugees. He provides a historical background, from League of Nations positions and traditional policies of Latin American states on asylum to the international regime provided by the United Nations and the role of the Inter-American System in it. The late cold war U.S. policies and problems are thoroughly analyzed by Michael S. Teitelbaum, *Latin Migration North: The Problem for U.S. Foreign Policy* (1984), and by contributors to Christopher Mitchell, ed., *Western Hemisphere Immigration and United States Foreign Policy* (1992).

The case of Mexico has been thoroughly studied, especially migration phenomena and issues regarding the United States. Two classic sociological studies are mentioned that provide thorough and enlightening analysis on the earlier historical period: Manuel Gamio, *Mexican Immigration to the United States: A Study of Human Migration and Adjustment* (1930), and Carey McWilliams, *North from Mexico: The Spanish Speaking People of the United States* (1949). A very good historical treatment is provided by Lawrence A. Cardoso, *Mexican Emigration to the United States, 1897–1931* (1980), which deals with the political, economic, and social factors. Among them was the specific matter of Mexican labor migration to the United States, much of it illegal under the circumstances of the times. Mark Reisler, *By the Sweat of Their Brow: Mexican Immigrant Labor in the United States, 1900–1940* (1976), is a scholarly examination of numerous facets of the subject. Reisler examines the costs and benefits for the immigrants themselves, their importance to U.S. agriculture and industry, the stereotyped views in the United States held about them, and issues in the United States over establishing limiting quotas. Reisler says that the story "is largely one of enduring poverty and isolation" of the migrants.

During World War II, with the vital U.S. need for agricultural and railway maintenance labor, the *bracero* ("field hand") program of "temporary guest workers" from Mexico was created, which continued in revised form until terminated in 1964. Thereafter Mexico remained the leading origin of agricultural labor under new U.S. rules for immigrants from all parts of the world. Richard B. Craig, *The Bracero Program: Interest Groups and Foreign Policy* (1971), addresses the domestic political processes in both states and the issues between them during the period from 1942 to 1964, when 4.5 million Mexican nationals contracted for work in the United States. An excellent, more narrowly focused study is by Barbara A. Driscoll, *The Tracks North: The Railroad Bracero Program of World War II* (1997). Arthur F. Corwin, *Immigrants—and Immigrants: Perspectives on Mexican Labor Migration to the United States* (1978), also addresses numerous issues regarding the Mexican labor migration phenomenon in a more general context. On an important related problem for Mexico, see the political-sociological inquiry by Harry E. Cross and James A. Sandos, *Across the Border: Rural Development in Mexico and Recent Migration to the United States* (1981). Jorge A. Bustamante, Clark W. Reynolds, and Raúl A. Hinojosa Ojeda, eds., *U.S.-Mexico Relations: Labor Market Interdependence* (1992), is the result of collaboration by Mexican and U.S. social scientists who address the subject within an analytic framework integrating elements of interdependence, economics security, law, policy, and migration studies. Peter G. Brown and Henry Shue, eds., *The Border that Joins: Mexican Migrants and the U.S. Responsibility* (1983), includes essays by eight contributors who discuss foreign workers, illegal entry, immigration, conditions in Mexico, historical and philosophical aspects, and policy alternatives.

Wayne A. Cornelius, *Immigration, Mexican Development Policy, and the Future of U.S.-Mexican Relations* (1981), is by the director of U.S.-Mexico Studies at the University of California, San Diego. Cornelius places Mexican decisions on emigration in the context of overall relations with the United States. Frank D. Bean, Rodolfo O. de la Garza, Bryan R. Roberts, and Sidney Weintraub, eds., *At the Crossroads: Mexico, Migration, and U.S. Policy* (1997), includes essays by noted scholars in the field who examine the characteristics, impact, and policy issues of Mexican immigration. Timothy J. Dunn, *The Militarization of the U.S.-Mexico Border, 1978–1992: Low-Intensity Conflict Doctrine Comes Home* (1995), deals with immigration and drugs in terms of U.S. security thinking. Sociologist Dunn argues that from 1978 to 1992 U.S. immigration and drug enforcement policies and practices in the border region were increasingly militarized in terms of the Pentagon's doctrine of "low-intensity conflict"; its implementation has often been accompanied by human rights violations. The framework is well conceived, the research thorough, the analysis is often subjective, and some of the assertions about low-intensity conflict doctrine are highly debatable. Alejandro Portes, *Latin Journey: Cuban and Mexican Migrants in the United States* (1985), and Silvia Pedraza-Bailey, *Political and Economic Migrants in America: Cubans and Mexicans* (1985), provide excellent scholarly social science analyses from the migrants' perspectives.

Patricia W. Fagen, *Exiles and Citizens: Spanish Republicans in Mexico* (1973), focuses especially on Spanish exiles considered to be professionals and intellectuals. Fagen examines their personal adjustments to Mexico (which was generally hospitable to them), and their impact on Mexico's development and cultural relations with Spain.

The circum-Caribbean has also been an area of fruitful research. Robert Pastor, ed., *Migration and Development in the Caribbean: The Unexplored Connection* (1985), has analyses by and debate among twenty contributors. They examine Caribbean migration and development in terms of emigration to the United States, asking if it is an effective "escape valve" for population pressures or if it results in the exit of too many talented and skilled people. Ransford W. Palmer, ed., *In Search of a Better Life: Perspectives on Migration from the Caribbean* (1990), brings together ten contributors who examine the factors behind Caribbean migration to the United States, Canada, and Great Britain and how migrants adapt to their new countries. Virginia R. Domínguez, *From Neighbor to Stranger: The Dilemma of the Caribbean Peoples in the United States* (1975), is a sympathetic treatment.

On Central American refugees' two-decade migration to the United States and problems after their arrival, see Elizabeth G. Ferris, *The Central American Refugees* (1987); Beatriz Manz, *Refugees of a Hidden War: The Aftermath of Counterinsurgency in Guatemala* (1988); and Susan Bibler Coutin, *Salvadoran Immigrants' Struggle for U.S. Residency* (2000). Michael L. Coniff, *Black Labor on a White Canal: Panama, 1904–1981* (1985), investigates the West Indians who helped build the canal and then "remained as an unwanted minority and built a defensive subculture to cope with American racism and exploitation, as well as Panamanian chauvinism." Michel S. Laguerre, *Diasporic Citizenship: Haitian Americans in Transnational America* (1998), investigates how Haitian immigrants adapted to U.S. society and their border-crossing practices in order to maintain relations with the homeland. The movement of people from the Dominican Republic to the United States and their transnational communities are described and explained by Eugenia Georges, *The Making of a Transnational Community: Migration, Development, and Cultural Change in the Dominican Republic* (1990); Sherri Grasmuck and Patricia R. Pessar, *Between Two Islands: Dominican International Migration* (1991); and Silvio Torres-Saillant and Ramona Hernández, *The Dominican Americans* (1998). For the policies of Dominican dictator Rafael Trujillo from the latter 1930s through the 1950s see C. Harvey Gardiner, *La política de inmigración del dictador Trujillo* (1979).

The Cuban experience presents a particularly complex case. Juan José Casasús, *La enmigración cubana y la independencia de la patria* (Havana 1953), is one of the most complete histories on the nineteenth century. From the vast literature on events following the Cuban Revolution of 1959 having to do with Cuba's cold war relations with the United States, see David W. Engstrom, *Presidential Decision Making Adrift: The Carter Administration and the Mariel Boatlift* (1997); Richard R. Fagen, Richard A. Brody, and Thomas J. O'Leary, *Cubans in Exile: Disaffection and the Revolution* (1968); two works by Felix Roberto Masud-Piloto, *From Welcomed Exiles to Illegal Immigrants: Cuban Migration to the U.S., 1959–1995* (1996), and *With Open Arms: Cuban Migration to the United States* (2 eds., 1988, 1995); and Mario A. Rivera, *Decision and Structure: U.S. Refugee Policy and the Mariel Crisis* (1991).

Migration to and from South America historically has been related as much to the outside world as to the United States and the other Americas. On Argentina, see George Reid Andrews, *The Afro-Argentines of Buenos Aires, 1800–1900* (1980); Alfredo E. Lattes and Zulema Reccini de Lattes, *Migraciones en la Argentina: estudio de las migraciones internas e internacionales, basado en datos censales, 1869–1960* (1970); Ronald C. Newton, *German Buenos Aires, 1900–1933: Social Change and Cultural Crisis* (1977); Jorge F. Sergi, *Historia de los italianos en la Argentina* (1940); Carl Solberg, *Immigration and Nationalism: Argentina and Chile*

(1970); and Robert Weisbrot, *The Jews of Argentina: From the Inquisition to Perón* (1979). On Brazil, see Cyrus B. Dawsey and James M. Dawsey, eds., *The Confederados: Old South Immigrants in Brazil* (1995); William Clark Griggs, *The Elusive Eden: Frank McMullan's Confederate Colony in Brazil* (1987); and Teiti Suzuki, *The Japanese Immigrant in Brazil* (1969). On Chile, see Carl Solberg, *Immigration and Nationalism: Argentina and Chile* (1970). On Peru, see two studies by C. Harvey Gardiner, *The Japanese and Peru, 1873–1973* (1975), and *Pawns in a Triangle of Hate: The Peruvian Japanese and the United States* (1981); and Watt Stewart, *Chinese Bondage in Peru: A History of the Chinese Coolie in Peru, 1849–1974* (1951). On Paraguay see two books by Joseph Winifield Fretz, *Immigrant Group Settlement in Paraguay: A Study in the Sociology of Colonization* (1962), and *Pilgrims in Paraguay: The Story of Mennonite Colonization in South America* (1953); Paul H. Lewis, *The Politics of Exile: Paraguay's Febrerista Party* (1968); and Norman R. Stewart, *Japanese Colonization in Eastern Paraguay* (1967). On Uruguay, see Saúl Sosnowski and Louise B. Popkin, *Repression, Exile, and Democracy: Uruguayan Culture* (1993).

The Drug Traffic

Drug trafficking has been an inter-American issue since the 1890s. But the problem was not of high priority until the sustained expansion of the "narcotraffic" beginning in the 1970s made it an immense transnational business enterprise with huge social consequences and that created major policy difficulties for the states involved. William O. Walker III has edited two authoritative works, essential reading for historical perspective. *Drug Control in the Americas* (2 eds., 1981, 1989) surveys the century-old inter-American drug control efforts to World War II. Walker compiled an original collection of forty-three essays on the history of drug cultures in Latin America, their place in individual societies, and the efforts of Latin American states and the United States to control them. *Drugs in the Western Hemisphere: An Odyssey of Cultures in Conflict* (1996) contains forty-six essays arranged chronologically to make up a comprehensive survey of the evolution of U.S.–Latin American drug policies from the turn of the century to the 1990s. The general argument is that the history is one of "adaptive drug cultures in competition with proscriptive cultures to create a legitimate place for themselves." Scott B. MacDonald, *Dancing on a Volcano: The Latin American Drug Trade* (1988), is a concise, balanced, informative, and serious study of the drug trade. MacDonald refrains from placing blame and recognizes the universal problem in the search for solutions. Bruce M. Bagley and William O. Walker III, eds., *Drug Trafficking in the Americas* (1995), is an informative encyclopedic compendium of twenty-eight chapters by established academic experts, talented newcomers, and experienced practitioners. They address U.S. drug policy, the international dimensions, and situations in all of the Latin American and Caribbean countries. Diego Garcia-Sayan, ed., *Narcotrafico: realidades y alternativas: conferencia internacional* (1990), brings together an impressive array of ninety-nine expert participants from governments, universities, and the professions at a conference sponsored by the Andean Commission of Jurists. They are from eleven countries in Latin America and Europe as well as from the United States. The discussion is exceptionally inclusive of the phenomenon.

Peter H. Smith, ed., *Drug Policy in the Americas* (1992), contains essays analyzing a number of elements: the magnitude and structure of the illicit international drug market, forms of therapy and treatment, the implications of legalization of the trade, the unintended consequences of antidrug policies, the way to balance policies dealing with both supply and demand, and the possibilities of regional collaboration. Fernando Mita Barrientos, *El fenómeno del narcotráfico: enfoque nacional e internacional* (1994), is by a former judge and professor of criminology. He presents a detailed treatment of the drug traffic, its social and economic causes and consequences, drug cartels, and juridical considerations. Chapters are devoted to the Latin American region and countries, the United States, Europe, Asia, and Africa.

Donald J. Mabry, ed., *The Latin American Narcotics Trade and U.S. National Security* (1989), is a collection of nine analyses by experts on the narcotraffic as a matter of U.S. national security. They emphasize Latin American social and political destabilization and the serious U.S. social problems as consequences of the drug trade. They address the failure of U.S. law enforcement agencies to reduce the flow of illegal drugs and congressional approaches. A particular concern is indicated about the increased role of the armed forces and concomitant issues of civil-military relations. Peter Dale Scott and Jonathan Marshall, *Cocaine Politics: Drugs, Armies, and the CIA in Central America* (1991), maintain that the war on drugs is largely a pretense inasmuch as the U.S. government, through CIA counterinsurgency activities, is one of the world's largest drug pushers. Alexandra Guáqueta y Francisco Thoumi, eds., *El rompecabezas de las drogas ilegales en Estados Unidos: una visión ecléctica* (1997), is a compilation by an economist and political scientist at the University of the Andes of eleven contributions from highly qualified Latin American and U.S. authors. They explore problems with illicit drugs in the United States—the major source of demand for the drugs that come from Latin America—and measures to deal with it. The thematic scope is thorough and the observations and conclusions are both critical and realistic.

For Latin American views of the Latin American side of the problem, see Elizabeth Joyce and Carlos Malamud, eds., *Latin America and the International Drug Trade* (1997); Jaime Malamud-Goti, *Smoke and Mirrors: The Paradox of the Drug Wars* (1992); and Rosa del Olmo, *Prohibir o domesticar: políticas de drogas en América Latina* (1992).

Diego García-Sayan, ed., *Coca, cocaina y narcotrafico: laberinto en los Andes* (1989), has sixteen articles addressing a variety of analytic perspectives on the Andean cocaine enterprise, with case studies of the individual states and societies. The contributors pay particular attention to the linkage between the drug traffic and problems of national development. Rensselaer W. Lee III, *The White Labyrinth: Cocaine and Political Power* (1989), is a survey of the main Latin American protagonists in the cocaine industry, with a focus on coca producers and the role of the Colombian cartels and guerrilla movements. Patrick L. Clawson and Renssalaer W. Lee III, *The Andean Cocaine Industry* (1996), follow the process of cocaine production from the cultivation of the coca fields to marketing in the United States. See also Scott B. MacDonald, *Mountain High, White Avalanche: Cocaine and Power in the Andean States and Panama* (1989), and Felipe E. MacGregor, *Coca and Cocaine: An Andean Perspective* (1993).

Country studies of the major South American producers are of note. Two books by by Sewall H. Menzell cover a wide range of individual states: *Cocaine Quagmire: Implementing the U.S. Anti-Drug Policy in the*

North-Andes-Colombia (1997), and *Fire in the Andes: U.S. Foreign Policy and Cocaine Politics in Bolivia and Peru* (1996). The South American states are also analyzed in F. LaMond Tullis, *Unintended Consequences: Illegal Drugs and Drug Policies in Nine Countries* (1995). On Bolivia, see Raul Barrios Morón, *Bolivia y los Estados Unidos: democracía, derechos, y narcotráfico, 1980–1982* (1989); Guillermo Bedregal Gutiérrez and Ruddy Viscarra Pando, *La lucha boliviano contra la agresión del narcotráfico* (1989); Eduardo A. Gamarra, *Entre la droga y la democracia: la cooperación entre Estados Unidos–Bolivia y la lucha contra narcotrafico* (1994); James Painter, *Bolivia and Coca: A Study in Dependency* (1994); Francisco E. Thoumi, *Political Economy and Illegal Drugs in Colombia* (1994); and Juan Tokatlian, *Drogas, dilemas y dogmas: Estados Unidos y la narcocriminalidad organizado en Colombia* (1995).

Ivelaw Lloyd Griffith, *Drugs and Security in the Caribbean: Sovereignty Under Siege* (1997), is an addition of the author to his more general work on Caribbean security by defining the concept to include drugs and drug trafficking, from a small-state perspective. Griffith incorporates demographic, macroeconomic, international trade and capital dependency, and international political variables, along with migration and the "brain drain" and susceptibility to traffickers, in a compelling manner.

References

Abecia Baldivieso, Valentin. *Las relaciones internacionales en la historia de Bolivia.* 2d ed. 3 vols. La Paz: Academia Nacional de Ciencias de Bolivia, Editorial Los Amigos del Libro, 1986. 1st ed. 1978. (Chap. 3)

Abel, Christopher, and Colin M. Lewis, eds. *Latin America, Economic Imperialism and the State: The Political Economy of the External Connection from Independence to the Present.* Dover, N.H.: Athlone Press, for Institute of Latin American Studies, University of London, 1985. (Chap. 2)

Adams, Jan S. *A Foreign Policy in Transition: Moscow's Retreat from Central America and the Caribbean, 1985–1992.* Durham, N.C.: Duke University Press, 1993. (Chap. 7)

Adams, Richard Newbold, and others. *Social Change in Latin America Today: Its Implications for United States Policy.* New York: Harper, for the Council on Foreign Relations, 1961. (Chap. 8)

Adelman, Alan, and Reid R. Reiding, eds. *Confrontation in the Caribbean Basin: International Perspectives on Security, Sovereignty and Survival.* Pittsburgh: Center for Latin American Studies, University of Pittsburgh, 1984. (Chaps. 2, 3)

Adelman, Jeremy, ed. *Colonial Legacies: The Problem of Persistence.* New York: Routledge, 1999. (Chap. 2)

Aggarwal, Vinod K. *Debt Games: Strategic Interaction in International Debt Rescheduling.* New York: Cambridge University Press, 1996. (Chap. 8)

Agosin, Manuel R., ed. *Direct Foreign Investment in Latin America.* Baltimore: Johns Hopkins University Press, for Inter-American Development Bank, 1995. (Chap. 8)

Aguayo Quesada, Sergio. *Myths and [Mis]Perceptions: Changing U.S. Elite Visions of Mexico.* Translated by Julián Brady. La Jolla, Calif.: Center for U.S.-Mexican Studies, University of California, San Diego, 1998. (Chap. 3)

Aguero, Felipe, and Jeffrey Stark, eds. *Fault Lines of Democratic Governance in the Americas.* Boulder: Lynne Rienner Publishers, for North-South Center, University of Miami, 1997. (Chap. 8)

Aguilar, Alonso. *Pan-Americanism from Monroe to the Present: A View from the Other Side.* New York: Monthly Review Press, 1968. (Chap. 6)

Aguilar, Luis E. *Cuba 1933, Prologue to Revolution.* Ithaca, N.Y.: Cornell University Press, 1972. (Chap. 3)

Aguilar Monteverde, Alonso. *El panamericanismo de la Doctrina Monroe a la Doctrina Johnson.* México: Cuadernos Americanos, 1965. (Chap. 5)

Alba, Víctor. *Alliance Without Allies: The Mythology of Progress in Latin America.* New York: Praeger, 1965. (Chap. 8)

_____. *Esquema histórico del communismo en Iberoamérica.* 3d ed. México: Ediciones Occidentales, 1960. 1st ed. 1954. (Chap. 2)

_____. *Historia del frente popular: análisis de una táctica política.* México: Libro Mex, 1959. (Chaps. 3, 8)

_____. *Nationalists Without Nations: The Oligarchy Versus the People in Latin America.* New York: Praeger, 1968. (Chap. 3)

Alemann, Roberto, and others. *Economic Development Issues: Latin America.* New York: Praeger, 1967. (Chap. 8)

Alexander, Robert J. *Communism in Latin America.* New Brunswick, N.J.: Rutgers University Press, 1957. (Chap. 8)

_____. *Trotskyism in Latin America.* Stanford: Hoover Institution, 1973. (Chap. 2)

Allison, Graham T. *Essence of Decision: Explaining the Cuban Missile Crisis.* Boston: Little, Brown, 1971. (Chap. 7)

Almeida, Paulo Roberto. *Relaçoes internacionais e política externa do Brasil.* Porto Alegre: Editora da Universidade Federal do Río Grande do Sul, 1998. (Chap. 3)

Alonso, Irma Tirado de, ed. *Trade, Industrialization, and Integration in Twentieth-Century Central America.* Westport, Conn.: Praeger, 1994. (Chap. 6)

_____. *Trade Issues in the Caribbean.* New York: Gordon and Breach Science Publishers, 1992. (Chap. 8)

Alonso Pineiro, Armando. *La trama de los 5000 dias: origines de las relaciones argentino-americanas.* Buenos Aires: Ediciones De Palma, 1986. (Chap. 7)

Altamira, Rafael. *España y el programa americanista.* Madrid, Editorial-América, 1917. (Chap. 4)

Alvarado Garaicoa, Teodoro. *El Dominio del Mar.* Guayaquil: Universidad de Guayaquil, 1968. (Chaps. 3, 6)

_____. *El mar territorial y el mar patrimonial.* Guayaquil: Universidad de Guayaquil, 1973. (Chap. 6)

_____. *La trascendencia de las reuniones interamericanos.* Guayaquil: Imprenta de la Universidad, 1949. (Chap. 6)

Alvarez, Alejandro. *Chile ante la segunda conferencia de La Haya.* Santiago de Chile: n.p., 1907. (Chap. 3)

_____. *La diplomacia de Chile durante la emancipación.* Santiago de Chile: Imprenta Barcelona, 1916. (Chap. 7)

_____. *Le droit international américain.* Paris: A. Pedone, Editeur, 1902. (Chap. 6)

_____. *International Law and Related Subjects from the Point of View of the American Continent.* Washington, D.C.: Carnegie Endowment for International Peace, 1922. (Chap. 6)

_____. *The Monroe Doctrine: Its Importance in the International Life of the States of the New World.* New York: Oxford University Press, 1924. (Chap. 5)

_____. *Rasgos generales de la historia diplomatica de Chile, 1810–1910.* Santiago de Chile: Imprenta Barcelona, 1911. (Chap. 3)

Ameringer, Charles D. *The Caribbean Legion: Patriots, Politicians, Soldiers of Fortune, 1946–1950.* University Park: Pennsylvania State University Press, 1996. (Chap. 7)

_____. *The Democratic Left in Exile: The Anti-Dictatorial Struggle in the Caribbean, 1945–1959.* Coral Gables, Fla.: University of Miami Press, 1974. (Chap. 7)

Amuchástegui Astrada, Armando. *Argentina-Chile: controversia y mediación.* Buenos Aires: Ediciones Ghersi, 1980. (Chap. 7)

Anderson, Thomas P. *Matanza: El Salvador's Communist Revolt of 1932.* Lincoln: University of Nebraska Press, 1971. (Chap. 3)

_____. *The War of the Dispossessed: Honduras and El Salvador, 1969.* Lincoln: University of Nebraska Press, 1981. (Chap. 7)

Andic, Fuat, Stephen Andic, and Douglas Dosser. *A Theory of Economic Integration for Developing Countries, Illustrated by Caribbean Countries.* London: George Allen and Unwin, 1971. (Chap. 6)

Andrews, George Reid. *The Afro-Argentines of Buenos Aires, 1800–1900.* Madison: University of Wisconsin Press, 1980. (Chap. 8)

Andrews, Gregg. *"Shoulder to Shoulder?" The American Federation of Labor, the United States, and the Mexican Revolution, 1910–1924.* Berkeley: University of California Press, 1991. (Chap. 8)

Anna, Timothy E. *Spain and the Loss of America.* Lincoln: University of Nebraska Press, 1983. (Chap. 7)

Antokoletz, Daniel. *Histoire de la diplomatie argentine.* 2 vols. Paris: A. Redone, 1914. (Chap. 3)

Ardouin, Beaurbrun. *Etudes sur l'histoire d'Haiti.* Port-au-Prince: Chéraquit, 1924–1930. (Chap. 7)

Arenal, Celestino del. *La política exterior de España hacia Iberoamérica.* Madrid: Editorial Complutense, 1994. (Chap. 4)

Arévalo, Juan José. *The Shark and the Sardines.* Translated by June Cobb and Raúl Osegueda. New York: Lyle Stuart, 1961. (Chap. 3)

Arismendi, Rodney. *Lenín, la revolución y América Latina.* Montevideo: Ediciones Pueblos Unidos, 1970. (Chap. 2)

Armony, Ariel C. *Argentina, the United States, and the Anti-Communist Crusade in Central America, 1977–1984.* Athens, Ohio: Ohio University Press, 1997. (Chap. 7)

Arnson, Cynthia. *Crossroads: Congress, the President, and Central America, 1976–1993.* 2d ed. University Park: Pennsylvania State University Press, 1993. 1st ed. 1989. (Chap. 7)

Arnson, Cynthia J., ed. *Comparative Peace Processes in Latin America*. Washington, D.C.: Woodrow Wilson Center Press; Stanford: Stanford University Press, 1999. (Chap. 7)

Arze Quiroga, Eduardo. *Las relaciones internacionales de Bolivia, 1825–1990*. La Paz and Cochabamba: Editorial Los Amigos del Libro, 1991. (Chap. 3)

Ashley, Timothy. *The Bear in the Back Yard: Moscow's Caribbean Strategy*. Lexington, Mass.: Lexington Books, 1987. (Chap. 7)

Asseff, Alberto Emilio. *Proyección continental de la Argentina de la geohistoria a la geopolítica nacional*. Buenos Aires: Editorial Pleamar, 1980. (Chap. 3)

Astiz, Carlos, ed. *Latin American International Politics: Ambitions, Capabilities, and the National Interest of Mexico, Brazil, and Argentina*. Notre Dame, Ind.: University of Notre Dame Press, 1969. (Chap. 3)

Atkins, G. Pope. *Encyclopedia of the Inter-American System*. Westport, Conn.: Greenwood Press, 1997. (Chap. 6)

_____. *Latin America and the Caribbean in the International System*. 4th ed. Boulder: Westview Press, 1999. 1st ed. 1977; 1st–3d eds. titled *Latin America in the International Political System*. (Chap. 2)

Atkins, G. Pope, ed. *South America into the 1990s: Evolving International Relationships in a New Era*. Boulder: Westview Press, 1990. (Chaps. 2, 3)

_____. *The United States and Latin America: Redefining U.S. Purposes in the Post–Cold War Era*. Austin, Tex.: Lyndon B. Johnson School of Public Affairs, University of Texas at Austin, 1992. (Chaps. 2, 5)

Atkins, G. Pope, and Larman C. Wilson. *The Dominican Republic and the United States: From Imperialism to Transnationalism*. Athens, Ga.: University of Georgia Press, 1998. (Chap. 3)

_____. *The United States and the Trujillo Regime*. New Brunswick, N.J.: Rutgers University Press, 1972. (Chap. 3)

Ayala, Segundo F. *Bolívar y el sistema interamericano: el ideal panamericano a traves de la historia de las conferencias interamericanas, desde el Congreso de Panamá hasta la unidécima conferencia interamericana, 1826–1964*. 3 vols. Quito: Imprenta Municipal, 1962–1964. (Chap. 6)

Aybar de Soto, José M. *Dependency and Intervention: The Case of Guatemala in 1954*. Boulder: Westview Press, 1978. (Chap. 7)

Ayearst, Morley. *The British West Indies: The Search for Self-Government*. New York: New York University Press, 1960. (Chap. 2)

Axline, W. Andrew. *Caribbean Integration: The Politics of Regionalism*. London: Francis Pinter, 1979. (Chap. 6)

Baer, M. Delal, Joseph T. Jockel, and Sidney Weintraub, eds. *NAFTA and Sovereignty: Trade-Offs for Canada, Mexico, and the United States*. Boulder: Westview Press, 1996. (Chap. 6)

Baer, Werner, and Donald V. Coes, eds. *United States Policies and the Latin American Economies*. New York: Praeger, 1990. (Chaps. 2, 8)

Baerrensen, Donald. *The Border Industrialization Program.* Lexington, Mass.: D. C. Heath, 1971. (Chap. 6)

Baerrensen, Donald W., Martin Carnoy, and Joseph Grunwald. *Latin American Trade Patterns.* Washington, D.C.: Brookings Institution, 1965. (Chap. 8)

Báez, Cecilio. *História diplomática del Paraguay.* 2 vols. Asunción: Imprenta Nacional, 1931–1932. (Chap. 3)

Báez Evertsz, Frank. *Braceros haitianos en República Dominicana.* Santo Domingo: Instituto Dominicano de Investigaciones Sociales, 1986. (Chap. 8)

Bagley, Bruce Michael, ed. *Contadora and the Diplomacy of Peace in Central America.* Boulder: Westview Press, with School of Advanced International Studies, Johns Hopkins University, 1989. (Chap. 7)

Bagley, Bruce Michael, and Sergio Aguayo Quezada, eds. *Mexico: In Search of Security.* Boulder: Lynne Rienner Publishers, for North-South Center, University of Miami, 1993. (Chap. 3)

Bagley, Bruce M., and William O. Walker III, eds. *Drug Trafficking in the Americas.* New Brunswick, N.J.: Transaction Publishers, for North-South Center, University of Miami, 1995. (Chap. 8)

Bagú, Sergio. *Argentina en el mundo.* México: Fondo de Cultura Económica, 1961. (Chap. 3)

Bahbah, Bishara. *Israel and Latin America: The Military Connection.* New York: St. Martin's Press; Washington, D.C.: Institute for Palestine Studies, 1986. (Chap. 8)

Bailey, Norman A. *Latin America in World Politics.* New York: Walker, 1967. (Chap. 2)

Baily, Samuel L. *The United States and the Development of South America, 1945–1975.* New York: New Viewpoints, 1976. (Chaps. 2, 5)

Baklanoff, Eric N. *Expropriations of U.S. Investments in Cuba, Mexico, and Chile.* New York: Praeger, 1975. (Chap. 8)

Ball, M. Margaret. *The OAS in Transition.* Durham, N.C.: Duke University Press, 1969. (Chap. 6)

Baloyra, Enrique. *El Salvador in Transition.* Chapel Hill, N.C.: University of North Carolina Press, 1982. (Chap. 7)

Bandeira, Moniz. *Presença dos Estados Unidos no Brasil: dois séculos de historia.* Río de Janeiro: Editora Civilização Brasileira, 1973. (Chap. 3)

Barber, Willard F., and C. Neale Ronning. *Internal Security and Military Power: Counterinsurgency and Civic Action in Latin America.* Columbus: Ohio State University Press, 1966. (Chap. 8)

Barberis, Julio A., and Eduardo A. Pigretti. *Régimen juridico del Río de la Plata.* Buenos Aires: Editorial Abeledo-Perrot, 1970. (Chap. 7)

Barcía Trelles, Camilo. *La Doctrina de Monroe y la cooperación internacional.* Madrid: Editorial Mundo Latino, 1931. (Chap. 5)

Barclay, Glen St. John. *Struggle for a Continent: The Diplomatic History of South America, 1917–1945.* London: Whitefriars Press, 1971. (Chap. 2)

314 REFERENCES

Bark, Dennis, ed. *The Red Orchestra: Instruments of Soviet Policy in Latin America and the Caribbean.* Stanford: Hoover Institution Press, 1986. (Chap. 4)

Barkin, David. *Las relaciones México–Estados Unidos.* México, D.F.: Universidad Nacional Autónoma de México, 1980. (Chap. 3)

Barral-Montferrat, Horace Dominique de. *De Monroe a Roosevelt, 1823–1905.* Paris: Nourrit, 1905. (Chap. 5)

Barrios Morón, Raúl. *Bolivia y los Estados Unidos: democracia, derechos, y narcotráfico, 1980–1982.* La Paz: HISBOL; FLACSO, 1989. (Chap. 8)

Barrios Morón, Raúl, and others. *Política exterior boliviano: tendencias y desafíos.* La Paz: UDAPEX, ILDIS, 1995. (Chap. 3)

Barrios Morón, Raúl, ed. *Bolivia, Chile y Perú: una opción cooperativa.* La Paz: UDAPEX, ILDIS, III, CAF, 1997. (Chap. 7)

Barros Borgoño, Luis. *The Problem of the Pacific and the New Policies of Bolivia.* Baltimore: Sun Job Printing Office, 1924. (Chap. 7)

Barros van Buren, Mario. *La diplomacia chilena en la Segunda Guerra Mundial.* Santiago: Empresa Editora Arquen, 1998. (Chap. 7)

———. *Historia diplomática de Chile, 1541–1938.* Barcelona: Ediciones Ariel, 1970. (Chap. 3)

Bartley, Russell H. *Imperial Russia and the Struggle for Latin American Independence, 1808–1828.* Austin: University of Texas Press, 1978. (Chap. 7)

Batstone, David, Eduardo Mendieta, Lois Ann Lorentzen, and Dwight N. Hopkins, eds. *Liberation Theologies, Postmodernity and the Americas.* New York: Routledge, 1997. (Chap. 8)

Bauer, K. Jack. *The Mexican War 1846–1848.* New York: Macmillan, 1974. (Chap. 7)

Baum, Daniel Jay. *The Banks of Canada in the Commonwealth Caribbean: Economic Nationalism and Multinational Enterprises of a Medium Power.* New York: Praeger, 1974. (Chap. 8)

Bean, Frank D., Rodolfo O. de la Garza, Bryan R. Roberts, and Sidney Weintraub. *At the Crossroads: Mexico, Migration, and U.S. Policy.* Lanham, Md.: Rowman and Littlefield, 1997. (Chap. 8)

Beck, Peter. *The Falkland Islands as an International Problem.* London: Routledge, 1988. (Chap. 7)

Beck, Robert J. *The Grenada Invasion: Politics, Law, and Foreign Policy Decisionmaking.* Boulder: Westview Press, 1993. (Chap. 7)

Becker, Bertha K., and Claudio A. G. Egler. *Brazil: A New Regional Power in the World Economy.* New York: Cambridge University Press, 1992. (Chap. 3)

Bedregal Gutiérrez, Guillermo, and Ruddy Viscarra Pando. *La lucha boliviano contra la agresión del narcotráfico.* La Paz: Editorial Los Amigos del Libro, 1989. (Chap. 8)

Behrman, Jack N. *The Role of International Companies in Latin America.* Lexington, Mass.: Lexington Books, 1972. (Chap. 8)

Belaunde, Víctor Andrés. *Bolívar and the Political Thought of the Spanish American Revolution*. Baltimore: Johns Hopkins Press, 1938. (Chap. 7)

———. *La vida international de Perú*. Lima: Imprenta Torres Aguirre, 1942. (Chap. 3)

Beltrán, Luís Ramiro, and Elizabeth Fox de Cardona. *Comunicación dominada: Estados Unidos en los medios de América Latina*. México: Instituto Latinoamericano de Estudios Transnacionales, 1980. (Chap. 8)

Bemis, Samuel Flagg. *The Latin American Policy of the United States*. New York: Harcourt Brace, 1943. (Chap. 5)

Benemelis, Juan F. *Castro, subversión y terrorismo en Africa*. Madrid: San Martín, 1988. (Chap. 3)

Benjamin, Jules Robert. *The United States and the Origins of the Cuban Revolution: An Empire of Liberty in an Age of National Liberation*. Princeton, N.J.: Princeton University Press, 1990. (Chap. 3)

Bennett, Douglas C., and Kenneth E. Sharpe. *Transnational Corporations Versus the State: The Political Eeconomy of the Mexican Auto Industry*. Princeton, N.J.: Princeton University Press, 1985. (Chap. 8)

Benton, Elbert Jay. *International Law and Diplomacy of the Spanish American War*. Baltimore: Johns Hopkins Press, 1908. (Chap. 7)

Bernstein, Harry. *Making an Inter-American Mind*. Gainesville, Fla.: University of Florida Press, 1961. (Chap. 8)

———. *Origins of Inter-American Interest, 1700–1812*. Philadelphia: University of Pennsylvania Press, 1945. (Chap. 2)

Berquist, Charles W. *Coffee and Conflict in Colombia, 1886–1910*. Durham, N.C.: Duke University Press, 1978. (Chap. 3)

Berryman, Philip. *Liberation Theology: Essential Facts About the Revolutionary Religious Movement in Latin America and Beyond*. Philadelphia: Temple University Press, 1987. (Chap. 8)

———. *Religious Roots and the Rebellion: Christians in the Central American Revolution*. Maryknoll, N.Y.: Orbis Books, 1984. (Chap. 8)

Betancourt, Ernesto. *Revolutionary Strategy*. New Brunswick, N.J.: Transaction Books, 1996. (Chap. 7)

Betancourt, Rómulo. *Venezuela: Oil and Politics*. Translated by Everett Baumann. Boston: Houghton Mifflin, 1979. (Chap. 8)

Bethel, Leslie, ed. *Colonial Latin America*. Vols. 1 and 2, *The Cambridge History of Latin America*. Cambridge: Cambridge University Press, 1984. (Chap. 2)

———. *The Independence of Latin America*. Vol. 3, *The Cambridge History of Latin America*. Cambridge: Cambridge University Press, 1987. (Chap. 7)

Beverina, Juan. *La guerra contra el imperio del Brasil: contribución al estudio de sus antecedentes y de las operaciones hasta Ituzaingo*. Buenos Aires: Taller Gráfico de L. Bernard, 1927. (Chap. 7)

_____. *La Guerra del Paraguay.* 7 vols. Buenos Aires: Establecimiento Graficó Ferrari Hermanos, 1921–1933. (Chap. 7)

_____. *Las invasiones inglesas al río de la plata (1806–1807).* 2 vols. Buenos Aires: Taller Gráfico de L. Bernard, 1939. (Chap. 7)

Bhana, Surendra. *The United States and the Development of the Puerto Rican Status Question, 1936–1968.* Lawrence: University Press of Kansas, 1975. (Chap. 2)

Bianchi, Andres, Robert Devlin, and Joseph Ramos. *External Debt in Latin America: Adjustment Policies and Renegotiation.* Boulder: Lynne Rienner Publishers, 1985. (Chap. 8)

Bianchi, William J. *Belize: The Controversy Between Guatemala and Great Britain over the Territory of British Honduras in Central America.* New York: Las Americas, 1959. (Chap. 7)

Bianchi Barros, Agustín. *Bosquejo historico de las relaciones chileno-norteamericanas durante la independencia.* Santiago de Chile: n.p., 1946. (Chap. 7)

Biles, Robert E., ed. *Inter-American Relations: The Latin American Perspective.* Boulder: Lynne Rienner Publishers, 1988. (Chap. 3)

Blachman, Morris J., William M. Leogrande, and Kenneth E. Sharpe, eds. *Confronting Revolution: Security Through Diplomacy in Central America.* New York: Pantheon Books, 1986. (Chap. 7)

Black, Jan Knippers. *Sentinels of Empire: The United States and Latin American Militarism.* Westport, Conn.: Greenwood Press, 1986. (Chap. 8)

_____. *United States Penetration in Brazil.* Philadelphia: University of Pennsylvania Press, 1977. (Chap. 3)

Blackburn, Robin. *The Making of New World Slavery: From the Baroque to the Modern, 1492–1800.* New York: Verso, 1997. (Chap. 8)

Blank, Stephen, and Jerry Haar. *Making NAFTA Work: U.S. Firms and the New North American Business Environment.* Boulder: Lynne Rienner Publishers, for North-South Center, University of Miami, 1997. (Chap. 6)

Blasier, Cole. *The Giant's Rival: The USSR and Latin America.* Rev. ed. Pittsburgh: University of Pittsburgh Press, 1988. 1st ed. 1983 (Chap. 4)

_____. *The Hovering Giant: U.S. Responses to Revolutionary Change in Latin America.* Rev. ed. Pittsburgh: University of Pittsburgh Press, 1985. 1st ed. 1976. (Chap. 8)

Blasier, Cole, and Carmelo Mesa-Lago, eds. *Cuba in the World.* Pittsburgh: University of Pittsburgh Press, 1979. (Chap. 3)

Blight, James G., Bruce J. Allen, and David A. Welch. *Cuba on the Brink: Castro, the Missile Crisis, and the Soviet Collapse.* New York: Pantheon Books, 1993. (Chap. 7)

Blight, James G., and Peter Kornbluh, eds. *Politics of Illusion: The Bay of Pigs Reexamined.* Boulder: Lynne Rienner Publishers, 1999. (Chap. 7)

Bloomfield, Louis M. *The British Honduras–Guatemala Dispute.* Toronto: Carswell, 1953. (Chap. 7)

Boersner, Demetrio. *Relaciones internacionales de América Latina: breve historia.* 4th ed. Caracas: Nueva Sociedád, 1990. 1st ed. 1982. (Chaps. 2, 3)

_____. *Venezuela y el Caribe: presencia cambiante.* Caracas: Monte Avila, 1978. (Chap. 3)

Boff, Clodovis, and Leonardo Boff. *Liberation Theology: From Confrontation to Dialogue.* Translated by Robert R. Barr. San Francisco: Harper and Row, 1986. (Chap. 8)

Bolton, Herbert E. *The Spanish Borderlands: A Chronicle of Old Florida and the Southwest.* New Haven, Conn.: Yale University Press, 1921. (Chap. 3)

Bonachea, Ramón L., and Marta San Martín. *The Cuban Insurrection, 1952–1959.* New Brunswick, N.J.: Transaction Books-Dutton, 1974. (Chap. 7)

Bond, Robert D., ed. *Contemporary Venezuela and Its Role in International Affairs.* New York: New York University Press, 1977. (Chap. 3)

Bonilla, Heraclio, and others. *La independencia en el Perú.* Lima: Instituto de Estudios Peruanos, 1972. (Chap. 7)

Bonino, José Míguez. *Faces of Latin American Protestantism: 1993 Carnahan Lectures.* Translated by Eugene L. Stockwell. Grand Rapids, Mich.: William B. Eerdmans, 1997. (Chap. 8)

Booth, John. *The End and the Beginning: The Nicaraguan Revolution.* Boulder: Westview Press, 1982. (Chap. 7)

Booth, John A., and Mitchell A. Seligson, eds. *Elections and Democracy in Central America.* Chapel Hill, N.C.: University of North Carolina Press, 1989. (Chap. 8)

Bosch García, Carlos. *Historia de las relaciones entre México y los Estados Unidos, 1819–1848.* 2d ed. México: Secretaría de Relaciones Exteriores, 1974. 1st ed. 1961. (Chap. 3)

_____. *Problemas diplomáticos del México independiente.* México, D.F.: El Colegio de México, 1947. (Chap. 3)

Bose, Christine E., and Edna Acosta-Belén, eds. *Women in the Latin American Development Process.* Philadelphia: Temple University Press, 1995. (Chap. 8)

Bouzas, Roberto, ed. *De espaldas a la prosperidad: América Latina y la economía internacional a fines de los ochenta.* Buenos Aires: Programa de Estudios Conjuntos sobre las Relaciones Internacionales de América Latina; Grupo Editor Latinoamericano, 1989. (Chap. 2)

Box, Pelham H. *The Origins of the Paraguayan War.* Urbana, Ill.: University of Illinois Press, 1930. (Chap. 7)

Boxer, Charles R. *The Portuguese Seaborne Empire, 1415–1825.* New York: Knopf, 1969. (Chap. 2)

Brack, Gene M. *Mexico Views Manifest Destiny, 1821–1846: An Essay on the Origins of the Mexican War.* Albuquerque, N.M.: University of New Mexico Press, 1975. (Chap. 7)

Brandt, Niels. *Das Interamerikanische Friedensystem: Idee und Wirklichkeit.* Hamburg: Hansischer Gildenverlag, 1971. (Chap. 6)

Brau, Salvador. *Historia de Puerto Rico.* Nueva York: D. Appleton, 1904. (Chap. 2)

Braveboy-Wagner, Jacqueline Anne. *The Caribbean in World Affairs: The Foreign Policies of the English-Speaking States.* 2d ed. Boulder: Westview Press, 1999. 1st ed. 1989. (Chap. 3)

——. *The Venezuelan-Guyana Border Dispute: Britain's Colonial Legacy in Latin America.* Boulder: Westview Press, 1984. (Chap. 7)

Braveboy-Wagner, Jacqueline Anne, with W. Marvin Will, Dennis J. Gayle, and Ivelaw L. Griffith. *The Caribbean in the Pacific Century: Prospects for Caribbean-Pacific Cooperation.* Boulder: Lynne Rienner Publishers, 1993. (Chaps. 2, 3)

Braveboy-Wagner, Jacqueline Anne, and Dennis J. Gayle, eds. *Caribbean Public Policy: Regional, Cultural, and Socioeconomic Issues for the 21st Century.* Boulder: Westview Press, 1997. (Chap. 3)

Brenner, Philip. *From Confrontation to Negotiation: U.S. Relations with Cuba.* Boulder: Westview Press, 1988. (Chap. 3)

Brock, Lothar. *Entwicklungsnationalismus und Kompradorenpolitik: Die Gründug de OAS und die Entwicklung der Abhangigkeit Lateinamerikas von den USA.* Maisenheim am Glan, FDR: Hain, 1975. (Chap. 6)

Brock, Philip L., Michael B. Connolly, and Claudio González-Vega, eds. *Latin American Debt and Adjustment: External Shocks and Macroeconomic Policies.* Westport, Conn.: Praeger, 1989. (Chap. 8)

Brodhead, Frank, and Edward S. Herman. *Demonstration Elections: U.S.-Staged Elections in the Dominican Republic, Vietnam, and El Salvador.* Boston: South End Press, 1984. (Chap. 8)

Brown, Jonathan C. *Oil and Revolution in Mexico.* Berkeley: University of California Press, 1993. (Chap. 8)

Brown, Peter G., and Henry Shue, eds. *The Border that Joins: Mexican Migrants and the U.S. Responsibility.* Totowa, N.J.: Rowman and Littlefield, 1983. (Chap. 8)

Bryan, Anthony T., ed. *The Caribbean: New Dynamics in Trade and Political Economy.* New Brunswick, N.J.: Transaction, for North-South Center, University of Miami, 1995. (Chap. 8)

Bryan, Anthony T., J. Edward Greene, and Timothy M. Shaw, eds. *Peace, Development, and Security in the Caribbean.* New York: St. Martin's Press, 1990. (Chaps. 2, 3)

Bryan, Anthony T., and Andrés Serbín, eds. *Distant Cousins: The Caribbean–Latin American Relationship.* New Brunswick, N.J.: Transaction, for North-South Center, University of Miami, 1994. (Chaps. 2, 3)

Brysk, Alison. *From Tribal Village to Global Village: Indian Rights and International Relations in Latin America.* Stanford: Stanford University Press, 2000. (Chap. 8)

Buchenau, Jurgen. *In the Shadow of the Giant: The Making of Mexico's Central American Policy, 1876–1930*. Tuscaloosa, Ala.: University of Alabama Press, 1996. (Chap. 3)

Bueno, Gerardo M., and Lorenzo Meyer, eds. *México–Estados Unidos*. México: El Colegio de México, 1987. (Chap. 3)

Buergenthal, Thomas, Robert Norris, and Dinah Shelton. *Protecting Human Rights in the Americas: Selected Problems*. 4th ed. Kehl, Germany; Arlington, Va.: N.P. Engel, 1995. 1st ed. 1973. (Chap. 8)

Bulmer-Thomas, Victor. *The Economic History of Latin America Since Independence*. New York: Cambridge University Press, 1994. (Chaps. 2, 8)

———. *The Political Economy of Central America Since 1920*. Cambridge: Cambridge University Press, 1987. (Chap. 2)

———. *Studies in the Economics of Central America*. New York: St. Martin's Press, 1998 (Chap. 2)

Bulmer-Thomas, Victor, ed. *Britain and Latin America: A Changing Relationship*. Cambridge: Cambridge University Press, 1989. (Chap. 4)

———. *The New Economic Model in Latin America and Its Impact on Income Distribution and Poverty*. Basingstoke, UK: Macmillan, in association with Institute of Latin American Studies, University of London, 1996. (Chap. 8)

Bulnes, Gonzalo. *Chile and Peru: The Causes of the War of 1879*. Santiago de Chile: Imprenta Universitaria, 1920. (Chap. 7)

———. *La Guerra del Pacífico*, 2d ed., 3 vols. Santiago de Chile: Editorial del Pacifico, 1955. 1st ed. 1912–1919. (Chap. 7)

Burden, W.A.M. *The Struggle for Airways in Latin America*. New York: Council on Foreign Relations, 1943. (Chap. 8)

Burkholder, Mark A., and Lyman L. Johnson. *Colonial Latin America*. 3d ed. New York: Oxford University Press, 1997. 1st ed. 1990. (Chap. 2)

Burn, William Laurence. *The British West Indies*. London: Hutchinson House, 1951. (Chap. 2)

Burns, Alan. *History of the British West Indies*. 2d ed. New York: Barnes and Noble, 1965. 1st ed. 1954. (Chap. 2)

Burns, E. Bradford. *At War in Nicaragua: The Reagan Doctrine and the Politics of Nostalgia*. New York: Harper and Row, 1987. (Chap. 7)

———. *Nationalism in Brazil: A Historical Survey*. New York: Praeger, 1968. (Chap. 3)

———. *The Unwritten Alliance: Rio-Branco and Brazilian-American Relations*. New York: Columbia University Press, 1966. (Chap. 3)

Burr, Robert N. *By Reason or Force: Chile and the Balancing of Power in South America, 1830–1905*. Berkeley: University of California Press, 1967. (Chap. 3)

———. *Our Troubled Hemisphere: Perspectives on United States–Latin American Relations*. Washington, D.C.: Brookings Institution, 1967. (Chap. 2)

_____. *The Stillborn Panama Congress: Power, Politics and Chilean-Colombian Relations During the War of the Pacific*. Berkeley: University of California Press, 1962. (Chap. 7)

Burrowes, Reynold A. *Revolution and Rescue in Grenada: An Account of the U.S.-Caribbean Invasion*. Westport, Conn.: Greenwood Press, 1988. (Chap. 7)

Bustamante, Jorge A., Clark W. Reynolds, and Raúl A. Hinojosa Ojeda, eds. *U.S.-Mexico Relations: Labor Market Interdependence*. Stanford: Stanford University Press, 1992. (Chap. 3)

Buxton, J., and N. Phillips, eds. *Case Studies in Latin American Political Economy*. New York: St. Martin's Press, 1999. (Chap. 3)

Byrne, Hugh. *El Salvador's Civil War: A Study of Revolution*. Boulder: Lynne Rienner Publishers, 1996. (Chap. 7)

Caballero, Manuel. *Latin America and the Comintern 1919–1943*. New York: Cambridge University Press, 1986. (Chaps. 2, 8)

Cabán, Pedro A. *Constructing a Colonial People: Puerto Rico and the United States, 1898–1932*. Boulder: Westview Press, 1999. (Chap. 2)

Cady, John Frank. *Foreign Intervention in the Rio de la Plata, 1838–1850: A Study of French, British and American Policy in Relation to the Dictator Juan Manuel Rosas*. Philadelphia: University of Pennsylvania Press, 1929. (Chap. 7)

Caicedo Castilla, José Joaquín. *El derecho internacional en el Sistema Interamericano*. Madrid: Ediciones Cultura Hispánica, 1970. (Chap. 6)

_____. *El Panamericanismo*. Buenos Aires: Ediciones R. Depalma, 1961. (Chap. 6)

Caillet-Bois, Ricardo R. *Cuestiones internacionales (1852–1966)*. Buenos Aires: Editorial Universitaria de Buenos Aires (EUDEBA), 1970. (Chap. 3)

_____. *Una tierra argentina: las islas Malvinas*. Buenos Aires: Peuser, 1948. (Chap. 7)

Calcagno, Alfredo Eric, ed. *Argentina hacia el 2000: desafíos y opciones*. Caracas: Editorial Nueva Sociedad, 1989. (Chap. 3)

Calder, Bruce. *The Impact of Intervention: The Dominican Republic During the U.S. Occupation of 1916–1924*. Austin, Tex.: University of Texas Press, 1984. (Chap. 7)

Callahan, James Morton. *American Foreign Policy in Mexican Relations*. New York: Macmillan, 1932. (Chap. 3)

_____. *Cuba and International Relations: A Historical Study in American Diplomacy*. Baltimore: Johns Hopkins Press, 1899. (Chaps. 3, 7)

Callcott, Wilfrid Hardy. *The Caribbean Policy of the United States, 1890–1920*. Baltimore: Johns Hopkins Press, 1942. (Chap. 5)

_____. *The Western Hemisphere: Its Influence on United States Policies to the End of World War II*. Austin: University of Texas Press, 1968. (Chap. 5)

Calogeras Pandía, João. *A política exterior do imperio*. 3 vols. Río de Janeiro: Conpanhia Editora Nacional, 1927–1928. (Chap. 3)

Calvert, Peter. *The International Politics of Latin America*. Manchester: Manchester University Press; New York: St. Martin's Press, 1994. (Chaps. 2, 3)

_____. *The Mexican Revolution, 1910–1914: The Diplomacy of Anglo-American Conflict*. Cambridge: Cambridge University Press, 1968. (Chap. 7)

Calvert, Peter, ed. *The Central American Security System: North-South or East-West?* Cambridge: Cambridge University Press, 1989. (Chap. 7)

Calvo Gamboa, Carlos. *Costa Rica en la segunda guerra mundial, 1939–1945*. San José: Editorial Universidad Estatala Distancia, 1985. (Chap. 7)

Camacho Omiste, Edgar. *Integración Andina*. La Paz: Editorial Amigos del Libro, 1975. (Chap. 6)

_____. *Política exterior independiente*. La Paz: [s.n.], 1989. (Chap. 3)

Camargo, Sonia de, and José María Vásquez Ocampo. *Autoritanismo e democracia na Argentina e Brasil (uma década de política exterior, 1973–1984)*. São Paulo: Editora Convívio, 1988. (Chap. 3)

Campos, Ricardo. *El Fondo Monetario Internacional y la deuda externa mexicana: estabilización y crisis*. 3d ed. Toluca, México: Universidad Autónoma del Estado de México, 1995. 1st ed. 1991. (Chap. 3)

Campos, Roberto de Oliveira. *Economia, planejamento e nacionalismo*. Río de Janeiro: APEC Editora, 1963. (Chap. 8)

_____. *O mundo que vejo e nao desejo*. Río de Janeiro: Livraria José Olympio Editora, 1976. (Chap. 8)

_____. *Reflections on Latin American Development*. Austin: University of Texas Press, 1967. (Chap. 8)

Canak, William L., ed. *Lost Promises: Debt, Austerity, and Development in Latin America*. Boulder: Westview Press, 1989. (Chap. 8)

Candelaria, Michael R. *Popular Religion and Liberation: The Dilemma of Liberation Theology*. Albany, N.Y.: State University of New York Press, 1990. (Chap. 8)

Carbajal, Carlos. *La penetración luso-brasileña en el Uruguay: ensayo histórico-sociológico*. Montevideo: Talleres Gráficos Prometeo, 1948. (Chap. 7)

Cárcano, Ramón J. *Guerra del Paraguay*. 2 vols. Buenos Aires: Ed. Domingo Viau, 1939–1942. (Chap. 7)

Cárdenas y Echarte, Raúl. *La política de los Estados Unidos en el continente americano*. La Habana: Sociedad Editorial Cuba Contemporánea, 1921. (Chap. 5)

Cardoso, Fernando Henrique, and Enzo Faletto. *Dependéncia y Desarrollo en América Latina*. México: Siglo XXI Editores, 1969; Translated by Marjory Mattingly Urquidi under the title *Dependency and Development in Latin America* (Berkeley: University of California Press, 1979). (Chap. 2)

Cardoso, Lawrence A. *Mexican Emigration to the United States, 1897–1931*. Tucson, Ariz.: University of Arizona Press, 1980. (Chap. 8)

Cardozo, Efraim. *Los derechos del Paraguay sobre los saltos del Guairá*. Asunción: Talleres Graficos, 1965. (Chap. 7)

Carey, James C. *Peru and the United States, 1900–1962.* Notre Dame, Ind.: University of Notre Dame Press, 1964. (Chap. 3)

Carey, John, ed. *The Dominican Republic Crisis, 1965.* Dobbs Ferry: Oceana Publications, 1967. (Chap. 7)

Carlisle, Douglas. *Venezuelan Foreign Policy: Its Organization and Beginning.* Lanham, Md.: University Press of America, 1978. (Chap. 3)

Carneiro, David. *Historia da Guerra Cisplatina.* São Paulo: Editora Nacional, 1946. (Chap. 7)

Carnero Checo, Genaro. *El Aguila Rampante: El imperialism yanqui sobre América Latina.* México: Ediciones Semanario Peruano, 1956. (Chap. 3)

Carnoy, Martin. *Industrialization in a Latin American Common Market.* Washington, D.C.: Brookings Institution, 1972. (Chap. 6)

Carothers, Thomas H. *In the Name of Democracy: U.S. Policy Toward Latin America in the Reagan Years.* Berkeley: University of California Press, 1991. (Chap. 8)

Carpio Castillo, Rubén. *Geopolítica de Venezuela.* Caracas: Editorial Ariel-Seix Barral Venezolano, 1981. (Chap. 3)

Carr, Raymond. *Puerto Rico: A Colonial Experiment.* New York: New York University Press, 1984. (Chap. 2)

Carreño, Alberto Maria. *La diplomacia extraordinaria entre México y los Estados Unidos, 1789–1947.* 2 vols. México: Editorial Jus, 1951. (Chap. 3)

_____. *México y los Estados Unidos de América: apuntaciones para la historia del acrecentamiento territorial de los Estados Unidos a costa de México desde la epoca colonial hasta nuestros días.* México: Imprenta de la Victoria, 1922. (Chap. 7)

Carreras, Charles. *United States Penetration of Venezuela and Its Effects on Diplomacy, 1895–1906.* New York: Garland, 1987. (Chap. 3)

Carrión Mena, Francisco. *Política exterior del Ecuador: evolución, teoria y practica.* Quito: Editorial Universitaria, 1986. (Chap. 3)

Casasús, Juan José. *La enmigración cubana y la independencia de la patria.* Havana: 1953. (Chap. 8)

Castañeda, Jorge G. *Mexico and the United Nations.* New York: Colegio de México and the Carnegie Endowment, 1958. (Chap. 3)

_____. *Utopia Unarmed: The Latin American Left after the Cold War.* New York: Alfred A. Knopf, 1993. (Chap. 8)

Castillero Pimental, Ernesto. *Panamá y los Estados Unidos.* Panamá: Editora Humanidad, 1953. (Chap. 6)

_____. *Política Exterior de Panamá.* Panamá: Impresora Panamá, 1961. (Chap. 3)

Castillo, José del, and others. *La Gulf + Western en Republica Dominicana.* Santo Domingo: Editora de la Universidad Autónoma de Santo Domingo, 1974. (Chap. 8)

Castro, Daniel, ed. *Revolution and Revolutionaries: Guerrilla Movements in Latin America.* Wilmington, Del.: Scholarly Resources, 1999. (Chap. 7)

Castro, Flávio Mendes de Oliveira. *História da organizaçao do Ministério das Relaçoes Exteriores*. Brasília: Editora Universidade de Brasília, 1983. (Chap. 3)

Castro, Max J., ed. *Free Markets, Open Societies, Closed Borders? International Migration and Immigration Policy in the Americas*. Boulder: Lynne Rienner Publishers, for North-South Center, University of Miami, 1998. (Chap. 8)

_____. *Trends in International Migration and Immigration Policy in the Americas*. Boulder: Lynne Rienner Publishers, for North-South Center, University of Miami, 1998. (Chap. 8)

Cavelier, Germán. *La política internacional de Colombia*. 4 vols. Bogotá: Editorial Esqueima, 1949–1959. (Chap. 3)

Cecena, José Luis. *México en la órbita imperial*. México, D.F.: Ed. Part. El Caballito, 1970. (Chap. 8)

Cepeda Ulloa, Fernando, and Rodrigo Pardo García-Peña. *Contadora: Desafio a la Diplomácia Tradicional*. Lima: Centro de Estudios Internacionales de la Universidad de Los Andes, 1985. (Chap. 7)

Cervo, Amado Luiz, and Clodoaldo Bueno. *Historia da política exterior do Brasil*. São Paulo: Atica, 1992. (Chap. 3)

Chadwick, French Ensor. *The Relations of the United States and Spain*. 2 vols. New York: C. Scribner's Sons, 1909, 1911. (Chap. 7)

Chamorro Zelaya, Pedro Joaquín. *Historia de la federación de la América Central, 1823–1840*. Madrid: Editorial Cultura Hispánica, 1951. (Chap. 6)

Charlier, Etienne D. *Aperçu sur la formation historique de la nation haitienne*. Port-au-Prince, Les Presses Libres, 1954. (Chap. 3)

Chaves, Julio César. *Historia de las relaciones entre Buenos Aires y el Paraguay, 1810–1813*. 2d ed. Asunción, Buenos Aires: Ediciones Nizza, 1959. (Chap. 7)

_____. *La revolución paraguaya de la independencia*. Buenos Aires: Talleres Graficos Lumen, Noseda, 1961. (Chap. 7)

Chayes, Abram. *The Cuban Missile Crisis: International Crises and the Role of Law*. New York: Oxford University Press, 1974. (Chap. 7)

Checa Drouet, Benigno. *La doctrina americans del uti possidetis de 1810*. Lima: Imprenta Gil, 1936. (Chap. 7)

Chilcote, Ronald H., and Joel C. Edelstein. *Latin America: Capitalist and Socialist Perspectives on Development and Underdevelopment*. Boulder: Westview Press, 1986. (Chap. 2)

Chilcote, Ronald H., and Joel Edelstein, eds. *Latin America: The Struggle with Dependency and Beyond*. New York: Halsted Press, 1974. (Chap. 2)

Child, Jack. *Antarctica and South American Geopolitics: Frozen Lebensraum*. New York: Praeger, 1988. (Chaps. 3, 6)

_____. *The Central American Peace Process, 1983–1991: Sheathing Swords, Building Confidence*. Boulder: Lynne Rienner Publishers, 1992. (Chap. 7)

_____. *Geopolitics and Conflict in South America: Quarrels Among Neighbors*. New York: Praeger, 1985. (Chaps. 3)

Child, Jack, ed. *Conflict in Central America: Approaches to Peace and Security.* New York: St. Martin's Press, 1986. (Chap. 7)

Child, John. *Unequal Alliance: The Inter-American Military System 1938–1978.* Boulder: Westview Press, 1980. (Chap. 8)

Cho, Key-Sung. *Organismos interamericanos: sus antecedentes, estructuras, funciones y perspectivas.* Quito: Ediciones Culturales, 1984. (Chap. 2)

Christian, Shirley. *Nicaragua: Revolution in the Family.* New York: Vintage Books, 1988. (Chap. 7)

Cirincione, Joseph, ed. *Central America and the Western Alliance.* New York: Holmes and Meier, for Carnegie Endowment for International Peace and International Institute for Strategic Studies, 1985. (Chap. 7)

Cisneros, Andrés, ed. *Política exterior argentina, 1989–1999: historia de un éxito.* Buenos Aires: Nuevohacer, Grupo Editor Latinoamericano, 1998. (Chap. 3)

Cisneros, Andrés, and Carlos Escudé, eds. *Historia general de las relaciones exteriores de la República Argentina* (volume titles vary). 14 vols. Buenos Aires: Centro de Estudios de Política Exterior, Consejo Argentina para las Relaciones Relaciones Internacionales; Nuevohacer, Grupo Editor Latinoamericano, Galerna, 1998–2000. (Chap. 3)

Cisneros Lavaller, Alberto. *América Latina: conflicto o cooperación.* Caracas: Proimagen, 1986. (Chap. 3)

Clark, Truman R. *Puerto Rico and the United States, 1917–1933.* Pittsburgh: University of Pittsburgh Press, 1975. (Chap. 2)

Clawson, Patrick L., and Renssalaer W. Lee III. *The Andean Cocaine Industry.* New York: St. Martin's Press, 1996. (Chap. 8)

Cleary, Edward L. *Crisis and Change: The Church in Latin America Today.* Maryknoll, N.Y.: Orbis Books, 1985. (Chap. 8)

————. *The Struggle of Human Rights in Latin America.* Westport, Conn.: Praeger, 1997. (Chap. 8)

Cleary, Edward L., and Hannah Stewart-Gambino, eds. *Conflict and Competition: The Latin American Church in a Changing Environment.* Boulder: Lynne Rienner Publishers, 1992. (Chap. 8)

————. *Power, Politics, and Pentecostals in Latin America.* Boulder: Westview Press, 1997. (Chap. 8)

Clendenen, Clarence Clemens. *Blood on the Border: The United States Army and the Mexican Irregulars.* New York: Macmillan, 1969. (Chap. 7)

————. *The United States and Pancho Villa: A Study in Unconventional Diplomacy.* Ithaca, N.Y.: Cornell University Press, for American History Association, 1961. (Chap. 7)

Cline, Howard F. *The United States and Mexico.* Rev. ed. Cambridge: Harvard University Press, 1963. 1st ed. 1953. (Chap. 3)

Cline, William R., and Enrique Delgado, eds. *Economic Integration in Central America.* Washington, D.C.: Brookings Institution, 1978. (Chap. 6)

Coatsworth, John H. *Central America and the United States: The Clients and the Colossus*. New York: Twayne Publishers, 1994. (Chap. 2)

Cobbs, Elizabeth A. *The Rich Neighbor Policy: Rockefeller and Kaiser in Brazil*. New Haven, Conn.: Yale University Press, 1992. (Chap. 8)

Cochrane, James D. *The Politics of Regional Integration: The Central American Case*. New Orleans: Tulane University Press, 1969. (Chap. 6)

Cockcroft, James D. *Latin America: History, Politics, and U.S. Policy*. 2d ed. Chicago: Nelson-Hall Publishers, 1996. 1st ed. 1989, titled *Neighbors in Turmoil: Latin America*. (Chaps. 3, 5)

Cockcroft, James D., Andre Gunder Frank, and Dale L. Johnson. *Dependence and Underdevelopment: Latin America's Political Economy*. Garden City, N.Y.: Anchor Books, 1972. (Chap. 2)

Coerver, Don M., and Linda B. Hall. *The United States and Latin America*. Albuquerque, N.M.: University of New Mexico Press, 1999. (Chaps. 2, 5)

Cohen, Martin A., ed. *The Jewish Experience in Latin America*. 2 vols. New York: American Jewish Historical Society, 1971. (Chap. 8)

Cohen Orantes, Isaac. *Regional Integration in Central America*. Lexington, Mass.: Lexington Books, 1972. (Chap. 6)

Colby, Gerard, with Charlotte Dennett. *Thy Will Be Done: The Conquest of the Amazon: Nelson Rockefeller and Evangelism in the Age of Oil*. New York: HarperCollins, 1995. (Chap. 8)

Cole, Julio Harold. *Latin American Inflation: Theoretical Interpretations and Empirical Results*. New York: Praeger, 1987. (Chap. 2)

El Colegio de México. *La frontera del norte: integración y desarrollo*. México, D.F.: El Colegio de México, 1981. (Chap. 3)

_____. *Lecturas de política exterior mexicana*. México, D.F.: El Colegio de México, 1970. (Chap. 3)

Coleman, Kenneth M., and George C. Herring, eds. *Understanding the Central American Crisis: Sources of Conflict, U.S. Policy, and Options for Peace*. 2d ed. Wilmington, Del.: Scholarly Resources, 1991. 1st ed. 1985 (Chap. 7)

Coll, Alberto, and Anthony C. Arend, eds. *The Falklands War: Lessons for Strategy, Diplomacy, and International Law*. Boston: Allen and Unwin, 1985. (Chap. 7)

Colli, Néstor S. *Rosas y el bloqueo anglo-francés*. Buenos Aires: Editora Patria Grande, 1978. 1st ed. 1963, titled *La política francesa en el Río de la Plata: Rosas y el bloqueo de 1838–1840*. (Chap. 7)

Collier, Simon. *Ideas and Politics of Chilean Independence, 1808–1833*. Cambridge: Cambridge University Press, 1967. (Chap. 7)

Collin, Richard H. *Theodore Roosevelt's Caribbean: The Panama Canal, the Monroe Doctrine, and the Latin American Context*. Baton Rouge: Louisiana State University Press, 1990. (Chap. 5)

Comisión Económica para América Latina y el Caribe; Banco Interamericano de Desarrollo. *La integración centroamericana y la institucionalidad regional.* México, D.F.: Comisión Económica para América y el Caribe, 1998. (Chap. 6)

Comitas, Lambros, and David Lowenthal, eds. *The Aftermath of Sovereignty: West Indian Perspectives.* Garden City, N.Y.: Anchor, 1973. (Chaps. 3, 6)

Conil Paz, Alberto A., and Gustavo E. Ferrari. *Argentina's Foreign Policy, 1930–1962.* Translated by Joseph J. Kennedy. Notre Dame, Ind.: University of Notre Dame Press, 1996. (Chap. 3)

Conn, Stetson, and Byron Fairchild. *The Western Hemisphere: The Framework of Hemispheric Defense* and *Guarding the United States and its Outposts.* Vol. 12, pts. 1, 2 of U.S. Department of the Army, Office of the Chief of Military History, *United States Army in World War II.* Washington, D.C.: Government Printing Office, 1960. (Chap. 8)

Connell-Smith, Gordon. *The Inter-American System.* London: Oxford University Press, 1966. (Chap. 6)

———. *The United States and Latin America: An Historical Analysis of Inter-American Relations.* New York: Halsted, 1974. (Chaps. 2, 5)

Connelly, Marisela, and Romero Cornejo Bustamante. *China–América Latina: génesis y desarollo de sus relaciones.* México, D.F.: El Colegio de México, 1992. (Chap. 4)

Conniff, Michael L. *Black Labor on a White Canal: Panama, 1904–1981.* Pittsburgh: University of Pittsburgh Press, 1985. (Chap. 8)

———. *Panama and the United States: The Forced Alliance.* Athens, Ga.: University of Georgia Press, 1992. (Chap. 3)

Connolly, Michael B., and John McDermott, eds. *The Economics of the Caribbean Basin.* New York: Praeger, 1985. (Chap. 2)

Consalvi, Simón Alberto. *Grover Cleveland y la controversia Venezuela–Gran Bretaña.* Washington, D.C.: Tierra de Gracia Editores, 1992. (Chap. 7)

———. *Un momento histórico de América Latina: Acapulco, 1987.* Caracas: Pomaire, 1988. (Chap. 6)

Córdova, Arnaldo. *La ideología de la Revolución Mexicana.* México: Ediciones Era, 1973. (Chap. 7)

Corkran, Herbert. *Patterns of International Cooperation in the Caribbean, 1942-1969.* Dallas: Southern Methodist University Press, 1972. (Chap. 2)

Corominas, Enrique Ventura. *Historia de las conferencias interamericanas.* Buenos Aires: Editorial Propulsion, 1959. (Chap. 6)

Cortés-Conde, Roberto, and Shane J. Hunt. *The Latin American Economies: Growth and the Export Sector, 1880–1930.* New York: Holmes and Meier, 1985. (Chap. 8)

Corwin, Arthur F. *Immigrants—and Immigrants: Perspectives on Mexican Labor Migration to the United States.* Westport, Conn.: Greenwood Press, 1978. (Chap. 8)

Cosio Villegas, Daniel. *The United States Versus Porfirio Díaz.* Translated by Nettie Lee Bensen. Lincoln, Nebr.: University of Nebraska Press, 1964. (Chap. 3)

Costa, Gino F. *Brazil's Foreign Policy: Toward Regional Dominance.* Boulder: Westview Press, 1989. (Chap. 3)

Costa, Licurgo. *Uma nova política para as Américas: Doutrina Kubitschek e OPA.* São Paulo: Maruns, 1960. (Chap. 8)

Cotler, Julio, and Richard Fagen, eds. *Latin America and the United States: The Changing Political Realities.* Stanford, Calif.: Stanford University Press, 1974. (Chap. 5)

Cottam, Martha L. *Images and Intervention: U.S. Policies in Latin America.* Pittsburgh: University of Pittsburgh Press, 1994. (Chap. 5)

Coutin, Susan Bibler. *Legalizing Moves: Salvadoran Immigrants' Struggle for U.S. Residency.* Ann Arbor: University of Michigan Press, 2000. (Chap. 8)

Crahan, Margaret E., ed. *Human Rights and Basic Needs in the Americas.* Washington, D.C.: Georgetown University Press, 1982. (Chap. 8)

Craig, Richard B. *The Bracero Program: Interest Groups and Foreign Policy.* Austin: University of Texas Press, 1971. (Chap. 8)

Cravey, Altha. *Women and Work in Mexico's Maquiladoras.* Lanham, Md.: Rowman and Littlefield Publishers, 1998. (Chap. 6)

Cross, Harry E., and James A. Sandos. *Across the Border: Rural Development in Mexico and Recent Migration to the United States.* Berkeley: University of California, Institute of Governmental Studies, 1981. (Chap. 8)

Crouse, Nellis Maynard. *The French Struggle for the West Indies, 1665–1713.* New York: Columbia University Press, 1943. (Chap. 2)

Cruz Monclova, Lidio. *Historia de Puerto Rico, Siglo XIX.* 3 vols., 3d ed. Río Piedras: Editorial Universitaria, Universidad de Puerto Rico, 1970–1971. 1st ed. 1952. (Chap. 2)

Cuello H., José Israel, and Julio E. Peynado. *La Gulf y Western en la reformismo.* Santo Domingo: Ediciones Taller, 1974. (Chap. 8)

Cuevas Cancino, Francisco M. *Del Congreso de Panamá a la Conferencia de Caracas, 1826–1954: El genio de Bolívar a través de la historia de las relaciones interamericanas.* 2 vols. Caracas: Ragon, 1955. (Chap. 6)

_____. *Roosevelt y la buena vecinidad.* México, D.F.: Fondo de la Cultura Económica, 1954. (Chap. 5)

Cullather, Nick. *Secret History: The CIA's Classified Account of Its Operations in Guatemala, 1952–1954.* Stanford Calif.: Stanford University Press, 1999. (Chap. 7)

Cumberland, Charles C. *Mexican Revolution: Genesis Under Madero.* Austin: University of Texas Press, 1952. (Chap. 7)

_____. *Mexican Revolution: The Constitutionalist Years.* Austin, Tex.: University of Texas Press, 1972. (Chap. 7)

Cummins, Lejeune. *Quijote on a Burro: Sandino and the Marines, a Study in the Formulation of Foreign Policy.* México: Imprenta Azteca, 1958. (Chap. 7)

Dabbs, Jack Aubrey. *The French Army in Mexico, 1861–1867: A Study in Military Government*. The Hague: Mouton, 1963. (Chap. 7)

Dallegri, Santiago. *El Paraguay y la Guerra de la Triple Alianza*. Buenos Aires: Instituto Amigos del Libro Argentino, 1964. (Chap. 7)

Danchev, Alex, ed. *International Perspectives on the Falklands Conflict: A Matter of Life and Death*. New York: St. Martin's Press, 1992. (Chaps. 6, 7)

Dantas, Francisco Clementino de San Tiago. *Política externa independente*. Río de Janeiro: Editora Civilição Brasileira, 1962. (Chap. 3)

D'Antonio, William V., and Fredrick B. Pike, eds. *Religion, Revolution, and Reform: New Forces for Change in Latin America*. New York: Praeger, 1964. (Chap. 8)

Dash, J. Michael. *Haiti and the United States: National Stereotypes and the Literary Imagination*. 2d ed. New York: St. Martin's Press, 1997. 1st ed. 1988. (Chap. 3)

Davies, Elizabeth W. *The Legal Status of British Territories: The West Indies and North Atlantic Region*. Cambridge: Cambridge University Press, 1995. (Chap. 2)

Davis, Darién J., ed. *Slavery and Beyond: The African Impact on Latin America and the Caribbean*. Wilmington, Del.: Scholarly Resources, 1995. (Chap. 8)

Davis, Harold Eugene, John J. Finan, and F. Taylor Peck. *Latin American Diplomatic History: An Introduction*. Baton Rouge: Louisiana State University Press, 1977. (Chap. 2)

Davis, Harold Eugene, Larman C. Wilson, and others. *Latin American Foreign Policies*. Baltimore: Johns Hopkins University Press, 1975. (Chap. 3)

Davis, William Columbus. *The Last Conquistadores: The Spanish Intervention in Peru and Chile, 1863–1866*. Athens, Ga.: University of Georgia Press, 1950. (Chap. 7)

Dawsey, Cyrus B., and James M. Dawsey, eds. *The Confederados: Old South Immigrants in Brazil*. Tuscaloosa, Ala.: University of Alabama Press, 1995. (Chap. 8)

Dawson, Frank Griffith. *The First Latin American Debt Crisis: The City of London and the 1822–25 Loan Bubble*. New Haven, Conn.: Yale University Press, 1990. (Chap. 8)

De Boni, L. A., ed. *A presençá italiana no Brasil*. 2 vols. Torino: Giovanni Agnelli, 1990. (Chap. 3)

Debray, Régis. *Che's Guerrilla War*. Harmondsworth, UK: Penguin, 1976. (Chap. 7)

———. *Strategy for Revolution: Essays on Latin America*. New York: Monthly Review Press, 1979. (Chap. 7)

DeConde, Alexander. *Herbert Hoover's Latin American Policy*. Stanford: Stanford University Press, 1951. (Chap. 5)

De Kadt, Emanuel, ed. *Patterns of Foreign Influence in the Caribbean*. London: Oxford University Press, 1972. (Chap. 2)

De la Garza, Rodolfo, and Jesús Velasco, eds. *Bridging the Border: Transforming Mexico-U.S. Relations*. Lanham, Md.: Rowman and Littlefield, 1997. (Chap. 3)

Delgado, Jaime. *España y México en el siglo diecinueve*. 2 vols. Madrid: Consejo de Investigaciones Científicas, 1950–1954. (Chap. 3)

Dell, Sidney. *The Central American Integration Programme*. London: Oxford University Press, 1966. (Chap. 6)

_____. *The Inter-Development Bank: A Study in Development Financing*. New York: Praeger, 1972. (Chap. 6)

_____. *A Latin American Common Market?* London: Oxford University Press, for Royal Institute of International Affairs, 1966. (Chap. 6)

Delpar, Helen. *The Enormous Vogue of Things Mexican: Cultural Relations Between the United States and Mexico, 1920–1935*. Tuscaloosa, Ala.: University of Alabama Press, 1992. (Chap. 8)

Dennis, William Jefferson. *Tacna and Arica: An Account of the Chile-Peru Boundary Dispute and the Arbitration by the United States*. New Haven, Conn.: Yale University Press, 1931. (Chap. 7)

Dent, David W. *The Legacy of the Monroe Doctrine: A Reference Guide to U.S. Involvement in Latin America and the Caribbean*. Westport, Conn.: Greenwood Press, 1998. (Chap. 5)

Dent, David W., ed. *Handbook of Political Science Research on Latin America: Trends from the 1960s to the 1990s*. Westport, Conn.: Greenwood Press, 1990. (Chap. 2)

_____. *U.S–Latin American Policymaking: A Reference Handbook*. Westport, Conn.: Greenwood Press, 1995. (Chap. 5)

Desch, Michael C. *When the Third World Matters: Latin America and the United States Grand Strategy*. Baltimore: Johns Hopkins University Press, 1993. (Chap. 5)

Desch, Michael, Jorge Domínguez, and Andrés Serbin. *From Pirates to Drug Lords: The Post–Cold War Caribbean Security Environment*. Albany, N.Y.: State University of New York Press, 1998.

Devlin, Robert. *Debt and Crisis in Latin America: The Supply Side of the Story*. Princeton, N.J.: Princeton University Press, 1989. (Chap. 8)

Dewitt, R. Peter, Jr. *The Inter-American Development Bank and Political Influence: With Special Reference to Costa Rica*. New York: Praeger, 1977. (Chap. 6)

Díaz Albonico, Rodrigo, ed. *Antecedentes, Balance y Perspectivas del Sistema Interamericano*. Santiago de Chile: Editorial Universitaria, 1977. (Chap. 6)

Díaz-Briquets, Sergio, ed. *Cuban Internationalism in Sub-Saharan Africa*. Pittsburgh: Duquesne University Press, 1989. (Chap. 7)

Díaz Cisneros, César. *Límites de la República Argentina: fundamentos histórico-jurídicos*. Buenos Aires: Editorial Depalma, 1944. (Chap. 7)

Dietz, James L., ed. *Latin America's Economic Development: Confronting Crisis*. 2d ed. Boulder: Lynne Rienner Publishers, 1995. 1st ed. 1987. (Chap. 8)

Dietz, James L., and Dilmus D. James, eds. *Progress Toward Development in Latin America: From Prebisch to Technological Autonomy*. Boulder: Lynne Rienner Publishers, 1990. (Chap. 2)

Dietz, James L., and James H. Street, eds. *Latin America's Economic Development: Institutionalist and Structuralist Perspectives*. Boulder: Lynne Rienner Publishers, 1987. (Chap. 2)

Diffie, Bailey W. *A History of Colonial Brazil, 1500–1792*. Edited by Edwin J. Perkins. Melbourne, Fla.: Krieger, 1987. (Chap. 2)

Dillon, G. M. *The Falklands, Politics, and War*. New York: St. Martin's Press, 1989. (Chap. 7)

Dinerstein, Herbert S. *The Making of a Missile Crisis: October 1962*. Baltimore: Johns Hopkins University Press, 1976. (Chap. 7)

Di Tella, Guido, and D. Cameron Watt, eds. *Argentina Between the Great Powers, 1939–1946*. London: Macmillan, 1990. (Chap. 7)

Dodd, Thomas J. *Managing Democracy in Central America: A Case Study of United States Election Supervision in Nicaragua, 1927–1933*. New Brunswick, N.J.: Transaction Publishers, for North-South Center, University of Miami, 1992. (Chap. 7)

Domínguez, Jorge I. *Cuba: Order and Revolution*. Cambridge: Harvard University Press, 1978. (Chap. 3)

――――. *Insurrection or Loyalty: The Breakdown of the Spanish American Empire*. Cambridge: Harvard University Press, 1980. (Chap. 7)

――――. *To Make a World Safe for Revolution: Cuba's Foreign Policy*. Cambridge: Harvard University Press, 1989. (Chap. 3)

Domínguez, Jorge I., ed. *Democratic Politics in Latin America and the Caribbean*. Baltimore: Johns Hopkins University Press, 1998. (Chap. 8)

――――. *The Future of Inter-American Relations*. New York: Routledge, 1999. (Chap. 2)

――――. *International Security and Democracy: Latin America and the Caribbean in the Post–Cold War Era*. Pittsburgh: University of Pittsburgh Press, 1998. (Chap. 2)

――――. *Latin America's International Relations and Their Domestic Consequences: War and Peace, Dependency and Autonomy, Integration and Disintegration*. New York: Garland Publishing, 1994. (Chap. 3)

――――. *Mexico's Political Economy: Challenges at Home and Abroad*. Beverly Hills, Calif.: Sage Publications, 1982. (Chap. 3)

Domínguez, Virginia R. *From Neighbor to Stranger: The Dilemma of the Caribbean Peoples in the United States*. New Haven, Conn.: Yale University Press, 1975. (Chap. 8)

Donnelly, Thomas, Margaret Roth, and Caleb Baker. *Operation Just Cause: The Storming of Panama*. Lexington, Mass.: Lexington Books, 1992. (Chap. 7)

Doran, Charles F., and Gregory P. Marchildon, eds. *The NAFTA Puzzle: Political Parties and Trade in North America*. Boulder: Westview Press, 1994. (Chap. 6)

Dosal, Paul J. *Doing Business with the Dictators: A Political History of United Fruit in Guatemala, 1899–1944*. Wilmington, Del.: Scholarly Resources, 1993. (Chap. 8)

Dos Santos, Theotonio. *La crisis norteamericana y América Latina*. Bogotá: Ediciones El Tigre de Papel, 1972. (Chap. 2)

_____. *Dependencia económica y cambio revolucionario en América Latina*. Caracas: Ed. Nueva Izquierda, 1970. (Chap. 2)

_____. *Imperialismo y empresas multinacionales*. Buenos Aires: Editorial Galerna, 1973. (Chap. 8)

Dozer, Donald Marquand. *Are We Good Neighbors? Three Decades of Inter-American Relations, 1930–1960*. Gainesville: University of Florida Press, 1959. (Chaps. 2, 5)

Drack, Gene M. *Mexico Views Manifest Destiny, 1821–1846*. Albuquerque, N.M.: University of New Mexico Press, 1975. (Chap. 3)

Drago, Mariano José. *El bloque francés de 1838 en el Río de La Plata*. Buenos Aires: El Ateneo, 1948. (Chap. 3)

Drake, Paul W. *The Money Doctor in the Andes: The Kemmerer Missions, 1923–1933*. Durham, N.C.: Duke University Press, 1989. (Chap. 3)

Drake, Paul W., ed. *Money Doctors, Foreign Debts, and Economic Reforms in Latin America from the 1890s to the Present*. Wilmington, Del.: Scholarly Resources, 1994. (Chap. 8)

Draper, Theodore. *Castroism: Theory and Practice*. New York: Praeger, 1965. (Chap. 3)

_____. *The Dominican Revolt: A Case Study in American Policy*. New York: Commentary, 1968. (Chap. 7)

Drekonja Kornat, Gerhard. *Colombia política exterior*. Bogotá: Universidad de los Andes, 1982. (Chap. 3)

Drekonja Kornat, Gerhard, and Juan G. Tokatlian, eds. *Teoría y práctica de la política exterior latinoamericana*. Bogotá: Universidad de los Andes, 1983. (Chap. 3)

Driscoll, Barbara A. *The Tracks North: The Railroad Bracero Program of World War II*. Austin: University of Texas Press, 1997. (Chap. 8)

Duncan, W. Raymond. *The Soviet Union and Cuba: Interests and Influence*. New York: Praeger, 1985. (Chap. 3)

Dunn, Hopeton S. *Globalization, Communications and Caribbean Identity*. New York: St. Martin's Press, 1995. (Chap. 8)

Dunn, Timothy J. *The Militarization of the U.S.-Mexico Border, 1978–1992: Low-Intensity Conflict Doctrine Comes Home*. Austin: University of Texas Press, 1995. (Chap. 8)

Dupuy, Alex. *Haiti in the New World Order: The Limits of the Democratic Revolution*. Boulder: Westview Press, 1997. (Chap. 3)

_____. *Haiti in the World Economy: Class, Race, and Underdevelopment Since 1700*. Boulder: Westview Press, 1989. (Chap. 3)

Duran, Esperanza. *European Interests in Latin America.* London: Routledge and Kegan Paul, for Royal Institute of International Affairs, 1985. (Chap. 4)

Dussell, Enrique. *History and the Theology of Liberation: A Latin American Perspective.* Maryknoll, N.Y.: Orbis Books, 1976. (Chap. 8)

———. *A History of the Church in Latin America: Colonialism to Liberation (1492–1979).* Grand Rapids, Mich.: William B. Eerdmans, 1981. (Chap. 8)

DuVal, Miles Percy. *Cadiz to Cathay: The Story of the Long Diplomatic Struggle for the Panama Canal.* 2d ed. Stanford: Stanford University Press, 1947. 1st ed. 1940. (Chap. 6)

Ealy, Lawrence O. *The Republic of Panama in World Affairs, 1903–1950.* Philadelphia: University of Pennsylvania Press, 1951. (Chap. 3)

———. *Yanqui Politics and the Isthmian Canal.* University Park, Pa.: Pennsylvania State University Press, 1971. (Chap. 6)

Earle, Robert L., and John D. Wirth, eds. *Identities in North America: The Search for Community.* Stanford: Stanford University Press, 1995. (Chap. 8)

Ebel, Roland H., Raymond Taras, and James D. Cochrane. *Political Culture and Foreign Policy in Latin America: Case Studies from the Circum-Caribbean.* Albany: State University of New York Press, 1991. (Chap. 3)

Echavarría, Juan José, and Alfredo L. Fuentes. *Relaciones económicas de Colombia con los países del Caribe insular.* Bogotá: Banco de la Republica, 1981. (Chap. 3)

Economic Commission for Latin America and the Caribbean. *Debt, Adjustment, and Renegotiation in Latin America: Orthodox and Alternative Approaches.* Boulder: Lynne Rienner Publishers, 1986. (Chap. 8)

———. *External Debt in Latin America: Adjustment Policies and Renegotiation.* Boulder: Lynne Rienner Publishers, 1985. (Chap. 8)

Edwards, Augustín. *La América Latina y la Liga de las Naciones.* Santiago de Chile: Editorial Universitaria, 1937. (Chap. 6)

Elkin, Judith Laikin, and Gilbert W. Merkx, eds. *The Jewish Presence in Latin America.* Boulder: Westview Press, 1988. (Chap. 8)

Engstrom, David W. *Presidential Decision Making Adrift: The Carter Administration and the Mariel Boatlift.* Lanham, Md.: Rowman and Littlefield, 1997. (Chap. 8)

Enrich, Silvia. *Historia diplomatica entre Espana e Iberoamerica en el contexto de las relaciones internacionales (1955–1985).* Madrid: Instituto de Cooperación Iberoamericana, 1989. (Chap. 4)

Enríquez Coyro, Ernesto. *El tratado entre México y los Estados Unidos de América sobre ríos internacionales: una lucha nacional de noventa años.* 2 vols. México: Universidad Nacional Autónoma de México, 1975, 1976. (Chap. 6)

Equizábel, Cristina, ed. *América Latina y la crisis centroamericana: en busca de una solución regional.* Buenos Aires: Programa de Estudios Conjuntos sobre las Relaciones Internacionales de América Latina (RIAL); Grupo Editor Latinoamericano, 1988.

Erfani, Julie A. *The Paradox of the Mexican State: Rereading Sovereignty from Independence to NAFTA.* Boulder: Lynne Rienner Publishers, 1995. (Chap. 3)

Erisman, H. Michael. *Cuba's Foreign Relations in a Post-Soviet World.* Gainesville: University of Florida Press, 2000. (Chap. 3)

_____. *Cuba's International Relations: The Anatomy of a Nationalistic Foreign Policy.* Boulder: Westview Press, 1985. (Chap. 3)

_____. *Pursuing Postdependency Politics: South-South Relations in the Caribbean.* Boulder: Lynne Rienner Publishers, 1992. (Chaps. 3, 6)

Erisman, H. Michael, and John M. Kirk, eds. *Cuban Foreign Policy Confronts a New International Order.* Boulder: Lynne Rienner Publishers, 1991. (Chap. 3)

Erisman, H. Michael, and John D. Martz, eds. *Colossus Challenged: The Struggle for Caribbean Influence.* Boulder: Westview Press, 1982. (Chaps. 2, 5)

Escobari Cusicanqui, Jorge. *El derecho al mar.* La Paz: Librería Juventud, 1964. (Chap. 3)

_____. *Historia diplomática de Bolivia: política internacional.* 4th ed. La Paz: Litografías e Imprentas Unidas, 1982. 1st ed. 1975. (Chap. 3)

Escoto Ochoa, Humberto. *Integración y desintegración de nuestra frontera norte.* México: Stylo, 1949. (Chap. 7)

Escudé, Carlos. *Foreign Policy Theory in Menem's Argentina.* Gainesville: University Press of Florida, 1997. (Chap. 3)

Espinosa, J. Manuel. *Inter-American Beginnings of U.S. Cultural Diplomacy, 1936–1948.* Washington, D.C.: U.S. Department of State, 1976. (Chap. 8)

Espinosa Moraga, Oscar. *Bolivia y el mar, 1810–1864.* Santiago de Chile: Editorial Nascimento, 1965. (Chap. 7)

_____. *El precio de la paz chileno-argentina, 1810–1869.* 3 vols. Santiago de Chile: Editorial Nascimento, 1969. (Chap. 7)

Etcheparaborda, Roberto. *Historia de las relaciones argentinas.* Buenos Aires: Editorial Pleamar, 1978. (Chap. 3)

Etchison, Don L. *The United States and Militarism in Central America.* New York: Praeger, 1975. (Chap. 8)

Etheredge, Lloyd S. *Can Governments Learn? American Foreign Policy and Central American Revolutions.* New York: Pergamon Press, 1985. (Chap. 5)

Etzioni, Minerva M. *The Majority of One: Towards a Theory of Regional Compatibility.* Beverly Hills: Sage Publications, 1970. (Chap. 6)

Evans, Henry Clay. *Chile and Its Relations with the United States.* Durham, N.C.: Duke University Press, 1927. (Chap. 3)

Evans, Luther Harris. *The Virgin Islands: From Naval Base to the New Deal.* Ann Arbor, Mich.: J. W. Edwards, 1945. (Chap. 2)

Evans, Peter. *Dependent Development: The Alliance of Multinational, State, and Local Capital in Brazil.* Princeton, N.J.: Princeton University Press, 1979. (Chap. 8)

Ewell, Judith. *Venezuela and the United States: From Monroe's Hemisphere to Petroleum's Empire.* Athens, Ga.: University of Georgia Press, 1996. (Chap. 3)

Fabela, Isidro. *Buena y mala vecinidad.* México, D.F.: Editorial Anérica Nueva, 1958. (Chap. 3)

_____. *Intervención.* México: Escuela Nacional de Ciencias Políticas y Sociales, 1959. (Chap. 3)

_____. *La historia diplomatica de la revolución mexicana.* México: Fondo de Cultura Económica, 1958. (Chap. 3)

_____. *Los precursores de la diplomacia mexicana.* México: Publicaciones de la Secretaría de Relaciones Exteriores, 1926. (Chap. 7)

Faber, Daniel. *Environment Under Fire: Imperialism and the Ecological Crisis in Central America.* New York: Monthly Review Press, 1993. (Chap. 8)

Fagen, Patricia W. *Exiles and Citizens: Spanish Republicans in Mexico.* Austin: University of Texas Press, 1973. (Chap. 8)

Fagen, Richard R., Richard A. Brody, and Thomas J. O'Leary. *Cubans in Exile: Disaffection and the Revolution.* Stanford: Stanford University Press, 1968. (Chap. 8)

Falcoff, Mark. *A Tale of Two Policies: U.S. Relations with the Argentine Junta, 1976–1983.* Philadelphia: Foreign Policy Research Institute, 1989. (Chap. 3)

Falk, Pamela. *Cuban Foreign Policy: Caribbean Tempest.* Lexington, Mass.: Lexington Books, 1986. (Chap. 3)

Farcau, Bruce W. *The Chaco War: Bolivia and Paraguay, 1932–1935.* Westport, Conn.: Praeger, 1996. (Chap. 7)

Farer, Tom J. *The Grand Strategy of the United States in Latin America.* New Brunswick, N.J.: Transaction, 1988. (Chap. 5)

Farer, Tom J., ed. *Beyond Sovereignty: Collectively Defending Democracy in the Americas.* Baltimore: Johns Hopkins University Press, 1996. (Chap. 8)

_____. *The Future of the Inter-American System.* New York: Praeger, 1988. (Chap. 6)

Farnsworth, David, and James McKenney. *U.S.-Panama Relations, 1903–1978: A Study in Linkage Politics.* Boulder: Westview Press, 1983. (Chap. 3)

Fatemi, Khosrow, ed. *The Maquiladora Industry: Economic Solution or Problem?* New York: Praeger, 1990. (Chap. 6)

_____. *U.S.-Mexican Economic Relations: Problems and Prospects.* New York: Praeger, 1988. (Chap. 3)

Fatemi, Khosrow, and Dominick Salvatore, eds. *The North American Free Trade Agreement.* Oxford: Pergamon, 1996. (Chap. 6)

Fauriol, Georges A., ed. *Security in the Americas.* Washington, D.C.: National Defense University Press, 1989. (Chap. 2)

Feinberg, Richard E., and Ricardo Ffrench-Davis, eds. *Development and External Debt in Latin America: Bases for a New Consensus.* Notre Dame, Ind.: University of Notre Dame Press, 1988. (Chap. 8)

Feller, Abraham H. *The Mexican Claims Commissions, 1923–1934: A Study in the Law and Procedures of International Tribunals.* New York: Macmillan, 1935. (Chap. 6)

Fenwick, Charles G. *The Organization of American States: The Inter-American Regional System.* Washington, D.C.: Kaufman, 1963. (Chap. 6)

Fermandois H., Joaquín. *Chile y el mundo, 1970–1973: la política exterior del gobierno de la Unidad Popular y el sistema internacional.* Santiago de Chile: Ediciones Universidad Católica de Chile, 1985. (Chap. 3)

Fernández, Carlos José. *La guerra del Chaco.* 4 vols. Buenos Aires and Asunción: n.p., 1955–1967, 1962. (Chap. 7)

Fernández, Damián J. *Cuba's Foreign Policy in the Middle East.* Boulder: Westview Press, 1988. (Chap. 3)

Fernández, Damián J., ed. *Central America and the Middle East: The Internationalization of the Crisis.* Miami: Florida International University Press, 1990. (Chaps. 4, 7)

Fernández, Raúl A. *The Mexican-American Border Region: Issues and Trends.* Notre Dame, Ind.: University of Notre Dame Press, 1989. (Chap. 3)

———. *The U.S.-Mexico Border: A Politico-Economic Profile.* Notre Dame, Ind.: University of Notre Dame Press, 1977. (Chap. 3)

Fernández, Ronald. *The Disenchanted Island: Puerto Rico and the United States in the Twentieth Century.* Westport, Conn.: Praeger, 1992. (Chap. 2)

Fernández-Shaw y Baldasano, Félix Guillermo. *La integración de Centroamérica.* Madrid: Ediciones Cultura Hispánica, 1965. (Chap. 6)

———. *La Organización de los Estados Americanos (O.E.A.): una nueva visión de América.* 2d ed. Madrid: Ediciones Cultura Hispánica, 1963. 1st ed. 1959. (Chap. 6)

Ferns, Henry Stanley. *Britain and Argentina in the Nineteenth Century.* Oxford: Clarendon Press, 1960. (Chap. 3)

Ferrari, Gustavo. *Conflicto y paz con Chile, 1898–1903.* Buenos Aires: Editorial Universitaria de Buenos Aires, 1968. (Chap. 7)

Ferrer, Aldo. *Economía internacional contemporanáo: rexto para latinoamericanos.* México: Fondo de Cultura Económica, 1976. (Chap. 2)

Ferrero Costa, Eduardo, ed. *Relaciones internacionales de Perú.* Lima: Centro Peruano de Estudios Internacionales, 1986. (Chap. 3)

Ferris, Elizabeth G. *The Central American Refugees.* New York: Praeger, 1987. (Chap. 8)

Ferris, Elizabeth G., and Jennie K. Lincoln, eds. *Latin American Foreign Policies: Global and Regional Dimensions.* Boulder: Westview Press, 1981. (Chap. 3)

Ffrench-Davis, Ricardo, and Stephany Griffith-Jones, eds. *Coping with Capital Surges: The Return of Finance to Latin America.* Boulder: Lynne Rienner Publishers, 1995. (Chap. 8)

Ffrench-Davis, Ricardo, and Ernesto Tironi, eds. *Latin America and the New International Economic Order.* London: Macmillan, 1982. (Chap. 6)

Fick, Carolyn E. *The Making of Haiti: The Saint Domingue Revolution from Below.* Knoxville: University of Tennessee Press, 1990. (Chap. 7)

Figari, Guillermo Miguel. *Pasado, presente y futuro de la política exterior argentina*. Buenos Aires: Editorial Biblos, 1993. (Chap. 3)

Finch, Elizabeth A. *The Politics of Regional Integration: A Study of Uruguay's Decision to Join LAFTA*. Liverpool: University of Liverpool, 1973. (Chap. 3)

Findling, John E. *Close Neighbors, Distant Friends: United States–Central American Relations*. Westport, Conn.: Greenwood Press, 1987. (Chaps. 2, 5)

Fishlow, Albert, and James Jones, eds. *The United States and the Americas: A Twenty-First Century View*. New York: W. W. Norton, 1999. (Chap. 2)

Fitch, Samuel. *The Armed Forces and Democracy in Latin America*. Baltimore: Johns Hopkins University Press, 1998. (Chap. 8)

Fitte, Ernesto J. *La agresión norteamericano a las Islas Malvinas*. Buenos Aires: Emece, 1966. (Chap. 7)

_____. *La disputa con Gran Bretaña por las islas del Atlántico sur*. Buenos Aires: Emecé Editores, 1968. (Chap. 7)

_____. *El precio de la libertad: La presión britanica en el proceso emancipador*. Buenos Aires: Emece Editores, 1965. (Chap. 7)

Fitzgibbon, Russell H. *Cuba and the United States, 1900–1935*. Menasha, Wisc.: George Banta, 1935. (Chap. 3)

Foner, Philip S. *A History of Cuba and Its Relations with the United States*. 2 vols. New York: International Publishers, 1962. (Chap. 7)

_____. *The Spanish-Cuban-American War and the Birth of American Imperialism, 1895–1902*. 2 vols. New York: Monthly Review Press, 1972. (Chap. 7)

_____. *United States Labor Movement and Latin America: A History of Workers' Response to Intervention, 1846–1919*. South Hadley, Mass.: Bergin and Garvey, 1988. (Chap. 8)

Fontaine, Roger W., and James D. Theberge, eds. *Latin America's New Internationalism: The End of Hemispheric Isolation*. New York: Praeger, 1976. (Chap. 2)

Fox, Annette Baker. *Freedom and Welfare in the Caribbean: A Colonial Dilemma*. New York: Harcourt Brace, 1949. (Chap. 2)

Francis, Michael. *The Limits of Hegemony: United States Relations with Argentina and Chile in World War II*. Notre Dame, Ind.: Notre Dame University Press, 1977. (Chap. 7)

Frank, Andre Gunder. *Capitalism and Underdevelopment in Latin America: Historical Studies of Chile and Brazil*. New York: Monthly Review Press, 1967. (Chap. 2)

_____. *Latin America: Underdevelopment or Revolution; Essays on the Development of Underdevelopment and the Immediate Enemy*. New York: Monthly Review Press, 1969. (Chap. 2)

_____. *Lumpenbourgeoise-Lumpendevelopment: Dependence, Class, and Politics in Latin America*. New York: Monthly Review Press, 1972. (Chap. 2)

_____. *World Accumulation, 1492–1789*. New York: Monthly Review Press, 1978. (Chap. 2)

Frank, Andre Gunder, and Barry Gills, eds. *The World System: Five Hundred or Five Thousand Years?* London: Routledge, 1996. (Chap. 2)

Frankel, Benjamin A. *Venezuela y los Estados Unidos (1810–1888).* Caracas: Ediciones de la Fundación John Boulton, 1997. (Chap. 3)

Franko-Jones, Patrice. *The Brazilian Defense Industry.* Boulder: Westview Press, 1992. (Chap. 8)

Frederick, Howard H. *Cuban-American Radio Wars: Ideology in International Telecommunications.* Norwood, N.J.: Ablex, 1986. (Chap. 8)

Freedman, Lawrence, and Virginia Gamba-Stonehouse, *Signals of War: The Falklands Conflict of 1982.* Princeton, N.J.: Princeton University Press, 1991. (Chap. 7)

Freithaler, William O. *Mexico's Foreign Trade and Economic Development.* New York: Praeger, 1968. (Chap. 3)

Fretz, Joseph Winifield. *Immigrant Group Settlement in Paraguay: A Study in the Sociology of Colonization.* North Newton, Kansas: Bethel College, 1962. (Chap. 8)

——. *Pilgrims in Paraguay: The Story of Mennonite Colonization in South America.* Scottsdale, Pa.: Herald Press, 1953. (Chap. 8)

Frieden, Jeffrey A. *Debt, Development, and Democracy: Modern Political Economy and Latin America, 1965–1985.* Princeton, N.J.: Princeton University Press, 1992. (Chap. 8)

Frieden, Jeffrey A., Manuel Pastor Jr., and Michael Tomz, eds. *Modern Political Economy and Latin America: Theory and Policy.* Boulder: Westview Press, 2000. (Chap. 2)

Friscia, August Blake, and Charles J.L.T. Kovaks. *Beyond the Lost Decade: Debt and Development in Latin America.* Boulder: Westview Press, 1993. (Chap. 8)

Fritsch, Winston. *External Constraints on Economic Policy in Brazil, 1889–1930.* Pittsburgh: University of Pittsburgh Press, 1988. (Chap. 3)

Frohman, Alicia. *Puentes sobre la turbulencia: la concertación política latinoamericana en los ochenta.* Santiago: Facultad Latinoamericana de Ciencias Sociales, 1990. (Chap. 3)

Frye, Alton. *Nazi Germany and the American Hemisphere, 1933–1941.* New Haven, Conn.: Yale University Press, 1967. (Chap. 4)

Fuller, Stephen M., and Graham A. Cosmos, *Marines in the Dominican Republic 1916–1924.* Washington, D.C.: History and Museums Division, Headquarters, U.S. Marine Corps, 1974. (Chap. 7)

Fundación Simón Bolívar, Centro de Estudios Internacionales Foro Interamericano. *La perestroika y la América Latina.* Bogotá: Tercer Mundo Editores, 1989. (Chap. 4)

Furlong, William L., and Margaret E. Scranton. *The Dynamics of Foreign Policymaking: The President, the Congress, and the Panama Canal Treaties.* Boulder: Westview Press, 1984. (Chap. 6)

Furtado, Celso. *Development and Underdevelopment*. Translated by Ricardo W. de Aguiar and Eric Charles Drysdale. Berkeley and Los Angeles, University of California Press, 1964. (Chap. 2)

_____. *Economic Development of Latin America: Historical Background and Contemporary Problems*. Translated by Suzette Macedo. 2d. ed. Cambridge: Cambridge University Press, 1976. 1st ed. 1970. (Chap. 2)

_____. *Obstacles to Development in Latin America*. Garden City, N.Y.: Anchor, 1970. (Chap. 2)

Furtak, Robert K. *Kuba und der Weltkommunismus*. Opladen: Westdeutscher Verlag, 1967. (Chap. 8)

Gaither, Roscoe B. *Expropriation in Mexico: The Facts and the Law*. New York: William Morrow, 1940. (Chap. 8)

Galeano, Eduardo. *Guatemala: Occupied Country*. Translated by Cedric Belfrage. New York: Monthly Review Press, 1969. (Chap. 7)

_____. *Open Veins of Latin America: Five Centuries of the Pillage of a Continent*. New York: Monthly Review Press, 1973. (Chap. 3)

Gamarra, Eduardo A. *Entre la droga y la democracia*. La Paz: ILDIS, 1994. (Chap. 8)

Gamba-Stonehouse, Virginia. *Falklands Conflict of 1982*. Princeton, N.J.: Princeton University Press, 1991. (Chap. 7)

_____. *The Falklands/Malvinas War: A Model for North-South Crisis Prevention*. Boston: Allen and Unwin, 1987. (Chap. 7)

Gambone, Michael D. *Eisenhower, Somoza, and the Cold War in Nicaragua, 1953–1961*. Westport, Conn.: Praeger, 1997. (Chap. 3)

Gamio, Manuel. *Mexican Immigration to the United States: A Study of Human Migration and Adjustment*. Chicago: University Press, 1930.

Garay Salamanca, Jorge. *América Latina ante el reordenamiento económico internacional*. Bogotá: Editorial Universidad Nacional, 1994. (Chap. 8)

Garber, Paul N. *The Gadsden Treaty*. Philadelphia: University of Pennsylvania Press, 1923. (Chap. 7)

Garcia Bauer, Carlos. *La controversia sobre el territorio de Belice y el procedimiento ex-aequeo*. Guatemala: Universidad de San Carlos de Guatemala, 1958. (Chap. 7)

García Cantú, Gastón. *Las invasiones norteamericanos en México*. 3d ed. México, D.F.: Ediciones Era, 1980. 1st ed. 1971. (Chap. 3)

García Jordán, Pilar. *Iglesia y poser en Perú contemporaneo, 1821–1919*. Cuzco: Centro de Estudios Regionales Andinos Bartolome de las Casas, 1991. (Chap. 8)

García Salazar, Arturo. *História diplomática del Perú*. Lima: A. J. Rivas Berrio, 1930. (Chap. 3)

García-Sayan, Diego, comp. *Narcotrafico: realidades y alternativas: conferencia internacional*. Lima: Comisión Andina de Juristas, 1990. (Chap. 8)

García-Sayan, Diego, ed. *Coca, cocaina y narcotráfico: laberinto en los Andes.* Lima: Comisión Andina de Juristas, 1989. (Chap. 8)

Gardiner, C. Harvey. *The Japanese and Peru, 1873–1973.* Albuquerque: University of New Mexico Press, 1975. (Chap. 8)

_____. *Pawns in a Triangle of Hate: The Peruvian Japanese and the United States.* Seattle: University of Washington Press, 1981. (Chap. 8)

_____. *La política de inmigración del dictador Trujillo.* Universidad Nacional Pedro Henríquez Ureña, 1979. (Chap. 8)

Gardner, Mary A. *The Inter-American Press Association: Its Fight for Freedom of the Press, 1926–1960.* Austin: University of Texas Press, 1967. (Chap. 8)

Garelli Farias, Miguel José. *La crisis internacional de 1962 y el bloqueo de Cuba.* México: Universidad Nacional Autónoma de México, 1967. (Chap. 7)

Garner, William R. *The Chaco Dispute: A Study of Prestige Diplomacy.* Washington, D.C.: Public Affairs Press, 1966. (Chap. 7)

Garrard-Burnett, Virginia, and David Stoll, eds. *Rethinking Protestantism in Latin America.* Philadelphia: Temple University Press, 1993. (Chap. 8)

Garré Copello, Belter. *El Tratado de Asunción y el Mercado Comun del Sur (MERCOSUR): los megabloques económicos y América austral.* Montevideo: Editorial Universidad, 1991. (Chap. 6)

Garrié Faget, Rodolfo. *Organismos militares interamericanos.* Buenos Aires: Ediciones Depalma, 1968. (Chap. 6)

Gauhar, Altaf, ed. *Regional Integration: The Latin American Challenge.* Boulder: Westview Press, 1985. (Chap. 6)

Gellman, Irwin F. *Good Neighbor Diplomacy: United States Policies in Latin America, 1933–1945.* Baltimore: Johns Hopkins University Press, 1979. (Chap. 5)

_____. *Roosevelt and Batista: Good Neighbor Diplomacy in Cuba, 1933–45.* Albuquerque: New Mexico University Press, 1973. (Chap. 3)

Georges, Eugenia. *The Making of a Transnational Community: Migration, Development, and Cultural Change in the Dominican Republic.* New York: Columbia University Press, 1990. (Chap. 8)

Gibson, Charles. *Spain in America.* New York: Harper and Row, 1966. (Chap. 2)

Gibson, Charles Robert. *Foreign Trade in the Economic Development of Small Nations: The Case of Ecuador.* New York: Praeger, 1971. (Chap. 3)

Gibson, Lay James, and Alfonso Corona Rentería, eds. *The U.S. and Mexico: Borderland Development and the National Economies.* Boulder: Westview Press, 1984. (Chap. 3)

Gil, Federico G. *Latin American–United States Relations.* New York: Harcourt Brace Jovanovich, 1971. (Chaps. 2, 5)

Gilbert, Dennis. *Sandinistas: The Party and the Revolution.* New York: B. Blackwell, 1988. (Chap. 7)

Gilderhus, Mark T. *Diplomacy and Revolution: U.S. Mexican Relations Under Wilson and Carranza.* Tucson: University of Arizona, 1977. (Chap. 7)

_____. *Pan American Visions: Woodrow Wilson in the Western Hemisphere, 1913–1921*. Tuscon: University of Arizona Press, 1986. (Chap. 5)

_____. *The Second Century: U.S.–Latin American Relations Since 1889*. Wilmington, Del.: Scholarly Resources, 1999. (Chaps. 2, 3, 5)

Gilio, Maria Esther. *The Tupamaro Guerrillas*. Translated by Anne Edmondson. New York: Saturday Review Press, 1972. (Chap. 7)

Glade, William P. *The Latin American Economies: A Study of Their Institutional Evolution*. New York: Van Nostrand, Reinhold, 1969. (Chap. 3)

Gleich, Albrecht von, and Diego Pizano Salazar, eds. *Colombia en la economía mundial*. Hamburg: Institut fur Iberoamerika-Kunde; Bogotá: C. Valencia, 1982. (Chap. 3)

Gleijeses, Piero. *The Dominican Crisis: The 1965 Constitutionalist Revolt and American Intervention*. Translated by Lawrence Lipson. Baltimore: Johns Hopkins University Press, 1978. (Chap. 7)

_____. *Shattered Hope: The Guatemalan Revolution and the United States, 1944–1954*. Princeton, N.J.: Princeton University Press, 1991. (Chap. 7)

Glick, Edward B. *Latin America and the Palestine Problem*. New York: Theodor Herzl Foundation, 1958. (Chap. 4)

Glinkin, Anatolii Nikolaevich. *Inter-American Relations from Bolívar to the Present*. Translated by Barry Jones. Moscow: Progress Publishers, 1990. (Chap. 2)

Glinkin, Anatolii N., Boris F. Martynov, and Petr P. Yakovlev. *U.S. Policy in Latin America: Postwar to Present*. Moscow: Progress Publishers, 1989. (Chap. 2)

Goebel, Julius Ludwig, Jr. *The Struggle for the Falkland Islands: A Study in Legal and Diplomatic History*. New Haven, Conn.: Yale University Press, 1927. (Chap. 7)

Goldhamer, Herbert. *The Foreign Powers in Latin America*. Princeton, N.J.: Princeton University Press, 1972. (Chaps. 2, 4)

Goldwert, Marvin. *The Constabulary in the Dominican Republic and Nicaragua: Progeny and Legacy of United States Intervention*. Gainesville: University of Florida Press, 1962. (Chap. 7)

Gómez de la Torre, Mario A. *Derecho constitucional interamericano*. 2 vols. Quito: Editorial Universitaria, 1964. (Chap. 6)

Gómez Robledo, Antonio. *La seguridad colectiva en el continente americano*. México, D.F.: Escuela Nacional de Ciencias Políticas y Sociales, 1959. (Chap. 6)

_____. *Las Naciones Unidas y el Sistema Interamericano: conflictas jurisdiccionales*. México, D.F.: Colegio de México, 1974. (Chap. 7)

Gómez-Robledo Verduzco, Alonso, ed. *Relaciones México–Estados Unidos: una visión interdisciplinaria*. México: Universidad Nacional Autonoma de México, 1981. (Chap. 3)

Goñi Garrido, Carlos M. *Crónica del conflicto chileno-argentino*. Buenos Aires: Ediar Editores, 1984. (Chap. 7)

González, Guadalupe, and Marta Tienda, eds. *The Drug Connection in U.S.-Mexican Relations*. San Diego: Center for U.S.-Mexican Studies, University of California, San Diego, 1989. (Chap. 3)

González Casanova, Pablo. *No intervención, autodeterminación y democracia en América Latina*. México: Siglo Veintiuno, 1983. (Chap. 6)

Goodman, David, and Anthony Hall, eds. *The Future of Amazonia: Destruction or Sustainable Development?* New York: St. Martin's Press, 1990. (Chap. 8)

Goodsell, Charles T. *American Corporations and Peruvian Politics*. Cambridge: Harvard University Press, 1974. (Chap. 8)

Gordon, Wendell Chaffee. *The Expropriation of Foreign-Owned Property in Mexico*. Washington, D.C.: American Council on Public Affairs, 1941. (Chap. 8)

Gorriti Ellenbogen, Gustavo. *Sendero: historia de la guerra milenaria en el Perú*. Lima: Editorial Apoyo, 1990. (Chap. 7)

Goslinga, Cornelis Ch. *The Dutch in the Caribbean and in the Guianas, 1680–1791*. Ed. Maria J. L. van Yperen. Assen, Netherlands: Van Gorcum, 1985. (Chap. 2)

_____. *The Dutch in the Caribbean and in Surinam, 1791/5–1942*. Assen, Netherlands: Van Gorcum, 1990. (Chap. 2)

_____. *The Dutch in the Caribbean and on the Wild Coast, 1580–1680*. Gainesville: University Press of Florida, 1971. (Chap. 2)

Gott, Richard. *Guerrilla Movements in Latin America*. London: Nelson, 1970. (Chap. 7)

Gouré, Leon, and Morris Rothenberg. *Soviet Penetration of Latin America*. Miami: University of Miami Press, 1975. (Chap. 4)

Grabendorff, Wolf, Heinrich-W. Krumwiede, and Jorge Todt. *Political Chcnge in Central America: Internal and External Dimensions*. Boulder: Westview Press, 1984. (Chap. 7)

Grabendorff, Wolf, and Riordan Roett, eds. *Latin America, Western Europe, and the U.S.: Reevaluating the Atlantic Triangle*. New York: Praeger, 1985. (Chaps. 2, 4)

Graham, Richard. *Britain and the Onset of Modernization in Brazil, 1850–1914*. Cambridge: Cambridge University Press, 1968. (Chap. 3)

_____. *Independence in Latin America: A Comparative Approach*. 2d ed. New York: McGraw-Hill, 1994. 1st ed. 1972. (Chap. 7)

Graham, Richard, ed. *Brazil and the World System*. Austin: University of Texas Press, 1991. (Chap. 3)

Granda Alva, German, Víctor Mate, and Mario Moreno. *La cooperación entre América y Europa*. Madrid: CIDEAL, 1988. (Chap. 4)

Grasmuck, Sherri, and Patricia R. Pessar. *Between Two Islands: Dominican International Migration*. Berkeley: University of California Press, 1991. (Chap. 8)

Grayson, George W. *The North American Free Trade Agreement: Regional Community and the New World Order*. Lanham, Md.: University Press of America, 1994. (Chap. 6)

_____. *Oil and Mexican Foreign Policy.* Pittsburgh: University of Pittsburgh Press, 1988. (Chap. 8)

_____. *The Politics of Mexican Oil.* Pittsburgh: University of Pittsburgh Press, 1981. (Chap. 8)

_____. *The United States and Mexico: Patterns of Influence.* New York: Praeger, 1984. (Chap. 3)

Green, David. *The Containment of Latin America: A History of the Myths and Realities of the Good Neighbor Policy.* Chicago: Quadrangle, 1971. (Chap. 5)

Green, Duncan. *Silent Revolution: The Rise of Market Economics in Latin America.* New York: Monthly Review Press, 1995. (Chap. 8)

Green, Roy, ed. *The Enterprise for the Americas Initiative: Issues and Prospects for a Free Trade Agreement in the Western Hemisphere.* Westport, Conn.: Praeger, 1993. (Chap. 6)

Grieb, Kenneth J. *The United States and Huerta.* Lincoln: University of Nebraska Press, 1969. (Chap. 7)

Griffin, Charles Carroll. *The United States and the Disruption of the Spanish American Empire: A Study on the Relations of the United States with Spain and the Rebel Spanish Colonies.* New York: Columbia University Press, 1937. (Chap. 7)

_____. *The United States and the Disruption of the Spanish Empire, 1810–1822.* New York: Columbia University Press, 1937. (Chap. 7)

Griffith, Ivelaw Lloyd. *Drugs and Security in the Caribbean: Sovereignty Under Siege.* University Park: Pennsylvania State University Press, 1997. (Chap. 8)

_____. *The Quest for Security in the Caribbean: Problems and Promises in Subordinate States.* Armonk, N.Y.: M. E. Sharpe, 1993. (Chap. 3)

Griggs, William Clark. *The Elusive Eden: Frank McMullan's Confederate Colony in Brazil.* Austin: University of Texas Press, 1987. (Chap. 8)

Grinspun, Ricardo, and Maxwell A. Cameron. *The Political Economy of North American Free Trade.* New York: St. Martin's Press, 1993. (Chap. 6)

Griswold del Castillo, Richard. *The Treaty of Guadalupe Hidalgo: A Legacy of Conflict.* Norman: University of Oklahoma Press, 1992. (Chap. 7)

Gross, Liza, in collaboration with Council on Hemispheric Affairs. *Handbook of Leftist Groups in Latin America and the Caribbean.* Boulder: Westview Press, 1995. (Chap. 7)

Grosse, Robert. *Multinationals in Latin America.* London: Routledge, 1989. (Chap. 8)

Grosse, Robert, ed. *Private Sector Solutions to the Latin American Debt Problem.* New Brunswick, N.J.: Transaction, 1992. (Chap. 8)

Grosse, Robert E., with Clarice Pechman. *Foreign Exchange Black Markets in Latin America.* Westport, Conn.: Praeger, 1994. (Chap. 8)

Grow, Michael. *The Good Neighbor Policy and Authoritarianism in Paraguay: United States Economic Expansion and Great Power Rivalry in Latin America During World War II.* Lawrence: Regents Press of Kansas, 1981. (Chap. 3)

Grugel, Jean. *Politics and Development in the Caribbean Basin: Central America and the Caribbean in the New World Order.* Bloomington: Indiana University Press, 1995. (Chap. 2)

Grunwald, Joseph, Miguel S. Wionczek, and Martin Carnoy. *Latin American Economic Integration and U.S. Policy.* Washington, D.C.: Brookings Institution, 1972. (Chap. 6)

Grunwald, Joseph, ed. *Latin America and World Economy: A Changing International Order.* Beverly Hills, Calif.: Sage Publications, 1978. (Chap. 2)

Guáqueta, Alexandra, and Francisco Thoumi, eds. *El rompecabezas de las drogas ilegales en Estados Unidos: una visión ecléctica.* Santafé de Bogotá: Ediciones Uniandes, 1997. (Chap. 8)

Guerra, José Guillermo. *La soberania chilena en las islas al sud del Canal Beagle.* Santiago de Chile: Imprenta Universitaria, 1917. (Chap. 7)

Guerra y Sánchez, Ramiro. *La guerra de los diez años, 1868–1878.* 2 vols. Habana: Cultural, 1950, 1952. (Chap. 7)

Guerrant, Edward O. *Roosevelt's Good Neighbor Policy.* Albuquerque: University of New Mexico Press, 1950. (Chap. 5)

Guevara, Ernesto Che. *Che Guevara on Guerrilla Warfare.* New York: Praeger, 1961. (Chap. 7)

———. *"Che" Guevara on Revolution: A Documentary Overview.* Edited by Jay Mallin. Coral Gables, Fla.: University of Miami Press, 1969. (Chap. 7)

———. *Che Guevara Speaks: Selected Speeches and Writings.* Ed. George Lavan. New York: Grove, 1970. (Chap. 7)

———. *Che: Selected Works of Ernesto Guevara.* Edited by Rolando E. Bonachea and Nelson P. Valdes. Cambridge: MIT Press, 1969. (Chap. 7)

———. *The Complete Bolivian Diaries of Che Guevara and Other Captured Documents.* Edited by Daniel James. New York: Stein and Day, 1968. (Chap. 7)

———. *El diario del Ché in Bolivia: noviembre 7, 1966 a octubre 7, 1967.* La Habana: Instituto del Libro, 1968. (Chap. 7)

———. *The Diary of Ché Guevara—Bolivia: November 7, 1966–October 7, 1967.* Edited by Robert Scheer. New York: Bantam, 1968. (Chap. 7)

———. *Guerrilla Warfare.* Edited by Brian Loveman and Thomas M. Davies Jr. 3d ed. Wilmington, Del.: Scholarly Resources, 1997. 1st ed. 1985. (Chap. 7)

———. *Obras Completas.* 5 vols. Buenos Aires: Editor Cepe, 1973–1974. (Chap. 7)

———. *Reminiscences of the Cuban Revolutionary War.* Translated by Victoria Ortíz. New York: Monthly Review Press, 1968.

———. *Venceremos! The Speeches and Writings of Che Guevara* (1968). Edited by John Gerassi. New York: Macmillan, 1969. (Chap. 7)

Guillén, Abraham. *El imperialismo del dólar: América Latina, revolución o alienación.* Buenos Aires: A. Peña Lillo, 1962. (Chap. 2)

_____. *Philosophy of the Urban Guerrilla: The Revolutionary Writings of Abraham Guillén.* Edited and translated by Donald C. Hodges. New York: Morrow, 1973. (Chap. 7)

Gumucio, Mariano Baptista. *Latinoamericanos y norteamericanos: cinco siglos de dos culturas.* La Paz: Editorial "Artística," 1987. (Chap. 8)

Gutiérrez, Gustavo. *Theology of Liberation: History, Politics, and Salvation.* Maryknoll: N.Y.: Orbis Books, 1973. (Chap. 8)

Gutman, Roy. *Banana Diplomacy: The Making of American Foreign Policy in Nicaragua, 1981–1987.* New York: Simon and Schuster, 1988. (Chap. 7)

Haar, Jerry, and Anthony T. Bryan, eds. *Canadian-Caribbean Relations in Transition: Trade, Sustainable Development and Security.* New York: St. Martin's Press, 1999. (Chap. 4)

Haar, Jerry, and Edgar Dosman, eds. *A Dynamic Partnership: Canada's Changing Role in the Americas.* New Brunswick, N.J.: Transaction, 1993. (Chap. 4)

Haglund, David G. *Latin America and the Transformation of U.S. Strategic Thought, 1936–1940.* Albuquerque: University of New Mexico Press, 1984. (Chap. 5)

Hahn, Walter F., ed. *Central America and the Reagan Doctrine.* Lanham, Md.: University Press of America, 1987. (Chap. 7)

Haines, Gerald K. *The Americanization of Brazil: A Study of U.S. Cold War Diplomacy in the Third World, 1945–1954.* Wilmington, Del.: Scholarly Resources, 1989. (Chap. 3)

Halebsky, Sandor, and Richard L. Harris, eds. *Capital, Power and Inequality in Latin America.* Boulder: Westview Press, 1995. (Chap. 8)

Hall, Linda B. *Oil, Banks, and Politics: The United States and Postrevolutionary Mexico, 1917–1924.* Austin: University of Texas Press, 1995. (Chap. 8)

Hall, Linda B., and Don M. Coerver. *Revolution on the Border: The United States and Mexico.* Albuquerque: University of New Mexico Press, 1988. (Chap. 7)

Hamilton, Nora, Jeffry A. Frieden, Linda Fuller, and Manuel Pastor Jr., eds. *Crisis in Central America: Regional Dynamics and U.S. Policy in the 1980s.* Boulder: Westview Press, 1988. (Chap. 7)

Hamman, Henry, ed. *Setting the North-South Agenda: United States–Latin American Relations in the 1990s.* Boulder: Lynne Rienner Publishers, for North-South Center, University of Miami, 1991. (Chaps. 2, 5)

Hanna, Alfred Jackson, and Kathryn Abbey Hanna. *Napoleon III and Mexico: American Triumph over Monarchy.* Chapel Hill: University of North Carolina Press, 1971. (Chap. 7)

Hansen, Niles. *The Border Economy: Regional Development in the Southwest.* Austin: University of Texas Press, 1981. (Chap. 3)

Hansen, Roger D. *Central America: Regional Integration and Economic Development.* Washington, D.C.: National Planning Association, 1967. (Chap. 6)

Hanson, Simon G. *Argentine Meat and the British Market*. Stanford: Stanford University Press, 1938. (Chap. 8)

_____. *Dollar Diplomacy Modern Style: Chapters in the Failure of the Alliance for Progress*. Washington, D.C.: Inter-American Affairs Press, 1971. (Chap. 8)

_____. *Economic Development in Latin America*. Washington, D.C.: Inter-American Affairs Press, 1951. (Chap. 8)

_____. *Five Years of the Alliance for Progress: An Appraisal*. Washington, D.C.: Inter-American Affairs Press, 1967. (Chap. 8)

Harbron, John D. *Canada and the Organization of American States*. Washington, D.C.: Canadian-American Committee, 1963. (Chap. 4)

Hardy, Chandra. *The Caribbean Development Bank*. Boulder: Lynne Rienner Publishers, 1995. (Chap. 6)

Haring, Clarence H. *The Spanish Empire in America*. New York: Oxford University Press, 1947. (Chap. 2)

Harrison, Lawrence E. *The Pan-American Dream: Do Latin America's Cultural Values Discourage True Partnership with the United States and Canada?* New York: Basic Books, 1997. (Chap. 8)

_____. *Underdevelopment Is a State of Mind: The Latin American Case*. Lanham, Md.: University Press of America, for Center for International Affairs, Harvard University, 1985. (Chap. 8)

Hart, Albert B. *The Monroe Doctrine: An Interpretation*. London: Duckworth, 1916. (Chap. 5)

Hart, John Mason. *Revolutionary Mexico: The Coming and Process of the Mexican Revolution*. Berkeley: University of California Press, 1987. (Chap. 8)

Hartlyn, Jonathan, Lars Schoultz, and Augusto Varas, eds. *The United States and Latin America in the 1990s: Beyond the Cold War*. Chapel Hill: University of North Carolina Press, 1992. (Chaps. 2, 5)

Hasbrouk, Alfred. *Foreign Legionaries in the Liberation of Spanish South America*. New York: Octagon Press, 1969. (Chap. 7)

Hayes, Margaret Daly. *Latin America and the U.S. National Interest: A Basis for U.S. Foreign Policy*. Boulder: Westview Press, 1984. (Chap. 5)

Healy, David. *Drive to Hegemony: The United States and the Caribbean, 1898–1917*. Madison: University of Wisconsin Press, 1988. (Chaps. 2, 5)

_____. *Gunboat Diplomacy in the Wilson Era: The U.S. Navy in Haiti, 1915–1916*. Madison: University of Wisconsin Press, 1976. (Chap. 7)

_____. *The United States in Cuba, 1898–1902: Generals, Politicians, and the Search for Policy*. Madison: University of Wisconsin Press, 1963. (Chap. 7)

Heer, David M. *Undocumented Mexicans in the United States*. New York: Cambridge University Press, 1990. (Chap. 3)

Heine, Jorge, ed. *A Revolution Aborted: The Lessons of Grenada*. Pittsburgh: University of Pittsburgh Press, 1990. (Chap. 7)

_____. *Time for Decision: The United States and Puerto Rico*. Lanham, Md.: North-South Publishing, 1983. (Chap. 2)

Heine, Jorge, and Leslie F. Manigat, eds. *The Caribbean and World Politics: Cross-Currents and Cleavages.* New York: Holmes and Meier, 1986. (Chap. 2)

Hellman, Ronald G., and H. J. Rosenbaum, eds. *Latin America: The Search for a New International Role.* New York: John Wiley and Sons, 1975. (Chap. 2)

Henelly, Alfred, and John Langan, eds. *Human Rights in the Americas: The Struggle for Consensus.* Washington, D.C.: Georgetown University Press, 1982. (Chap. 8)

Henry, Paget, and Carl Stone, eds. *The Newer Caribbean: Decolonization, Democracy, and Development.* Philadelphia: Institute for the Study of Human Issues, 1983. (Chap. 3)

Herman, Donald L. *The Comintern in Mexico.* Washington, D.C.: Public Affairs Press, 1974. (Chap. 8)

Herman, Donald L. ed. *The Communist Tide in Latin America.* Austin: University of Texas Press, 1973. (Chap. 2)

Hernández, José M. *Cuba and the United States: Intervention and Militarism, 1868–1933.* Austin: University of Texas Press, 1993. (Chap. 7)

Herrarte, Alberto. *La unión de Centroamérica: tragedia y esperanza: ensayo político-social sobre la realidad de Centro América.* 2d ed. Guatemala: Editorial del Ministro de Educación Publica, 1964. 1st ed. 1955. (Chap. 6)

Herrera, Felipe. *Desarrollo e integración.* Santiago de Chile: Editorial Emision, 1986. (Chap. 6)

———. *Nacionalismo latinoamericano.* Santiago de Chile: Editorial Universitaria, 1967. (Chap. 8)

———. *Nacionalismo, regionalismo, internacionalismo: América Latina en el contexto internacional.* Buenos Aires: Banco Interamericano de Desarrollo, 1970. (Chap. 3)

Herrero, Pedro Pérez, and Nuria Tabanera, eds. *España/América Latina: un siglo de políticas culturales.* Madrid: AIETI/Síntesis; OEI, 1993. (Chap. 4)

Herzog, Lawrence A., ed. *Changing Boundaries in the Americas: New Perspectives on the U.S.-Mexican, Central American, and South American Borders.* San Diego: Center for U.S.-Mexican Studies, University of California, San Diego. 1992. (Chap. 3)

Hey, Jeanne A. K. *Theories of Dependent Foreign Policy and the Case of Ecuador in the 1980s.* Columbus: Ohio State University Press, 1995. (Chap. 3)

Higgins, Trumbull. *The Perfect Failure: Kennedy, Eisenhower, and the CIA at the Bay of Pigs.* New York: Norton, 1987. (Chap. 7)

Hill, Eduardo, and Luigi Einaudi, eds. *América Latina y el nuevo order economico internacional.* Santiago de Chile: Corporación de Promoción Universitaria, 1979. (Chap. 6)

Hill, Howard Copeland. *Roosevelt and the Caribbean.* Chicago: University of Chicago Press, 1927. (Chap. 5)

Hill, Lawrence F. *Diplomatic Relations Between the United States and Brazil.* Durham, N.C.: Duke University Press, 1932. (Chap. 3)

Hill, Roscoe R. *Fiscal Intervention in Nicaragua.* New York: n.p., 1933. (Chap. 7)

Hilton, Stanley E. *Brazil and the Great Powers, 1930–1939: The Politics of Trade Rivalry.* Austin: University of Texas Press, 1975. (Chap. 3)

_____. *Brazil and the Soviet Challenge, 1917–1947.* Austin: University of Texas Press, 1991. (Chap. 3)

_____. *Hitler's Secret War in South America, 1939–1945: German Military Espionage and Allied Counterespionage in Brazil.* Baton Rouge: Louisiana State University Press, 1981. (Chap. 3)

Hirschman, Albert O. *A Bias for Hope: Essays on Development and Latin America.* New Haven, Conn.: Yale University Press, 1971. (Chap. 8)

_____. *Journeys Toward Progress: Studies of Economic Policy Making in Latin America.* New York: Twentieth Century Fund, 1963. (Chap. 3)

Hirschman, Albert O., ed. *Latin American Issues.* New York: Twentieth Century Fund, 1961. (Chap. 8)

Hirst, Monica, and Roberto Russell. *Democracia y política exterior: los casos de Argentina y Brazil.* Buenos Aires: Facultad Latinoamericana de Ciencias Sociales Programa Buenos Aires, 1987. (Chap. 3)

Hodges, Donald C. *Intellectual Foundations of the Nicaraguan Revolution.* Austin: University of Texas Press, 1986. (Chap. 7)

_____. *The Latin American Revolution: Politics and Strategy from Afro-Marxism to Guevarism.* New York: William Morrow, 1974. (Chap. 7)

Hogan, J. Michael. *The Panama Canal in American Politics: Domestic Advocacy and the Evolution of Policy.* Carbondale: Southern Illinois University Press, 1986. (Chap. 6)

Hogan, William. *The Panama Canal in American Politics: Domestic Advocacy and the Evolution of Policy.* Carbondale: Southern Illinois University Press, 1986. (Chap. 6)

Hollerman, Leon. *Japan's Economic Strategy in Brazil: Challenge for the United States.* Lexington, Mass.: D. C. Heath, 1988. (Chap. 3)

Honey, Martha. *Hostile Acts: U.S. Policy in Costa Rica in the 1980s.* Gainesville, Fla.: University Press of America, 1994. (Chap. 3)

Hood, Miriam. *Gunboat Diplomacy, 1895–1905: Great Power Pressure in Venezuela.* 2d ed. Boston: Allen and Unwin, 1983. 1st ed. 1977. (Chap. 7)

House, John. *Frontier on the Rio Grande: A Political Geography of Development and Social Deprivation.* New York: Oxford University Press, 1982. (Chap. 3)

Houston, John A. *Latin America in the United Nations.* New York: Carnegie Endowment for International Peace, 1956. (Chap. 3)

Hufbauer, Gary Clyde, and Jeffrey J. Schott. *NAFTA: An Assessment.* Washington, D.C.: Institute for International Economics, 1993. (Chap. 6)

_____. *North American Free Trade: Issues and Recommendations.* Washington, D.C.: Institute for International Economics, 1992. (Chap. 6)

_____. *Western Hemisphere Economic Integration.* Washington, D.C.: Institute for International Economics, 1994. (Chap. 6)

Huggins, Martha K. *Political Policing: The United States and Latin America.* Durham, N.C.: Duke University Press, 1998. (Chap. 8)

Huguet Santos, Montserrat, Antonio Niño Rodríguez, and Pedro Pérez Herrero, eds. *La formación de la imagen de América Latina en España, 1898–1989.* Madrid: Organización de Estados Iberoamericanos para la Educación, la Ciencia y la Cultura, 1992. (Chap. 4)

Humphrey, John P. *The Inter-American System: A Canadian View.* Toronto: Macmillan, 1942. (Chap. 4)

Humphreys, Robert Arthur. *Latin America and the Second World War.* 2 vols. London: University of London Athlone Press, 1982. (Chap. 7)

Humphreys, Robert Arthur, and John Lynch, eds. *The Origins of the Latin American Revolutions, 1808–1826.* New York: Alfred A. Knopf, 1965. Revised edition edited by John Lynch under the title *Latin American Revolutions, 1808–1826: Old and New World Origins* (Norman: University of Oklahoma Press, 1994). (Chap. 7)

Hundley, Norris. *Dividing the Waters: A Century of Controversy Between the United States and Mexico.* Berkeley: University of California Press, 1966. (Chap. 6)

Hunt, Alfred N. *Haiti's Influence on Antebellum America.* Baton Rouge: Louisiana State University Press, 1988. (Chap. 3)

Hutchinson, Lincoln. *The Panama Canal and International Trade Competition.* New York: Macmillan, 1915. (Chap. 6)

Iglesias, Enrique V. *Reflections on Economic Development: Toward a New Latin American Consensus.* Baltimore: Johns Hopkins University Press and Inter-American Development Bank, 1993. (Chap. 8)

Immerman, Richard H. *The CIA in Guatemala: The Foreign Policy of Intervention.* Austin: University of Texas Press, 1982. (Chap. 7)

Ince, Basil A., ed. *Contemporary International Relations of the Caribbean.* St. Augustine and Trinidad: Institute of International Relations, University of the West Indies, 1979. (Chaps. 2, 3)

Ingram, George M. *Expropriation of U.S. Property in South America: Nationalization of Oil and Copper Companies in Peru, Bolivia and Chile.* New York: Praeger, 1974. (Chap. 8)

Inman, Samuel Guy. *Inter-American Conferences, 1826–1954: History and Problems.* Edited by Harold Eugene Davis. Washington, D.C.: University Press, 1965. (Chap. 6)

_____. *Latin America: Its Place in World Life.* Rev. ed. New York: Harcourt, Brace, 1942. 1st ed. 1937. (Chap. 2)

_____. *Problems in Pan Americanism.* New York: George H. Doran, 1925. (Chap. 6)

Institute for European–Latin American Relations (IRELA). *La UE y México: una nueva relación política y económica.* Madrid: IRELA, 1997. (Chap. 8)

Institute for European–Latin American Relations (IRELA) and Inter-American Development Bank (IDB). *Foreign Direct Investment in Latin America: Perspectives of the Major Investors.* Madrid: IRELA, 1998. (Chap. 8)

Instituto Mexicana de Comercio Exterior. *El comercio exterior de México.* 3 vols. México: Siglo Veintiuno Editores, 1982. (Chap. 3)

Inter-American Economic and Social Council. *Hemispheric Cooperation and Integral Development: Report for the Secretary General.* Washington, D.C.: General Secretariat of the Organization of American States, 1982. (Chap. 8)

Inter-American Institute of International Legal Studies, *The Inter-American System: Its Development and Strengthening.* Dobbs Ferry, N.Y.: Oceana Publications, 1966. (Chap. 6)

Ireland, Gordon. *Boundaries, Possessions, and Conflicts in Central and North America, and the Caribbean.* Cambridge: Harvard University Press, 1941. (Chap. 7)

_____. *Boundaries, Possessions, and Conflicts in South America.* Cambridge: Harvard University Press, 1938. (Chap. 7)

Irish, Donald P., ed. *Multinational Corporations in Latin America.* Athens: Ohio University Press, 1978. (Chap. 8)

Irvin, George, and Stuart Holland, eds. *Central America: The Future of Economic Integration.* Boulder: Westview Press, 1989. (Chap. 6)

Jackson, D. Bruce. *Castro, the Kremlin, and Communism in Latin America.* Baltimore: Johns Hopkins Press, 1969. (Chap. 3)

Jacobini, H. B. *A Study of the Philosophy of International Law as Seen in Works of Latin American Writers.* The Hague: Martimes Nijhoff, 1954. (Chap. 6)

Jaguaribe, Hélio. *El nuevo escenario internacional.* México: Fondo de Cultura Económica, 1985. (Chap. 2)

_____. *Political Development: A General Theory and a Latin American Case Study.* New York: Harper and Row, 1973. (Chap. 2)

C.L.R. *The Black Jacobeans: Toussaint L'Ouverture and the San Domingo Revolution.* 2d ed. New York: Vintage Books, 1963. 1st ed. 1938. (Chap. 7)

Jauberth, H. Rodrigo, Gilberto Castañeda, Jesús Hernández, and Pedro Vúscovic. *The Difficult Triangle: Mexico, the United States, and Central America.* Boulder: Westview Press, 1992. (Chap. 7)

Jenkins, Rhys Owen. *Dependent Industrialization in Latin America: The Automotive Industry in Argentina, Chile, and Mexico.* New York: Praeger, 1977. (Chap. 3)

_____. *Transnational Corporations and the Latin American Automobile Industry.* Pittsburgh: University of Pittsburgh Press, 1986. (Chap. 8)

Jenks, Leland Hamilton. *Our Cuban Colony: A Study in Sugar.* New York: Vanguard Press, 1928. (Chap. 8)

Jensen, Poul. *The Garrotte: The United States and Chile, 1970–1973.* 2 vols. Aarhus, Denmark: Aarhus University Press, 1989. (Chap. 7)

Johannsen, Robert W. *To the Halls of Montezuma: The Mexican View in the American Imagination.* New York: Oxford University Press, 1985. (Chap. 7)

Johnson, Cecil. *Communist China and Latin America, 1959–1967.* New York: Columbia University Press, 1970. (Chap. 4)

Johnson, Haynes B. *The Bay of Pigs: The Leaders' Story of Brigade 2506.* New York: W. W. Norton, 1964. (Chap. 7)

Johnson, John J. *A Hemisphere Apart: The Foundations of United States Policy Toward Latin America.* Baltimore: Johns Hopkins University Press, 1990. (Chap. 5)

Johnson, Kenneth F., and Miles W. Williams. *Illegal Aliens in the Western Hemisphere: Political and Economic Factors.* New York: Praeger, 1981. (Chap. 8)

Johnson, Roberta Ann. *Puerto Rico: Commonwealth or Colony?* New York: Praeger, 1980. (Chap. 2)

Johnson, Willis Fletcher. *The History of Cuba.* 5 vols. New York: B. F. Buck, 1920. (Chap. 7)

Johnstone, Ian. *Rights and Reconciliation: Strategies in El Salvador.* Boulder: Lynne Rienner Publishers, 1995. (Chap. 7)

Jonas, Susanne. *The Battle for Guatemala: Rebels, Death Squads, and U.S. Power.* Boulder: Westview Press, 1991. (Chap. 7)

_____. *Of Centaurs and Doves: Guatemala's Peace Process.* Boulder: Westview Press, 1998. (Chap. 7)

Jones, Chester Lloyd. *Caribbean Interests of the United States.* New York: D. Appleton, 1916. (Chaps. 2, 5)

Jones, Chester Lloyd, Henry Kittredge Norton, and Peter Thomas Moon. *The United States and the Caribbean.* Chicago: University of Chicago Press, 1929. (Chap. 5)

Jordan, David C. *Revolutionary Cuba and the End of the Cold War.* Lanham, Md..: University Press of America, 1993. (Chap. 3)

Jorden, William J. *Panama Odyssey.* Austin: University of Texas Press, 1984. (Chap. 6)

Jorge, Antonio, and Jorge Salazar-Carrillo, eds. *The Latin American Debt.* New York: St. Martin's Press, 1992. (Chap. 8)

Jose, James R. *An Inter-American Peace Force Within the Framework of the Organization of American States: Advantages, Impediments, Implications.* Metuchen, N.J.: Scarecrow Press, 1970. (Chap. 6)

Joslin, D. *A Century of Banking in Latin America.* London: Oxford University Press, 1963. (Chap. 8)

Joyce, Elizabeth, and Carlos Malamud, eds. *Latin America and the International Drug Trade.* New York: St. Martin's Press, 1997. (Chap. 8)

Kagan, Robert. *A Twilight Struggle: American Power and Nicaragua, 1977–1990.* New York: Free Press, 1996. (Chap. 7)

Kamman, William. *A Search for Stability: United States Diplomacy Toward Nicaragua, 1925–1933.* Notre Dame, Ind.: University of Notre Dame Press, 1968. (Chap. 7)

Kane, William E. *Civil Strife in Latin America: A Legal History of U.S. Involvement.* Baltimore: Johns Hopkins University Press, 1972. (Chap. 7)

Kaplowitz, Donna Rich. *Anatomy of a Failed Embargo: U.S. Sanctions Against Cuba.* Boulder: Lynne Rienner Publishers, 1998. (Chap. 7)

Kaplowitz, Donna Rich, ed. *Cuba's New Ties to a Changing World.* Boulder: Lynne Rienner Publishers, 1993. (Chap. 3)

Karlsson, Weine, Ake Magnusson, and Carlos Vidales, eds. *Suecia-Latinoamérica: relaciones y cooperación.* Stockholm: Latinamerika-Institutet, 1993. (Chap. 4)

Karnes, Thomas L. *The Failure of Union: Central America, 1824–1975.* 2d ed. Tempe: Arizona State University Press, 1976. 1st ed. 1961. (Chap. 6)

Karol, K. S. *Guerrillas in Power: The Course of the Cuban Revolution.* New York: Hill and Wang, 1970. (Chaps. 3, 8)

Katz, Friedrich. *The Secret War in Mexico: Europe, the United States, and the Mexican Revolution.* Chicago: University of Chicago Press, 1981. (Chap. 7)

Kaufman, Edy. *Crisis in Allende's Chile: New Perspectives.* New York: Praeger, 1988. (Chap. 3)

_____. *The Superpowers and Their Spheres of Influence: The United States and the Soviet Union in Eastern Europe and Latin America.* London: Croom Helm, 1976. (Chap. 2)

Kaufman, Edy, Yoram Shapira, and Joel Barromi. *Israeli–Latin American Relations.* New Brunswick, N.J.: Transaction, 1979. (Chap. 4)

Kaufmann, William W. *British Policy and the Independence of Latin America, 1804–1828.* New Haven, Conn.: Yale University Press, 1951. (Chap. 7)

Kay, Cristóbal. *Latin American Theories of Development and Underdevelopment.* New York: Routledge Chapman and Hall, 1989. (Chap. 2)

Kelly, Philip L. *Checkerboards and Shatterbelts: The Geopolitics of South America.* Austin: University of Texas Press, 1997. (Chap. 3)

Kelly, Philip, and Jack Child, eds. *Geopolitics of the Southern Cone and Antarctica.* Boulder: Lynne Rienner Publishers, 1988. (Chap. 3)

Kelsey, Carl. *The American Intervention in Haiti and the Dominican Republic.* Philadelphia: American Academy of Political and Social Science, 1922. (Chap. 7)

Kemble, Hohn Haskell. *The Panama Route, 1848–1869.* Berkeley: University of California Press, 1943. (Chap. 6)

Kenworthy, Eldon, ed. *America/Américas: Myth in the Making of U.S. Policy Toward Latin America.* University Park: Pennsylvania State University Press, 1995. (Chap. 5)

Keogh, Dermot, ed. *Church and Politics in Latin America.* New York: St. Martin's Press, 1990. (Chap. 8)

Kepner, Charles David, Jr., and Jay Henry Soothill. *The Banana Empire: A Case Study of Economic Imperialism.* New York: Vanguard Press, 1935. (Chap. 8)

Kinney, Douglas. *National Interest/National Honor: The Diplomacy of the Falklands Crisis.* New York: Praeger, 1989. (Chap. 7)

Kinsbruner, Jay. *Independence in Spanish America: Civil Wars, Revolutions, and Underdevelopment.* 3d ed. Albuquerque: University of New Mexico Press, 2000. 1st ed. 1973. (Chap. 7)

Kirk, John M. *José Martí: Mentor of the Cuban Nation.* Gainesville: University Press of Florida, 1983. (Chap. 7)

Kirk, John M., and Peter McKenna. *Canada-Cuba Relations: The Other Good Neighbor Policy.* Gainesville: University Press of Florida, 1997. (Chap. 3)

Kirkpatrick, F. A. *South America and the War.* Cambridge: Cambridge University Press, 1918. (Chap. 7)

Klak, Thomas, ed. *Globalization and Neoliberalism: The Caribbean Context.* Lanham, Md.: Rowman and Littlefield, 1997. (Chap. 2)

Klepak, Hal P. *Canada and Latin American Security.* Quebec: Méridien, 1994. (Chap. 4)

Klepak, Hal P., ed. *Natural Allies? Canadian and Mexican Perspectives on International Security.* Montreal: McGill-Queen's University Press, 1996. (Chap. 3)

Knauth, Lothar. *Confrontación transpacífica: El Japón y el nuevo mundo hispánico, 1542–1639.* México: Universidad Nacional Autónoma de México, 1972. (Chap. 2)

Knight, Alan. *The Mexican Revolution.* 2 vols. Cambridge, UK: Cambridge University Press, 1986. (Chap. 7)

———. *U.S.-Mexican Relations 1910–1940: An Interpretation.* San Diego: Center for Mexican Studies, University of California, San Diego, 1987. (Chap. 3)

Knight, Franklin W. *The Caribbean: The Genesis of a Fragmented Nationalism.* 2d ed. New York: Oxford University Press, 1990. 1st ed. 1978. (Chap. 3)

Knight, Melvin M. *The Americans in Santo Domingo.* New York: Vanguard Press, 1928. (Chap. 7)

Kohl, James, and John Litt, eds. *Urban Guerrilla Warfare in Latin America.* Cambridge: MIT Press, 1974. (Chap. 7)

Kolinski, Charles J. *Independence or Death! The Story of the Paraguayan War.* Gainesville: University Presses of Florida, 1965. (Chap. 7)

Kornbluh, Peter. *The Price of Intervention: Reagan's War Against the Sandinistas.* Washington, D.C.: Institute of Policy Studies, 1987. (Chap. 7)

Korzeniewicz, Roberto Patricio, and William C. Smith, eds. *Latin America in the World Economy.* Westport, Conn.: Greenwood Press, 1996. (Chap. 2)

Koutoudjian, Adolfo. *Geopolítica tridimensional Argentina: reflexiones para el siglo XXI.* Buenos Aires: Eudeba, 1999. (Chap. 3)

Kraus, Herbert. *Die Monroe-Doktrin, in ihren Beziehungen zur amerikanischen Diplomatie und zum Voelkerrecht.* Berlin: Gutentag, 1913. (Chap. 5)

Kreckler, Luis Maria. *La diplomacia empresarial: una nueva forma de política exterior.* Buenos Aires: Editorial Depalma, 1997. (Chap. 3)

Krenn, Michael L. *U.S. Policy Toward Economic Nationalism in Latin America, 1917–1929.* Wilmington, Del.: Scholarly Resources, 1990. (Chaps. 3, 5)

Krieg, William L. *Ecuadorian-Peruvian Rivalry in the Upper Amazon.* 2d ed. Washington, D.C.: U.S. Department of State, 1986. 1st ed. 1979. (Chap. 7)

Krieger Vasena, Adalbert, and Javier Pasos. *Latin America: A Broader World Role.* London: Ernest Benn, 1973. (Chaps. 2, 8)

Kruszewski, Zbigniew Anthony, and William Richardson. *Mexico and the Soviet Bloc: The Foreign Policy of a Middle Power.* Boulder: Westview Press, 1990. (Chap. 3)

Kryzanek, Michael J. *Leaders, Leadership, and U.S. Policy in Latin America.* Boulder: Westview Press, 1992. (Chap. 8)

_____. *U.S.–Latin American Relations.* 3d ed. Westport, Conn.: Praeger, 1996. 1st ed. 1985. (Chap. 5)

Kryzanek, Michael J., and Howard J. Wiarda. *The Politics of External Influence in the Dominican Republic.* New York and Stanford: Praeger and Hoover Institution Press, 1988. (Chap. 3)

Kuczynski Godard, Pedro-Pablo. *Latin American Debt.* Baltimore: Johns Hopkins University Press, 1988. (Chap. 8)

Kumar, Chetan. *Building Peace in Haiti.* Boulder: Lynne Rienner Publishers, 1998. (Chap. 7)

Kumar, U. Shiv. *U. S. Interventionism in Latin America: Dominican Crisis and the OAS.* New Delhi: Radiant Publisher, 1987. (Chap. 7)

Kutzner, Gerhard. *Die Organisation der Amerikanischen Staaten (OAS).* Hamburg: Hansischer Gildenverlag, Heitmann, 1970. (Chap. 6)

Lael, Richard L. *Arrogant Diplomacy: U.S. Policy Toward Colombia, 1903–1922.* Wilmington, Del.: Scholarly Resources, 1987. (Chap. 3)

LaFeber, Walter. *Inevitable Revolutions: The United States in Central America.* 2d ed. New York: W. W. Norton, 1993. 1st ed. 1983. (Chap. 2)

_____. *The Panama Canal: The Crisis in Historical Perspective.* 2d ed. New York: Oxford University Press, 1989. 1st ed. 1979. (Chap. 6)

Lafer, Celso. *O Brasil e a crise mundial: paz, poder e política externa.* São Paulo: Editora Perspectiva, 1984. (Chap. 3)

Lagos Matus, Gustavo, ed. *Las relaciones entre América Latina, Estados Unidos y Europa Occidental.* Santiago de Chile: Editorial Universitaria, 1979. (Chap. 2)

Laguerre, Michel S. *Diasporic Citizenship: Haitian Americans in Transnational America.* New York: St. Martin's Press, 1998. (Chap. 8)

Lamborn, Alan C., and Stephen P. Mumme. *Statecraft, Domestic Politics, and Foreign Policy Making: The El Chamizal Dispute.* Boulder: Westview Press, 1988. (Chap. 6)

Lang, James. *Inside Development in Latin America: A Report from the Dominican Republic, Colombia, and Brazil.* Chapel Hill: University of North Carolina Press, 1988. (Chap. 3)

Langley, Lester D. *America and the Americas: The United States in the Western Hemisphere.* Athens: University of Georgia Press, 1989. (Chaps. 2, 5)

_____. *The Banana Wars: United States Intervention in the Caribbean, 1898–1934*. Lexington: University Press of Kentucky, 1983. (Chap. 7)

_____. *The Cuban Policy of the United States: A Brief History*. New York: John Wiley and Sons, 1968. (Chap. 3)

_____. *Mexico and the United States: The Fragile Relationship*. Boston: Twayne Publishers, 1991. (Chap. 3)

_____. *Struggle for the American Mediterranean: United States–European Rivalry in the Gulf-Caribbean, 1776–1904*. Athens: University of Georgia Press, 1976. (Chaps. 2, 5)

_____. *The United States and the Caribbean in the Twentieth Century*. 4th ed. Athens: University of Georgia Press, 1989. 1st ed. 1980. (Chaps. 2, 3, 5)

Langley, Lester D., and Thomas D. Schoonover. *The Banana Men: American Mercenaries and Entrepreneurs in Central America, 1880–1930*. Lexington: University Press of Kentucky, 1995. (Chap. 8)

Lansberger, Henry A. *Church and Social Change in Latin America*. Notre Dame, Ind.: Notre Dame University Press, 1970. (Chap. 8)

Lascano, Víctor. *Argentine Foreign Policy in Latin America*. Coral Gables, Fla.: University of Miami Press, 1941. (Chap. 3)

Latané, John Holladay. *The United States and Latin America*. Rev. ed. Garden City, N.J.: Doubleday, Page, 1920. 1st ed. titled *The Diplomatic Relations of the United States and Spanish America* (1900). (Chap. 2)

Latorre Cabal, Hugo. *The Revolution of the Latin American Church*. Translated by Frances Kellan Hendricks and Beatrice Berler. Norman: University of Oklahoma Press, 1978. (Chap. 8)

Lattes, Alfredo E., and Zulema Reccini de Lattes. *Migraciones en la Argentina: estudio de las migraciones internas e internacionales, basado en datos censales, 1869–1960*. Buenos Aires: Instituto Torcuato de Tella, 1970. (Chap. 8)

Lavrin, Asunción. *Women, Feminism, and Social Change in Argentina, Chile and Uruguay*. Lincoln: University of Nebraska Press, 1995. (Chap. 8)

Leacock, Ruth. *Requiem for Revolution: The United States and Brazil, 1961–1969*. Kent, Ohio: Kent State University Press, 1990. (Chap. 3)

Lee, Rensselaer W., III. *The White Labyrinth: Cocaine and Political Power*. New Brunswick, N.J.: Transaction, 1989. (Chap. 8)

Léger, Jacques Nicholas. *Haiti, Her History and Her Detractors*. New York: Neale Publishing, 1907. (Chap. 3)

Lehman, Kehman D. *Bolivia and the United States: A Limited Partnership*. Athens: University of Georgia Press, 1999. (Chap. 3)

Leiken, Robert S., ed. *Central America: Anatomy of Conflict*. New York: Pergamon Press, 1984. (Chap. 7)

Lemco, Jonathan. *Canada and the Crisis in Central America*. New York: Praeger, 1991. (Chap. 7)

LeoGrande, William M. *Our Own Backyard: The United States in Central America, 1977–1992.* Chapel Hill: University of North Carolina Press, 1998. (Chap. 7)

Leonard, Thomas M. *Central America and the United States: The Search for Stability.* Athens: University of Georgia Press, 1991. (Chaps. 2, 3, 5)

Leonard, Thomas M., ed. *United States-Latin American Relations, 1850–1903: Establishing a Relationship.* Tuscaloosa: University of Alabama Press, 1999. (Chaps. 3, 5)

Lévesque, Jacques. *The USSR and the Cuban Revolution: Soviet Ideological and Strategical Perspectives, 1959–77.* Translated by Deanna Drendel Lebouef. New York: Praeger, 1979. (Chaps. 3, 4)

Levin, Boleslav. *Los movimientos de emanipación en Hispanoamerica y independencia de los Estados Unidos.* Buenos Aires: Raigal, 1952. (Chap. 7)

Levine, Barry B., ed. *El desafío neoliberal: el fin del tercermundismo en América Latina.* Bogotá: Grupo Editorial Norma, 1992. (Chap. 6)

Levine, Daniel H., ed. *Churches and Politics in Latin America.* Chapel Hill: University of North Carolina Press, 1986. (Chap. 8)

Levinson, Jerome, and Juan de Onís. *The Alliance that Lost Its Way: A Critical Report on the Alliance for Progress.* Chicago: Quadrangle Books, 1970. (Chap. 8)

Lewis, Colin. *Latin America in the World Economy.* Boulder: Lynne Rienner Publishers, 1990. (Chap. 2)

Lewis, Gordon K. *Grenada: The Jewel Despoiled.* Baltimore: Johns Hopkins University Press, 1987. (Chap. 7)

———. *The Growth of the Modern West Indies.* London: Allen and Unwin, 1966. (Chap. 2)

———. *Puerto Rico: Freedom and Power in the Caribbean.* New York: Monthly Review Press, 1963. (Chap. 2)

———. *The Virgin Islands: A Caribbean Lilliput.* Evanston, Ill.: Northwestern University Press, 1972. (Chap. 2)

Lewis, Paul H. *The Politics of Exile: Paraguay's Febrerista Party.* Chapel Hill: University of North Carolina Press, 1968. (Chap. 8)

Li, He. *Sino-Latin American Economic Relations.* New York: Praeger, 1991. (Chap. 4)

Lieuwen, Edwin. *Arms and Politics in Latin America.* Rev. ed. New York: Praeger, 1961. 1st ed. 1960. (Chap. 8)

———. *Petroleum in Venezuela: A History.* Berkeley: University of California Press, 1954. (Chap. 8)

Liévano Aguirre, Indalecio. *Bolivarismo y Monroismo.* Bogotá: Tercer Mundo Editores, 1987. (Chap. 6)

Lincoln, Jennie K., and Elizabeth G. Ferris, eds. *The Dynamics of Latin American Foreign Policies.* Boulder: Westview Press, 1984. (Chap. 3)

Lipsey, Richard G., and Patricio Meller. *Western Hemisphere Trade Integration: A Canadian–Latin American Dialogue.* New York: St. Martin's Press, 1997. (Chap. 6)

Liss, Sheldon B. *A Century of Disagreement: The Chamizal Conflict, 1864–1964.* Washington, D.C.: University Press of America, 1965. (Chap. 6)

_____. *Diplomacy and Dependency: Venezuela, the United States, and the Americas.* Salisbury, N.C.: Documentary Publications, 1978. (Chap. 3)

Lobo, Helio. *O Panamericanismo e o Brasil.* São Paulo: Companhia Editora Nacional, 1939. (Chap. 3)

Lockey, Joseph Byrne. *Essays in Pan Americanism.* Berkeley: University of California Press, 1939. (Chap. 2)

_____. *Pan Americanism: Its Beginnings.* New York: Macmillan, 1920. (Chap. 6)

Lockmiller, David Alexander. *Magoon in Cuba: A History of the Second Intervention, 1906–1909.* Chapel Hill: University of North Carolina Press, 1938. (Chap. 7)

Logan, John A. *No Transfer: An American Security Principle.* New Haven, Conn.: Yale University Press, 1961. (Chap. 5)

Logan, Rayford W. *The Diplomatic Relations of the United States with Haiti, 1776–1891.* Chapel Hill: University of North Carolina Press, 1941. (Chap. 3)

_____. *Haiti and the Dominican Republic.* New York: Oxford University Press, 1968.

Longley, Kyle. *The Sparrow and the Hawk: Costa Rica and the United States During the Rise of José Figueres.* Tuscaloosa: University of Alabama Press, 1997. (Chap. 3)

Lorey, David E. *The U.S.-Mexican Border in the Twentieth Century.* Wilmington, Del.: Scholarly Resources, 1999. (Chap. 3)

Loveman, Brian. *Por la Patria: Politics and the Armed Forces in Latin America.* Wilmington, Del.: Scholarly Resources, 1999. (Chap. 8)

Loveman, Brian, and Thomas M. Davies Jr., eds. *Politics of Antipolitics: The Military in Latin America.* 3d ed. Wilmington, Del.: Scholarly Resources, 1997. 1st ed. 1978. (Chap. 8)

Lowenfeld, Andreas F., ed. *Expropriation in the Americas: A Comparative Law Study.* New York: Dunnellen, 1971. (Chap. 8)

Lowenthal, Abraham F. *The Dominican Intervention.* Cambridge: Harvard University Press, 1972. (Chap. 7)

_____. *Partners in Conflict: The United States and Latin America.* Rev. ed. Baltimore: Johns Hopkins University Press, 1990. 1st ed. 1987. (Chap. 5)

Lowenthal, Abraham F., ed. *Exporting Democracy: The United States and Latin America.* Baltimore: Johns Hopkins University Press, 1991. (Chap. 8)

Lowenthal, Abraham F., and Gregory F. Treverton, eds. *Latin America and the United States in a New World.* Boulder: Westview Press, 1994. (Chaps. 2, 3, 5)

Lowenthal, David. *The West Indies Federation.* New York: Columbia University Press, 1961. (Chap. 2)

Lozano de Rey, Ester, and Pilar Marulanda de Galofre. *Como se hace la política exterior en Colombia.* Bogotá: Ediciones Tercer Mundo, 1982. (Chap. 3)

Lozoya, Jorge, and Jaime Estévez, eds. *Latin America and the New International Economic Order.* New York: Pergamon, 1980. (Chap. 6)

Lynch, Edward A. *Religion and Politics in Latin America.* New York: Praeger, 1991. (Chap. 8)

Lynch, John. *Spanish Colonial Administration, 1782–1810: The Intendant System in the Viceroyalty of the Rio de la Plata.* London: Athlone Press, 1958. (Chap. 2)

Lynch, John, ed. *Latin American Revolutions, 1808–1826: Old and New World Origins.* Norman: University of Oklahoma Press, 1994. Revised edition edited by Robert Arthur Humphreys and John Lynch, *The Origins of the Latin American Revolutions, 1808–1826.* New York: Alfred A. Knopf, 1965. (Chap. 7)

Mabry, Donald J., ed. *The Latin American Narcotics Trade and U.S. National Security.* New York: Greenwood Press, 1989. (Chap. 8)

McAnany, Emile G., and Kenton T. Wilkinson, eds. *Mass Media and Free Trade: NAFTA and the Cultural Industries.* Austin: University of Texas Press, 1997. (Chap. 6)

Macauley, Neill. *The Sandino Affair.* Chicago: Quadrangle Books, 1967. (Chap. 7)

McBeth, B. S. *Juan Vicente Gómez and the Oil Companies in Venezuela, 1908–1935.* New York: Cambridge University Press, 1983. (Chap. 8)

McCann, Frank D., Jr. *The Brazilian-American Alliance, 1937–1945.* Princeton, N.J.: Princeton University Press, 1973. (Chap. 3)

McClintock, Cynthia. *Revolutionary Movements in Latin America: El Salvador's FMLN and Peru's Shining Path.* Washington, D.C.: United States Institute of Peace Press, 1998. (Chap. 7)

McCoy, Alfred W., and Alan A. Block, eds. *War on Drugs: Studies in the Failure of U.S. Narcotics Policy.* Boulder: Westview Press, 1992. (Chap. 8)

McCullough, David. *The Path Between the Seas: The Creation of the Panama Canal, 1870–1914.* New York: Simon and Schuster, 1977. (Chap. 6)

MacDonald, Gordon J., Daniel L. Nielson, and Marc A. Stern, eds. *Latin American Environmental Policy in International Perspective.* Boulder: Westview Press, 1996. (Chap. 8)

MacDonald, Scott B. *Dancing on a Volcano: The Latin American Drug Trade.* New York: Praeger, 1988. (Chap. 8)

———. *Mountain High, White Avalanche: Cocaine and Power in the Andean States and Panama.* Westport, Conn.: Greenwood Press, 1989. (Chap. 8)

MacDonald, Scott B., Jane Hughes, and Uwe Bott, eds. *Latin American Debt in the 1990s: Lessons from the Past and Forecasts for the Future.* New York: Praeger, 1991. (Chap. 8)

Mace, Gordon, and Louis Bélanger, eds. *The Americas in Transition: The Contours of Regionalism.* Boulder: Lynne Rienner Publishers, 1999. (Chaps. 2, 6)

Mace, Gordon, and Jean-Philippe Thérien, eds. *Foreign Policy and Regionalism in the Americas.* Boulder: Lynne Rienner Publishers, 1999. (Chaps. 3, 6)

McGann, Thomas Francis. *Argentina, the United States, and the Inter-American System, 1880–1914.* Cambridge: Harvard University Press, 1957. (Chap. 3)

MacGregor, Felipe E. *Coca and Cocaine: An Andean Perspective.* Westport, Conn.: Greenwood Press, 1993. (Chap. 8)

Machado, Manuel A., Jr. *Aftosa: A Historical Survey of Foot-and-Mouth Disease and Inter-American Relations.* Albany: State University of New York Press, 1969. (Chap. 8)

Machado y Ortega, Luis. *La enmienda Platt.* Havana: Imprenta "El Siglo XX," 1922. (Chap. 7)

McIntyre, W. D. *Colonies into Commonwealth.* New York: Walker, 1967. (Chap. 6)

Mack, Gerstle. *The Land Divided: A History of Panama and Other Isthmian Canal Projects.* New York: Knopf, 1944. (Chap. 6)

McKinney, Joseph A. *Created from NAFTA: The Structure, Function, and Significance of the Treaty's Related Institutions.* Armonk, N.Y.: M. E. Sharpe, 2000. (Chap. 6)

MacLachlan, Colin M. *Spain's Empire in the New World: The Role of Ideas in Institutional and Social Change.* Berkeley: University of California Press, 1988. (Chap. 2)

McWilliams, Carey. *North from Mexico: The Spanish Speaking People of the United States.* New York: Lippincott, 1949. (Chap. 8)

Madariaga, Salvador de. *The Fall of the Spanish-American Empire.* London: Hollis and Carter, 1947. (Chap. 7)

———. *Latin America Between the Eagle and the Bear.* New York: 1962. (Chap. 2)

———. *The Rise of the Spanish American Empire.* London: Hollis and Carter, 1947. (Chap. 2)

Maeztu, Ramiro de. *Defensa de la Hispanidad.* 4th ed. Madrid: Cultura Española, 1941. 1st ed. 1934. (Chap. 4)

Magnet, Alejandro. *Origines y antecedentes del panamericanismo.* Santiago de Chile: Talleres Graficos Horizonte, 1945. (Chap. 6)

Maingot, Anthony P. *The United States and the Caribbean: Challenges of an Asymmetrical Relationship.* Boulder: Westview Press, 1994. (Chaps. 2, 3, 5)

———. *U.S. Power and Caribbean Sovereignty: Geopolitics in a Sphere of Influence.* Boulder: Lynne Rienner Publishers, 1988. (Chaps. 2, 3, 5)

Maira, Luis. *América Latina y la crisis hegemonía norteamericana.* Lima: DESCO, 1982. (Chap. 5)

Maira, Luis, ed. *El Sistema Internacional y América Latina: Una nueva era de hegemonia norteamericana?* Buenos Aires: Programa de Estudios Conjuntos Sobre los Relaciones Internacionales de America Latina (RIAL); Grupo Editor Latinoamericano, 1986. (Chaps. 2)

Major, John. *Prize Possession: The United States and the Panama Canal: 1903–1979.* New York: Cambridge University Press, 1993. (Chap. 6)

Malamud-Goti, Jaime. *Smoke and Mirrors: The Paradox of the Drug Wars.* Boulder: Westview Press, 1992. (Chap. 8)

Manchester, Alan K. *British Preeminence in Brazil, Its Rise and Decline.* Chapel Hill: University of North Carolina Press, 1933. (Chap. 3)

Manning, William Ray. *Early Diplomatic Relations Between the United States and Mexico.* Baltimore: Johns Hopkins Press, 1916. (Chap. 3)

Manrique, Nelson. *Campesinado y nación: las guerrillas indígenas en la guerra con Chile.* Lima: Centro de Investigación, 1981. (Chap. 7)

Manz, Beatriz. *Refugees of a Hidden War: The Aftermath of Counterinsurgency in Guatemala.* Albany: State University of New York Press, 1988. (Chap. 8)

Marcella, Gabriel, and Richard Downes, eds. *Security Cooperation in the Western Hemisphere: Resolving the Ecuador-Peru Conflict.* Boulder: Lynne Rienner Publishers, for North-South Center, University of Miami, 1998. (Chap. 7)

Marichal, Carlos. *A Century of Debt Crisis in Latin America: From Independence to the Great Depression, 1820–1930.* Princeton, N.J.: Princeton University Press, 1989. (Chap. 8)

Márques Fuentes, Manuel, and Octavio Rodríguez Araujo. *El Partido Comunista Mexicana: en el periodo de la Internacional Comunista, 1919–1943.* 2d ed. México: Ediciones "El Caballito," 1981. 1st ed. 1973. (Chap. 8)

Marsh, Margaret A. *The Bankers in Bolivia: A Study in American Foreign Investment.* New York: Vanguard Press, 1928. (Chap. 8)

Marshall, Don D. *Caribbean Political Economy at the Crossroads: NAFTA and Regional Developmentalism.* New York: St. Martin's Press, 1998. (Chap. 6)

Martí, José. *Inside the Monster: Writings on the United States and American Imperialism.* Edited by Philip S. Foner. New York: Monthly Review Press, 1975. (Chap. 7)

———. *Our America: Writings on Latin America and the Struggle for Cuban Independence.* Edited by Philip S. Foner, translated by Elinor Randall. New York: Monthly Review Press, 1977. (Chap. 7)

Martin, David. *Tongues of Fire: The Explosion of Protestantism in Latin America.* Oxford, UK: Basil Blackwell, 1990. (Chap. 8)

Martin, Edwin McCammon. *Kennedy and Latin America.* Lanham, Md.: University Press of America, 1994. (Chap. 5)

Martin, John Bartlow. *Overtaken by Events: The Dominican Crisis from the Fall of Trujillo to the Civil War.* Garden City, N.Y.: Doubleday, 1966. (Chap. 3)

Martin, Percy Alvin. *Latin America and the War.* Baltimore: Johns Hopkins Press, 1925. (Chap. 7)

Martin, Percy F. *Maximilian in Mexico: The Story of the French Intervention, 1861–1867.* New York: Charles Scribner's Sons, 1914. (Chap. 7)

Martinez, Aníbal. *Chronology of Venezuelan Oil.* London: Allen and Unwin, 1969. (Chap. 8)

Martínez, Oscar J. *Troublesome Border.* Tucson: University of Arizona Press, 1988. (Chap. 3)

———. *U.S.-Mexican Borderlands: Historical and Contemporary Perspectives.* Wilmington, Del.: Scholarly Resources, 1996. (Chap. 3)

Martínez, Ricardo A. *De Bolívar a Dulles: El Panamericanismo, doctrina y práctica imperialista.* México: Editorial Nueva, 1959. (Chap. 6)

Martínez Ortiz, Rafael. *Cuba: Los primeros años de independencia.* 3d ed. 2 vols. Paris: Le Livere Libre, 1929. 1st ed. 1911. (Chap. 3)

Martz, John D. *Politics and Petroleum in Ecuador.* New Brunswick, N.J.: Transaction, 1987. (Chap. 8)

Martz, John D., ed. *United States Policy in Latin America: A Decade of Crisis and Challenge.* Lincoln: University of Nebraska Press, 1995. (Chap. 5)

———. *United States Policy in Latin America: A Quarter Century of Crisis and Challenge, 1961–1986.* Lincoln: University of Nebraska Press, 1988. (Chap. 5)

Martz, John D., and Lars Schoultz, eds. *Latin America, the United States, and the Inter-American System.* Boulder: Westview Press, 1980. (Chaps. 2, 3, 5)

Masters, Ruth D., ed. *Handbook of International Organizations in the Americas.* Washington, D.C.: Carnegie Endowment for International Peace, 1945. (Chap. 6)

Masterson, Daniel M. *Militarism and Politics in Latin America: Peru from Sánchez Cerro to Sendero Luminoso.* Westport, Conn.: Greenwood Press, 1991. (Chap. 8)

Masterson, Daniel M., John F. Bratzel, and Sayaka Funada. *Japanese in Latin America, 1800 to the Present.* Boulder: Westview Press, 1998. (Chap. 3)

Masud-Piloto, Felix Roberto. *From Welcomed Exiles to Illegal Immigrants: Cuban Migration to the U.S., 1959–1995.* Lanham, Md.: University Press of America, 1996. (Chap. 8)

———. *With Open Arms: Cuban Migration to the United States.* Rev. ed. Lanham, Md.: Rowman and Littlefield, 1995. 1st ed. 1988. (Chap. 8)

Masur, Gerhard. *Nationalism in Latin America.* New York: Macmillan, 1966. (Chap. 3)

Maxwell, Kenneth R. *Conflicts and Conspiracies: Brazil and Portugal, 1750–1808.* New York: Cambridge University Press, 1973. (Chap. 2)

May, Ernest R. *The Making of the Monroe Doctrine.* Cambridge: Harvard University Press, 1975. (Chap. 5)

May, Herbert K. *Problems and Prospects of the Alliance for Progress.* New York: Praeger, 1968. (Chap. 8)

May, Robert. *The Southern Dream of Caribbean Empire, 1854–1861.* Athens: University of Georgia Press, 1989. (Chap. 5)

Mayer, Frederick W. *Interpreting NAFTA: The Science and Art of Political Analysis.* New York: Columbia University Press, 1998. (Chap. 6)

Mecham, J. Lloyd. *A Survey of United States–Latin American Relations.* Boston: Houghton Mifflin, 1965. (Chaps. 2, 3, 5)

_____. *The United States and Inter-American Security, 1889–1960.* Austin: University of Texas Press, 1961. (Chap. 6)

Medina Castro, Manuel. *Estados Unidos y América Latina: siglo XIX.* Habana: Casa de las Américas, 1968. (Chap. 2)

Medina Quiroga, Cecilia. *The Battle of Human Rights: Gross, Systematic Violations and the Inter-American System.* Dordrecht; Boston: M. Nijhoff, 1988. (Chap. 8)

Meléndez, Edgardo. *Puerto Rico's Statehood Movement.* Westport, Conn.: Greenwood Press, 1988. (Chap. 2)

Meléndez, Edwin, and Edgardo Meléndez, eds. *Colonial Dilemma: Critical Perspectives on Contemporary Puerto Rico.* Boston: South End Press, 1993. (Chap. 2)

Meller, Patricio, ed. *The Latin American Development Debate: Neostructuralism, Neomonetarism, and Adjustment Processes.* Boulder: Westview Press, 1991.

Méndez Asensio, Luis. *Contadora.* México: Plaza y Valdés, 1987. (Chap. 7)

Méndez Pereira, Octavio. *Bolívar y las relaciones interamericanas.* Panamá: Imprenta Nacional, 1960. (Chap. 3)

Mendonça, Renato de. *Fronteira em marcha: ensaio de uma geopolítica brasileira.* Río de Janeiro: Livraria São José, 1956. (Chap. 3)

Menzel, Sewall H. *Cocaine Quagmire: Implementing the U.S. Anti-Drug Policy in the North-Andes-Colombia.* Lanham, Md.: University Press of America, 1997. (Chap. 8)

Mercado, R. *El Partido Comunista del Perú: Sendero Luminoso.* Lima: Ediciones de Cultura Popular, 1982. (Chap. 7)

Mercier Vega, Luis. *Guerrillas in Latin America.* New York: Praeger, 1969. (Chap. 7)

Merk, Frederick, with Lois Bannister Merk. *The Monroe Doctrine and American Expansionism: 1843–1849.* New York: Knopf, 1966. (Chap. 7)

Mesa-Lago, Carmelo, ed. *Cuba After the Cold War.* Pittsburgh: University of Pittsburgh Press, 1993. (Chap. 7)

Mesa-Lago, Carmelo, and June Belkin, eds. *Cuba in Africa.* Pittsburgh: University of Pittsburgh Press, 1982. (Chaps. 3, 7)

Meyer, Carrie A. *The Economics and Politics of NGOs in Latin America.* Westport, Conn.: Praeger, 1999. (Chap. 8)

Meyer, Lorenzo. *Las empresas transnacionales de México.* México: El Colegio de México, 1974. (Chap. 3)

_____. *Mexico and the United States in the Oil Controversy, 1917–1942.* Translated by Muriel Vasconcellos. Austin: University of Texas Press, 1977. (Chap. 8)

Meyer-Lindenberg, Herman. *El procedimiento interamericano para consolidar la paz.* Bogotá: Taller Grafico "Mundo al Día," 1941. (Chap. 6)

Middlebrook, Kevin J., ed. *Electoral Observation and Democratic Transitions in Latin America.* San Diego: Center for U.S.-Mexican Studies, University of California, San Diego, 1998. (Chap. 8)

Middlebrook, Kevin, and Carlos Rico, eds. *The United States and Latin America in the 1980s: Contending Perspectives on a Decade of Crisis.* Pittsburgh: University of Pittsburgh Press, 1986. (Chap. 2)

Milenky, Edward S. *Argentina's Foreign Policies.* Boulder: Westview Press, 1978. (Chap. 3)

———. *The Politics of Regional Organization in Latin America: The Latin American Free Trade Association.* New York: Praeger, 1973. (Chap. 6)

Miller, Hugh Gordon. *The Isthmian Highway: A Review of the Problems of the Caribbean.* New York: MacMillan, 1929. (Chap. 6)

Miller, Nicola. *Soviet Relations with Latin America, 1959–1987.* New York: Cambridge University Press, 1989. (Chap. 4)

Miller, Rory. *Britain and Latin America in the Nineteenth and Twentieth Centuries.* London: Longman, 1993. (Chap. 4)

Millett, Allan R. *The Politics of Intervention: The Military Occupation of Cuba 1906–1909.* Columbus: Ohio State University Press, 1968. (Chap. 7)

Millett, Richard L., and Michael Gold-Biss, eds. *Beyond Praetorianism: The Latin American Military in Transition.* Boulder: Lynne Rienner Publishers, for North-South Center, University of Miami, 1996. (Chap. 8)

Millett, Richard L., and W. Marvin Will, eds. *The Restless Caribbean: Changing Patterns in International Relations.* New York: Praeger, 1979. (Chaps. 2, 3)

Millington, Herbert. *American Diplomacy and the War of the Pacific.* New York: Columbia University Press, 1948. (Chap. 7)

Millis, Walter. *The Martial Spirit: A Study of Our War with Spain.* Boston: Houghton Mifflin, 1931. (Chap. 7)

Millor, Manuel R. *Mexico's Oil: Catalyst for a New Relationship with the U.S.?* Boulder: Westview Press, 1982. (Chap. 8)

Miner, Dwight C. *The Fight for the Panama Route: The Story of the Spooner Act and the Hay-Herrán Treaty.* New York: Columbia University Press, 1940. (Chap. 6)

Miranda, Roger, and William Ratliff. *The Civil War in Nicaragua: Inside the Sandinistas.* New Brunswick, N.J.: Transaction, 1993. (Chap. 3)

Mita Barrientos, Fernando. *El fenómeno del narcotráfico: enfoque nacional e internacional.* La Paz, Bolivia: AVF Producciones, 1994. (Chap. 8)

Mitchell, Christopher, ed. *Western Hemisphere Immigration and United States Foreign Policy.* University Park: Pennsylvania State University Press, 1992. (Chap. 8)

Mitchell, Harold. *Europe in the Caribbean: The Policies of Great Britain, France and the Netherlands Toward Their West Indian Territories.* Edinburgh: T. and A. Constable, 1963. (Chap. 2)

Modak, Frida, ed. *25 años de relaciones América Latina-Estados Unidos.* México: Sociedad Cooperativa Publicaciones Mexicanas, 1988. (Chap. 3)

Moffett, George D., III. *The Limits of Victory: Ratification of the Panama Canal Treaties.* Ithaca, N.Y.: Cornell University Press, 1985. (Chap. 6)

Molineu, Harold. *U.S. Policy Toward Latin America: From Regionalism to Globalism.* 2d ed. Boulder: Westview Press, 1990. 1st ed. 1986. (Chap. 5)

Mols, Manfred, Manfred Wilhelmy, and Hernán Gutiírres, eds. *América Latina y el sudeste asia: perfiles de cooperación regional.* Santiago de Chile: Instituto de Estudios Internacionales, Universidad de Chile, 1995. (Chap. 6)

Montague, Ludwell Lee. *Haiti and the United States, 1714–1938.* Durham, N.C.: Duke University Press, 1940. (Chap. 3)

Montalvo-Barbot, Alfredo. *Political Conflict and Constitutional Change in Puerto Rico, 1898–1952.* Lanham, Md.: University Press of America, 1997. (Chap. 2)

Montaner y Bello, Ricardo. *Historia diplomática de la independencia de Chile.* Santiago de Chile: Editorial Andres Bello, 1941. (Chap. 3)

Montgomery, Tommie Sue. *Revolution in El Salvador: From Civil Strife to Civil Peace.* 2d ed. Boulder: Westview Press, 1995. 1st ed. 1982. (Chap. 7)

Montgomery, Tommie Sue, ed. *Peacemaking and Democratization in the Western Hemisphere.* Boulder: Lynne Rienner Publishers, for North-South Center, University of Miami, 2000. (Chap. 7)

Moore, Carlos. *Castro, the Blacks, and Africa.* Los Angeles: Center for Afro-American Studies, University of California at Los Angeles, 1993. (Chap. 3)

Moore, John N. *The Secret War in Central America: Sandinista Assault on World Order.* Frederick, Md.: University Publications of America, 1987. (Chap. 7)

Morales Abarzua, Carlos. *La Internacional Socialista: America Latina y el Caribe.* Buenos Aires: Michka, 1986. (Chap. 9)

Morales Carrión, Arturo. *Puerto Rico: A Political and Cultural History.* New York: Norton, 1983. (Chap. 2)

Moran, Theodore H. *Multinational Corporations and the Politics of Dependence: Copper in Chile.* Princeton, N.J.: Princeton University Press, 1975. (Chap. 8)

Morawetz, David. *The Andean Group: A Case Study in Economic Integration Among Developing Countries.* Cambridge: MIT Press, 1974. (Chap. 6)

Mordecai, John. *Federation of the West Indies.* Evanston, Ill.: Northwestern University Press, 1968. (Chaps. 2)

Morello, Augusto Mario, ed. *El MERCOSUR: aspectos institucionales y económicos.* La Plata, Argentina: Librería Editora Platense, 1993. (Chap. 6)

Moreno, Dario. *U.S. Policy in Latin America: The Endless Debate.* Gainesville: University Press of Florida, 1990. (Chap. 5)

Moreno, Laudelino. *Historia de las relaciones interestatuales de Centroamérica.* Madrid: Compañia Ibero-Americana de Publicaciones, 1928. (Chap. 2)

Moreno Guerra Luis, *Integración fronteriza: el ejemplo del Ecuador y Colombia.* Quito: AFESE, ILDIS, 1996. (Chap. 7)

Moreno Guerra, Luis. *Orígines y evolución del Sistema Interamericano.* México, D.F.: Secretaría de Relaciones Exteriores, 1977. (Chap. 6)

Moreno Pino, Ismael. *Orígines y evolución del Sistema Interamericano.* Tlatelolco, México: Secretaría de Relaciones Exteriores, 1977. (Chap. 6)

Morley, Morris H. *Imperial State and Revolution: The United States and Cuba, 1952–1986.* New York: Cambridge University Press, 1988. (Chap. 3)

_____. *Washington, Somoza, and the Sandinistas: State and Regime in U.S. Policy Toward Nicaragua, 1969–1981.* New York: Cambridge University Press, 1994. (Chap. 7)

Morner, Magnus, with the collaboration of Harold Sims. *Adventurers and Proletarians: The Story of Migrants in Latin America.* Pittsburgh: University of Pittsburgh Press, 1985. (Chap. 8)

Morris, Michael A. *Caribbean Maritime Security.* New York: St. Martin's Press, 1994. (Chap. 6)

_____. *International Politics and the Sea: The Case of Brazil.* Boulder: Westview Press, 1979. (Chap. 6)

Morris, Michael A., and Victor Millán, eds. *Controlling Latin American Conflicts: Ten Approaches.* Boulder: Westview Press, 1983. (Chap. 7)

Morris, Nancy. *Puerto Rico: Culture, Politics, and Identity.* Westport, Conn.: Praeger, 1995. (Chap. 2)

Morzone, Luis Antonio. *Soberania territorial argentino.* 2d ed. Buenos Aires: Ediciones de Palma, 1982. 1st ed. 1978. (Chap. 7)

Moses, Bernard. *The Establishment of Spanish Rule in America.* New York: G. P. Putnam's Sons, 1898. (Chap. 2)

_____. *The Intellectual Background of the Revolution in South America, 1810–1824.* New York: Printed by Order of the Trustees, 1926. (Chap. 7)

_____. *South America on the Eve of Emancipation.* New York: G. P. Putnam's Sons, 1908. (Chap. 2)

_____. *Spain's Declining Power in South America, 1730–1806.* Berkeley: University of California Press, 1919. (Chap. 2)

_____. *The Spanish Dependencies in South America.* 2 vols. New York: Harper, 1914. (Chap. 2)

Mower, Alfred Glenn, Jr. *The European Community and Latin America: A Case Study in Global Role Expansion.* Westport, Conn.: Greenwood Press, 1982. (Chap. 4)

_____. *Regional Human Rights: A Comparative Study of the West European and Inter-American Systems.* New York: Greenwood Press, 1991. (Chap. 8)

Moya Pons, Frank. *La dominación haitiana, 1822–1844.* Santiago, R.D.: Universidad Católica Madre y Maestre, 1978.

Moyano, Marie José. *Argentina's Lost Patrol: Armed Struggle, 1969–1979.* New Haven, Conn.: Yale University Press, 1995. (Chap. 7)

Mujal-León, Eusebio M. *European Socialism and the Conflict in Central America.* New York: Praeger, 1989. (Chaps. 4, 7)

Mujal-León, Eusebio M., ed. *The USSR and Latin America: A Developing Relationship.* Boston: Unwin Hyman, 1988. (Chap. 4)

Muñoz, Heraldo. *Las relaciones exteriores del gobierno militar chileno.* Santiago de Chile: Ediciones del Ornitorrinco, 1986. (Chap. 3)

Muñoz, Heraldo, and Carlos Portales. *Elusive Friendship: A Survey of U.S.-Chilean Relations.* Boulder: Lynne Rienner Publishers, 1991. (Chap. 6)

Muñoz, Heraldo, ed. *El fin del fantasma: las relaciones interamericanos después de la Guerra Fría.* Santiago de Chile: Hachette, 1992. (Chap. 2)

Muñoz, Heraldo, ed. *Environment and Diplomacy in the Americas.* Boulder: Lynne Rienner Publishers, 1992. (Chap. 8)

_____. *From Dependency to Development.* Boulder: Westview Press, 1981. (Chap. 2)

Muñoz, Heraldo, and Francisco Orrego Vicuña, eds. *La cooperación regional en América Latina: diagnostico y proyección futuras.* México, D.F.: El Colegio de México; Universidad de Chile, 1987. (Chap. 6)

Muñoz, Heraldo, and Robin L. Rosenberg, eds. *Difficult Liaison: Trade and Environment in the Americas.* New Brunswick, N.J.: Transaction, for North-South Center, University of Miami; and Organization of American States, 1993. (Chap. 8)

Muñoz, Heraldo, and Joseph S. Tulchin, eds. *Latin American Nations in World Politics.* 2d ed. Boulder: Westview Press, 1996. 1st ed. 1984. (Chap. 3)

Munro, Dana G. *The Five Republics of Central America: Their Political and Economic Development and Their Relations with the United States.* New York: Oxford University Press, 1918. (Chaps. 2, 3, 5)

_____. *Intervention and Dollar Diplomacy in the Caribbean, 1900–1921.* Princeton, N.J.: Princeton University Press, 1964. (Chaps. 2, 3, 5, 7)

_____. *Pan America and the War.* Boston: World Peace Foundation, 1934. (Chap. 7)

_____. *The United States and the Caribbean Area.* Boston: World Peace Foundation, 1934. (Chaps. 2, 3, 5)

_____. *The United States and the Caribbean Republics, 1921–1933.* Princeton, N.J.: Princeton University Press, 1974. (Chaps. 2, 3, 5, 7)

Munro, Dana G., and others. *Latin America in World Affairs, 1914–1940.* Philadelphia: University of Pennsylvania Press, 1941. (Chaps. 2, 3)

Murch, Arvin. *Black Frenchmen: The Political Integration of the French Antilles.* Cambridge, Mass.: Schenkman, 1971. (Chap. 2)

Murphy, Martin F. *Dominican Sugar Plantations: Production and Foreign Labor Integration.* New York: Praeger, 1991. (Chap. 3)

Musgrove, Peggy B., ed. *Mexico and the United States: Studies in Economic Interaction.* Boulder: Westview Press, 1985. (Chap. 3)

Mytelka, Lynn Krieger. *Regional Development in a Global Economy: The Multinational Corporation, Technology, and Andean Integration.* New Haven, Conn.: Yale University Press, 1979. (Chap. 8)

Nathan, James A., ed. *The Cuban Missile Crisis Revisited.* New York: St. Martin's Press, 1992. (Chap. 7)

Needler, Martin C. *The United States and the Latin American Revolution.* Boston: Allen and Bacon, 1969. (Chap. 8)

Nerval, Gaston (pseudonym for Raúl Díaz de Medina). *Autopsy of the Monroe Doctrine: The Strange Story of Inter-American Relations.* New York: Macmillan, 1934. (Chap. 5)

Neumann, William L. *Recognition of Goverments in the Americas.* Washington, D.C.: Foundation for Foreign Affairs, 1947. (Chap. 8)

Newfarmer, Richard, ed. *From Gunboats to Diplomacy: New U.S. Policies for Latin America.* Baltimore: Johns Hopkins University Press, 1984. (Chap. 5)

Newfarmer, Richard S., ed. *Profits, Progress and Poverty: Case Studies of International Industries in Latin America.* Notre Dame, Ind.: Notre Dame University Press, 1985. (Chap. 8)

Newton, Arthur P. *The European Nations in the West Indies, 1493–1688.* London: Adam and Charles Black, 1933. (Chap. 2)

Newton, Ronald C. *German Buenos Aires, 1900–1933: Social Change and Cultural Crisis.* Austin: University of Texas Press, 1977. (Chap. 8)

———. *The "Nazi Menace" in Argentina, 1931–1947.* Stanford: Stanford University Press, 1992. (Chap. 7)

Newton, Wesley Phillips. *The Perilous Sky: U.S. Aviation Diplomacy and Latin America, 1919–1931.* Coral Gables, Fla.: University of Miami Press, 1978. (Chap. 8)

Niblo, Stephen R. *War, Diplomacy, and Development: The United States and Mexico, 1938–1954.* Wilmington, Del.: Scholarly Resources, 1995. (Chap. 3)

Nicholson, Norman L. *Canada in the American Community.* Princeton, N.J.: Van Nostrand, 1963. (Chap. 4)

Niess, Frank. *A Hemisphere to Itself: A History of U.S.–Latin American Relations.* Translated by Harry Drost. London: Zed Books, 1990. (Chaps. 2, 5)

Nieto-Navia, Rafael. *Introducción al sistema interamericano de protección a los derechos humanos.* Bogotá: Temis, 1993. (Chap. 6)

Nieto-Navia, Rafael, ed. *El corte y el sistema interamericanos de derechos humanos.* San José: Corte Interamericano de Derechos Humanos, 1994. (Chap. 8)

Nishijima, Shoji, and Peter H. Smith, eds. *Cooperation or Rivalry? Regional Integration in the Americas and the Pacific Rim.* Boulder: Westview Press, 1996. (Chap. 6)

Nugent, Daniel, ed. *Rural Revolt in Mexico and U.S. Intervention.* San Diego: Center for U.S.-Mexican Studies, University of California, San Diego, 1988. (Chap. 7)

Nugent, Jeffrey B. *Economic Integration in Central America*. Baltimore: Johns Hopkins University Press, 1974. (Chap. 6)

Nuñez, Benjamin. *Dictionary of Afro-Latin American Civilization*. Westport, Conn.: Greenwood Press, 1980. (Chap. 8)

Nunn, Frederick M. *The Time of the Generals: Latin American Professional Militarism in World Perspective*. Lincoln: University of Nebraska Press, 1992. (Chap. 8)

_____. *Yesterday's Soldiers: European Military Professionalism in South America, 1890–1940*. Lincoln: University of Nebraska Press, 1983. (Chap. 8)

Nye, Joseph A. *Central American Integration*. New York: Appleton-Century Crofts, 1967. (Chap. 6)

O'Brien, Thomas F. *The Century of U.S. Capitalism in Latin America*. Albuquerque: University of New Mexico Press, 1999. (Chap. 8)

_____. *The Revolutionary Mission: American Business in Latin America, 1900–1945*. Cambridge: Cambridge University Press, 1996. (Chap. 8)

Offner, John L. *An Unwanted War: The Diplomacy of the United States and Spain over Cuba, 1895–1898*. Chapel Hill: University of North Carolina Press, 1992. (Chap. 7)

Ogelsby, J.C.M. *Gringos from the Far North: Essays in the History of Canadian–Latin American Relations, 1866–1968*. Toronto: Macmillan of Canada, 1976. (Chap. 4)

Ojeda Gómez, Mario. *Alcances y límites de la política exterior de México*. México: El Colegio de México, 1976. (Chap. 3)

_____. *México: El surgimiento de una política exterior activa*. México, D.F.: Secretaría de Educación Pública, 1986. (Chap. 3)

Oliveira, Gesner. *Brasil-FMI: frustracões e perspectivas*. São Paulo: Bienal, 1993. (Chap. 3)

Oliveira Lima, Manuel de. *Historia diplomática do Brasil: reconhecimento do imperio*. 2d ed. Río de Janeiro and Paris: H. Garnier, 1902. 1st ed. 1901. (Chap. 3)

_____. *O movimento da independencia, 1821–1822*. São Paulo: Weiszfolg Irmaos, 1922. (Chap. 7)

Oliveres, Ramón. *El imperialismo yanqui en América: la dominación política y económica del continente*. Buenos Aires: 1952. (Chap. 3)

Oliveri, Ernest J. *Latin American Debt and the Politics of International Finance*. Westport, Conn.: Praeger, 1992. (Chap. 8)

Olmo, Rosa del. *Prohibir o domesticar: políticas de drogas en América Latina*. Caracas: Editorial Nueva Sociedad, 1992. (Chap. 8)

O'Neill, Edward A. *Rape of the American Virgins*. New York: Praeger, 1972. (Chap. 2)

Orlove, Benjamin, ed. *The Allure of the Foreign: Imported Goods in Postcolonial Latin America*. Ann Arbor: University of Michigan Press, 1997. (Chap. 8)

368

REFERENCES

Orme, William A., Jr. *Understanding NAFTA: Mexico, Free Trade, and the New North America.* 2d ed. Austin: University of Texas Press, 1996. 1st ed. titled *Continental Shift: Free Trade and the New North America* (1993). (Chap. 6)

Oswald, J. Gregory, and Anthony J. Strover, eds. *The Soviet Union and Latin America.* New York: Praeger, 1970. (Chap. 4)

Otero, Gustavo Adolfo. *Sociología del nacionalismo en Hispano-América.* Quito: Ediciones del Grupo América, 1947. (Chap. 3)

Ott, Thomas O. *The Haitian Revolution, 1789–1801.* Knoxville, Tenn.: University of Tennessee Press, 1973. (Chap. 7)

Packenham, Robert A. *The Dependency Movement: Scholarship and Politics in Development Studies.* Cambridge: Harvard University Press, 1992. (Chap. 2)

———. *Liberal America and the Third World: Political Development Ideas in Foreign Aid and Social Science.* Princeton, N.J.: Princeton University Press, 1973. (Chap. 8)

Painter, James. *Bolivia and Coca: A Study in Dependency.* Boulder: Lynne Rienner Publishers, 1994. (Chap. 8)

Painter, Michael, and William H. Durham, eds. *The Social Causes of Environmental Destruction in Latin America.* Ann Arbor: University of Michigan Press, 1994. (Chap. 8)

Palacios, Marco. *El café en Colombia (1850–1970): Una historia económica, social y política.* 2d ed. México, D.F.: El Colegio de México, 1983. Originally published as *Coffee in Colombia, 1850–1970: An Economic, Social, and Political History* (New York: Cambridge University Press, 1980). (Chap. 3)

Palmer, Bruce, Jr. *Intervention in the Caribbean: The Dominican Crisis of 1965.* Lexington: University Press of Kentucky, 1989. (Chap. 7)

Palmer, David Scott, ed. *The Shining Path of Peru.* New York: St. Martin's Press, 1992. (Chap. 7)

Palmer, Ransford W. *Caribbean Dependence on the United States Economy.* New York: Praeger, 1979. (Chap. 2)

Palmer, Ransford W., ed. *In Search of a Better Life: Perspectives on Migration from the Caribbean.* New York: Praeger, 1990. (Chap. 8)

———. *U.S.-Caribbean Relations: Their Impact on Peoples and Culture.* Westport, Conn.: Praeger, 1998. (Chap. 8)

Paquette, Robert L., and Stanley L. Engerman, eds. *The Lesser Antilles in the Age of European Expansion.* Gainesville: University Press of Florida, 1996. (Chap. 2)

Pardo, Rodrigo, and Juan G. Tokatlian. *Política exterior colombiana: de la subordinación a la autonomía?* Bogotá: Tercer Mundo Editores, 1988. (Chap. 3)

Pares, Richard. *War and Trade in the West Indies, 1739–1763.* Oxford: Clarendon Press, 1936. (Chap. 2)

———. *Yankees and Creoles: The Trade Between North America and the West Indies Before the American Revolution.* London: Longmans, 1968. (Chap. 2)

Pariset, Georges. *Historique sommaire du conflit anglo-vénézuélien en Guyane; des origines au traité d'arbitrage, 1493–1897*. Paris: Berger-Levrault, 1898. (Chap. 7)

Parker, James W. *Latin American Underdevelopment: A History of Perspectives in the United States, 1877–1965*. Baton Rouge: Louisiana State University Press, 1995. (Chap. 2)

Parkinson, F. *Latin America, the Cold War, and the World Powers, 1945–1973*. Beverly Hills, Calif.: Sage Publications, 1974. (Chap. 2)

Parks, E. Taylor. *Colombia and the United States, 1765–1934*. Durham, N.C.: Duke University Press, 1935. (Chap. 3)

Parra Sandoval, Rodrigo, ed. *Dependencia externa y desarrollo politico en Colombia*. Bogotá: Imprenta Nacional, 1970. (Chap. 3)

Parry, J. H. *The Spanish Seaborne Empire*. New York: Knopf, 1966. (Chap. 2)

Parry, J. H., P. M. Sherlock, and Anthony P. Maingot. *A Short History of the West Indies*. 4th ed. New York: St. Martin's Press, 1987. 1st ed., by Parry and Sherlock, 1956. (Chap. 2)

Pastor, Manuel, Jr. *The International Monetary Fund and Latin America: Economic Stabilization and Class Conflict*. Boulder: Westview Press, 1987. (Chap. 6)

Pastor, Robert A. *Condemned to Repetition: The United States and Nicaragua*. Princeton, N.J.: Princeton University Press, 1987. (Chap. 7)

_____. *Whirlpool: U.S. Foreign Policy Toward Latin America and the Caribbean*. Princeton, N.J.: Princeton University Press, 1992. (Chap. 5)

Pastor, Robert A., ed. *Democracy in the Americas: Stopping the Pendulum*. New York: Holmes and Meier, 1989. (Chap. 8)

_____. *Migration and Development in the Caribbean: The Unexplored Connection*. Boulder: Westview Press, 1985. (Chap. 8)

Pastor, Robert A., and Jorge Castañeda. *Limits to Friendship: The United States and Mexico*. New York: Knopf, 1988. (Chap. 3)

Paterson, Thomas G. *Contesting Castro: The United States and the Triumph of the Cuban Revolution*. New York: Oxford University Press, 1994. (Chap. 7)

Paus, Eva, ed. *Struggle Against Dependence: Nontraditional Export Growth in Central America and the Caribbean*. Boulder: Westview Press, 1988. (Chap. 8)

Pavlov, Yuri. *Soviet-Cuban Alliance: 1959–1991*. Boulder: Lynne Rienner Publishers, 1996. (Chap. 3)

Paxson, Frederic L. *The Independence of the South American Republics: A Study in Recognition and Foreign Policy*. Philadelphia: Ferris and Leach, 1903. (Chap. 7)

Payne, Anthony J. *The Politics of the Caribbean Community, 1961–1979: Regional Integration Among New States*. New York: St. Martin's Press, 1980. (Chap. 6)

Payne, Anthony J., Paul Sutton, and Tony Thorndike. *Grenada: Revolution and Invasion*. New York: St. Martin's Press, 1984. (Chap. 7)

Payne, Douglas, Mark Falcoff, and Susan Kaufman Purcell. *Latin America: U.S. Policy After the Cold War*. New York: Americas Society, 1991. (Chap. 5)

Payne, Richard J. *Opportunities and Dangers of Soviet-Cuban Expansion: Toward a Pragmatic U.S. Policy.* Albany: State University of New York Press, 1988. (Chap. 3)

Pedraza-Bailey, Silvia. *Political and Economic Migrants in America: Cubans and Mexicans.* Austin: University of Texas Press, 1985. (Chap. 8)

Pellicer, Olga, ed. *La política exterior de México: desafíos en los ochenta.* México, D.F.: Centro de Investigación y Docencia Económicas, 1983. (Chap. 3)

Pellicer de Brody, Olga. *México y la revolución cubana.* México: El Colegio de México, 1972. (Chap. 3)

Pereyra, Carlos. *El mito de Monroe.* Madrid: Editorial América, 1914. (Chap. 5)

_____. *Rosas y Thiers: la diplomacia europea en el Río de la Plata, 1838–1850.* Madrid: Editorial América, 1919. (Chap. 7)

Pérez, Louis A., Jr. *Cuba and the United States: Ties of Singular Intimacy.* Athens: University of Georgia Press, 1990. (Chap. 3)

_____. *Cuba Between Empires, 1878–1902.* Pittsburgh: University of Pittsburgh Press, 1983. (Chap. 7)

_____. *Cuba Under the Platt Amendment, 1902–1934.* Pittsburgh: University of Pittsburgh Press, 1986. (Chap. 7).

_____. *Intervention, Revolution, and Politics in Cuba, 1913–1921.* Pittsburgh: University of Pittsburgh Press, 1978. (Chap. 7)

_____. *The War of 1898: The United States and Cuba in History and Historiography.* Chapel Hill: University of North Carolina Press, 1999. (Chap. 7)

Pérez Concha, Jorge. *Ensayo histórico-crítico de las relaciones diplomáticas del Ecuador con los estados limítrofes.* 2 vols. Quito: Editorial Casa de la Cultura Ecuatoriana, 1961, 1964. (Chap. 7)

Pérez Herrero, Pedro, and Nuria Tabanera, eds. *España/América Latina: un siglo de políticas culturales.* Madrid: Síntesis, 1993. (Chap. 4)

Perina, Rubén M., and Roberto Russell, comps. *Argentina en el mundo (1973–1987).* Buenos Aires: Grupo Editor Latinoamericano, 1988. (Chap. 3)

Perkins, Dexter. *A History of the Monroe Doctrine.* Boston: Little, Brown, 1963. (Chap. 5)

_____. *The Monroe Doctrine, 1823–1826.* Cambridge: Harvard University Press, 1927. (Chap. 5)

_____. *The Monroe Doctrine, 1826–1867.* Baltimore: Johns Hopkins University Press, 1933. (Chap. 5)

_____. *The Monroe Doctrine, 1867–1907.* Baltimore: Johns Hopkins University Press, 1937. (Chap. 5)

Perkins, Whitney T. *Constraint of Empire: The United States and Caribbean Interventions.* Westport, Conn.: Greenwood Press, 1981. (Chap. 7)

Perry, William. *Contemporary Brazilian Foreign Policy: The International Strategy of an Emerging Power.* Beverley Hills, Calif.: Sage Publications, 1976. (Chap. 3)

Perry, William, and Peter Wehner, eds. *The Latin American Policies of U.S. Allies: Balancing Global Interests and Regional Concerns.* New York: Praeger, 1985. (Chap. 4)

Peruse, Roland I. *Haitian Democracy Restored 1991–1995.* Lanham, Md.: University Press of America, 1995. (Chap. 7)

Peterson, Harold F. *Argentina and the United States, 1810–1960.* Albany: State University of New York Press, 1964. (Chap. 3)

Petin, Hector. *Les Etats-Unis et la Doctrine de Monroe.* Paris: A. Rousseau, 1900. (Chap. 5)

Petras, James F. *Politics and Social Structure in Latin America.* New York: Monthly Review Press, 1970. (Chap. 2)

Petras, James F., and Morris Morley. *The United States and Chile: Imperialism and the Overthrow of the Allende Government.* New York: Monthly Review Press, 1975. (Chap. 7)

Petras, James F., Morris Morley, and Steven Smith. *The Nationalization of Venezuelan Oil.* New York: Praeger, 1977. (Chap. 8)

Petras, James F., and Maurice Zeitlin. *Latin America: Reform or Revolution?* Greenwich, Conn.: Fawcett Publications, 1968. (Chap. 2)

Petras, James F., ed. *Latin America: From Dependence to Revolution.* New York: John Wiley, 1973. (Chap. 2)

Phelps, Dudley Maynard. *Migration of Industry to South America.* New York: McGraw-Hill, 1936. (Chap. 8)

Philip, George. *Oil and Politics in Latin America: Nationalist Movements and State Companies.* Cambridge: Cambridge University Press, 1982. (Chap. 8)

Pike, Fredrick B. *Chile and the United States, 1880–1962.* Notre Dame, Ind.: University of Notre Dame Press, 1963. (Chap. 3)

_____. *FDR's Good Neighbor Policy: Sixty Years of Generally Gentle Chaos.* Austin: University of Texas Press, 1995. (Chap. 5)

_____. *Hispanismo, 1898–1936: Spanish Conservatives and Liberals and Their Relations with Spanish America.* Notre Dame, Ind.: University of Notre Dame Press, 1971. (Chap. 4)

_____. *The United States and the Andean Republics: Peru, Bolivia, and Ecuador.* Cambridge: Harvard University Press, 1977. (Chap. 3)

_____. *The United States and Latin America: Myths and Stereotypes of Civilization and Nature.* Austin: University of Texas Press, 1992. (Chap. 5)

Pilar Arguelles, Maria del. *Morality and Power: The U.S. Colonial Experience in Puerto Rico from 1898–1948.* Lanham, Md.: University Press of America, 1995. (Chap. 2)

Pinelo, Adalberto J. *The Multinational Corporation as a Force in Latin American Politics: A Case Study of the International Petroleum Company in Peru.* New York: Praeger, 1973. (Chap. 8)

Piñero, Norberto. *La política internacional argentina.* Buenos Aires: Libreria y Casa Editora de J. Menéndez e Hijo, 1924. (Chap. 3)

Pinochet de la Barra, Oscar. *La antártica chilena.* 4th ed. Santiago de Chile: Andres Bello, 1976. 1st ed. 1948. (Chap. 3)

Pinto, Aníbal. *Hacia nuestra independencia económia.* Santiago de Chile: Editorial del Pacífico, 1953. (Chap. 2)

Pitman, Frank Wesley. *The Development of the British West Indies, 1700–1763.* New Haven, Conn.: Yale University Press, 1917. (Chap. 2)

Pittman, Howard T. *Geopolitics in the ABC Countries: A Comparison.* 5 vols. Ph.D. dissertation, American University, Washington, D.C., 1981. (Chap. 3)

Platt, D.C.M. *Latin America and the British Trade, 1806–1914.* London: Adam and Charles Black, 1972. (Chap. 8)

Platt, D.C.M., ed. *Business Imperialism: An Inquiry Based on British Experience in Latin America.* Oxford: Clarendon Press, 1977. (Chap. 8)

Pletcher, David M. *The Diplomacy of Annexation: Texas, Oregon, and the Mexican War.* Columbia: University of Missouri Press, 1973. (Chap. 7)

Plummer, Brenda Gayle. *Haiti and the Great Powers, 1902–1915.* Baton Rouge: Louisiana State University Press, 1988. (Chaps. 3, 7)

————. *Haiti and the United States: The Psychological Moment.* Athens: University of Georgia Press, 1992. (Chap. 3)

Poitras, Guy. *The Ordeal of Hegemony: The United States and Latin America.* Boulder: Westview Press, 1990. (Chaps. 2, 5)

La política exterior de México. Special issues of *Foro Internacional* 6, nos. 2, 3 (octubre-diciembre 1965, enero-marzo 1966).

La política exterior de México: la práctica de México en el derecho internacional. México: Editorial Esfinge, 1969. (Chap. 3)

Pons Muzzo, Gustavo. *Estudio Historico sobre el Protocolo de Río de Janeiro: el Ecuador, país amazónica.* Lima: n.p., 1994. (Chap. 7)

Poole, Bernard L. *The Caribbean Commission.* Columbia: University of South Carolina Press, 1951. (Chap. 2)

Portales, Carlos, ed. *El sistema internacional y América Latina: El mundo en transición y América Latina.* Buenos Aires: Programa de Estudios Conjuntos Sobre los Relaciones Internacionales de America Latina (RIAL); Grupo Editor Latinoamericano, 1989. (Chap. 2)

Portell-Vilá, Herminio. *Historia de Cuba en sus relaciones con los Estados Unidos y España.* 4 vols. Havana: Jesús Montero, 1938–1941. (Chap. 3)

Portes, Alejandro. *Latin Journey: Cuban and Mexican Migrants in the United States.* Berkeley: University of California Press, 1985. (Chap. 8)

Postma, Johannes M. *The Dutch in the Atlantic Slave Trade, 1600–1815.* New York: Cambridge University Press, 1990. (Chap. 8)

Poulson, Barry W., T. Noel Osborn, and Hugo B. Margaín, eds. *U.S.-Mexico Economic Relations.* Boulder: Westview Press, 1979. (Chap. 3)

Powell, Philip W. *Tree of Hate: Propaganda and Prejudices Affecting United States Relations with the Hispanic World.* New York: Basic Books, 1971. (Chap. 5)

Prat Guy, Gastón de. *Política internacional del grupo latinoamericano*. Buenos Aires: Abeledo-Perrot, 1967. (Chap. 6)

Prebisch, Raúl. *Capitalismo periférico: crisis y transformación*. México, D.F.: Fondo de Cultura Económica, 1981. (Chap. 2)

_____. *Change and Development: Latin America's Great Task*. New York: Praeger, 1971. (Chap. 2)

_____. *The Economic Development of Latin America and Its Principal Problems*. New York: United Nations, 1950. (Chap. 2)

_____. *Nueva política comercial para el desarrollo*. México, D.F.: Fondo de Cultura Económica, 1964. (Chap. 2)

_____. *Towards a Dynamic Development Policy for Latin America*. New York: United Nations, 1963. (Chap. 2)

Prevost, Gary, and Harry Vanden, eds. *The Undermining of the Sandinista Revolution*. New York: St. Martin's Press, 1997. (Chap. 7)

Price, Glen W. *Origins of the War with Mexico: The Polk-Stockton Intrigue*. Austin: University of Texas Press, 1967. (Chap. 7)

Price-Mars, Jean. *La République d'Haiti et la République Dominicaine*. Port-au-Prince: n.p., 1953. (Chap. 7)

Prizel, Ilya. *Latin America Through Soviet Eyes: The Evolution of Soviet Perceptions During the Brezhnev Era 1964–1982*. New York: Cambridge University Press, 1990. (Chap. 4)

Programa de Relaciones Politicas y de Cooperacion al Desarrollo Europa/America Latina (PREAL). *Europa-América Latina, el desafio de la cooperación*. Madrid: Editorial P. Iglesias, 1988. (Chap. 4)

Programa de Seguimiento de las Políticas Exteriores Latinoamericanas (PROSPEL). *Anuario de Políticas Exteriores Latinoamericanas*. 8 vols., title varies. Edited by Heraldo Muñoz. Buenos Aires: Grupo Editor Latinoamericano, 1985–1988; Caracas: Editorial Nueva Sociedad, 1989–1990. Title changed to *Anuario de Políticas Exteriores Latinoamericanas y del Caribe*. Edited by Alberto van Klaveren. Santiago: Universidad de Chile, 1997. (Chaps. 2, 3)

Proudfoot, Mary. *Britain and the United States in the Caribbean: A Comparative Study in Methods of Development*. New York: Praeger, 1954. (Chap. 2)

Puentes, Gabriel A. *La intervención francesa en el Río de la Plata: federales, unitarios y románticos*. Buenos Aires: Ediciones Teoría, 1958. (Chap. 7)

Puig, Juan Carlos, ed. *América Latina: políticas exteriores comparadas*. Buenos Aires: Grupo Editor Latinoamerinano, 1984. (Chap. 3)

Purcell, Susan Kaufman, ed. *México in Transition: Implications for U.S. Policy— Essays from Both Sides of the Border*. New York: Council on Foreign Relations, 1988. (Chap. 2)

_____. *Mexico–United States Relations*. New York: Praeger, 1981. (Chap. 3)

Purcell, Susan Kaufman, and Robert M. Immerman, eds. *Japan and Latin America in the New Global Order*. Boulder: Lynne Rienner Publishers, 1992. (Chaps. 2, 4)

Purcell, Susan Kaufman, and Françoise Simon, eds. *Europe and Latin America in the World Economy*. Boulder: Lynne Rienner Publishers, 1995. (Chap. 4)

Puyana de Palacios, Alicia. *Economic Integration Among Unequal Partners: The Case of the Andean Group*. New York: Pergamon Press, 1982. (Chap. 6)

Querejazu Calvo, Roberto. *La Guerra del Pacífico: síntesis histórica de sus antecedentes, desarrollo y consecuencias*. Cochabamba: Editorial Los Amigos del Libro, 1983. (Chap. 7)

_____. *Masamaclay: historia política, diplomática y militar de la guerra del Chaco*. 2d ed. La Paz: Los Amigos del Libro, 1975. 1st ed. 1965. (Chap. 7)

Quesada, Vicente G. *Historia diplomática hispanoamericana*. 3 vols. Buenos Aires: La Cultura Argentina, 1918–1920. (Chaps. 2, 3)

Quijano, Anibal. *Nationalism and Capitalism in Peru: A Study of Neo-Imperialism*. New York: Monthly Review Press, 1971. (Chap. 8)

Quirk, Robert E. *An Affair of Honor: Woodrow Wilson and the Occupation of Vera Cruz*. Lexington: University of Kentucky Press, 1962. (Chap. 7)

Quiroz, Alfonso W. *Domestic and Foreign Finance in Modern Peru, 1850–1950: Financing Visions of Development*. Pittsburgh: University of Pittsburgh Press, 1993. (Chap. 8)

Raat, W. Dirk. *Mexico and the United States: Ambivalent Vistas*. Athens: University of Georgia Press, 1992. (Chap. 3)

Rabe, Stephen G. *Eisenhower and Latin America: The Foreign Policy of Anticommunism*. Chapel Hill: University of North Carolina Press, 1988. (Chap. 5)

_____. *The Most Dangerous Area in the World: John F. Kennedy Confronts Communist Revolution in Latin America*. Chapel Hill: University of North Carolina Press, 1999. (Chap. 8)

_____. *The Road to OPEC: United States Relations with Venezuela, 1919–1976*. Austin: University of Texas Press, 1982. (Chap. 8)

Radu, Michael, and Vladimir Tismaneanu. *Latin American Revolutionaries: Groups, Goals, Methods*. Washington, D.C.: Pergamon-Brassey Publishers, for Foreign Policy Research Institute, 1990. (Chap. 7)

_____. *Revolutionary Organizations in Latin America: A Handbook*. Boulder: Westview Press, 1988. (Chap. 7)

Rama, Carlos. *La imagen de los Estados Unidos en la América Latina: de Simón Bolívar a Salvador Allende*. México: Secretaria de Educación Pública, 1975. (Chap. 3)

Ramírez, Socorro, Luis Alberto Restrepo, and Maria Emma Mejía. *Colombia entre la inserción y el aislamiento: la política exterior colombiana en los años noventa*. Santafé de Bogotá: Universidad Nacional; Siglo del Hombre Editores, 1997. (Chap. 3)

Randall, Laura. *The Political Economy of Mexican Oil.* New York: Praeger, 1989. (Chap. 8)

Randall, Laura, ed. *The Political Economy of Latin America in the Postwar Period.* Austin: University of Texas Press, 1997. (Chaps. 2, 3)

Randall, Stephen J. *Colombia and the United States: Hegemony and Interdependence.* Athens: University of Georgia Press, 1992. (Chap. 3)

_____. *The Diplomacy of Modernization: Colombian American Relations, 1920–1940.* Toronto: University of Toronto Press, 1977. (Chap. 3)

Randall, Stephen J., and Graeme S. Mount. *The Caribbean Basin: An International History.* New York: Routledge, 1998. (Chaps. 2, 3)

Rangel, Carlos. *The Latin Americans: Their Love-Hate Relationship with the United States.* 2d ed. New Brunswick, N.J.: Transaction, 1987. 1st ed. 1977. (Chaps. 3, 8)

Rapaport, Mario. *Gran Bretaña, Estados Unidos y las clases dirigentes argentinas: 1940–1945.* Buenos Aires: Editorial de Belgrano, 1981. (Chap. 7)

_____. *El labertino argentino: política internacional en un mundo conflictivo.* Buenos Aires: Eudeba, 1997. (Chap. 3)

Ratliff, William E. *Castroism and Communism in Latin America, 1959–1976: The Varieties of Marxist-Leninist Experience.* Washington, D.C.: American Enterprise Institute for Public Policy Research, 1976. (Chap. 8)

Rebolledo, Alvaro. *Reseña histórico-política de la comunicación interoceánica, con especial referencia a la separación de Panamá y a los arreglos entre los Estados Unidos y Colombia.* San Francisco: Editorial Hispano-América, 1930. (Chap. 6)

Rebolledo, Miguel. *México y los Estados Unidos.* México and Paris: Vda. de C. Bouret, 1917. (Chap. 3)

Reisler, Mark. *By the Sweat of Their Brow: Mexican Immigrant Labor in the United States, 1900–1940.* Westport, Conn.: Greenwood Press, 1976. (Chap. 8)

Resio Trejo, Alvaro. *Historia de las relaciones ruso-argentinas.* Buenos Aires: Talleres Graficos Ayacucho, 1946. (Chap. 3)

Reuter, Bertha Ann. *Anglo-American Relations During the Spanish-American War.* New York: Macmillan, 1924. (Chap. 7)

Revert, Eugene. *Les Antilles.* Paris: Armand Colin, 1954. (Chap. 2)

Reynolds, Clark W., and Carlos Tello, eds. *U.S.-Mexico Relations: Economic and Social Aspects.* Stanford: Stanford University Press, 1983. (Chap. 3)

Rippy, J. Fred. *British Investments in Latin America, 1822–1949: A Case Study in the Operations of Retarded Regions.* Minneapolis: University of Minnesota Press, 1959. (Chap. 8)

_____. *The Capitalists and Colombia.* New York: Vanguard Press, 1931. (Chap. 8)

_____. *Latin America and the Industrial Age.* 2d ed. New York: G. P. Putnam, 1947. 1st ed. 1944. (Chap. 2)

_____. *Latin America in World Politics.* 3d ed. New York: F. S. Crofts, 1938. 1st ed. 1928. (Chap. 2)

_____. *The United States and Mexico*. 2d ed. New York: Knopf, 1931. 1st ed. 1926. (Chap. 3)

Ritter, Archibald R. M., and John M. Kirk, eds. *Cuba in the International System: Normalization and Integration*. New York: St. Martin's Press, 1995. (Chap. 3)

Rivas, Raimundo. *Historia diplomática de Colombia, 1810–1934*. Bogotá: Imprenta Nacional, 1961. (Chap. 3)

_____. *Relaciones internacionales entre Colombia y los Estados Unidos, 1810–1850*. Bogotá: Imprenta Nacional, 1915. (Chap. 3)

Rivera, Mario A. *Decision and Structure: U.S. Refugee Policy and the Mariel Crisis*. Lanham, Md.: University Press of America, 1991. (Chap. 8)

Rives, George Lockhart. *The United States and Mexico, 1821–1848*. 2 vols. New York: Scribner, 1913. (Chap. 3)

Roa, Jorge. *Los Estados Unidos y Europa en Hispano America: interpretación política y económica de la Doctrina Monroe, 1823–1933*. Habana: Cultural, 1935. (Chap. 3)

Roberts, W. Adolphe. *The Caribbean: The Story of Our Sea of Destiny*. Indianapolis: Bobbs-Merrill, 1940. (Chap. 2)

Robertson, William Spence. *France and Latin American Independence*. Baltimore: Johns Hopkins Press, 1939. (Chap. 7)

_____. *Hispanic-American Relations with the United States*. Edited by David Kinley. New York: Oxford University Press, for Carnegie Endowment for International Peace, 1923. (Chaps. 2, 5)

Robinson, Cecil, ed. and trans. *The View from Chapultepec: Mexican Writers on the Mexican-American War*. Tucson: University of Arizona Press, 1989. (Chap. 7)

Robinson, William I. *A Faustian Bargain: U.S. Intervention in the Nicaraguan Elections and American Foreign Policy in the Post–Cold War Era*. Boulder: Westview Press, 1992. (Chap. 7)

Rochlin, James F. *Canada as a Hemisphere Actor*. Toronto: McGraw Hill-Ryerson, 1992. (Chap. 4)

_____. *Discovering the Americas: The Evolution of Canadian Foreign Policy Towards Latin America*. Vancouver: University of British Columbia Press, 1994. (Chap. 4)

_____. *Redefining Mexican "Security": Society, State, and Region Under NAFTA*. Boulder: Lynne Rienner Publishers, 1997. (Chap. 3)

Rodley, Nigel S., and C. Neale Ronning, eds. *International Law in the Western Hemisphere*. The Hague: Martinus Nijhoff, 1974. (Chap. 6)

Rodrígues, José Honorio. *Aspiracoes nacionais: interpretecao historico-político*. São Paulo: Fulgor, 1965. (Chap. 3)

_____. *Brazil and Africa*. Translated by Richard A. Mazzara and Sam Hileman. Berkeley: University of California Press, 1965. (Chap. 3)

_____. *Interêsse nacional e política externa.* Río de Janeiro: Editora Civilização Brasileira, 1966. (Chap. 3)

Rodrígues, José Honorio, and Ricardo A. S. Seitenfus. *Una historia diplomática do Brasil, 1531–1945.* Río de Janeiro: Editora Civilização Brasileira, 1995. (Chap. 3)

Rodríguez, José Egidio. *Imagen y política international.* Caracas: Editorial Ateneo de Caracas, 1987. (Chap. 3)

Rodríguez, José Ignacio. *Estudio historico sobre el origin, desenvolvimiento y manisfestaciones practicas de la idea de la anexión de la Isla de Cuba a los Estados Unidos.* Havana: Imprenta de la Propaganda Literaria, 1900. (Chap. 7)

Rodríguez, Linda Alexander, ed. *Rank and Privilege: The Military and Society in Latin America.* Wilmington, Del.: Scholarly Resources, 1994. (Chap. 8)

Rodríguez Beruff, Jorge, and Humberto García Muñiz, eds. *Security Problems and Policies in the Post–Cold War Caribbean.* New York: St. Martin's Press, 1996. (Chap. 2)

Rodríguez Larretta, Aureliano. *Orientación de la política internacional en América Latina.* 2 vols. Montevideo: Peña, 1938. (Chap. 3)

Rodriguez O., Jaime E. *The Independence of Spanish America.* New York: Cambridge University Press, 1998. (Chap. 7)

Rodríguez O., Jaime E., and Kathryn Vincent, eds. *Common Border, Uncommon Paths: Race and Culture in U.S.-Mexican Relations.* Wilmington, Del.: Scholarly Resources, 1997. (Chap. 8)

_____. *Myths, Misdeeds, and Misunderstandings: The Roots of Conflict in U.S.-Mexican Relations.* Wilmington, Del.: Scholarly Resources, 1997. (Chaps. 3, 7)

Roett, Riordan, ed. *Mercosur: Regional Integration, World Markets.* Boulder: Lynne Rienner Publishers, 1998. (Chap. 6)

_____. *Mexico and the United States: Managing the Relationship.* Boulder: Westview Press, 1988. (Chap. 3)

_____. *Mexico's External Relations in the 1990s.* Boulder: Lynne Rienner Publishers, 1991. (Chap. 3)

Roig de Leuchsenring, Emilio. *Cuba y los Estados Unidos, 1805–1898.* Havana: Cultural, 1949. (Chap. 7)

_____. *Historia de la enmienda Platt: una interpretación de la realidad cubana.* 2 vols. Havana: Cultural, 1935. (Chap. 7)

Rojas, Armando. *Historia de las relaciones diplomaticas entre Venezuela y los Estados Unidos, 1810–1899.* 2 vols. Caracas: Ediciones de la Presidencia de la Republics, 1979. (Chap. 3)

Rojas Aravena, Francisco. *Costa Rica: política exterior y crisis centroamericana.* Heredia: Universidad Nacional de Costa Rica, Escuela de Relaciones Internacionales, 1990. (Chap. 3)

Rojas Aravena, Francisco, ed. *Costa Rica y el sistema internacional.* San José: Fundación Friedrich Ebert en Costa Rica; Caracas: Editorial Nueva Sociedad, 1990. (Chap. 3)

Rojas Sandford, Robinson. *El imperialismo yanqui en Chile*. Santiago de Chile, 1971. (Chap. 7)

Romanova, Ninaida Ivanova. *La expansión económica de Estados Unidos en América Latina*. Moscú: Editorial Progreso, 1965. (Chap. 2)

Romero, Agustín M. *Malvinas: la política exterior de Alfonsín y Menem*. Buenos Aires: Editorial de Belgrano, 1999. (Chap. 7)

Ronning, C. Neale. *Diplomatic Asylum: Legal Norms and Political Reality in Latin American Relations*. The Hague: Nijhoff, 1957. (Chap. 8)

_____. *Law and Politics in Inter-American Diplomacy*. New York: John Wiley and Sons, 1963. (Chap. 6)

Ronning, C. Neale, ed. *Intervention in Latin America*. New York: Knopf, 1970. (Chap. 7)

Ronning, C. Neale, and Albert P. Vannucci, eds. *Ambassadors in Foreign Policy: The Influence on U.S.-Latin American Policy*. New York: Praeger, 1987. (Chap. 5)

Roorda, Eric Paul. *The Dictator Next Door: The Good Neighbor Policy and the Dominican Republic, 1930–1945*. Durham, N.C.: Duke University Press, 2000. (Chap. 3)

Rosenberg, Mark B., ed. *The Changing Hemispheric Trade Environment: Opportunities and Obstacles*. Miami: Florida International University, 1991. (Chap. 8)

Rosenberg, Robin L. *Spain and Central America: Democracy and Foreign Policy*. New York: Greenwood Press, 1992. (Chap. 4)

Ross, Stanley R., ed. *Views Across the Border: The United States and Mexico*. Albuquerque: University of New Mexico Press, 1978. (Chap. 3)

Roussin, Marcel. *Le Canada et le Systéme Interaméricain*. Ottawa: Editions de l'Université d'Ottawa, 1959. (Chaps. 4, 6)

Rout, Leslie B. *Politics of the Chaco Peace Conference, 1935–39*. Austin: University of Texas Press, 1970. (Chap. 7)

Rout, Leslie B., and John F. Bratzel. *The Shadow War: German Espionage and United States Counterespionage in Latin America During World War II*. Frederick, Md.: University Publications of America, 1986. (Chap. 7)

Rowe, Leo Stanton. *The United States and Porto Rico*. New York: Longmans, Green, 1903. (Chap. 2)

Roy, Joaquin, ed. *The Reconstruction of Central America: The Role of the European Community*. Boulder: Lynne Rienner Publishers, for North-South Center, University of Miami, 1992. (Chap. 7)

Roy, Joaquín, and Albert Galinsoga Jordá, eds. *The Ibero-American Space: Dimensions and Perceptions of the Special Relationship Between Spain and Latin America*. Miami, Fla.: Iberian Studies Institute, University of Miami; Mérida, Spain: Jean Monnet Chair for European Integration, University of Lleida, 1997. (Chap. 3)

Rubenstein, Richard L., and John K. Roth, eds. *The Politics of Latin American Liberation Theology: The Challenge to U.S. Public Policy.* Washington, D.C.: Washington Institute Press, 1988. (Chap. 8)

Rubert deVentós, Xavier. *The Hispanic Labyrinth: Spain's Encounter with Latin America.* Translated by Mary Ann Newman. New Brunswick, N.J.: Transaction, 1990. (Chap. 2)

Rudenko, Boris Timofeevich, Nikolai Matveevich Lavrov, and Moisei Samuilovich Al'perovich. *Cuatro estudios sobre la Revolución Mexicana.* 2d ed. México, D. F.: Ediciones Quinto Sol, 1984. 1st ed. 1960. (Chap. 7)

Ruilova, Leonardo. *China Popular en América Latina.* Quito: Instituto Latinoamericano de Investigaciones Sociales, 1978. (Chap. 4)

Ruíz García, Enrique. *La estrategia mundial del petróleo: una teoría del poder, una teoría de la dependencia.* México: Editorial Nueva Imagen, 1982. (Chap. 8)

Ruíz Moreno, Isidro J. *Historia del las relaciones exteriores argentinas, 1810–1955.* Buenos Aires: Editorial Perrot, 1961. (Chap. 3)

_____. *La neutralidad Argentina en la Segunda Guerra Mundial.* Buenos Aires: Emecé Editores, 1997. (Chap. 7)

Russell, Roberto. *Nuevos rumbos en la relación Unión Soviética–América Latina.* Buenos Aires: Grupo Editor Latinoamericano, 1990. (Chap. 4)

Russell, Roberto, and others. *Temas de política exterior latinoamericana: el caso uruguayo.* Buenos Aires: Grupo Editor Latinoamericano, 1986. (Chap. 3)

Russell, Roberto, ed. *Enfoques teóricos y metodológicos para el estudio de política exterior.* Buenos Aires: Grupo Editor Latinoamericano, 1992. (Chap. 3)

_____. *Política exterior y toma de decisiones en América Latina.* Buenos Aires: Grupo Editor Latinoamericano, 1990. (Chap. 3)

_____. *El Sistema Internacional y América Latina: La agenda internacional en los años '90.* Buenos Aires: Programa de Estudios Conjuntos Sobre los Relaciones Internacionales de America Latina (RIAL); Grupo Editor Latinoamericano, 1990. (Chap. 3)

Russell-Wood, A.J.R., ed. *From Colony to Nation: Essays on the Independence of Brazil.* Baltimore: Johns Hopkins University Press, 1978. (Chap. 7)

Ryan, David. *U.S.-Sandinista Diplomatic Relations: Voice of Intolerance.* New York: St. Martin's Press, 1995. (Chap. 7)

Ryan, Henry Butterfield. *The Fall of Che Guevara: A Story of Soldiers, Spies, and Diplomats.* New York: Oxford University Press, 1998. (Chap. 7)

Rydjord, John. *Foreign Interest in the Independence of New Spain: An Introduction to the War for Independence.* Durham, N.C.: Duke University Press, 1935. (Chap. 7)

Sabaté Lichtschein, Domingo. *Problemas argentinos de soberanía territorial.* 3d ed. Buenos Aires: Abeledo-Perrot, 1985. 1st ed. 1976. (Chap. 7)

Saborio, Sylvia, ed. *The Premise and Promise: Free Trade in the Americas.* New Brunswick, N.J.: Transaction, 1992. (Chap. 6)

Saddy, Fehmy, ed. *Arab–Latin American Relations: Energy, Trade, and Investment.* New Brunswick, N.J.: Transaction, 1983. (Chap. 8)

Sáenz, Vicente. *Rompiendo cadenas, las del imperialismo en Central América y en otros repúblicas del continente.* 3d ed. Buenos Aires: Palestra, 1961. 1st ed. 1933. (Chap. 3)

St. John, Ronald Bruce. *The Foreign Policy of Peru.* Boulder: Lynne Rienner Publishers, 1992. (Chap. 3)

Saito, Hiroshi. *O japonés no Brasil.* São Paulo: Editóra "Sociologia e Política," 1961. (Chap. 8)

Salazar Sparks, Juan, con coloboración de Pilar Alamos, Luz O'Shea, and Manfred Wilhelmy. *Chile y la comunidad del Pacifico.* Santiago de Chile: Editorial Universitaria, 1999. (Chap. 3)

Salgado, Germánico. *Ecuador y la integración económica de América Latina.* Buenos Aires: Instituto Para la Integración de América Latina, Banco Interamericano de Desarrollo, 1970. (Chap. 3)

Salinas Baldivieso, Carlos Alberto. *Historia diplomática de Bolivia.* Sucre: Editorial Charcas, 1938. (Chap. 3)

Salinas Carranza, Alberto. *La expedición punitiva.* México: Bota, 1936. (Chap. 7)

Salmon, C. *Caribbean Confederation.* London: Cassell, 1888. (Chap. 2)

_____. *Depression in the West Indies.* London: Cassell, 1884. (Chap. 2)

Salum-Flecha, Antonio. *Historia diplomática del Paraguay de 1869–1938.* Asunción: EMASA, 1972. (Chap. 3)

Salum-Flecha, Antonio, and others. *Política internacional, economía e integración.* Asunción: Editorial Araverá, 1985. (Chap. 3)

Sánchez G., Walter, and Teresa Pereira L., eds. *Cientocincuenta años de política exterior chilena.* Santiago: Instituto de Estudios Internacionales de la Universidad de Chile, 1977. (Chap. 3)

Sanderson, Steven E. *The Politics of Trade in Latin American Development.* Stanford: Stanford University Press, 1992. (Chap. 8)

Sandford, Gregory, and Richard Vigilante. *Grenada: The Untold Story.* Lanham, Md.: Madison Books, 1984. (Chap. 7)

Sater, William F. *Chile and the United States: Empires in Conflict.* Athens: University of Georgia Press, 1990. (Chap. 7)

_____. *Chile and the War of the Pacific.* Lincoln: University of Nebraska Press, 1986. (Chap. 7)

Saunders, Sol. *Mexico: Chaos on Our Doorstep.* Lanham, Md.: Madison Books, 1986. (Chap. 3)

Scenna, Miguel Angel. *Argentina-Brazil: cuatro siglos de rivalidad.* Buenos Aires: Ediciones La Bastilla, 1975. (Chap. 7)

Scheetz, Thomas. *Peru and the International Monetary Fund.* Pittsburgh: University of Pittsburgh Press, 1986. (Chap. 6)

Scheman, L. Ronald. *The Inter-American Dilemma: The Search for Inter-American Cooperation at the Centennial of the Inter-American System*. New York: Praeger, 1988. (Chap. 6)

Scheman, L. Ronald, ed. *The Alliance for Progress: A Retrospective*. New York: Praeger, 1988. (Chap. 8)

Schmidt, Hans. *The United States Occupation of Haiti, 1915–1934*. New Brunswick, N.J.: Rutgers University Press, 1971. (Chap. 7)

Schmitt, Karl M. *Communism in Mexico: A Study in Political Frustration*. Austin: University of Texas Press, 1965. (Chap. 8)

_____. *Mexico and the United States, 1821–1973: Conflict and Coexistence*. New York: Wiley and Sons, 1974. (Chap. 3)

Schneider, Ronald M. *Brazil: Foreign Relations of a Future World Power*. Boulder: Westview Press, 1976. (Chap. 3)

_____. *Communism in Guatemala, 1944–1954*. New York: Praeger, 1958. (Chap. 7)

Schoenhals, Kai P., and Richard A. Melanson. *Revolution and Intervention in Grenada: The New Jewel Movement, the United States, and the Caribbean*. Boulder: Westview Press, 1985. (Chap. 7)

Schoonover, Thomas. *The French in Central America: Culture and Commerce, 1820–1930*. Wilmington, Del.: Scholarly Resources, 1999. (Chap. 4)

Schoonover, Thomas David. *Germany in Central America: Competitive Imperialism, 1821–1929*. Tuscaloosa: University of Alabama Press, 1998. (Chap. 4)

Schoultz, Lars. *Beneath the United States: A History of U.S. Policy Toward Latin America*. Cambridge: Harvard University Press, 1998. (Chap. 5)

_____. *Human Rights and United States Policy Toward Latin America*. Princeton, N.J.: Princeton University Press, 1981. (Chap. 8)

_____. *National Security and United States Policy Toward Latin America*. Princeton, N.J.: Princeton University Press, 1987. (Chap. 5)

Schoultz, Lars, William C. Smith, and Augusto Varas, eds. *Security, Democracy, and Development in U.S.–Latin American Relations*. New Brunswick, N.J.: Transaction, for North-South Center, University of Miami, 1994. (Chap. 8)

Schuler, Friedrich E. *Mexico Between Hitler and Roosevelt: Mexican Foreign Relations in the Age of Lázaro Cárdenas, 1934–1940*. Albuquerque: University of New Mexico Press, 1998. (Chap. 7)

Schulz, Donald E., and Deborah Sundloff Schulz. *The United States, Honduras, and the Crisis in Central America*. Boulder: Westview Press, 1994. (Chap. 7)

Schulz, Donald E., and Douglas H. Graham, eds. *Revolution and Counterrevolution in Central America and the Caribbean*. Boulder: Westview Press, 1984. (Chap. 7)

Schwoch, James. *The American Radio Industry and Its Latin American Activities, 1900–1939*. Urbana: University of Illinois Press, 1990. (Chap. 8)

Scott, Peter Dale, and Jonathan Marshall. *Cocaine Politics: Drugs, Armies, and the CIA in Central America*. Berkeley: University of California Press, 1991. (Chap. 8)

Scranton, Margaret E. *The Noriega Years: U.S.-Panamanian Relations, 1981–1990*. Boulder: Lynne Rienner Publishers, 1991. (Chap. 3)

Seara Vázquez, Modesto. *Política exterior de México*, 3d ed. México: Harper and Row Latinoamericana, 1985. 1st ed. 1968. (Chap. 3)

Seckinger, Ron. *The Brazilian Monarchy and the South American Republics, 1822–1831: Diplomacy and State Building*. Baton Rouge: Louisiana State University Press, 1984. (Chap. 3)

Sedoc-Dahlberg, Betty, ed. *The Dutch Caribbean: Prospects for Democracy*. New York: Gordon and Breach Science Publishers, 1990. (Chap. 2)

Seidel, Robert N. *Progressive Pan Americanism: Development and United States Policy Toward South America*. Ithaca, N.Y.: Cornell University Press, 1973. (Chap. 6)

Selcher, Wayne A. *The Afro-Asian Dimension of Brazilian Foreign Policy, 1956–1972*. Gainesville: University of Florida Press, 1974. (Chap. 3)

_____. *Brazil's Multilateral Relations: Between First and Third Worlds*. Boulder: Westview Press, 1978. (Chap. 3)

Selcher, Wayne A., ed. *Brazil in the International System: The Rise of a Middle Power*. Boulder: Westview Press, 1981. (Chap. 3)

Seligson, Mitchell A., and John A. Booth, ed. *Elections and Democracy in Central America, Revisited*. Chapel Hill: University of North Carolina Press, 1989. (Chap. 8)

Sepúlveda, Bernardo, and Antonio Chumacero. *La inversión extranjera en México*. México: Fondo de Cultura Económica, 1973. (Chap. 8)

Sepúlveda, Bernardo, and others. *Las empresas transnacionales en México*. México: El Colegio de México, 1974. (Chap. 8)

Sepúlveda, César. *Las fuentes del derecho internacional americano: una encuesta sobre los métodos de creación de reglas internacionales en el Hemisferio Occidental*. 2d ed. México: Editorial Porrúa, 1975. 1st ed. 1969. (Chap. 6)

_____. *El Sistema Interamericano: genesis, integración, decadencia*. 2d ed. México, D.F.: Editorial Porrua, 1974. (Chap. 7)

Serbin, Andrés. *Caribbean Geopolitics: Toward Security Through Peace?* Translated by Sabet Ramírez. Boulder: Lynne Rienner Publishers, 1990. (Chap. 3)

_____. *Sunset Over the Islands: The Caribbean in an Age of Global and Regional Challenges*. New York: St. Martin's Press, 1998. (Chap. 2)

Serbin, Andrés, and Anthony Bryan, eds. *El Caribe hacia el 2000: desafíos y opciones*. Caracas: Editorial Nueva Sociedad, 1991. (Chap. 3)

Serbin, Andrés, and Anthony Bryan, comps. *Vecinos indiferentes: el Caribe de habla inglesa y América Latina*. Caracas: Editorial Nueva Sociedad, 1990. (Chap. 3)

Sergi, Jorge F. *Historia de los italianos en la Argentina*. Buenos Aires: Il Mattino de Italia, 1940. (Chap. 8)

Shafer, Robert Jones, and Donald Mabry. *Neighbors—Mexico and the United States: Wetbacks and Oil*. Chicago: Nelson Hall, 1981. (Chap. 8)

Shapira, Yoram. *Mexican Foreign Policy Under Echeverria*. Beverly Hills: Sage Publications, for Center for Strategic and International Studies, 1978. (Chap. 3)

Shapiro, Samuel, ed. *Cultural Factors in Inter-American Relations*. Notre Dame, Ind.: University of Notre Dame Press, 1968. (Chap. 8)

Shavit, David. *The United States in Latin America: A Historical Dictionary*. Westport, Conn.: Greenwood Press, 1992. (Chap. 5)

Shaw, Royce Q. *Central America: Regional Integration and National Political Development*. Boulder: Westview Press, 1979. (Chap. 6)

Shea, Donald R. *The Calvo Clause: A Problem of Inter-American and International Law and Diplomacy*. Minneapolis: University of Minnesota Press, 1955. (Chap. 6)

Shepherd, Philip L. *The Honduran Crisis and Economic Assistance*. Boulder: Westview Press, 1989. (Chap. 8)

Sherman, William Roderick. *The Diplomatic and Commercial Relations of the United States and Chile, 1820–1914*. Boston: Richard G. Badger, Publisher, 1926. (Chap. 3)

Sherrill, Charles H. *Modernizing the Monroe Doctrine*. Boston: Houghton Mifflin, 1916. (Chap. 5)

Shurbutt, T. Ray, ed. *United States–Latin American Relations, 1800–1850: The Formative Generations*. Tuscaloosa: University of Alabama Press, 1991. (Chaps. 3, 5)

Sigmund, Paul E. *Liberation Theology at the Crossroads: Democracy or Revolution?* New York: Oxford University Press, 1990. (Chap. 8)

_____. *Multinationals in Latin America: The Politics of Nationalization*. Madison, Wisc.: University of Wisconsin Press, 1980. (Chap. 8)

_____. *The United States and Democracy in Chile*. Baltimore: Johns Hopkins University Press, 1993. (Chap. 7)

Silva, Rafael Euclides. *Derecho territorial ecuatoriano*. Guayaquil: Universidad de Guayaquil, 1962. (Chap. 7)

Silva-Michelena, José A., ed. *Latin America: Peace, Democratization, and Economic Crisis*. Tokyo: United Nations University, 1988. (Chap. 7)

_____. *Los factores de la paz*. Tokyo: United Nations University; Caracas: Instituto Latinoamericano de Investigaciones Sociales, 1987. (Chap. 7)

_____. *Paz, seguridad y desarrollo en América Latina*. Caracas: Instituto Latinoamericano de Investigaciones Sociales, 1987. (Chap. 7)

Singletary, Otis A. *The Mexican War*. Chicago: University of Chicago Press, 1960. (Chap. 7)

Sistema Económico Latinoamericano. *América Latina y el Caribe ante el nuevo escenario europeo*. Caracas: Editorial Nueva Sociedad, 1993. (Chap. 6)

_____. *La economía mundial y el desarrollo de América Latina y el Caribe*. Caracas: Editorial Nueva Sociedad, 1988. (Chap. 2)

_____. *Relaciones económicas internacionales de América Latina*. Caracas: Editorial Nueva Sociedad, 1987. (Chap. 2)

_____. *Políticas de ajuste: financiamiento del desarrollo en América Latina*. Caracas: Editorial Nueva Sociedad, 1987. (Chap. 8)

Sklair, Leslie. *Assembling for Development: The Maquila Industry in Mexico and the United States*. 2d ed. San Diego: Center for U.S.-Mexican Studies, University of California, San Diego, 1993. 1st ed. 1989. (Chap. 6)

Slater, Jerome. *Intervention and Negotiation: The United States and the Dominican Revolution*. New York: Harper and Row, 1970. (Chap. 7)

_____. *The OAS and United States Foreign Policy*. Columbus: Ohio State University Press, 1967. (Chap. 6)

_____. *A Reevaluation of Collective Security: The OAS in Action*. Columbus: Ohio State University Press, 1965. (Chap. 6)

Smetherman, Bobbie B., and Robert M. Smetherman. *Territorial Seas and Inter-American Relations: With Case Studies of the Peruvian and U.S. Fishing Industries*. New York: Praeger, 1974. (Chap. 6)

Smith, Christian. *Resisting Reagan: The U.S. Central American Peace Movement*. Chicago: University of Chicago Press, 1996. (Chap. 7)

Smith, Clint E. *Inevitable Partnership: Understanding Mexico-U.S. Relations*. Boulder: Lynne Rienner Publishers, 2000. (Chap. 3)

Smith, Gaddis. *The Last Years of the Monroe Doctrine, 1945–1993*. New York: Hill and Wang, 1994. (Chap. 7)

Smith, Joseph. *Illusions of Conflict: Anglo-American Diplomacy Toward Latin America, 1865–1896*. Pittsburgh: University of Pittsburgh Press, 1979. (Chap. 2)

_____. *Unequal Giants: Diplomatic Relations Between the United States and Brazil, 1889–1930*. Pittsburgh: University of Pittsburgh Press, 1991. (Chap. 3)

Smith, Justin H. *The War with Mexico*. 2 vols. New York: Macmillan, 1919. (Chap. 7)

Smith, O. Edmund, Jr. *Yankee Diplomacy: U.S. Intervention in Argentina*. Dallas: Southern Methodist University Press, 1953. (Chap. 7)

Smith, Peter H. *Talons of the Eagle: Dynamics of U.S.–Latin American Relations*. 2d ed. New York: Oxford University Press, 1999. 1st ed. 1996. (Chaps. 2, 5)

Smith, Peter H., ed. *The Challenge of Integration: Europe and the Americas*. Miami, Fla.: North-South Center, University of Miami, 1993. (Chaps. 4, 6)

_____. *Cooperation or Rivalry: Regional Integration in the Americas and the Pacific Rim*. Boulder: Westview Press, 1996. (Chap. 6)

_____. *Drug Policy in the Americas*. Boulder: Westview Press, 1992. (Chap. 8)

Smith, Robert Freeman. *The United States and Revolutionary Nationalism in Mexico, 1916–1932*. Chicago: University of Chicago Press, 1972. (Chap. 3)

Smith, Robert Freeman, ed. *The United States and the Latin American Sphere of Influence.* 2 vols. Malabar, Fla.: Krieger Publishing, 1981–1983. (Chap. 2)

Smith, Wayne S., ed. *The Russians Aren't Coming: New Soviet Policy in Latin America.* Boulder: Lynne Rienner Publishers, 1992. (Chap. 4)

Smith, William C., Carlos H. Acuña, and Eduardo A. Gamarra, eds. *Latin American Political Economy in the Age of Neoliberal Reform: Theoretical and Comparative Perspectives for the 1990s.* New Brunswick, N.J.: Transaction, for North-South Center, University of Miami, 1994. (Chap. 8)

Soares, Alvaro Teixeira. *O Brasil no conflicto ideologico global, 1937–1979.* Río de Janeiro: Civilizacão Brasileira, 1980. (Chap. 3)

Sobel, Richard, ed. *Public Opinion in U.S. Foreign Policy: The Controversy over Contra Aid.* Lanham, Md.: Rowman, 1993. (Chap. 7)

Solari, Aldo E. *El tercerismo en el Uruguay: Ensayo.* Montevideo: Editorial Alfa, 1965. (Chap. 3)

Solberg, Carl. *Immigration and Nationalism: Argentina and Chile.* Austin: University of Texas Press, 1970. (Chap. 8)

Solow, Barbara L., ed. *Slavery and the Rise of the Atlantic System.* New York: Cambridge University Press; Cambridge, Mass.: W.E.B. DuBois Institute for Afro-American Research, 1991. (Chap. 8)

Somavía, Juan, ed. *Cooperación política regional para la democracia.* México: Instituto Latinoamericano de Estudios Transnacionales, 1986. (Chap. 8)

Sommi, Luis V. *Los capitales alemanes en la Argentina: historia de su expansión.* Buenos Aires: Editorial Claridad, 1945. (Chap. 8)

Sonntag, Heinz Rudolf. *Duda/certeza, crisis: La evolución de las ciencias sociales de América Latina.* Caracas: Nueva Sociedad, 1988. (Chap. 2)

Sosnowski, Saúl, and Louise B. Popkin. *Repression, Exile, and Democracy: Uruguayan Culture.* Translated by Louise B. Popkin. Durham, N.C.: Duke University Press, 1993. (Chap. 8)

Spener, David, and Kathleen Staudt. *The U.S.-Mexico Border: Transcending Divisions, Contesting Identities.* Boulder: Lynne Rienner Publishers, 1998. (Chap. 3)

Spenser, Daniela. *The Impossible Triangle: Mexico, Soviet Russia, and the United States in the 1920s.* Durham, N.C.: Duke University Press, 1999. (Chap. 3)

Spykman, Nicholas J. *America's Strategy in World Politics.* New York: Harcourt, Brace, 1942. (Chap. 5)

Stallings, Barbara, and Robert Kaufman. *Debt and Democracy in Latin America.* Boulder: Westview Press, 1989. (Chap. 8)

Stallings, Barbara, and Gabriel Székely, eds. *Japan, the United States, and Latin America: Toward a Trilateral Relationship in the Western Hemisphere.* Baltimore: Johns Hopkins University Press, 1993. (Chaps. 2, 4)

Stein, Stanley J., and Barbara H. Stein. *The Colonial Heritage of Latin America: Essays on Economic Development in Perspective.* New York: Oxford University Press, 1970. (Chap. 2)

Stern, Steve J., ed. *Shining and Other Paths: War and Society in Peru, 1980–1995.* Durham, N.C.: Duke University Press, 1998. (Chap. 7)

Stevens, Willy J., ed. *América Latina se ha quedado sola.* Bogotá: Fundación Santillana para Iberoamerica, 1989. (Chap. 6)

Steward, Dick. *Money, Marines, and Mission: Recent U.S.–Latin American Policy.* Lanham, Md.: University Press of America, 1980. (Chap. 5)

_____. *Trade and Hemisphere: The Good Neighbor Policy and Reciprocal Trade.* Columbia: University of Missouri Press, 1975. (Chap. 8)

Stewart, Norman R. *Japanese Colonization in Eastern Paraguay.* Washington, D.C.: National Academy of Sciences, 1967. (Chap. 8)

Stewart, Watt. *Chinese Bondage in Peru: A History of the Chinese Coolie in Peru, 1849–1974.* Durham, N.C.: Duke University Press, 1951. (Chap. 8)

Stoetzer, O. Carlos. *The Organization of American States.* 2d ed. Westport, Conn.: Praeger, 1993. 1st ed. 1965. (Chap. 6)

Stoll, David. *Is Latin America Turning Protestant? The Politics of Evangelical Growth.* Berkeley: University of California Press, 1990. (Chap. 8)

Street, John. *Artigas and the Emancipation of Uruguay.* Cambridge: Cambridge University Press, 1959. (Chap. 7)

Stuart, Graham H., and James L. Tigner. *Latin America and the United States.* 6th ed. Englewood Cliffs, N.J.: Prentice-Hall, 1975. 1st ed. 1922. (Chaps. 2, 3, 5)

Suchlicki, Jaime, ed. *Cuba, Castro, and Revolution.* Coral Gables, Fla.: University of Miami Press, 1972. (Chap. 3)

Sunkel, Osvaldo, con colaboración de Pedro Paz. *El subdesarrollo latinoamericano y la tería del desallollo.* México: Siglo Veintiuno Editores, 1970. (Chap. 2)

Sunkel, Osvaldo, ed. *Development from Within: Toward a Neostructuralist Approach for Latin America.* Boulder: Lynne Rienner Publishers, 1993. (Chap. 8)

Sutton, Paul, ed. *Europe and the Caribbean.* London: Macmillan, 1991. (Chaps. 2, 4)

Suzuki, Teiiti. *The Japanese Immigrant in Brazil.* Tokyo: University of Tokyo Press, 1969. (Chap. 8)

Swansbrough, Robert H. *The Embattled Colossus: Economic Nationalism and United States Investors in Latin America.* Gainesville: University Presses of Florida, 1976. (Chap. 8)

Syzmanski, A. *The Logic of Imperialism.* New York: Praeger, 1981. (Chap. 2)

Talbot, Robert. *A History of Chilean Boundaries.* Ames: Iowa State University Press, 1974. (Chap. 7)

Tamayo, Jesús. *Zonas fronterizas.* México, D.F.: Centro de Investigación y Docencia Economicas, 1983. (Chap. 3)

Tancer, Shoshana Baron. *Economic Nationalism in Latin America: The Quest for Economic Independence.* New York: Praeger, 1976. (Chap. 3)

Tansill, Charles Callan. *The Purchase of the Danish West Indies.* Baltimore: Johns Hopkins Press, 1932. (Chap. 2)

_____. *The United States and Santo Domingo, 1798–1873: A Chapter in Caribbean Diplomacy.* Baltimore: Johns Hopkins University Press, 1938. (Chap. 3)

Tarazona-Sevillano, Gabriela, with John B. Reuter. *Sendero Luminoso and the Threat of Narcoterrorism.* New York: Praeger, 1990. (Chap. 7)

Taylor, Philip B., Jr. *Law and Politics in Inter-American Diplomacy.* New York: John Wiley and Sons, 1963. (Chap. 6)

Teitelbaum, Michael S. *Latin Migration North: The Problem for U.S. Foreign Policy.* New York: Council on Foreign Relations, 1984. (Chap. 9)

Tello, Manuel. *México: una posición internacional.* México: Mortíz, 1972. (Chap. 3)

Theberge, James D. *The Soviet Presence in Latin America.* New York: Crane, Russak, 1974. (Chap. 4)

Thomas, Ann Van Wynen, and A. J. Thomas Jr. *Non-Intervention: The Law and Its Import in the Americas.* Dallas: Southern Methodist University Press, 1956. (Chap. 6)

_____. *The Organization of American States.* Dallas: Southern Methodist University Press, 1963. (Chap. 6)

Thomas, A. J., Jr., and Ann Van Wynen Thomas, eds. *The Dominican Republic Crisis 1965.* Dobbs Ferry, N.Y.: Oceana Publications, for Association of the Bar of the City of New York, 1967. (Chap. 7)

Thomas, David Y. *One Hundred Years of the Monroe Doctrine, 1823–1923.* New York: Macmillan, 1923. (Chap. 5)

Thomas, Hugh. *Cuba: The Pursuit of Freedom.* New York: Harper and Row, 1971. (Chap. 3)

_____. *The Slave Trade: The Story of the Atlantic Slave Trade: 1440–1870.* New York: Simon and Schuster, 1997. (Chap. 8)

Thorndike, Tony. *Grenada: Politics, Economics and Society.* Boulder: Lynne Rienner Publishers, 1985. (Chap. 3)

Thornton, John. *Africa and the Africans in the Making of the Atlantic World, 1400–1680.* Cambridge: Cambridge University Press, 1992. (Chap. 8)

Thorp, Rosemary, and Geoffrey Bertram. *Peru, 1880–1977: Growth and Policy in an Open Economy.* New York: Columbia University Press, 1968. (Chap. 8)

Thorp, Rosemary, and Laurence Whitehead, eds. *Latin American Debt and the Adjustment Crisis.* Pittsburgh: University of Pittsburgh Press, 1987. (Chap. 8)

Thorup, Cathryn L., ed. *The United States and Mexico: Face to Face with New Technology.* New Brunswick, N.J.: Transaction, 1987. (Chap. 3)

Thoumi, Francisco E. *Political Economy and Illegal Drugs in Colombia.* Boulder: Lynne Rienner Publishers, 1994. (Chap. 8)

Timm, Charles A. *The International Boundary Commission, United States and Mexico.* Austin: Bureau of Research in the Social Sciences, University of Texas, 1941. (Chap. 7)

Tischendorf, Alfred Paul. *Great Britain and Mexico in the Era of Porfiro Díaz.* Durham, N.C.: Duke University Press, 1961. (Chap. 3)

Tokatlian, Juan. *Drogas, dilemas y dogmas: Estados Unidos y la narcocriminalidad organizado en Colombia.* Santa fe de Bogotá: CEI: TM Editores, 1995. (Chap. 8)

Tokatlian, Juan G., ed. *Teoría y práctica de la política exterior latinoamericana.* Bogotá: Universidad de los Andes, 1983. (Chap. 3)

Tomassini, Luciano, ed. *El sistema internacional y América Latina: nuevas formas de concertación regional en América Latina.* Buenos Aires: Programa de Estudios Conjuntos Sobre los Relaciones Internacionales de America Latina (RIAL); Grupo Editor Latinoamericano, 1990. (Chap. 3)

———. *Transnacionalización y desarrollo nacional en América Latina.* Buenos Aires: Grupo Editor Latinoamericano, 1984. (Chap. 8)

Tomassini, Luciano, ed. *Las relaciones internacionales de América Latina.* México: Fondo de Cultura Económica, 1981. (Chaps. 2, 3)

Tomassini, Luciano, ed., con colaboración de Carlos J. Moneta and Augusto Varas. *El sistema internacional y América Latina: La política internacional en un mundo postmoderno.* Buenos Aires: Programa de Estudios Conjuntos Sobre los Relaciones Internacionales de America Latina (RIAL); Grupo Editor Latinoamericano, 1991. (Chap. 2)

Tondel, Lyman M., Jr., ed. *The Inter-American Security System and the Cuban Crisis.* Dobbs Ferry, N.Y.: Oceana Publications, 1964. (Chap. 7)

———. *The Panama Canal.* Dobbs Ferry, N.Y.: Oceana Publications, 1965. (Chap. 6)

Topic, Steven C. *Trade and Gunboats: The United States and Brazil in the Age of Empire.* Stanford: Stanford University Press, 1998. (Chaps. 3, 8)

Topik, Steven C., and Allen Wells, eds. *The Second Conquest of Latin America: Coffee, Henequen, and Oil During the Export Boom, 1850–1930.* Austin: University of Texas Press, 1998. (Chap. 8)

Toro Hardy, Alfredo. *Venezuela, Democracia y Política Exterior.* Caracas: Proimagen, 1986. (Chap. 3)

Torres, Blanca. *México en la segunda guerra mundial.* México: El Colegio de México, 1979. (Chap. 7)

Torres Ramírez, Blanca. *Las relaciones cubano-sovieticas, 1959–1968.* México: El Colegio de México, 1971. (Chap. 3)

Torres-Salliant, Silvio, and Ramona Hernández. *The Dominican Americans.* Westport, Conn.: Greenwood Press, 1998. (Chap. 8)

Torriente, Cosme de la. *Fin de la dominación de España en Cuba.* Havana: Imprenta El Siglo XX, 1948. (Chap. 7)

Trask, David F. *The War with Spain in 1898.* New York: Macmillan, 1981. (Chap. 7)

Travis, Ira Dudley. *The History of the Clayton-Bulwer Treaty.* Ann Arbor, Mich.: Michigan Political Science Association, 1900. (Chap. 6)

Trias, Vivian. *Historia del imperialismo norteamericano.* 3 vols. Buenos Aires: A. Peña Lillo, 1975–1977. (Chap. 2)

Trias Monge, José. *Puerto Rico: The Trials of the Oldest Colony in the World.* New Haven, Conn.: Yale University Press, 1997. (Chap. 2)

Triska, Jan F., ed. *Dominant Powers and Subordinate States: The United States in Latin America and the Soviet Union in Eastern Europe.* Durham, N.C.: Duke University Press, 1986. (Chap. 2)

Tugwell, Franklin. *The Politics of Oil in Venezuela.* Stanford: Stanford University Press, 1975. (Chap. 8)

Tulchin, Joseph S. *The Aftermath of War: World War I and U.S. Policy Toward Latin America.* New York: New York University Press, 1971. (Chap. 5)

_____. *Argentina and the United States: A Conflicted Relationship.* Boston: Twayne Publishers, 1990. (Chap. 3)

Tulchin, Joseph S., and Ralph H. Espach, eds. *Security in the Caribbean Basin: The Challenge of Regional Cooperation.* Boulder: Lynne Rienner Publishers, 2000. (Chap. 2)

Tulchin, Joseph S., ed., with Andrew Rudman. *Economic Development and Environmental Protection in Latin America.* Boulder: Lynne Rienner Publishers, 1991. (Chap. 8)

Tulchin, Joseph S., Andrés Serbin, and Rafael Hernández, eds. *Cuba and the Caribbean: Regional Issues and Trends in the Post–Cold War Era.* Wilmington, Del.: Scholarly Resources, 1997. (Chap. 2)

Tullis, F. LaMond. *Unintended Consequences: Illegal Drugs and Drug Policies in Nine Countries.* Boulder: Lynne Rienner Publishers, 1995. (Chap. 8)

Turner, Frederick C. *The Dynamic of Mexican Nationalism.* Chapel Hill: University of North Carolina Press, 1968. (Chap. 3)

Turnier, Alain. *Les Etats Unis et le marché haitien.* Washington, D.C.: n.p., 1955, 1957. (Chap. 3)

Tussie, Diana. *The Inter-American Development Bank.* Boulder: Lynne Rienner Publishers, 1994. (Chap. 6)

Tussie, Diana, ed. *Latin America in the World Economy: New Perspectives.* New York: St. Martin's Press, 1983. (Chap. 2)

Ugarte, Manuel. *The Destiny of a Continent.* New York: Alfred A. Knopf, 1925. (Chap. 3)

Ulloa, Berta. *Revolución Mexicana, 1910–1920.* 2d ed. México: Secretaria de Relaciones Exteriores, 1985. 1st ed. 1963. (Chap. 7)

Universidad Central del Ecuador, Escuela de Ciencias Internacionales. *El Ecuador y los problemas internacionales.* Quito: Universidad Central del Ecuador, 1989. (Chap. 3)

Uribe, Antonio José. *Anales diplomáticos y consulares de Colombia.* 6 vols. Bogotá: Imprenta Nacional, 1900–1920. (Chap. 3)

_____. *Colombia y los Estados Unidos de América: El canal interoceanico.* Bogotá: Imprenta Nacional, 1925. (Chap. 6)

Urquidi, Víctor L. *The Challenge of Development in Latin America.* New York: Praeger, 1964. (Chap. 2)

——. *Free Trade and Economic Integration in Latin America.* Translated by Marjorie M. Urquidi. Berkeley: University of California Press, 1962. (Chap. 2)

Urrutia, Francisco José, *Le continent américain et le droit international.* Paris: Rousseau, 1928. (Chap. 6)

——. *La evolución del principio de arbitraje en América: La Sociedad de Naciones.* Madrid: Editorial América, 1920. (Chap. 6)

Uruguayan Institute of International Law. *Uruguay and the United Nations.* New York: Carnegie Endowment for International Peace, 1958. (Chap. 3)

Vacchino, Juan Mario. *Integración latinoamericana de la ALALC a la ALADI: una salida para los problemas de su desarrollo.* Buenos Aires: Ediciones de Palma, 1983. (Chap. 6)

Vacs, Aldo César. *Discreet Partners: Argentina and the USSR Since 1917.* Translated by Michael Joyce. Pittsburgh: University of Pittsburgh Press, 1984. (Chap. 3)

Vaky, Viron P., and Heraldo Muñoz. *The Future of the Organization of American States.* New York: Twentieth Century Fund Press, 1993. (Chap. 6)

Valdés, Juan Gabriel. *Pinochet's Economists: The Chicago School of Economics in Chile.* New York: Cambridge University Press, 1995. (Chap. 8)

Valois Arce, Daniel. *Reseña historica sobre los limites de Colombia y Venezuela.* Medellín: Editorial Bedout, 1970. (Chap. 7)

Vanderlaan, Mary B. *Revolution and Foreign Policy in Nicaragua.* Boulder: Westview Press, 1986. (Chap. 3)

Varas, Augusto. *Militarization and the International Arms Race in Latin America.* Boulder: Westview Press, 1985. (Chap. 8)

Varas, Augusto, ed. *Hemispheric Security and U.S. Policy in Latin America.* Boulder: Westview Press, 1989. (Chaps. 2, 5)

——. *Jaque de la democracia: orden internacional y violencia política en América Latina.* Buenos Aires: Grupo Editor Latinoamericano, 1990. (Chap. 8)

——. *Soviet–Latin American Relations in the 1980s.* Boulder: Westview Press, 1987. (Chap. 4)

Vargas Carreño, Edmundo. *América Latina y los problemas contemporáneos del derecho del mar.* Santiago de Chile: Editorial Andrés Bello, 1973. (Chap. 6)

Vasconcelos, José. *Bolivarismo y Monroeismo.* Santiago: Universidad de Chile, 1937. (Chap. 6)

Vásquez, Carlos, and Manuel García y Griego. *México frente a los Estados Unidos: un ensayo historico, 1776–1980.* México: El Colegio de México, 1982. (Chap. 3)

Vásquez, Carlos, and Manuel García y Griego, eds. *Mexican-U.S. Relations: Conflict and Convergence.* Los Angeles: University of California Press, 1983. (Chap. 3)

Vázquez, Josefina Zoraida, and Lorenzo Meyer. *The United States and Mexico.* Chicago: University of Chicago Press, 1985. (Chap. 3)

Vásquez, Luis Ospina. *Industria y protección en Colombia, 1810–1930.* Medellín: E.S.F., 1955. (Chap. 3)

Vázquez Carrizosa, Alfredo. *Las relaciones de Colombia y Venezuela: La historia atormentada de dos naciones.* Bogotá: Ediciones Tercer Mundo, 1983. (Chap. 7)

Vega, Bernardo. *Kennedy y los Trujillo.* Santo Domingo: Fundación Cultural Dominicana, 1991.

_____. *Trujillo y las fuerzas armadas norteamericanos.* Santo Domingo: Fundación Cultural Dominicana, 1992. (Chap. 3)

Veneroni, Horacio Luis. *Estados Unidos y las fuerzas armadas de América Latina.* Buenos Aires: Ediciones Periferia, 1971. (Chap. 8)

Ventós, Xavier Rubert de. *The Hispanic Labyrinth: Spain's Encounter with Latin America.* Translated by Mary Ann Newman. New Brunswick, N.J.: Transaction, 1990. (Chap. 4)

Vera Castillo, Jorge. *La politica exterior chilena durante el gobeirno del Presidente Salvador Allende, 1970–1973.* Santiago de Chile: Instituto de Estudios de las Relaciones Internacionales Contemporáneas, 1987. (Chap. 3)

Vianna, Hélio. *Historia diplomática do Brazil.* 2d ed. São Paulo: Ediçoñes Melhoramentos, 1961. 1st ed. 1958. (Chap. 3)

Vicens Vives, Jaime, ed. *Historia de España y América.* 5 vols.; 2d ed. Barcelona: Editorial Vicens Vives, 1971. 1st ed. 1957–1959. (Chaps. 2, 4)

Villalobos R., Sergio. *El Beagle, historia de una controversia.* Santiago de Chile: Editorial Andrés Bello, 1979. (Chap. 7)

Vivas Gallardo, Freddy. *Venezuela en la sociediad de las naciones, 1920–1939.* Caracas: Universidad Central de Venezuela, 1981. (Chap. 3)

Vivot, Alfredo N. *La doctrina Drago.* Buenos Aires: Coni Hermanos, 1911. (Chap. 6)

Volski, Victor. *América Latina: petróleo e independencia.* Buenos Aires: Editorial Cartago, 1966. (Chap. 8)

Wagner de Reyna, Alberto. *Historia diplomática del Perú, 1900–1945.* Lima: Ediciones Peruanas, 1964. (Chap. 3)

Walker, Thomas W., ed. *Nicaragua in Revolution.* New York: Praeger, 1982. (Chap. 7)

_____. *Reagan Versus the Sandinistas: The Undeclared War on Nicaragua.* Boulder: Westview Press, 1987. (Chap. 7)

Walker, William O., III. *Drug Control in the Americas.* Rev. ed. Albuquerque: University of New Mexico Press, 1989. 1st ed. 1981. (Chap. 8)

Walker, William O., III, ed. *Drugs in the Western Hemisphere: An Odyssey of Cultures in Conflict.* Wilmington, Del.: Scholarly Resources, 1996. (Chap. 8)

Wallerstein, Immanuel. *The Modern World System.* 3 vols. New York: Academic Press, 1974, 1980; San Diego: University of California at San Diego, 1989. (Chap. 2)

Warren, Harris Gaylord. *The Sword Was Their Passport: A History of American Filibustering in the Mexican Revolution.* Baton Rouge: Louisiana State University Press, 1943. (Chap. 7)

Watson, Bruce W., and Peter G. Tsouras, eds. *Operation Just Cause: The U.S. Intervention in Panama.* Boulder: Westview Press, 1990. (Chap. 7)

Watson, Hilbourne A., ed. *The Caribbean in the Global Political Economy.* Boulder: Lynne Rienner Publishers, 1994. (Chaps. 2, 3)

Weber, Cynthia. *Faking It: U.S. Hegemony in a "Post-Phallic" Era.* Minneapolis: University of Minnesota Press, 1999. (Chap. 5)

Weber, David J. *The Mexican Frontier, 1821–1846: The American Southwest Under Mexico.* Albuquerque: University of New Mexico Press, 1982. (Chap. 7)

Weber, David J., and Jane M. Rausch, eds. *Where Cultures Meet: Frontiers in Latin American History.* Wilmington, Del.: Scholarly Resources, 1994. (Chap. 8)

Weinstein, Martin, ed. *Revolutionary Cuba in the World Arena.* Philadelphia: Institute for the Study of Human Issues, 1979. (Chap. 3)

Weintraub, Sidney. *Free Trade Between Mexico and the United States?* Washington, D.C.: Brookings Institution, 1984. (Chap. 3)

_____. *A Marriage of Convenience: Relations Between Mexico and the United States.* New York: Oxford University Press, 1990. (Chap. 6)

Weintraub, Sidney, ed. *Free Trade in the Western Hemisphere.* Entire issue of *Annals of the American Academy of Political and Social Science* 526 (March 1993). (Chap. 6)

_____. *Integrating the Americas: Shaping Future Trade Policy.* New Brunswick, N.J.: Transaction, for North-South Center, University of Miami, 1994. (Chap. 6)

Weis, W. Michael. *Cold Warriors and Coups d'Etat: Brazilian-American Relations, 1945–1964.* Albuquerque: University of New Mexico Press, 1993. (Chap. 3)

Weisbrot, Robert. *The Jews of Argentina: From the Inquisition to Perón.* Philadelphia: Jewish Publication Society of America, 1979. (Chap. 8)

Welch, Richard E., Jr. *Response to Revolution: The United States and the Cuban Revolution, 1959–1961.* Chapel Hill: University of North Carolina Press, 1985. (Chap. 3)

Welles, Sumner. *Naboth's Vineyard: The Dominican Republic, 1844–1924.* 2 vols. New York: Payson and Clarke, 1928. (Chap. 3)

Wells, Henry. *The Modernization of Puerto Rico.* Cambridge: Harvard University Press, 1969. (Chap. 2)

Wesson, Robert G. *The United States and Brazil: Limits of Influence.* New York: Praeger, 1981. (Chap. 3)

Wesson, Robert G., ed. *Communism in Central America and the Caribbean.* Stanford: Hoover Institution, 1982. (Chap. 2)

_____. *U.S. Influence in Latin America in the 1980s.* New York: Praeger, 1982. (Chap. 2)

Wesson, Robert G., and Heraldo Muñoz, eds. *Latin American Views of U.S. Policy.* New York: Praeger, 1986. (Chap. 3)

Westergaard, Waldemar. *The Danish West Indies Under Company Rule (1671–1754).* New York: Macmillan, 1917. (Chap. 2)

Whitaker, Arthur P. *Nationalism in Latin America.* Gainesville: University of Florida Press, 1962. (Chap. 3)

_____. *The United States and Argentina.* Cambridge: Harvard University Press, 1954. (Chap. 3)

_____. *The United States and South America: The Northern Republics.* Cambridge: Harvard University Press, 1948. (Chap. 3)

_____. *The United States and the Independence of Latin America, 1800–1830.* Baltimore: Johns Hopkins University Press, 1941. (Chap. 7)

_____. *The United States and the Southern Cone: Argentina, Chile, and Uruguay.* Cambridge: Harvard University Press, 1976. (Chap. 3)

_____. *The Western Hemisphere Idea: Its Rise and Decline.* Ithaca, N.Y.: Cornell University Press, 1954. (Chap. 5)

Whitaker, Arthur P., and others. *Latin America and the Enlightenment.* 2d ed. Ithaca, N.Y.: Cornell University Press, 1961. 1st ed. 1942. (Chap. 2)

Whitaker, Arthur P., and David C. Jordan, eds. *Nationalism in Contemporary Latin America.* New York: Free Press, 1966. (Chap. 3)

White, Richard Alan. *Paraguay's Autonomous Revolution, 1810–1840.* Albuquerque: University of New Mexico, 1978. (Chap. 7)

Whitehead, Laurence, ed. *The International Dimensions of Democratization: Europe and the Americas.* Oxford: Oxford University Press, 1996. (Chap. 8)

Whiting, Van R., Jr. *The Political Economy of Foreign Investment in Mexico: Nationalism, Liberalism, and Constraints on Choice.* Baltimore: Johns Hopkins University Press, 1992. (Chap. 8)

Wiarda, Howard J. *The Democratic Revolution in Latin America: History, Politics, and U.S. Policy.* New York: Holmes and Meier, 1990. (Chap. 8)

_____. *Finding Our Way? Toward Maturity in U.S.–Latin American Relations.* Washington, D.C.: American Enterprise Institute for Public Policy Research, 1987. (Chap. 5)

_____. *Iberia and Latin America: New Democracies, New Policies, New Models.* Lanham, Md.: Rowman and Littlefield, 1996. (Chap. 4)

Wiarda, Howard J., ed. *The Iberian–Latin American Connection: Implications for U.S. Foreign Policy.* Boulder: Westview Press, 1986. (Chap. 4)

Wickham-Crowley, Timothy P. *Exploring Revolution: Essays on Latin American Insurgency and Revolutionary Theory.* Armonk, N.Y.: M. E. Sharpe, 1991. (Chap. 7)

_____. *Guerrillas and Revolution in Latin America: A Comparative Study of Insurgents and Regimes Since 1956.* Princeton, N.J.: Princeton University Press, 1992. (Chap. 7)

Wilgus, A. Curtis, ed. *The Caribbean: British, Dutch, French, United States.* Gainesville: University of Florida Press, 1958. (Chap. 2)

_____. *The Caribbean: Contemporary International Relations.* Gainesville: University of Florida Press, 1957. (Chaps. 2, 3)

_____. *The Caribbean: Current United States Relations.* Gainesville: University of Florida Press, 1966. (Chaps. 2, 3, 5)

_____. *The Caribbean: Its Hemispheric Role.* Gainesville: University of Florida Press, 1967. (Chaps. 2, 3)

Wilhelms, Saskia K. S. *Haitian and Dominican Sugarcane Workers in Dominican Batayes: Patterns and Effects of Prejudice, Stereotypes, and Discrimination.* (Boulder: Westview Press, 1995). (Chap. 8)

Wilhelmy, Manfred, ed. *La formación de la política exterior: los paises desarrolados y América Latina.* Buenos Aires: Grupo Editor Latinoamericano, 1987. (Chap. 3)

Williams, Edward J. *The Rebirth of the Mexican Petroleum Industry: Developmental Directions and Policy Implications.* Lexington, Mass.: Lexington Books, 1979 (Chap. 8)

Williams, Felicity. *La Internacional Socialista y América Latina: Una Visión Crítica.* México: Universidad Autónoma Metropolitana, 1984. (Chap. 8)

Williams, Mary Wilhelmine. *Anglo-American Isthmian Diplomacy, 1815–1915.* Washington, D.C.: American Historical Association, 1916. (Chap. 6)

Williamson, John, ed. *Latin American Adjustment: How Much Has Happened?* Washington, D.C.: Institute for International Economics, 1990. (Chap. 8)

Wilson, Joe F. *The United States, Chile and Peru in the Tacna and Arica Plebiscite.* Lanham, Md.: University Press of America, 1979. (Chap. 7)

Wilson, Larman C., and David W. Dent. *Historical Dictionary of Inter-American Organizations.* Lanham, Md.: Scarecrow Press, 1997. (Chap. 6)

Winkler, Max. *Investments of United States Capital in Latin America.* Boston: World Peace Foundation, 1928. (Chap. 8)

Wionczek, Miguel S., ed. *Latin American Economic Integration: Experiences and Prospects.* New York: Frederick, 1966. (Chap. 6)

Wionczek, Miguel S., ed., in collaboration with Luciano Tomassini. *Politics and Economics of External Debt Crisis: The Latin American Experience.* Boulder: Westview Press, 1985. (Chap. 8)

Wirth, John D. *Latin American Oil Companies and the Politics of Energy.* Lincoln of Nebraska: University Press, 1985. (Chap. 8)

Wolpin, Miles D. *Cuban Foreign Policy and Chilean Politics.* Toronto: D. C. Heath, 1972. (Chap. 3)

Wood, Bryce. *Aggression and History: The Case of Ecuador and Peru.* New York: Columbia University Press, 1978. (Chap. 7)

_____. *The Dismantling of the Good Neighbor Policy*. Austin: University of Texas Press, 1985. (Chap. 5)

_____. *The Making of the Good Neighbor Policy*. New York: Columbia University Press, 1961. (Chap. 5)

_____. *The United States and Latin American Wars, 1932–1942*. New York: Columbia University Press, 1966. (Chap. 7)

Woods, Randall Bennett. *The Roosevelt Foreign-Policy Establishment and the "Good Neighbor": The United States and Argentina, 1941–1945*. Lawrence: Regents Press of Kansas, 1979. (Chap. 7)

Woodward, Ralph Lee, ed. *Central America: Historical Perspectives on the Contemporary Crisis*. Westport, Conn.: Greenwood Press, 1988. (Chap. 2)

Worcester, Donald E. *Sea Power and Chilean Independence*. Gainesville: University of Florida Press, 1962. (Chap. 7)

Wright, Harry K. *Foreign Enterprise in México: Laws and Policies*. Chapel Hill: University of North Carolina Press, 1971. (Chap. 8)

Wright, Philip Green. *The Cuban Situation and Our Treaty Relations*. Washington, D.C.: Brookings Institution, 1931. (Chap. 7)

Wright, Winthrop R. *British-Owned Railways in Argentina: Their Effect on the Growth of Economic Nationalism, 1854–1948*. Austin: University of Texas Press, 1974. (Chap. 8)

Wrong, Hume. *Government of the West Indies*. Oxford: Clarendon Press, 1923. (Chap. 2)

Wythe, George. *The United States and Inter-American Relations: A Contemporary Appraisal*. Gainesville: University of Florida Press, 1964. (Chaps. 2, 5)

Ycaza Tigerino, Julio. *Originalidad de Hispanoamérica*. Madrid: Ediciones de Cultura Hispánica, 1952. (Chap. 4)

Yepes, Jesús María. *Del Congreso de Panamá a la Conferencia de Caracas, 1826–1954: El genio de bolívar a través de la historia de las relaciones Interamericanas*. 2 vols. Caracas: Cromotip, 1955. (Chap. 6)

_____. *La panaméricanisme au point de vue historique, juridique et politique*. Paris: Les Éditions Internationales, 1936. (Chap. 6)

Yundt, Keith W. *Latin American States and Political Refugees*. New York: Praeger, 1998. (Chap. 8)

Zamora R., Augusto. *El conflicto Estados Unidos–Nicaragua, 1979–1990*. Managua: Fondo Editorial CIRA, 1996. (Chap. 7)

Zarate, Juan Carlos. *Forging Democracy: A Comparative Study of the Effects of U.S. Foreign Policy on Central American Democratization*. Boulder: Westview Press, 1994. (Chap. 8)

Zavala, Silvio Arturo. *Programa de historia de América en la época colonial*. 2 vols. México: Instituto Panamericano de Geografía e Historia, 1961. Abridgement in English: Max Savelle. *The Colonial Period in the History of the New World: Program of the History of the New World*. México: Instituto Panamericano de Geografía e Historia, 1961. (Chap. 2)

Zorilla, Luis G. *Historia de las relaciones entre México y los Estados Unidos de America, 1800–1958.* México: Editorial Porrúa, 1965. (Chap. 3)

Zook, David H. *The Conduct of the Chaco War.* New Haven, Conn.: Bookman Associates, 1960. (Chap. 7)

_____. *Zarumilla-Marañón: The Ecuador-Peru Dispute.* New York: Bookman Associates, 1964. (Chap. 7)

Zubieta, Pedro A. *Apuntaciones sobre las primeras misiones diplomáticas de Colombia (primero y segundo períodos—1808–1810–1830).* Bogotá: Imprenta Nacional, 1924. (Chap. 7)

Notes

CHAPTER 1

1. Bryce Wood, "Area Studies," *International Encyclopedia of the Social Sciences*, vol. 1 (New York: Macmillan and Free Press, 1968), 401–407.

2. With the onset of the cold war, the global system came to be widely perceived as consisting of the First World of industrialized and noncommunist states, the Second World of Communist states, and the Third World of nonaligned and developing states. Latin Americanists generally recognized the artificiality of forcing the region into a category that was only partially accurate in describing its characteristics. Latin America had thrown off the "yolk of colonialism" in a much earlier period (for the most part), and had complex and differentiated patterns of alignment and nonalignment and of processes and stages of development. See G. Pope Atkins, *Latin America and the Caribbean in the International System* (Boulder: Westview Press, 1999), 261–267.

3. Some evaluations of the state of Latin American and Caribbean IR research over time are: Jorge I. Domínguez, "Consensus and Divergence: The State of the Literature on Inter-American Relations in the 1970s," *Latin American Research Review* 13:1 (1978), 87–126; Alberto Cisneros-Lavaller, "Old Wine in New Bottles: An Essay on the Study of Inter-American Relations," *New Scholar* 8 (1982), 267–288; Abraham F. Lowenthal, "Research in Latin America and the Caribbean on International Relations and Foreign Policy: Some Impressions," *Latin American Research Review* 18:1 (1983), 154–174; Alberto van Klaveren, "The Analysis of Latin American Foreign Policies: Theoretical Perspectives," chap. 1 in *Latin American Nations in World Politics,* ed. Heraldo Muñoz and Joseph Tulchin (Boulder: Westview Press, 1984); Luciano Tomassini, Carlos Juan Moneta, and Augusto Varas, *La política internacional en un mundo postmoderno* (Buenos Aires: Grupo Editor Latinoamericano, 1991), last chapter; and Heraldo Muñoz, "The Dominant Themes in Latin American Foreign Relations," chap. 1 in *Latin American Nations in World Politics,* 2d ed., ed. Heraldo Muñoz and Joseph Tulchin (Boulder: Westview Press, 1996). Of particular interest is the book-length treatment edited by Rubén Perina, *El Estudio de las Relaciones Internacionales en América Latina y el Caribe* (Buenos Aires: Grupo Editor Latinoamerica, 1985).Of a more general nature, contributors to Charles Wagley, ed., *Social Science Research on Latin America:*

Report of a Seminar (New York: Columbia University Press, 1964) make representative reference to IR. Christopher Mitchell, ed., *Changing Perspectives in Latin American Studies: Insights from Six Disciplines* (Stanford: Stanford University Press, 1988) refers to IR in the introduction and individual chapters, especially those on political science and economics and to a lesser degree on history, sociology, and anthropology. An important contribution is the collection edited by David W. Dent, *Handbook of Political Science Research on Latin America: Trends from the 1960s to the 1990s* (Westport, Conn.: Greenwood Press, 1990), in which Part 2 (four chapters) is devoted to IR; the introduction by Dent and Part 1 on comparative politics are also of interest to IR scholars. The premier bibliographic source in Latin American Studies is Library of Congress, Hispanic Division, *Handbook of Latin American Studies*, 57 vols. (Cambridge, Mass.: Harvard University Press; Gainesville: University of Florida Press; Austin, Tex.: University of Texas Press, 1935–2000). Beginning with vol. 26 (1964) volumes alternate coverage between social sciences and humanities. See especially the introductory essays written over the years to the section on international relations, and, also of interest, those on comparative politics, history, economics, sociology, and anthropology. Also of an analytic nature, dealing in a general way with IR in earlier decades, is the classic bibliographic source, Samuel Flagg Bemis and Grace Gardner Griffin, *Guide to the Diplomatic History of the United States, 1775–1921* (Washington, D.C.: Library of Congress, 1935), which has considerable reference to Latin America. David F. Trask, Michael C. Meyer, and Roger R. Trask, eds., *A Bibliography of United States–Latin American Relations Since 1810: A Selected List of Eleven Thousand Published References* (Lincoln: University of Nebraska Press, 1968); and Michael C. Meyer, ed., *Supplement* (Lincoln: University of Nebraska Press, 1979) make up a monumental effort. Although nonanalytic and sketchily annotated, this work is so well organized and exceptionally thorough that, taken in concert with the above sources, it assists understanding the development of the study of Latin American IR.

4. Wood, "Area Studies," 402.

5. This is the conclusion reached by William Thompson in his especially helpful survey of the early literature: "The Regional Subsystem," in *International Studies Quarterly* 17 (March 1973), 89–117. The matter is discussed at some length in G. Pope Atkins, *Latin America and the Caribbean in the International System* (Boulder: Westview Press, 1999), chap. 2, from which these remarks are taken.

6. Atkins, *Latin America and the Caribbean in the International System*, 28; supporting evidence and argument follow, pp. 28–41. Five fundamental levels developed early in the literature: (1) the overall Latin American region; (2) subregions within the region (such as the circum-Caribbean and the Southern Cone of South America, among others); (3) the individual states making up the

region; (4) the larger western hemispheric inter-American system; and (5) the global international system and the constituent parts in which Latin American states and societies participate. Transnational phenomena were also a part of the early literature and have increasingly been included in the above levels of analysis.

7. This statement may be disputed. Mark T. Berger, *Under Northern Eyes: Latin American Studies and U.S. Hegemony in the Americas, 1898–1990* (Bloomington: Indiana University Press, 1995), arguing from a world-system perspective, sees in the evolution of Latin American studies in the U.S. academic activity profoundly complementing continuous imperial policies. Earlier, Susanne Bodenheimer, a leading advocate of neo-Marxist dependency theory, had argued in a similar manner in a fifty-three-page monograph, *The Ideology of Developmentalism: The American Paradigm-Surrogate for Latin American Studies* (Beverly Hills: Sage, 1971). My complaint with these positions is that they leave little room for the existence of scholarly complexity and diversity. Many political scientists in the field of comparative politics would also challenge the claim, arguing that a true understanding of a state's foreign policy requires knowledge of domestic structures and processes from a more general comparative perspective. This view should be subsumed as a part of the study but not as an overarching consideration.

8. A superb intellectual history of the study of IR is provided by William C. Olson and A.J.R. Groom, *International Relations Then and Now: Origins and Trends in Interpretation* (London: HarperCollins Academic, 1991). Focusing exclusively on theories, James E. Dougherty and Robert L. Pfaltzgraff Jr., *Contending Theories of International Relations: A Comprehensive Survey*, 3d ed. (New York: Harper and Row, 1990), is a particularly thorough treatment. Recommended as a survey from a current perspective is Paul R. Viotti and Mark V. Kauppi, *International Relations Theory: Realism, Pluralism, Globalism*, 2d ed. (New York: Macmillan, 1993); as is the book of more subjective contemplations by Fred Halliday, *Rethinking International Relations* (Vancouver: University of British Columbia, 1994). Also useful are M. P. Sullivan, *International Relations: Theories and Evidence* (Englewood Cliffs, N.J.: Prentice-Hall, 1976); T. Taylor, ed., *Approaches and Theory in International Relations* (London and New York: Longmans, 1978); P. M. Morgan, *Theories and Approaches to International Politics: What Are We to Think?* (New Brunswick, N.J.: Transaction, 1981); J. C. Garnett, *Commonsense and the Theory of International Politics* (Albany: State University of New York Press, 1984); Martin Hollis and Steve Smith, *Explaining and Understanding International Relations* (Oxford: Clarendon Press, 1990); and Jurgen Martin Gabriel, *Worldviews and Theories of International Relations* (New York: St. Martin's Press, 1994). Well-conceived multiauthored collections with broad theoretical treatments are James Der Derian, ed., *International Theory: Critical Investigations* (New York: New York University Press, 1995); Booth and

Smith, eds., *International Theory Today* (1995); and Scott Burchill and Andrew Linklater, with Richard Devetak, Mathew Paterson, and Jacqui True, *Theories of International Relations* (New York: St. Martin's Press, 1996). Also of note is the collection of analytic bibliographical essays edited by Margot Light and A.J.R. Groom, *International Relations Theory: A Handbook of Current Theory* (London: Francis Pinter, 1985). Two current college textbooks—Daniel S. Papp, *Contemporary International Relations: Frameworks for Understanding,* 3d ed. (New York: Allen and Bacon, 1997) and Chris Brown, *Understanding International Relations* (New York: Macmillan, 1997)—offer clear explanations of IR theories within their thematic treatments. Evaluations of the often contentious theoretical debates include Quincy Wright, *The Study of International Relations* (New York: Appleton-Century-Crofts, 1955), a brilliant survey by a leading IR scholar; Stanley Hoffmann, ed., *Contemporary Theory in International Relations* (Englewood Cliffs, N.J.: Prentice-Hall, 1960), a multiauthored appraisal that Hoffmann characterizes as a "wrecking operation"; Klaus Knorr and James N. Rosenau, eds., *Contending Approaches to International Politics* (Princeton, N.J.: Princeton University Press, 1969); the autobiographical essays brought together by J. N. Rosenau, ed., *In Search of Global Patterns* (New York: Free Press, 1976); K. J. Holsti, *The Dividing Discipline: Hegemony and Diversity in International Theory* (Boston: Allen and Unwin, 1985); Richard Ned Lebow and Thomas Risse-Kappen, eds., *International Relations Theory and the End of the Cold War* (New York: Columbia University Press, 1995); and Michael W. Doyle and G. John Ikenberry, eds., *New Thinking in International Relations Theory* (Boulder: Westview Press, 1997).

9. Michael Haas, ed., *International Systems: A Behavioral Approach* (New York: Chandler, 1974), 2.

10. K. J. Holsti, *International Politics: A Framework for Analysis,* 5th ed. (Englewood Cliffs: Prentice-Hall, 1988), 4.

11. See Jack Child, *Geopolitics and Conflict in South America* (New York: Praeger, 1985), chap. 2.

12. G. Pope Atkins, *Encyclopedia of the Inter-American System* (Westport, Conn.: Greenwood Press, 1997), 56.

13. See the discussions of these disciplinary matters by Olson and Groom, *International Relations Then and Now,* chap. 4; and by Scott Burchill in Burchill, Linklater, and others, *Theories of International Relations,* 4–7.

14. Child, *Geopolitics and Conflict in South America,* 22–23.

15. Among the most notable prewar realists were Frederick Schuman in the United States, who authored the long-lived influential textbook, *International Politics* (New York: McGraw-Hill, 1933; 7th ed. 1969); and Edward H. Carr in Great Britain, author of *The Twenty Years Crisis, 1919–1939* (London: Macmillan, 1939; 2d ed. 1946), a classic, erudite, and even more influential contribution to IR.

16. Morgenthau set forth his axioms in a classic work: *Politics Among Nations* (New York: Alfred A. Knopf, 1948). The sixth edition, edited after Morgenthau's death by his former student and prominent realist, Kenneth Thompson, was issued thirty-six years later (New York: Random House, 1984).

17. The "rational actor" model has not been restricted to the realist school. Others with different values underlying their preferences for state purposes and policies use the rationalist language of strategic setting and external challenges, state interest and capability, and the need for effective and purposeful action. Many of those with idealist inclinations also think within the framework of an interstate system and state interests but, in contrast to realists, seek to reform IR and the way policymakers rationally thought about and used power. Governments themselves tend to explain and defend their decisions in its terms. International political economists adopt rationalist concepts in their concern with policies based on macroeconomic models and goals that stress the interrelationship of economic policies and the international political and economic systems. Rationalist assumptions at microlevels create contradictions and problems of predictability, so that microtheory economists are more prone to investigate other explanations of human behavior (such as psychological and social processes) than are macrotheorists. Numerous international historians and many journalists also base their analyses and commentaries on rational model tenets.

18. Morgenthau, "The Intellectual and Political Functions of Theory," in *International Theory*, ed. Der Derian, 36–52.

19. Some historians, especially in Great Britain, attempted to steer a course between what they saw as atheoretical history and ahistorical behavioralism. A study by F. S. Northedge and M. J. Grieve, *A Hundred Years of International Relations* (New York: Praeger, 1971) illustrates this approach. They indicated dissatisfaction with orthodox diplomatic history, which, they said, could not see the wider framework of the international political system, and jargon-laden social science analysis, whose abstractions missed the "living realities of state behavior." Central to their historical study was the assumption that an international system exists, in constant process of change and evolution, that comprises an important but not exclusive determinant of state behavior. It may be noted that a significant number of pioneer British and U.S. IR scholars began professional life as historians. They became discouraged with their colleagues' refusal to recognize historical patterns of behavior.

20. For a full discussion, see Atkins, *Latin America and the Caribbean in the International System*, chap. 1. James N. Rosenau, ed., *International Politics and Foreign Policy* (New York: Free Press, 1961, 1969) was influential in drawing the distinction between foreign policy and international politics; the two editions are different enough to be considered separate volumes. World regions as foci for subsystem analysis lagged behind the global concept but then flourished for a

time. The end of the cold war revived regionalism and the literature on it. Among the early efforts were Gavin Boyd, ed., *Regionalism and Global Security* (Lexington, Mass.: Lexington Books, 1984); Louis J. Cantori and Steven L. Spiegel, eds., *The International Politics of Regions* (Englewood Cliffs, N.J.: Prentice-Hall, 1970), which includes Latin America as one of five regions discussed and compared; Richard A. Falk and Saul Mendlovitz, eds., *Regional Politics and World Order* (San Francisco: W. H. Freeman, 1973); Werner Feld and Gavin Boyd, *Comparative Regional Systems* (New York: Pergamon, 1980), with an excellent chapter on Latin America by Yale H. Ferguson; Bruce M. Russett, *International Regions and the International System* (Chicago: Rand McNally, 1967); Ronald Yalem, *Regional Subsystems and World Politics* (Tucson: University of Arizona Press, 1970). Recent work, which tends to emphasize political economy and formal institutions, includes Edward D. Mansfield and Helen V. Milner, eds., *The Political Economy of Regionalism* (New York: Columbia University Press, 1997); Louise Fawcett and Andrew Hurrell, eds., *Regionalism in World Politics: Regional Organization and World Order* (New York: Oxford University Press, 1995); and A. Gamble and A. Payne, eds., *Regionalism and World Order* (London: Macmillan, 1996).

21. The peace research movement was a form of "scientific idealism." It was adopted by scholars who applied objective behavioralism in the service of normative purposes—finding solutions to problems of international conflict and its resolution. They sought to be "policy-relevant" and to bring "conscience into science" by combining political and social values with methodological rigor to scientifically design solutions to world problems and recommend or implement policies designed to facilitate world peace and justice. Many peace researchers argued that past research had tended to serve the interests of powerful states rather than to facilitate world peace. Michael Banks notes that peace research has identified factors that undermine realism, particularly the multiplicity of parties involved in conflict, including nonstate actors. Banks, "The Inter-Paradigm Debate," in Light and Groom, *International Relations*, 16.

22. Early seminal insights were provided by Richard C. Snyder, H. W. Bruck, and Burton Sapin, eds., *Foreign Policy Decision-Making: An Approach to the Study of International Politics* (New York: Free Press of Glencoe, 1962). Snyder, Bruck, and Sapin had collaborated for a number of years in the field—an example is their coauthored monograph, *Decision-Making as an Approach to the Study of Politics* (Princeton, N.J.: Organization Behavior Section, Princeton University, 1954). A highly influential pioneer work by a psychologist was Robert Jervis, *Perception and Misperception in International Politics* (Princeton, N.J.: Princeton University Press, 1976). Later, Martha Cottam, *Foreign Policy Decision Making: The Influence of Cognition* (Boulder: Westview Press, 1987) offered a good review of the political psychology literature; and Charles F. Hermann, Charles W.

Kegley Jr., and James N. Rosenau edited a collection of sophisticated analyses on comparative foreign policy analysis, *New Directions on Foreign Policy* (Boston: Allen and Unwin, 1987). Recently, Laura Neak, Jeanne A. K. Hey, and Patrick J. Haney, *Foreign Policy Analysis: Continuity and Change in Its Second Generation* (Englewood Cliffs, N.J.: Prentice-Hall, 1995) reviewed the evolution of the subject and examined the state of the study as of the late 1990s.

23. For an excellent synopsis, see Viotti and Kauppi, *International Relations Theory*, 60–67. The leading neorealist scholar has been Kenneth N. Waltz. See especially his *Man, the State, and War* (New York: Columbia University Press, 1959) and *Theory of International Politics* (Reading, Mass.: Addison-Wesley, 1979). In contrast, in a major book, Hedley N. Bull, *The Anarchical Society: A Study of World Order* (New York: Columbia University Press) subtly linked the "reality" of a quasi-anarchic international system with the need for a cooperative world community.

24. Also virtually ignored was the "English School" of IR that appeared after World War II. Drawing inspiration from the classical tradition, it made little impact on the study of Latin American–Caribbean IR. But it had a profound and enduring influence on the study of IR in British universities and should be acknowledged as an important effort. Martin Wight, professor of international relations at the London School of Economics and Political Science and founder of the English School, drew a sharp distinction between international and political theory (i.e., philosophy). He asserted that no tradition of international theory existed to equal that of political theory, because the latter's focus on the state as the central concept had led to a scholarly reluctance to think beyond an essentially domestic paradigm. Wight argued that international theory could not be other than a philosophy of history, which was best suited to deal with the nature of foreign policy, the working of the interstate system, the concern for survival in that system, and the concepts of world society and universal human rights. Wight identified three classical traditions as making up his philosophical framework: Realism (Machiavellian *realpolitik*), Rationalism (Grotian legalism), and Revolutionism (Kantian idealism). See Wight, "Why Is There No International Theory?" in *International Theory: Critical Investigations*, ed. Der Derian, 15–35; and Wight, *International Theory: The Three Traditions* (New York: Holmes and Meier, 1992), with an introduction by Hedley Bull (Wight's renowned student). Two prominent British scholars—Halliday, *Rethinking International Relations*, 24–27; and Smith, "The Self Images of a Discipline," 8–9, 11–13—offer cogent explications and criticism. They see strengths in the historical approach, emphasis on traditions of Western thought, and normative analytic and ethical concerns. But they find fault with (1) the limited view of IR as consisting of only the three transhistorical themes of diplomacy, law, and war, which neglects economic and social elements; (2) the false dichotomy of

political versus international theory, which ignores classical theories going beyond a narrow focus on the state; and (3) the too-easy dismissal of other IR paradigms and methods.

25. See V. Kubalkova and A. A. Cruikshank, *Marxism-Leninism and the Theory of International Relations* (Boston: Routledge and Kegan Paul, 1980).

26. For further discussion, see Chapter 2 of this volume and Atkins, *Latin America and the Caribbean in the International System*, 67–72.

27. Fernando Henrique Cardoso, "The Consumption of Dependency Theory in the United States," *Latin American Research Review* 12:3 (1977), 7–24. Cogent critiques of the theory are made by David Ray, "The Dependency Model of Latin American Underdevelopment: Three Basic Fallacies," *Journal of Inter-American Studies* 15 (February 1973), 4–20; Tony Smith, "The Underdevelopment of Development Literature: The Case of Dependency Theory," *World Politics* 31 (January 1979), 247–288; and Philip J. O'Brien, "Dependency Revisited," Occasional Papers, Institute of Latin American Studies, University of Glasgow, Scotland (1984).

28. This section is based on the fuller discussion in Atkins, *Latin America and the Caribbean in the International System*, 18–19, 40–41, 72–77.

29. A highly influential early work was Robert O. Keohane and Joseph S. Nye Jr., eds., *Transnational Relations and World Politics* (Cambridge, Mass.: Harvard University Press, 1972), followed by Keohane and Nye, *Power and Interdependence: World Politics in Transition* (Boston: Little, Brown, 1977). Also among the earlier important works were John W. Burton, *World Society* (New York: Cambridge University Press, 1972); J. Galtung, *The True Worlds: A Transnational Perspective* (New York: Free Press, 1980); Richard W. Mansbach, Yale H. Ferguson, and Donald E. Lampert, *The Web of World Politics: Non-State Actors in the Global System* (Englewood Cliffs, N.J.: Prentice-Hall, 1976), which includes a chapter on the Latin American region; Richard W. Mansbach and John W. Vasquez, *In Search of Theory: A New Paradigm for Global Politics* (New York: Columbia University Press, 1981); Edward L. Morse, *Modernization and the Transformation of International Relations* (New York: Free Press, 1976); and James N. Rosenau, *The Study of Global Interdependence: Essays on the Transnationalization of World Affairs* (London: Frances Pinter, 1980).

30. Some works that broadly analyze transnationalization and globalization in the new era from various perspectives are: Michael Banks and Martin Shaw, eds., *State and Society in International Relations* (New York: St. Martin's Press, 1991); Hans-Henrik Holm and George Sorensen, *Whose World Order? Uneven Globalization and the End of the Cold War* (Boulder: Westview Press, 1995); Thomas Risse-Kappen, ed., *Bringing Transnational Relations Back In: Non-State Actors, Domestic Structures and International Institutions* (Cambridge: Cambridge University Press, 1995); James N. Rosenau, *Along the Domestic-Foreign Frontier: Exploring Governance in a Turbulent World* (Cambridge: Cambridge University

Press, 1997); and Martin Shaw, *Global Society and International Relations: Sociological Concepts and Political Perspectives* (Cambridge, UK: Polity Press, 1994). See also the helpful discussion in Viotti and Kauppi, *International Relations Theory*, 7–8, chap. 3.

31. Stephen D. Krasner, "International Political Economy," in *Oxford Companion to Politics of the World* (New York: Oxford University Press, 1993), 453–460.

32. Robert O. Keohane was an important leader in the development of structural liberalism. See his *After Hegemony: Cooperation and Discord in the World Political Economy* (Princeton, N.J.: Princeton University Press, 1984). See David A. Baldwin, ed., *Neorealism and Neoliberalism: The Contemporary Debate* (New York: Columbia University Press, 1993).

33. Banks, "The Inter-Paradigm Debate," 16.

34. Dina A. Zinnes, *Contemporary Research in International Relations: A Perspective and a Critical Assessment* (New York: Free Press, 1976).

35. If anyone may be identified as the founder of formal theory in IR, it is the security analyst, Thomas Schelling. Beginning with his classic *The Strategy of Conflict* (Cambridge, Mass.: Harvard University Press, 1960), Schelling's work had continuing impact on IR behavioralist researchers, at least until the 1980s. Schelling sought to improve rational strategic decisional processes with game theory analysis applied to cold war situations. But he was more modest about methodological claims than his formalist descendants, warning security analysts to beware of overemphasizing mathematical models. Formal theory does not have the same hold in Britain as in the United States. The leading proponent is Michael Nicholson, *Formal Theories in International Relations* (New York: Cambridge University Press, 1989), who estimates that about 30 percent of the study of IR is amenable to formal theorizing. But Nicholson also sees the field as a simplex divided between mathematical and discursive approaches. See also Michael Nicholson, *Causes and Consequences in International Relations: A Conceptual Study* (New York: Cassell Academic, 1996), a further defense of a social scientific approach to IR based on the design of natural science.

36. Robert Bates, "Area Studies and the Discipline: A Useful Controversy," *PS: Political Science and Politics* 30:2 (June 1997), 166–169. See Barbara Geddes, "Uses and Limitations of Rational Choice," in *Latin America in Comparative Perspectives: New Approaches to Methods and Analysis,* ed. Peter H. Smith (Boulder: Westview Press, 1995).

37. Stephen M. Walt, "Rigor or Rigor Mortis? Rational Choice and Security Studies," *International Security* 23:4 (spring 1999), 4–48. Donald Green and Ian Shapiro, with reference to U.S. political science in general, had earlier applied their own mathematical skills to test formalist outcomes. They concluded that too often ill-conceived assumptions were asserted so as to validate formalist-rational choice method and prior mathematical formulations. See their

NOTES

Pathologies of Rational Choice Theory: A Critique of Applications in Political Science (New Haven, Conn.: Yale University Press, 1995). Walt reached the same general conclusion. All three authors called for theoretical and methodological pluralism and advocated problem-oriented over method-driven political science.

38. See Jane S. Jaquette, "Rewriting the Scripts: Gender in the Comparative Study of Latin American Politics," in *Latin America in Comparative Perspective,* ed. Peter H. Smith.

39. Mark A. Neufeld, *The Restructuring of International Relations* (New York: Cambridge University Press, 1995). Neufeld provides a good guide to the varied literature on the subject.

40. J. Ann Tickner, "You Just Don't Understand: Troubled Engagements Between Feminists and IR Theorists," *International Studies Quarterly* 41 (1997), 611–632. This is a particularly clear and helpful summary, which also refers to principal feminist works.

41. A generally accepted way of depicting the evolution of the study of IR since the end of World War I, when it was first organized as a separate field of study, has been as a succession of "phases" within which "great debates" have occurred between "schools" of competing paradigms. The collective suggestion (with variations) is the following: In each of the first three phases, specific theoretical schools were dominant: idealism in the 1920s and most of the 1930s, realism from the late 1930s into the 1950s, and behavioralism in the 1950s and 1960s. The first great debate was between realists and idealists; the second was between behavioralists and traditionalists (the combination of idealists and realists). The third debate was part of the fourth phase that emerged in the 1970s and involved neorealism, pluralism, and neo-Marxism (it has been called the "interparadigm debate"). A fifth and current phase began in the late 1980s in which postpositivist theorists have precipitated the fourth great debate by challenging the central assumptions about the very nature of past paradigms and disputing their assumptions about the very nature of knowledge and theory. The summary in this chapter of the development of IR reflects the view that, although the above approach reveals a great deal about the theoretical substance and controversies in IR, it has certain flaws that limit its usefulness. The process of theoretical development has been more complex and less precise than intimated. The various phases and debates have not been so sharply delineated nor their consequences as universal as suggested. The range of theoretical and conceptual diversity within each period is broader than indicated—some important paradigms have been largely ignored, and most of those identified have in fact lacked internal cohesion and constituted "schools" of defensive contention more than reflective argumentation. See the discussion by Steve Smith, "The Self Images of a Discipline: A Genealogy of International Relations Theory," in *International Theory Today,* ed. Ken Booth and Steve Smith (University Park: Pennsylvania State University Press, 1995), 13–17.

42. James Rosenau bluntly and clearly states the matter: "Most students of IR are political scientists and most inquiries focus on one or another political aspect of IR. The number of sociologists, anthropologists, psychologists, economists, and historians who specialize in international exchanges is small, both within each of their disciplines and within international studies itself. However regrettable the fragmentation of IR and its dominance by political scientists, this state of affairs can be explained. The most developed of the social sciences, especially economics and psychology, are so preoccupied with their paradigms that their practitioners are disinclined to look for collaborative work with colleagues in the less developed social sciences. Such an attitude is further reinforced by a reward structure wherein advancement tends to go to those who make a mark through disciplinary research than to those who engage in interdisciplinary or multidisciplinary inquiry." James N. Rosenau, "International Relations," in *Oxford Companion to Politics of the World* (New York: Oxford University Press, 1993), 456.

43. Rosenau, "International Relations," says, with respect to the end of the cold war, whether the "unrelenting pace of change will lead to a convergence around fewer approaches remains to be seen. The history and complexity of IR, however, make it seem very doubtful that any single conception of the dynamics of global politics will come to unify the study and teaching of global affairs." Papp, *Contemporary International Relations,* 11–12, says that this state of affairs should not be surprising and probably not discouraging; the field of IR is too large for even its principal elements to be captured in a single set of concepts or unified by a particular method or theory. For a recent and articulate defense of the idea of autonomy, see Donald J. Puchala, "Visions of a Weberian Moment: Our Discipline Looks Ahead," *International Studies Perspectives* 1:2 (August 2000), 133–144. Puchala argues that "International Relations is a full-fledged, full-blown, autonomous, legitimate and accomplished academic discipline, and ought not be thought of as a subfield of political science or any other of the social sciences." See also Michael Brecher, "International Studies in the Twentieth Century and Beyond: Flawed Dichotomies, Synthesis, Cumulation," *International Studies Quarterly* 43 (1999), 213–264, which is Brecher's presidential address to the International Studies Association.

44. This section is based on G. Pope Atkins, "Patterns of International Relations Research," in *Handbook of Political Science Research on Latin America,* ed. David W. Dent, chap. 14.

45. J. Gregory Oswald, ed. and tr., *Soviet Image of Contemporary Latin America* (Austin: University of Texas Press, 1970), is a compilation and translation of forty-seven Soviet Russian writings on the contemporary Latin American scene. Although not much IR is included, the introduction is a valuable discussion of the general objectives and achievements of Soviet research that have implications for IR.

46. An appendix to Dent, ed., *Handbook of Political Science Research on Latin America*, carefully prepared by David Dent, is an extensive directory of major social science research centers and institutes in Latin America and the Caribbean. See also Lowenthal, "Research in Latin America and the Caribbean on International Relations and Foreign Policy," which comments on numerous institutions where IR research is conducted. Roberto Russell, ed., *Enfoques teóricos y metodológicos para el estudio de política exterior* (Buenos Aires: Grupo Editor Latinoamericano, 1992), surveys the literature and the evolution and state of IR studies in Argentina, Brazil, Colombia, and Mexico.

CHAPTER 2

1. See, in the companion volume to this handbook, G. Pope Atkins, *Latin America and the Caribbean in the International System*, 4th ed. (Boulder: Westview Press, 1999), chaps. 2 and 3.

2. The term "inter-American system" is used here to mean the regularized structures and processes of inter-American relations within the boundaries of the Western Hemisphere. The same nomenclature, Inter-American System (with capital letters), refers to the formal hemispherewide organizations among the American states that originated in 1889, a subject treated in Chapter 6.

3. See Shlomo Avineri, ed., *Karl Marx on Colonialism and Modernization: His Despatches and Other Writings on China, India, Mexico, the Middle East and North Africa* (New York: Doubleday, 1968).

4. Aníbal Quijano and Immanuel Wallerstein, "Americanity as a Concept, or the Americas in the Modern World System," *International Social Science Journal* 134 (November 1992), 549–557, is a concise summary of the authors' view of the critical position of the Americas in the world-system.

CHAPTER 3

1. See G. Pope Atkins, *Latin America and the Caribbean in the International System* (1999), chap. 4, for further discussion on the subject of this chapter.

2. Heraldo Muñoz, "The Dominant Themes in the Study of Latin America's Foreign Relations," *World Affairs* 8 (fall 1987).

3. Other insightful articles on the subject are Muñoz, "The Dominant Themes in the Study of Latin America's Foreign Relations"; Alberto van Klaveren, "Enteniendo las políticas exteriores latinoamericanas: modelo para armar," *Estudios Internacionales* 25:98 (abril/junio 1992), 169–216; Luciano Tomassini, "El análisis de la política exterior," *Estudios Internacionales* 21:84 (Octubre/Diciembre 1988), 498–559; Jeanne A. K. Hey, "Three Building Blocks in a Theory of Latin American Foreign Policy," *Third World Quarterly* 18,

631–657; and Kenneth M. Coleman and Luis Quiros-Varela, "Determinants of Latin American Foreign Policies: Bureaucratic Organizations and Development Strategies," in Ferris and Lincoln, *Latin American Foreign Policies*.

4. For a full discussion of research trends and specific studies, as well as references for individual states, see Damián J. Fernández, "Central America and the Caribbean," chap. 16 in *Handbook of Political Science Research on Latin America: Trends from the 1960s to the 1990s*, ed. David W. Dent (Westport, Conn.: Greenwood Press, 1990).

5. For a full discussion of research trends and specific studies since 1960 in South America, as well as references for individual states, see Michael J. Francis and Timothy J. Power, "South America," chap. 17 in *Handbook of Political Science Research on Latin America*, ed. David W. Dent.

6. For a full discussion of research trends and specific studies, see Dale Story, "Mexico's International Relations," chap. 15 in *Handbook of Political Science Research on Latin America*, ed. David W. Dent.

CHAPTER 4

1. See the companion volume to this handbook, G. Pope Atkins, *Latin America and the Caribbean in the International System* (4th ed., 1999), chap. 5.

CHAPTER 5

1. G. Pope Atkins, *Latin America and the Caribbean in the International System* (4th ed., 1999), companion volume to this handbook, devotes chapter 6 to U.S. policies.

CHAPTER 6

1. The companion volume to this handbook, G. Pope Atkins, *Latin America and the Caribbean in the International System* (4th ed., 1999), deals with these matters in chapters 7, 8, and 9.

2. This paragraph is based on and taken from G. Pope Atkins, "Introduction," in *Encyclopedia of the Inter-American System* (Westport, Conn.: Greenwood Press, 1997). In that introduction I discuss my position that, although the nineteenth-century Spanish-American initiatives provided certain important historical antecedents, the Inter-American American System was so fundamentally different that it should not be considered an extension of the former efforts (p. 7).

CHAPTER 7

1. For further discussion of these phenomena, see the companion volume to this handbook: G. Pope Atkins, *Latin America and the Caribbean in the International System* (Boulder, Colo.: Westview Press, 1999), pp. 301–312 and chap. 12.

CHAPTER 8

1. Many of the phenomena addressed are essentially domestic matters extended to international proportions. The general rule of judgment for studies to be included was that they devote substantial attention to interstate or transnational processes. Those cast only or mostly in domestic terms were excluded. For further discussion of the subjects included in this chapter, see G. Pope Atkins, *Latin America and the Caribbean in the International System* (Boulder: Westview Press, 1999), chapters 10–15.

2. I have written elsewhere the following: The assortment of transnational actors is highly diverse. It has included international business enterprises and multinational corporations, international non-governmental organizations of all kinds (educational foundations, humanitarian and voluntary organizations, and professional associations, to name but a few categories), international political party associations and labor movements, the Holy See and the transnational Roman Catholic Church network, other churches, immigrants and refugees, travelers and tourists, communications media, entertainment and sports enterprises, educational institutions, the accompanying business people, journalists, artists, entertainers, athletes, educators, students, scientists, and a wide range of other individuals; as well as pirates, privateers, buccaneers, revolutionaries, terrorists, guerrilla groups, mercenaries, drug traffickers, and organized criminal elements. . . . Transnational actors have engaged in a wide variety of activities and transactions having multiple effects and immense consequences. Goods, money, people, organizations, information, ideas, images, beliefs, doctrines, and popular culture flow across and transcend state boundaries, creating their own political, economic, ethnic, social, and cultural patterns that are by and large not subject to state control. Most phenomena are closely identified with domestic society. Most issues are not appropriate for the use of state force or necessarily responsive to diplomacy (Atkins, *Latin America and the Caribbean in the International System*, 75).

3. Heraldo Muñoz, "The Dominant Themes in Latin American Foreign Relations," in *Latin American Nations in World Politics*, 2d ed., ed. Heraldo Muñoz and Joseph Tulchin (Boulder: Westview Press, 1996), 8. For general treatments of these matters, with references to the Latin American region, see

Jan Knippers Black, *Development in Theory and Practice* (Boulder: Westview Press, 1991); Richard A. Higgot, *Political Development Theory* (New York: St. Martin's Press, 1983); and Heraldo Muñoz, ed., *From Dependency to Development: Strategies to Overcome Underdevelopment and Inequality* (Boulder: Westview Press, 1981).